The Best Test Preparation for the

TOEFL

Test of English as a Foreign Language

Richard X. Bailey, M.F.A.
Coordinator of ESL Program
Ocean County College, Toms River, New Jersey

Sundari Seetharaman, M.A.
Former Assistant Professor of English
Vaishnav College for Women, University of Madras,
Madras, India

Carole A. Gavin, Ed.D.
ESL Program Coordinator
Burlington County College, Pemberton, New Jersey

Neelima Shukla, M.A.
Former Associate Professor of English
Arts and Commerce College—Idar, Gujarat, India

Joyce Penfield, Ph.D.
Associate Professor of Language Education
Rutgers University, New Brunswick, New Jersey

Ramya Subramanian, M.A.
Coordinator of ESL/NEL Services
Newark Public Library, Newark, New Jersey

Lorraine H. Teller, M.A.
Adult High School English/Writing Teacher, ESL Program
New Brunswick Adult Learning Center,
New Brunswick, New Jersey

RESEARCH & EDUCATION ASSOCIATION
61 Ethel Road West • Piscataway, New Jersey 08854

The Best Test Preparation for the
TEST OF ENGLISH AS A FOREIGN
LANGUAGE (TOEFL)

Printed in the United States of America

Library of Congress Catalog Card Number 98-65416

International Standard Book Number 0-87891-784-5

Research & Education Association
61 Ethel Road West
Piscataway, New Jersey 08854

REA supports the effort to conserve and
protect environmental resources by
printing on recycled papers.

CONTENTS

Chapter 1

Introduction to TOEFL

Chapter 1

About Research & Education Association

Research & Education Association (REA) is an organization of educators, scientists, and engineers specializing in various academic fields. Founded in 1959 with the purpose of disseminating the most recently developed scientific information to groups in industry, government, high schools, and universities, REA has since become a successful and highly respected publisher of study aids, test preps, handbooks, and reference works.

REA's Test Preparation series includes study guides for all academic levels in almost all disciplines. Research & Education Association publishes test preps for students who have not yet completed high school, as well as high school students preparing to enter college. Students from countries around the world seeking to attend college in the United States will find the assistance they need in REA's publications. For college students seeking advanced degrees, REA publishes test preps for many major graduate school admission examinations in a wide variety of disciplines, including engineering, law, and medicine. Students at every level, in every field, with every ambition can find what they are looking for among REA's publications.

Unlike most test preparation books—which present only a few practice tests which bear little resemblance to the actual exams — REA's series presents tests that accurately depict the official exams in both degree of difficulty and types of questions. REA's practice tests are always based upon the most recently administered exams, and include every type of question that can be expected on the actual exams.

REA's publications and educational materials are highly regarded and continually receive an unprecedented amount of praise from professionals, instructors, librarians, parents, and students. Our authors are as diverse as the subjects and fields represented in the books we publish. They are well-known in their respective fields and serve on the faculties of prestigious universities throughout the United States.

About the Computer-Based TOEFL

This book will provide you with an accurate and complete representation of the paper-and-pencil version of the TOEFL (Test Of English as a Foreign Language), with information and sample questions to help you prepare for the new computer-based test. As of July 1998, the TOEFL will be administered exclusively as a Computer-Based Test (CBT), and some sections will utilize Computer-Adaptive Testing (CAT). We will discuss computer-adaptive testing in greater detail a bit later, but it is important to note here that while the format of the test is changing, the skills the TOEFL is intended to measure are not. According to research conducted by the test administrators, there is no significant difference between the scores of students who take a paper-and-pencil version of the test and those who take CAT versions. Therefore, a good score on our paper-and-pencil exams should translate into a good score on the Computer-Based Test. In addition, the test administrators are preparing an accordance table, so that schools will be able to accurately compare scores from students who take paper-and-pencil exams with those who take computer-based tests.

The diagnostic test and the six sample tests are based on the most recently administered paper-and-pencil TOEFL examinations. Our reviews are designed to ensure that you possess the skills required to do well when taking the actual test. You are allowed 1 hour and 55 minutes to complete each sample test. Following each test you will find an answer key with detailed explanations that are designed to help you understand the test material.

Some editions of this book include two audiocassettes, containing the six sample listening tests. **If this book does not contain these cassettes, you should have a friend read the Listening Comprehension material to you, from the transcripts located in the back of this book.** This will help you improve your listening skills and prepare you for the Listening Comprehension portion of the TOEFL.

About the Test

Who takes the test?

People who are not native speakers of English will take the TOEFL if they plan to attend an undergraduate school in the United States, Canada, the United Kingdom, or in a country where English is the language of instruction, because most schools in these countries require TOEFL scores from foreign applicants. According to TOEFL administrators, in the 1996-97 academic year approximately 953,000 people registered to take the examination.

Who administers the test?

The TOEFL was developed and is administered by the Educational Testing Service (ETS). The questions for the TOEFL are crafted by language specialists who follow standardized procedures that ensure high-quality work. All questions are reviewed by many people, revised as necessary, and then are administered in trial test situations, before being compiled into a test format. According to ETS, the tests are then reviewed, using specific procedures, to ensure that they are free from cultural bias and that they will properly measure students' knowledge. ETS also coordinates test site instructors.

When and where is the test given?

TOEFL is administered in 170 countries, at Sylvan Technology Centers®.

To receive information on upcoming administrations of the TOEFL, ask your guidance counselor or contact the TOEFL test service at:

Educational Testing Service
TOEFL Registration Office
P.O. Box 6152
Princeton, NJ 08541-6152
USA

Test Center Information:
1-800-GO-TOEFL

Website:
http://www.toefl.org

What is the test used for?

The Test Of English as a Foreign Language is used to measure your verbal skills in English, as well as your understanding of spoken English. It is used at over 2,300 colleges and universities in the U.S. and Canada as an admission requirement for non-native speakers of English, and may also be used for academic placement. Often, educational institutions will also use the scores to determine eligibility for scholarships and other forms of financial aid. The TOEFL is also used as a means of evaluating English proficiency by many government agencies and licensing boards.

What is a Computer-Adaptive Test (CAT)?

As of July 1998, some sections of the TOEFL Computer-Based Test (CBT) will be computer-adaptive. This means that you will use a computer to take the test, and the software will determine which questions to ask based on your performance on the previous questions. In this way, the test will customize itself to your level of ability. A correct response will be followed by a more difficult question, and an incorrect response will be followed by an easier question. Difficult questions increase your score in greater increments than medium or easier questions.

In the traditional paper-and-pencil test, every examinee sees the same questions. Because of the adaptive nature of the CAT, and the large pool of questions that are available, different examinees will be asked different questions. However, the questions have been designed to meet content and difficulty specifications that will allow an equitable comparison of scores.

Pros and Cons of Computer-Adaptive Testing

There are several advantages to computer-adaptive testing. First, you will receive your unofficial scores for the multiple-choice sections on the day you take your test, rather than several weeks later. Second, the CAT is offered much more frequently than the paper-and-pencil version, and you may register just a few days in advance. In addition, the testing venue is quieter and more orderly than traditional testing locations.

Unfortunately, there are also some important disadvantages to the CAT. People who are unfamiliar with computers may find the testing environment intimidating. While no computer skills are required, an unusual environment may have a negative psychological impact on your preparedness. In addition, you must answer the questions in the order in which they are presented. You cannot skip a question and return to it later — or return to an earlier question to change your answer — as you could with a paper-and-pencil test. This is significant because it eliminates the important test-taking strategy of answering the easier questions first and returning to the more difficult questions if you have time. Finally, because of the nature of adaptive testing, the majority of the questions you encounter will be challenging to you.

What's New About the TOEFL?

The most obvious difference between the paper-and-pencil version of the TOEFL and the computer-based test is the fact that the test will be administered by a computer. In order to prepare candidates for this change, the testing software provides a thorough tutorial covering how to use the computer's mouse, how to click, how to scroll, and how to navigate through the computer-based testing interface. Because of this exhaustive tutorial, the most significant changes involve new types of questions that are unique to the computer-based format. Examples of these question types can be found in the section of this introduction that explain each review. In addition, the computer-based TOEFL requires an essay. Some sample essay topics are included in this introduction to help you prepare for this new section. When you take the actual exam, you will be given the option of either typing or handwriting your essay. Typing your essay offers the advantage of being able to revise as you write it. Keep in mind, however, that you have only 30 minutes to compose your essay, so if you type slowly, you may not have enough time to adequately express your ideas.

How to Use this Book

What do I study first?

Before you do anything else, you should take the diagnostic test, which appears after this introduction. After you complete this test, you will be able to determine what areas are causing you difficulty by referring to the diagnostic chart. These problem areas are what you should begin to study first, so that you can strengthen your weaknesses. The diagnostic test is described in more detail in the *About the Diagnostic Test* section.

After you have thoroughly studied the areas with which you are having problems, you may want to retake the diagnostic test to gauge your improvement in these areas. When you feel comfortable with the areas which have previously caused you difficulty, you should then begin reviewing and preparing for each section of the TOEFL.

When should I start studying?

It is never too early for you to start studying for the TOEFL—the earlier the better. You should start studying as soon as possible so that you will be able to learn more. Make sure you take our diagnostic test before you start studying, so that you can determine your weaknesses and begin working on them immediately. Using the diagnostic test, the diagnostic chart, and its cross-referencing system (described in the *About the Diagnostic Test* section) can help you strengthen your problem areas before you run out of time to study. Last-minute studying is not an efficient way to study and does not allow you to learn the material which you will need to know for the exam.

How else can I improve my English speaking and writing skills while preparing for the test?

In addition to using the diagnostic test to determine your problem areas, make sure you study all of the reviews. The reviews will cover the information you will need to know for the exam. You should also test yourself by completing as many of the practice tests as you possibly can.

Besides using this book, there is one way you can familiarize yourself with written English—READ! Reading will help you improve your writing skills because you will become acquainted with correct structure and phrasing in written English. You should read newspaper and magazine articles. Read the college admissions material and college catalogs of the schools to which you are applying. You should also read books of interest to you. Just make sure you read, read, **READ**!

There are many ways you can familiarize yourself with spoken English. If you are in your car, turn on the radio. Listening to radio newscasts and weather reports can also help prepare you for the test. You should watch television documentaries, go to lectures, and even go to the movies. Doing all of these things will help hone your perception of spoken English and will help prepare you for the Listening Comprehension section, and may even aid in building your vocabulary.

Format for the Computer-Based TOEFL

The computer-based TOEFL consists of four sections. These sections are:

Section 1: Listening Comprehension – In this computer-adaptive section, your ability to respond to and understand spoken English will be tested. A tape recording of a series of dialogues and short talks will be played for you. You will then have to choose the best answer based on the spoken questions. When you take the sample tests, take the Listening sections for Tests 1-6 by using the provided tapes. If you have purchased the book without the tapes, have a friend read the transcripts located in the back of the book.

Section 2: Structure and Written Expression – This computer-adaptive section will test your knowledge of the structure and grammar of the English language. The items in this section will include a number of sentences that contain errors. You will be required to find the mistakes and correct them by choosing the right answer. Other sentences will be incomplete. For these, you must choose the answers that correctly complete the sentence.

Section 3: Reading Comprehension and Vocabulary – The Reading Comprehension section will have several short paragraphs. You must read the paragraphs and then answer questions that will be based upon what you have just read. This section of the TOEFL CBT is not computer adaptive.

Section 4: Writing – The Writing section measures your ability to write clearly in English. You will be assigned a topic on which to write, and you will have the option of typing or handwriting your essay. This section of the TOEFL CBT is not computer adaptive.

New Computer-Based Question Types

Most of the questions on the TOEFL CBT will be the same as those presented in the practice exams in this book. However, there are also some new types of questions created specifically for the CBT. Examples of some of these new question types can be found on the next pages. Even though there are some differences in the format of these questions, the skills they test have not changed. Keep this in mind when you encounter a new question type on the actual exam. These new question types are just using the power of the computer to test the same information in different ways.

New Listening, Structure and Reading Question Types

Sample Question 1

Some questions will require you to choose two correct answers. For example:

Which two states were the last admitted into the United States of America?

Click on 2 answers

☐ New Jersey
☒ Alaska
☐ Wyoming
☒ Hawaii

Sample Question 2

Some questions will ask you to match words with their appropriate categories. For example:

What is the appropriate category for each word?

Click on a word. Then click on the box where it belongs.

bicycle   write   pretty

verb   noun   adjective

Sample Question 3

Some questions require you to find a word or phrase in a passage and answer some questions about it. For example:

Many people find the study of English grammar intimidating. There are so many rules to follow. A good reference book, such as *REA's Handbook of English: Grammar, Style, and Writing* can help make sense of them, but there is no substitute for daily reading. Newspaper and magazine articles are a great place to start. Joseph Conrad, whose first language was Polish, learned English by reading newspapers, and then gave English literature some of its finest works.	Look at the word them in the passage. Click on the word or phrase in the bold text to which this word refers.

Essay Questions For the Computer-Based TOEFL

The computer-based TOEFL requires an essay. You may want to practice writing essays on the topics listed below. Then have a friend or teacher read them and point out areas in which you may need additional work.

Sample Essay Topics

1) What, in your opinion, is the greatest crisis facing the world in the 21st Century?

2) The impact of computers on our lives grows stronger with each passing year. What is the most significant benefit of this growth? What is the most significant drawback?

You will have the option of handwriting or typing your essay. If you do not feel comfortable typing on a computer, you should handwrite your essay. You will have only thirty minutes to compose your essay, so you should not let your typing skills stand in the way of clearly expressing your ideas. However, if you are comfortable typing on a computer, typing your essay offers the advantage of being able to revise as you write.

Some other question types appear new at first, but are just slightly different representations of old question types. Even if a question looks different from anything you've seen before, the skills it tests will not be. If you pay attention to *what* a question asks rather than *how* it asks, you'll do fine.

About the Diagnostic Test

You should use the diagnostic test in conjunction with the reviews to gauge your strengths and weaknesses in order to best prepare for the TOEFL. The diagnostic test will look just like the practice tests in this book. It will contain the same sections and the same amount of questions as the practice tests. Although the diagnostic test is a timed test, you may choose not to time it. It is not as important to time the diagnostic test as it is to time the practice tests, since you are only gauging your strengths and weaknesses in different areas of the test. Unlike the Listening Comprehension sections in the practice tests, the diagnostic Listening Comprehension section is not recorded on tape. Instead, have a friend read the material to you from the transcripts provided at the back of the book.

Once you have completed the diagnostic test and have determined which questions you answered incorrectly, you can use the cross-referencing system to determine your problem areas. If you follow the directions for using the cross-referencing system (found in the table after the diagnostic test) you will be guided to the review section that corresponds with your problem area. This will make your preparation for the TOEFL much easier.

About the Review Sections

Although the format and delivery system of the TOEFL is changing, the content of the test is not. Therefore, our reviews will still provide everything you need to understand the concepts behind the questions which will be asked in the TOEFL. They will help you to prepare for the actual test. They contain study tips on how to choose the best answer quickly and accurately. Also, there will be many drills that will help you in studying for the TOEFL. You should use the reviews in conjunction with the diagnostic test and its cross-referencing table, which can show you what areas you need to study the most.

Listening Comprehension Review: The Listening Comprehension section will be discussed, in great detail, in this review. It will illustrate for you the different forms of questions that may appear in this section of the TOEFL. It will also review some aspects of American culture that may be discussed in the Listening Comprehension section. Through using this review, you will learn how to listen for key words and phrases. A number of study-tips have been included to help you concentrate more effectively and choose the correct answer quickly.

Structure and Written Expression Review: This review will describe for you the grammar and structure of English in a clear way. The review will help you learn how to pick out errors in sentences and to replace them with correct choices. It will also help you become familiar with the basic rules of English grammar.

Reading Comprehension and Vocabulary Review: An extensive vocabulary list containing some of the words you will most likely encounter on the TOEFL has been included. Definitions with many drills are also included to help you learn and remember these words. Using the sample reading passages, you can learn to pick out topic sentences, make inferences, and determine content.

Scoring the Exam

What is a passing score for the TOEFL?

There is no specific "passing grade" on the TOEFL. Every school looks at many factors, of which your TOEFL score is only one, in determining whether or not you will be admitted. Every school has a different set of admissions standards. You should check with the school to which you are applying to find out what range of TOEFL scores will be acceptable for admission.

How is the TOEFL scored?

The scoring range has been revised for the TOEFL CBT, and it may be some time before the schools to which you are applying adapt to this change. For this reason, our practice exams retain the scoring scales used in the paper-and-pencil version of the TOEFL.

You will receive three section scores, one for each section of the TOEFL, and a total score. Only correct answers are counted, and there is no penalty for wrong answers. Each section will be given a raw score, which is the total number of correct answers for a particular section. The raw scores are then converted into a scaled score which is what is reported on your score report. Scaled scores for each section can range from 20 to 68, while the total scaled score can range from 200 to 677. You should keep in mind that a total score below 400 is considered fairly low, while a score above 600 is considered advanced.

Under the new scoring system, individual sections will be scored on a 0-30 scale, except for the essay portion of the exam, which will be scored on a scale of 0-6. The highest possible scaled score on the TOEFL CBT is a 300. When you receive your scores for the TOEFL CBT, they will appear much lower than your scores on our practice exams. This is because of the change in the scoring scale. Remember, a score of 677 on the paper-and-pencil version of the exam is roughly equivalent to a score of 300 on the TOEFL CBT.

Your 0-6 essay score will be the average of two scores given by two qualified readers. If there is a difference of more than one point in the scores of these two readers, a third reader will independently score your essay. Note that a score of 0 is reserved for essays that are blank, incoherent, or written on a topic other than the one assigned.

How do I score my practice tests?

To determine your score on any of the practice tests, you should perform the following procedure, using the given table.

Count your number of correct answers (your raw score) in the Listening Comprehension section. Go to the *Raw Score Conversion Table* which follows. Under the column marked *Number of Correct Answers*, find the score range that includes your number of correct answers. From the numbers you have just found, move to the right, and under the column marked *Listening Comprehension*, find the score range that corresponds to your number of correct answers.

RAW SCORE CONVERSION TABLE

Number of Correct Answers (Raw Score)	Listening Comprehension	Structure and Written Expression	Reading Comprehension and Vocabulary
60			
57-59			66-67
54-56			64-65
51-53			61-63
48-50	64-68		59-60
45-47	61-63		56-58
42-44	58-60		54-56
39-41	55-57		52-54
36-38	53-55	63-68	50-51
33-35	51-52	58-62	48-49
30-32	49-50	54-57	45-47
27-29	47-49	51-53	43-45
24-26	46-47	48-50	41-42
21-23	44-45	45-47	38-40
18-20	42-43	42-44	35-37
15-17	40-41	38-41	32-34
12-14	37-39	35-37	30-31
9-11	33-36	30-34	28-29
6-8	30-32	26-29	25-27
3-5	27-29	22-25	23-24
0-2	24-26	20-21	20-22

For example, say you had 40 correct answers in the Listening Comprehension section. Looking under the *Number of Correct Answers* column, you would find that 40 falls under the score range of 39-41. Then, you would move to the right, to the *Listening Comprehension* column, and find that the score range 39-41 corresponds to the score range of 55-57 in the *Listening Comprehension* column.

Repeat this procedure for the last two sections of the test. When you determine your score range for each of the sections, mark the range below:

	Your Score	Example
Listening Comprehension	_____	55 - 57
Structure and Written Expression	_____	48 - 50
Reading Comprehension and Vocabulary	_____	61 - 63

When you have determined your score range for each section, add together the first number of each score range (mark this below). Then add together the last number of each score range (mark this below).

Add first numbers

_____ + _____ + _____ = _____

Example (using numbers above):

55 + 48 + 61 = 164

Add last numbers

_____ + _____ + _____ = _____

Example (using numbers above):

57 + 50 + 63 = 170

When this is done, you will have determined the total score range. The total score range is the sum of the first numbers and the sum of the last numbers. Example: the total score range for the numbers above is 164-170.

Now, you must multiply each sum by $^{10}/_3$.

Example:

$$164 \times {}^{10}/_3 = 546.66 \text{ (round to nearest whole number)} = 547$$

$$170 \times {}^{10}/_3 = 566.66 \text{ (round to nearest whole number)} = 567$$

When this is done, you will have determined your total score range. Make sure to round the total score range to the nearest whole number.

Example: Your total score range is 547-567.

Studying for the TOEFL

At first glance, the TOEFL may appear to be primarily a test of written English. However, the TOEFL not only tests your written English ability, but it also tests your ability to understand spoken English. By using the tests contained in this book, you will be able to develop your abilities in both of these areas.

It is important for you to discover the time and place for studying that works best for you. Some students may set aside a certain number of hours every morning to study, while others may choose to study at night before going to sleep. Other students may study during the day, while waiting in a line, or they may even listen to English tapes while doing chores. Only you will be able to know when and where your studying is most effective. The most important factor to keep in mind is consistency. Use your time wisely. Work out a study routine—and stick to it!

You may want to follow a schedule similar to the one below. (Depending on how long before the exam you begin to study, you may want to add to this schedule or condense it.)

Study Schedule

Week	Study Plan
1	Take the diagnostic test to determine your problem areas, and use the cross-referencing system to determine what to study. Begin studying the areas which the cross-referencing system has directed you to study in the reviews.
2	Retake the diagnostic test to gauge improvement. Continue to study and strengthen your weak areas.
3	Study the Listening Comprehension Review.
4	Study the Structure and Written Expression Review.

5	Study the Reading Comprehension Review.
6	Study the Vocabulary List and quiz yourself on the spelling, the pronunciation, and the definition of each word.
7	Take Practice Examination 1 and review all incorrect answers.
8	Take Practice Examination 2 and review all incorrect answers.
9	Take Practice Examination 3 and review all incorrect answers.
10	Take Practice Examination 4 and review all incorrect answers.
11	Take Practice Examination 5 and review all incorrect answers.
12	Take Practice Examination 6 and review all incorrect answers.

Again, make sure to utilize the diagnostic test and its cross-referencing system. They will save you time and energy when you are studying. By using them, you will discover what you need to study most, so that you don't waste valuable time reviewing things that you already know.

When you take the practice tests, you should sit down at a quiet table and time yourself. Try to make the conditions as much like a test center as possible by removing all distractions. Afterwards, you should check each answer and thoroughly review the reasoning behind each question that you missed. You should not review too much at one time. Concentrate on each of your problem areas individually, until you feel comfortable with your ability in each of those areas.

Keep track of your scores! You will be able to gauge your progress and discover general weaknesses in particular sections. You may find it very helpful to work with someone else, particularly on the verbal sections. If possible, you should find a friend or classmate who is also taking the test. You may even find it convenient to ask a native speaker of English to help you practice.

The more rules of English that you naturally incorporate and utilize, the better you will do—both on the test and in real conversations. For instance, if you can manage to avoid breaking the structure of sentences into its components (past participles, gerunds, etc.), by all means do so. Try to use sentence structure only to show yourself why an answer is different from what you had expected. Each time you learn about a new structure in the review, create as many sentences as you can with this new structure. You will then be able to use the new information automatically.

TOEFL Test-Taking Tips

You may be unfamiliar with computer-based tests, such as the TOEFL CBT. Computer-adaptive testing has eliminated many of the traditional test-taking strategies, such as answering the easier questions first and returning to the more difficult questions later. However, new strategies have evolved that take the place of traditional ones. The most important of these strategies are listed below:

• **Take the Tutorial**

Even if you have some computer experience, pay attention to the tutorial that introduces the TOEFL CBT. This tutorial will teach you how to use the features and characteristics of the computer system to your advantage. As with any software package, there are some aspects of the testing system that are unique to the CBT environment. It is not in your best interest to learn about these features in the middle of a timed test.

• **Use Your Time Wisely**

Keep in mind that this is a timed test, and check your time regularly. As with any standardized test, you should not spend too much time on any one question. If you do not know the answer to a question, try to make an educated guess by eliminating as many of the answer choices as possible, and move on to the next question.

• **Answer Every Question in Each Section**

Because the number of questions answered is calculated into your overall score, it is in your best interest to answer every question. If you are running out of time, you will be better served by guessing, even random guessing, than by leaving the last questions unanswered.

• **Pay Particular Attention to the First Questions of Each Section**

The adaptive testing engine makes major score adjustments based on your answers to the first few questions of each section, and uses subsequent questions to "fine tune" your score. While you should not spend an undue amount of time on these questions, you should be aware that they are potentially more important than later questions, and treat them accordingly.

- **Use the "Answer Confirm" Button to Your Advantage**

It is very easy to get into the habit of choosing an answer and automatically clicking on the "Answer Confirm" button. This is a dangerous tendency. Be absolutely sure that you have clicked on the appropriate answer choice before confirming.

- **Learn as Much as You Can About the Test Before Your Test Date**

If you have access to a computer with a CD-ROM drive, obtain the TOEFL Sampler from Educational Testing Service. It is available free of charge until February 1999. The Sampler CD contains the same type of tutorials that you will see on the day you take the exam. If you do not have access to a computer, order the *TOEFL Information Bulletin for Computer-Based Testing*. Finally, if you have access to the Internet, periodically check the TOEFL website. This will provide the most up-to-date information.

The Day of the Test

On the day of the test, you should wake up early (it is hoped after a decent night's rest) and have a good breakfast. Make sure you dress comfortably, so that you are not distracted by being too hot or too cold while taking the exam. You should plan on arriving at the test center early. By being early, you will spare yourself the anxiety of being late for the test. It will also allow you to collect your thoughts and to relax before taking the exam.

Before you leave for the test center, make sure that you have your admission ticket and your signed photo file record with a recent photograph of yourself attached. In order to be admitted to the test center, you must also have a valid passport. Your passport must bear your signature and a recognizable photograph of yourself. If your passport does not meet these requirements, or if you do not have one, or if you think you may be exempt from presenting a certain form of identification, you should consult your *Bulletin of Information for TOEFL and TSE* for exact requirements.

You may want to wear a watch to the test center; however, only ordinary watches will be permitted. Watches with alarms, calculator functions, flashing lights, beeping sounds, etc., will not be allowed in the test center. In addition, no food will be allowed into the examination room.

During the Test

When you arrive at the test center, you will be assigned a seat, in the examination room, by a member of the test center staff. You will not receive a break during the examination. If you need to use the rest room, or if you become ill, you may leave the examination room, but you must first give the test supervisor your identification documents before you leave the room. If you do leave the room, you will not be allowed to make up any lost time. Start working on the Tutorials. If you do not have much experience working at a computer, the Tutorials will help ease any anxiety you may be feeling. In a clear, step-by-step method, they will provide all the computer knowledge you need to do well on the exam.

After the Test

When you have completed your exam, go home and take a well-deserved rest.

Chapter 2

The Diagnostic Test

Now that you have some background information concerning the TOEFL, you are ready to take the diagnostic test. This test is designed to help you identify where your strengths and weaknesses lie. You will want to use this information to help you study for the TOEFL. It is a complete TOEFL test, so take this test in the same way you would take the actual TOEFL. Situate yourself in a quiet room so that there will be no interruptions and keep track of the time allotted for each section. For the Diagnostic Listening Section, use the transcripts located in the back of this book. You may want a friend to read them to you as you take the Listening Section. When you are finished with the test, refer to the charts that follow to evaluate your performance.

Test of English as a Foreign Language
DIAGNOSTIC TEST
ANSWER SHEET

Section 1:
Listening Comprehension

1. Ⓐ Ⓑ Ⓒ Ⓓ
2. Ⓐ Ⓑ Ⓒ Ⓓ
3. Ⓐ Ⓑ Ⓒ Ⓓ
4. Ⓐ Ⓑ Ⓒ Ⓓ
5. Ⓐ Ⓑ Ⓒ Ⓓ
6. Ⓐ Ⓑ Ⓒ Ⓓ
7. Ⓐ Ⓑ Ⓒ Ⓓ
8. Ⓐ Ⓑ Ⓒ Ⓓ
9. Ⓐ Ⓑ Ⓒ Ⓓ
10. Ⓐ Ⓑ Ⓒ Ⓓ
11. Ⓐ Ⓑ Ⓒ Ⓓ
12. Ⓐ Ⓑ Ⓒ Ⓓ
13. Ⓐ Ⓑ Ⓒ Ⓓ
14. Ⓐ Ⓑ Ⓒ Ⓓ
15. Ⓐ Ⓑ Ⓒ Ⓓ
16. Ⓐ Ⓑ Ⓒ Ⓓ
17. Ⓐ Ⓑ Ⓒ Ⓓ
18. Ⓐ Ⓑ Ⓒ Ⓓ
19. Ⓐ Ⓑ Ⓒ Ⓓ
20. Ⓐ Ⓑ Ⓒ Ⓓ
21. Ⓐ Ⓑ Ⓒ Ⓓ
22. Ⓐ Ⓑ Ⓒ Ⓓ
23. Ⓐ Ⓑ Ⓒ Ⓓ
24. Ⓐ Ⓑ Ⓒ Ⓓ
25. Ⓐ Ⓑ Ⓒ Ⓓ
26. Ⓐ Ⓑ Ⓒ Ⓓ
27. Ⓐ Ⓑ Ⓒ Ⓓ
28. Ⓐ Ⓑ Ⓒ Ⓓ
29. Ⓐ Ⓑ Ⓒ Ⓓ
30. Ⓐ Ⓑ Ⓒ Ⓓ

31. Ⓐ Ⓑ Ⓒ Ⓓ
32. Ⓐ Ⓑ Ⓒ Ⓓ
33. Ⓐ Ⓑ Ⓒ Ⓓ
34. Ⓐ Ⓑ Ⓒ Ⓓ
35. Ⓐ Ⓑ Ⓒ Ⓓ
36. Ⓐ Ⓑ Ⓒ Ⓓ
37. Ⓐ Ⓑ Ⓒ Ⓓ
38. Ⓐ Ⓑ Ⓒ Ⓓ
39. Ⓐ Ⓑ Ⓒ Ⓓ
40. Ⓐ Ⓑ Ⓒ Ⓓ
41. Ⓐ Ⓑ Ⓒ Ⓓ
42. Ⓐ Ⓑ Ⓒ Ⓓ
43. Ⓐ Ⓑ Ⓒ Ⓓ
44. Ⓐ Ⓑ Ⓒ Ⓓ
45. Ⓐ Ⓑ Ⓒ Ⓓ
46. Ⓐ Ⓑ Ⓒ Ⓓ
47. Ⓐ Ⓑ Ⓒ Ⓓ
48. Ⓐ Ⓑ Ⓒ Ⓓ
49. Ⓐ Ⓑ Ⓒ Ⓓ
50. Ⓐ Ⓑ Ⓒ Ⓓ

Section 2:
Structure and
Written Expression

1. Ⓐ Ⓑ Ⓒ Ⓓ
2. Ⓐ Ⓑ Ⓒ Ⓓ
3. Ⓐ Ⓑ Ⓒ Ⓓ
4. Ⓐ Ⓑ Ⓒ Ⓓ
5. Ⓐ Ⓑ Ⓒ Ⓓ
6. Ⓐ Ⓑ Ⓒ Ⓓ
7. Ⓐ Ⓑ Ⓒ Ⓓ

8. Ⓐ Ⓑ Ⓒ Ⓓ
9. Ⓐ Ⓑ Ⓒ Ⓓ
10. Ⓐ Ⓑ Ⓒ Ⓓ
11. Ⓐ Ⓑ Ⓒ Ⓓ
12. Ⓐ Ⓑ Ⓒ Ⓓ
13. Ⓐ Ⓑ Ⓒ Ⓓ
14. Ⓐ Ⓑ Ⓒ Ⓓ
15. Ⓐ Ⓑ Ⓒ Ⓓ
16. Ⓐ Ⓑ Ⓒ Ⓓ
17. Ⓐ Ⓑ Ⓒ Ⓓ
18. Ⓐ Ⓑ Ⓒ Ⓓ
19. Ⓐ Ⓑ Ⓒ Ⓓ
20. Ⓐ Ⓑ Ⓒ Ⓓ
21. Ⓐ Ⓑ Ⓒ Ⓓ
22. Ⓐ Ⓑ Ⓒ Ⓓ
23. Ⓐ Ⓑ Ⓒ Ⓓ
24. Ⓐ Ⓑ Ⓒ Ⓓ
25. Ⓐ Ⓑ Ⓒ Ⓓ
26. Ⓐ Ⓑ Ⓒ Ⓓ
27. Ⓐ Ⓑ Ⓒ Ⓓ
28. Ⓐ Ⓑ Ⓒ Ⓓ
29. Ⓐ Ⓑ Ⓒ Ⓓ
30. Ⓐ Ⓑ Ⓒ Ⓓ
31. Ⓐ Ⓑ Ⓒ Ⓓ
32. Ⓐ Ⓑ Ⓒ Ⓓ
33. Ⓐ Ⓑ Ⓒ Ⓓ
34. Ⓐ Ⓑ Ⓒ Ⓓ
35. Ⓐ Ⓑ Ⓒ Ⓓ
36. Ⓐ Ⓑ Ⓒ Ⓓ
37. Ⓐ Ⓑ Ⓒ Ⓓ
38. Ⓐ Ⓑ Ⓒ Ⓓ
39. Ⓐ Ⓑ Ⓒ Ⓓ
40. Ⓐ Ⓑ Ⓒ Ⓓ

Section 3:
Reading Comprehension
and Vocabulary

1. Ⓐ Ⓑ Ⓒ Ⓓ
2. Ⓐ Ⓑ Ⓒ Ⓓ
3. Ⓐ Ⓑ Ⓒ Ⓓ
4. Ⓐ Ⓑ Ⓒ Ⓓ
5. Ⓐ Ⓑ Ⓒ Ⓓ
6. Ⓐ Ⓑ Ⓒ Ⓓ
7. Ⓐ Ⓑ Ⓒ Ⓓ
8. Ⓐ Ⓑ Ⓒ Ⓓ
9. Ⓐ Ⓑ Ⓒ Ⓓ
10. Ⓐ Ⓑ Ⓒ Ⓓ
11. Ⓐ Ⓑ Ⓒ Ⓓ
12. Ⓐ Ⓑ Ⓒ Ⓓ
13. Ⓐ Ⓑ Ⓒ Ⓓ
14. Ⓐ Ⓑ Ⓒ Ⓓ
15. Ⓐ Ⓑ Ⓒ Ⓓ
16. Ⓐ Ⓑ Ⓒ Ⓓ
17. Ⓐ Ⓑ Ⓒ Ⓓ
18. Ⓐ Ⓑ Ⓒ Ⓓ

19. Ⓐ Ⓑ Ⓒ Ⓓ
20. Ⓐ Ⓑ Ⓒ Ⓓ
21. Ⓐ Ⓑ Ⓒ Ⓓ
22. Ⓐ Ⓑ Ⓒ Ⓓ
23. Ⓐ Ⓑ Ⓒ Ⓓ
24. Ⓐ Ⓑ Ⓒ Ⓓ
25. Ⓐ Ⓑ Ⓒ Ⓓ
26. Ⓐ Ⓑ Ⓒ Ⓓ
27. Ⓐ Ⓑ Ⓒ Ⓓ
28. Ⓐ Ⓑ Ⓒ Ⓓ
29. Ⓐ Ⓑ Ⓒ Ⓓ
30. Ⓐ Ⓑ Ⓒ Ⓓ
31. Ⓐ Ⓑ Ⓒ Ⓓ
32. Ⓐ Ⓑ Ⓒ Ⓓ
33. Ⓐ Ⓑ Ⓒ Ⓓ
34. Ⓐ Ⓑ Ⓒ Ⓓ
35. Ⓐ Ⓑ Ⓒ Ⓓ
36. Ⓐ Ⓑ Ⓒ Ⓓ
37. Ⓐ Ⓑ Ⓒ Ⓓ
38. Ⓐ Ⓑ Ⓒ Ⓓ
39. Ⓐ Ⓑ Ⓒ Ⓓ

40. Ⓐ Ⓑ Ⓒ Ⓓ
41. Ⓐ Ⓑ Ⓒ Ⓓ
42. Ⓐ Ⓑ Ⓒ Ⓓ
43. Ⓐ Ⓑ Ⓒ Ⓓ
44. Ⓐ Ⓑ Ⓒ Ⓓ
45. Ⓐ Ⓑ Ⓒ Ⓓ
46. Ⓐ Ⓑ Ⓒ Ⓓ
47. Ⓐ Ⓑ Ⓒ Ⓓ
48. Ⓐ Ⓑ Ⓒ Ⓓ
49. Ⓐ Ⓑ Ⓒ Ⓓ
50. Ⓐ Ⓑ Ⓒ Ⓓ
51. Ⓐ Ⓑ Ⓒ Ⓓ
52. Ⓐ Ⓑ Ⓒ Ⓓ
53. Ⓐ Ⓑ Ⓒ Ⓓ
54. Ⓐ Ⓑ Ⓒ Ⓓ
55. Ⓐ Ⓑ Ⓒ Ⓓ
56. Ⓐ Ⓑ Ⓒ Ⓓ
57. Ⓐ Ⓑ Ⓒ Ⓓ
58. Ⓐ Ⓑ Ⓒ Ⓓ
59. Ⓐ Ⓑ Ⓒ Ⓓ
60. Ⓐ Ⓑ Ⓒ Ⓓ

TOEFL

DIAGNOSTIC TEST

Section 1:
LISTENING COMPREHENSION

TIME: 35 Minutes
50 Questions

Part A

> **DIRECTIONS**: In Part A have your friend read the short conversations and the question about what was said. **Your friend should read the conversation just one time.** Therefore, you must listen carefully to understand what your friend says. After you hear a conversation and the question about it, read the four possible answers in the test and decide which one is the best answer to the question you heard. Then, on your answer sheet, find the number of the question and fill in the space that corresponds to the answer you have chosen.

1. (A) The woman will drive her car.
    (B) The man will drive his car.
    (C) They will take a bus because neither of them want to drive.
    (D) The man will drive the woman's car.

2. (A) The man is wearing an ugly tie.
    (B) The man's tie does not match his shirt.
    (C) Although she does like the man's tie, she likes his other one better.
    (D) The man is wearing the tie she likes best.

3. (A) In a field
    (B) In a shopping mall
    (C) In the town where the man spent his childhood
    (D) In a ball park

4. (A)   Her piano playing sounded very bad.
    (B)   She thought that she practiced enough.
    (C)   She didn't practice at all last week.
    (D)   Although she knows she didn't practice as much as she should have, she didn't think her piano playing sounded bad.

5. (A)   She will not have a piece of chocolate cake.
    (B)   The woman will decide that she doesn't like chocolate cake after all.
    (C)   She will have a very large slice of chocolate cake.
    (D)   The woman will have a tiny slice of chocolate cake.

6. (A)   She read the book and thought it was great.
    (B)   She did not read the book at all.
    (C)   She started reading the book, but stopped because she didn't like it.
    (D)   She wanted to buy that book, but could not find it in the store.

7. (A)   Go make his purchase at another flower shop
    (B)   Leave the flower shop, angry that there was a problem with his order
    (C)   Wait for the flowers he ordered to be in stock again
    (D)   Buy a dozen red, long-stemmed roses instead of the flowers he originally ordered

8. (A)   She will wait a week and buy the medium-sized shirt.
    (B)   She will buy the large-sized shirt.
    (C)   She will buy the small-sized shirt.
    (D)   She decided that she doesn't like the shirt.

9. (A)   That the food at the restaurant was awful.
    (B)   He liked the food, but found the waiter to be unsatisfactory.
    (C)   The service at the restaurant was great.
    (D)   He doesn't think they should eat there again.

10. (A)   In a department store
    (B)   In a grocery store
    (C)   In a kitchen
    (D)   In a bakery

11. (A) They cannot afford a television right now.
    (B) They might be able to buy a new television if they put all their funds together.
    (C) They have to pull some strings to buy a T.V.
    (D) They have to find out another source of income in order to be able to afford it.

12. (A) Fifteen
    (B) Ten
    (C) Five
    (D) Twenty-five

13. (A) In a film studio
    (B) In a frame store
    (C) In a gift shop
    (D) In a photo-processing laboratory

14. (A) The woman cannot make him work overtime.
    (B) He was counting the woman's hours of work.
    (C) He doesn't feel like working either.
    (D) He was depending on the woman to finish the work.

15. (A) He is a lucky man.
    (B) He is happy without a job.
    (C) He is an easygoing person.
    (D) He does not need a job.

16. (A) Checking a train timetable
    (B) Waiting for a train
    (C) Waiting for a friend
    (D) Making an announcement

17. (A) Sunday
    (B) Monday
    (C) Tuesday
    (D) The woman's birthday

18. (A) The woman should start an independent business.
    (B) The woman should not interfere in his duties.
    (C) Linda is his only business partner.
    (D) The woman does not have an attitude for business.

19. (A) The man
    (B) The woman
    (C) Kathy
    (D) Johnny

20. (A) Nineteen years
    (B) Ten years
    (C) One year
    (D) One hundred years

21. (A) They met a different person by mistake.
    (B) Rich men in this town don't talk to anyone.
    (C) Donald has changed since he became rich.
    (D) Donald is rich, though he never went to school.

22. (A) Ms. Emerson has very good references.
    (B) Ms. Emerson's work is prompt.
    (C) Ms. Emerson hired good decorators.
    (D) Ms. Emerson would be the most proper person for the decorating job.

23. (A) Bill never prayed.
    (B) Bill's friend victimized him.
    (C) Bill sympathized with his friend.
    (D) Bill's friend prayed for him.

24. (A) She is cooking.
    (B) She is typing.
    (C) She is having her dinner.
    (D) She is helping the man.

25. (A) From the personal telephone book
    (B) From the directory
    (C) From the operator
    (D) From the woman

Part B

26. (A) She did not have a window.
    (B) She did not want to.
    (C) She was in a meeting.
    (D) It was snowing.

27. (A) He wanted to go skiing.
    (B) The office was too cold.
    (C) The roads became treacherous.
    (D) The roads were plowed often.

28. (A) If they put in at least five hours
    (B) If it snowed heavily
    (C) If it snowed lightly
    (D) If they closed the building

29. (A) She needed the money.
    (B) She loved her job.
    (C) Her boss would not let her.
    (D) She had to close the building.

30. (A) A penny
    (B) Snow
    (C) A new car
    (D) A full paycheck

31. (A) Dr. Downs' health
    (B) The books they have to buy for their course
    (C) Man's proposal
    (D) Fifty dollars

32. (A) Two
    (B) Three
    (C) Five
    (D) Fifty

33. (A) Because he is very strict
    (B) Because all his students are rich
    (C) Because these books are not expensive
    (D) Because he wants to discuss them in detail

34. (A) They intend to borrow them from the library.
    (B) They intend to get them from Dr. Downs.
    (C) They intend to share the books.
    (D) They intend to drop out of the course.

35. (A) She wants the man to buy three books and she herself would buy two books.
    (B) She would buy the books she likes and the man should buy the rest.
    (C) She would pay the man $50 for sharing.
    (D) Each one of them should pay half of the total amount for the books and divide them at the end of the course.

36. (A) She bought it from an auction.
    (B) She bought it in Nepal.
    (C) She bought it from a friend.
    (D) She bought it from an antique shop.

37. (A) Less than twenty-five dollars
    (B) More than one hundred dollars
    (C) Five dollars
    (D) Ten dollars

38. (A) The idol that the woman has
    (B) Traditional art products of Oriental countries
    (C) Tickets to Nepal
    (D) Natural cosmetics

39. (A) You can buy inexpensive things there.
    (B) Nepal is amazing.
    (C) The tickets to the Orient are easily available.
    (D) They have interesting cultures.

40. (A) The man
    (B) The woman
    (C) The travel agent
    (D) Their friends

Part C

> **DIRECTIONS**: In Part C your friend will read some short talks as well as some questions referring to them. **Your friend should read the talks and the questions about them just one time.** They will not be written out for you. Therefore, you must listen carefully to understand what your friend says.
>
> After you hear a question, read the four possible answers in the test and decide which one is the best answer to the question you heard. Then, on your answer sheet, find the number of the question and fill in the space that corresponds to the answer you have chosen.

41. (A) Workers Property Act
    (B) Workers Progress Appropriations
    (C) Works Progress Administration
    (D) Works Property Administration

42. (A) April 1935
    (B) May 1935
    (C) 1941
    (D) 1977

43. (A) 2 hours
    (B) 8 hours
    (C) 11 hours
    (D) 30 hours

44. (A) April 1935
    (B) May 1935
    (C) 1941
    (D) 1977

45. (A) $30 billion
    (B) $11.4 billion
    (C) $8 billion
    (D) $2 billion

46. (A) Language was the first invention of mankind.
    (B) Man depends a lot on language.
    (C) Man could not have made most of his inventions, if there was no language.
    (D) There are so many languages in the world.

47. (A) Communication through language is unlimited.
    (B) Only man uses language
    (C) There are no other means of communication.
    (D) Man's inventions are limited.

48. (A) Man would have to use war signals.
    (B) Man would have to stop inventing things.
    (C) Man would not be able to live with his fellow beings.
    (D) The world would be a place without universities, big businesses, and newspapers.

49. (A) It is passed on to the next generation in genes.
    (B) It is stored in computers.
    (C) It is passed on to the next generation through language.
    (D) The younger people start their research before the older people die.

50. (A) Facial expressions
    (B) Printed word
    (C) Universities
    (D) Language, man's greatest invention

STOP

If time still remains, you may review work only in this section.
When the time allotted is up, you may go on to the next section.

Section 2:
STRUCTURE AND WRITTEN EXPRESSION

TIME: 25 Minutes
        40 Questions

DIRECTIONS: Questions 1-15 are incomplete sentences. Beneath each sentence are four words or phrases marked (A), (B), (C), and (D). Choose the **one** word or phrase which best completes the sentence. Then, on your answer sheet, find the number of the question and fill in the space that corresponds to the answer you have chosen.

---

1. Amateur bird-watchers _____ provide scientists with a lot of information about birds.
   - (A) able to
   - (B) are able
   - (C) are helpful in
   - (D) help to

2. _____ indoor pollution we must focus on the sources of pollution rather than on ventilation.
   - (A) We must control
   - (B) Controlling
   - (C) To control
   - (D) For control

3. The space programs of the U.S. are run by NASA which _____ in 1958 with its headquarters in Washington, D.C.
   - (A) was established
   - (B) is established
   - (C) to be established
   - (D) established

4. Michelson, _____ carried out experiments on the speed of light, was the first American to receive a Nobel Prize in science.
   - (A) always
   - (B) who
   - (C) that
   - (D) which

5. Newton pointed out _____ man-made objects could be made to orbit the earth.
   (A) the possibility
   (B) that it is possible
   (C) that
   (D) the fact

6. While there is _____ single newspaper with a large national circulation, many magazines have a national readership.
   (A) not
   (B) no
   (C) no one
   (D) not any one

7. At the time of its completion, Disneyland was _____ expensive than had been expected.
   (A) very
   (B) much
   (C) very much
   (D) much more

8. _____ being the outer protective covering of the body, the skin performs many other necessary functions.
   (A) Beside
   (B) Besides
   (C) Just as
   (D) Similar

9. My friend believes that research is a group effort and _____ do I.
   (A) as
   (B) the same
   (C) so
   (D) too

10. Author Ursula LeGuin has won awards for her stories of _____ adult and children's books.
    (A) the two
    (B) both
    (C) together
    (D) also

11. Aristotle held that women needed separate educational institutions because of _____ distinctive functions in life.
    (A) one's
    (B) his
    (C) her
    (D) their

12. It was indeed a merry Christmas for Mrs. and Mr. Smith as they were joined by their daughters, _____, and their grandchildren.
    (A) their husbands
    (B) whose husbands
    (C) sons-in-law
    (D) son-in-laws

13. Clothes do _____ provide protection and maintain modesty; they define the status of the wearer.
    (A) help in
    (B) more than
    (C) unlike
    (D) much

14. _____ Egyptian pyramids, the Mayan pyramids served as temples.
    (A) Just as
    (B) Same as
    (C) Unlike
    (D) Contrary to

15. *Don Juan,* _____ by Warner Bros. in 1926, was the first feature film to have a sound track.
    (A) to be made
    (B) to be done
    (C) made
    (D) done

DIRECTIONS: In questions 16-40 each sentence has four underlined words or phrases marked (A), (B), (C), and (D). Choose the **one** word or phrase which is incorrect and must be changed to make the sentence correct. Then, on your answer sheet, find the number of the question and fill in the space that corresponds to the answer you have chosen.

16. Insect blood should be green, yellow, or colorless.
      A   B   C   D

17. Folk artists are people who know that to express their creativity naturally without
                             A   B   C   D
any formal training in art.

18. Some parents let their children to explore in and around the home as that is one
                A   B   C   D
way of learning unconsciously.

19. If he was not an insurance agent, he would now be publishing poetry.
      A   B   C   D

20. Daedalus wished that he was able to fly and so he made a pair of wings for himself.
                      A   B   C   D

21. Only few historical films show their characters wearing authentic period costumes.
      A   B   C   D

22. It is by now a well-attested fact of which the major advantage of microwave
    A   B
cooking is the speed with which food is cooked.
        C   D

23. President Kennedy <u>hopes</u> to see man <u>land</u> on the moon but did not live to see the
    hoped
            A   B   C

    <u>hope</u> realized.
     D

24. The Pilgrim Fathers <u>went to Holland</u> before sailing to America on the *Mayflower*,
                    A   B⃝

    <u>in 1602</u>, <u>weren't they?</u>
     C   D

25. <u>As</u> my babysitter was ill, my friend <u>promised</u> to <u>watch</u> my baby <u>for mine</u>.
     A   B   C   D⃝

26. I was able to buy a <u>copy</u> of Cooper's complete <u>work</u> at a bargain price, <u>from</u> a
                  A   B C⃝   D

    store dealing in old books.

27. When he <u>sighted</u> land, <u>a little</u> did Columbus <u>know</u> that he was <u>discovering</u> a new
                              A⃝   B   C   D

    continent.

28. While <u>in some</u> parts of the world it is jewelry that indicates high <u>economic status</u>,
         A   B

    <u>in the other</u>, <u>it is</u> fur coats.
     C   D

29. This student is <u>cleverer</u> <u>than</u> diligent <u>but</u> <u>that</u> will not do.
    more clever
                      A   B   C D

30. <u>Instead of</u> all the <u>hard work</u> she was <u>made to do</u>, Cinderella never <u>complained to</u>
     A⃝   B   C   D

    her father.

31.   The mother asked her son what did he want for his birthday.
                              A   B   C D

32.   Efforts to save the brown pelican have been successful, and experts feel that the
                       for n A   B
        bird need not longer be on the endangered list.
               C   D

33.   It is little known that Alexander Graham Bell was associated with the National
               A   B
        Geographic Society, devoting a great deal of his time and energy to them.
                                        C   D

        has proven
34.   Research has prove that culture-specific texts pose a comprehension problem to
                       A   B   C
        readers from other cultures.
               D

                                        at
35.   I wish rather that I were browsing in a library than doing chores around the house.
               A   B   C   D

36.   The Romantic poet Keats died by tuberculosis at a very young age.
                                A   B   C D

37.   I need a room all to myself as for studying in peace and quiet.
               A   B   C   D

                                                        past
38.   My friend told she would meet me at the library if she did not get delayed at work.
                    A   B   C D

39.   Hand-crafting flutes from Boston have become popular with flutists all over the
               A   B   C   D
        world.

40. In regions, where it is too much hot, people use draped clothing instead of tailored
           A   B   C
    clothing for a freer flow of air.
           D

STOP

If time still remains, you may review work only in this section.
When the time allotted is up, you may go on to the next section.

Section 3:
READING COMPREHENSION AND VOCABULARY

TIME: 55 Minutes
60 Questions

DIRECTIONS: In this section you will read several passages. Each one is followed by several questions about it. You are to choose the best answer to each question, marked (A), (B), (C), and (D). Then, on your answer sheet, find the number of the question and fill in the space that corresponds to the answer you have chosen.

Questions 1–10 refer to the following passage:

1   Highly talented artists sometimes spend months duplicating the paintings of the old masters. These copies are so perfect that it is virtually impossible to tell them from the real thing. This is a serious problem in the art world. Tests can show if the paints are old or new, but most chemical tests require a fair-sized paint sample. A new test solves this problem. The
5 exquisitely narrow beam of a laser is used to vaporize a hundred-thousandth of a square inch of pigment surface. This tiny sample, invisible to the naked eye, is large enough for a spectroscope to "fingerprint" a paint by disclosing what elements it contains, and in what proportions.

1.   The main idea of this passage is
    (A)   painting duplication.
    (B)   master artists.
    (C)   paint analysis.
    (D)   testing paintings for authenticity.

2.   In the third sentence the word "this" refers to
    (A)   telling copies from real paintings.
    (B)   who painted which paintings.
    (C)   why painting copies are made.
    (D)   kinds of paints used.

3.   According to this passage
    (A)   most chemical tests require a fair-sized paint sample.

     (B)   there is only one way to determine the age and composition of paint.

     (C)   old and new paints test the same and differences cannot be shown.

     (D)   all tests require a large-sized sample.

4.   According to the passage,
     (A)   a spectroscope can determine paint composition.
     (B)   a spectroscope can determine where paint was bought.
     (C)   a spectroscope can determine the artist's identity if unknown.
     (D)   a spectroscope is an old machine.

5.   The next paragraph in this discussion most likely would talk about
     (A)   how art is bought and sold.
     (B)   prices of artists' paints.
     (C)   an example of how the spectroscope is used by art dealers.
     (D)   prices of paintings.

6.   In line 5 "exquisitely" means which of the following?
     (A)   Precisely
     (B)   Beautifully
     (C)   Fashionably
     (D)   Pleasantly

7.   A hundred-thousandth of a square inch is represented by which of the following?
     (A)   100,000
     (B)   1,000
     (C)   .001
     (D)   .00001

8.   In line 6 "naked" most nearly means
     (A)   unclothed.
     (B)   unaided.
     (C)   unseeing.
     (D)   unable.

9.   In the second line, "them" refers to
     (A)   artists.
     (B)   copies.
     (C)   months.
     (D)   masters.

10. From this passage, one could infer that paint analysis is necessary in the art world because
   (A) dealers need detailed records of paint composition.
   (B) forgers are adept at copying originals.
   (C) the abilities of the old masters have been lost.
   (D) spectroscopic analysis needs to be tested many times before it can be proven.

Questions 11–20 refer to the following passage:

1   Around the year 1500, scientists and scholars engaged in bitter debates over the origin of fossils. One group held the modern view that fossils were the remains of prehistoric plants and animals. This group was opposed by another which declared that fossils were either freaks of nature or creations of the devil. Some of these people held that fossils were relics
5   of the biblical flood and that they were the remains of men who perished in that disaster. But, over the past two centuries, less than seven human generations, scientists have begun to study and to understand the history of life on this planet. Progress has been impressive. Nearly 200,000 species of fossil organisms have been discovered and described; the evolutionary continuum that links life to that of earlier epochs has been extended far into the geologic past,
10   and great strides have been taken toward deciphering the timing and nature of the major events in the development of life on Earth.

11. In line 1, "bitter" most nearly means
   (A) heated.
   (B) sour.
   (C) acrid.
   (D) sweet.

12. In which century did scientists begin to start understanding the history of life on this planet?
   (A) Fifteenth century
   (B) Sixteenth century
   (C) Seventeenth century
   (D) Eighteenth century

13. According to one of the groups, fossils were which of the following?
   (A) Strange rock formations
   (B) Remains of demons
   (C) Creations of God
   (D) Scientific pranks

14. In line 4, "relics" most nearly means
     (A)   remains.
     (B)   scientists.
     (C)   epochs.
     (D)   events.

15. The next paragraph that would likely follow would be about
     (A)   witchcraft.
     (B)   biblical disasters.
     (C)   geological epochs.
     (D)   biological processes.

16. This passage leads one to believe that a generation is
     (A)   10–15 years.
     (B)   16–18 years.
     (C)   18–20 years.
     (D)   26–30 years.

17. One could infer that the author feels that progress in this area has been
     (A)   not important.
     (B)   not possible.
     (C)   not measurable.
     (D)   significant.

18. "Nearly," as it is used in this paragraph, means the same as
     (A)   almost.
     (B)   more than.
     (C)   exactly.
     (D)   far more than.

19. A replacement for the word "epochs," as it is used in this paragraph, is
     (A)   biologies.
     (B)   geological periods.
     (C)   chemicals.
     (D)   stars.

20.   The major idea of this paragraph deals with
      (A)   history.
      (B)   biological forms.
      (C)   the Earth.
      (D)   the history of life.

Questions 21–30 refer to the following passage:

1   Consumers who believe a company is well run and shows promise of doing well in the
stock market will invest in that company's stock. If the company shows a profit, the investor
will receive a dividend check. Buying United States Savings Bonds is another well-known
way of investing money. Some companies offer a dividend reinvestment plan: the profits,
5   instead of being sent to the investor in the form of a check, can be reinvested automatically
in the company's stock. To encourage this practice, companies offer several incentives. For
example, if the dividend is too small to buy a whole share, most companies allow the investor
to purchase part of a share until enough dividends accumulate for a whole share. In addition,
some companies offer shareholders a discount off the market price of their stock. A five
10   percent discount is the usual rate. Finally, about 70 percent of companies charge no fee if the
stockholder wishes to purchase more shares for cash.

21.   According to the passage, "consumers" are which of the following?
      (A)   Artists
      (B)   Presidents
      (C)   Companies
      (D)   Investors

22.   If a company is managed well and has a bright future, investors will
      (A)   buy company stock.
      (B)   sell company stock.
      (C)   dump company stock.
      (D)   discount company stock.

23.   What is another investment plan besides stock according to the passage?
      (A)   Antique cars
      (B)   Cash
      (C)   Savings bonds
      (D)   Gold

24.   What is the normal discount percentage for dividend reinvestment?
      (A)   50%
      (B)   15%

(C)   5%

(D)   .5%

25.   In line 6, "incentives" most nearly means
    (A)   inducements.
    (B)   dividends.
    (C)   companies.
    (D)   stockholders.

26.   Approximately what percentage of companies do not charge a fee for cash purchases?
    (A)   Seven percent
    (B)   Seventeen percent
    (C)   Seventy percent
    (D)   Seven hundred percent

27.   Which of the following is an incentive to reinvest dividends?
    (A)   Purchase of partial shares
    (B)   Purchase of a new car
    (C)   Purchase of a fur coat
    (D)   Purchase of a new home

28.   What can be inferred about the author's attitude toward investment?
    (A)   He warns everyone against doing it.
    (B)   He thinks it is a good idea.
    (C)   He thinks people should invest in art instead.
    (D)   He thinks it steals money from the elderly.

29.   In line 9, "their" refers to
    (A)   checks.
    (B)   dividends.
    (C)   shareholders.
    (D)   companies.

30.   When will a shareholder receive a dividend check?
    (A)   When the stock is sold
    (B)   When the company closes down
    (C)   When the company makes a profit
    (D)   When the shareholders vote on it

Questions 31–40 refer to the following passage:

1   Jupiter is the largest planet in the solar system and a member of the Jovian planets. Exploring spacecraft have found Jupiter to be a whirling ball of liquid hydrogen topped with a uniquely colorful atmosphere which is mostly hydrogen and helium, but also contains small amounts of methane, ammonia, ethane, acetylene, phosphene, germanium, tetrahydride, and
5   possibly hydrogen cyanide.

Jupiter's "Great Red Spot" was first discovered in 1664. It is a tremendous atmospheric storm, similar to an Earth hurricane rotating counterclockwise. The color of this storm has diminished over the years, so that only a faint outline remains.

Jupiter rotates at a dizzying pace, once every 9 hours and 50 minutes. It takes the
10   massive planet 12 Earth-years to complete a revolution around the Sun.

31.   In what century was the "Great Red Spot" discovered?
(A)   Fifteenth century
(B)   Sixteenth century
(C)   Seventeenth century
(D)   Eighteenth century

32.   If the time is 10:30 p.m. on Earth, at what time will Jupiter complete one rotation?
(A)   12:30 p.m.
(B)   12:30 a.m.
(C)   8:20 p.m.
(D)   8:20 a.m.

33.   In line 8, "diminished" most nearly means
(A)   increased.
(B)   lessened.
(C)   brightened.
(D)   grown.

34.   Jupiter's "colorful" atmosphere occurs
(A)   near the center of the planet.
(B)   only near the "Great Red Spot."
(C)   near the upper atmosphere.
(D)   only in the lower atmosphere.

35.   How did scientists learn the composition of Jupiter's atmosphere?
(A)   Telescopes
(B)   Satellites
(C)   Aliens
(D)   Guesses

36. From information in the passage, one can infer that Jupiter has some Earth-like
     (A)   air.
     (B)   water.
     (C)   atmospheric disturbances.
     (D)   dirt.

37. "Jupiter rotates at a dizzying pace" implies that a person accustomed to Earth's
     rotational speed would
     (A)   never fall down.
     (B)   easily stand straight and tall.
     (C)   experience no uneasiness.
     (D)   be quite uncomfortable on Jupiter.

38. The listing of elements and gases found on Jupiter indicates
     (A)   there are similar elements and gases on Jupiter and on Earth.
     (B)   no common elements and gases exist on Earth and Jupiter.
     (C)   there are liquids on Earth but none on Jupiter.
     (D)   there are only solids on Jupiter.

39. The word "massive" as it is used in the passage refers to
     (A)   Earth's size.
     (B)   Jupiter's size.
     (C)   Jupiter's rotational speed.
     (D)   Jupiter's color.

40. As it used in the selection, "uniquely" refers to
     (A)   the unique size of the planet Jupiter.
     (B)   the difference between Jupiter's rotation on its axis and its revolution around
           the sun.
     (C)   Jupiter's atmosphere and its color.
     (D)   the elements of Jupiter's atmosphere.

Questions 41–50 refer to the following passage:

1   Tests are a yardstick. Schools use them to measure, and then improve, education.
Some tests indicate that schools need to strengthen courses or change teaching techniques.
Other tests compare students by schools, school districts, or cities. Tests can determine how
well your child is doing. That's very important.

5   Most of the tests your child will take are "teacher-made." That is, teachers design
them. These tests are associated with the grades on report cards. They help measure a
student's progress, telling the teacher and student whether he or she is keeping up with the
class, needs extra help or, perhaps, is far ahead of the other students.

41.   This article was written for which of the following?
      (A)   Students
      (B)   Grandparents
      (C)   Teachers
      (D)   Parents and guardians

42.   The analogy used is that tests are like
      (A)   a report card.
      (B)   a musical instrument.
      (C)   a measuring stick.
      (D)   a game.

43.   "Teacher-made" refers to
      (A)   tests.
      (B)   report cards.
      (C)   schools.
      (D)   comparisons.

44.   The passage implies that the common characteristic shared by all tests is that they
      compare students by
      (A)   cities.
      (B)   knowledge level.
      (C)   school districts.
      (D)   schools.

45.   The term "strengthen courses" in this article means
      (A)   change course textbooks.
      (B)   change courses so that curriculum presentation is more effective.
      (C)   get a better teacher.
      (D)   give more homework.

46.   What do schools use tests for?
      (A)   To improve education
      (B)   To weed out problem children
      (C)   To keep students busy
      (D)   To measure teachers' progress

47.   What information do tests give teachers?
      (A)   Which students are potential troublemakers
      (B)   Which students need help

     (C)   Which students are good athletes

     (D)   Which students will become actors

48.   The author of this passage implies
     (A)   all tests should be called off..
     (B)   teachers need to develop better tests.
     (C)   tests are necessary.
     (D)   tests are inaccurate.

49.   In line 6, "associated" most nearly means
     (A)   related.
     (B)   unrelated.
     (C)   competing.
     (D)   fighting.

50.   The paragraph that would most likely follow would be about
     (A)   the ability of tests to help children who are having difficulties.
     (B)   the use of tests in the working world.
     (C)   the need for multiple-choice tests.
     (D)   the course requirements of various school districts.

Questions 51–60 refer to the following passage:

1   Creosote is a black, tarry liquid that comes from the condensation of wood gases which are not burned in the combustion process. There is no way to prevent the formation of creosote, but it can be minimized by avoiding smoldering fires, burning seasoned hardwoods, and using interior chimneys.

5   Creosote is dangerous only when it is allowed to accumulate in large amounts. It can then become the fuel for a chimney fire.

51.   In line 2, "combustion" refers to
     (A)   burning.
     (B)   condensing.
     (C)   forming.
     (D)   accumulating.

52.   When can creosote be a hazard?
     (A)   When it heats up
     (B)   When it is placed in water
     (C)   When it is allowed to accumulate
     (D)   When it is not burned in the combustion process

53. According to the passage,
    (A) creosote can be eliminated.
    (B) creosote formation cannot be prevented.
    (C) creosote is a helpful by-product.
    (D) creosote does not occur normally.

54. Creosote is which of the following?
    (A) Solid
    (B) Liquid
    (C) Gas
    (D) Catalyst

55. In line 5, "accumulate" most nearly means
    (A) lessen.
    (B) aggrandize.
    (C) shake down.
    (D) build-up.

56. The main idea of this passage is
    (A) uses of creosote.
    (B) ways to manufacture creosote.
    (C) burning creosote.
    (D) the properties and dangerous nature of creosote.

57. "Minimized" as used in this passage means the same as
    (A) made larger.
    (B) reduced.
    (C) kept in certain areas.
    (D) allowed to grow.

58. The conditions for development of creosote require
    (A) heat.
    (B) combustion.
    (C) intense cold.
    (D) moderate cold.

59. According to the passage, chimney fire is
    (A) uncontained.
    (B) raging.

(C)   hotter than 520 degrees Fahrenheit.

(D)   preventable.

60.   In line 3, smoldering refers to

    (A)   creosote.

    (B)   hard woods.

    (C)   fire.

    (D)   liquid.

STOP

If time still remains, you may review work only in this section.

DIAGNOSTIC TEST

ANSWER KEY

SECTION 1: LISTENING COMPREHENSION

1.	(B)	14.	(D)	26.	(A)	39.	(D)
2.	(C)	15.	(C)	27.	(C)	40.	(A)
3.	(C)	16.	(B)	28.	(D)	41.	(C)
4.	(D)	17.	(D)	29.	(A)	42.	(A)
5.	(D)	18.	(B)	30.	(D)	43.	(D)
6.	(C)	19.	(A)	31.	(B)	44.	(C)
7.	(D)	20.	(D)	32.	(C)	45.	(B)
8.	(A)	21.	(C)	33.	(D)	46.	(C)
9.	(B)	22.	(D)	34.	(C)	47.	(A)
10.	(B)	23.	(B)	35.	(D)	48.	(D)
11.	(B)	24.	(A)	36.	(B)	49.	(C)
12.	(A)	25.	(C)	37.	(A)	50.	(D)
13.	(D)			38.	(B)		

SECTION 2: STRUCTURE AND WRITTEN EXPRESSION

1.	(D)	11.	(D)	21.	(A)	31.	(B)
2.	(C)	12.	(C)	22.	(B)	32.	(C)
3.	(A)	13.	(B)	23.	(A)	33.	(D)
4.	(B)	14.	(C)	24.	(D)	34.	(A)
5.	(C)	15.	(C)	25.	(D)	35.	(A)
6.	(B)	16.	(B)	26.	(B)	36.	(B)
7.	(D)	17.	(B)	27.	(A)	37.	(B)
8.	(B)	18.	(B)	28.	(C)	38.	(A)
9.	(C)	19.	(A)	29.	(A)	39.	(A)
10.	(B)	20.	(A)	30.	(A)	40.	(B)

SECTION 3: READING COMPREHENSION AND VOCABULARY

1.	(D)	16.	(D)	31.	(C)	46.	(A)
2.	(A)	17.	(D)	32.	(D)	47.	(B)
3.	(A)	18.	(A)	33.	(B)	48.	(C)
4.	(A)	19.	(B)	34.	(C)	49.	(A)
5.	(C)	20.	(D)	35.	(B)	50.	(A)
6.	(A)	21.	(D)	36.	(C)	51.	(A)
7.	(D)	22.	(A)	37.	(D)	52.	(C)
8.	(B)	23.	(C)	38.	(A)	53.	(B)
9.	(B)	24.	(C)	39.	(B)	54.	(B)
10.	(B)	25.	(A)	40.	(C)	55.	(D)
11.	(A)	26.	(C)	41.	(D)	56.	(D)
12.	(D)	27.	(A)	42.	(C)	57.	(B)
13.	(B)	28.	(B)	43.	(A)	58.	(B)
14.	(A)	29.	(D)	44.	(B)	59.	(D)
15.	(C)	30.	(C)	45.	(B)	60.	(C)

Detailed Explanations of Answers

DIAGNOSTIC TEST

Section 1:
LISTENING COMPREHENSION

Part A

1. **(B)** The question asks: "What will they probably do about driving to the movies?" The answer is (B), The man will drive his car. When the man asked the woman who was driving, she responded "...I don't have enough gas in my car."

2. **(C)** The question asks: "What is the woman trying to say?" The answer is (C), Although she does like the man's tie, she likes his other one better. When the man asked the woman if she liked his tie, she responded, "Yes, but I prefer the one you wore yesterday." She meant that although she did indeed like his tie, she did not like it as much as the one he wore the day before.

3. **(C)** The question asks: "Where did this conversation probably take place?" The answer is (C), In the town where the man spent his childhood. When asked if the shopping mall was new, the man's response was, "Probably. When I was a kid there was a field here. We would come and play ball after school." The man remembers playing ball in the field where the shopping mall now stands.

4. **(D)** The question asks: "What does the woman mean?" The answer is (D), Although she knows she didn't practice as much as she should have, she didn't think her piano playing sounded bad. When asked if she practiced last week, she responded, "...I probably should have practiced more, but I really didn't think it sounded that bad."

5. **(D)** The question asks: "What will the woman probably do?" The answer is (D), The woman will have a tiny slice of chocolate cake. When asked if she would like a piece

of chocolate cake, the woman responded, "...I suppose a tiny slice wouldn't really hurt." She will have a tiny piece although she is on a diet.

6. **(C)**   The question asks: "What does the woman mean?" The answer is (C), She started reading the book, but stopped because she didn't like it. When asked if she had read the book yet, the woman replied, "I started reading that book, but I couldn't get into it." She meant that although she did begin reading the book, she was unable to finish it because it was not to her liking.

7. **(D)**   The questions asks: "What will the man probably do?" The answer is (D), Buy a dozen red, long-stemmed roses instead of the flowers he originally ordered. Upon hearing that the flowers he originally ordered were no longer in stock, he asked, "Well, do you have any red, long-stemmed roses in stock?" He was willing to buy the roses instead of the other flowers he ordered.

8. **(A)**   The question asks: "What will the woman probably do?" The answer is (A), She will wait a week and buy the medium-sized shirt. The woman said, "I love this shirt..." and then stated that neither the small nor large size fit her properly. The man said that they didn't have that shirt in a medium, but suggested that "...if you wait a week, that size will be shipped to us."

9. **(B)**   The questions asks: "What does the man think about the restaurant?" The answer is (B), He liked the food, but found the waiter to be unsatisfactory. The woman said, "The food at that restaurant was very good, but I thought the service was poor..." and the man said, "Yes, we should have left the waiter a smaller tip."

10. **(B)**   The question asks: "Where did this conversation probably take place?" The answer is (B), In a grocery store. The woman said "I have to get the milk, butter and eggs in aisle 8...will you please go and get the flour, oatmeal and chocolate chips?" Out of the choices provided, "In a grocery store" would be the only place where all of those items could be found in their respective aisles.

11. **(B)**   The question asked was, "What does the man mean?" The correct answer is (B), They might be able to buy a new television if they put all their funds together. When the woman asked, "Do you think we can afford a new television right now?" the man answered, "May be. If we pool all our resources together." "To pool resources together" means to put money together.

12. **(A)**   The question asked was, "How many total invitations does the woman have to send?" The correct answer is (A), Fifteen. When the man asked, "Did you send all the

invitations today?" the woman answered, "I sent ten of them today and I will send five tomorrow. Then I will be done." Ten plus five makes it fifteen.

13. **(D)**   The question asked was, "Where did this conversation take place?" The correct answer is (D), In a photo-processing laboratory. The woman wanted to get a film developed. The only place she could get it done would be in a photo developing laboratory.

14. **(D)**   The question asked was, "What does the man imply?" The correct answer is (D), He was depending on the woman to finish the work. The woman told him that she was not inclined to work overtime. And he responded, "You can't do that to me. I am counting on you to finish this work today." "To count on someone" means to depend or rely on someone.

15. **(C)**   The question asked was, "What is the man's opinion about Shawn?" The correct answer is (C), He is an easygoing person. The man said, "...He is a happy-go-lucky man." "Happy-go-lucky" means easygoing.

16. **(B)**   The question asked was, "What are these people doing?" The correct answer is (B), Waiting for train. The woman said, "They said the train is 15 minutes late. It has been more than half an hour since then." The man responded, "All we can do is to wait." Obviously, the train is late and they are waiting for it.

17. **(D)**   The question asked was, "On what day did this conversation take place?" The correct answer is (D), The woman's birthday. The man said, "Many, many happy returns of the day. And here is a small birthday gift for you from all of us."

18. **(B)**   The question asked was, "What does the man mean?" The correct answer is (B), The woman should not interfere in his duties. When the woman asked, "Are you going to grant a day off for Linda?" the man retorted, "Will you please mind your own business?" "To mind one's business" means not to interfere in anyone's affairs.

19. **(A)**   The question asked was, "Who baked the cake?" The correct answer is (A), The man. The man said, "Can we eat the cake now? I would like to see how successful my first attempt at baking is."

20. **(D)**   The question asked was, "About how long ago was the building built?" The correct answer is (D), One hundred years. The man said, "...It was built in the last decade of the nineteenth century." The last decade of the nineteenth century was about a hundred years ago.

21. **(C)**   The question asked was, "What does the man mean?" The correct answer is (C), Donald has changed since he became rich. The man said, "He (Donald) is not the same man that went to school with us." "Not to remain the same" means to change.

22. **(D)**   The question asked was, "What does the woman think about Ms. Emerson?" The correct answer is (D), Ms. Emerson would be the most proper person for the decorating job. When the man asked, "Do you think we should hire Ms. Emerson for this decorating job?" the woman answered, "She would be a perfect choice." She was not referring directly to Ms. Emerson's references, promptness, or decorators.

23. **(B)**   The question asked was, "What does the man mean?" The correct answer is (B), Bill's friend victimized him. The man said, "He fell prey to his friend's show of sympathy." "To fall prey to" means to be victimized by.

24. **(A)**   The question asked was, "What is the woman doing?" The correct answer is (A), She is cooking. When the man asked, "Can you help me with some typing?" the woman answered, "Let me finish making this soup. Then, let's have dinner. After dinner, I can do all the typing." So at the moment the woman is cooking.

25. **(C)**   The question asked was, "How did the man find Dr. James's number?" The correct answer is (C), From the operator. The man said, "…you said that his number was in our telephone book; it was not. I couldn't find it in the directory either. At last I called the operator and got it."

Part B

26. **(A)**   The question asked was, "Why could the woman not answer the man's question?" The correct response is (A), She did not have a window." When asked if she knew if it was snowing she replied, "No, I have been in my office all morning and I do not have a window."

27. **(C)**   The question was "Why did the man have to leave if it snowed?" The correct response is (C), The roads became treacherous. The man told the woman, "I live over an hour away and the roads can get very bad when it snows." Treacherous means bad or dangerous in this context.

28. **(D)**   The question was "Under what conditions would the employees get paid if it snowed?" The correct response is (D), If they closed the building. The man's response to the woman's inquiry about leaving early was "Only if they decide to close the building."

Although "If it snowed heavily" they might decide to close the building, it is not guaranteed.

29. **(A)**   The question asked was "Why did the woman not want to leave early?" The correct answer is (A), She needed the money. She says, "I could always take the work home with me, but I cannot afford to go without pay." "Pay" in this case refers to her paycheck or the money she would receive for working.

30. **(D)**   The question asked was "What did the man say he needed?" The correct response is (D), A full paycheck. He tells the woman, "I need every penny of my paycheck." This is another way of saying that he needs to get all the money that he normally gets in his paycheck.

31. **(B)**   The question asked was, "What are these people concerned about?" The correct answer is (B), The books they have to buy for their course. The conversation started with the man asking, "Did you see the list of books for this course?" Then he asked, "Are you going to buy them?" And the woman answered, "I don't know. These books are expensive. And I don't have a lot of money on me." So their concern is buying the books.

32. **(C)**   The question asked was, "How many books do they have to buy?" The correct answer is (C), Five. The woman said, "Dr. Downs said that he expects us to have the first five on the list."

33. **(D)**   The question asked was, "Why does Dr. Downs want his students to have these five books on the list?" The correct answer is (D), Because he wants to discuss them in detail. The woman said, "Dr. Downs said he expects us to have the first five on the list. He is going to discuss them in detail."

34. **(C)**   The question asked was, "How do these people plan to solve their problems about books?" The correct answer is (C), They intend to share the books. The woman mentioned that she did not have enough money to buy the books, as they are expensive. The man asked, "How about sharing them with me?" The woman responded, "Sounds good." So they intended to solve the problem by sharing the books.

35. **(D)**   The question asked was, "How does the woman want to share the books?" The correct answer is (D), Each one of them should pay half of the total amount for the books and divide them at the end of the course. The woman said, "I would rather do it this way; we pay fifty-fifty for the books now. And at the end of the course you can take the books you find more interesting and I can take the ones I like."

36. **(B)**   The question asked was, "From where did the woman get the idol?" The correct answer is (B), She bought it in Nepal. When the man asked, "...Did you buy it from an antique auction." The woman answered, "No. I bought this in Nepal last summer."

37. **(A)**   The question asked was, "How much did the woman pay for the idol?" The correct answer is (A), Less than twenty-five dollars. When the man asked, "...Is this very expensive?" the woman answered, "You won't believe the price I paid for it. It is less than twenty-five dollars."

38. **(B)**   The question asked was, "What could be sold for hundreds of dollars?" The correct answer is (B), Traditional art products of the Oriental countries. During the conversation, the woman said, "In some of the Oriental countries, the traditional art products are so beautiful, they could be easily sold for hundreds of dollars."

39. **(D)**   The question asked was, "Why does the woman recommend a trip to the Oriental countries?" The correct answer is (D), They have interesting cultures. When the man mentioned that he was planning a trip to the Oriental countries, the woman said, "You must take it. Many of the countries are not very advanced technologically, but they have very interesting cultures...."

40. **(A)**   The question asked was, "Who is planning a trip to the Oriental countries?" The correct answer is (A), The man. In the conversation the man mentioned, "...Actually I was planning a trip to the Orient myself."

Part C

41. **(C)**   "What does WPA stand for?" The correct response is (C), Works Progress Administration. This is given in the first line of the paragraph.

42. **(A)**   "When was the Emergency Relief Appropriations Act begun?" The correct response is (A), April 1935. May 1935 was when the Works Progress Administration was begun. 1941 is when the WPA ended. 1977 relates to nothing in the paragraph.

43. **(D)**   "How many hours per week did the WPA employ people for?" The correct response is (D), 30 hours. This information was given in the second line of the reading with "The WPA employed people from the relief roles for 30 hours of work a week at pay double the relief payment but less than private employment."

44. **(C)**   The question asked was "When did the WPA program end?" The correct response is (C), 1941. This questions tests the ability to order and recognize chronological events.

45. **(B)**   The question was "How much did the WPA program cost?" The correct response is (B), $11.4 billion. In this question you must recognize the monetary units and organize the numbers you heard in the passage.

46. **(C)**   The question asked was, "For what reason is language the greatest invention of mankind?" The correct answer is (C), Man could not have made most of his inventions, if there was no language. In the beginning of the talk, the speaker said, "If I had to name a single great invention of mankind, I would say language. There has been no greater invention; because if there was no language, most of man's inventions would not have been made."

47. **(A)**   The question asked was, "What makes language the greatest means of communication?" The correct answer is (A), Communication through language is unlimited. In the talk you heard, "Though there are other means of communication like signals in war, signs made with hands, and facial expressions, they are not as powerful as language. The communication possible through these means is limited." This means that language is the most powerful means of communication as it is unlimited.

48. **(D)**   The question asked was, "What would be the condition of the world if there was no printed word?" The correct answer is (D), The world would be a place without universities, big businesses, and newspapers. The last sentence of the talk was, "There would be no universities, no business contracts, no political treaties, and no newspapers, if we did not have the printed word."

49. **(C)**   The question asked was, "How does the knowledge gained by one generation become the basis for the inventions of the next?" The correct answer is (C), It is passed on to the next generation through language. In the talk you heard, "Knowledge gained by one generation could become the basis of inventions of the next generation only because of language."

50. **(D)**   The question asked was, "What was the main topic of the talk?" The correct answer is (D), Language, man's greatest invention. In the beginning of the talk, the speaker made a statement that language is the greatest invention of mankind. And every sentence in the talk supported that statement.

Section 2:
STRUCTURE AND WRITTEN EXPRESSION

1.　**(D)**　(D) is the right answer; the causative verb **help** requires as its object an infinitive. (A) Lacks a finite verb to complete the sentence. (B) Lacks the preposition **to** to complete the sentence. (C) Lacks a finite verb to complete the sentence.

2.　**(C)**　(C) is the right answer; the infinitive expresses purpose with **indoor pollution** as its object. (A) The clause is not required here. (B) The participle does not help to complete the sentence. (D) **For control** does not adequately express purpose; it needs the preposition **of.**

3.　**(A)**　(A) is the finite past tense verb in the passive voice that completes the adjectival subordinate clause beginning with **which.** (B) The present tense does not agree with **1958.** (C) lacks a finite verb to complete the subordinate clause beginning with **which;** it also expresses futurity and is inappropriate here. (D) The finite past tense is not in the passive voice.

4.　**(B)**　(B) The relative pronoun **who** helps complete the adjectival subordinate clause **who carried out experiments on the speed of light.** (A) The adverb does not help complete the subordinate clause. (C) The relative pronoun **that** cannot refer to proper nouns. (D) The relative pronoun **which** is not used to refer to persons.

5.　**(C)**　(C) is the right answer; the conjunction **that** joins the main clause **Newton pointed out** and the subordinate clause **man-made objects could be made to orbit the earth.** (A) The noun will not help join the main clause and subordinate clause. (B) The clause will not help join the main clause and the subordinate clause. (D) **The fact** is a noun, not a conjunction.

6.　**(B)**　(B) is the right answer; the adjective **no** along with the adjective **single** qualifies newspaper. (A) Forms a negative with **is** but the sentence will be incomplete without the indefinite article **a.** (C) The numeral **one** is redundant. (D) The numeral **one** is redundant.

7.　**(D)**　(D) is the right answer; the comparative degree (with intensifier) is qualifying the adjective **expensive.** (A) **Very** is an intensifier, not an adjective in the comparative degree. (B) is an adjective in the positive degree and not appropriate here. (C) is an adjective in the positive degree with an intensifier and is not appropriate here.

8.   **(B)**   (B) is the right answer; the adverb **besides** means **in addition to** and modifies **being.** (A) is a preposition meaning **next to.** (C) is an adverb expressing likeness in two things. (D) is an adjective expressing similarity between two things.

9.   **(C)**   (C) is the right answer; the adverb modifying **do** stands for the idea already stated: **believes that research is a group effort.** To avoid repetition of the idea, this is the normal order of words: so + V + subject. This is the usual form for expressing affirmative agreement. (A) **As** is an adjective that can qualify **I** but not the verb **do.** (B) **the same** is a pronoun and so can't modify the verb **do.** (D) is an adverb that can modify **do** but cannot appear at the beginning of a clause; we may say **I do too.**

10.   **(B)**   (B) is the right answer because it completes the correlative conjunction pair: **both...and.** (A) is not correct because it means that the author won the awards for only two books. (C) is incorrect because it attempts to use **together** as an adjective, an incorrect form. (D) **Also** is used to add on, but nothing is there to add on to.

11.   **(D)**   (D) is the right answer; the possessive plural pronoun agrees with **women.** (A) The possessive pronoun **one's** can agree with the indefinite pronoun **one** but not with **women.** (B) The possessive pronoun **his** is in the singular and is masculine; it cannot agree with the feminine plural **women.** (C) The possessive pronoun **her** is feminine, singular and so cannot agree with **women.**

12.   **(C)**   (C) is the right answer; it collectively forms an item in the series of people related to Mrs. and Mr. Smith; the right plural form of son-in-law is sons-in-law. (A) **Their** must refer to Mrs. and Mr. Smith; **their husbands** is illogical here. (B) The relative pronoun **whose** introduces a clause; there is no verb to complete it. (D) is the wrong plural form of son-in-law; **son** must be pluralized not **law.**

13.   **(B)**   (B) is the right answer; **more than** here denotes something additional to **provide** and **maintain** which is stated in the subordinate clause **they define the status of the wearer.** (A) must be followed by participle verbs (providing, maintaining) and makes no connection between the two clauses, **clothes...modesty** and **they...wearer.** (C) is an adjective/adverb of quantity; not required here. (D) is an adjective/adverb of quantity; not required here.

14.   **(C)**   (C) is the right answer; **unlike** means **different from** and is appropriate to the sentence. (A) Needs a finite verb to complete a clause (e.g., Just as the Egyptian pyramids **did**). (B) **Same** is an adjective stating a similarity between two things. (D) Means completely opposed to, not suitable to the sentence; the Mayan and Egyptian pyramids have similarities and differences.

15. **(C)** (C) is the right answer; the past participle meaning produced is in agreement with the tense and meaning of the sentence. (A) is indicative of future; not compatible with 1926. (B) is indicative of future. (D) is not right as the word **done** denotes performing something, not producing something.

16. **(B)** (B) is the answer. **Should be** denotes an obligation. The answer should be **could be** which denotes possibility of any one of the three colors. (A) is a noun functioning as an adjective to qualify the noun **blood** and form a compound noun. (C) Expresses a choice of any of the three colors. (D) is an adjective qualifying **blood** and complementing **was.**

17. **(B)** (B) is the answer. **That** is a conjunction that introduces a nominal clause, so it is not appropriate here. It should be **know how, how** denoting **the ability to express.** (A) is a relative pronoun that introduces an adjectival clause. (C) The possessive pronoun relates **creativity** to **artist.** (D) is an adverb modifying the infinitive **to express.**

18. **(B)** (B) is the answer. The causative verb **let** must be followed by an infinitive without **to.** The answer should be **explore.** (A) The possessive pronoun relates **children** to **parents.** (C) is a conjunction meaning **because** joining the clauses **some...home** and **that...unconsciously.** (D) is a finite verb of the subordinate clause **that...unconsciously.**

19. **(A)** (A) is the answer. **If** introduces a conditional sentence; **be publishing** indicates the present. A hypothetical statement contrasting with present circumstances must be expressed by **were.** (B) is the right form of the indefinite article to precede a noun beginning with a vowel sound. (C) is the right form of verb to express consequence of present hypothetical statement. (D) is the adverbial of time.

20. **(A)** (A) is the answer. A wish must be expressed by **were** not by **was.** (B) is a conjunction denoting that the clause **he...** is a result of **Daedalus...fly.** (C) The indefinite article is appropriate as **pair of wings** has not been particularized or differentiated in the context. (D) is the indirect object of the verb **made.** Since the object is the same person as the one in the subject, the reflexive pronoun has been used.

21. **(A)** (A) is the answer. **Few** when it is not preceded by **a** or **only a** means **not many, not enough. A few, only a few** mean a small number (unspecified). Since the word **only** is already in the sentence, the answer must be **only a few.** (B) The possessive pronoun relates **characters** to **films.** (C) is an adjective qualifying the compound noun **period costume.** (D) is an adjective qualifying **costume** to form a compound noun.

22. **(B)**   (B) is the answer. **Of which** denotes part of a whole and so is inappropriate with reference to **fact.** The answer should be **that,** the conjunction which will connect the two clauses **it...fact** and **the major...speed.** (A) is an impersonal pronoun referring to the real subject **fact.** (C) is a finite verb predicating the subject **advantage** in the clause **the major...speed.** (D) is the finite (passive) predicating the subject **food** in the clause **with...cooked.**

23. **(A)**   (A) is the answer. (i) Kennedy is not living anymore. So we must use the past tense. **Hopes** is simple present tense. (ii) The **hoping** was at a time before man landed on the moon, which has already taken place. An event/occurrence in the past and preceding another past event must be expressed in the past perfect. So **had hoped** would be appropriate here. (B) is an adjectival past participle qualifying **hope.** (C) is a definite article used with the noun **hope** as the noun has been particularized earlier in the context. (D) is an adjectival past participle qualifying **realized.**

24. **(D)**   (D) is the answer. **Weren't they** is not the right form of the tag question. The finite forms of **to be** (am, are, is, was, were, will, shall) and the modals (could, would, should) in the main clause, must use, in the tag question, a finite form of **to do,** that will agree with person, number, and tense of the main verb.

25. **(D)**   (D) is the answer. **Mine** is a possessive pronoun and so cannot function as the object of **promised.** The answer should be **me.** (A) is a conjunction, meaning **because,** connecting the two clauses **my babysitter was ill** and **my friend....** (B) is a finite verb predicating **friend** in the clause, **my friend....** (C) is the infinitive object of the verb **promised.**

26. **(B)**   (B) is the answer. **Work** can be pluralized to denote objects of art. The answer must be **works.** (A) is the appropriate indefinite article. Here it means **one.** (C) is the preposition normally used to relate the item purchased to the price paid for it. (D) is a preposition indicating the source of **purchase.**

27. **(A)**   (A) is the answer. (i) **A little** is an adjective of quantity to denote a small measure. (ii) **A little + did + S** is not the normal order. The answer should be the adverb **little,** which when used with verbs of knowing, thinking, feeling means **not at all.** In this sense, **Little + did + S** is the normal order. (B) is a conjunction connecting the two clauses. **Little did Columbus know** and **he was...continent.** (C) is the finite verb singular, in agreement with subject **he** and past tense in agreement with **sighted** in the clause **when he sighted land.** (D) The indefinite article used as **continent** has not been differentiated in the context.

28. **(C)** (C) is the answer. The singular, **the other,** does not contrast with the plural **some parts** in the clause **while…jewelry.** The answer should be **others.** The article **the** is not required as the sentence does not specify which other parts. (A) is a conjunction connecting the two clauses: **in some…jewelry** and **in…coats.** (B) is an adjective qualifying the noun **status.** (D) is the finite verb predicating the subject **it,** in the clause **in others…coats.**

29. **(A)** (A) is the answer. **Cleverer** is the comparative form of **clever** but it is not appropriate here. When comparing two qualities in a person, the predominant quality is always denoted by **more.** The answer should be **more clever.** (B) is the conjunction used to compare two unequal qualities. (C) is a contrastive conjunction connecting the clauses **this…diligent** and **that will not do.** (D) is a demonstrative pronoun referring to the state of being **more clever than diligent.**

30. **(A)** (A) is the answer. **Instead of** meaning **in the place of** is inappropriate here. The answer should be **in spite of** denoting a contrast between two events/states. (B) The definite article is used because **work** has been differentiated later in the context. (C) The past tense is in agreement with **complained.** (D) is a preposition of direction relating **father** and **complaint.**

31. **(B)** (B) is the answer. **Aux + S + V** is the normal order of questions. In reported speech the question must be embedded in a statement, **S + V.** The answer should be **he wanted.** (A) is a possessive adjective qualifying **son.** (C) Denotes purpose. (D) is a possessive adjective qualifying **birthday.**

32. **(C)** (C) is the answer. **Not** is an adverb used with verbs for negation. The answer must be **no longer; no** is an adjective, negatively qualifying the adjective that follows it. (A) is a definite article used to differentiate **pelican** from **other birds.** (B) is present perfect in agreement with the present tense of **feel** in the clause **experts…list.** (D) is a preposition used to locate objects on a surface such as **paper/list.**

33. **(D)** (D) is the answer. **Them** is a plural pronoun and therefore cannot refer to the singular noun **National Geographic Society.** The answer should be the singular pronoun **it.** (A) is an adverb modifying **known.** (B) is a singular verb agreeing with a single subject, **Alexander Graham Bell.** (C) is a possessive adjective qualifying the noun **time.**

34. **(A)** (A) is the answer. **Has prove** is a nonexistent form. The answer should be **has proved.** The present perfect tense denotes that the result of the **research** is still valid. (B) The plurality is in agreement with the absence of the indefinite article **a** before it and the plural verb following it. (C) is a preposition of directionality relating **readers** to **problem.** (D) is a preposition denoting the source of **readers.**

35. **(A)** (A) is the answer. **Wish rather** is a nonexistent form. The answer should be **had rather,** which denotes a preference for something, **browsing in a library,** over another, **doing chores.** (B) is a present participle complementing **were.** (C) is a preposition used with reference to three-dimensional locations. (D) is the object of **doing.**

36. **(B)** (B) is the answer. **By** denotes an active agent. The appropriate preposition here is **of** or **from,** both denote the cause of death, tracing the origin of the cause to **tuberculosis.** (A) is a finite verb predicating the subject **Keats.** (C) Denotes a point in time. (D) The indefinite article is used because **age** has not been specified.

37. **(B)** (B) is the answer. **As** is not required here. **For** denotes purpose. The answer should be **for.** (A) The indefinite article is appropriate as **room** has not been differentiated in the context. (C) The subject's experience of a state (peace, quiet) is indicated by the preposition **in.** (D) is a conjunction joining **peace** and **quiet.**

38. **(A)** (A) is the answer. **Told** must be followed by an object denoting the person spoken to. **Said** does not require such an object, unless it is **said to.** The answer should be **said.** (B) **Would** in reported speech indicates futurity. (C) is a preposition indicating specific location. (D) **Library** is not differentiated in the sentence but the **friends** have a shared knowledge of it, so **the** is appropriate.

39. **(A)** (A) is the answer. A present participle verb before a noun denotes that the noun is the actor of the action denoted by the present participle verb. The past participle denotes that the noun following it is acted on (passive receiver). The answer should be **hand-crafted.** (B) The preposition is used to denote the source of something. (C) is a plural finite verb in agreement with the plural subject **flutes.** (D) is a definite pronoun used to refer to a noun that is the only one of its kind.

40. **(B)** (B) is the answer. **Much** is an adjective of quantity that can only qualify noncount nouns nonassertively (don't have much time) or denote a large part of a noncount noun (much of the time/work/money). Since it cannot qualify another adjective, it is inappropriate here. The answer should be **too hot.** (A) is a relative adverb introducing the adverbial clause **where...hot.** (C) is a past participle adjective qualifying **clothing.** (D) is a preposition denoting purpose.

Section 3:
READING COMPREHENSION
AND VOCABULARY

1. **(D)**   While (A), (B), and (C) are all part of the answer, only (D) is the most complete answer. (A) "painting duplication," (B) "master artists," and (C) "paint analysis" are all mentioned, but the majority of the paragraph deals with the "new test" for authenticity.

2. **(A)**   "Telling copies from real paintings" is correct. (B) "who painted which paintings" is not an issue. (C) "why painting copies are made" is never discussed in the paragraph. (D) "kinds of paints used" comes later in the passage.

3. **(A)**   "Most chemical tests require a fair-sized paint sample" is verbatim from the fourth sentence. (B) "there is only one way to determine the age and composition of paint" is disproved by the fact that "a new test solves this problem," which infers that more than one other test exists. (C) "old and new paints test the same" is disproved by the words "Tests can show if the paints used are old or new." (D) "all tests require a large-sized sample" is refuted by the word "most" in the fourth sentence, followed by the description of the sample size needed for spectroscopic analysis.

4. **(A)**   "A spectroscope can determine paint composition" is synonymous with the words "is large enough for a spectroscope to 'fingerprint' a paint by disclosing what elements it contains and in what proportions." (B) "A spectroscope can determine where paint was bought" and (C) "A spectroscope can determine the artist's identity if unknown" are not mentioned in the passage and are therefore incorrect. (D) "A spectroscope is an old machine" is clearly incorrect by virtue of the fact that it is defined as an "exquisitely narrow beam of laser, used to vaporize a hundred-thousandth of a square inch of pigment surface," and laser technology is a relatively new technology.

5. **(C)**   The passage discusses the use of the spectroscope in authenticity determination. The next logical step in the process would be an example of how art dealers incorporate the use of the spectroscope into their business. (A) "how art is bought and sold," (B) "prices of artists' paints," and (D) "prices of paintings" would not provide a logical narrative progression from this passage.

6. **(A)**   "Precisely" is the correct choice. In order to vaporize only a hundred-thousandth of an inch of paint, the laser must be precise in its target. Whether the laser is

"beautiful," "fashionable," or "pleasant" will have no bearing on how much of the painting will be destroyed.

7. **(D)**   A hundred-thousandth is written out as .00001. (A) "100,000" would be written as a hundred-thousand. (B) "1,000" is written as a thousand. (C) ".001" is written as a thousandth.

8. **(B)**   In this sentence, "naked" most nearly means "unaided." To be invisible to the naked eye means that it cannot be seen without the use of a magnifying implement. Naked also means (A) "unclothed," but not in the context of this paragraph. (C) "unseeing" and (D) "unable" are not synonymous in any way.

9. **(B)**   "Them" refers to "copies." The second line reads, "These copies are so perfect that it is virtually impossible to tell them from the real thing." (A) "artists," (C) "months," and (D) "masters" are all referred to in the first sentence, but it is the copies that are talked about in the second sentence.

10. **(B)**   "Forgers are adept at copying originals" is the correct response. The paragraph states that, "These copies are so perfect that it is virtually impossible to tell them from the real thing. This is a serious problem in the art world." Because forgery is such a problem, a way of verifying a painting was necessary, but it needed to cause minimal destruction to the painting. So, paint analysis was necessary because the forgers were capable of perfectly duplicating originals.

11. **(A)**   "Heated" is the correct response. Since "bitter" normally refers to taste, answers (B) and (D) seem logical choices, but in the context of the paragraph it is not taste that is being discussed. Choice (C) "acrid" means a sharp, pungent taste or smell. Choice (A) "heated" is the best choice. "Heated" also means fervid or passionate.

12. **(D)**   The "Eighteenth century" is the correct choice. To answer this question two things must be done. First, the time period must be found. The second paragraph says, "But over the past two centuries, less than seven human generations, scientists have begun to study and understand the history of life on this planet." Two centuries back would be 200 years, which means the start of understanding would have begun in the 1700s. Once this is known, you have to know also that centuries are always one over the years they represent (i.e. Twentieth century is the 1900s, Nineteenth century is the 1800s, etc.). Because debate began in the 1500s does not mean that understanding was taking place, so (B) "Sixteenth century" would not be a correct choice.

13. **(B)** "Remains of demons" is the correct choice. The passage does not mention (A) "Strange rock formations" nor (D) "Scientific pranks," so both of these choices can be eliminated. Choice (C) "Creations of God" could be correct, but it is not the best choice. The passage states, "This group was opposed by another which declared that fossils were either freaks of nature or creations of the devil." Because of this line, choice (B) is the best answer.

14. **(A)** "Remains" is the correct choice. "Relics" is not referring to (B) "scientists," (C) "epochs," or (D) "events" that were mentioned within the paragraph. This is just a question of vocabulary knowledge and "relics" most nearly means "remains."

15. **(C)** "Geological epochs" is the correct choice. Choices (A) "witchcraft" and (B) "biblical disasters" were both mentioned in the passage, but the transition sentence at the end of the reading would lead one to believe that (C) "geological epochs" was to be the next topic discussed. Choice (D) "biological processes" was never mentioned in the passage, so it is unlikely that it would follow.

16. **(D)** If you divide 200 years ("over the past two centuries") by "seven human generations" you get approximately 29 years; therefore, (D) "26–30 years," is the best answer.

17. **(D)** The words "progress has been impressive" leads one to choose "significant," a synonym for impressive. The author believes that progress has been impressive, and therefore possible. Answers (A) "not important," (B) "not possible," and (C) "not measurable" are incorrect.

18. **(A)** "Nearly," used to describe the close to 200,000 species of fossil organisms, is synonymous with "almost." It is not (B) "more than" 200,000, (C) "exactly" 200,000, or (D) "far more than" 200,000 species.

19. **(B)** The dictionary defines "epochs" as a geological period of time marked by new development and crucial changes. (A) "biologies" is a less specific term and therefore incorrect. (C) "chemicals" is not mentioned at all and therefore is incorrect, as is (D) "stars."

20. **(D)** Choice (A) "history" is too general. (B) "biological forms" is also too general and does not take history into consideration. (C) "the Earth" is not a specific answer. (D) "the history of life" incorporates both ideas of passage of time and life forms.

21. **(D)** "Investors" is the correct answer. Choices (A) "Artists," (B) "Presidents," and (C) "Companies" are all types of consumers, but the question asked specifically for the paragraph's definition of a consumer. The only consumers that the author deals with are investors.

22. **(A)** "Buy company stock" is the correct answer. "If a company is managed well and has a bright future..." is synonymous with "Consumers who believe a company is well run and shows promise of doing well in the stock market..." The answer would then appear at the end of the sentence which is "...will invest in that company's stock." The other three answer choices are all incorrect and refer to what investors would do if they did not believe a company was doing well.

23. **(C)** "Savings bonds" is the correct choice. This is taken straight from the passage. "Buying United States Savings Bonds is another well-known way of investing money." None of the other choices (A) "Antique cars," (B) "Cash," or (D) "Gold" are mentioned in the paragraph as viable options for investment.

24. **(C)** "5%" is the correct choice. This is taken straight from the passage; "A five percent discount is the usual rate." Answer choice (A) "50%" is written as "fifty percent." Choice (B) "15%" is written as "fifteen percent." Choice (D) ".5%" is written as "five-tenths of a percent."

25. **(A)** "Inducements" is the correct choice. An incentive is anything that causes a desired response, in this case, the reinvestment of dividends. The other three choices are all items that appeared within the reading. None of them are correct responses to the question.

26. **(C)** "Seventy percent" is the correct answer. The answer to this question is straight out of the text, "Finally, about 70 percent of companies charge no fee if the stockholder wishes to purchase more shares with cash." The other choices appear numerically as (A) 7 percent, (B) 17 percent, and (D) 700 percent.

27. **(A)** "Purchase of partial shares" is the correct choice. To answer this question, you need to know the meaning of "incentives." Question 25 answers that. The answer is then in the following sentence, "For example, if the dividend is too small to buy a whole share, most companies allow the investor to purchase part of a share until enough dividends accumulate for a whole share." The other three choices listed, may be incentives for the purchase of more stock, but none of them are mentioned in the paragraph.

28. **(B)** "He thinks it is a good idea" is the correct response. The author of this passage never states an overt opinion on the subject of reinvestment. To answer it, first look at your four answer choices. Choices (C) and (D) can be eliminated immediately since no where in the passage does the author mention art or theft of money. Of the two remaining choices (A) is not the best choice because the author never states anything negative about reinvestment and only offers positive information about it. Because he only mentions the good parts of reinvestment, it can be inferred that he thinks it is a good idea.

29. **(D)** "Companies" is the correct response. In the sentence, "In addition, some companies offer shareholders a discount off the market price of their stock," the companies are offering a discount off of their stock, not the shareholder's. This, therefore, eliminates choice (C). Choices (A) and (B) are not even mentioned in the sentence, and there is no indication that they are offering a discount.

30. **(C)** "When the company makes a profit" is the correct answer. The answer to this question is taken directly from the reading. "If the company shows a profit, the investor will receive a dividend check." Choices (A), (B), and (D) are not mentioned in the paragraph.

31. **(C)** "Seventeenth century" is the correct response. To answer this question also look at the response to question 12. The answer can be ascertained directly from the reading. "Jupiter's 'Great Red Spot' was first discovered in 1664." The year 1664 falls in the seventeenth century.

32. **(D)** "8:20 a.m." is the correct response. This is a simple addition problem. You need to know that a rotation takes 9 hours and 50 minutes. With that information it is simply a matter of adding that to 10:30 p.m. You also need to know that after 11:59 p.m. it becomes 12:00 a.m.

33. **(B)** "Lessened" is the correct response. If you do not know the meaning of the word, there is a context clue provided. "The color of this storm has diminished over the years, so that only a faint outline remains." If only a faint outline remains, then the storm has not (A) "increased," (C) "brightened," or (D) "grown."

34. **(C)** "Near the upper atmosphere" is the correct answer. The answer to this question is found in the following sentence: "Exploring spacecraft have found Jupiter to be a whirling ball of liquid hydrogen topped with a uniquely colored atmosphere which is mostly hydrogen and helium, but also contains small amounts of methane, ammonia, ethane, acetylene, phosphene, germanium, tetrahydride, and possibly hydrogen cyanide."

If Jupiter is "topped" with a colorful atmosphere, that atmosphere would occur in the upper portions of the planet.

35. **(B)** "Satellites" is the correct answer. The answer is found in the same sentence as the answer to the previous question. You need to know that "exploring spacecraft" does not refer to (C) "aliens," but instead (B) "satellites." Choices (A) and (D) are not mentioned in the passage.

36. **(C)** "Atmospheric disturbances" is implied in the passage by "similar to an Earth hurricane." (A) "air" is incorrect, as Jupiter's atmosphere is stated as mostly hydrogen and helium, and Earth's atmosphere is mostly hydrogen, oxygen, and some carbon. (B) "water" is incorrect as water contains hydrogen and oxygen. Hydrogen is evident in Jupiter's atmosphere. Oxygen is not. (D) "dirt" is incorrect since solid masses such as dirt are never mentioned in the passage, and there is no way to deduce this information.

37. **(D)** "Dizzying pace" indicates that an Earth person would be quite uncomfortable on Jupiter. (A) "never fall down" is incorrect as a "dizzying pace" might cause a person to fall down. (B) "easily stand straight and tall" is incorrect as a "dizzying pace" might inhibit this. (C) "Experience no uneasiness" is incorrect as the "dizzying pace" would cause "uneasiness."

38. **(A)** Since the gases listed on Jupiter are the same gases known to exist on Earth, only (A) "there are similar elements and gases on Jupiter and on Earth" is correct. The passage states there are liquids on Jupiter, so (C) is false. The passage does not state that there are no solids on Jupiter, so (D) is false. (B) "No common elements and gases exist on Earth and Jupiter" is disproved by the listing of common elements and gases such as hydrogen, helium, methane, ammonia, ethane, acetylene, phosphene, germanium tetrahydride, and possibly hydrogen cyanide.

39. **(B)** The word "massive" is used as an adjective, and the noun it describes is "Jupiter," thereby signifying that it is Jupiter's size that is massive. (A) "Earth's size" is incorrect because the words "Largest of the solar system's planets, Jupiter" clearly states that the sentence refers to Jupiter, not Earth. (C) "Jupiter's rotational speed" is incorrect. Massive refers to the planet's size, not the planet's speed. (D) "Jupiter's color" is incorrect, for the word "massive" refers to size, not color.

40. **(C)** "Jupiter's atmosphere and its colors" is the correct answer as "uniquely" is used as an adverb to modify the adjective "colorful" describing Jupiter's atmosphere. (A) "size" and (B) "rotation and revolution" are excluded, and therefore incorrect answers. (D) "elements of Jupiter's atmosphere" are not unique, although their color is.

41. **(D)** "Parents and guardians" is the correct answer in light of the sentence "Tests can determine how well your child is doing," showing the article was written for parents and guardians. (A) "students" is incorrect as paragraph one clearly says to its audience, "your child." (B) "grandparents" is also incorrect because, although grandparents may sometimes be guardians, this choice is too restrictive. (C) "teachers" is also incorrect because paragraph one does not say "your students."

42. **(C)** The first sentence uses the analogy "Tests are a yardstick," making "a measuring stick" the correct answer. (A) "a report card" is incorrect as it is said to be associated with tests, not analogous to tests. (B) "a musical instrument" and (D) "a game" are incorrect as they are not analogous to a test nor are they ever mentioned in the passage.

43. **(A)** The sentence "Most of the tests your child will take are 'teacher-made'," makes "tests" correct. (B) "report cards" is incorrect as it is associated with tests and grades, but not teacher-made as much as student-generated and teacher-reported. (C) "schools" is incorrect because they are not teacher-made but rather district-built and supported. (D) "comparisons" is incorrect as they are teacher-interpreted, not teacher-made.

44. **(B)** Since the passage "telling the teacher and student whether he or she is keeping up with the class, needs extra help or, perhaps, is far ahead of the other students" presents more than one comparison, only (B) "knowledge level" is correct. (A) "cities," (C) "schools districts," and (D) "schools" are all incorrect as they are only part of the whole answer encompassed by the words correct choice.

45. **(B)** As textbooks, personnel changes, and homework are not mentioned in the passage, only (B), the idea of changing the curriculum, is correct. The words "change teaching techniques" refers to changing teaching methods, not to (C) "getting a better teacher." (A) "change course textbooks" and (D) "give more homework" are incorrect as they are not mentioned in the passage. While it is possible that changing teachers, textbooks, or the amount of homework will be part of a curriculum change, each of these choices individually is too restrictive for use in defining "strengthen courses."

46. **(A)** "To improve education" is the correct choice. The answer to this question is taken straight from the passage. "Schools use them to measure, and then improve, education. Although choice (D) "Measure teachers' progress" seems like a possible choice, the passage does not discuss teachers' progress, but instead discusses teaching techniques.

47. **(B)** "Which students need help" is the correct choice. The answer to this question appears in the final sentence of the passage. "They help measure a student's progress,

telling the teacher and student whether he or she is keeping up with the class, needs extra help, or, perhaps, is far ahead of the other students."

48. **(C)** "Tests are necessary" is the correct response. Since the author speaks only of the positive aspects of tests, it can be assumed that his position is positive toward tests. If his opinion is positive then choices (A) "All tests should be called off" is another way of saying tests should be eliminated, and (D) "Tests are inaccurate" cannot be correct choices. These are both negative opinions of tests. The passage does not judge the quality of tests, but rather the need for tests, therefore, choice (B) "Teachers need to develop better tests" is incorrect.

49. **(A)** "Related" is the correct answer. This is a straight vocabulary question. There are no context clues to help in answering this question. You need to know that "associated" most nearly means "related."

50. **(A)** "The ability of tests to help children who are having difficulties" is the correct answer. The last sentence of this passage would be the transition sentence for the next paragraph. Since this last sentence deals with the ability of tests to help students, it can be assumed that the next paragraph would build on this information. None of the other choices is mentioned, except to support the idea that tests are necessary.

51. **(A)** "Burning" is the correct choice. Combustion is synonymous with burning. The sentence even mentions wood being burned. So, you are given a context clue as to the meaning of combustion. The other choices are not synonyms for combustion.

52. **(C)** "When it is allowed to accumulate" is the correct answer. The answer to this question is directly from the sentence, "Creosote is dangerous only when it is allowed to accumulate in large amounts." Choice (B) "When it is placed in water" is not mentioned in the passage. Choices (A) and (D) are not complete enough to offer the best possible choices.

53. **(B)** "Creosote formation cannot be prevented" is the correct response. The answer to this question appears in the following sentence, "There is no way to prevent the formation of creosote, but it can be minimized by avoiding smoldering fires, burning seasoned hardwoods, and using interior chimneys." Choice (A) is the opposite of what was said in the passage. Choice (D) is a contradiction to what was said. Finally, choice (C) is never mentioned.

54. **(B)** "Liquid" is the correct answer. The answer to this question is found in the first sentence, "Creosote is a black, tarry liquid that comes from the condensation of wood gases which are not burned in the combustion process."

55. **(D)** "Build-up" is the correct choice. The context clue of "large amounts" eliminates one of the possible choices, (A) "lessen." Choices (B) and (C) do not make sense within the context of the passage. That leaves choice (D) as the correct choice.

56. **(D)** (A) "uses of creosote" are never mentioned, except to say that it could be fuel. How it is manufactured, (B), and how it burns, (C), are mentioned in passing. The main idea of the passage is the nature and dangers of creosote (D).

57. **(B)** The passage tells how to reduce the formation of creosote, thereby minimizing its production. (A) "made larger" is the antonym of this concept, and therefore correct. (C) "kept in certain areas" refers to location, as "minimized" refers to size, so it is incorrect. (D) "allowed to grow" is the exact opposite of minimized, therefore, it is incorrect.

58. **(B)** The passage tells us that creosote is formed from the black, tarry liquid not burned off during combustion, thereby making (B) the correct answer. Cold, in any degree, is never mentioned, thereby eliminating (C) and (D); and (A), "heat," is not all that is needed for creosote formation.

59. **(D)** The chimney fire would be caused by the creosote. If the creosote did not accumulate, no fire would start. While the fire could be raging (B), and might be (A) uncontained, or (C) "hotter than 520 degrees fahrenheit," it could not start if it did not accumulate.

60. **(C)** The word "smoldering" in this passage is used as an adjective for fire. While it could also be used with the words (A) "creosote," (B) "hardwoods," and (D) "liquids," that is not the case in this passage.

DIAGNOSTIC CHART

> **DIRECTIONS**: After taking the diagnostic test and determining your correct and incorrect answers, find the number of the question that you answered incorrectly on each of the three charts. **Be sure to look in the appropriate section of each chart.** This will direct you to a review area that can help you with that type of question in the future. Often, a question will be cited in more than one topic area.

Demonstration:

STEP 1: You answered question #13 incorrectly on Section 2, the Structure and Written Expression Section. Look for all of the #13's in the second column of all three reviews.

STEP 2: You will then find that there is a #13 listed in the *Listening Comprehension Review Chart* under the topic "Expressing Contrast.

STEP 3: There is also a #13 in the second column of the *Structure & Written Expression Review Chart* under the topic "Subject-verb-pronoun agreement."

STEP 4: Finally, there is a #13 in the first column of the *Reading Comprehension & Vocabulary Review Chart* under the topic "Cause and effect, compare and contrast."

STEP 5: Refer to those topic areas in the reviews that were recommended in the chart. See the page number by each topic listed on the chart.

The same procedure applies if you answer a question incorrectly in the Listening Comprehension section of the diagnostic test. This time, remember that you are only checking the **Section 1** column of all the review charts.

Finally, if you answer a question incorrectly in the Reading Comprehension and Vocabulary section of the diagnostic test, refer to the **Section 3** column of all of the review charts.

LISTENING COMPREHENSION REVIEW CHART

Review Area and Page Number	Section 1: Listening Comprehension	Section 2: Structure and Written Expression	Section 3: Reading Comprehension and Vocabulary
Words or phrases that are different in appearance but similar in meaning—p. 84			7, 12, 24
Homonyms—Words that are similar in sound or spelling but different in meaning (example: sun vs. son)—p. 84	23		
Inferences from the given information—p. 85	14, 16, 17, 21, 23		1, 6, 8, 9, 10, 11, 14, 18, 19, 21, 22, 25, 27, 29, 31, 33, 34, 35, 36, 37, 38, 44, 45, 49, 51, 52, 55, 57
Selecting answers based on partial information—p. 86	14, 17, 23		1, 9, 18, 19, 25, 27, 29, 33, 34, 35, 36, 37, 38, 44, 45
Selecting answers that require mathematical calculations—p. 86	12, 32		7, 16, 32
The many ways of expressing negativity in English—p. 86	25		
U.S. holidays—pp. 88–89		12	
Sequence of events as presented in short talks—p. 89	34		
U.S. idioms—p. 89	4, 6, 11, 14, 15, 18, 27, 30		
U.S. university life—pp. 90–93	31		
Phrasal verbs—pp. 93-96			48
Selective listening—pp. 100	3, 10, 13, 17, 24, 25, 37, 40, 42, 45		
The importance of details in mini-talks—p. 100	19, 31, 36, 37, 38, 40, 41, 42, 44, 45, 47, 48		3, 4, 16
Ways of expressing the future tense—p. 101–102	1, 8		
Expressing future completion—p. 103			
Expressing two past actions—p. 106-107		28	

Area and Page Number	Section 1:	Section 2:	Section 3:
Expressing time: sequence—p.107	24		
Expressing possession—p. 108	1		
Comparisons—p. 110		29, 40	
Expressing advice—p. 112-113	22		
Expressing a preference—p. 115	2		
Expressing an obligation—p. 116	14, 33		
Making a suggestion—pp.117	39		
Giving a reason or making a conclusion—pp. 118–119	27, 46, 47		10
Expressing contrast—pp. 119-120		6, 13, 28	
Adding information—pp. 120–122		9	
Expressing real conditions—p. 122–124	28, 46, 48		
Expressing imaginary conditions—pp. 124-125		19	
Making a polite request—p. 128	18		
Focusing on or emphasizing information—p. 1228–129	47		
Explaining what the speaker means in a dialogue—pp. 136–137	4, 6, 11, 15 18, 23	28	
Identifying the topic of conversation in a dialogue—pp. 137–138	31, 50		
Describing a past event—p. 138	20	3, 4, 14, 24	
Location of the speakers in a dialogue—pp. 139–140	3, 10, 13, 16, 26		
Guess the future or make inferences about it—pp. 141–142	5, 7, 8		5, 15, 50
Computing or inferring time—p.142	16, 20		12, 16, 32
Identifying a cause—pp. 143-144	33, 46, 49		
Identifying feelings—pp. 144-145			17
Giving advice or making a suggestion—pp. 146–147	35		
Identifying an attitude—pp.149-150	9, 14, 15		

STRUCTURE & WRITTEN EXPRESSION REVIEW CHART

Review Area and Page Number	Section 1: Listening Comprehension	Section 2: Structure and Written Expression	Section 3: Reading Comprehension and Vocabulary
Verbs—pp. 173		1, 5, 40	60
Subjects—p. 173		40	60
Prepositions—pp. 173–174		6, 15, 24, 25, 26, 30, 31, 32, 33, 34, 35, 36, 37, 38, 39, 40	60
"Because" vs. "Because of"—p.176	33	11	
Verb tenses—pp. 178–190		1, 3, 4, 14, 19, 20, 24, 25, 33, 34, 36, 38	
Passive voice—p. 191		3, 6, 7, 17, 22, 30, 34, 38	
Verbals—p. 192–193		2, 16, 17, 18, 19, 22, 23, 27, 31, 32, 34, 35, 37, 39	
Subject-verb-pronoun agreement—pp. 195–197		1, 2, 9, 11, 13, 17, 20, 22, 23	2, 21, 39, 43, 60
Correlative conjunctions—p. 201		10	
Articles—pp. 205–208		19, 21, 26, 27, 30, 32, 36, 37, 38, 39	
Plural nouns—p. 208–210		12, 21, 26	
The possessive case—p. 210–211		11, 17, 18, 26	

READING COMPREHENSION & VOCABULARY REVIEW CHART

Review Area and Page Number	Section 1: Listening Comprehension	Section 2: Structure and Written Expression	Section 3: Reading Comprehension and Vocabulary
Skimming the passages—p. 217			32
Reading the passages— p. 217–218			32
Scanning the answers— p. 218–219			32
Finding the main idea in a passage—pp. 220–222	50		1, 20, 56
Noticing and remembering specific facts contained in the passage— pp. 222–225	36, 37, 38, 39, 40, 41, 42, 43, 44, 45, 46		12, 13, 22, 23, 26, 30, 39, 40, 46, 47, 52, 53, 54, 58, 59
Making an inference—p. 225–229	21, 44, 48, 50		10, 37, 44, 45
Cause and effect Compare and contrast—p. 231	28, 29, 48, 49	7, 13, 28, 29	42
Recognizing the author's attitude—pp. 231-235	39		17, 28, 41, 48
Connector words—pp. 236-237		9, 20, 23, 29	

Chapter 3

Listening
Comprehension Review

Chapter 3

LISTENING COMPREHENSION REVIEW

    I.   HINTS FOR PREPARATION
    II. TEST TAKING HINTS
    III. TEST CONTENT
        • Statements
        • Dialogues
        • Short Talks

I. HINTS FOR PREPARATION

> ➤ Hint 1   **Be familiar with the test.**

The Listening Comprehension section will be the first section you will be required to take. It has a total of 50 questions, and all the questions are oral and played to you from a tape recorder. The multiple-choice answers are all written on the test. You must choose the best answer to each spoken question. The test administrator will give you 35 minutes to complete the section, so you will have to learn to work quickly. Follow these study tips in addition to taking the practice exams so that you will become more familiar with the Listening Comprehension section. The more familiar you become with this section, the less time it will take you to choose the correct answer.

There are three parts to the Listening Comprehension test. These are:

A. **Dialogues** (25 questions): You will hear an informal conversation between a man and a woman. Usually each person speaks only once. A third voice (man or woman) then asks a question about their conversation. You must select the written statement which ANSWERS THE QUESTION.

B. **Extended Conversations** (15 questions): You will hear two people having a conversation. A third voice then asks four or five questions about the mini-talk. You must select the written statement which ANSWERS THE QUESTION.

C. **Short Talks** (10 questions): You will hear one person talking. A second voice will then ask four or five questions about the talk. You must select the written statement which ANSWERS THE QUESTION.

➤ Hint 2   **Recognize the correct answer.**

The correct answer usually uses a vocabulary word or a structure which is close in meaning to the original statement, but which LOOKS VERY DIFFERENT. Often the correct answer will use a different noun, verb, or sentence structure.

Example:	**Structural Difference**
You will hear:	She has so many students she can hardly grade all the papers in time.
Correct choice:	There are many students in her class.

Example:	**Opposite**
You will hear:	I am as quiet as I can be.
Correct choice:	I never make any noise.

Example:	**Vocabulary Difference**
You will hear:	Jane wanted to go to the beach on Saturday, but she has homework due on Monday.
Correct choice:	Jane is unable to go to the beach.

➤ Hint 3   **Recognize the wrong answers.**

The test may use words which have the same pronunciation but different meanings or spellings.

Example:	**"sun" vs. "son"**
You will hear:	The sun is out today.
Wrong answer:	Her son went out to play.

The test may use words that have a similar pronunciation but do NOT MEAN the same thing. Be careful of teens vs. tens (13 vs. 30, 15 vs. 50).

Example: **"thirteen" vs. "thirty"**

You will hear: The teacher has thirteen students in the class.

Wrong answer: Thirty students are in the class.

Example: **"work" vs. "walk"**

You will hear: If you work fast, you can make it in time.

Wrong answer: You must walk quickly to get there on time.

The test may use statements that are the opposite of what was said.

Example:

You will hear: I used to live in Chicago.

Wrong answer: I live in Chicago now.

The test may use statements that might be true in life but were not mentioned on the tape by the speaker.

Example:

You will hear: Ben promised Carol a letter.

Wrong answer: Ben made promises easily.

➤ Hint 4   **Be prepared to infer meaning.**

Some statements or answers go beyond their direct meaning. They require a cultural inference. You will need to know the culture and some terms to select the correct answer. In the example below, you must infer that if coffee cups are presented, people are going to drink coffee, not tea, lemonade or water.

Example:

You will hear: Please put the coffee cups on the breakfast table.

Correct answer: Coffee will be served with breakfast.

> **Hint 5** | **Be prepared to choose answers with partial information.**

Some answers include ONLY PART of the information which the speaker mentions on the tape. Some of the information given in the statement is NOT present in the answer.

Example:

You will hear: Linda sold her uncle's house after his death.

Correct answer: Linda's uncle died.

> **Hint 6** | **Be prepared to make mathematical calculations.**

The speaker will give you the information, but the correct answer requires some simple calculations.

Example:

You will hear: The cookies are two dollars per pound. I bought three pounds.

Correct answer: I paid $6.00.

> **Hint 7** | **Be familiar with forms of measurement in the United States.**

It is good to remember some general facts. Remember that when the speakers refer to temperature, they are using Fahrenheit even though they won't directly say Fahrenheit. Here are some helpful things to remember:

1 meter – a little more than a yard
80 degrees – hot weather
90 degrees – very hot weather
32 degrees – cold weather (water freezes)
98.6 degrees – normal body temperature

Example:

You will hear: His temperature was 103 degrees.

Correct answer: He needed to see a doctor because he was very sick.

Remember that some forms of measurement can be expressed in many different ways. The speaker on the tape may use one word, but the answer may appear written in a different form. For example:

a dollar – a bill – a buck

a couple of dollars – $2.00 – two dollars
a dozen – 12
a pound – lb. – 16 ounces
4 quarts – 4 qts. – 1 gallon

Example:

You will hear: The eggs were three dollars a dozen. I bought thirty-six.

Correct answer: I paid $9.00.

| ➤ Hint 8 | **Remember that negatives are expressed in many ways in English.** |

Negatives can be expressed in English by using sentence structure or a conjunction or a vocabulary word or prefix. For example:

Sentence structure: "She can't sing."
Conjunction: "She can't do anything, but sing."
Vocabulary word: "She sings in monotone."
Prefix: "She is unable to sing."

Example: **"but" – "not" – "un-"**

You will hear: The computer will be available any time but one o'clock.

Correct answer: The computer will not be available at one o'clock.

Correct answer: The computer is unavailable at one o'clock.

| ➤ Hint 9 | **Know the geography of the United States.** |

You need to know which states are found in what is referred to as "the North," "the East," "New England," "the West," and "the South." It's also important to remember that the climate in the West and South is usually hot or moderate all year, while the climate in the North and East is warm during the summer but very cold during the winter.

Example:

You will hear: She's living in New York right now, but she wants to move to Texas.

Correct answer: She wants to live in the South.

> Hint 10 | **Know the seasons of the year and the months that go with them.**

Summer – June 21 through September 20 (warm/hot climate)

Fall – September 21 through December 20 (warm/cool climate)

Winter – December 21 through March 20 (cold climate)

Spring – March 21 through June 20 (rainy/moderate climate)

> Hint 11 | **Know the typical university schedules in the United States.**

Each university or college decides its own schedules. However, there are some traditional schedules. Here is one:

Fall semester – (14 weeks) September through part of December

Semester break – (4 weeks) the free period at the end of December and beginning of January when no classes are held

Spring semester – (14 weeks) part of January through part of May

Spring break – (1 week) vacation time in the middle of spring semester which may or may not occur during the Christian holiday of Easter

Summer session – courses offered during June, July, or August for 4, 6, or 8 weeks each

> Hint 12 | **Know the major holidays in the United States.**

Classes do not meet on some of these holidays. You will need to know what these holidays celebrate in order to answer some questions on the TOEFL exam. Here are some major holidays:

Labor Day – the first Monday in September – a national holiday in celebration of working people. Schools and colleges usually begin their fall semester the day after Labor Day.

Halloween – October 31 – a fun holiday for all. Children dress up as ghosts, or witches, or other characters and go to houses to receive candy. Adults have parties.

Thanksgiving – the fourth Thursday in November – a national celebration of thanks for surviving difficult weather and other conditions in the settling of the United States. This holiday often includes the Friday, Saturday, and Sunday which follow it.

Christmas – December 25 – a Christian holiday celebrating the birth of Christ which is celebrated nationally. Most businesses and schools are closed this day. Campuses are usually closed also.

New Year's – January 1 – a big celebration of the beginning of the year. Many businesses are closed and many parties last until January 2.

Valentine's Day – February 14 – a celebration of love for boyfriends, girlfriends, married couples, and close relatives. Schools do not close for this holiday.

Mother's Day – the second Sunday in May – tribute to mothers.

Memorial Day – the last Monday in May – a national holiday in celebration of all those who have died in military service to the United States.

Father's Day – the third Sunday in June – tribute to fathers.

Independence Day – July 4 – celebration of the independence of the United States. Many parades, flags, and evening fireworks displays appear on this day.

➤ Hint 13	**Remember the sequence of events referred to in mini-talks.**

Mini-talks often mention inventions or discoveries. Remember the sequence of events in these discoveries because questions sometimes ask for this sequence. For example:

"What was the first discovery that Salk made?"

➤ Hint 14	**Guess the meaning of metaphoric idioms.**

Sometimes idioms are really metaphors. They are words which have extended their concrete meaning. If you don't know an idiomatic expression, make a guess based on what you already know about the words. For example:

"Just stick to your subject." – "stick" means don't leave your subject

"Sam bugged me." – "bugged" means bothered or annoyed

Example:

You will hear: John tried to get at the root of the problem.

Correct answer: John wanted to understand the cause of the problem.

➤ Hint 15	**Know something about daily life in the United States.**

Sometimes terms will be used which carry cultural information. You will need to know the meaning of the term in order to select the correct answer. Many culturally based terms are used during the listening comprehension test.

Example: (A football game is divided into four quarters.)

You will hear: The football game started at two o'clock, and they arrived just in time for the third quarter.

Correct answer: They were very late.

Example: (A "round-trip ticket" – going to a place and returning to the place of origin)

You will hear: "I'd like a round-trip ticket from Chicago to Atlanta."

Correct answer: "I want a ticket to Atlanta and back to Chicago.

Some terms are important to know:

COMMUNICATIONS:

telephone operator – the person who handles calls personally

answering machine – the machine which plays a recorded message when the person does not answer the phone and on which you leave your message for that person

a collect call – the person receiving the call agrees to pay for it

person-to-person – the operator makes the call and the caller pays for the call only if the exact person requested answers

call waiting – a common system in which a telephone conversation is interrupted by another call without cutting off the first call

to be on hold – to wait for someone to return to your call without hanging up or being cut off

to fax – to send an exact copy of a picture or typed message by telephone

---

➤ Hint 16 | **Know something about university life in the United States.**

It is important to know common campus terms and what they mean. These terms are often used in the listening comprehension test. Here are some common terms and definitions:

COURSES:

to register – to complete the paperwork to enter a class

an I.D. – identification card which permits you to use university services (the library, the recreation facilities, etc.)

to be closed out of a class – you can't take a class because the maximum number of students have already registered for it

to drop a course – to cancel a course which you registered for. You may receive your money back if you do it early.

to withdraw from a course – to officially cancel your enrollment at the beginning of a course

to take an incomplete – **I** – to not receive a grade for a course because you failed to complete all the requirements due to illness or other legitimate reasons. You will be given a period of time to complete the requirements.

to cut a class – to fail to appear in class without the instructor's permission.

to audit a class – to sit in a class and participate without paying or receiving a grade

a transcript – an exact record of the courses you have taken and the grades received which may also have a grade point average

G.P.A. – **grade point average** – your average based on all the courses you have taken in your degree program

a major – the primary concentration of courses in a field of study. All students must have a major.

FEES:

a term bill – the total amount you owe the university for one semester, including tuition, fees, and library charges

tuition – amount you pay for courses

student fees – amount you are required to pay for student services even if you never use these services

room and board – amount you pay for living and eating in a dormitory or other residence

HOUSING:

roommate – **dorm mate** – the person you share a room with

the dorm – **dormitory** – a building where students live which is supervised and owned by the university

co-ed dorm – a dorm which has females on one floor and males on another floor

R.A. – **resident advisor** – the person on each floor who helps keep peace, organize educational events, and act as a counselor to ease student adjustment

off-campus housing – places of living which are NOT supervised or owned by the university and therefore do not follow the same restrictions

sorority house/fraternity house – a place of residence which serves also as a close social group or club. These houses are located either on the campus or nearby.

HEALTH:

university health center or clinic – a center where students receive health care inexpensively

to have a physical – to assure your health or identify problems

to get a shot – to receive an injection of medicine

FOOD:

a cafeteria – an eating place where food is already prepared and you select what you want and then pay a certain price for each separate item

a snack bar – a quick eating place where you order food at a counter, wait for it to be prepared, pay for it, and take it to your table to eat

a diner – a restaurant open 24 hours a day in which a waitress or waiter takes your order and brings food to you at your table

a vending machine – a machine that sells snacks and drinks: soda, hot drinks, candy, potato chips, and occasionally fruit/sandwiches

a grease truck – on some campuses you can buy food at a snack bar inside a van or truck which is parked close to your class

a sub-shop – a place where you can buy sandwiches prepared as you wish very quickly

a deli – delicatessen – a place where you can buy meat, cheese, and other prepared food prepared as you wish into sandwiches

to order out – to order food by phone and have it delivered to your home

to take out – to order food in a restaurant, but take it out of the store and eat it somewhere else

LIBRARY:

card catalogue – the system of organization in the library which identifies books, authors, and topics using a number system. You use the number to locate the books in the library. Some card catalogues are now also on computer.

reference desk – a place where librarians stay to give you information and help on how to use the library

due date – the date a book must be returned to a library

a fine – the amount you must pay if you do not return a book by its due date

the stacks – the place where books are stored. In some universities, students may not be permitted in this area.

to be on reserve – books which can only be loaned for a few hours are "on reserve"

to check out – charge out – to borrow a book from the library

to recall – to request the return of a book which has been borrowed by another person

SPORTS:

the gym – gymnasium – where indoor sports are played

halftime – a long break in the middle of a football game in which players take a rest and the audience receives entertainment

time out – a short break requested by one of the teams

touchdown – a goal scored in football

> ► Hint 17   **Know phrasal verbs and their meanings.**

Phrasal verbs ("come in," "turn on," and so forth) are very common on all three parts of the listening comprehension test. Remember that these two or three little words make ONE meaning. They often do NOT appear together. Nouns or even clauses can separate them. Try to memorize the most common phrasal verbs so that you will be prepared. (See list.)

Example:

You will hear: When Larry's friend drove too fast, he got pulled over by a policeman.

Correct answer: Larry's friend was ticketed for speeding by a policeman.

Here are some phrasal verbs to remember:

BRING IN – to carry inside
It's raining. Bring your bike in now.

BRING OUT – to reveal or expose
Her colorful blouse brought out the best in her.

BRING UP – to mention; to take care of
John brought the subject of drugs up.
She was brought up by her grandmother.

BURN OUT – to become mentally exhausted
The man was burned out by his job.

CALL OFF – to cancel
There was a bad storm so they called the party off.

CATCH UP – to bring up to date; to come from behind
I am so far behind that I won't catch up with my work for months.

CLEAR UP – to end the confusion
Perhaps more information would clear the problem up.

COME ABOUT – to happen
None of us can understand how the plane crash came about.

COME ACROSS – to accidentally find
I came across your name in a newspaper article I was reading.

COME AROUND – to change one's opinion or position
He's stubborn now but if you give him time, he'll come around.

COME BY – to get possession of
I'd really like a hat like that. How did you come by that?

COME OUT – to be disclosed or to result
I got a good grade on my TOEFL exam. Everything came out well.

COME UP – to introduce or mention
The topic of peace is very popular. It comes up often in our conversations.

CUT OFF – to disconnect on the telephone; to remove by cutting
I was cut off while talking to my brother.
Mary cut too much of her hair off.

DO OVER – to repeat
My professor asked me to do the experiment over.

DROP OFF – to return
Please drop the book off at my office tomorrow.

FILL OUT – to write information
You need to fill the application out and return it to me tomorrow.

GIVE UP – to stop or surrender
He finally gave up smoking.

GET ACROSS – to make clear
He can lecture well. He knows how to get his point across.

GET AHEAD – to surpass another
Competition forces people to try to get ahead of one another.

GET ALONG WITH – to play or work well with
Tom and Bill argue all the time; they don't get along well with each other.

GET BEHIND – to delay
If you don't practice every day, you can get behind.

GET ON WITH – to continue
I have had enough of the delay. Let's get on with the lecture.

GET ONE'S POINT ACROSS – to communicate
He can lecture well. He knows how to get his point across.

GET OUT OF – to remove someone
It's time for a test. Please get your notebooks out.

GET OVER – to recover or return to normal
Bill is angry now but don't worry. He'll get over it.

GET THROUGH – to finish; to endure
If you eat a good breakfast, it will help you get through the day.

GO AHEAD WITH – to continue
You have my permission to go ahead with the experiment.

HAND IN – to submit
The students handed their reports in at the end of the semester.

HOLD ON – to wait
Hold on a minute, please. I want to check your account.

KEEP RIGHT ON …ING – to continue
She told him to stop but he just kept right on singing.

KEEP UP WITH – to continue at the same level or pace.
She runs faster than he does. He can't keep up with her.

LOOK OUT FOR – to guard or protect
The cat looked out for her kittens whenever a dog came near.

LOOK OVER – to review or examine
Could you look this report over and give me your opinion?

LOOK UP TO – to admire
I always looked up to my older sister when I was young.

MAKE SURE OF – to ascertain
If John calls, make sure you tell him about the meeting tomorrow.

MAKE UP – to resolve a personal quarrel; to compensate for a mistake or error
They quarreled and then made up and forgot their disagreement.
You can make up the homework you missed if you see me on Friday.

MAKE UP YOUR MIND – to decide
He was very uncertain. He couldn't make up his mind where to go on vacation.

MIX UP – to confuse [A MIX-UP]
Be careful. Don't mix up our names in the future.

PASS OVER – to overlook or ignore
He was passed over for a promotion. He didn't get a raise.

PICK UP – to give a ride
We'll pick you up at 7:00 tonight.

PUT OFF – to delay or procrastinate
Don't put off for tomorrow what you can do today.

RUN INTO – to accidentally meet
I was downtown and happened to run into my friend Bob.

RUSH AROUND – to be in a hurry
During the holiday season it's common to find people rushing around the stores.

SEE TO – to assure
I'm sorry my son broke your window. I'll see to it that he pays for it.

SIT IN ON – to audit or attend but not pay
I got permission to sit in on the class.

TAKE OFF – to remove or deduct
The teacher took ten points off for each wrong answer.

TAKE ON – to accept work
I always admire someone who is willing to take on the job of leadership.

TAKE OVER – to take control of
The students took over the building during a student demonstration.

TRY OUT – to attempt
As soon as you return home, try out your new can opener.

TURN OUT – to produce
The plant turned out more spare parts than in any previous quarter.

TURN UP – to appear unexpectedly
She couldn't find her purse, but later it turned up in the closet.

USE UP – to deplete
She needed to buy more detergent because hers was all used up.

II. TEST TAKING HINTS

You will want to follow these suggested tips while you are taking the test.

➤ Hint 1	**Use selective listening. Guess what the topic is related to BEFORE the speaker begins.**

Work fast. Use each free second on the tape. Guard your time.

For example, as soon as you have answered a question, go on to the answers of the next question and quickly skim the four choices for clues. Guess what the statement or dialogue may be related to. You will have about four or five seconds to use in this way.

Then, as soon as the speakers on the tape begin to say the statement or dialogue, stop looking at the answers and concentrate ONLY on listening.

> **DIRECTIONS**: Look at the four choices below and make some guesses of what TOPIC may be used by the speaker on the tape.

    (A) 2:00
    (B) 1:30
    (C) 5:00
    (D) 3:45

Guess: TIME

Now try this exercise on the answers given below. Work as quickly as you can.

---

1.   (A) John accused the school.
        (B) John uses his car to get to school.
        (C) John walks to school every day.
        (D) John doesn't need a car to get to school.

Guess: JOHN, SCHOOL, TRANSPORTATION

---

2.   (A) I don't think that geometry is hard.
        (B) I like geometry better than algebra.
        (C) Algebra isn't difficult for me.
        (D) Algebra is easier for me than geometry.

Guess: GEOMETRY, ALGEBRA, COMPARISON (EASY OR DIFFICULT)

3.　(A)　He never walks to the library at night.
　　(B)　There is only one librarian here at night.
　　(C)　The library is the only place to study.
　　(D)　He never works in the library in the daytime.

Guess:　HE, LIBRARY, NIGHT OR DAY

4.　(A)　I told you to see a lot of museums.
　　(B)　You've taught me a great deal here.
　　(C)　People say that you know this place well.
　　(D)　Many museums are like this one, you know.

Guess:　PLACE, MUSEUM

5.　(A)　Sandra checked with her son's dentist.
　　(B)　Sandra sent her son for a checkup.
　　(C)　Sandra paid her son's dentist.
　　(D)　Sandra wrote a note to the dentist's son.

Guess:　SANDRA, SON, DENTIST, ACTION

6.　(A)　I have no typewriters.
　　(B)　We just left the typewriter shop.
　　(C)　I just found a typewriter.
　　(D)　I went out to get some typewriters.

Guess:　I/WE, TYPEWRITER, QUANTITY

7.　(A)　He fixes bicycles.
　　(B)　He raises sheep.
　　(C)　He sells chairs.
　　(D)　He's a gardener.

Guess:　HE, OCCUPATION/ACTION

8.　(A)　In a department store
　　(B)　In a bank
　　(C)　At a tourist bureau
　　(D)　At a hotel

Guess:　A PLACE OF BUSINESS

---

9. (A) You should believe everything you read.
   (B) She thinks the book is excellent.
   (C) She wonders which newspaper he reads.
   (D) Reaction to the book has been varied.

Guess: SHE, READING, BOOK OR NEWSPAPER

---

10. (A) The winter has just begun.
    (B) Once it starts, it'll snow a lot.
    (C) They're ready for the snow.
    (D) It has been snowing for some time.

Guess: WINTER, SNOW

---

11. (A) Bob did not wear a ring because he was single.
    (B) Bob wore a ring because he was married.
    (C) Bob was single, but he wore a ring.
    (D) Bob was married, but he did not wear a ring.

Guess: BOB, RING, SINGLE OR MARRIED

---

12. (A) Mrs. Smith is a teacher.
    (B) Mrs. Smith is a doctor.
    (C) Mrs. Smith is a lawyer.
    (D) Mrs. Smith is a dentist.

Guess: MRS. SMITH, PROFESSION

---

13. (A) Samuel Johnson
    (B) Mao Tse Tung
    (C) Abraham Lincoln
    (D) Charles De Gaulle

Guess: FAMOUS PERSON, LEADERS

---

14. (A) Very shortly
    (B) After everyone has finished
    (C) Tomorrow night
    (D) In a few days

Guess: TIME, COMPLETION

---

15. (A) 200 years
     (B) 400 years
     (C) 2,000 years
     (D) 4,000 years

Guess: LENGTH OF TIME

➤ Hint 2   **Don't get discouraged if you can't understand the first few questions.**

Sometimes the more difficult questions are at the beginning. Sometimes you need time to adjust to the speaker on the tape. If you don't understand the beginning, don't be discouraged. Continue listening and trying. The questions may become easier.

➤ Hint 3   **If you don't know which choice is the correct answer, use the process of elimination.**

Eliminate answers that do not use the same noun, verbs, or synonyms of those nouns and verbs of the voice on the tape.

Pay close attention to the VERBS which the speaker uses. TOEFL questions focus on the meaning in the VERB more often than the subject of the sentence.

It is common to find a one-word VERB in the written answer and a two-word or three-word verb or synonym used by the speaker on the tape.

➤ Hint 4   **When you listen to the mini-talk, remember the: YEAR, NAMES OF PEOPLE, PLACE, OR IMPORTANT FACTS AND EVENTS.**

Sometimes questions will ask you details about the mini-talk. In order to answer these questions you need to remember the year, name of a person, place, or important event which was mentioned in the mini-talk.

➤ Hint 5   **Pay attention to the relationship between two speakers.**

III. TEST CONTENT

Statements

Statements are used to express MEANING in language. You will find the following types of statements and meanings within the conversations of the Listening Comprehension section of the TOEFL:

Express Time:
  Future
  Future Completion
  Duration/Quality of Time
  Habitual Past
  Two Past Actions
  Sequence
Compare:
  Difference or Similarities
  Double Comparison
Expressing Possession
Express Advice:
  Present
  Past
Express an Inference
Express a Preference
Express an Obligation
Make a Suggestion

Give a Reason or Make a Conclusion
Expressing a Contrast
Add Information
Express Real Conditions
Imagine a Condition:
  Present
  Past
Describe
Qualify Negatively
Make a Polite Request
Focus on or Emphasize Information:
  Passive
  Noun Clause
"Get" + Adjective
Stress Importance
Cause Someone to Do Something
"Promise," "Tell," "Ask" Someone

Examples of these statements are discussed below.

| ➤ Statement Type 1 | **Expressing time: Future** |

Language Needed: will/'ll + VERB
                   am/is/are going to + VERB
                   am/is/are about to + VERB
                   am/is/are on the verge of + VERB ing
                   am/is/are VERB ing + TIME ADVERB

Examples: I will leave the house.
                   I'll leave the house.
                   I'm going to leave the house.
                   I'm on the verge of leaving the house.
                   I'm leaving the house tomorrow.

Structures Used: Future Tense; Present Progressive + Time Adverb

Remember: Future time is not always expressed by future tense.

NOW YOU PRACTICE:

Find the best choice which has the same meaning as the statement. You can cover up the answer or study the answer to get familiar with the best **meaning** of the statement.

You will hear: John lives in an apartment now, but next year he'll leave to live in a house.

    (A) John lives in a house now.
    (B) John is leaving his house.
    (C) John will move from his apartment.
    (D) John wants to leave his house.

Answer: C

PRACTICE:

You will hear: I have to hurry now because I'm about to miss my bus.

    (A) I must meet Harry on the bus.
    (B) If I'm late, the bus will leave without me.
    (C) The bus often comes late.
    (D) I don't want to take the bus because I'm in a hurry.

Answer: B

PRACTICE:

You will hear: I was about to drop out of school when my loan application was approved.

    (A) I dropped off the loan application.
    (B) I almost stopped attending school.
    (C) School attendance dropped sharply.
    (D) I didn't go to school because my financial aid wasn't approved.

Answer: B

| ➤ Statement Type 2 | **Expressing time: Future completion** |

Language Needed: will/'ll have + Past Participle
will/'ll have been VERB + ing for

Examples: By the end of the summer, he'll have completed his biology course.
By this time next year, I'll have been studying English for two years.

Structures Used: Future Perfect, Future Perfect Progressive

NOW YOU PRACTICE:
You will hear: I will already have finished eating by the time you arrive.

(A)   When you come, I'll eat.
(B)   It's time to eat.
(C)   When you come, I'll no longer be hungry.
(D)   I'll need time to eat when you arrive.

Answer: C

PRACTICE:
You will hear: They will have been married for 50 years by 1996.

(A)   They've been married for 50 years.
(B)   In 1996, they will get married.
(C)   They'll celebrate their 50th wedding anniversary this year.
(D)   They got married in 1946.

Answer: D

PRACTICE:
You will hear: By March, we'll have been attending English classes for four months.

(A)   We haven't been in English class for four months yet.
(B)   We'll attend English class in March.
(C)   Four months ago, we began English classes.
(D)   We march to our English class.

Answer: A

> **Statement Type 3** | **Expressing time: Duration/quality of time**

Language Needed: already, still, since, for, yet, ever since, often, frequently

Examples: She's (has) already gone to the dance.
She hasn't returned from the dance yet.
She's (is) still at the dance.
She's (has) been at the dance for two hours.
She's (has) been dancing for two hours.

Structures Used: Present Perfect, Past Perfect Progressive, Present + still

---

NOW YOU PRACTICE:
You will hear: She's gone to the party already?

    (A) I didn't know she left for the party.
    (B) Isn't she ready for the party?
    (C) Has she returned from the party yet?
    (D) She sang a song at the party?

Answer: A

PRACTICE:
You will hear: Mr. White has been living in his apartment building since 1970.

    (A) Mr. White has left his apartment building.
    (B) Mr. White still lives in the same building.
    (C) Mr. White has spent half his income.
    (D) Mr. White no longer lives in the same apartment building.

Answer: B

PRACTICE:
You will hear: Carol has been playing the guitar longer than I have.

    (A) Carol used to practice a lot.
    (B) Carol started guitar before I did.
    (C) Carol practices longer than I do.
    (D) Carol had practiced a long time.

Answer: B

> ➤ Statement Type 4   **Expressing time: Habitual past**

Language Needed: used to

Examples: I used to read *The New York Times* every day.

Remember: The meaning implied is that the action is completed.

                   He used to smoke cigarettes. — He doesn't smoke now.

NOW YOU PRACTICE:
You will hear: I used to live in Chicago.

     (A)   I didn't like Chicago.
     (B)   I'm leaving Chicago.
     (C)   I couldn't adjust to Chicago.
     (D)   I don't live in Chicago now.

Answer: D

PRACTICE:
You will hear: Jim didn't used to drive a car.

     (A)   Jim doesn't use a car.
     (B)   Jim didn't buy a used car.
     (C)   Jim drives a car now.
     (D)   Jim was using a car.

Answer: C

PRACTICE:
You will hear: Jack used to walk to school every day but now he has his own car.

     (A)   Jack accused the school.
     (B)   Jack uses his car to get to school.
     (C)   Jack walks to school every day.
     (D)   Jack doesn't need a car to get to school.

Answer: B

> ► Statement Type 5   **Expressing time: Two past actions**

Language Needed: when, while, before, after

Examples: She hasn't seen him since he left.
                      He'd (had) already lived there for two years when I joined him.

Structures Used: Past Perfect + Simple Past
                     Present Perfect + Simple Past

PRESENT PERFECT	TIME MARKER + SIMPLE PAST
Main Clause	Subordinate Clause

PAST PERFECT	TIME MARKER + SIMPLE PAST
Main Clause	Subordinate Clause

Remember: Usually the subjects of each clause are different.
                 Clauses can go in either order, but time markers stay attached to
                 the clause with simple past.
                 Past perfect always refers to the oldest action of the two.

NOW YOU PRACTICE:

You will hear: He regretted he'd already agreed to go to a movie when Louise told
                 him about the special opera showing today.

    (A)   Louise told him how special the opera was.
    (B)   He agreed to go to the opera tonight.
    (C)   He would've preferred to go to the opera.
    (D)   Louise went to a movie with him.

Answer: C

PRACTICE:

You will hear: Since she went to study abroad, I haven't heard anything from her.

    (A)   Cynthia is studying abroad.
    (B)   She hasn't heard from me since I went abroad.
    (C)   She hasn't written or phoned.
    (D)   She is studying biology.

Answer: C

PRACTICE:

You will hear: When it began to rain, we had already started walking.

  (A) We were caught in the rain.
  (B) We avoided the rain.
  (C) We were outside all morning.
  (D) We began to leave when it rained.

Answer: A

| ► Statement Type 6 | **Expressing time: Sequence** |

Language Needed: while, when, as, as soon as, after, before, until, by the time, whenever, as/so long as, since, once

Examples: She read the newspaper while she ate lunch.
             She always reads the newspaper when she eats lunch.
             She stopped reading the newspaper as soon as the bell rang.
             She always read the newspaper after the bell rang.
             She finished reading the newspaper before the bell rang.
             She read the newspaper until the bell rang.
             She had finished reading the newspaper by the time the bell rang.
             She always reads the newspaper whenever she eats lunch.
             She eats lunch as she reads the newspaper.
             She's been reading the newspaper since she began eating lunch.
             She begins to read the newspaper once she begins to eat lunch.

| MAIN CLAUSE | | TIME MARKER + SUBORDINATE CLAUSE |

or

| TIME MARKER + SUBORDINATE CLAUSE | | MAIN CLAUSE |

NOW YOU PRACTICE:

You will hear: She reads novels whenever she has a chance.

  (A) She likes novels a lot.
  (B) She doesn't get a chance to read.
  (C) She rarely reads novels.
  (D) She reads novels by chance.

Answer: A

PRACTICE:
You will hear: After he finished his education, he worked as a lawyer.

    (A) He studied after working.
    (B) He studied while he worked as a lawyer.
    (C) He completed his education.
    (D) He stopped studying and became a lawyer.

Answer: C

PRACTICE:
You will hear: He flew to Europe as soon as he had the time.

    (A) He never had time to go to Europe.
    (B) He flew sooner than he expected.
    (C) He went to Europe once he had a chance.
    (D) He flew immediately to Europe.

Answer: C

► Statement Type 7   **Comparisons: Difference or Similarity**

Language Needed: better than, worse than, the best, the worst, the most, the least

Structures used: Comparative, Superlative, Equalative

more ADJECTIVE than	or	ADJECTIVE + er than

    John is more occupied than Mary.
    John is busier than Mary.

the most ADJECTIVE	or	the ADJECTIVE + est

    John is the most occupied person I know.
    John is the busiest person I know.

more and more ADJECTIVE	or	ADJECTIVE + er and ADJECTIVE + er

    John is more and more occupied.
    John is busier and busier.

NOUN is the same as NOUN	or	NOUN is like NOUN

        or   NOUN and NOUN are alike (the same)

His house is the same as her apartment.
His house is like her apartment.
His house and her apartment are alike (the same).

NOW YOU PRACTICE:

You will hear: Jim is a better teacher than his friend Jack.

(A) Jim's teaching surpasses that of Jack.
(B) Jack is bigger than his friend Jim.
(C) Jim has better friends than Jack.
(D) The students like Jack better than Jim.

Answer: A

PRACTICE:

You will hear: Sue is a more elegant dancer than Joe, although she has more difficulty than he in keeping balance.

(A) Sue's balance is better than Joe's.
(B) Elegance is part of Joe's dancing.
(C) Sue's style is better than Joe's.
(D) Joe's dancing is unbalanced.

Answer: C

PRACTICE:

You will hear: The newspaper of the school is thorough, but the school yearbook is less comprehensive.

(A) The newspaper coverage is comprehensive.
(B) The yearbook is not easy to read.
(C) The newspaper is like the yearbook.
(D) The newspaper isn't published anymore.

Answer: A

Comparisons: Double Comparison

Language Needed: the more ..., the more

Structure Used: Comparative

the ADJECTIVE + er, the ADJECTIVE + er

> The older you get, the wiser you become.
> The older, the wiser.

the more ADJECTIVE, the more ADJECTIVE

> The more advanced you become, the more quickly you get a raise.

the more ...., the more ....

> The more he advances, the more he gets raises.

NOW YOU PRACTICE:

You will hear: The harder he worked, the farther behind he got.

(A) His working hard did not help him keep up.
(B) He worked harder when he was in the back.
(C) His hard work delayed him.
(D) He needs to work more often.

Answer: A

PRACTICE:

You will hear: The longer we study, the sleepier we get.

(A) They studied long and slept little.
(B) The got sleepy because they hadn't studied.
(C) Studying makes them sleepy.
(D) Sleeping helped them study.

Answer: C

PRACTICE:

You will hear: The more he explained, the more confused I became.

(A) His explanations confused me.
(B) He explained more than I could tolerate.
(C) He was confused.
(D) His talking never confused anyone.

Answer: A

> ➤ **Statement Type 8**   **Expressing possession**

Language Needed: my, your, his, her, our, your, their, mine, yours, his, hers, ours, yours, theirs

Structure Used: Possessive pronoun, noun, or adjective

Examples: Give me the name of your neighbor.
Give me your neighbor's name.
We are excited about Mary's coming to visit us.

NOW YOU PRACTICE:
You will hear: Mike can't remember the name of the neighbor who borrowed his shovel.

(A) Mike doesn't know the name of the shovel.
(B) Mike doesn't like to borrow shovels.
(C) Mike doesn't know his neighbor's name.
(D) Mike's neighbor lent him a shovel.

Answer: C

PRACTICE:
You will hear: His studying after midnight became a habit.

(A) He couldn't study after midnight.
(B) His studies lasted until midnight.
(C) He studied after midnight all the time.
(D) After midnight, he went to sleep.

Answer: C

PRACTICE:
You will hear: She often saw the man's cat in the street.

(A) She saw the man in the street.
(B) The man saw her in the street.
(C) The cat which belongs to the man was often in the street.
(D) She liked the man's cat.

Answer: C

> ➤ Statement Type 9 | **Expressing advice: Present**

Language Needed: would be better if, might be better if, had/'d better, should, ought to, need to

Examples:
It would be better if you drove slowly.
It might be better if you drove slowly.
You'd better drive slowly.
You should drive slowly.
You ought to drive slowly.
You need to drive slowly.

NOW YOU PRACTICE:

You will hear: It would be better if he studied before he took the test.

(A) He should study before he takes the test.
(B) He studied and then he took the test.
(C) He took the test before he studied.
(D) He feels ill and can't study.

Answer: A

PRACTICE:

You will hear: You'd better hurry or you'll be late for school.

(A) I bet you were in a hurry.
(B) You might be late for school.
(C) Don't worry about school.
(D) You're always late for school.

Answer: B

PRACTICE:

You will hear: It might be better if you didn't phone me.

(A) You need to phone me.
(B) It would be better if you phoned me.
(C) You didn't phone me.
(D) You shouldn't phone me.

Answer: D

Expressing advice: Past

Language Needed: should have

Examples: We worried about you. You should have called us.
                 You should have saved your money. Now you can't buy anything.

Remember: "Should have" always refers to something the subject DID NOT do.

PRACTICE:

You will hear: Joe should have sold the car after having it for ten years, but he didn't.

    (A) Joe sold his car after ten years.
    (B) Joe hasn't had a car for ten years.
    (C) Joe has been driving the same car for over ten years.
    (D) Joe seldom drove his car.

Answer: C

PRACTICE:

You will hear: I know that Louise should have been at the play, but some relatives dropped in.

    (A) Louise brought her relatives to the play.
    (B) Louise didn't want to come to the play.
    (C) Louise didn't make it to the play.
    (D) Louise was late.

Answer: C

PRACTICE:

You will hear: I told you that you shouldn't have gone to that movie.

    (A) I told you the movie would be good.
    (B) You really shouldn't go to that movie.
    (C) Let's go to that movie.
    (D) You made a mistake by going to that movie.

Answer: D

> **Statement Type 10** | **Expressing an inference**

Language Needed: should, should have, must, must have

Examples: The train is supposed to arrive at 9:00. It should be here any minute.
I don't know why the plan is delayed. It should have landed
30 minutes ago.
You haven't had breakfast. You must be hungry.
You look very tired. You must have worked hard today.

NOW YOU PRACTICE:
You will hear: The cake is very sweet. You must have used plenty of sugar.

(A) I like sweet cakes.
(B) If you use plenty of sugar, the cake is better.
(C) You put a lot of sugar in the cake.
(D) To make a sweet cake, you need a lot of sugar.

Answer: C

PRACTICE:
You will hear: Jim should have returned home by now, but unfortunately he had a
problem at work.

(A) Jim isn't home.
(B) Jim returned home with his problems.
(C) Jim doesn't work very often.
(D) It is unfortunate that Jim isn't employed.

Answer: A

PRACTICE:
You will hear: Your son is playing with a well-known band. You must be very
happy.

(A) Your son is happy in the band.
(B) You are happy to see your son play in the band.
(C) Your son needs to make you happy.
(D) You ought to permit your son to play in the band.

Answer: B

| Statement Type 11 | **Expressing a preference** |

Language Needed: ...'d like, prefer, ...'d rather

Examples: I'd like some coffee with milk.
I prefer coffee with milk.
I'd rather have coffee with milk.

NOW YOU PRACTICE:
You will hear: I'd like a different one, please.

(A) I don't like differences.
(B) I don't want the same one.
(C) I prefer the same kind.
(D) I like differences in color.

Answer: B

PRACTICE:
You will hear: I'd rather not say what my yearly salary is.

(A) I want to make more per year.
(B) I don't want to tell you how much I make per year.
(C) I'll tell you what I earn.
(D) I prefer to earn more.

Answer: B

PRACTICE:
You will hear: She'd rather go home with her roommate than stay on campus during Thanksgiving break.

(A) She goes home with her roommate often.
(B) She likes to live on campus during holidays.
(C) She goes home with her roommate and then stays on campus.
(D) She prefers visiting a friend to staying on campus.

Answer: D

> ➤ Statement Type 12 | **Expressing an obligation**

Language Needed: must, need to, has/have to, has/have/'ve got to, is/are required
to, is/are supposed to, is/are expected to

Examples: I must go to school.
I need to go to school.
I have to go to school.
I've got to go to school.
I'm required to go to school.
I'm supposed to go to school.
I'm expected to go to school.

NOW YOU PRACTICE:
You will hear: She's got to go to register for classes this afternoon.

    (A) Classes begin today.
    (B) She must sign up for classes.
    (C) Registration is all day long.
    (D) She goes to class every afternoon.

Answer: B

PRACTICE:
You will hear: Drivers are supposed to carry a valid driver's license with them at
all times.

    (A) Drivers are opposed to having their license with them.
    (B) Cars are easy to drive once you obtain your license.
    (C) Drivers don't need any identification.
    (D) A valid driver's license is required of all drivers.

Answer: D

PRACTICE:
You will hear: She's doing so well that she doesn't have to spend more time studying.

    (A) Studying takes a lot of time.
    (B) She must not study more.
    (C) She doesn't need to study more.
    (D) She's not doing so well.

Answer: C

> ➤ Statement Type 13   **Making a suggestion**

Language Needed: how about, why don't we, let's, shall we

Examples: How about going out to lunch today?
             Why don't we go out to lunch today?
             Let's go out to lunch today.
             Shall we go out to lunch today?

NOW YOU PRACTICE:
You will hear: Why don't we go to the new movie in town?

   (A) Why isn't the movie showing?
   (B) I didn't know there was a new movie in town.
   (C) Let's go to the movie.
   (D) Don't go to the movie.

Answer: C

PRACTICE:
You will hear: How about a game of ping-pong?

   (A) How long does the game last?
   (B) I don't know how to play ping-pong.
   (C) Would you like to play ping-pong?
   (D) Give me a ping-pong lesson.

Answer: C

PRACTICE:
You will hear: Why not sit in on the class?

   (A) Let's sit in the front row.
   (B) Let's audit the class.
   (C) Let's look for the class.
   (D) There's a seat in the class.

Answer: B

> ➤ **Statement Type 14** | **Giving a reason or making a conclusion**

Language Needed: since, because, when, as, now that, so long as, inasmuch as, so that, due to the fact that, therefore, consequently

Examples: Since the two men couldn't agree, they're going to court.
Because the two men couldn't agree, they're going to court.
When the two men couldn't agree, they went to court.
As the two men couldn't agree, they went to court.
Now that the two men can't agree, they will have to go to court.
So long as the two men can't agree, they went to court.
Inasmuch as the two men couldn't agree, they went to court.
Due to the fact that the two men couldn't agree, they went to court.
The two men couldn't agree; therefore, they went to court.
The two men couldn't agree; consequently, they went to court.

Structures Used: Intensifiers

| such + ADJECTIVE + NOUN + that |

| such a + ADJECTIVE + NOUN |

| so + ADJECTIVE + that |

It was such nice weather that we went to the beach.
It was such a sunny day that we went to the beach.
The weather was so nice that we went to the beach.

NOW YOU PRACTICE:
You will hear: I've registered for my courses so I'd like to pick up my I.D. card.

   (A) I have a good idea.
   (B) I want to get my I.D. card.
   (C) I want to buy books for my courses.
   (D) I know how to register.

Answer: B

PRACTICE:
You will hear: The test was so difficult that Jane could hardly pass it.

(A) Jane couldn't pass the exam.
(B) Jane's taste was difficult.
(C) Jane barely passed the exam.
(D) Jane was happy to take the test.

Answer: C

PRACTICE:
You will hear: The test was so long that I could barely finish in time.

(A) The test wasn't long.
(B) The test wasn't easy.
(C) There wasn't much time for the test.
(D) There weren't many questions on the test.

Answer: C

► Statement Type 15	**Expressing a contrast**

Language Needed: but, although, even though, while, despite, in spite of,
on the other hand, however, nevertheless, but yet, yet

Examples: I took an aspirin but I still have a headache.
Although I took an aspirin, I still have a headache.
Even though I took an aspirin, I still have a headache.
While I took an aspirin, I still have a headache.
Despite taking an aspirin, I still have a headache.
In spite of taking an aspirin, I still have a headache.
I took an aspirin; on the other hand, I still have a headache.
I took an aspirin; however, I still have a headache.
I took an aspirin; nevertheless, I still have a headache.
I took an aspirin; but yet I have a headache.
I took an aspirin; yet I have a headache.

NOW YOU PRACTICE:

You will hear: I'd like to stay on campus during break even though the dorms may be closed.

    (A) The dorms are close by.
    (B) I like living in the dorms.
    (C) I don't want to leave campus during vacation.
    (D) The dorms are closed in May.

Answer: C

PRACTICE:

You will hear: Despite what Sue thought, the concert was a success.

    (A) Sue taught about the concert.
    (B) Sue didn't think the concert was good.
    (C) Sue wasn't able to go to the concert.
    (D) Sue thought the concert was great.

Answer: B

PRACTICE:

You will hear: Joe was still confused even though the teacher explained the math problem twice.

    (A) Joe didn't understand the math problem.
    (B) Joe confused the teacher.
    (C) Joe explained the problem.
    (D) Joe stole the answer.

Answer: A

  ▶ **Statement Type 16**   **Adding information**

Language Needed: and, moreover, furthermore, in addition, besides, also, not only......but also, both......and

Examples: It was raining hard and there was a strong wind.
It was raining hard; moreover, there was a strong wind.
It was raining hard; furthermore, there was a strong wind.
It was raining hard; in addition, there was a strong wind.
It was raining hard; besides, there was a strong wind.
It was raining hard; also, there was a strong wind.
It was not only raining hard but also there was a strong wind.
It was both raining hard and there was a strong wind.

Structures Used: Elliptical

AFFIRMATIVE STATEMENT......and so do/does/am/is/are

or

AFFIRMATIVE STATEMENT......do/does/am/is/are too

or

NEGATIVE STATEMENT......and neither do/does/am/is/are

or

NEGATIVE STATEMENT......and do/does/am/is/are + n't either

My mother is here and so is my sister.
My mother is here and my sister is too.
My mother isn't here and neither is my sister.
My mother isn't here and my sister isn't either.

NOW YOU PRACTICE:
You will hear: Not only was his lecture uninteresting, but it was also inaccurate.

(A)   The lecture was about cures.
(B)   The lecture was only offered once.
(C)   The lecture was boring.
(D)   The lecture was about interest rates.

Answer: C

PRACTICE:
You will hear: Mark took the bus to school and so did Jim.

(A)   Mark took the bus but Jim didn't take it.
(B)   Mark sewed a shirt.
(C)   Both Mark and Jim took the bus to school.
(D)   Mark didn't go to school.

Answer: C

PRACTICE:

You will hear: The president of the college appreciates the work of the faculty and so do the students.

(A) The president appreciates the work of the students.
(B) The president assigns work to the professors.
(C) Both the students and the president value their teachers.
(D) Only the students appreciate the faculty.

Answer: C

PRACTICE:

You will hear: Jim always likes to eat ice cream and Mary does too.

(A) Both Mary and Jim enjoy ice cream.
(B) Jim likes ice cream more than Mary does.
(C) Jim screams and so does Mary.
(D) Mary doesn't like to eat ice cream.

Answer: A

PRACTICE:

You will hear: Neither John nor his sister studied law.

(A) John and his sister were both law students.
(B) John didn't study law and his sister didn't either.
(C) John brought his sister a legal report.
(D) John is a lawyer but his sister isn't.

Answer: B

➤ Statement Type 17 | **Expressing real conditions**

Language Needed: if, or, so that, unless, until, only if, providing (that), provided (that), in case (that), in the event (that), even if, otherwise, whether or not, without, by

Examples: If you don't study, you'll fail the exam.
You'd better study or you will fail the exam.
You'd better study so that you'll pass the exam.
Unless you study, you won't pass the exam.
Only if you study, will you pass the exam.
Provided that you study, you'll pass the exam.
In the event that you study, you'll pass the exam.

Whether you study or not, you will probably pass the exam.
*Even if you study, you may not pass the exam.
You'd better study; otherwise, you won't pass the exam.
By studying, you'll pass the exam.
Without studying, you won't pass the exam.

Remember: *"Even if" poses a negative condition.

NOW YOU PRACTICE:

You will hear: By practicing the piano daily, you will improve your ability to play many types of music.

    (A) Practice makes pretty hands.
    (B) You are able to play different music.
    (C) Daily practice improves your music.
    (D) Practice never makes a perfect player.

Answer: C

PRACTICE:

You will hear: If that course isn't required, I won't take it.

    (A) I want to take the course.
    (B) The course isn't required.
    (C) I don't want to take that course.
    (D) Of course, it's required.

Answer: C

PRACTICE:

You will hear: You'd better study or you will fail your exam.

    (A) You need to study in order to pass your test.
    (B) It's better to study than take a test.
    (C) I'm sure you'll pass the test.
    (D) Many students failed the test.

Answer: A

PRACTICE:

You will hear: Without your assistance, the project will not get finished.

    (A)   The projected assistance is necessary.
    (B)   Your assistants will finish the project.
    (C)   Your assistance will be finished.
    (D)   Your help is necessary.

Answer: D

| ➤ Statement Type 18 | **Imagining a condition: Present** |

Language Needed: would'/d......if, could......if, might......if

Examples: I would (I'd) teach him, if he asked me.
              I could teach him, if he asked me.
              I might teach him, if he asked me.

Structures Used: Subjunctive

NOW YOU PRACTICE:

You will hear: I'd be glad to go over your grades if you made an appointment with
                my secretary.

    (A)   Your grades exceeded my expectations.
    (B)   My secretary will provide you with grades.
    (C)   My secretary was appointed to a better position.
    (D)   You need an appointment to discuss your grades.

Answer: D

Imagining a condition: Past

Language Needed: would've, if PAST PERFECT, could've, if PAST PERFECT,
                  might've, if PAST PERFECT

Examples: I would've come, if I'd (had) known you were home.
              I could've come, if I'd (had) known you were home.
              I might've come, if I'd (had) known you were home.

Structures Used: Past Subjunctive, Inverted Helping Verb-Subject

| IF CLAUSE = auxiliary verb + subject | | MAIN CLAUSE |

Had I known you were home, I would've come over.
Should you have complained, I could've taken action.

PRACTICE:

You will hear: We would've looked for you, if we'd known you were going to be there.

(A)   We didn't know you were there so we didn't look for you.
(B)   We looked for you but we didn't find you.
(C)   You knew we were coming.
(D)   We looked for you but didn't find you.

Answer: A

PRACTICE:

You will hear: Had I known you were coming, I would've invited my mother and father to meet you.

(A)   I had known of your arrival before.
(B)   Your mother and father told me of your arrival.
(C)   I didn't know you would be here.
(D)   I wanted to meet your mother and father.

Answer: C

PRACTICE:

You will hear: If he had had more time, he could've visited all of his friends.

(A)   He knew he needed to visit his friends.
(B)   He didn't have enough time to see his friends.
(C)   He couldn't visit his friends because they didn't have time.
(D)   He had lots of time to visit his friends.

Answer: B

➤ Statement Type 19	**DESCRIPTIONS**

Language Needed: who, which, whose, that

Examples: The man who (that) I saw was Mr. Jones.
The movie which (that) we saw was good.
The student whose composition I read is a good writer.

Structures Used: Relative Clause

NOUN	Rel. Clause Marker + RELATIVE CLAUSE	VERB PHRASE

NOUN	VERB PHRASE	Rel. Clause Marker + RELATIVE CLAUSE

The student who I like sits in the front of the room.
I like the student who sits in the front of the room.

NOW YOU PRACTICE:

You will hear: Mary searched high and low for her can opener which she finally found in the dishwasher.

(A) The can opener was in the dishwasher.
(B) Mary washed dishes.
(C) Mary was opening cans all day.
(D) Mary finally got the can open.

Answer: A

PRACTICE:

You will hear: Paul mentioned a book (that) I had never heard of.

(A) Paul gave me a strange look.
(B) I couldn't hear what Paul said.
(C) I didn't recognize the name of the book.
(D) Paul read a book to me.

Answer: C

PRACTICE:

You will hear: I'll never forget the woman whose child was always crying.

(A) I forgot who the woman was.
(B) I forgot who the child was.
(C) I'll never forget the child who cried.
(D) I'll always remember the woman with the unhappy child.

Answer: D

➤ **Statement Type 20** | **Qualifying negatively**

Language Needed: never, hardly ever, barely, seldom, scarcely, rarely

Examples: Never have I missed a day of work.
                 Hardly ever have I missed a day of work.
                 Barely have I missed a day of work.
                 Seldom have I missed a day of work.
                 Scarcely have I missed a day of work.
                 Rarely have I missed a day of work.

Structure Used: Neg. MARKER + AUXILIARY + SUBJECT

NOW YOU PRACTICE:

You will hear: Seldom have I agreed with my brother.

(A) My brother and I are alike.
(B) My brother agrees with me.
(C) I seldom see my brother.
(D) My brother and I don't agree.

Answer: D

PRACTICE:

You will hear: Hardly ever has the mail arrived before 10:00 in the morning.

(A) The mail rarely arrives after 10:00.
(B) The mail has not yet arrived.
(C) The mail almost always arrives after 10:00.
(D) I never see the mailman in the morning.

Answer: C

PRACTICE:

You will hear: Never have I known Pat to be dishonest.

(A) Pat is very honest.
(B) Pat doesn't know she is honest.
(C) I never knew Pat before.
(D) Pat is not always honest.

Answer: A

> **➤ Statement Type 21**   **Making a polite request**

Language Needed: would you mind, could you, do you mind, kindly, can you,
I'd prefer it if you...

NOW YOU PRACTICE:

You will hear: Would you mind picking me up?

    (A) Please remember my name.
    (B) Please give me a ride.
    (C) Don't point at me.
    (D) Jim phones me.

Answer: B

PRACTICE:

You will hear: May I turn in my paper on Thursday?

    (A) Did I turn in my assignment on Thursday?
    (B) May I take my turn in class on Thursday?
    (C) I'd like to give you my paper.
    (D) I'll take my paper home on Thursday.

Answer: C

PRACTICE:

You will hear: I'd rather you finish talking before class begins.

    (A) Talk during class.
    (B) Finish the class.
    (C) Talk before the class.
    (D) Class is beginning.

Answer: C

➤ Statement Type 22	**Focusing on or emphasizing information: Passives**

Structure Used: | OBJECT OF ACTION | | ACTION | | (by + AGENT) |

Examples:
I was invited by John.
I didn't want to be invited.
I liked being invited.
I liked having been invited.
I was happy to have been invited.

NOW YOU PRACTICE:

You will hear: Your participation in the class would be preferred, but it isn't required.

(A) You can participate in class if you want to.
(B) You prefer to participate in class.
(C) Class is not obligatory.
(D) You should study the principles of the class.

Answer: A

PRACTICE:

You will hear: The teachers were told to report their grades to the chair of the department.

(A) Departmental chairs collected student grades.
(B) Teachers told students their grades.
(C) Grades were reported to the teachers.
(D) The chair of each department reported grades.

Answer: A

PRACTICE:

You will hear: A suit and tie are required at the dance.

(A) Everyone must wear formal attire.
(B) The dance will suit everyone.
(C) You look nice in a suit and tie.
(D) The dance is at a suitable time.

Answer: A

Focus on or emphasize information: Noun clause focus

Language Needed: what..., where..., the fact that

Examples: What he is, is a complete fool.
             Where we found the key was in the drawer.
             The fact that he sold you a book for less, is nothing unusual.
             What I find hard to understand is why you need my help.

Structures Used:

WHAT + CLAUSE WHERE	+	VERB PHRASE

THE FACT THAT + CLAUSE	+	VERB PHRASE

THAT + CLAUSE	+	VERB PHRASE

NOW YOU PRACTICE:

You will hear: What I really don't understand is why the thief denied he stole the ring.

   (A) I don't understand the denial.
   (B) It seems someone didn't understand.
   (C) I understand why the thief stole a ring.
   (D) I don't deny you understand.

Answer: A

PRACTICE:

You will hear: What Mary is really trying to do is to complete her courses and lab work by May.

   (A) Mary isn't sure what she may do.
   (B) Mary is working on an incomplete course.
   (C) Mary wants to finish courses and lab work.
   (D) Mary may take two courses.

Answer: C

PRACTICE:

You will hear: That he was required to buy health insurance surprised the entering student.

   (A) The student surprised everyone by accepting the insurance policy.
   (B) The student thought that health insurance was necessary.
   (C) The student didn't know that he had to buy health insurance.
   (D) Health insurance is a prize students receive.

Answer: C

| ► Statement Type 23 | **"get" + adjective** |

Language Needed: bored, interested in, worried, fired, dressed, lost, used to,
                  tired, married, confused, amused by

Examples: They got bored with the class.
           She got interested in biology.
           I got worried because he was late.
           We got used to her loud voice.
           Tomorrow they will get married.
           Don't get confused by her.
           Mary got dressed early in the morning.
           Be careful. You can easily get lost in New York.

NOW YOU PRACTICE:
You will hear: She finally got used to living abroad.

    (A) She used to live abroad.
    (B) She has lived abroad a long time.
    (C) She became accustomed to life abroad.
    (D) She got bored overseas.

Answer: C

PRACTICE:
You will hear: We can leave as soon as I get finished with my work.

    (A) We'll leave before I finish my work.
    (B) We can't leave my work.
    (C) Once I finish my work we can leave.
    (D) I can work soon.

Answer: C

PRACTICE:
You will hear: He got fired because he came to work late.

    (A) He lost his job.
    (B) He got angry because he was late.
    (C) They gave him a new job.
    (D) He always got to work late.

Answer: A

> ➤ Statement Type 24   **Stressing importance**

Language Needed: demand, insist, request, ask (that + CLAUSE), recommend, suggest, it is important, it is necessary, it is crucial

Remember: The verb in the clause which follows "that" will be in a subjunctive form:

I demand that he sit down. (not: "sits down")

NOW YOU PRACTICE:
You will hear: He demanded that he be given a raise.

(A) He insisted upon a raise.
(B) He wanted to give me a raise.
(C) He raised his hand.
(D) He was given a raise.

Answer: A

PRACTICE:
You will hear: I requested that she see a doctor.

(A) I requested a doctor.
(B) I asked to see a doctor.
(C) She asked to see a doctor.
(D) She saw a doctor because I advised her today.

Answer: D

PRACTICE:
You will hear: It is essential that no one be admitted without a student I.D. card.

(A) No one with a student I.D. card may come.
(B) Only those with student I.D. cards may enter.
(C) Students don't need their I.D. cards.
(D) It isn't important to have your I.D. card.

Answer: B

> **Statement Type 25** | **Causing someone to do something**

Language Needed: get + someone + to do something
                           make + someone + do something
                           have + someone + do something

Examples: I'll get Jim to fix the door.
                     I'll make Jim fix the door.
                     I'll have Jim fix the door.

NOW YOU PRACTICE:
You will hear: She just had a company paint her car.

(A) She had visitors.
(B) She painted her car.
(C) She was required to paint her car.
(D) Some workers painted her car.

Answer: D

PRACTICE:
You will hear: Mary got Carol to read the children a book.

(A) Carol read a book to the children.
(B) Mary got to read to the children.
(C) Mary read the children a book.
(D) Mary caught Carol reading a book to the children.

Answer: A

PRACTICE:
You will hear: The teacher made Gary play a long song.

(A) Gary made a long song.
(B) The teacher sang a long song.
(C) The teacher made a new song.
(D) Gary had to play a long song.

Answer: D

> Statement Type 26   **"Promising," "telling," "asking," "someone," something**

Language Needed: promise
tell + someone + something
ask

NOW YOU PRACTICE:

You will hear: Ben promised his girlfriend, Carol, a letter.

(A) Ben and Carol agreed to write each other.
(B) Ben made promises easily.
(C) Ben never phoned Carol.
(D) Ben planned to write Carol.

Answer: D

PRACTICE:

You will hear: Sally told her brother to feed the cats while she was away.

(A) Sally fed the cats for her brother.
(B) Sally went away with the cats.
(C) Sally's brother fed the cats.
(D) Sally doesn't tell her brother what to do.

Answer: C

PRACTICE:

You will hear: Bob asked the professor to show him how to do the experiment.

(A) The professor watched Bob do the experiment.
(B) Bob can do the experiment by himself.
(C) The experiment will be demonstrated by Bob.
(D) Bob needed help with the experiment.

Answer: D

Dialogues

Dialogues are followed by a question about the content of the dialogue. The questions follow a pattern. It will help you to recognize the types of questions which are asked. This section will give you practice in recognizing the types of questions asked after the dialogues.

> ➤ Question Type 1 | **Be familiar with the test.**

Typical questions: What are the speakers doing?

What have the speakers been asked to do?

What does the speaker want to do?

What does the man want the woman to do?

DIRECTIONS: Read the dialogue and then choose the answer which best answers the question asked by the third voice.

NOW YOU PRACTICE:
You will hear:
Man's voice: Mary asked if we could pick her up this afternoon.
Woman's voice: I'll see. I'm not sure we'll have room.
Third voice: What does Mary want them to do?

(A) Give her a ride
(B) Make her feel better
(C) Drop her friends by to her
(D) Give her room in their house

Answer: A

PRACTICE:
You will hear:
Woman's voice: I need to get a copy of my transcript. Can you tell me where the Registrar's Office is?
Man's voice: Just follow me. I'm going there myself.
Third voice: What does the woman need to do?

(A) Register for a class
(B) Apply for a job
(C) Get an official copy of her grades
(D) See a friend

Answer: C

Cultural tip: Official copies (transcripts) of grades are usually sent by the Registrar's Office rather than by the student. This is what makes them official.

PRACTICE:
You will hear:

Man's voice:	It's sunny and warm. Stop studying and come to the beach with me.
Woman's voice:	Why not?
Third voice:	What is the woman probably going to do?

    (A) Study with the man
    (B) Stay home and study
    (C) Go to the beach with the man
    (D) Study at the beach

Answer: C

► **Question Type 2** | **Explain the meaning.**

Many times you will be asked to tell what a speaker means. You must provide a paraphrase (another statement) which tells the meaning.

Typical question: What does the man (the woman) mean?

NOW YOU PRACTICE:
You will hear:

Man's voice:	We worked hard for the event to make it a success.
Woman's voice:	I've never seen such a crowd. You must be very tired.
Third voice:	What does the woman mean?

    (A) She was looking for many people.
    (B) She agrees that the event was a success.
    (C) She didn't see many people.
    (D) She is surprised that the man is tired.

Answer: B

PRACTICE:
You will hear:

Woman's voice:	What's going on upstairs?
Man's voice:	I don't know. It sounds like they're coming through the ceiling.
Third voice:	What does the man mean?

(A) Someone fell down the stairs.
(B) The ceiling is collapsing.
(C) There is a lot of noise upstairs.
(D) He doesn't like his apartment.

Answer: C

> **Question Type 3** | **Identify the topic of conversation.**

Typical questions: What are they discussing?

What do they say about ....?

What are these people talking about?

NOW YOU PRACTICE:
You will hear:
Man's voice: How did you like the coverage of the missile launching?
Woman's voice: Unfortunately, I was too busy to see a paper today.
Third voice: What are these people talking about?

(A) A speech on television
(B) A lecture at work
(C) A radio show
(D) An article in a newspaper

Answer: D

PRACTICE:
You will hear:
Woman's voice: Did you notice that the museum has several portraits on display about the French Revolution?
Man's voice: Yes, I noticed some pottery there also.
Third voice: What are the man and the woman discussing?

(A) Architecture
(B) A history class
(C) Student paintings
(D) An exhibit

Answer: D

PRACTICE:

You will hear:

Woman's voice: What do you think about the tornado that touched down ten miles from here last night?

Man's voice: You think that's something? I used to live in a place that had dust storms every week.

Third voice: What topic are they discussing?

    (A) The clouds
    (B) Housing construction
    (C) The countryside
    (D) The weather

Answer: D

Cultural tip: Tornados are common in certain areas of the United States, such as, the Midwest and South. Dust storms are only found in the desert (the southwestern part of the United States). Dust storms are fast winds that whip up the sand.

➤ **Question Type 4** | **Describe a past event or happening.**

Typical question: What happened to the man (the woman)?

NOW YOU PRACTICE:

You will hear:

Woman's voice: Joe's in a real bad mood today. What's wrong with him?

Man's voice: His job was taken over by a fellow worker.

Third voice: What happened to Joe?

    (A) He got a pay raise.
    (B) He fainted.
    (C) He got sick at work.
    (D) He lost some of his responsibility.

Answer: D

PRACTICE:

You will hear:

Woman's voice: Hello, Mr. Black's office. Can I help you?

Man's voice: Yes, I just called a few minutes ago and I got cut off. Could I speak with Mr. Black now?

Third voice: What happened to the man?

    (A) He got disconnected.
    (B) He hurt himself.

(C) He fainted.

(D) He caught a cold.

Answer: A

Cultural tip: It is common business etiquette to answer the phone by greeting and identifying the location or business and offering assistance. The other speaker then responds with his/her request.

PRACTICE:

You will hear:

Woman's voice: I didn't see you in class this afternoon.

Man's voice: No, I was in my lab this morning. One minute I was setting up an experiment and the next I passed out.

Third voice: What happened to the man?

    (A) He fainted.

    (B) He helped the teacher.

    (C) He came to biology class.

    (D) He set up an experiment in one minute.

Answer: A

| ➤ Question Type 5 | **State the location of the speakers.** |

Typical questions: Where did this conversation take place?

                           Where are they?

NOW YOU PRACTICE:

You will hear:

Man's voice: Could you tell me where I could find the aspirin and the toothpaste?

Woman's voice: It's in aisle B, near the lotion.

Third voice: Where did this conversation probably take place?

    (A) In a cafeteria

    (B) In a restaurant

    (C) In a church

    (D) In a drug store

Answer: D

Cultural tip: You can buy aspirin and toothpaste also in a grocery store or supermarket in the United States.

PRACTICE:

You will hear:

Woman's voice: Let's go get in line to eat. I'm hungry.

Man's voice: Me too. I wish we could go someplace that we could sit down and get served by a waitress.

Third voice: Where are they probably going?

    (A) To a restaurant
    (B) To a student cafeteria
    (C) To a grocery store
    (D) To a book store

Answer: B

*Cultural tip: Restaurants usually have a host or hostess who seats people and a waiter or waitress who takes your order. Cafeterias only have food servers. Customers enter a line and choose from the prepared food they see before them. They pay the cashier when they reach the end of the line.

PRACTICE:

You will hear:

Man's voice: Can you help me find some information about Martin Luther King, Jr. for a history assignment?

Woman's voice: Sure. You can look under "King" in the card catalogue or you can use our computer system.

Third voice: Where does this conversation probably take place?

    (A) In the student lounge
    (B) In the bookstore
    (C) In the health center
    (D) In the library

Answer: D

*Cultural tip: Many libraries now have their book reference system on a computer. Many students look up references by using a computer.

> Question Type 6 | **Guess the future or infer.**

You will be asked to guess what might happen next.

Typical questions: What is the man probably going to do?

What does the man want to do?

What will the man do next?

What can we probably conclude about…?

NOW YOU PRACTICE:
You will hear:

Woman's voice: I understand that you're planning to move off-campus next semester, Tom.

Man's voice: I plan to rent a one-bedroom apartment with my friend, Jim, if we can save enough money for a rental deposit.

Third voice: What does Tom plan to do?

    (A) Move into a dorm
    (B) Save his money
    (C) Visit his friend, Jim
    (D) Rent an apartment

Answer: D

*Cultural tip: On-campus housing is usually in a dorm. Off-campus housing is in an apartment or a sorority or fraternity house. Sometimes "off-campus" housing is located close to or even on campus.

PRACTICE:
You will hear:

Man's voice: What time are you going to register?

Woman's voice: The class is very popular so I need to be there early to make sure I get a place.

Third voice: What will the woman probably do to prevent from getting closed out of the class?

    (A) See the Dean
    (B) Go early
    (C) Insist on her needs
    (D) Stand in front of others

Answer: B

PRACTICE:

You will hear:

Woman's voice: I'm hungry and it's too late to go out to get anything.

Man's voice: Why don't we order out for pizza?

Third voice: What will they probably do next?

    (A) Wait until tomorrow

    (B) Phone a pizza restaurant to deliver food to them

    (C) Ask a friend to stop by with a pizza

    (D) Go to bed

Answer: B

*Cultural tip: Pizza places often have a delivery system. You can call in your order by phone and someone brings the food directly to your door 20 minutes later. Restaurants usually don't have this system. However, you can call in an order to a restaurant and go yourself to get the food and eat it in your home. This is called "carry out," "take out," or "an order to go."

| ➤ Question Type 7 | **Compute or infer time.**

Sometimes you will be asked to compute time given the information provided by the speaker.

Typical questions: How much ...?

                            How many ...?

                            How long ...?

NOW YOU PRACTICE:

You will hear:

Man's voice: I haven't had fast food for a long time. How much is a hamburger and soda now?

Woman's voice: They used to only cost a couple of dollars, but now the price has doubled.

Third voice: How much is a hamburger and a soda now?

    (A) $2.00

    (B) $1.00

    (C) $4.00

    (D) $2.50

Answer: C

PRACTICE:
You will hear:
Man's voice: Where have you been? I've been looking all over for you.
Woman's voice: I went to buy a dozen donuts but got twice that number because they were on sale.
Third voice: How many donuts did the man buy?

    (A) 20
    (B) 12
    (C) 24
    (D) 2

Answer: C

PRACTICE:
You will hear:
Woman's voice: What are you planning to do this summer?
Man's voice: I'm going to take a month's vacation in Bermuda.
Third voice: How long will the woman stay?

    (A) All summer long
    (B) For four weeks
    (C) One year
    (D) Through the spring

Answer: B

> **Question Type 8** | **Identify the cause.**

Typical questions: Why did (n't)...?

    Why might the woman (the man)...?

    Why is the woman (the man) ...ing?

NOW YOU PRACTICE:
You will hear:
Man's voice: Did you watch the football game today? It was fantastic.
Woman's voice: No, I had my hands full with the children.
Third voice: Why didn't the woman know about the football game?

    (A) She hurt her hands.
    (B) She was washing clothes.

(C) She doesn't like football.

(D) She was busy taking care of children.

Answer: D

PRACTICE:

You will hear:

Man's voice: Would you like to go see a play tonight with me? I have front row seats.

Woman's voice: I'd love to but I have a test tomorrow and I haven't prepared for it yet.

Third voice: Why didn't the woman accept the invitation?

(A) She had to study.

(B) She doesn't like plays.

(C) She's in love with someone else.

(D) She likes to sit in the back.

Answer: A

PRACTICE:

You will hear:

Woman's voice: Good afternoon, Dr. Smith's office.

Man's voice: Hello, this is Tom Greer. Could you please tell Dr. Smith I'll be delayed? My car won't start.

Third voice: Why was the man going to be late?

(A) He couldn't find the classroom.

(B) He forgot the apartment.

(C) His car broke down.

(D) He wasn't feeling well.

Answer: C

> **Question Type 9** | **Identify feelings.**

Typical question: How does the man (the woman) feel?

NOW YOU PRACTICE:

You will hear:

Woman's voice: Be careful of Joe today. He's been shouting at everyone who enters his office.

Man's voice: I'll approach him very cautiously.

Third voice: How is Joe feeling?

    (A) Cautious
    (B) Angry
    (C) Apathetic
    (D) Stimulated

Answer: B

PRACTICE:
You will hear:
Man's voice: Hi, Sue. What's happening?
Woman's voice: I was hoping I would get the job I applied for, but I didn't.
Third voice: How does Sue feel?

    (A) Elated
    (B) Disappointed
    (C) Indifferent
    (D) Confused

Answer: B

PRACTICE:
You will hear:
Woman's voice: I'm really glad summer is here. Now I can go camping in the Rockies.
Man's voice: That's funny. I was planning the same thing. Why don't we try to go together.
Third voice: How does the man feel?

    (A) Insulted
    (B) Angry
    (C) Uninterested
    (D) Friendly

Answer: D

*Cultural tip: The Rockies are located in the northwestern part of the United States. This is a mountainous region which has many trees and rivers. Some people in the United States like to vacation in such areas and stay outside in tents. This is referred to as "camping."

> **Question Type 10** | **Give advice or make a suggestion.**

Typical questions: What is the man (the woman) recommending?
What advice does the man give the woman?

NOW YOU PRACTICE:
You will hear:
Man's voice: I've been working on this all day and I can't get it right.
Woman's voice: I hardly think you should start all over.
Third voice: What is the woman recommending?

    (A) That the man think harder
    (B) That the man begin again
    (C) That the man stop
    (D) That the man continue

Answer: D

PRACTICE:
You will hear:
Man's voice: Hello, Mary. Would you like to join us? We've just been seated.
Woman's voice: Thank you. Why don't we all take the special? I'm famished.
Third voice: What does the woman suggest they do?

    (A) Buy a textbook
    (B) Play a game
    (C) Order the same meal
    (D) Listen to the concert

Answer: C

*Cultural tip: Many restaurants offer two or three "specials" during each meal. If you order the special, you pay a little less and you can get served more quickly.

PRACTICE:
You will hear:
Man's voice: John's new red car now has two big dents in the side.
Woman's voice: He should have been more careful with his car.
Third voice: What does the woman suggest?

    (A) That John was careless.
    (B) That John needs a car.
    (C) That John prevented an accident.
    (D) That John is a very cautious driver.

Answer: A

PRACTICE:
You will hear:

Woman's voice: I'm upset. I'd planned to go to Boston by plane, but the seats are all sold out.

Man's voice: What's the problem? You could go by train and pay even less.

Third voice: What does the man suggest?

(A) The woman can go by car.
(B) The woman may take a train.
(C) The man will enjoy the train.
(D) The man needs to solve his problem.

Answer: B

> **Question Type 11** **Identify the profession of the speaker.**

Typical question: Who is the man speaking to?

NOW YOU PRACTICE:
You will hear:

Woman's voice: May I help you?

Man's voice: Yes, I'd like some help in locating these references which were put on reserve.

Third voice: Who is the man speaking to?

(A) A police officer
(B) A telephone operator
(C) A librarian
(D) A waitress

Answer: C

*Cultural tip: Books or articles which are popular are often put "on reserve" by a professor. They cannot be checked out of the library, but can be borrowed for an hour or two.

PRACTICE:
You will hear:

Woman's voice: Could you help me? I was stopped at this light and that yellow car hit my car, putting this dent in it.

Man's voice: O.K. Show me your driver's license, car registration and proof of insurance and fill out this accident form.

Third voice: Who is the man?

    (A) A professor
    (B) A police officer
    (C) A dean of students
    (D) A librarian

Answer: B

*Cultural tip: If a police officer stops a driver, he usually asks for three forms of identification: a driver's license (proof of permission to drive), car registration (proof of car inspection and ownership), and car insurance (proof of insurance coverage). Most of these are required of all drivers in every state in the United States.

PRACTICE:
You will hear:

Man's voice:	Good morning. Can I help you?
Woman's voice:	Yes, I'd like to have my current balance and to withdraw fifty dollars from my savings account.
Third voice:	Who is the woman speaking to?

    (A) A teacher
    (B) A waiter
    (C) A mail clerk
    (D) A bank clerk

Answer: D

*Cultural tip: Banks have very good computers in the United States. They can usually give you a balance quickly. Many people have different types of accounts. The most common accounts are checking accounts (which allow you to write checks for payment) and savings accounts (which pay you a little extra for letting the bank store your money).

> ➤ Question Type 12 | **Express an attitude or feeling.**

PRACTICE:
You will hear:

Woman's voice:	I think I'll have lunch in the cafeteria. I like their macaroni and cheese.
Man's voice:	The chicken salad is good but there's nothing like home cooking.
Third voice:	What does the man think of the food in the cafeteria?

    (A) He doesn't like it.
    (B) He prefers his own cooking.

(C) He enjoys it.
(D) He doesn't have any preference.

Answer: B

*Cultural tip: "Home cooking" refers to food that is prepared in a home by a non-professional individual. "Eating out" refers to food that is prepared by a restaurant. "Ordering out" refers to food that is prepared by a restaurant but eaten in one's home.

PRACTICE:
You will hear:
Woman's voice: Are you taking a computer class?
Man's voice: Yes. I'm worried that I won't do as well as the others in the class.
Third voice: How does the man feel about having to take the class?

    (A) Uncertain
    (B) Uninterested
    (C) Ill
    (D) Impressed

Answer: A

PRACTICE:
You will hear:
Woman's voice: Did you happen to hear the President's speech on television last night?
Man's voice: Boy, did I. I could give a more exciting speech if I were sleeping.
Third voice: What did the man think of the lecture?

    (A) It was too boring.
    (B) It was very informative.
    (C) It was incoherent.
    (D) It was useless.

Answer: A

*Cultural tip: The President of the United States will often give a speech on television in the evening a few times each year.

EXERCISE: SCAN AND GUESS

The purpose of this exercise is to practice guessing and to do it fast. Guessing can help prepare you for the question which appears on the tape.

DIRECTIONS: Each question below has four answers which look like answers to a question asked after you hear a short dialogue between two speakers. SCAN the four answers very quickly and GUESS the TOPIC of the dialogue and what QUESTION is going to be asked.

POSSIBLE TOPICS TO IDENTIFY:

- A place (in or towards)
- An action/activity
- An event
- A type of ...
- Amount of time
- Quantity
- Evaluation
- Cause

- Reason or purpose
- Emotions or feelings
- Activity
- Topic
- Current, past, future action
- Money
- Advice
- Requirements

Allow yourself only a few seconds per question. Cover up the answer until you have guessed your own and then look and compare your answer.

Example:
You will see:
- (A) In a store
- (B) In a classroom
- (C) In a church
- (D) In a hospital

Answer:
Guess the topic: A place
Guess the question: Where are the speakers?
Where does this conversation probably take place?

NOW YOU BEGIN:

1. (A) A lecture
   (B) A meeting with the president
   (C) A telephone conversation
   (D) A news program on television

GUESS THE TOPIC AND QUESTION

Topic: Type of speech
Question: What are they talking about?

---

2. (A) Two or three days
   (B) About a month
   (C) More than a week
   (D) Exactly two weeks

GUESS THE TOPIC AND QUESTION

Topic: Amount of time
Question: How long ...?

3. (A) To a grocery store
   (B) To the church
   (C) To a cafe
   (D) To a drugstore

GUESS THE TOPIC AND QUESTION

Topic: Towards a place
Question: Where is the speaker probably going?
            Where would he (they) like to go?

4. (A) Six
   (B) Sixteen
   (C) Sixty
   (D) Sixty-one

GUESS THE TOPIC AND QUESTION

Topic: Number
Question: How many ...?

5. (A) He got a pay raise.
   (B) He fainted.
   (C) He got sick.
   (D) He didn't get promoted.

GUESS THE TOPIC AND QUESTION

Topic: Event or action
Question: What happened?

6.   (A) At 9:00
      (B) All the time
      (C) At 7:00
      (D) At 10:00

GUESS THE TOPIC AND QUESTION

Topic: Time
Question: When will ...?

---

7.   (A) Write a check.
      (B) Join a club.
      (C) Phone a friend.
      (D) Write a note.

GUESS THE TOPIC AND QUESTION

Topic: Action
Question: What were they asked to do?
            What are they going to do?

---

8.   (A) You'd better take the subway.
      (B) I can tell you a quick way to get there.
      (C) My son always uses the bus.
      (D) If you take the train, it'll be cheaper.

GUESS THE TOPIC AND QUESTION

Topic: Advice
Question: What does the speaker recommend?
            How should you ...?

---

9.   (A) In a drugstore
      (B) In a restaurant
      (C) In a cafe
      (D) In a church

GUESS THE TOPIC AND QUESTION

Topic: Place
Question: Where does this conversation probably take place?

---

10. (A) He'll tell Phil when he sees him.
    (B) He wants to make sure there is room.
    (C) He's not sure he can find a room.
    (D) He doesn't have enough information.

GUESS THE TOPIC AND QUESTION

Topic: Reason
Question: Why does the speaker ...?
           What did the man tell the woman?

---

11. (A) For two hours
    (B) From one to three hours
    (C) One whole day
    (D) All morning

GUESS THE TOPIC AND QUESTION

Topic: Length of time
Question: How long will ...?
           How long did ...?

---

12. (A) Disappointed
    (B) Angry
    (C) Depressed
    (D) Happy

GUESS THE TOPIC AND QUESTION

Topic: Emotions
Question: How does the man (the woman) feel?

---

13. (A) She was looking for a man.
    (B) She agrees the event was a success.
    (C) She didn't find her friend.
    (D) She is surprised that the man was fired.

GUESS THE TOPIC AND QUESTION

Topic: Undefined
Question: What does the woman (the man) mean?

---

14. (A) A mail carrier
    (B) An author
    (C) A police officer
    (D) A clerk

GUESS THE TOPIC AND QUESTION

Topic: Occupation
Question: What is probably the man's (the woman's) profession?
          Who is the man (the woman) probably speaking to?

15. (A) Take a picture
    (B) Tour the city
    (C) Visit a friend
    (D) Go out for lunch

GUESS THE TOPIC AND QUESTION

Topic: Action
Question: What is the man (the woman) probably going to do?
          What does the man (the woman) probably want to do?

16. (A) Architecture
    (B) A history class
    (C) Student paintings
    (D) An art exhibit

GUESS THE TOPIC AND QUESTION

Topic: Subject/topic
Question: What are they discussing?
          What do they want to discuss?

17. (A) He apologized nicely.
    (B) He complained bitterly.
    (C) He accepted graciously.
    (D) He argued strongly.

GUESS THE TOPIC AND QUESTION

Topic: Past actions
Question: What did the man do?
          What was the man's reaction to what the woman said?

18. (A) He's stealing from the woman.
    (B) He's withdrawing money from a bank.
    (C) He's trying to help the woman.
    (D) He's answering the woman's questions.

GUESS THE TOPIC AND QUESTION

Topic: Current action
Question: What is the man probably doing?

---

19. (A) He was pleased.
    (B) He wasn't sure how he felt.
    (C) He was bored.
    (D) He found it childish.

GUESS THE TOPIC AND QUESTION

Topic: Evaluation or reaction
Question: How did the man feel about ...?

---

20. (A) $5.00
    (B) $5.50
    (C) $3.50
    (D) $15.00

GUESS THE TOPIC AND QUESTION

Topic: Money
Question: How much ...?

---

21. (A) Go to the mountains
    (B) Stay home
    (C) Go to the beach
    (D) Go to the city

GUESS THE TOPIC AND QUESTION

Topic: Future action
Question: What will the man (the woman) probably do?
          What would the man (the woman) like to do?

---

22. (A) Black with sugar
    (B) Black with cream and sugar
    (C) Decaffeinated
    (D) Light and sweet

GUESS THE TOPIC AND QUESTION

Topic: A kind of coffee
Question: How does the man (the woman) like their coffee?

---

23. (A) Take a bath
    (B) Pick up the room
    (C) Vacuum the carpet
    (D) Get dressed

GUESS THE TOPIC AND QUESTION

Topic: Future action
Question: What is the man (the woman) probably going to do?
          What does the man (the woman) intend to do?
          What would the man (the woman) like to do?

---

24. (A) Observing the moon
    (B) Attending an outdoor opera
    (C) Looking for a lost cat
    (D) Planning a party

GUESS THE TOPIC AND QUESTION

Topic: Current action
Question: What are they probably doing?

---

25. (A) He's impressed by her.
    (B) He doesn't like her.
    (C) He finds her pleasant.
    (D) He thinks she's strange.

GUESS THE TOPIC AND QUESTION

Topic: Evaluation
Question: What does the man think of the woman?

---

26. (A) Go to a hospital
    (B) Take two aspirin and sleep
    (C) Get plenty of rest in bed
    (D) Forget about it

GUESS THE TOPIC AND QUESTION

Topic: Advice
Question: What did the man advise the woman to do?
           What advice did the man give to the woman?
           What will the woman probably do?

27. (A) Give her a hand.
    (B) Recommend a job to her.
    (C) Invite their friends to help out.
    (D) Give her a donation.

GUESS THE TOPIC AND QUESTION

Topic: Actions
Question: What does the woman probably want the man to do?
           What will the woman probably do?

28. (A) She didn't follow directions.
    (B) She started too late.
    (C) Her car broke down.
    (D) She got nervous and panicked.

GUESS THE TOPIC AND QUESTION

Topic: Cause
Question: Why might the woman ...?
           What happened to the woman?

29. (A) The man detained her.
    (B) She finished shopping because she had time.
    (C) She is happy that she could shop.
    (D) She didn't find time to finish.

GUESS THE TOPIC AND QUESTION

Topic: Undefined
Question: What does the woman mean?
           What was the woman implying?

30. (A) Application procedures
    (B) How to register
    (C) How to apply for a visa
    (D) Admission requirements

GUESS THE TOPIC AND QUESTION

Topic: Requirements
Question: What are they discussing?
          What does the man (the woman) need to know?

Short Talks

TOPICS:

In short talks you will find one person giving a talk on a topic or two people having a long conversation. Below are topics commonly discussed in these short talks.

One-Person Narratives

Topics given by one person usually are on the following:

1. **Historical period of the United States**
   - the pioneers
   - the exploration
   - the discovery of gold in California
   - the Civil War
   - the abolition of slavery
   - immigration
   - World War I
   - the Great Depression
   - the Civil Rights struggle of the 1960s
   - World War II

2. **Geographical locations or regions in the United States**
   - Ellis Island (where immigrants were processed)
   - the Redwoods in California (ancient trees)
   - the Rocky Mountains
   - New York City
   - Niagara Falls

3. **Important historical figures or heroes in the United States**
   • George Washington
   • Abraham Lincoln
   • John F. Kennedy
   • Martin Luther King, Jr.
   • Sojourner Truth
   • Susan B. Anthony
   • Helen Keller

4. **Scientific topics**
   • The greenhouse effect: Changes in weather patterns
   • Whales: the dying species
   • Whales: extinction of the blue whale
   • Geology: how earthquakes are formed

5. **Campus services**
   • Health center/clinic
   • Student center
   • Plays or movies
   • Newspaper

6. **News and weather report**

7. **Advertisement**

Two-People/Long Conversation

   Two people have a long conversation about informal topics or about something specific to the context, or about a report on the topics mentioned above.

Some possible conversations:

1. A university lecture
2. Old friends meet in a cafeteria one day
3. Two students talk about a test they just took
4. A student calls a professor to get permission to take a class
5. A policeman interviews a man about a car accident
6. A student asks a departmental secretary questions about procedures in the department
7. Two people talk about a report or lecture in class

QUESTIONS TO ANTICIPATE:

The tape will ask you five or six separate questions after the short talk. These questions ask you about the main topic and details of the short talk.

Possible questions

| ➤ Question 1 | **Remember titles, names, clients, customers.** |

1.   Actors/Listeners:

WHO IS/DOES/DID...?
WHO IS THIS REPORT INTENDED FOR?

___

| ➤ Question 2 | **Remember the sequence of events given by the speaker.** |

2.   Process/Procedure:

HOW DID...?
HOW WAS ... DISCOVERED/INVENTED?

___

| ➤ Question 3 | **This question is almost always present. Think of the topic of the mini-talk before you begin listening to the question.** |

3.   Main Idea/Topic:

WHAT IS THE MAIN TOPIC OF THIS TALK?
WHAT ARE THE SPEAKERS DISCUSSING?

___

| ➤ Question 4 | **Remember specific dates and quantities from the short talk. Many times you will need to compute your answer.** |

4.   Time/Dates:

WHEN WAS ... DISCOVERED/INVENTED?
WHEN ...?
WHAT ARE THE HOURS?
HOW LONG ...?

For example:

"She decided to buy two dozen eggs."

How many eggs did the woman buy?

Answer: 24

➤ Question 5	**This question may ask what purpose does an item serve or what type of object is mentioned in a passage**

5. Purpose:

WHAT DOES THE ... DO?
WHAT TYPE OF ...?

For example:

"She hit the nail into the board

What type of tool did she use?

Answer: a hammer

➤ Question 6	**Location may not be mentioned more than once OR it may not be mentioned at all. Usually the vocabulary gives you a hint of the location. Listen to the frequent vocabulary terms and guess the location.**

6. Location:

WHERE IS ... LOCATED?
WHERE ARE THE SPEAKERS?

➤ Questions 7-8	**You will need to guess the motivation or reason for actions. The speaker will not tell you WHY, but the question will ask you the reason for someone's action. You will need to infer to answer this question.**

7. Importance:

WHAT WAS IMPORTANT ABOUT ...?

WHAT WAS SIGNIFICANT ABOUT ...?
WHAT DOES THE SPEAKER THINK IS MOST INTERESTING ABOUT ...?

8. Cause/Reason:

WHY DID ...?
WHY IS/ARE ... ING?

➤ Question 9 | **Remember what type of problem the speaker or speakers is referring to. The problem may not be stated, but hints will be given as to what it is**

9. Problem/Event:

WHAT IS THE PROBLEM?
WHAT HAPPENED TO ...?

For example:

"There is water filling up the basement."

What is the problem?

Answer: A water pipe broke

➤ Question 10 | **The speakers sometimes make suggestions for solving a problem. These problems may not be stated, but you can determine the answer by listening to how a speaker reacts or what is said**

10. Suggestion/Recommendation/Reaction:

WHAT DOES THE SPEAKER RECOMMEND (SUGGEST) TO ...?
WHAT ADVICE DOES THE MAN GIVE THE WOMAN?
HOW DID THE SPEAKER REACT TO THE INFORMATION/REPORT?

For example:

"I cannot believe you let him treat you that way!"

What advice will the man probably give?

Answer: Leave her boyfriend

► Question 11	**This type of question will ask you to choose an appropriate description of something that was mentioned by the speaker**

11. Description:

HOW CAN YOU DESCRIBE ...?
HOW WAS ... DESCRIBED?
WHAT IS ... MADE OF?

For example:

"I think pigs roll in the mud all day."

How would the man describe pigs?

Answer: Dirty

EXERCISE: YOU GUESS THE QUESTIONS

DIRECTIONS: Below are some brief short talks. Read the short talk and guess some questions which might be asked. You can cover up the questions and then guess. After you guess some questions, uncover the questions and see if you guessed close.

EXAMPLE:
You will hear:

Early man came to the Americas from Asia over the Bering Strait. Thousands of years later after big animals had become extinct, these peoples stopped roaming and began to settle in an area now known as the U.S. Southwest. One favorite area in what is now New Mexico was called Canyon del Muerto. No one knows exactly when the first people arrived in the Canyon del Muerto but a tree-ring dates their arrival at about 306 A.D. These early people were primarily farmers rather than nomadic hunters, although they still depended to some extent on game animals for food. They established their homes in the shelter of the many caves in the canyon and farmed the canyon bottom. Corn was their major crop. They gathered pinyon nuts and sunflower seeds for food.

Possible Questions:
1. How did early man come from Asia to the Americas?
2. What is the main topic of this report?
3. When did people first arrive in Canyon del Muerto?
4. Where is Canyon del Muerto located?
5. Why did nomadic hunters become farmers and settle in one place?

NOW YOU PRACTICE:

You will hear:

Woman's voice: This week we've been studying about the various differences between the planets. Did you know that Mars actually gets patches of early morning fog in its valleys?

Man's voice: Yes and yesterday I read about the ring particles that surround Saturn. Apparently, they can't form into a moon or drift away from each other. They just stay held in place by the gravitational pull of Saturn and its satellites.

Woman's voice: Did you know that most of this was learned from the research done by Pioneer, a spacecraft launched in the 1970s?

Man's voice: It IS amazing what science has taught us. Wonders will never cease!

Possible questions:
1. What is the outer part of Saturn made of?
2. When was the spacecraft Pioneer launched?
3. What is the main topic of this discussion?
4. Why is gravity important to Saturn?
5. How does the man feel about the contributions of science?

PRACTICE:

You will hear:

The United States of America has a republican or representative form of government. The citizens choose or elect individuals to represent them at the local, state, and federal levels of government. These representatives are responsible for expressing the concerns of those they represent. They are guided by the Constitution, a document of principles written in 1787 to meet the needs of the people. A few additions have been amended since that time, but the Constitution has not changed basically since it was first written. It states the rights of the people living in the U.S.A. No law can be passed which interferes with these rights because the Constitution is the supreme law which was created to protect "life, liberty and the pursuit of happiness."

Possible questions:
1. What type of government does the United States have?
2. When was the Constitution written?
3. What is the topic of the report?
4. What was the purpose of the Constitution?

PRACTICE:

You will hear a woman's voice:

The Smith Health Center is available for all graduate and undergraduate students. It is located in the center of campus next to the Student Center. We have three doctors and five nurses on staff to serve you. If you plan to work on campus, you will be required to have us certify that you are healthy. We treat about 2,000 patients per year for everything from colds to broken bones. We encourage you to bring your problems to us early and to educate yourself about your health. We practice the old saying that an ounce of prevention is worth a pound of cure.

Possible questions:
1. Who does the Smith Health Center serve?
2. How many patients are served by the Center each year?
3. What does the woman mean by the old saying: An ounce of prevention is worth a pound of cure?
4. Where is the health service located?
5. How do you think the woman feels about the Center?

PRACTICE:
You will hear:

Woman's voice:	Good morning, Biology Department.
Man's voice:	Hello, my name is John Blackman and I'm calling for a friend of mine who would like to enter the biology program. Could you tell me something about admission requirements and the application procedure he would have to follow? He would be coming from another country?
Woman's voice:	Sure. He first needs to fill out an application for admission. He must provide the scores on two major tests and a transcript of his grades. If he is admitted, he will then have to provide proof of finances and obtain a visa. I recommend that you begin by sending him a school catalogue and an application packet. When would you like to pick these up?
Man's voice:	I'll come by today, if that's O.K.
Woman's voice:	Fine. I'll be here until 4:30.

Possible questions:
1. Who is the man probably talking to?
2. What are they discussing?
3. It's now 1:00. How much longer will the woman be in?
4. Why did the man phone the woman?
5. What does the woman recommend to the man?

Chapter 4

Structure and Written Expression Review

Chapter 4

STRUCTURE AND WRITTEN EXPRESSION REVIEW

I. USING THE STUDY TIPS
II. SENTENCE CONTENT
III. VERB TENSES
IV. VERBALS
V. SUBJECT-VERB-PRONOUN AGREEMENT
VI. WORD USAGE ERROR AREAS

I. USING THE STUDY TIPS

Certain types of sentence structure errors are usually tested in the TOEFL. If you are prepared for and alert to these areas, you will have the tools needed to become more confident in taking the Structure and Written Expression section of TOEFL.

This review section will not give a complete grammatical review of the English language. Many excellent books have been written which analyze the structure of English and its many exceptions. It is the aim of this section to organize, in a methodical way, the strategic error areas that you can use as a checklist when attempting to eliminate incorrect choices. English grammar can be intricate and confusing. This review section will alert you to item errors and will focus on the grammatical points tested in this section of TOEFL.

PLAN FOR TOEFL STRUCTURE AND WRITTEN EXPRESSION QUESTIONS: NINE-STEP STUDY TIPS

Multiple-choice TOEFL Structure and Written Expression questions can be tricky *even if* you know the correct answer. The following Nine-Step Plan is an approach to help you methodically answer these multiple-choice questions.

STEP 1   Read the question carefully for both meaning and structure, noting any errors which you recognize immediately.

STEP 2   Think of what the answer might be before you look at the answer choices. When you think of the answer first and then find that answer among the choices, that answer is very likely to be correct.

STEP 3   Read the choices and try to select the correct answer. However, do not expect to recognize the correct answer immediately. Remember—do not panic. Your plan as a TOEFL test taker should always be to try to "figure out" the correct answer.

STEP 4   Even if you think (A) or (B) is the correct answer, thoughtfully read and consider the remaining choices so that you are absolutely certain that (A) or (B) is truly correct.

STEP 5   Eliminate incorrect choices. Have a system for noting the potential correct answer, possibly by circling the letter in your test booklet, and for eliminating wrong answers, possible by putting an "x" over the letter of the choice. Whatever your system is, do not make marks on the answer sheet. Write in the test booklet only.

STEP 6   Remember the five error areas that are explained in this review section. Carefully look at the whole sentence and the way it is put together.

STEP 7   Remember to assume that all punctuation, capitalization, and spelling on the test are correct, and to ignore anything that cannot be corrected by the choices offered. Sometimes we think something is an error when it is not. Perhaps that "something" in the question could have been written differently, but since it is not an error that can be corrected by one of the choices, do not waste your time.

STEP 8   Select your answer after narrowing down your choices; pick the one you think is best. Always try to eliminate choices before selecting an answer and marking it on your answer sheet.

STEP 9   If you have absolutely no idea what the correct answer may be, even after considering all the choices, guess. There is no penalty for guessing on the TOEFL test, and you have a 25% chance that the answer is correct. Guess quickly, and do not change your mind unless you have a logical reason for doing so. First guesses tend to be, at least in part, some form of analysis. If, however, in reviewing your guess you discover other considerations that suggest your first guess was perhaps not the best, then by all means change your answer.

QUESTIONS YOU MAY ASK ABOUT THE TOEFL STRUCTURE AND WRITTEN EXPRESSION SECTION

QUESTION: "WHAT TYPES OF QUESTIONS SHOULD I EXPECT?"

TYPE 1

The first 15 questions are Type 1. Type 1 is a sentence completion, multiple-choice section where you must determine what piece will complete the sentence "puzzle." You must determine whether you are looking for the form of a verb, noun, adverb, or a combination of all three.

The directions for Type 1 begin as follows: "Questions 1-15 are incomplete sentences." This means that a word or words have been taken out of the normal order of the sentence. You need to find the missing piece of the sentence.

The directions continue... "Beneath each sentence you will see four words or phrases, marked (A), (B), (C), or (D). Choose the one word or phrase that best completes the sentence."

An example will be printed after the directions and before the actual exam questions.

TYPE 2

Questions 16 to 40 are complete sentences with one word or phrase underlined. Here you do not have to select a piece to complete the sentence. Rather, you have to recognize which one of the four parts underlined is incorrect.

The directions for the Type 2 begin as follows: "In questions 16-40 each sentence has four underlined words or phrases. The four underlined parts of the sentence are marked (A), (B), (C), and (D)."

The directions continue... "Identify the ONE underlined word or phrase that must be changed in order for the sentence to be correct."

An example will be printed after the directions and before the actual exam questions.

TEST TIME MANAGEMENT

QUESTION: "SHOULD I READ THE SECTION DIRECTIONS AND EXAMPLES?"

You will be familiar with the two types of questions by the time you complete this review section. Since the directions and sample questions are part of the timed part of the test, you should only glance at them for a few seconds to refresh your memory before you move on to the actual test questions.

QUESTION: "HOW MUCH TIME SHOULD I SPEND ON EACH QUESTION?"

You must complete 40 questions in 25 minutes. That gives you a little more than half a minute to spend on each question. The first 15 questions, Type 1, require you to read a sentence plus four choices. You may want to spend more time on these questions because there is more reading material. The last 25 questions, Type 2, only require the reading of the test question. Therefore, these might require slightly less time.

You may only spend a few seconds or some questions; however, your goal should be to work at a steady pace throughout the test and then go back to the questions you may have had difficulty with.

QUESTION: "SHOULD I KEEP TRACK OF TEST TIME?"

You should use a watch to keep track of the time so that, at the end of the test section, you will not be disappointed and frustrated because you did not have the time to consider some test items.

QUESTION: "HOW SHOULD I APPROACH DIFFICULT QUESTIONS?"

All questions are worth the same number of points toward your score. You will get as much credit for an easy question on which you may spend a few seconds as you will for a very difficult question on which you may spend over a minute.

If you encounter a difficult question, eliminate choices you think are correct by putting an "x" through the letter in your test booklet. Put a question mark, "?", in front of the number of the question so that you know to go back to it after you have considered the rest of the questions. When you return to the difficult questions, don't bother reconsidering the choices you have already eliminated.

If you have made a valid attempt at answering the questions and you cannot eliminate any of the choices, guess and move on to the next question since your time is limited.

QUESTION: "SHOULD I WORK THROUGH THE SECTION WITHOUT STOPPING?"

It is very difficult to work constantly, at the same level of productivity, for the entire 25 minutes. The switch in types of questions, from Type 1 to Type 2, is an appropriate time for you to plan a break, perhaps a break of ten seconds, when you can raise your head, put down your pencil, take a deep breath, and relax the tense muscles in your neck, shoulders, and back.

CATEGORIES OF ERROR

Think of the TOEFL Structure and Written Expression test items as divided into the following five categories of error:

SENTENCE CONTENT

Certain parts of speech are needed to form a correct English sentence. Sentence content errors are made because the test-taker did not know what ingredients were needed to create a complete sentence.

VERB TENSES

Verb tenses tell the reader the time during which the action of the sentence takes place. Verb tense errors are made because the test-taker did not know the correct time focus needed by the verb form.

EXAMPLE: The house <u>was painted</u> yesterday. (past tense)

VERBALS

Verbals show that English is an economical language because it allows a verbal, which looks like a verb, to act like a noun, adjective, or adverb. Verbal errors are made because the test-taker did not know the role of the verbal in the sentence.

EXAMPLE: <u>Writing</u> a paper is not as easy as you might think.

AGREEMENT

Agreement errors occur between the number and gender of nouns and the verb, as well as between the noun and pronoun. Agreement errors are made because other words are often placed between the two words that should agree and this may distract and mislead the test-taker from knowing which words should agree.

WORD USAGE

Small errors in word choice or word formation can lead to a misunderstanding of language expression. It is important to learn the small elements that connect the basic meaning of the sentence to make your ideas logical and accurate.

II. SENTENCE CONTENT

PARTS OF SPEECH

As a TOEFL test-taker, particularly in this section, you must be alert to all the possible roles of a word within a sentence. A word's role is its "function" in a sentence. The role a word serves in one sentence may be different from the role the same word serves in another sentence. Following are the eight roles a word may serve in a sentence.

PART OF SPEECH	FUNCTION	EXAMPLES
A. NOUN	A person, place, or thing	girl, dress, Mary, John
B. PRONOUN	A substitute for a noun	he, she, it, I, them
C. VERB	Expresses action	sing, dance
D. ADJECTIVE	Describes a noun or pronoun	silent, calm, anxious, eager
E. ADVERB	Modifies a verb, adjective, or adverb	quietly, fast, calmly
F. PREPOSITION	Shows the relationship between the noun or pronoun and another word	around, to, in, during, for
G. CONJUNCTION	Joins two words or groups	and, or, but
H. INTERJECTION	Displays feelings	Oh!, Wow!

A SENTENCE

The most important skill you can learn for the TOEFL Structure and Written Expression section is how to identify a sentence's subjects and verbs. Type 1 questions involve the selection of correct forms of subjects and verbs to make complete sentences. If you have difficulty recognizing a complete sentence, this part of the test will be very difficult for you.

A complete sentence contains at least one subject and one verb. The subject and the verb form the basis of the sentence. Extra words added to sentences do not change the subject and the verb. It is essential to IDENTIFY THE VERB IN THE SENTENCE FIRST. Why? Recognizing the verb first is easier because there are fewer possible words for verbs than there are for subjects. The verb is the *action* being performed in a sentence.

The following parts of speech are NOT verbs, so you should not include them when looking for the verbs:

INFINITIVE—the combination of the word "to" plus a verb, such as "to sing" or "to dance." This is not part of the verb in the sentence.

ADVERB—words that describe the verb are not part of the verb. The words "not," "never," "quickly," and "very" are some adverbs.

All forms of the verb **"BE"** are verbs: **AM, IS, ARE, WAS, WERE,** and **BEEN.** Verbs also include words that substitute for **BE,** such as **BECOME, APPEAR, SEEM,** and **FEEL.**

VERBS: MAIN AND HELPING

Main verbs tell the action or activity being performed. Helping verbs are used with main verbs to: (a) show "tense," the time of an action (present, past, or future), and (b) show meaning that cannot be expressed by the main verb alone.

Helping verbs always come before the main verb, although sometimes another word, such as an adverb, may come between the helping verb and the main verb. The following words are examples of helping verbs: **CAN, COULD, MAY, MIGHT, MUST, SHALL, SHOULD, WILL,** and **WOULD.**

A VERB INCLUDES THE MAIN VERBS PLUS ALL THE HELPING VERBS.

In the sentence, "I should have helped her," the complete verb is "should have helped." In the sentence "I will have a piece of cake, thank you," the complete verb is "will have."

Sentences can contain one, two, or three helping verbs with the main verb.

A complete verb with all of its helping verbs is called a finite verb.

SUBJECTS

The person or thing performing the action or activity is the subject. The following types of words are NOT subjects:

ADJECTIVES—words that describe a noun are not part of the subject.

WORDS THAT SHOW OWNERSHIP OR POSSESSION—words like "hers" or "his" are not part of the subject.

A sentence consists of a person or thing doing an action, or, in other words, a subject plus a verb.

PREPOSITIONS

Prepositions are small words that show the relationship between one word and another. Prepositions in the following sentences show the position of the paper in relation to the desk, the book, his hand, and the door.

The paper is "on" the desk.

The paper is "under" the book.

The paper is "in" his hand.

The paper is "by" the door.

COMMON PREPOSITIONS

ABOUT	AT	BY	IN	ONTO	TOWARD
ABOVE	BEFORE	CONCERNING	INSIDE	OUT	UNDER
ACROSS	BEHIND	DESPITE	INTO	OVER	UNTIL
AFTER	BELOW	DOWN	LIKE	SINCE	UP
AGAINST	BENEATH	DURING	NEAR	THROUGH	UPON
ALONG	BESIDE	EXCEPT	OF	THROUGHOUT	WITH
AMID	BETWEEN	FOR	OFF	TILL	WITHIN
AMONG	BEYOND	FROM	ON	TO	WITHOUT
AROUND					

Prepositions are found in phrases. Each prepositional phrase begins with a preposition and ends with a noun or pronoun. This is an important fact because if a word is part of a prepositional phrase, it cannot be the subject or the verb of the sentence. Verbs are not in prepositional phrases, and the noun or pronoun that is the object of the preposition cannot be the main subject.

QUESTION: "WHAT SHOULD I DO WHEN A TEST SENTENCE IS EXTREMELY LONG WITH DIFFICULT VOCABULARY?"

Cross out the prepositional phrases and within the few words left will be the subjects and verbs.

EXAMPLE: The early phase of the Bronze Age on the mainland ended about 2000 B.C. with military conquest of the area by invaders from the north.

This sentence has 24 words, but only one subject and one verb. Cross out the prepositional phrases and you'll see how easy it is to find the subject and verb.

The following sentence has 22 words, but no verb. Cross out the prepositional phrases and the infinite phrase, and you will find the subject.

The wing design of the U-2 <u>permitting</u> long distance <u>gliding</u> without engine power
                               A   B
<u>to reduce</u> the likelihood of detection <u>from the ground</u>.
  C   D

The subject of the sentence is "design," but the sentence has no complete verb. The test-taker must ask, what does the wing design do? The answer shows that the error lies in (A) "permitting" which should be "permits," a finite verb. (B) is correct because it is a verb form used as a noun. The clue is the adjective "long-distance." (C) gives the purpose of the wing design, and (D) tells where there is the likelihood of detection. If there are two or more clauses (clauses are subject-verb patterns), you must check to see if the clauses are combined correctly.

There are two basic ways to combine clauses:

A. Keep them as independent clauses that can stand alone and join them with a coordinating conjunction, such as: and, but, or, nor, for.

EXAMPLE: Jean looked everywhere but she could not find her velvet pillow.

B. Keep at least one as an independent clause and make the others dependent clauses using subordinate conjunctions.

EXAMPLE: She loved Michael dearly, but did not love his dog.

QUESTION: "WHAT ARE SOME OF THE WAYS TO MAKE A CLAUSE (SUBJECT-VERB PATTERN) DEPENDENT?"

A dependent clause that describes a word is an **adjective clause.** An adjective clause is introduced by a relative pronoun.

WHO	WHOM	WHOSE	
WHICH	THAT	WHERE	WHEN

Dependent clauses and their subjects and verbs must be in complete sentences.

EXAMPLE 1: The issue could be a paramount one in the decade to come.

EXAMPLE 2: Whenever I eat garlic, I feel better.

In example 1, a complete idea is expressed. The verb is "could be" and the subject is "issue." This is an independent clause.

In example 2, the first verb "eat" and its subject "I" are introduced by the subordinating conjunction "whenever," making that a subordinate clause. The verb "feel" and the subject "I" stand alone as an independent clause, making this a complete sentence.

Is each of the following a sentence?

I cannot insist enough that the man whom you are dating is a liar and a thief.
S1   V1   S2   S3   V3   V2

S1 and V1 form the independent main clause. The subordinate clause is introduced by "that." There is an adjective clause introduced by the relative pronoun "whom" within the subordinate clause.

Most Americans to purchase a colored television, regardless of what the cost might be.

This is not a complete sentence. "Regardless of" introduces the subordinate clause with the subject "cost" and the verb "might be." "To purchase" is not a verb; it is an infinitive. The main verb is missing.

Although many of his friends have come.

The subject "many" and verb "have come" are introduced by a subordinate conjunction "although," making this a subordinate clause, not a sentence. Remember that you need an independent clause, a subject and verb not introduced by a subordinating word, to have a sentence.

BECAUSE vs. BECAUSE OF

BECAUSE + subject + verb

BECAUSE OF + noun or pronoun

<u>Because</u> the situation did not improve, the boss decided to call a gathering of her employees.

<u>Because of</u> the worsening situation, the boss decided to call a gathering of her employees.

EXAMPLE: <u>Because</u> his conduct at the campaign, Bazaine <u>was found guilty</u> of
            A   B

treason and received a death sentence, <u>which was commuted</u> to imprisonment
                                        C

<u>for 20 years</u>.
   D

(A) is the error. "Because" is not followed by a subject and verb, only by a noun. If it is followed by a noun, it should be "because of." (B) is a correct passive verb form. (C) is a description of the death sentence, a relative pronoun and passive verb. (D) tells the length of imprisonment.

APPOSITIVES

A noun or noun substitute used without a verb to explain or describe the noun beside it is called an appositive.

EXAMPLES:

Sue, our leader, took us to the museum.

    ("leader" is the appositive)

Two students, Beth and I, were chosen for the activity.

    ("Beth" and "I" are the appositives)

EXAMPLES:

1. Agathocles, _____, was exiled twice for attempting to overthrow the aristocratic government.
    (A) a tyrant of Syracuse who
    (B) a tyrant of Syracuse
    (C) as a tyrant of Syracuse, he
    (D) whose tyrant of Syracuse

ANSWER: (B) explains who Agathocles was without using a relative pronoun, as in answers (A) and (D). (C) gives extra words that confuse the meaning of the sentence.

2. _____, Vincent van Gogh lived a tumultuous life in the southern part of France.
    (A) Despite the famous French impressionist
    (B) A famous French impressionist who is
    (C) A famous French impressionist
    (D) He is a famous French impressionist

ANSWER: (D) gives a subject and a verb—it is an independent clause, not an appositive. Although it explains who van Gogh was, it should be treated as a complete sentence and combined with the next complete sentence by a conjunction. This, however, is not one of the answers, so it is not correct. (A) is a prepositional phrase introduced by "despite" and does not explain who van Gogh was. (B) gives a relative pronoun and that is not necessary. (C) is the correct choice.

EXERCISES: PRACTICE WHAT YOU HAVE LEARNED ABOUT "SENTENCE CONTENT"

> **DIRECTIONS:** Choose the best word or phrase which would complete the sentence.

1. _____ reflect the principles of American adolescence during the 1950s.
    (The sentence has one main verb, "reflect," but no subject. It needs a subject.)
    (A) Students go to school
    (B) Whether the country's high schools
    (C) Why students go to school
    (D) The country's high schools

ANSWER: Only (D) is a subject. (A) is a subject and verb, (B) has an introductory word, "whether," that makes the subject and the verb "reflect" into a dependent clause, and (C) has an introductory word, as well as a subject and a verb.

2.   This _____ the only correct answer on the test.
       ("This" is the subject. A verb is needed.)
       (A) which
       (B) is
       (C) being
       (D) as

ANSWER: (A) and (D) are not verbs. (C) "being" is not a finite verb and cannot be used as a main verb. (B) is the only choice.

3.   The common name applied to large seabirds of the family *Diomedeidae*
       _____ the albatross, of which 13 species can be found from the Antarctic region north to the tropics.
       ("Name" is the subject. A verb is needed.)
       (A) to be
       (B) being
       (C) is
       (D) has been

ANSWER: "Applied" and the phrase that follows it describe "the common name," so "applied" is a past participle used as an adjective. It is not the verb of the sentence. "Can be found" is not the main verb; rather, it is the verb of the preposition. So the sentence needs a verb.

(A) and (B) are not verbs. "To be" is an infinitive, and "being" is a participle, not a complete, finite verb. (D) is the present perfect tense. (C) is correct because it is the simple present tense appropriate for definitions.

III. VERB TENSES

An understanding of verb tenses is critical when taking the TOEFL Structure and Written Expression section. Considering the many tenses there are in any language, this is not undue emphasis on verb tenses. Though there are many tenses that can be tested, and many intricate exceptions, do not become overwhelmed with the extensive range of the verb tenses. Complete understanding of verb tense is a goal, but is not needed to do relatively well on the TOEFL Structure and Written Expression section.

SIMPLE TENSES

1.   Simple Present
       — a general statement of fact:
Example: The earth is a sphere.

       — a habitual activity:
Example: I always skip breakfast.

— a statement of something existing at the time of speaking:
Example: I hear you.

2.   Simple Past
       — an activity begun and completed at a particular time in the past:
Example: I went to college last year.

       — "After" and "before" clauses:
Examples: After she left, I went directly to bed.
           They arrived before I did.

3.   Simple Future/be going to
       — future activity:
Examples: I will do that later.
           I am going to do that later.

PERFECT TENSES

1.   Present Perfect
       — an activity begun in the past and continued into the present when used
with since or for:
       since + a particular time
       for + a duration of time
Examples: I have studied French for ten years.
           She has studied Spanish since 1989.

       — a repeated activity:
Example: I have read four books this month.

       — an activity that happened at an unspecified time in the past:
Example: I have already visited China.

       — an activity in a time clause to emphasize it has been completed before the
main clause action begins:
Example: I will go to the movies after I have finished all my homework.

2.   Past Perfect
       — a completed activity before another activity in the past:
Example: They had already left by the time I arrived.

3.   Future Perfect
       — an activity to be completed before another activity in the future:
Example: They will have left by the time I arrive.

Perhaps the most tedious activity of a learner of English is learning the parts of irregular verbs. For this TOEFL Structure and Written Expression section, you will generally need to select the correct verb tense. Incorrect verb forms are occasionally given for problem irregular verbs, such as rise/raise and lie/lay.

Review the following verbs so you will feel confident when you are dealing with verb tenses on the structure section. As an aid to learning, verbs with three different forms are indicated by a (+) and verbs with all forms the same are indicated by a (=). The remaining unmarked verbs have one different form.

IRREGULAR VERB FORMS

KEY

+	Three different forms	
=	Three forms that are the same	
(Unmarked verbs have only one different form)		

	Simple	Past	Past Participle
+	arise	arose	arisen
+	awake	awoke	awoken
+	be	was, were	been
+	bear	bore	born/borne
	beat	beat	beaten
	become	became	become
+	begin	began	begun
	bend	bent	bent
=	bet	bet	bet
=	bid	bid	bid
	bind	bound	bound
+	bite	bit	bitten
	bleed	bled	bled
+	blow	blew	blown
+	break	broke	broken
	breed	bred	bred
	bring	brought	brought
=	broadcast	broadcast	broadcast
	build	built	built
=	burst	burst	burst
	buy	bought	bought

	Simple	Past	Past Participle
=	cast	cast	cast
	catch	caught	caught
+	choose	chose	chosen
	cling	clung	clung
	come	came	come
=	cost	cost	cost
	creep	crept	crept
=	cut	cut	cut
	dig	dug	dug
+	do	did	done
+	draw	drew	drawn
+	drink	drank	drunk
+	drive	drove	driven
+	eat	ate	eaten
	fall	fell	fallen
	feed	fed	fed
	feel	felt	felt
	fight	fought	fought
	find	found	found
=	fit	fit	fit
	flee	fled	fled
+	fly	flew	flown
+	forget	forgot	forgotten
+	forgive	forgave	forgiven
+	forsake	forsook	forsaken
+	freeze	froze	frozen
+	get	got	got(ten)
+	give	gave	given
+	go	went	gone
	grind	ground	ground
+	grow	grew	grown

	Simple	Past	Past Participle
	hang	hung	hung
	have	had	had
	hear	heard	heard
+	hide	hid	hidden
=	hit	hit	hit
	hold	held	held
=	hurt	hurt	hurt
	keep	kept	kept
=	knit	knit	knit
+	know	knew	known
	lay	laid	laid
	lead	led	led
	leave	left	left
	lend	lent	lent
=	let	let	let
+	lie	lay	lain
	lose	lost	lost
	make	made	made
	mean	meant	meant
	meet	met	met
+	mistake	mistook	mistaken
	pay	paid	paid
=	put	put	put
=	quit	quit	quit
=	read	read	read
=	rid	rid	rid
+	ride	rode	ridden
+	ring	rang	rung
+	rise	rose	risen
	run	ran	run
	say	said	said

	Simple	Past	Past Participle
+	see	saw	seen
	seek	sought	sought
	sell	sold	sold
	send	sent	sent
=	set	set	set
+	shake	shook	shaken
=	shed	shed	shed
	shine	shone	shone
	shoot	shot	shot
+	shrink	shrank	shrunk
=	shut	shut	shut
+	sing	sang	sung
+	sink	sank	sunk
	sit	sat	sat
	sleep	slept	slept
	slide	slid	slid
	sling	slung	slung
=	slit	slit	slit
+	speak	spoke	spoken
	speed	sped	sped
	spend	spent	spent
	spin	spun	spun
=	spit	spit	spit
=	split	split	split
=	spread	spread	spread
+	spring	sprang	sprung
	stand	stood	stood
+	steal	stole	stolen
	stick	stuck	stuck
	sting	stung	stung
	strike	struck	struck

	Simple	Past	Past Participle
+	strive	strove	striven
+	swear	swore	sworn
	sweep	swept	swept
+	swim	swam	swum
	swing	swung	swung
+	take	took	taken
	teach	taught	taught
+	tear	tore	torn
	tell	told	told
	think	thought	thought
+	throw	threw	thrown
=	thrust	thrust	thrust
	understand	understood	understood
+	wake	woke	woken
+	wear	wore	worn
+	weave	wove	woven
	weep	wept	wept
	win	won	won
	wind	wound	wound
	wring	wrung	wrung
+	write	wrote	written

EXERCISE: TEST YOURSELF

DIRECTIONS: Read the simple verb form and then fill in the appropriate past and past participle verb forms.

IRREGULAR VERB FORMS

Simple	Past	Past Participle
arise		
awake		
be		
bear		
beat		
become		
begin		
bend		
bet		
bid		
bind		
bite		
bleed		
blow		
break		
breed		
bring		
broadcast		
build		
burst		
buy		
cast		
catch		
choose		
cling		

Simple	Past	Past Participle
come		
cost		
creep		
cut		
dig		
do		
draw		
drink		
drive		
eat		
fall		
feed		
feel		
fight		
find		
fit		
flee		
fly		
forget		
forgive		
forsake		
freeze		
get		
give		
go		
grind		
grow		
hang		
have		
hear		
hide		

Simple	Past	Past Participle
hit		
hold		
hurt		
keep		
knit		
know		
lay		
lead		
leave		
lend		
let		
lie		
lose		
make		
mean		
meet		
mistake		
pay		
put		
quit		
read		
rid		
ride		
ring		
rise		
run		
say		
see		
seek		
sell		
send		

Simple	Past	Past Participle
set		
shake		
shed		
shine		
shoot		
shrink		
shut		
sing		
sink		
sit		
sleep		
slide		
sling		
slit		
speak		
speed		
spend		
spin		
spit		
split		
spread		
spring		
stand		
steal		
stick		
sting		
strike		
strive		
swear		
sweep		
swim		

Simple	Past	Past Participle
swing		
take		
teach		
tear		
tell		
think		
throw		
thrust		
understand		
wake		
wear		
weave		
weep		
win		
wind		
wring		
write		

LOOK AT THESE!

Correct Verb Form: The following test items focus on the form of the verb used incorrectly.

1. <u>Before we returned</u> from <u>the tour</u> of the city, someone <u>had took</u> our car, and we
      A   B   C
<u>had to walk</u> back to our hotel.
    D

(Note: "had took" is the incorrect form of the past participle "taken.")

2. The towel <u>that</u> you see <u>laying</u> on the ground <u>by</u> the pool <u>belongs</u> to the lifeguard.
           A   B   C   D

(Note: See the difference between the verb usage of lie-lying and lay-laying.)

3.   Most of Jersey City _____ in a low and swampy area.
       (A)   lays
       (B)   lies
       (C)   is lying
       (D)   are laying

ANSWER: (B) is correct because the sentence needs the present tense of the verb "lie" which means "is located" and has an intransitive meaning because it is not done to anything or anyone else. (A) is the verb "lay" which means to place or put down. (C) and (D) are in the progressive tense, an incorrect tense for a description of an area.

PROGRESSIVE TENSES

1.   Present Progressive
       — a planned or intended future event or activity:
Example: Jocelyne is leaving for her vacation tomorrow.

       — an activity in progress at the time of speaking:
Example: Jerry is watching a show on television.

       —a general activity in progress during the next day, week, month, or year, though not actually going on at the time of speaking:
Example: Claudine is trying to improve her grades.

2.   Past Progressive
       — a past activity in progress when another activity occurred:
Example: At six o'clock last evening, I was eating dinner.
              (activity of eating was in progress when six o'clock occurred)

       — two past activities in progress at the same time:
Example: While I was answering the phone, he was getting the mail.

3.   Future Progressive
       — a future activity that will be in progress:
Example: He will be looking for her tomorrow.

4.   Present Perfect Progressive
       — duration of an activity that began in the past and continued to the present, and is used with time words like "since," "for," "all year ":
Example: He has been travelling all summer.

       — duration of a more general activity that began in the past and continued to the present; does not mention time:
Example: He has been studying hard.

5. Past Perfect Progressive
   — the length of a past activity that was going on before another past activity:
Example: When she finally arrived, I <u>had been waiting</u> for her for two hours.
   — an activity in progress right before another activity in the past:
Example: Her hair was wind-blown because she <u>had been walking</u> in the park.

6. Future Perfect Progressive
   — a future activity that has been in progress and is continuing into the future:
Example: She <u>will have been looking</u> for the right material for her drapes for three years.

PASSIVE VOICE

If the subject is acted upon, the verb is passive.

To make a verb passive, add the past participle to the form of "be."

The active voice is the preferred form in English because it is more forceful and direct.

EXAMPLE: *The Thinker* was sculpted by Rodin.

The passive voice is used to emphasize the receiver of the action as the focus of interest.

PRESENT, PASSIVE: They are led.

PAST, PASSIVE: They were led.

FUTURE, PASSIVE: They will be led.

PRESENT PERFECT: They have been led.

PAST PERFECT: They had been led.

FUTURE PERFECT: They will have been led.

SHORT EXERCISE: Find the element in the following sentence where the passive voice is expressed incorrectly.

The first <u>man-made</u> <u>orbiting earth satellite</u> <u>had launched</u> by the U.S.S.R. <u>in 1957</u>.
A   B   C   D

ANSWER: (C) is the correct answer. (Note: Satellites-rockets cannot launch themselves.) The word "by" is your clue to the possible need for a passive voice. (C) is the element of the sentence where the passive voice should be expressed with the verb "was launched."

IV. VERBALS

GERUNDS/INFINITIVES/PARTICIPLES

When taking the TOEFL, you can sometimes tell if a word is a noun or a verb or some other part of speech by just looking at the word. In most cases, however, the test-taker has to see how a certain word fits into a sentence pattern before it can be called a "noun" or a "verb." In the following two sentences, the word "glow" is used in different ways:

Lights glow in the distance.
The glow of the light brightened her face.

"Glow" is a verb in the first sentence because it comes in a verb **position** in the sentence pattern; but in the second sentence, "glow" is a noun because it comes in a **subject position.** The position of words is very important. "The dog bit Mary" is very different from saying that "Mary bit the dog." Some words can even be in four positions:

I "lean" in the direction of that opinion.	(verb position)
The "lean" of the Tower of Pisa is well known.	(noun position)
The "lean" swimmers stood on the blocks.	(adjective position)
Remember to eat "lean."	(adverb position)

Since position in the sentence is very important, you need to be alert to **verbals** when looking for subjects and verbs in sentences. Because verbals look like verbs, you must be able to recognize them and not confuse them with verbs. Verbals are **infinitives, gerunds,** or **participles.** These are forms of verbs that, when placed in certain positions in the sentence pattern, will act like nouns or adjectives.

The girl was "singing."	("singing" in verb position = **main verb** used with "was")
"Singing" was her hobby.	("singing" in the subject position = **gerund**)
The "singing" girl won a medal.	("singing" in the adjective position = **participle**)
"To sing" in a theatre was her desire	("to sing" in the subject position = **infinitive**)

Although nouns (such as book, girl) and pronouns (such as I, she, they) are the most common subjects, gerunds (singing, running, eating) are commonly used for subjects ("Singing" was her hobby). Infinitives (to sing, to swim, to eat) are also used as subjects ("To sing" in a theatre was her desire).

Gerunds and participles look alike because they both end in "-ing" ("The singing cheered him" and "The singing bird sat in the tree"), but the only way to tell them apart is by their position in the sentence.

In these sentences, which are gerunds (subjects) and which are participles (modifiers of nouns)?

The washing machine is new.   (participle)
The washing should take about five minutes.   (gerund)
Earning money gives a person self-respect.   (gerund)
Her earning power was reduced after her accident.   (participle)

Notice that gerunds, like nouns, may be modified by adjectives and prepositional phrases:

The first "running" of the race was in July 1988.
The sudden and fierce "rushing" of the wind blew over the shack.

Gerunds may also act like nouns in other ways. They may be objects or objects of prepositions. Again, the way you can tell the difference between the verb and the verbal is by the position in the sentence pattern:

John is "running" the race again.   (running is part of the verb)
The thought of "running" again made him feel tired. (as object of preposition)
Sandra likes "running."   (as object of verb)

Notice that you would still have good sentences if you substituted nouns for the two gerunds.

The participles reviewed so far all ended in "-ing." These are called **present participles** because they come from verbs in the present tense ("The car is rolling"). When participles come from verbs in the past tense, they are called **past participles** ("The player was injured"). Past participles are also commonly used to modify subjects. Notice the position of the participle before you decide whether it is being used as part of the verb or being used to modify the subject.

EXERCISES: PRACTICE WHAT YOU HAVE LEARNED ABOUT "VERBALS"

> **DIRECTIONS:** Choose the best word or phrase which would complete the sentence.

1. Oil of bay, _____ from the leaves of a tropical American bay tree commonly called the bayberry, is used in the distilling of bay rum.
   (A) make
   (B) makes
   (C) making
   (D) made

ANSWER: (D) is the answer because it is the past participle used to describe the oil of bay. The description is set aside from the main clause of the sentence by commas. (A) is not correct because it is the present tense, plural form of the verb and does not agree in number with the subject, even if the sentence needed a verb. (B) is not correct because it is the present tense, singular form of the verb, but the sentence does not need a finite verb. (C) is not correct because it is the present participle, inappropriate for the description form needed in this sentence.

2.   After _____ his flight training, American astronaut Alan Bean was sta-
tioned in Jacksonville.
(A) completes
(B) completed
(C) completing
(D) complete

ANSWER: (C) is the correct answer because there is an independent clause, and
the dependent present participle following "after" is needed to describe what Bean
did before being stationed in Jacksonville. (A), (B), and (D) are all finite verbs that
need a subject, and there is no subject following "after."

3.   The sight of the American flag _____ inspired him to
write the poem, "The Star Spangled Banner."
(A) still flown over the fort at daybreak
(B) still flew over the fort at daybreak
(C) still flying over the fort at daybreak
(D) still flies over the fort at daybreak

ANSWER: (C) is the correct answer because the main verb of the sentence is
"inspired" and the subject "sight" needs a present participle to describe it. (A) is the
past participle which is not correct with the present word "still." (B) is the past tense
of the verb, and a finite conjugated verb is not correct here. (D) is the present tense
of the verb, and a finite conjugated verb is not correct here.

4.   If you expect to move in a few years, _____ may be more
economical than buying one.
(A) there is a rented home
(B) having rented a home
(C) you will need to rent a home that
(D) renting a home

ANSWER: (D) is the answer because it is the gerund that serves as the subject of
the verb of the independent clause "may be." It also parallels the comparison to
"buying one." "If you expect to move in a few years" serves as the dependent clause.
(A) creates an incorrect phrasing of the independent clause by adding another
subject and verb. (B) creates an incorrect time frame—by placing the rental in a
questionable time period; the reader is unsure if it is the future, past, or present. (C)
creates an incorrect comparison by saying the home should be more economical, not
the act of renting that should be economical.

V. SUBJECT-VERB-PRONOUN AGREEMENT

This is a common testing area for TOEFL because it is such a common error in the English language.

SUBJECT-VERB AGREEMENT

Extra words must be eliminated so that you can check to see if the subjects and verbs agree.

For Type 2 questions in particular, check to make sure that all subjects and verbs agree. Since locating the subject and verb is your first step in every item, you are almost there.

DIRECTIONS: Choose the best choice which completes the sentence.

---

1. In the same century a type of beagle with some of the characteristics _____ in the southern United States.

    (A) were known
    (B) was known
    (C) known
    (D) are known

ANSWER: (B) is the answer since this sentence needs a verb that agrees with the singular subject "type." (A) is not correct because it is the plural form of the verb and the subject is singular. (C) is the past participle form of the verb and the sentence needs a finite verb. (D) is not correct because it is the plural form of the verb and the subject is singular.

DIRECTIONS: Choose the word or phrase which is grammatically incorrect.

---

1. <u>Many</u> relics <u>from</u> the Roman period <u>has been unearthed</u> <u>throughout</u> the
      A   B   C   D
    country.

ANSWER: (C) is the answer because the verb form is singular when the subject "relics" is in the plural form. (A) is correct because it is a counting adjective and "relics" must be counted. (B) is correct because the expression is something "from" a particular time period. (D) is correct because it is a preposition that explains where the relics have been unearthed.

2.   This country's fertile land, together <u>with</u> the fertile land of <u>other</u> countries,
                                      A   B
   <u>are being used</u> in a <u>worldwide</u> crop utilization project.
        C   D

ANSWER: (C) is the answer since this sentence needs a verb that agrees with the singular subject "land." (A) is used correctly because it is the expression "together with" that adds to the subject. (B) is the correct adjective "other" to refer to countries. (D) is the correct adjective to describe the project.

   The following collective nouns use singular verbs:

   one of   everyone   everything
   each of   everybody   neither
   every   somebody

   The following words use "is" although they end with an "s" and may seem plural:

   United States
   statistics
   physics
   mathematics
   economics
   news

   The following expressions also use "is":

   Time Expressions: Two minutes is better than nothing.
   Distance Expressions: Three miles is a good distance for a morning walk.
   Money Expressions: Fifty dollars is a lot of money for a blouse.

DIRECTIONS: Choose the best phrase or word which is grammatically incorrect.

---

1.   People who <u>gets</u> a lot done <u>know</u> <u>ahead of</u> time <u>what is important</u> to them.
                   A   B   C   D

ANSWER: (A) is the answer because the verb form "gets"—present tense, singular form—does not agree with "people" which is plural. (B) is correct because it is the present tense, plural form for the subject "people." (C) is correct because it is the correct wording of the phrase "ahead of time." (D) is the correct noun clause that serves as the direct object of the verb "know."

2.   <u>According to</u> the philosophy of the German George Wilhelm Friedrich Hegel,
          A
   art, religion, and philosophy <u>is</u> the <u>bases</u> of the <u>highest</u> spiritual development.
                                  B   C   D

ANSWER: (B) is the answer because the verb is not correct. The subject is a compound subject—art, religion, and philosophy—so the verb should be plural, "are." (C) is correct because it is the plural form of "basis," and the plural form is needed due to the compound subject. (D) is correct because the superlative form is used with "the."

3.   <u>A</u> book <u>on</u> mathematics <u>are going</u> to help out <u>when</u> the time comes.
     A   B   C   D

ANSWER: (C) is the answer because the verb is not correct. The subject is "book" so the verb should be singular, "is." Even if the word "mathematics" had been the subject, it should be treated as singular. (A) is correct because reference is made to any book on mathematics. (B) is correct because books are "on" or about a particular subject. (D) is correct because it gives the correct time frame.

4.   The three elements <u>of</u> speed, strength, <u>and</u> technique <u>is</u> vital <u>to</u> karate expertise.
                          A   B   C   D

ANSWER: (C) is the answer because the subject is "the three elements" followed by a prepositional phrase explaining what the three elements are—speed, strength, and technique—so the verb should be plural, "are." (A) is correct because the preposition introduces what the three elements are. (B) adds the third element. (D) is the correct preposition following "vital."

5.   <u>In</u> the Gothic Cathedral of Boyeux <u>is</u> Romanesque sections <u>dating from the</u>
     A   B   C

    <u>twelfth century.</u>
        D

ANSWER: (B) is the answer because the verb is not in the correct number. The subject is "Romanesque sections" a plural subject, which requires a plural verb. The correct plural verb form should be "are." (A) is correct because it is a correct expression to say where something is located. (C) is correct because "dating" tells from when the sections date. (D) tells from what century the sections date.

VI. WORD USAGE ERROR AREAS

Word Form Errors: Prefixes and Suffixes

Word form errors are made when the sentence includes a verb or adjective form used incorrectly as a noun, or a noun form used incorrectly as an adjective or verb. There is a very logical way to recognize if the word is in its proper form.

Basic knowledge of the English language, especially a familiarity with its numerous prefixes, can help build vocabulary and also strengthen spelling. For example, if one knows that "inter" means "between" and "intra" means "within," one is not likely to spell "intramural" "intermural." (The former means within the limits or limits of a city, college, etc.)

The following table lists some common Latin and Greek prefixes which are part of the foundation of the English language.

PREFIX	MEANING	EXAMPLE
ab-, a-, abs-	away, from	abstain
ad-	to, toward	adjacent
ante-	before	antecedent
anti-	against	antidote
bi-	two	bisect
cata-, cat-, cath-	down	cataclysm
circum-	around	circumlocution
contra-	against	contrary
de-	down, from	decline
di-	twice	diatonic
dis-, di-	apart, away	dissolve
epi-, ep-, eph-	upon, among	epidemic
ex-, e-	out of, from	extricate
hyper-	beyond, over	hyperactive
hypo-	under, down, less	hypodermic
in-	in, into	instill
inter-	among, between	intercede
intra-	within	intramural
meta-, met-	beyond, along with	metaphysics
mono-	one	monolith
non-	no, not	nonsense
ob-	against	obstruct
para-, par-	beside	parallel
per-	through	permeate

pre-	before	prehistoric
pro-	before	project
super-	above	superior
tele-, tel-	across	television
trans-	far	transpose
ultra-	beyond	ultraviolet

A suffix is a syllable added to a word that affects its meaning. When a suffix is added to a word, it does not change its meaning radically, but it does change the job it has in a sentence.

EXAMPLES:

1. The struggle for survival is the most basic of all natural instincts.
    (adding suffix -al to verb *survive*)

2. The fact that he had not been to see her lay like a weight on his conscience.
    (adding suffix -t to verb *weigh*)

3. The general form of African government today is democracy.
    (adding suffix -ment to verb *govern*)

Learn to recognize these "Suffixes for Nouns."

SUFFIX	MEANING	EXAMPLE
-acy	quality of being or having	candidacy, diplomacy
-age	collection of, condition of	salvage, carriage
-al	pertaining to, having the character of	refusal, denial
-an	pertaining to, one concerned with	artisan, partisan
-ance	quality of	fragrance, romance
-ancy	quality of	buoyancy, vagrancy
-ar	pertaining to	scholar
-ard	one who subscribes to excess	drunkard
-ation	action or process of	determination, imagination
-dom	state or condition of being	freedom, kingdom
-ence	quality of being	patience, diligence
-ency	quality of being	emergency, efficiency
-er	a person or thing connected with	laborer, worker
-ess	used to form feminine	hostess, tigress

-hood	state of being	statehood, motherhood
-ice	condition, quality, or act	avarice, malice
-ism	belief in	schism, communism
-ite	one connected with	Israelite, plebiscite
-ity	quality of	security, celebrity
-ment	result of	bombardment, department
-ness	state or quality of being	kindness, sadness
-or	state of	tutor, dictator
-ship	condition of	ambassadorship, partnership
-sion	act of	diversion, conversion
-th	result of action	growth, wealth
-tion	act of	dedication, celebration
-ty	state of being	modesty, frailty

Learn to recognize these "Suffixes for Adjectives."

SUFFIX	MEANING	EXAMPLE
-able	capable of	movable, repairable
-ac	pertaining to	maniac, cardiac
-al	having the character of	terminal, thermal
-ar	pertaining to	circular, cellular
-ary	connected with	imaginary, sedentary
-ful	possessing the quality of	hasteful, spiteful
-ible	able to be	visible, reversible
-ic	pertaining to	anemic, caloric
-ical	pertaining to	comical, historical
-ile	pertaining to, capable of	sterile, fertile
-ish	having the quality of	mannish, boyish
-ive	tending to	secretive, evasive
-less	without	endless, countless
-ous	full of	gracious, spacious
-ulent	abounding in	succulent, fraudulent
-y	quality of	nosy, greedy

Learn to recognize these "Suffixes for Verbs."

SUFFIX	MEANING	EXAMPLE
-ate	characterized by	facilitate, dedicate
-en	to make	deepen, thicken
-ify	to make	quantify, qualify
-ize (ise)	to make, to do something, to subject to	criticize, fertilize

Learn to recognize these "Suffixes for Adverbs"

SUFFIX	MEANING	EXAMPLE
-ly	in a specified manner	commonly, quietly
-fold	having specified number of parts	tenfold, manifold
-ward	toward	inward, outward
-wise	in a specified manner	lengthwise, otherwise

WORD CHOICE ERRORS

Correlative Conjunctions

The following words go together:

either.........................or

neither ....nor

not only ....but (also)

whether......................or

both...........................and

Also note that if an adjective follows one, an adjective must follow the other. If a noun follows one, a noun or pronoun must follow the other.

EXAMPLE:

1. Illustrator Mercer Mayer has won awards for his drawings of _____ adult and children's books.
   (A) the two
   (B) both
   (C) together
   (D) also

ANSWER: (B) is correct because it completes the correlative conjunction pair: both... and. (A) is not correct because it means that the illustrator won the awards for only two books. (C) is incorrect because it attempts to use "together" as an adjective, an incorrect form. (D) "also" is used to add on, but nothing is there to add on to.

Parallel Structures

Parallel structure is the same form of two or more grammatically related elements. Whenever words or phrases are joined by a coordinating conjunction (and, but, or, nor), they should have the same form.

EXAMPLE:

1. The review was very critical of the film, citing the poor photography, weak plot, and _____.
    (A) also including the boring dialogue
    (B) boring dialogue
    (C) while the dialogue was boring
    (D) but the dialogue was boring

ANSWER: (B) is a noun form, just like "photography" and "plot," the other areas criticized by the review. Connect the same elements with "and," which is supplied. The other answers begin with conjunctions which would make the sentence confusing and incorrect. Oppose two different ideas with "but." "While" indicates an importance of time. "Also" includes another idea which may be similar or different.

Comparison of Adjectives

Adjectives and adverbs have three forms that show a greater or lesser degree of the characteristic of the basic word: the positive, the comparative, and the superlative. The basic word is called the positive. The comparative is used to refer to two persons, things, or groups. The superlative is used to refer to more than two people, things, or groups; it indicates the greatest or least degree of the quality named. Most adjectives of one syllable become comparative by adding "er" to the ending and become superlative by adding "est" to the ending. In adjectives ending with "y", the "y" changes to "i" before adding the endings.

Examples of comparison of adjectives:

POSITIVE	COMPARATIVE	SUPERLATIVE
little	littler, less	littlest, least
happy	happier	happiest
late	later	latest
brave	braver	bravest
lovely	lovelier	loveliest
long	longer	longest

friendly	*friendlier*	friendliest
fast	*faster*	fastest
shrewd	*shrewder*	shrewdest
tall	*taller*	tallest

Adjectives of two or more syllables usually form their comparative degree by adding "more" (or "less") and form their superlative degree by adding "most" (or "least").

Examples of comparison of adjectives of two or more syllables:

POSITIVE	COMPARATIVE	SUPERLATIVE
handsome	more handsome less handsome	most handsome least handsome
timid	more timid less timid	most timid least timid
tentative	more tentative less tentative	most tentative least tentative
valuable	more valuable less valuable	most valuable least valuable
endearing	more endearing less endearing	most endearing least endearing

Some adjectives are irregular; their comparatives and superlatives are formed by changes in the words themselves.

Examples of comparison of irregular adjectives:

POSITIVE	COMPARATIVE	SUPERLATIVE
good many	better	best
much some	more	most
bad	worse	worst
little	less	least
far	farther further	farthest furthest

DEFINITION: *farther* — referring to a physical distance.
further — referring to a differing degree, time, or quality.

Adverbs are compared in the same way as adjectives of more than one syllable: by adding "more" (or "less") for the comparative degree and "most" (or "least") for the superlative.

Examples of comparison of adverbs:

POSITIVE	COMPARATIVE	SUPERLATIVE
easily	more easily	most easily
	less easily	least easily
quickly	more quickly	most quickly
	less quickly	least quickly
truthfully	more truthfully	most truthfully
	less truthfully	least truthfully

Some adverbs are irregular; some add "er" or "est."

Examples of comparison of irregular adverbs:

POSITIVE	COMPARATIVE	SUPERLATIVE
little	less	least
well	better	best
far	farther	farthest
badly	worse	worst
fast	faster	fastest
soon	sooner	soonest
much	more	most
hard	harder	hardest
close	closer	closest

The comparative and superlative indicate not only the differences in the degree of the quality named, but also in the number of things discussed.

Use the comparative to compare two things:

Mary is the <u>more lazy</u> of the two.

I've tasted <u>creamier</u> cheese than this.

James is the <u>shorter</u> of the two boys.

Of the two, I like Gail <u>better</u>.

My teacher is <u>kinder</u> than yours.

This book is <u>more interesting</u> than that one.

Use the superlative to compare more than two things:

Mary is the laziest girl I know.

This is the creamiest cheese I've ever tasted.

James is the shortest boy in the class.

Of those five people, I liked Gail best.

My teacher is the kindest in the school.

This book is the most interesting of the three.

There are some words to which comparison does not apply, since they already indicate the highest degree of a quality.

Here are some examples:

immediately	superlative	first
last	very	unique
uniquely	universally	perfect
perfectly	exact	complete
correct	dead	deadly
preferable	round	perpendicularly
square	third	supreme
totally	infinitely	immortal

ERRORS TO AVOID IN COMPARISON

Do not combine two superlatives:

NO: That was the <u>most bravest</u> thing he ever did.

YES: That was the <u>bravest</u> thing he ever did.

NO: He grew up to be the <u>most handsomest</u> boy in the town.

YES: He grew up to be the <u>most handsome</u> boy in the town.

Do not combine two comparatives:

NO: Mary was <u>more friendlier</u> than Susan.

YES: Mary was <u>friendlier</u> than Susan.

NO: The puppy was <u>more timider</u> last week.

YES: The puppy was <u>more timid</u> last week.

COMPARISON WITH "OTHER," "ELSE" OR "OF ALL"

A common mistake when comparing members of a group is to forget to indicate that the item being held up for comparison is still a part of the rest of the group to which it is being compared. The addition of "other" or "else" to the comparative makes this relationship more clear. If the superlative is used, adding "of all" makes the meaning more definite and emphatic.

NO: She is a better piano player than any pianist in our group.
(Is she part of the group?)

YES: She is a better piano player than any <u>other</u> pianist in our group.
(It is now clear that she is a member of the group.)

NO: Our dog is smarter than any on the block.
(Does the dog live on the block?)

YES: Our dog is smarter than any <u>other</u> on the block.
(Now it is obvious that the dog lives on the block.)

NO: Your car is the fastest car in the neighborhood.
(Whose neighborhood?)

YES: Your car is the fastest <u>of all</u> the cars in the neighborhood.
(Your car belongs in the neighborhood.)

CONFUSION WITH ADVERBS AND ADJECTIVES

There are two categories of verbs after which an adjective form is used instead of an adverb form. When using these verbs, it is easy to make a mistake and use an adverb instead of an adjective since, logically, the modifier seems to refer to the verb, but actually it refers to the subject.

Use an adjective after:

1.   Forms of the verb "to be" and other nonaction verbs such as:

seem	appear	become
remain	prove	

The boy was studious. (studious boy)

She appears happy. (happy girl)

The prediction proved incorrect. (incorrect prediction)

Jim remained depressed. (depressed Jim)

2.   Verbs of the senses such as:

taste	feel	look
smell	sound	

Marianne feels sick. (sick Marianne)

That apple tastes good. (good apple)

Those girls look beautiful. (beautiful girls)

The music sounded crisp and clear. (crisp and clear music)

The cake smelled appetizing. (appetizing cake)

NO: Those girls look beautifully. (wrong)
Those girls are beautifully. (illogical)

YES: She appears happy.
She is happy. (logical)

NO: I feel badly. (wrong)
I am badly. (illogical)

YES: The rose smells sweet.
The rose is sweet. (logical)

YES: The music sounded crisp and clear.
The music is crisp and clear. (logical)

Sometimes the modifier refers to the verb, describing or clarifying the manner of the action. In this case, the adverbial form must be used.

She <u>felt cautiously</u> for the light switch.   (cautiously felt)

The music <u>sounded loudly</u> in her ears.   (loudly sounded)

Her parents <u>appeared immediately</u> after she called.   (immediately appeared)

THE ARTICLES—LIMITING ADJECTIVES

The most commonly used adjectives are the shortest—the articles "a," "an," and "the" that signal nouns. <u>A</u> and <u>an</u> are called <u>indefinite articles</u> because they refer to any unspecified member of a group or class. <u>The</u> is called a <u>definite article</u> because it refers to a specific member of a group or class. Articles function as adjectives because they limit a noun or pronoun.

<u>Indefinite articles — "a" "and" "an"</u>		<u>Definite article — "the"</u>	
a pen	a refrigerator	the pen	(a specific pen)
a tree	a secretary	the tree	(a specific tree)
an onion	an error	the error	(a specific error)

"A" is used before words beginning with a consonant sound, and "an" before words with a vowel sound. This is an important distinction; it is not the spelling that determines whether to use "a" or "an," but the sound.

an umbrella	BUT	a university
a radio	BUT	an R.C.A. record
an hour	BUT	a human being

ERRORS TO AVOID IN USING THE ARTICLE

Do not use <u>the</u> before "both":

NO: Let's see <u>the both</u> of them on Saturday.
YES: Let's see <u>both</u> of them on Saturday.

NO: He helped <u>the both</u> of them out of the car.
YES: He helped <u>both</u> of them out of the car.

Do not use <u>a</u> or <u>an</u> after phrases ending with "of," such as "kind of," "sort of," "type of," "manner of ":

NO: What <u>kind of a</u> car did he buy?
YES: What <u>kind of</u> car did he buy?

NO: He was not that <u>sort of a</u> person.
YES: He was not that <u>sort of</u> person.

The following possessive forms of pronouns, "my," "our," "your," "her," "his," "its," "their" are also limiting adjectives. They help to define or limit the noun or the pronoun. Indefinite, demonstrative, interrogative and relative pronouns also function as adjectives when they modify a noun or pronoun.

Take <u>this</u> road.

Will you hand me <u>some</u> silverware?

<u>Whose</u> sweater is this?

That was <u>my</u> paper which won.

The girl <u>whose</u> purse was stolen was very upset.

NUMBER—PLURAL NOUNS

Most nouns can be singular or plural. The usual plural form adds "s" to the end of the word:

desk	desks	book	books
girl	girls	lamp	lamps
guest	guests	idea	ideas
letter	letters	smile	smiles

However, there are many exceptions to this guideline. After "y" preceded by a consonant, "y" changes to "i" and "es" is added:

forty	forties	ecstasy	ecstasies
lady	ladies	category	categories
country	countries	sky	skies
baby	babies	secretary	secretaries
cabby	cabbies	berry	berries
economy	economies	fairy	fairies

If the final "y" is preceded by a vowel, no change is made and the plural is formed by adding "s":

money	moneys	decoy	decoys
buy	buys	guy	guys
attorney	attorneys	abbey	abbeys
valley	valleys	boy	boys
volley	volleys	monkey	monkeys

If the last sound in the word is "s," "z," "ch," "sh," or "x," an "es" is added. The "es" is added so the word can be easily pronounced.

class	classes	branch	branches
box	boxes	dish	dishes
kiss	kisses	fish	fishes
fox	foxes	ranch	ranches
watch	watches	match	matches

However, if the "ch" is pronounced "k," only "s" is added:

stomach	stomachs
monarch	monarchs
epoch	epochs

Often the final "fe" or "f" in one syllable words becomes "ves":

half	halves
wife	wives
life	lives
leaf	leaves
hoof	hooves
calf	calves

There are exceptions, of course:

chief	chiefs
roof	roofs

Many nouns have plural forms that are irregular:

child	children	goose	geese
sheep	sheep	cherub	cherubim
mouse	mice	deer	deer
series	series	man	men
foot	feet	ox	oxen

For nouns ending in "o," add "s" or "es" to form the plural. These spellings must be memorized individually.

solo, solos	tomato, tomatoes
piano, pianos	potato, potatoes
studio, studios	

Finally, there are a number of foreign words that have become part of the language that retain their foreign plural form. There is a trend that Anglicizes the spelling of some of these plural forms by adding "s" to the singular noun. In the list that follows, the letter(s) in parentheses indicate the second acceptable spelling as listed by *Webster's New Collegiate Dictionary*.

axis	axes
radius	radii (radiuses)
bureau	bureaux (s)
plateau	plateaux (s)
larva	larvae (s)
vertebra	vertebrae (s)
crisis	crises
parenthesis	parentheses
criterion	criteria (s)
phenomenon	phenomena (s)
vortex	vortices (es)
matrix	matrices (es)
memorandum	memorandums (a)
stratum	strata
symposium	symposia (s)
appendix	appendices (es)

As you can see, there are many peculiarities associated with plural formation. It is advisable to have a dictionary on hand to check plural forms.

THE POSSESSIVE CASE

The possessive case of nouns is formed by adding an apostrophe and an "s" to words that do not end with an "s" or a "z" sound:

a fox's cunning	anyone's choice
the girl's dress	the tree's leaves
somebody's letter	the mother's hope
the room's color	the men's store
the children's game	the M. D.'s charges

one's desire	anybody else's way
nobody's business	our school's record
Jeannie's grades	Mr. Smith's hopes

The preference is to add only an apostrophe to words when they end in an "s" or "z" sound :

a lioness' strength	the lynx' tail
the boys' bicycles	the crocus' growth
the girls' dresses	the Roberts' address
Burns' poems	the hostess' gown
for goodness' sake	Dickens' story
M.D.s' theories	the Jones' house

However, it is also acceptable to add "s" if the sound is not unpleasant or difficult to pronounce:

	a lioness's strength	the lynx's tail
	Burns's poems	crocus's growth
	the Roberts's address	the hostess's gown
	Dickens's story	the Jones's house
NOT	the boys's bicycles	the girls's dresses
	for goodness's sake	the M.D.s's theories

It is the sound that determines whether to add ('s) or only (').

THE "OF" PHRASE

When the possessive form refers to an animate object, such as a person, the addition of (') or ('s) to the noun is the standard procedure. However, an "of" phrase is most often preferred when the possession refers to an inanimate object.

Chapter 5

Reading Comprehension and Vocabulary Review

Chapter 5

READING COMPREHENSION AND VOCABULARY REVIEW

I. READING COMPREHENSION
- **Effective Reading Tips**
- **Basic Questions**
- **Additional Tips**

II. VOCABULARY
- **Problem Situations**
- **Context Clues**
- **Vocabulary Word List**
- **Vocabulary Drills with Answer Key**

The Reading Comprehension and Vocabulary section of the TOEFL is designed to measure your comprehension of standard written English.

This section has 60 questions and asks you questions based on reading passages. You are given 55 minutes to answer all these questions.

This review will present examples and explanations for the types of problems you will face. It will also provide methods and strategies to help you solve these problems.

I. READING COMPREHENSION

This portion of the test measures how well you can read. There are usually five to six reading passages. Each passage usually contains from one to three paragraphs. At the end of each passage there are questions related to that passage. There are a total of 60 reading questions.

The first passage that you read will usually be the simplest in terms of its length, content, and vocabulary. The next passage will usually be more difficult and so on until you reach the last passage which is usually the most difficult.

Time is in short supply! The reading portion of the test has been designed so that most students will NOT have enough time to read all of the passages carefully and answer all of the questions.

In order to best prepare for this portion of the exam, there are two things to know:

HOW DO YOU READ EFFECTIVELY?

1. Skim the passage and the questions.

2. Read the passage.

3. Scan to answer questions.

WHAT ARE THE SIX BASIC QUESTIONS COMMONLY ASKED?

1. What is the main idea of the passage?

2. What facts were stated in the passage?

3. What new ideas can be inferred from the passage?

4. What might be discussed before or after the passage?

5. What is the author's attitude towards the subject?

6. What is the meaning of the word or phrase?

Effective Reading Tips

There are strategies and techniques which have proven to be successful. They improve overall comprehension, and they are particularly effective in providing the types of information which are needed to answer the reading questions.

Let's look at each and decide how and why it works.

> ➤ Reading Tip | **Skim the Passage and the Questions.**

Skimming is a quick technique that takes only seconds. It gives a general idea of the passage. We can understand a passage better if we know the general subject it will discuss before we read it. We can also answer questions with more success if we have a general understanding of what those questions will ask. When we skim the questions, we read ONLY the questions and not the answer choices. We want to know the general information they will ask for. We don't need to remember them exactly; that will come later. Knowing the general subject and the general questions gives us a head start.

Skimming is a simple way to find the important ideas that will be discussed. It can also help us to identify the major idea of the passage. There are two different ways to skim a passage.

The reading passages have two basic structures:

One long paragraph.

Two or more shorter paragraphs.

If the passage is constructed in one long paragraph, read:

The first two sentences and the last sentence of the paragraph.

Then skim the questions.

If the passage is constructed of two or more paragraphs, read:

The first sentence of each paragraph.

Then skim the questions.

> ➤ Reading Tip | **Read the Passage.**

This is simple. This is where the real comprehension occurs. There are a number of techniques to improve both comprehension and test scores.

1. **PACE YOURSELF.** There are usually five or six reading passages with questions in the reading portion of the test. Try to spend no more than 9 or 10 minutes to complete each passage and its questions. And remember the first passage is usually easier than the second and so on. Extra time will be needed for the later passages.

2. **READ IDEAS NOT WORDS.** A good reader does not move slowly, one word at a time. He reads phrases. He reads sentences. He reads ideas. He recognizes subjects…their actions…and their results. He recognizes main ideas and sees how they are supported and how they are organized.

3. **USE CONTEXT CLUES TO UNDERSTAND DIFFICULT WORDS.** Many times when we read a passage, we will find words whose meaning is not clear. Luckily, the sentence that the word is in and the other sentences in the passage will often provide information that helps to explain what that word means. We call this information context clues. There are many types of context clues and with them we can increase our understanding of particular words and thereby increase our general understanding of the passage.

NOTE: A full discussion of context clues will be given in the vocabulary review section.

> **► Reading Tip** | **Scan to Answer Questions**

Once we have completed steps 1 and 2, we can then begin to deal with the reading material.

Scanning is a quick way of finding specific words in a passage. Those specific words mark the location in the passage where we can find the information we need to answer a question. Scanning is not reading! When we scan, our eyes move very quickly through the sentences and paragraphs. We have only one purpose: find the key word. Once we have found the key word, we begin to read for the information we need to answer the question.

Let's look at a passage.

There are many important resort areas in the state of New Jersey. They include popular ski areas in the northern part of the state, and the river and forest wilderness of the pinelands in the central region, but both these areas draw a relatively small number of tourists compared to the coastal resorts which attract millions each year to their beaches for sand, sea, and sun. Probably the best known of these resorts are Long Beach Island, which provides activity for the whole family; Atlantic City, whose casinos provide the excitement of gambling and nightlife; and Cape May, a small town which has carefully preserved its rich history and architecture, and which is today home to some of the finest restaurants in the country.

Key words in questions will indicate where to look for answers!

EXAMPLES:

1. The **pinelands** is famous for what physical features?

2. A **family man** would probably choose which beach resort?

3. A **gourmet** would probably choose which beach resort?

Scan quickly through the passage and find where the key words are located. The information needed to answer each question is nearby. Repeat the key word in your mind as you scan.

Let's look at the passage again. The **key words** will be in bold face and the essential information will be underlined.

There are many important resort areas in the state of New Jersey. They include popular ski areas in the northern part of the state, and the river and forest wilderness of the **pinelands** in the central region, but both these areas draw a relatively small number of tourists compared to the coastal resorts which attract millions each year to their beaches for sand, sea, and sun. Probably the best known of these resorts are Long Beach Island, which provides activity for **the whole family**; Atlantic City, whose casinos provide the excitement of gambling and nightlife; and Cape May, a small town which has carefully preserved its rich history and architecture, and which is today home to some of the finest **restaurants** in the country.

QUESTION #1:   Once we find the key word "pinelands," we can quickly find the answer. "Physical features?"
ANSWER: "river and forest wilderness."

QUESTION #2:   A "family man" wants a resort which provides activities for the "whole family."
ANSWER: "Long Beach Island" provides those activities.

QUESTION #3:   The first two questions were fairly easy to answer, but the last question required you to know what a "gourmet" is. The key word "gourmet" is never mentioned in the passage, but if you know what the word means: a person who is an expert in fine food and dining, then scanning still provides the answer. We see "the finest restaurants" and we know these would interest a gourmet.
ANSWER: "Cape May...home to some of the finest restaurants" provides our answer.

The three basic techniques which we have discussed will help you to read with greater speed and comprehension, and they will provide you with effective ways to answer the questions which the reading portion of the TOEFL will ask. But to be fully prepared for this section of the test, it is essential that you develop an understanding and a familiarity with the types of questions you will be asked and to practice the use of our reading techniques upon them.

Basic Questions

Let's look at six basic questions asked on the test.

Basic Question 1:   What is the main idea of the passage?

Good writing is carefully organized around an important idea. This idea controls all of the other ideas within the passage. Sometimes this main idea is clearly stated in one or two sentences in the passage BUT not always. Sometimes it is not directly mentioned in the passage at all.

Let's look at an example:

Marge sure knows how to have a party. I got there at nine o'clock and the place was already jumping. People were laughing and shouting as waiters ran back and forth from the kitchen with trays loaded down with lobster and caviar. A Mexican band was performing on the patio and a long line of people were doing the "conga." I didn't see who was the first person to jump into the pool with his clothes on, but before long everyone at the party had joined in. People tell me it was around midnight when Michael Jackson showed up, but I really couldn't tell you for sure. I don't remember anything after that French girl and I opened our second bottle of champagne in the jacuzzi.

One main idea controls all of the facts, examples, and discussion in this passage:

Marge's party was a lot of fun.

In this passage the first sentence "Marge sure knows how to have a party." gives us a very clear indication of what that main idea is, but it is not exactly the main idea. Marge's general ability to plan and give parties is not the central idea. The main idea of a passage will **sometimes** be stated in the first or second sentence of the passage.

Many times the main idea is not directly stated in the passage. But even without that first sentence the main idea is clear. Look at the examples presented:

...the place was jumping...people laughing and shouting...trays loaded with lobster and caviar...a Mexican band...people dancing...people jumping into the pool...and Michael Jackson too.

All of these examples point to only one central idea: The party was fun.

Let's look at another example:

Life in Colorado was changed overnight by the gold rush of 1859. Miners needed supplies and, at first, depended upon the foodstuffs imported from the Midwest. Flour cost as much as $50 a barrel, but hungry miners were willing to pay these inflated prices. Further, because many of these Fifty-niners had farming backgrounds, they turned to agriculture after they were unable to survive in the mines. These people found the land fertile and began to farm the land. They did not plant crops for survival but rather to sell. At this point agriculture in Colorado changed from subsistence to commercial farming.

The first sentence of this paragraph gives us important information about the central idea, but it is not the central idea. The first sentence is too general. Read the passage again and try to decide what idea controls the discussion.

Yes, "Life in Colorado was changed by the gold rush," but the passage does not discuss all the ways "life" was changed. The passage discusses only one aspect of life in Colorado which changed: agriculture. The controlling idea is

Farming in Colorado was changed suddenly by the gold rush.

Let's look at the **important supporting ideas.**

Life in Colorado was changed overnight by the gold rush of 1859. Miners needed supplies and, at first, **depended upon the foodstuffs** imported from the Midwest. **Flour cost** as much as $50 a barrel, but **hungry miners were willing to pay** these inflated prices. Further, because many of **these Fifty-niners had farming backgrounds,** they **turned to agriculture** after they were unable to survive in the mines. These people found the **land fertile** and **began to farm** the land. They did not **plant crops** for survival but rather to sell. At this point **agriculture in Colorado changed** from subsistence to **commercial farming.**

All of these supporting ideas point in only one direction.

NOT: Life in Colorado

NOT: The gold rush

NOT: Farming in Colorado

BUT: ...**How farming was changed by the gold rush in Colorado**

REMEMBER: The first and last sentences of each paragraph are very important. They usually point towards the main idea.

Once we know what the main idea is, we will be able to answer many questions. The TOEFL reading comprehension exam uses information connected to the main idea to ask many different types of questions.

EXAMPLES:

1.   What would be a good title for this passage?

   (A)   Farming in Colorado
   (B)   The Gold Rush of '59
   (C)   The Real Gold Grew Out of the Ground
   (D)   Go West, Young Man

All of these ideas are connected to the passage, but only one is a good title. To choose the best answer we must know that the main idea is not farming, nor the gold rush but the relationship between the two. The best title is (C) because it mentions both.

2.   What is the author's main purpose?

    (A) To discuss Colorado's interesting history
    (B) To show that farming is sometimes better than mining
    (C) To show that the Gold Rush was an exciting time to be alive
    (D) To show the effects of the Gold Rush upon agriculture in Colorado

All of these ideas were in the passage, but only one of them was the main purpose. The author's main purpose is always to clearly express and to support his main idea. The main purpose of this passage is (D).

RELATED QUESTIONS:

    What is the subject of the passage?

    What is the topic of the passage?

    What is the emphasis of the passage?

    What is the controlling idea?

The answer to all of these questions can be found in the main idea.

Basic Question 2:   What specific facts were stated in the passage?

    Let's look at an example.

Coral reef communities are normally classified in two ways: live bottom or patch reef. The live bottom community, also known as hardground, is generally found closest to shore in tidal passes, under bridges, and short distances seaward of the intertidal zone. It usually occupies fossil reef formations, limestone, and other rocky substrates. Animal and plant life are not consistent from reef to reef, but are usually visually dominated by octocorals, algae, and sponges.

This passage appears to be quite difficult. The reason it appears so difficult is because of the technical words which it uses. It is not necessary to know every word in a passage in order to understand it.

Read the passage again and see if you can answer these questions.

1.   What is the general subject of the discussion?

2.   How many types of reef communities are there?

3.   Which type of reef community is discussed?

4.   Where is this type of reef found?

5.   What does it occupy?

6.   What plants and animals dominate?

To read with understanding it is necessary to understand how a basic sentence in written English works.

There is a SUBJECT and there is a VERB.

The SUBJECT is	a person	The VERB is	an action
	a place		a state of being
	a thing		
	an idea		

To put it simply: SOMEONE OR SOMETHING **DOES** SOMETHING!

or

SOMEONE OR SOMETHING **IS** SOMETHING!

"Bob eats hamburgers."

| Subject | BOB |
| Verb | EATS |

"Bob is a policeman."

| Subject | BOB |
| Verb | IS |

Every sentence contains at least one idea. To understand that idea, we must know what the subject is and what the subject does.

Let's look at the passage again. The subjects will be shown in **bold face** and the verbs will be <u>underlined</u>.

Coral reef communities <u>are</u> normally <u>classified</u> in two ways: live bottom or patch reef. The **live bottom community,** also known as hardground, <u>is</u> generally <u>found</u> closest to shore in tidal passes, under bridges, and short distances seaward of the intertidal zone. **It** usually <u>occupies</u> fossil reef formations, limestone, and other rocky substrates. **Animal and plant life** <u>are not</u> consistent from reef to reef, but <u>are</u> usually visually <u>dominated</u> by octocorals, algae, and sponges.

Understanding this passage is much easier now even with the technical vocabulary. Try answering these questions:

1. How are reef communities classified?

2. Where is the live bottom community found?

3. What does it usually occupy?

4. What types of plants and animals visually dominate the reefs?

If we understand the subject and the verb of each sentence, the information that follows is easier to understand and even when the vocabulary is very difficult.

Let's look at the passage again. This time we will look for the important information which follows the verbs. The verbs will be underlined and the factual information will be in bold face.

Coral reef communities <u>are normally classified</u> in two ways: **live bottom or patch reef.** The live bottom community, also known as hardground, <u>is generally found</u> closest to shore **in tidal passes, under bridges, and short distances seaward of the intertidal zone.** It usually <u>occupies</u> **fossil reef formations, limestone, and other rocky substrates.** Animal and plant life <u>are</u> **not consistent** from reef to reef, but <u>are</u> usually visually <u>dominated by</u> **octocorals, algae, and sponges.**

---

1. How are reef communities classified?

   Live bottom or patch reef

2. Where is the live bottom community found?

   In tidal passes, under bridges, and seaward of the intertidal zone

3. What does it usually occupy?

   Fossil reef formations, limestone, and rocky substrates

4. What types of plants and animals visually dominate the reefs?

   Octocorals, algae, and sponges

By understanding the structure and organization of a sentence, we can understand the idea it expresses even when the meanings of many words in that sentence are unclear.

BE CAREFUL OF REVERSE QUESTIONS!

Many times the questions will ask not only what was discussed but also **what wasn't discussed.** Let's look at an example.

Chicago, the windy city, as it is sometimes called, has always possessed its own unique style. Its citizens are justly proud of its long, glorious, and slightly notorious history. Its reputation, deservedly or not, is known throughout the world. Mention Al Capone, prohibition, or a mobster with a machine gun and only one city comes to mind.

A reverse question would ask you this:

According to the passage, Chicago's history has **NOT** been

(A) developed over many years.
(B) filled with glory.
(C) somewhat notorious.
(D) carefully recorded.

Our key word is "history." When we scan quickly for the word, we see that it is described as "long, glorious, and slightly notorious." The choices we are given have been slightly changed, but we can see (A), (B), and (C) are used in the passage to describe Chicago's history. (D) "Carefully recorded" has NOT been mentioned. It is the correct choice.

Here's another example.

> According to the passage, Chicago quickly comes to mind to people all over the world EXCEPT when you mention

    (A)   windy city.
    (B)   Al Capone.
    (C)   prohibition.
    (D)   gangsters.

The key words in this question are "all over the world." Three examples are mentioned after this phrase. They are (B), (C), and (D). (A) "windy city" is mentioned at the beginning of the passage, but it is not a specific example which causes people throughout the world to think of Chicago. (A) is correct.

Basic Question 3:   What new ideas can be inferred from the passage?

In question 2 we were asked to find facts, data, and other types of information which were stated in the passage. But in basic question 3 we have to take the next step. We have to develop new ideas which are based upon the facts that we have read. These new ideas are called inferences.

Let's look at an example.

THE SMOKING GUN!

FACT: Mr. Murphy was found dead on the kitchen floor.

FACT: There was a bullet hole in his chest.

We know this information is correct.

Do we **know for sure** that he was killed by the bullet?

When we make an inference, we have to study the facts carefully and decide what new idea can be formed.

From the facts that we know, decide which inference concerning Murphy's death would be most reasonable.

INFERENCE 1:   Murphy was shot and killed by a bullet to the chest.

INFERENCE 2:   Murphy was shot in the chest and was probably killed by that bullet.

INFERENCE 3:   Murphy was shot and now he is dead.

The only difference between 1 and 2 is the word "probably." If you chose 2, then you are correct. What's wrong with 1?

Well....do we know for sure that the bullet killed him? NO!

Do we know for sure he was alive when he was shot? NO!

The problem with 1 is that it leaves no room for questions or possibilities and there are both.

Number 2 is a good inference because it uses the correct word "probably" to describe the relationship between the facts.

Inference 3, "Murphy was shot and now he is dead," was a trick! It is not really an inference. Number 3 does not give us new information. It only gives us the facts which we already knew. An inference must give us new information.

Now read the whole story.

THE SMOKING GUN!

Mrs. Brown, who lives in the apartment next to the Murphys', was watching the eleven o'clock news as usual when she heard what sounded like gunshots from the apartment next door. She told the police, "Oh, it was a terrible noise and it sounded just like a gunshot. I was frightened to death. I didn't know what to do. I just sat there like a rock for several minutes listening before I went to wake up my husband, who's always in bed by nine. I was in the bedroom shaking him, trying to wake him up, when the second gunshot was fired. My God, the noise even rattled the open windows. Finally he sat up in bed and looked at me. I told him what I had heard and asked him if we should call the police. He didn't want to call the police until he was sure something was really wrong. 'Come on, woman! Let's see if everyone is okay,' he said. The door to their apartment was open. My husband called out, 'Mr. Murphy?' I heard Mary, I mean Mrs. Murphy, say, 'In here.' When we walked into the kitchen, we saw her, poor dear. She was standing there over his body with a gun in her hand. He lay there in a pool of blood. If you ask me, I say the dirty rat got what he deserved. My husband called the police immediately."

When we look at a statement of fact, we can say that it is either true or false. But when we look at an inference, we have to judge it in a different way. We can say that it is:

ALMOST CERTAIN	The world will not end tomorrow.
VERY PROBABLE	It will rain in New York this summer.
PROBABLE	You will lose you car keys someday.
POSSIBLE	You will meet a movie star.
UNLIKELY	You will live to be 90 years old.
VERY UNLIKELY	You will live to be 100 years old.
ALMOST IMPOSSIBLE	You will win the lottery this week.

Let's look at several inferences connected to the passage and decide if they are weak or strong.

INFERENCE: Mr. Brown wakes up earlier than Mrs. Brown most mornings.

PROBABLE   WHY? We know from the passage that she stays up and watches the eleven o'clock news most nights. We know that he is asleep by nine o'clock. He probably wakes up earlier.

INFERENCE: Mrs. Brown and Mr. Murphy were best friends.

VERY UNLIKELY   WHY? Look at Mrs. Brown's last statement. "If you ask me, I say the dirty rat got what he deserved." Mrs. Brown is not sad about the death. She call Mr. Murphy a "dirty rat."

> **DIRECTIONS:** Look at the inferences listed below and decide if they are weak or strong. Find clues from the passage to support your ideas.

1. Mrs. Brown would be a good person to have with you in an emergency.

2. Mr. Brown would be a good person to have with you in an emergency.

3. We can be fairly sure that the second shot was fired several minutes after the first.

4. The murder happened on a winter night.

5. Mr. Brown and Mr. Murphy were close friends.

6. Mrs. Brown and Mrs. Murphy were close friends.

7. Mr. Brown is a cautious man.

8. Mr. Brown saw smoke coming out of the gun that Mrs. Murphy was holding.

9. Mrs. Murphy was in a state of shock when they found her.

10. Mrs. Brown knows a lot more about the Murphys and their problems than she tells the police.

Let's discuss each inference and the information from the passage which shows it to be weak or strong.

INFERENCES:

1. UNLIKELY/VERY UNLIKELY. Mrs. Brown would NOT be a good person to have with you in an emergency. When she heard the gunshot, she says, "I was frightened to death. I didn't know what to do. I just sat there like a rock for several minutes..." In an emergency people have to make decisions quickly and then to act quickly. Mrs. Brown is not able to do either.

2. PROBABLE/VERY PROBABLE. Faced with a dangerous situation Mr. Brown was able to quickly make a decision and to act upon that decision. He didn't want to call the police until he had the facts. Once he saw Mr. Murphy dead on the floor, he immediately called the police.

3. UNLIKELY. The inference says, "We can be fairly sure that the second shot was fired several minutes after the first." The key phrase in this inference is "fairly sure." Can we be fairly sure? No, we can't! The only evidence we have is what Mrs. Brown tells us. She says it was several minutes but we can't be sure that she is correct. We know that the first gunshot surprised and frightened her. She was so upset that she could hardly move. Being in such a state of fear, it would be difficult for her to judge accurately the passage of time. It may have seemed like a few minutes to her, but it could have been a much longer or much shorter period of time.

4. UNLIKELY. There is only one small clue to indicate what season of the year it is. Did you find it? Mrs. Brown gives the clue when she says, "My God, the noise (of the gunshot) even rattled the open windows." If the windows are open, then it is unlikely that it is winter.

5. VERY UNLIKELY. There is no real discussion concerning the relationship between the two men, but we can still be very sure that they were NOT good friends. When the Browns go next door to see what is wrong, Mr. Brown pauses at the door and calls out, "Mr. Murphy?" In American culture when good friends are speaking to one another, they almost never use each other's family name when calling out to them.

6. PROBABLE. There are many indications of their friendship. Mrs. Brown refers to her as "Mary" and when they come into the kitchen with Mr. Murphy dead on the floor, she is not worried about him but rather her. "We saw her, poor dear," she says. "Poor dear" was holding a gun but the "dirty rat" is dead on the floor. If they were not close friends, her reaction would have been completely opposite.

7. POSSIBLE. This is a difficult problem to judge because we are given information that could point in two different directions. He hesitates to call the police until he is really sure that something is wrong. This indicates some caution. But then he says, "Come on, woman! Let's see if everyone is okay." He says this just after his wife has told him she heard gunshots. A cautious man probably would not have done this. The inference is **possible** but we can't be sure.

8. VERY UNLIKELY. Smoke comes out of the barrel of a gun for only a few seconds after it is fired. Mr. Brown is still asleep when the second shot is fired. They then have to get up and walk to the next apartment, stand and call at the door, and walk through the living room into the kitchen before they see the gun. This would indicate a minimum of one minute and most likely two or three. By that time it is very unlikely that smoke could still be seen.

9. UNLIKELY. There is very little evidence to describe her mental and emotional condition either way. The only real clues we have that she is NOT in a state of shock come from several facts. When Mr. Brown calls out, she answers him in a reasonable way, "In here." We see her standing over the body. She is not crying or moaning. She is simply standing there. We can't be sure, but she does not appear to be in a state of shock.

10. VERY PROBABLE. We know that they are next-door neighbors. Mrs. Brown could probably hear them when they had an argument. It appears that she and Mrs. Murphy were good friends and good friends tell each other their problems. But the strongest clue comes when Mrs. Brown says, "If you ask me, I say the dirty rat got what he deserved." She has formed a very strong opinion about Mr. Murphy, so strong in fact that she says he deserves to die. If she did not know a lot more about them and their problems, she would not have formed such a strong opinion.

Basic Question 4:   What might be discussed before or after the passage?

This is a very difficult question for most students to answer. The reason why it is so difficult is that most students never ask themselves this question. Their major problem is understanding the passage which is difficult enough all by itself. Why should they think about "What might come before?" or "What might come next?"?

The purpose of writing is to express ideas. Many times those ideas are complicated. Good writers know that their ideas have to be carefully organized.

Once the pattern of the organization is understood, it is easy to know what would come before and what would come after.

There are many ways to organize these ideas.

Let's look at some examples.

Order of importance

Problem: Imagine you have a brother whom you love very much but whom you haven't seen for many years. In the years you have been away, you have become very rich. You are flying home for his birthday party, and you have decided to buy him three presents:

(A) a beautiful watch
(B) a trip to Hawaii
(C) a brand new Mercedes-Benz 540 sport coupe

You want him to enjoy his party and you want him to appreciate each of his presents, but you can't decide which gift to give him first, which second and which last.

There is only one **effective** way to give him the presents. Decide which present should be given first and so on.

REMEMBER: We want him to appreciate all three gifts.

The gifts must be organized this way:

First, the watch

Second, the trip

Last, the Mercedes

What happens if we give the trip first? Your brother will love it. But how will he feel when he gets the watch next? He will feel let down because the first gift was better than the second. The pattern has to follow from good to better to best. This pattern is called order of importance. In this example it moves from least important to most important.

Process

PROBLEM: Your Aunt Mary went to Florida to see her sister. Uncle Harry, her husband, is having his boss come over for dinner. Unfortunately, Uncle Harry is a terrible cook. He calls you for help. You know a wonderful way to make lasagna. How do you explain it to him so he can prepare it properly? How do we organize the steps?

Making lasagna is a PROCESS. There is only way to organize a process: STEP BY STEP.

What is done first?

What is done second?

What is done next?

And so on until the process is complete.

General to specific which is to say from large idea to small idea.

PROBLEM: The year is 2345 and you are visiting a faraway planet. You have met a resident of this planet and you have become friends. You want to tell him about your home town. His only knowledge of earth is its general location in the universe. Where do you begin your discussion?

Begin with the general and move to the specific.

1. Solar system
2. Planet
3. Continent
4. Country
5. State
6. City
7. Street
8. House
9. Room

If the passage is moving from GENERAL TO SPECIFIC, then we can determine what would be discussed before and after the passage.

A passage discussing California would probably have a discussion about the United States coming before it, and the passage would probably be followed by a discussion of cities in California.

Cause and effect

This is another common method of organization. It would follow this pattern:

General Discussion of > Discussion > Discussion > Discussion
Problem or Situation   of Causes   of Effects   of Solutions

If the subject of the passage is the "effects of drug abuse," then a discussion of its causes would have come before and possible solutions would be discussed after the effects.

Compare and contrast

Usually you don't have one without the other. When we **compare**, we examine how two things are similar or the **same**. When we **contrast**, we examine how two things are **different**.

Usual Pattern: Discussion of   then   Discussion of
                      likenesses   differences

There are many different ways to organize information. We have discussed the most common methods. There are other methods but they all follow a pattern. The pattern will be logical. It will make sense. Listed below are some other common patterns.

Most to Least	Far to Near
Least to Most	Near to Far
Large to Small	Left to Right
Small to Large	Morning to Night

Basic Question 5:   What is the author's attitude towards a subject?

The author, like any person, has an opinion about a subject. He or she might consider it to be: right or wrong, good or bad, sad or happy, wise or silly. Very seldom do we have an opinion of something without having some emotional feeling concerning the same subject. The emotional feeling can be strong or weak or anywhere in between.

An author's attitude is this combination: OPINION and EMOTION.

How can we recognize the author's attitude?

There are two types of clues:

1.   The selection of specific facts mentioned in the passage.

2.   Choice of specific words used in the passage.

Let's look at an example.

Roger and Mary were happily married for many years. Their children are all grown and have moved out of the house. With the children gone, Mary felt bored and lonely and that her life was without purpose. She wanted to find a job but Roger told her that was silly since he earned a good living and he didn't want people to think that he couldn't support his family. Sitting around the house all day with nothing to do but eat and watch television, Mary began to put on weight. She would have a drink before dinner. Roger had been under a lot of pressure at his job. He spent long hours at work and when he got home, he was too tired to do anything but eat and go to sleep. Some nights he would have to work late and when he got home he found Mary almost drunk. They began to argue constantly. Last month they got a divorce. Who is to blame?

MARY'S OPINION: Roger is to blame for the divorce.

ROGER'S OPINION: Mary is to blame for the divorce.

There are facts to support each opinion but a writer will select those facts which help show his opinion is strong. Here are some facts. Look at them carefully and decide which opinion they support.

FACTS:

1. Mary was gaining weight and not taking care of her appearance.
2. Roger didn't try hard enough to understand Mary's problems.
3. Roger was under a lot of pressure at work.
4. Roger never wanted to do anything after work.
5. Mary was often drunk when Roger came home.
6. Everyone has the right to try to enjoy themselves.
7. Roger had to work long hours; he needed to rest when he got home.
8. Roger's pride made Mary's life empty.

These facts don't change but each side in the argument selects only those facts which support its opinion.

MARY'S OPINION: 2, 4, 6, 8   ROGER'S OPINION: 1, 3, 5, 7

An author has many words to choose from when stating his ideas. His attitude towards a subject will determine which words he will select.

> **DIRECTIONS**: Look at some examples and decide what are the authors' attitudes concerning the same subject: **SNAKES**.

Author 1: "Like a thin ribbon of many colors, it glides softly through the grass and calmly disappears before our eyes."

Author 2: "The cold beady eyes of the deadly assassin are watchful. It lurks hidden, ready to strike and devour its prey."

Author 3: "This limbless scaled reptile has a long tapering body. One of its many unusual characteristics is that it is known to exist in all types of habitat except for the polar regions."

Who hates snakes?

Who loves snakes?

Who considers them an interesting subject for study?

Read the sentences again and notice the highlighted words.

Author 1: "Like a **thin ribbon** of **many colors**, it **glides softly** through the grass and **calmly disappears** before our eyes."

Author 2: "The **cold beady eyes** of the **deadly assassin** are watchful. It **lurks hidden**, ready to **strike** and **devour** its prey."

Author 3: "This **limbless scaled reptile** has a **long tapering body**. One of its many **unusual characteristics** is that it is known to **exist** in all types of **habitat** except for the polar regions."

Each author chose different words to refer to the snake.

1. **thin ribbon**

2. **deadly assassin**

3. **limbless scaled reptile**

How is the snake described?

1. **many colors...glides softly...calmly disappears**

2. **cold beady eyes...lurks hidden...strike and devour**

3. **long tapering body...unusual characteristics...exists...habitat**

Author 1 has chosen words to show that the snake is a beautiful creature with graceful movements.

"thin ribbon...many colors...glides softly...calmly disappears"

ATTITUDE: Snakes are wonderful creatures.

Author 2 has chosen words to make the snake appear dangerous and evil.

"cold beady eyes...deadly assassin...lurks hidden...strike and devour"

ATTITUDE: Snakes are terrible creatures.

Author 3 gives us the scientific facts. The only opinion that he gives is that the snake has "many unusual characteristics" which can indicate to us that he finds snakes interesting.

ATTITUDE: Snakes are scientifically interesting.

REMEMBER: By examining the author's choice of words and facts, we can determine his attitude

Basic Question 6:   What is the meaning of the word or phrase?

The reading portion of the TOEFL will ask you questions related to the meaning of specific words in the passages. The questions will ask you to choose a suitable replacement for a word or phrase.

Let's look at a passage.

Mr. Brown's odious habits were disgusting to strangers and even more so to his co-workers who, day after day, were forced to watch and listen as he scratched, belched, and spit. He was a walking collection of nasty gestures and poor manners. In addition to this, he was an insult to the olfactory sense of anyone who by bad luck happened to have a nose.

A replacement question might ask:

1.   In the first sentence, the word "odious" could best be replaced by which of the following?

    (A) Unpleasant
    (B) Evil
    (C) Hateful
    (D) Foul smelling

Vocabulary questions such as the one above can be answered in two different ways:

1.   Using our knowledge of vocabulary.

2.   Using context clues to discover the meaning of an unknown word.

You might know simply by looking at the word "odious" that it means: deserving hatred or repugnance. But this will NOT usually be the case. The meaning of many words will be unclear to you, but there are ways to solve this problem. There are many context clues given in the passage which help us to understand what the word means. Context clues can come from the facts and grammar which surround the word whose meaning we seek

Let's look at the passage again.

Mr. Brown's <u>odious</u> habits were **disgusting** to strangers and even more so to his co-workers who, day after day, were forced to watch and listen as he **scratched, belched, and spit.** He was a walking collection of **nasty gestures and poor manners.** In addition to this, he was an insult to the olfactory sense of anyone who by bad luck happened to have a nose.

The grammatical structure of the first sentence shows us that "odious" is an adjective which modifies "habits." If we know something about these "habits," we will have a good clue towards understanding "odious."

What specifically are the habits?

1. Scratched

2. Belched

3. Spit

How would you describe these habits?

How would you feel if you had to watch someone doing this every day?

By answering these questions we begin to see that these habits are "Not nice." But when we look at the answer choices, we see that all of the choices are "not nice." We need to be more specific and more exact.

In the first sentence, his "habits" are described as "disgusting to strangers and co-workers." The second sentence says, "nasty gestures."

When we look at the answer choices, we are able to eliminate certain ones.

(D) Foul smelling. At the end of the passage there is a discussion about how Mr. Brown smells but this is not related to his habits and has nothing to do with "odious." It is incorrect.

(B) Evil. This choice is **too strong.** "Evil" causes harm or injury to others. His habits cause unhappiness to those around him but they do not cause harm or injury. It is incorrect.

We have to decide which word is best: unpleasant or hateful. Both are related to "odious" in meaning but one is a much better replacement. The most important context clues are "disgusting and nasty" and the examples themselves. A disgusting and nasty habit such as spitting is more than "unpleasant"; the correct answer is "Hateful."

Try another example on your own.

In the last sentence of the passage, what does the word "olfactory" mean? There are several context clues to help you understand its meaning. Read the sentence carefully.

This is only a brief discussion of how we can use context clues to discover the meaning of words. In the Vocabulary Review section, we will discuss with explanations and examples all of the various context clues.

Additional Tips

It is impossible to include in any review a discussion of all the problems which may face a student taking the TOEFL, but there are elements in the test that we can be sure will appear.

Two different ideas are often joined together in one sentence. The word that joins these two ideas expresses their relationship to one another. To increase comprehension, it is essential to understand that relationship, but that can only be done when we understand the meaning of the connecting word.

SIMPLE CONNECTORS: The most simple of the two types of connectors are called "coordinating conjunctions." Most students will easily recognize and understand the meaning of these basic connectors:

AND	OR	BUT
FOR	SO	YET
NOR		

"AND" means the addition of both ideas.

EXAMPLE: Bob **and** Sally went to the party. (These two people went to the party.)

"OR" means there is a choice of only one.

EXAMPLE: Bob **or** Sally will go to the party. (Only one person will go. If Bob then not Sally. If Sally then not Bob.)

"BUT" and "YET" have the same basic meaning. They both are used to show the differences in the ideas being joined.

EXAMPLE: Fred has a lot of money, but his car is very old. (We know that Fred has a lot of money. We expect his car to be new. His car is not new. These ideas contrast with one another. They are different ideas.)

"FOR" and "SO" are opposites which are used to show the correct relationship between a cause and an effect. There are two possibilities:

CAUSE	"SO"	EFFECT
EFFECT	"FOR"	CAUSE

EXAMPLE: <u>Marta broke her leg</u> **so** <u>she went to the hospital</u>.

CAUSE	EFFECT

EXAMPLE: <u>Jose worked day and night</u> **for** <u>he needed money badly</u>.

EFFECT	CAUSE

"NOR" performs the same basic function as "AND" but it is used with negative ideas.

EXAMPLE: Bob will go home and Mary will too.

EXAMPLE: Bob will not go home nor will Mary.

CONFUSING CONNECTORS: While most students recognize and understand these conjunctions, they are often confused by the connectors we call: conjunctive adverbs. But there is an easy way to understand what they mean because most of them share a common meaning with one of the seven basic conjunctions. For example, the connector "nevertheless" serves the same basic function as "but."

The lists below will group the confusing connectors which share a common meaning with one of the simple connectors.

AND	BUT/YET	SO
ALSO	HOWEVER	CONSEQUENTLY
BESIDES	NEVERTHELESS	HENCE
FURTHERMORE	NONETHELESS	THEREFORE
MOREOVER	STILL	THUS
IN ADDITION	ALTHOUGH	ACCORDINGLY

MODALS

A clear understanding of how modals function to change the meaning of a sentence is essential for developing your reading comprehension.

Let's look at a basic sentence and see how it and its meaning will change with the addition of a modal.

BASIC SENTENCE:	ERIC FLIES AIRPLANES.
Ability:	Eric **can** fly an airplane.
Possibility:	Eric **could** fly an airplane.
Slight	Eric **may** fly an airplane.
Possibility:	Eric **might** fly an airplane.
Permission:	**Can** Eric fly the airplane?
	Could Eric fly the airplane?
	May Eric fly the airplane?
	Might Eric fly the airplane?
Obligation:	Eric **should** fly an airplane.
	Eric **ought** to fly an airplane.
Necessity:	Eric **must** fly the airplane.
	Eric **has to** fly the airplane.
Prohibition:	Eric **must** not fly the airplane.
No Necessity:	Eric **does not have** to fly the airplane.

Inference:	Eric **must** fly an airplane since he is a pilot.
Preference:	Eric **would rather** fly an airplane than drive a bus.
Past habit:	Eric **would** fly his airplane every Saturday before the accident happened.
Advisability:	Eric **had better** fly his plane before the storm comes.

II. VOCABULARY

Your knowledge of English vocabulary will be tested within the Reading Comprehension passages. The questions dealing with vocabulary will refer to the line number in which the word appears. You have to choose from among the four answer choices the word or phrase that best keeps the meaning of the original sentence

Sometimes, the meaning of the word and the best choice to replace it will be clear to you, but many times the meaning of the word will not be clear. To solve this problem, we can use clues inside the sentence. These clues are called "context clues." Not every sentence will provide enough clues to allow us to determine the meaning of the words, but many times they will.

Problem Situations

In the reading portion of the test, you will face vocabulary questions. You will have an advantage because you can use the entire passage to find context clues to help you understand the meaning of words which are tested.

There are four main problem situations. We will discuss each situation and explain the strategies that can be used to manage them.

SITUATION 1

You are familiar with the word. You are familiar with the answer choices. You think you know the correct choice.

You have to be careful. A single word can have many meanings. Often, these meanings will be very similar to one another, but only one will be correct.

Let's look at an example using the word "collect."

EXAMPLE 1: Many animals <u>collect</u> seeds and nuts for the winter.

    (A) pick up
    (B) organize
    (C) store
    (D) need

EXAMPLE 2: She wanted to <u>collect</u> her thoughts before she spoke to her boss.
    (A) pick up
    (B) organize
    (C) store
    (D) need

The correct answer for #1 is (A) "pick up." It would be very easy to choose (C) "store" because animals store food after they collect it, but it is not the best replacement. (D) "need" fits into to survive the winter, but "need" and "collect" are not synonyms. (B) "organize" makes no sense in the context of the sentence.

The correct answer for #2 is (B) "organize." Her thoughts need to be arranged and organized before she speaks to her boss. In this example, the word does **not** mean "pick up" as it did in the first example.

SITUATION 2

You understand the meaning of the word, but you are not sure which answer choice is correct.

There are no context clues to help you understand the meaning of answer choices. You need to deal with them quickly and to take your chances. Follow these simple rules.

1. Eliminate the choices you know are incorrect.

2. Don't choose a word because it looks like or sounds like the word. These words are often used to confuse or to trick you. They are usually not the correct choice.

3. After going through steps one and two, make your best guess. Many times, your first choice will be the best.

4. Don't waste valuable time.

SITUATION 3

You don't understand the meaning of the word. You don't know the meanings of the answer choices.

You can often discover the meaning of a word by using context clues, but if you have no idea what an answer choice means, you face an unsolvable problem. Waste no time! Take a guess and move to the next question.

SITUATION 4

The meaning of the word is not clear, but you are familiar with the answer choices and their meanings.

Use context clues in the sentence to help you discover the meaning of a word. This is the most common problem situation you will face, and there are many ways to manage it which are explained below.

Context Clues

Context clues come in many shapes and forms. They include examples, synonyms, antonyms, grammatical structures, and the general idea of a sentence or passage. What type of clue they are doesn't matter. What matters is being able to use whatever information you can to discover the meaning.

DIRECTIONS: Read the examples below and underline what you think are context clues. Then try to write a definition for the underlined word.

---

1. The war caused tremendous <u>turmoil</u> but, eventually, order and calm were restored to the nation.

Definition:

2. The drug was widely used and was considered <u>innocuous</u>; however, recent studies indicate many harmful side-effects can occur with its usage.

Definition:

3. She had been <u>sterilized</u> as a young girl, so now it was impossible for her to have children even if she wanted to.

Definition:

4. There was no <u>malice</u> in her heart towards the murderer, for she had forgiven him years before.

Definition:

In the examples above, the connecting words give us information about the relationship between ideas. If we understand the relationship and we understand one idea, then we can often understand the other idea. Important context clues are in **bold face** below.

---

1. The war caused tremendous <u>turmoil</u> **but**, eventually, **order and calm were restored** to the nation.

Definition:

2. The drug was widely used and was considered <u>innocuous</u>; **however**, recent studies **indicate many harmful side-effects can occur with its usage.**

Definition:

3. She had been <u>sterilized</u> as a young girl, **so** now **it was impossible for her to have children** even if she wanted to.

Definition:

4. There was no <u>malice</u> in her heart towards the murderer, **for** she **had forgiven** him years before.

Definition:

DISCUSSION

1. The connector "but" indicates ideas that contrast or are different. The second idea is "order and calm." The first idea must be different or opposite. "Turmoil" means disorder, chaos, or confusion.

2. In this sentence we have the word "however" which functions the same way as "but," so again we have contrasting ideas. On one side, we see "harmful side- effects," so on the other side we can assume there is no harm or danger. "Innocuous" means to cause no harm.

3. The connector used is "so" which shows a relationship of cause-and-effect. The result or effect is that she can't have children. The cause is something which prevents having children. "Sterilized" is a medical procedure which prevents a woman from becoming pregnant.

4. "For" indicates a cause-and-effect relationship, but it is the opposite of "so." After "so" we have the result. After "for" we have the cause. What is the result of having "forgiven him"? No malice. Malice means anger, ill will or bad intentions towards someone.

Let's look at some more sentences.

DIRECTIONS: Again, look for context clues and then try to write a definition for the underlined word.

1. <u>Vulgar</u> habits, such as spitting, belching, or wiping your nose without a handkerchief, are considered most inappropriate in public.

Definition:

2. The state's most impressive <u>attractions</u>, including the Empire State Building, Radio City Music Hall, and the Museum of Modern Art, are the recipients of millions of eager tourists each year.

Definition:

The two sentences include examples of the underlined words.

1. <u>Vulgar</u> habits, **such as spitting, belching, or wiping your nose without a handkerchief,** are considered most inappropriate in public.

Definition:

2. The city's most impressive <u>attractions</u>, **including the Empire State Building, Radio City Music Hall, and the Museum of Modern Art,** are the recipients of millions of eager tourists each year.

Definition:

DISCUSSION

By looking at the examples that follow the underlined word, we can get a much better idea of what that word means.

1. We see in "vulgar" is an adjective which modifies "habits." We then see the specific habits that are considered "vulgar" in public: spitting, belching, or wiping your nose without a handkerchief. These are not considered to be proper actions when done in public. Someone who does them in public does not have good manners. "Vulgar" means having the qualities of being rude, unpleasant, or disgusting.

2. The examples that follow "attractions," the Empire State Building, Radio City Music Hall, and the Museum of Modern Art, give us important clues. When we put these clues together with "eager tourists," we can guess that "attractions" are famous places where tourists go.

Another important source of information can come from **relative clauses.** An easy way to spot them is to look for the relative pronouns that introduce them: **who, whom, which, that,** and **whose.** Relative clauses provide information about the noun they modify.

Let's look at some examples.

DIRECTIONS: Find the key words that introduce the clause. Underline the clause. What information does it give about the noun in front of it? Try to write a definition.

---

1. The <u>gizmo</u>, which regulates the valves and the choke mechanism, must be carefully installed.

Definition:

2. The <u>benefactress</u>, who gave huge sums of money to schools and hospitals in our city, died recently.

Definition:

DISCUSSION

1. What kind of thing "regulates the valves and the choke mechanism?"

Answer: Some kind of mechanical device.

2. What kind of person "gave huge sums of money to schools and hospitals"?

Answer: Someone who is very generous with her money.

There are many different types of context clues. Look at the information that surrounds the words. It can help you understand the word's meaning.

Vocabulary Word List

The following list consists of approximately 500 commonly used words that are tested in the Reading Comprehension and Vocabulary section of the test. Study these words as best you can and then complete the following 25 exercises.

There are a few ways to go about studying this section. Choose the one with which you feel most comfortable.

1. Study 25 words a day for three weeks. Then, take the exercises, check your answers, and look up the words you missed in the list.

2. Complete the drills first, check the answers, and then study the words in the list that you missed.

3. Study each word and example sentence. Make up a sentence using the word, and then take the exercises.

4. Every day before the day of the test, try to use the words you missed in the exercises in conversations with your friends and family.

abandon, *v.* to leave alone or to give up. The baby wolf was abandoned in the woods when its mother was killed.

abate, *v.* to decrease or diminish. For three terrible days, the heat of the sun never abated.

abet, *v.* to help or aid. The stranger abetted the lost child by taking him to the police station.

abhor, *v.* to hate something. Everyone abhors war and the loss of life it causes.

abject, *adj.* hopeless or miserable. The abject poverty in many slums is a major cause of crime within our cities.

absorbent, *adj.* having the quality of holding water. The paper towels were almost as absorbent as the sponge.

abundance, *n.* an amount greater than needed. There is an abundance of oil in Saudi Arabia.

accessory, *n.* an extra or added part. A beautiful handbag is an important accessory to a woman's clothes.

accommodation, *n.* something supplied for convenience. Temporary accommodations were provided to the refugees.

accomplice, *n.* someone who helps another to break the law. The bank robber claims to have acted alone, but the police believe he had an accomplice.

accomplish, *v.* to achieve. Everyone wishes to accomplish something important in his life.

accost, *v.* to bother or threaten. A woman walking alone in the city can be accosted at any time.

accru, *v.* to build up over time. As a result of his wise investments in stocks and bonds, he had accrued a fortune by the age of 80.

accumulate, *v.* to build up, to collect. If a room is not used, dust begins to accumulate.

acrid, *adj.* having an unpleasant, irritating quality. The acrid smoke from the chemicals burned his eyes.

acuity, *n.* sharpness of perception. Visual acuity is important to an airline pilot.

adapt, *v.* to change. Many wild animals cannot adapt to life in a zoo.

admonish, *v.* to advise or to warn against. Parents must admonish their children about the use of drugs.

adroitly, *adv.* with easy skill and ability. A great soccer player like Pele could adroitly pass the ball to a teammate.

advantage, *n.* benefit. One advantage of not smoking is that you save a lot of money.

advocate, *v.* to propose or to support. Many doctors advocate a balanced diet that includes only a small amount of red meat.

affluent, *adj.* rich or wealthy. An affluent society should take care of its poor and needy.

aggravate, *v.* to make worse. He aggravated his sore elbow by trying to play tennis.

agile, *adj.* able to move quickly and easily. A deer in the woods is the most agile of runners.

agitate, *v.* to cause trouble and upset. The husband's rudeness so agitated his wife that she decided to divorce him.

ailment, *n.* physical or mental problem. Coughing is a common ailment for people who work in coal mines.

akin, *adj.* like or similar to. Riding a motorcycle is akin to riding a bicycle, only more dangerous.

alleviate, *adj.* to fix or remedy a problem or condition. Winning a million dollars in the lottery would alleviate many of his financial problems.

allure, *n.* the ability to strongly attract. The allure of easy money and little work attracts many to a life of crime.

amateur, *n.* a nonprofessional. An amateur should never try to fix a problem that concerns electrical wiring.

ambiguous, *adj.* unclear. The clues found by the detective were so ambiguous that he had no idea who had committed the crime.

amicable, *adj.* friendly. An amicable man like Joe has many friends and belongs to many clubs.

ample, *adj.* more than enough. We had ample time to answer all of the questions and to finish the test with ease.

analyst, *n.* person who carefully studies data in order to reach a conclusion. An analyst determined that a rare poison had been added to the dead man's wine.

anchor, *v.* to hold in position. Only a steel chain with a great weight can anchor a large ship.

anguish, *n.* great worry or concern. The death of his beautiful wife caused the young man great anguish.

angular, *adj.* to have sharp, pointed angles. His long pointed nose and chin gave his face a very angular appearance.

anomaly, *n.* something unusual or strange. The many reports of UFOs are an anomaly science has yet to explain.

antique, *adj.* old or old-fashioned. The antique chair had been made in 1745.

apex, *n.* the highest point. At the apex of his career, he had great wealth and power.

apparatus, *n.* device or machine. A chemistry lab is equipped with an apparatus to allow students to perform experiments.

appreciable, *adj.* noticeable or substantial. For weeks, there was no appreciable change in his illness until doctors began to administer antibiotics.

approximate, *adj.* not exact but close to the amount or number. No one knows for sure exactly how many people live in China, but the approximate number is one billion.

arduous, *adj.* difficult. Sailing alone across an ocean is an arduous task.

argue, *v.* to strongly support an idea. He argued that the money should be spent for health care and not for weapons.

arouse, *v.* to excite. Sharks are aroused by the smell of blood in water.

arrogance, *n.* state of being unconcerned about other peoples' feelings or thoughts. The man showed his arrogance by pushing his way to the front of the line and demanding that he be served first.

artifact, *n.* object made in the past. Scientists dig in the ruins of ancient cities in order to find artifacts from past cultures.

aspire, *v.* to desire or to long for. The young actor aspired to someday being a famous movie star.

assert, *v.* to say that something is true or correct. Columbus asserted that the world was round and not flat as most people believed in his time.

assuage, *v.* to ease or to relieve. His mother tried to assuage his fears by holding his hand and whispering that everything would be all right.

atop, *prep.* on top of. A radio tower was placed atop the building.

attain, *v.* to reach a goal or position. We can attain our dreams with hard work and dedication.

audacious, *adj.* bold, daring, willing to risk danger. Many believed that Lindbergh's audacious plan to cross the Atlantic alone in a single-engine plane was impossible.

augment, *v.* to add to. He had to take a second job at night to augment his low salary.

authentic, *adj.* real. The jewels in her necklace were so large that many believed they were not authentic.

automaton, *n.* machine which performs jobs normally done by humans. Automatons will be used in space flights to distant planets because of the many years the journeys will take.

aversion, *n.* dislike. She has a strong aversion to most insects, but she hates flies most of all.

bail, *n.* money required to get someone out of jail while they await their trial. His friends were penniless, so he had to ask his father for the money to pay his bail.

ban, *v.* to make illegal. Many drugs have been banned after it was found that they caused dangerous side-effects.

barricade, *v.* to be surrounded with walls for protection. The murderer barricaded himself in the house and threatened to shoot anyone who came near him.

basis, *n.* the foundation, what we build upon. A good education is the basis for a successful career.

become, *v.* to develop or grow. A small seed can become a great tree.

behavior, *n.* conduct or actions. The student's rude and noisy behavior was unacceptable to his teacher.

bewilder, *v.* to confuse. He was bewildered by many of the difficult questions asked in the test.

blame, *n.* guilt or fault. A careless cigarette smoker was to blame for the forest fire.

blandishment, *n.* something that tends to coax or to allure. The star basketball player was offered many blandishments to sign a new contract with his team.

blight, *n.* disease or curse, or a run-down condition. The blight of many of our inner cities is caused by poor economic conditions.

blizzard, *n.* a strong snowstorm with high winds. Anyone traveling in the Rocky Mountains in January can expect to experience a blizzard.

blunder, *n.* a bad mistake. Trying to cheat on the test was a real blunder that caused him to fail the course.

brand name, *n.* product with company's name upon it. Brand-names, such as the Sony Walkman, are sold throughout the world.

breadthwise, *adv.* in relation to something's width. When they measured the refrigerator breadthwise, they found it would not fit through the door.

bribe, *n.* the illegal act of giving money to someone in order to influence their actions. The man tried to give the policeman a bribe so that he wouldn't get a speeding ticket.

bring about, *v.* to cause to happen. Water pollution can bring about the destruction of many animal species.

brittle, *adj.* easily broken. When we grow older, our bones may become brittle.

cabal, *n.* a secret group whose objective is to cause political turmoil or violence. A small cabal of powerful businessmen caused the revolution.

callous, *adj.* having no feeling. The hangman's job forces him to be callous.

canal, *n.* structure designed to carry liquids. A canal was built across the desert to provide water for the new city.

capacious, *adj.* having a large area. It was a huge house and the capacious dining room could seat 100 guests.

captive, *n.* one who is held hostage or imprisoned. The captives were bound in chains and housed in an old prison.

castigate, *v.* to strongly criticize. The politician was castigated for having lied about his love affair.

category, *n.* division or class within a larger group. Snakes are usually divided into two categories, poisonous or nonpoisonous.

cessation, *n.* an ending or completion. With the cessation of the war, refugees returned to their homes and began to rebuild their homes.

chaos, *n.* total confusion. The effects of the earthquake created chaos in the city.

characteristic, *n.* an aspect or feature. Blond hair is an uncommon characteristic for Asian people.

chasm, *n.* a deep hole. The explosion caused a chasm in the side of the mountain.

chilly, *adj.* somewhat cold. Days begin to turn chilly in late October.

chore, *n.* a small job or an unpleasant task. Washing the dishes each night after supper is a real chore if you have worked all day.

clumsy, *adj.* awkward in actions or movements. Everyone appears clumsy the first time they ice-skate.

coerce, *v.* to try to force one to do or say something against their will. The convict tried to coerce the witness by threatening to kill her if she didn't lie to the judge and jury.

cogent, *adj.* convincing or persuasive. His speech was so powerful and his ideas so cogent that everyone agreed that his plan was best.

commerce, *n.* the activity of business and trade. Commerce between the two countries has increased because of the new trade policy.

compassion, *n.* sympathy for the problems of others. The nurse's compassion for her patients made them love her.

composite, *n.* something formed by the combination of different elements or substances. Salt is a composite of sodium and chloride.

compulsory, *adj.* required, necessary, or mandatory. Compulsory education in the U.S. requires every child to attend school until the age of 16.

concentration, *n.* a gathering or collection. The highest concentration of big-game animals can be found in national parks.

concoct, *v.* to create by mixing things together. He concocted a bad-tasting drink by mixing milk and apple juice.

condone, *v.* to approve of or to forgive an action. The judge condoned the woman's actions by saying she acted in self-defense.

confidant, *n.* one to whom secrets can be told. She was not only his wife but also his closest confidant and therefore knew all of his deepest secrets.

confide, *v.* to tell someone secret or personal information. The boy confided to his mother that he had broken the window by accident.

confine, *v.* to limit movement to a small area. After the accident, he was confined to a wheelchair for many weeks.

confiscate, *v.* to take or seize goods because of criminal activity. If police find drugs in your car, they will confiscate the drugs, your money, and your car.

congeal, *v.* to change from liquid to solid. The milk that was left in the glass overnight slowly began to congeal.

congenial, *adj.* friendly and pleasant to be with. They were such congenial people that everyone wished to attend their parties.

conscientious, *adj.* careful to fulfill responsibilities. Since the lives of many people are in their hands, doctors and airline pilots have to be conscientious.

consequence, *n.* results of an action. There is strong evidence to indicate that there are many harmful consequences of smoking cigarettes.

consummate, *v.* to perfect or complete. Their long romance and long affair was consummated in marriage.

contaminate, *v.* to make dirty or impure. Water in the bay was contaminated by oil leaking from the ship.

contingent, *adj.* likely but not certain to happen. Payment of the money was contingent upon delivery of the goods.

conventional, *adj.* common or usual. In Japan, wood is the conventional material used to build houses.

core, *n.* the center, the heart. We eat most of the apple, but we usually leave the core.

corroborate, *v.* to confirm or support what someone else has said. Mr. Brown's explanation of what caused the accident was corroborated by a policeman who saw it happen.

create, *v.* to make for the very first time. The Bible says that God created the world in six days and then rested on the seventh.

credulous, *adj.* trusting or unsuspecting. A credulous person is often the first to be robbed and cheated.

creed, *n.* one's belief or faith. The creed that we follow helps us to determine which actions are good and which are evil.

cruel, *adj.* lacking human kindness, mean or vicious. It is a cruel wife who will hit her husband.

cryptic, *adj.* difficult to understand. The note that was found in the bottle was too cryptic to understand.

culpable, *adj.* guilty of some wrong action. If the owner of a dog allows it to run free, then the owner is culpable for any damage that dog does.

cut down, *v.* to reduce. He wanted to cut down on the number of cigarettes that he smoked each day.

dangle, *v.* to hang down. The windstorm knocked over trees and utility poles; the electric wires that dangled down were a real danger.

decade, *n.* period of ten years. The decade from 1960 to 1969 was called the "Sexy Sixties" in the U.S.

decency, *n.* the moral state of good behavior. Decency demands that we do the right thing whether we want to or not.

decrepit, *adj.* old and in poor condition. The house was so decrepit that it would be cheaper to tear it down and start again rather than try to repair it.

defect, *n.* a flaw or imperfection. His job was to find any product with a defect and see that it was corrected.

deficiency, *n.* something needed but not present. In the past, sailors who had no fresh vegetables suffered from vitamin deficiencies and became ill.

deliberately, *adv.* to do something on purpose with a clear understanding of the consequences. He deliberately slammed the door in his boss's face.

dependable, *adj.* can be relied upon. American cars are very dependable and seldom break down.

depict, *v.* to describe or characterize. In the movie, he was depicted as kind and gentle, but his family knew the truth.

deprecate, *v.* to criticize or belittle. Thomas Edison's efforts to create a light bulb were deprecated by many experts and called impossible until he achieved success.

deprive, *v.* to prevent from having. A child whose parents have died is often deprived of the love that he needs.

deride, *v.* to strongly criticize. Critics derided the writer's new book as being poorly written and filled with lies.

desire, *n.* a strong wish or want. Everyone has a desire for health, happiness, and sometimes a piece of chocolate.

destiny, *n.* fate or the future. A fortune-teller claims to be able to know our destiny.

detect, *v.* to notice or to find. The doctors gave her a blood test, but they could not detect any signs of disease.

deterioration, *n.* the state of declining or decaying. The deterioration of a person's mind and body is a normal result of growing old.

determinant, *n.* important factor that affects the result. Lack of exercise is a major determinant in weight gain.

deviate, *v.* to change course. If we never deviate from our normal activities, our lives will be boring.

devise, *v.* to conceive, design, or create. He devised a new method to change sea water to fresh water.

diagnosis, *n.* the conclusion reached by a doctor as to the cause of a problem. After a thorough examination which included several tests, the doctor was able to make a diagnosis: she had a bad cold.

digress, *v.* to turn away from the main subject of attention. To be an effective writer, we must organize our thoughts and never digress too far from our main idea.

diligent, *adj.* hard-working. The diligent way he performed his work earned him many promotions.

diminutive, *adj.* small. Her voice was so soft and diminutive that it was difficult to hear what she said.

discern, *v.* to discover or to be able to tell the difference between two things. Only an expert could discern which painting was the original and which was the fake.

discontinue, *v.* to stop. The sale of many toys has been discontinued because of their danger to children.

disposal, *n.* having the property to get rid of or to eliminate. The garbage disposal unit failed to operate as the salesman promised it would.

dissect, *v.* to cut something up in order to study it. Sandy refused to dissect the frog and so failed the biology course.

disseminate, *v.* to send out. The object of the meeting was to disseminate as many ideas as possible throughout the company about the new project.

dissolvable, *adj.* the ability to break down and disappear in a liquid. The pharmacist assured the customer that the tablets were dissolvable in liquid.

divulge, *v.* to give secret or personal information. Mrs. Haddy was angry that her sister Sylvia divulged her secrets to the neighborhood gossip.

documentation, *n.* written evidence or proof. Mr. Monroe was distraught that no documentation could be found to prove his innocence.

dominant, *adj.* strongest or most powerful. It was clearly evident that the dominant male of the pack of wolves had no intention of stalking prey at the moment.

drought, *n.* a long period of time with little or no rainfall. Because of the long drought and dry conditions in the western states, many homes were destroyed by fire.

dubious, *adj.* doubtful or uncertain. Fred was not hired for the position because of his dubious reputation.

durable, *adj.* able to last a long time. The label on the uniform stated that the fabric was durable and stain resistant.

eccentric, *adj.* odd or unusual. Jonathan was considered by the local community to be an eccentric inventor whose creations were useless.

ecosystem, *n.* the complex of living things and their environment which functions as a single unit or a whole. Many local scientists have warned about the effects of pollution on the fragile ecosystem of the bay.

effects, *n.* the results or consequences. The effects of his recent medical treatments are not yet known.

elicit, *v.* to draw out. The inspector was determined to elicit as much information as he could from each suspect.

elucidate, *v.* to explain or clarify. Marcus was always proud of his ability to elucidate on the more difficult passages in the chemistry book.

elusive, *adj.* difficult to find, catch, or see. The Zodiac Killer has remained elusive to the New York City Police Department for months now.

emerge, *v.* to come out of. Maria has emerged as one of the most talented female basketball players the school has ever had.

emit, *v.* to send out. The residents of Pleasant Park have been complaining about the foul odors being emitted by the new recycling center in town.

emulate, *adj.* to copy or to follow. Many children like to emulate their parents in some ways.

energetically, *adv.* to act with vigor. When Billy's father promised him ten dollars to rake the fall leaves, Billy energetically completed the task.

enervate, *v.* to weaken or to exhaust. The task of climbing three flights of stairs enervated the elderly woman so much that she had to rest for an hour.

enhance, *v.* to make better or clearer. The attractive pink eyeglass frames enhanced the color of her eyes.

ensnare, *v.* to trap or entangle. As the township administrator, she had no intention of becoming ensnared in the local corruption scandal.

ensue, *v.* to follow. With the help of his college counselor, Carlos was determined to ensue the career path he had chosen.

enterprise, *n.* a business venture. The dream of launching the enterprise soon collapsed when the two businessmen realized the cost of their venture.

enticement, *n.* something which attracts or lures. The enticement of winning a vacation in Hawaii for two weeks caused Lisa to fill out 15 entry forms for the contest.

equivocal, *adj.* uncertain or vague. Jason repeated the same equivocal answer when his father asked where he was going: "Out," he would say.

erosion, *n.* the process of wearing away caused by wind or water. The retired couple could not fulfill their dream of building a home near the beach because of erosion along the coast.

essential, *adj.* necessary or most important. It is essential that each student pass every exam in order to receive credit for the course.

esteem, *n.* honor or respect. General Tindal was held in high esteem by the soldiers because of his courage.

evidence, *n.* facts or data which support an idea. Enough evidence was gathered to indict three employees with illegally tampering with government documents.

evolve, *v.* to change. His ideas on life in the twentieth century evolved into one of the most complex philosophies she had ever read before.

exacting, *adj.* carefully precise. The professor's exacting instructions for the final paper dismayed the students.

examiner, n. one who carefully inspects. The claims examiner rejected the customer's request for payment of medical treatment due to restrictions in the policy.

exasperate, v. to annoy a person until they reach a state of confusion or anger. Manny's wife exasperated him so much that he backed into a neighbor's fence with his car.

excessive, adj. more than is needed. The doctor reminded Martha once again that her weight was excessive and thus dangerous to her health.

exempt, v. to release from a commitment. Jimmy was exempted from gym class for a week after running into the fence while playing baseball.

exhaust, v. to tire out or to use up completely. The gambler exhausted his family's savings and sold their house to pay off his debts.

exist, v. to be alive. Scholars consider William Faulkner to be one of the greatest American writers who ever existed.

exorbitant, adj. extremely high priced. They were selling hot dogs for the exorbitant price of $10 apiece.

exotic, adj. unusual or uncommon. Mary always considered her friend Susan's taste in clothing to be exotic.

expensive, adj. costly or high priced. When the Martins heard how expensive the new house was, they were shocked and decided not to buy it.

explicit, adj. clear and specific. Norma considered her instructions explicit and could not understand why her husband kept overcooking the pasta for dinner.

explore, v. to investigate or to search through new territory. He explored the passages of the cave.

expose, v. to uncover or to reveal. The political scandal was exposed on Friday, and on Saturday morning it was on the front page of every newspaper in the city.

extensive, adj. covering a large area or amount. The Pacific Ocean covers an extensive portion of Earth.

extinct, adj. no longer alive. Dinosaurs have been extinct for millions of years.

extravagant, adj. excessive or lavish. Owning a house with 24 bedrooms is extravagant even for a rich person.

facile, adj. easy or simple. For some complex problems, there are no facile solutions.

facilitate, v. to aid or assist. Automatic doors facilitate the movement of handicapped people who use wheelchairs.

fail, v. unable to succeed. He was sure that his plan could not fail.

fall short, v. to produce results which are below a certain standard or goal. They had hoped to raise $1,000 for charity, but they fell short of that amount.

falter, v. to stumble or to momentarily hesitate. At first he was winning the race, but as the pain in his leg increased, he began to falter.

fascinate, *v.* to strongly attract someone's interest. Children are fascinated by toys and games.

feebleness, *n.* weakness. With old age comes a gradual loss of hearing and a general state of feebleness.

feud, *n.* an argument or quarrel which has lasted a long time. The two families had a feud for so long that no one was quite sure how the argument had started.

flee, *v.* to try to escape from some danger. The war in Vietnam caused thousands of farmers to flee their homes.

flimsy, *adj.* weak, easily broken. A kite is a flimsy toy which can be easily damaged by a high wind.

follow, *v.* to come after. A dinner party later that afternoon will follow the wedding ceremony.

forbearance, *n.* patience or tolerance. Forbearance is a necessary quality for parents with small children.

foremost, *adj.* first or most important. Water is of foremost importance when traveling across a desert.

foresee, *v.* to see what will happen in the future. Fortune-tellers claim to foresee the future, but most simply want our money.

forfeit, *v.* to lose or to surrender. If you don't vote, then you are forfeiting your rights to participate in our democratic process of elections.

foster, *v.* to help to grow with care and support. Sunlight and water help to foster the growth of plants.

fraction, *n.* a part of the whole. The Christian population in Egypt makes up only a small fraction of the total population there.

fraud, *n.* the attempt to cheat people with lies and deception. If someone tries to sell you a watch on the street, be careful it isn't a fraud.

fret, *v.* to worry. Don't fret over how you will do in the test; study hard and hope for the best.

fugitive, *n.* someone trying to escape the law. Sometimes it takes years, but most fugitives are eventually caught and sent back to jail.

futile, *adj.* useless or hopeless. He made a futile attempt to put out the fire, but the building burned to the ground.

genealogy, *n.* study of one's family and relatives in the past. Many people study their genealogy to see if they are related to famous people.

generic, *adj.* common or unusual. A generic brand of aspirin is much cheaper than one with a brand name, even though they are the same product.

genuinely, *adv.* honestly. Even after he apologized for the insults, she didn't believe that he was genuinely sorry for his behavior.

germinate, *v.* to begin to grow. It takes two weeks after the seeds have been planted for them to begin to germinate.

get across, *v.* to explain an idea so that it is understood. It seemed like a simple concept to the professor, but no matter how he tried to explain it, he could not get it across to his students.

get rid of, *v.* to remove, destroy, or throw away. The vaccines that doctors have developed since 1850 have helped to get rid of many dangerous diseases.

gist, *n.* the essential part or a summary. He told her he didn't have time for all the details; he just wanted the gist of the story.

glitter, *v.* to sparkle with light, to shine. On a clear night, the stars glitter like diamonds.

globose, *adj.* shaped like a globe or a sphere. The shape of the fat man's stomach was globose.

greed, *n.* the extreme desire to possess more than is needed. The man's greed for money and power caused him to lose his friends.

grievance, *n.* a complaint or an objection. If a worker has a grievance, he should discuss it with his supervisor before he files a written complaint.

group, *n.* a collection of things. Many animals live in groups in order to help them survive.

grudge, *n.* a feeling of resentment caused by an action in the past. It was a grudge match between the two boxers who had fought before and who felt mutual hatred.

guarantee, *n.* an assurance for the fulfillment of a condition. The VCR came with a 12-month guarantee on all parts and service.

hamper, *v.* to bother or hinder. Rain and snow hampered the construction of the new building.

handicap, *n.* problem or disability that limits actions. Being unable to hear is a handicap that many people have to overcome.

haphazard, *adj.* in a careless or disorganized fashion. She was such a haphazard driver that she had four accidents in four days.

harsh, *adj.* hard or cruel. Slapping a child with your hand is a harsh way to make the child behave.

hectic, *adj.* confused or chaotic. Traffic is most hectic at 5:00 p.m. when everyone is leaving work.

hold, *v.* to argue or propose. Many geographers held that the world was flat until Columbus proved that it was round by sailing to America.

hilarious, *adj.* extremely funny or humorous. The audience in the theater thought the movie was so hilarious that they couldn't stop laughing.

hoax, *n.* a joke or deception meant to fool people. Mary's boyfriend pretended to be a policeman, but she knew it was a hoax when she heard his voice.

humid, *adj.* weather condition of very wet or moist air. Summer is more humid than winter because warm air can carry more moisture than cold air.

hypothesis, *n.* prediction or guess. With careful experiments, scientists can usually determine if a hypothesis is correct or not.

ignorant, *adj.* lacking knowledge. People who do not go to school are ignorant of the many cultures and societies that exist in the world.

illuminate, *v.* to brighten with light or to clarify. Street lights help to illuminate dark roads.

imaging, *n.* the process of producing a picture or image. The powerful imaging produced by the telescope allowed the scientists to see the planet in much clearer detail.

immature, *adj.* not yet adult or fully grown. An immature bird can't fly.

imminent, *adj.* approaching, near, about to happen. The residents who remained in the city were in imminent danger from the approaching storm.

impede, *v.* to hinder, restrict, or delay. Doctors had to operate to remove the obstacle which impeded the flow of blood to his heart.

impediment, *n.* obstacle or barrier. Nervousness is often an impediment to learning to speak a new language.

impinge, *v.* to infringe or to intrude upon something. The long hours he had to spend at work impinged upon the time he could be with his family.

inaugurate, *v.* to begin. A ceremony took place to inaugurate the opening of the new bridge.

inception, *n.* the beginning. At the inception of the company, there were only two employees; a year later, there were a hundred.

incessant, *adj.* constant or continuous. He had to leave the city to escape the incessant noise of the traffic.

incisive, *adj.* a clear, sharp understanding. His incisive ideas helped them to find a solution which others had failed to find.

inconsequential, *adj.* of no real importance. We do a thousand inconsequential actions each day which our minds quickly forget after having done them.

index, *v.* to put into a list or catalog. Every magazine purchased by the library is carefully indexed.

indict, *v.* to be brought to trial and accused. The wife, who was found holding the gun, was indicted for the murder of her husband.

induce, *v.* to cause to happen. Doctors often prescribe drugs that induce sleep.

indurate, *v.* to make unfeeling or hard. Unlike copper, which is soft, steel is an extremely indurate metal.

inept, *adj.* lacking the necessary skill or ability. She was a skillful writer, but her nervousness made her totally inept as a speaker.

infamous, *adj.* famous for bad actions. Hitler was an infamous dictator who caused the deaths of millions of people.

inferior, *adj.* of low quality. Shoppers prefer fresh vegetables rather than frozen ones which are inferior in taste.

infest, *v.* to occupy or spread over in a troubling way. The apartment was infested with bugs and had to be sprayed before the people could move in.

inflammable, *adj.* having the ability to burn easily. Petroleum is an inflammable substance.

inhabit, *v.* to normally live in or occupy a particular place. Camels inhabit the dry regions of the earth because of their ability to go long periods without water.

injustice, *n.* a wrong action done to someone. To purposely damage or destroy the property or goods of others is an injustice.

inquisitive, *adj.* curious. Children are inquisitive because they want to know why and how things happen.

integrate, *v.* to combine with or to unite together. In the early 1960s, schools in America were integrated so that black and white children could attend classes together.

intentionally, *adv.* done on purpose. The fire was no accident; it had been intentionally started.

interactive, *adj.* acting with or in response to another. An interactive exchange of ideas between countries is the best way to prevent wars.

intrepid, *adj.* adventurous or fearless. Early American pioneers had to be intrepid to face the dangers of the wilderness.

intricate, *adj.* complex or complicated. A wristwatch is a very intricate machine.

intruder, *n.* a person who enters without permission. An intruder broke the lock on their back door and entered their house while they were sleeping.

invalid, *n.* one unable to live normally because of an illness or handicap. The invalid had been confined to a wheelchair since the car accident.

investment, *n.* money used for income or profit. He bought land in Florida in hopes that it would increase in value, but his investment never paid off.

irritation, *n.* an annoyance or problem. A piece of sand in your eye can be a painful irritation.

jilt, *v.* to abandon one's lover. After waiting an hour in a restaurant for her boyfriend to appear, she knew she had been jilted.

lack, *n.* the absence of something. The lack of rain caused the grass to die.

lament, *v.* to express great sorrow, to cry and moan. For many years, the mother lamented the death of her son.

lapses, *n.* periods of omissions or errors. The lapses in his memory were caused by a blow to the head.

leisure, *adj.* free time. He likes to swim and play golf in his leisure time.

lengthwise, *adv.* in relation to something's length. The tree, measured lengthwise, was 100 feet long.

license, *n.* legal document which allows an action to be performed. To be legally married, a young couple must first apply for a marriage license.

limb, *n.* an arm or leg on a person, or a branch on a tree. A shark bit off one of the swimmer's limbs.

litter, *v.* to dirty with trash or garbage. People who litter our streets with trash cost the state millions of dollars each year to collect that trash.

loathe, *v.* to hate or despise. George Bush loathes broccoli, which he was forced to eat as a child.

locate, *v.* to exist in a particular spot. Paris is located in France.

longitudinal, *adj.* moving from top to bottom. The ship was moving in a longitudinal direction from north to south.

loot, *v.* to steal. When the electricity went off, people began to loot the shops along the darkened street.

luminous, *adj.* filled with light. The full moon was so luminous that the night seemed like day.

maintain, *v.* to keep in proper condition. A car has to be maintained to stay in good condition.

malign, *v.* to injure someone by saying bad things about him. His good name was maligned by the story in the newspaper which called him a liar.

masonry, *n.* blocks or bricks jointed together with cement. The masonry of ancient Egyptians can be seen in their pyramids.

massive, *adj.* very large, huge. A whale is a massive mammal.

mature, *adj.* adult or fully grown. The grapes are picked as soon as they mature.

meddle, *v.* to interfere in the business of others. The young husband told his mother-in-law not to meddle in his affairs.

melancholy, *adj.* sad or unhappy. The song was so melancholy that it made the audience cry.

menace, *v.* to put in danger or at risk. Air pollution is a menace to our health.

merge, *v.* to join or combine together. The two small companies merged to form one large company.

metabolism, *n.* the processes by which energy is provided for life. Our metabolism slows when we go to sleep.

meticulous, *adj.* precise and careful about even the smallest detail. She was so meticulous with her house that she even scrubbed and waxed the garage floor.

migrate, *v.* to travel from place to place. Every year, the photography club gathers at the state park to photograph birds that migrate south for the winter.

molest, *v.* to bother or physically assault. One of the fears parents have is that their children will be molested.

morbid, *adj.* concerned with death and dying. Sally was so morbid at times that many of her friends stopped calling her.

mundane, *adj.* common or ordinary. The professor always tried to persuade his students from living a mundane life.

mutual, *adj.* in conjunction with another. A mutual feeling of resentment and anger built up between the couple after only two years of marriage.

nadir, *n.* the lowest point. He considered the six months he lived in New York City without a job or a decent place to live as the nadir of his existence.

neglect, *v.* to fail to provide what is needed. Rita caught the flu and her doctor admonished her for neglecting to eat and rest properly during the winter months.

negligent, *adj.* responsible for improper actions. Dan's electricity was turned off yesterday because he was negligent in paying his monthly bill.

negligible, *adj.* unimportant or insignificant. At the office meetings, Debbie felt her opinions were considered negligible by her co-workers, and so she decided not to speak up any more.

nomadic, *adj.* having the characteristic of moving from place to place without a fixed pattern. As a child, Howard resented his family's nomadic lifestyle because he was never able to develop lasting friendships.

non-trademark, *n.* product with no company name on it. His father always advised him against buying appliances with non-trademarks.

notorious, *adj.* famous for wrong actions. Luiz was notorious for borrowing money and failing to pay it back.

objective, *n.* goal or purpose. Her main objective was to find her own apartment to live in as soon as possible.

obscure, *adj.* not well known. Alex always enjoyed the obscure writings of the early philosophers.

obsolete, *adj.* no longer of any use. The customer knew the record player would soon become obsolete, but he bought it anyway.

occurrence, *n.* event or happening. The repeated occurrence of missing funds at the bank baffled the investigators.

ominous, *adj.* menacing or threatening. The large black clouds looked ominous, and so the baseball game was cancelled.

omit, *v.* to leave out. Betty was hurt when she heard her name was omitted from Ana's wedding invitation list.

orbit, *n.* circular pattern of movement around another object. Christopher won second prize at the science fair for his detailed diagram of the orbit of the planets.

orb-like, *adj.* shaped like a globe or ball. Mrs. Sanwell left the room in a huff when her guests described her fat pet poodle as being orb-like.

ordeal, *n.* a painful or difficult experience. Mr. Thompson considered his visit to the dentist such a frightening ordeal that he vowed never to go back.

origin, *n.* the place where something began. Cindy was determined to find the origin of the rumors circulating about her in the office.

ostensibly, *adv.* as it appears, apparently. Ostensibly, he was honest about his past, but she didn't trust him.

output, *n.* what was produced. The production manager was troubled over the recent drop in output by his employees.

pact, *n.* an agreement. Before Jerry moved, he made a pact with his best friend that they would meet at Hadley's park on Jerry's eighteenth birthday.

palatable, *adj.* eatable or good tasting. Mike and Sara agreed that their dinner at the new restaurant was just about palatable.

paralyze, *v.* to cause something to be unable to move. Some predators will paralyze their prey with poison and then devour them.

parasitic, *adj.* the quality of living off others. This parasitic species of fish was called "bloodsucker" by local fisherman.

patent, *n.* legal right of ownership. Tom was advised to obtain a patent for his latest invention.

penetratable, *adj.* can be entered. The commander realized the fort was penetratable and ordered his troops to attack the weak point.

penetrate, *v.* to enter into. Since the spilled wine penetrated the upholstery, Lydia decided to purchase a new couch.

perforated, *adj.* filled with holes. Jeffrey grimaced when the doctor told him he had a perforated ulcer.

perilous, *adj.* dangerous. Since the path was so muddy and steep, the hikers decided it was too perilous to continue and turned back.

perish, *v.* to die. Abe watched Loretta's love letters perish as he placed each one of them into the fireplace.

perpetual, *adj.* lasting forever. Margaret hoped that her neighbor's sunrise visits would not become a perpetual problem.

persist, *v.* to continue an action despite obstacles. Mr. Price persisted in eating a breakfast of eggs and sausage every morning in spite of his high cholesterol readings.

pessimist, *n.* one who expects the worst will happen. Mary came to be known as the pessimist in her family because she always found something to worry about.

petition, *n.* a written request. Many angry residents circulated a petition to repeal the large tax increases in the state.

phenomenon, *n.* an unusual event or occurrence. Many consider the aurora borealis to be a spectacular phenomenon of nature.

phlegmatic, *adj.* showing no feeling or energy. Having studied for two straight days without stopping to sleep, he appeared phlegmatic as he sat at his desk with the test before him.

placate, *v.* to make peace with an enemy. He tried to placate his angry wife by bringing her flowers.

plea, *n.* a request, usually with strong emotion. The Red Cross made an urgent plea for blood donors to aid the victims of the fire.

plethora, *n.* a large amount of variety. She said it was just a dinner party, but when he saw the plethora of food and drink, he knew it was a real feast.

pollute, *v.* to make dirty. Exhaust from cars pollutes our air.

ponder, *v.* to think carefully. Great men often ponder the eternal questions of why we were born and why we must die.

postpone, *v.* to delay an action until a later time. The class picnic had to be postponed because of the heavy rain.

precede, *v.* to come before. Fall precedes winter.

predator, *n.* a creature that survives by attacking and eating another creature. The most feared of all marine predators is the great white shark.

predetermine, *v.* to decide the outcome or result before it occurs. She hoped to predetermine the questions she would be asked in the test so that she would be better prepared.

prelude, *n.* what comes before. The dark skies and the sound of distant thunder were a prelude to the storm.

premise, *n.* an unproven idea which is the basis for research. His theory was based on the premise that animals could be taught to speak.

prescription, *n.* a written order of medicine given by a doctor. The prescription stated that the antibiotics were to be taken three times a day.

prevalent, *adj.* common in many areas. Colds are most prevalent during the winter months.

prior, *adj.* before or previous to. He graduated from high school three years prior to entering college.

probe, *n.* a careful study to discover information. The detective began to probe through the dark house with his flashlight.

prolific, *adj.* abundant or productive. He was such a prolific writer that he was able to complete a novel every three weeks.

promulgate, *v.* to promote or to publicize an idea. In the late 1800s, many activists began to promulgate the idea that women should be given the right to vote.

prosecute, *v.* to seek punishment for breaking the law. The banker was prosecuted for stealing money from his own bank.

prudent, *adj.* careful. It is considered prudent to a married man to have life insurance.

purify, *v.* to make pure or clean. Charcoal filters in the air conditioner were used to purify the air coming into the house.

quality, *n.* a feature or characteristic. One quality common to all societies is the love and care given to children.

random, *adj.* with no pattern or organization. The numbers for the lottery are chosen at random.

raze, *v.* to demolish or destroy. It took the bulldozer only one hour to raze the old building into a pile of bricks.

recede, *v.* to go back to a previous state. After the high tide caused by the rain and storm, the water slowly began to recede to its normal level.

receptive, *adj.* open to new ideas. His father was very old-fashioned, so he was not receptive to new ideas.

recite, *v.* to read aloud. Most children learn the alphabet by reciting it many times.

recluse, *n.* one who wishes to live alone. The old recluse lived deep in the woods, ten miles from the nearest neighbor.

reconcile, *v.* to make peace. When a husband and wife cannot reconcile their differences, a divorce is likely to occur.

refine, *v.* to make better by removing impurities. Petroleum has to be refined before it can be used as fuel.

remnant, *n.* something left behind. The only remnant left of the ancient city is a pile of rocks.

repel, *v.* to fight off. Fire will not repel wild animals.

repugnant, *adj.* having a quality that repels people because of its unpleasant nature. To many people, snakes are considered the most repugnant of creatures.

resolute, *adj.* very determined to do something. A resolute person will endure any hardship to reach his or her goal.

retard, *v.* to slow down the progress of an action. Lacking a proper diet, the growth of many children is retarded.

revenue, *n.* money collected from taxes or by a business. The government receives the revenue needed to operate by taxing people and companies.

ridicule, *v.* to make fun of. The student was ridiculed by his classmates for giving the wrong answer in class.

ripe, *adj.* mature, fully grown, or ready to eat. A green banana is usually not ripe enough to eat.

rivalry, *n.* competition. In the Olympic Games, there is a rivalry between many nations.

sagacity, *n.* wisdom or great knowledge. Through long years of experience and study, the old man had acquired a sagacity about the ways of men.

savage, *n.* one who is not civilized or educated. Savages in the jungles of the Amazon use primitive stone tools.

scarce, *adj.* in short supply, hard to find. Diamonds and gold have always been scarce; that is part of the reason they are so valuable.

scatter, *v.* to throw in many directions. The strong wind scattered the leaves across the yard.

schedule, *v.* to assign a particular time for an event to occur. He was scheduled to see the doctor at 10:00 a.m. and the dentist at 1:00 p.m.

scorn, *v.* to ridicule or to express great contempt. The man who ran away from the battle was scorned by the other soldiers who had fought.

scrutiny, *n.* a careful investigation or examination. The liar hoped that the story he had told the police would pass their scrutiny.

seasoned, *adj.* having been changed by age or experience. Wood should be seasoned before it is used in construction.

secure, *adj.* safe. Due to long-range missiles and nuclear bombs, no place on Earth is truly secure.

seemingly, *adv.* apparently. Seemingly, the stranger had knocked at the door to get directions into town.

seize, *v.* to quickly grab and hold. The policeman seized all of the drugs and money found in the apartment.

selective, *adj.* careful when making a choice. We have to be very selective when purchasing a used car.

self-reliance, *n.* to depend upon oneself. Camping in the woods is a good test of self-reliance.

senility, *n.* mental condition of confusion caused by old age. Everyone reaches a state of senility if they live long enough.

shatter, *v.* to break into many pieces. The window was shattered by a rock.

shield, *v.* to protect from outside harm. A mother bear will shield her young from any danger.

shrewd, *adj.* very clever. A shrewd man knows both his strengths and his weaknesses.

simulate, *v.* to copy or imitate. Pilots often practice in a machine which simulates the problems they might face when flying.

situate, *v.* to locate. Los Angeles is situated in California.

skeins, *n.* the coiled or wound lengths of cloth upon a reel. She spent hours looking through the skeins of silk to find the material she wanted for her dress.

skeptical, *adj.* unbelieving. We should always be skeptical when someone tells us they know an easy way to make money.

sleazy, *adj.* of low quality. The hotel room was so sleazy that not even the rats wanted to be there.

sluggish, *adj.* slow in movement. Bob's mind and actions are very sluggish when he first wakes up in the morning.

soluble, *adj.* able to dissolve or melt in water or liquids. Sugar is soluble in water.

soothe, *v.* to ease or to calm. Cool water is soothing on a hot day.

species, *n.* a class of animals. A new species of animal was discovered by the zoologist.

specific, *adj.* particular or designated. The judge wanted the defendant to give a specific answer to the question: yes or no.

spill, *v.* to overturn so that liquid escapes. Despite his years of experience as a waiter, Walter managed to spill the wine on the king.

sporadic, *adj.* occurring at odd intervals. At sporadic times, the sky was lit by flashes of lightning.

spurn, *v.* to reject. She would never forget how her boyfriend spurned her for another woman.

squash, *v.* to stop or to destroy. He squashed the bug with his shoe.

stable, *adj.* steady and not easily changed. They couldn't build the skyscraper there because the ground was not stable enough to support the great weight.

stagnant, *adj.* not flowing or moving. Mosquitoes will breed in stagnant water.

static, *adj.* not changing. She felt her life had grown too static; she wanted to make some changes.

stimulate, *v.* to cause action. The ideas in the book stimulated his imagination.

strain, *n.* tension or stress. The worries that he faced each day on his job caused him great strain.

strangulation, *n.* death caused by blocking the passage of air into the lungs. Strangulation often occurs at the end of a rope.

stun, *v.* to daze or to shock. He was stunned to find out that his uncle had died and left him a million dollars.

subject, *v.* to cause to experience or to submit to. A traveler is subject to the laws of the country in which he is traveling.

subordinate, *v.* to put under the control of higher power. The employees were surprised to hear that the company subordinated Bob, a long-time employee, to Stan, the new employee.

substance, *n.* matter or material. Vivian was unsure of the substance in the package, so she threw the package out.

suffocation, *n.* death caused by lack of oxygen. The famous mystery writer revealed that his next novel will be about the death of a prominent politician by suffocation.

supercede, *v.* to displace. Judy Cameron superceded Beatrice Mills as the president of the Women's Club on campus.

surmise, *v.* to assume. Many students surmised that the history class would be difficult merely by the stern look on their professor's face.

surname, *n.* family name. By changing his surname to Walters, Albert Waltinchizsky thought he could become a famous actor.

survive, *v.* to continue to live. No one can survive without food or water.

symbolize, *v.* to represent or to stand for. Since the American flag symbolizes freedom to many, Americans are proud to display it on the Fourth of July.

sympathy, *n.* feelings of understanding for the problems of others. Many people in the neighborhood like to visit the elderly woman because of her great sympathy and concern for others.

synchronize, *v.* to align or to match the movement of two. It took great skill for the two skaters to synchronize their movements during the performance.

taciturn, *adj.* quiet and shy. Jean complains that her husband is so taciturn that she can't even have an argument with him.

tactile, *adj.* related to the sense of touch. The curators of the state museum were pleased that the tactile activities delighted the children who visited the exhibit.

tailor, *v.* to design to fit particular needs. Many passengers on the cruise ship had such a good time that they swore the trip was tailored especially for them.

take after, *v.* to appear similar to someone else in terms of their looks or actions. Because Ernie gestures wildly when he speaks, people say he takes after his father.

tangible, *adj.* touchable or real. Marissa insisted on some tangible evidence from her friend before she would believe her husband was cheating on her.

tentative, *adj.* temporary or uncertain. A tentative schedule was set up for the employees until the new business was fully operational.

tenuous, *adj.* vague or weak. She felt her husband's tenuous grasp of their marital problems would lead them to divorce.

terminate, *v.* to bring to an end or to stop. Teresa was distraught when she learned her position at the company would be terminated.

terse, *adj.* short or brief. She abruptly hung up the phone after Kurt's terse reply.

therapy, *n.* treatment provided to restore good health. After the accident, Randy received three weeks of physical therapy and was soon back at his job.

tolerant, *adj.* open to many ideas. The class discussions were often lively and controversial due to the instructor's tolerant attitude.

track, *v.* to follow something's movements. The hunter's adept ability to silently track the movements of his prey brought him many awards.

tract, *n.* an area or region. City officials plan to turn the tract of land along the river into a park.

tranquility, *n.* a state of complete rest and peace. Many people spend all their lives seeking peace and tranquility.

transact, *v.* to engage in or to accomplish. Simon hated the daily grind of transacting with business leaders, so he quit and became a sculptor.

transcribe, *v.* to write down what was said. Fortunately, many of the poet's last words were transcribed by his wife.

trauma, *n.* a severe injury or a state of emotional distress. Visiting her mother-in-law in Florida every summer was such a trauma for Annie that she scheduled a month-long visit at a health resort every fall.

traverse, *v.* to cross. Because the bridge was traversed by so many people traveling into the city, it was finally closed for repairs.

trivial, *adj.* unimportant. He thought her complaints were trivial and left the room.

tumble, *v.* to fall down or to roll. Mrs. Benthill shrieked as she watched her new vase tumble to the floor and shatter.

tumult, *n.* chaos or upheaval. The sudden cancellation of the concert caused such a tumult in the crowd that extra police were called to the site.

turmoil, *n.* confusion. The turmoil over her daughter's upcoming wedding gave Mrs. Windman constant headaches.

ultimate, *adj.* the highest, the best, the most important. Bernie's ultimate goal was to become president of the company by the age of 40.

unique, *adj.* unlike anything else. His paintings were so unique that he was given a one-man show at a gallery on Fifth Avenue.

unreliable, *adj.* cannot be trusted. Pete's plumbing business finally went bankrupt because of his unreliable service.

utilitarian, *adj.* serving the needs of many people. Frank was honored at a special banquet for his generous support of utilitarian causes.

vacillate, *v.* to hesitate or to waver. Archie impatiently drummed his fingers on the table as his wife vacillated between ordering chicken or seafood for dinner.

vary, *v.* to change. The teacher always varied her lesson plans in order to keep her students stimulated and motivated.

venture, *n.* a gamble or risk. Mr. Stanton refused to financially support his son's latest business venture.

verify, *v.* to check that something is true or correct. Every statement by the bank teller about the robbery was verified by witnesses standing in the lobby.

vibrant, *adj.* full of life. Emma had such a vibrant personality that no one could believe she was 82 years old.

vibrate, *v.* to move in a back-and-forth motion. Charlie's washing machine would vibrate so loudly in the spin cycle that his neighbors constantly complained to the landlord.

vigorously, *adv.* showing great energy or life. Shirley spent an hour vigorously scrubbing her kitchen floor before her dinner guests arrived.

volatile, *adj.* explosive or unsteady. After the shooting of an innocent victim, the crowds in the streets became volatile and citizens were advised to stay at home.

vulnerable, *adj.* open to danger or damage. A woman walking alone at night on a deserted street is vulnerable to an attack.

warranty, *n.* a written guarantee. Arthur searched and searched through the box but could not find the warranty that was supposed to come with his new car radio.

wither, *v.* to die slowly because of a lack of water. On the fifth day of no rain, Bernice's flowers began to wither and die.

wrath, *n.* great anger. His wrath was so great that many employees refused to go near his office.

zone, *n.* a specific region or area. Because of an attack by a bear on campers, the area was declared a danger zone and visitors were denied access to it.

Vocabulary Drills

The following drills will help build your vocabulary. Complete the drills and find the answers beginning on page 296. If there are any words you do not know, you may want to use a dictionary or a thesaurus after you complete each drill.

DRILL 1

> **DIRECTIONS:** Match the below word list to their appropriate synonym (words **similar** in meaning) or antonym (words **opposite** in meaning) found below the word list.

1. remnant
2. squash
3. strain
4. tentative
5. sympathy
6. substance
7. vibrant
8. morbid
9. sluggish
10. diagnosis

11. anomaly
12. zone
13. dominant
14. inferior
15. appreciable
16. negligible
17. inconsequential
18. origin
19. inception
20. canal

Synonyms
A. examination ____
B. struggle ____
C. region ____
D. noticeable ____
E. source ____
F. fragment ____
G. irregularity ____
H. start (noun) ____
I. flatten ____
J. insignificant ____
K. matter ____
L. waterway ____

Antonyms
A. permanent ____
B. cheerful ____
C. submissive ____
D. unconcern ____
E. superior ____
F. drab ____
G. energetic ____
H. significant ____

DRILL 2

DIRECTIONS: Match the following words to their appropriate synonym or antonym listed below.

1. automaton
2. mundane
3. digress
4. maintain
5. cessation
6. capacious
7. clumsy
8. inept
9. amateur
10. injustice

11. trauma
12. therapy
13. loot
14. elicit
15. infamous
16. notorious
17. tangible
18. elusive
19. unique
20. atop

Synonyms
A. remedy ____
B. inequality ____
C. extract ____
D. plunder ____
E. detectable ____
F. stray ____
G. disturbance ____
H. on ____
I. robot ____
J. unusual ____
K. preserve ____

Antonyms
A. beginning ____
B. competent ____
C. honorable ____
D. small ____
E. noble ____
F. straightforward ____
G. graceful ____
H. exciting ____
I. expert

DRILL 3

> **DIRECTIONS:** Match the following words to their appropriate synonym or antonym listed below.

1. output
2. prosecute
3. promulgate
4. abandon
5. discontinue
6. indict
7. subject
8. shield
9. expose
10. exempt

11. subordinated
12. seemingly
13. ostensibly
14. genuinely
15. authentic
16. selective
17. impeded
18. facilitate
19. impinged
20. hampered

Synonyms
A. apparently ____
B. excuse ____
C. blocked ____
D. guard ____
E. product ____
F. evidently ____
G. stop ____
H. intruded ____
I. announce ____
J. honestly ____
K. genuine ____
L. submit ____

Antonyms
A. defend ____
B. helped ____
C. clear (verb) ____
D. rescue ____
E. conceal ____
F. hinder ____
G. indiscriminate ____
H. dominated ____

DRILL 4

> **DIRECTIONS:** Match the following words to their appropriate synonym or antonym listed below.

1.	nadir	11.	terse
2.	apex	12.	disposal
3.	self-reliance	13.	stable
4.	contingence	14.	vacillate
5.	parasitic	15.	tenuous
6.	advocated	16.	stimulate
7.	petition	17.	ecosystem
8.	indurate	18.	lapses
9.	volatile	19.	senility
10.	inflammable	20.	persist

Synonyms
A. summit ____
B. dependent ____
C. combustible ____
D. infirmity ____
E. mistakes ____
F. possibility ____
G. ask ____
H. lowest point ____
I. hardened ____
J. discarding ____
K. environment ____
L. waver ____

Antonyms
A. opposed ____
B. stable ____
C. stifle ____
D. quit ____
E. wordy ____
F. dependence ____
G. solid ____
H. changeable ____

DRILL 5

1. transact
2. penetrate
3. skeptical
4. mutual
5. durable
6. recite
7. random
8. get across
9. spill
10. probe

11. refine
12. behavior
13. prevalent
14. divulge
15. get rid of
16. deviate
17. prior
18. static
19. turn to
20. recluse

Synonyms

A. investigation ____
B. widespread ____
C. stray ____
D. perform ____
E. shared ____
F. narrate ____
G. drop ____
H. convey ____
I. rely on ____
J. conduct (noun) ____
K. improve ____

Antonyms

A. convinced ____
B. subsequent ____
C. flimsy ____
D. conceal ____
E. withdraw ____
F. regular ____
G. preserve ____
H. active ____
I. socialite ____

DRILL 6

> **DIRECTIONS:** Match the following words to their appropriate synonym or antonym listed below.

1.	foresee	11.	extravagant
2.	globose	12.	held
3.	orb-like	13.	derided
4.	angular	14.	abhorred
5.	decrepit	15.	menaced
6.	agile	16.	argue
7.	longitudinal	17.	quality
8.	resolute	18.	track
9.	breadthwise	19.	characteristic
10.	lengthwise	20.	species

Synonyms

A. trait ____
B. breed ____
C. threatened ____
D. anticipate ____
E. globular ____
F. sharp-cornered ____
G. clutched ____
H. trait ____
I. round ____
J. path ____
K. up and down ____

Antonyms

A. loved ____
B. across ____
C. doubtful ____
D. awkward ____
E. frugal ____
F. admired ____
G. agree ____
H. vertical ____
I. sturdy ____

DRILL 7

> **DIRECTIONS:** Match the following words to their appropriate synonym or antonym listed below.

1. perish
2. composite
3. scarce
4. tract
5. masonry
6. utilitarian
7. acuity
8. tactile
9. imaging
10. surname

11. genealogy
12. jilted
13. spurn
14. consummate
15. documentation
16. corroborate
17. turmoil
18. tranquil
19. inaugurated
20. ridiculed

Synonyms
A. region ____
B. portray ____
C. useful ____
D. inducted ____
E. sharpness ____
F. die ____
G. construction ____
H. concrete ____
I. combination ____
J. last name ____
K. evidence ____
L. ancestry ____
M. fulfill ____

Antonyms
A. welcomed (verb) ____
B. praised ____
C. abundant ____
D. turbulent ____
E. respect ____
F. refute ____
G. order ____

DRILL 8

DIRECTIONS: Match the following words to their appropriate synonym or antonym listed below.

1. imminent
2. chaos
3. conventional
4. traverse
5. prelude
6. depict
7. compulsory
8. trivial
9. prudent
10. eradicate

11. blizzard
12. captive
13. surmise
14. deprecate
15. fraction
16. extensive
17. rivalry
18. bring about
19. intricate
20. prolific

Synonyms
A. describe ____
B. eliminate ____
C. piece ____
D. comprehensive ____
E. guess ____
F. criticize ____
G. produce ____
H. snowstorm ____
I. cross (verb) ____
J. hostage ____
K. fruitful ____

Antonyms
A. significant ____
B. distant ____
C. simple ____
D. unorthodox ____
E. order ____
F. friendship ____
G. voluntary ____
H. finale ____
I. foolish ____

DRILL 9

1. schedule
2. pessimist
3. equivocal
4. decrepit
5. negligent
6. ultimate
7. taciturn
8. evolve
9. loathe
10. bribe

11. verify
12. haphazard
13. tolerant
14. credulous
15. induce
16. confide
17. luminous
18. sporadic
19. callous
20. flee

Synonyms
A. escape ____
B. glowing ____
C. trusting ____
D. utmost ____
E. payoff ____
F. reveal ____
G. plan ____
H. develop ____
I. random ____
J. confirm ____

Antonyms
A. talkative ____
B. love ____
C. careful ____
D. robust ____
E. optimist ____
F. strict ____
G. clear ____
H. tender ____
I. steady ____
J. prevent ____

DRILL 10

DIRECTIONS: Match the following words to their appropriate synonym or antonym listed below.

1. generic
2. specific
3. non-trademark
4. expensive
5. brand name
6. exotic
7. patent
8. asset
9. prescription
10. accommodation

11. license
12. situated
13. barricaded
14. located
15. synchronize
16. concocted
17. devise
18. ponder
19. condone
20. create

Synonyms
A. blocked ____
B. common ____
C. permit ____
D. design (verb) ____
E. generic ____
F. label ____
G. lodge ____
H. formulated ____
I. copyright ____
J. positioned ____
K. written direction ____
L. coordinate ____

Antonyms
A. forget ____
B. cheap ____
C. destroy ____
D. general ____
E. native ____
F. lost ____
G. liability ____
H. disapprove ____

DRILL 11

> **DIRECTIONS:** Match the following words to their appropriate synonym or antonym listed below.

1.	chore	11.	compassion
2.	flimsy	12.	raze
3.	deterioration	13.	take after
4.	tumult	14.	pact
5.	detect	15.	diligent
6.	scatter	16.	commerce
7.	menace	17.	pollute
8.	incisive	18.	hectic
9.	soothe	19.	eccentric
10.	discern	20.	hoax

Synonyms
A. sympathy ____
B. comprehend ____
C. frantic ____
D. task ____
E. penetrating ____
F. prank ____
G. exchange ____
H. treaty ____
I. threat ____
J. decay ____

Antonyms
A. lazy ____
B. sturdy ____
C. build ____
D. gather ____
E. overlook ____
F. serenity ____
G. differ ____
H. typical ____
I. cleanse ____
J. upset ____

DRILL 12

DIRECTIONS: Match the following words to their appropriate synonym or antonym listed below.

1. lament
2. malign
3. grudge
4. postpone
5. tranquil
6. infest
7. extinct
8. molest
9. condone
10. meticulous
11. shrewd
12. facile
13. repel
14. placate
15. tumble
16. synchronize
17. inhabit
18. vary
19. concoct
20. confiscate

Synonyms

A. resentment ____
B. calm (verb) ____
C. delay ____
D. fall ____
E. dwell ____
F. clever ____
G. assault ____
H. match ____
I. infect ____
J. create ____
K. seize ____

Antonyms

A. difficult ____
B. celebrate ____
C. attract ____
D. living ____
E. maintain ____
F. praise ____
G. careless ____
H. stormy ____
I. disapprove ____

DRILL 13

DIRECTIONS: Match the following words to their appropriate synonym or antonym listed below.

1. hypothesis
2. defect
3. cogent
4. shatter
5. limb
6. retard
7. cryptic
8. obscure
9. diminutive
10. incessant

11. omit
12. esteem
13. cut down
14. reconcile
15. erosion
16. blame
17. simulate
18. perforated
19. perilous
20. explicit

Synonyms
A. copy ____
B. constant ____
C. diminish ____
D. theory ____
E. reunite ____
F. unclear ____
G. dangerous ____
H. flaw ____
I. branch ____
J. deterioration ____

Antonyms
A. include ____
B. quicken ____
C. mend ____
D. sealed ____
E. vindicate ____
F. unconvincing ____
G. obvious ____
H. big ____
I. ambiguous ____
J. scorn (noun) ____

DRILL 14

DIRECTIONS: Match the following words to their appropriate synonym or antonym listed below.

1. emit
2. grievance
3. assuage
4. feud
5. aversion
6. exasperate
7. hilarious
8. dissect
9. revenue
10. blandishment

11. leisure
12. contaminated
13. scorn
14. brittle
15. ominous
16. dubious
17. ignorant
18. fret
19. perpetual
20. chasm

Synonyms

A. threatening ____
B. crevasse ____
C. doubtful ____
D. analyze ____
E. complaint ____
F. worry ____
G. flattery ____
H. dislike ____
I. comical ____
J. emanate ____
K. relaxation ____

Antonyms

A. purified ____
B. truce ____
C. sturdy ____
D. informed ____
E. sporadic ____
F. soothe ____
G. aggravate ____
H. loss ____
I. admire ____

DRILL 15

> **DIRECTIONS:** Match the following words to their appropriate synonym or antonym listed below.

1.	effects	11.	deficiency
2.	blight	12.	feebleness
3.	allure	13.	prevalence
4.	merger	14.	lack
5.	consequences	15.	irritation
6.	tailored	16.	soluble
7.	adapt	17.	dissolvable
8.	illuminate	18.	exorbitant
9.	aggravate	19.	penetrable
10.	confine	20.	absorbent

Synonyms
A. adjust ____
B. passable ____
C. plague ____
D. fragility ____
E. results ____
F. dissoluble ____
G. alliance ____
H. suited ____
I. solvent ____
J. predomination ____
K. bibulous ____

Antonyms
A. surplus ____
B. causes ____
C. abundance ____
D. obscure ____
E. repel ____
F. release ____
G. alleviate ____
H. pleasure ____
I. cheap ____

DRILL 16

DIRECTIONS: Match the following words to their appropriate synonym or antonym listed below.

1.	enhance	11.	placate
2.	seize	12.	terminate
3.	coerce	13.	drought
4.	audacious	14.	exhaust
5.	harsh	15.	creed
6.	wither	16.	futile
7.	greed	17.	molest
8.	bewilder	18.	castigate
9.	obsolete	19.	decade
10.	culpable	20.	integrate

Synonyms
A. severe ____
B. outdated ____
C. intensify ____
D. combine ____
E. drain ____
F. discontinue ____
G. ten years ____
H. compel ____
I. belief ____
J. wilt ____
K. bold ____

Antonyms
A. flood ____
B. release ____
C. worthy ____
D. clarify ____
E. defend ____
F. compliment (verb) ____
G. innocent ____
H. agitate ____
I. release ____

DRILL 17

DIRECTIONS: Match the following words to their appropriate synonym or antonym listed below.

1. accrued
2. ample
3. approximate
4. abated
5. accumulate
6. investment
7. dependable
8. unreliable
9. affluent
10. antique

11. phenomenon
12. desire
13. enticement
14. fact
15. occurrence
16. destiny
17. fascinate
18. predetermine
19. synchronize
20. disseminate

Synonyms
A. reliable ____
B. captivate ____
C. wish ____
D. event ____
E. fate ____
F. collected ____
G. match ____
H. irresponsible ____
I. miracle ____
J. predestine ____
K. contribution ____

Antonyms
A. insufficient ____
B. poor ____
C. modern ____
D. repellent ____
E. exact ____
F. disperse ____
G. increased ____
H. assemble ____
I. fiction

DRILL 18

DIRECTIONS: Match the following words to their appropriate synonym or antonym listed below.

1. chilly
2. assert
3. fraud
4. dangle
5. vulnerable
6. ban
7. purify
8. aspire
9. fascinate
10. glitter

11. lush (adj.)
12. blunder
13. sagacity
14. lament
15. cabal
16. cryptic
17. culpable
18. elucidate
19. enervate
20. decency

Synonyms

A. aim ____
B. trickery ____
C. affirm ____
D. shrewdness ____
E. illuminate ____
F. suspend ____
G. enthrall ____
H. sparkle ____
I. error ____
J. conspiracy ____

Antonyms

A. permit ____
B. arid ____
C. obvious ____
D. celebrate ____
E. vulgarity ____
F. warm ____
G. innocent ____
H. strengthen ____
I. pollute ____
J. impenetrable ____

DRILL 19

DIRECTIONS: Match the following words to their appropriate synonym or antonym listed below.

1. abetted
2. analyst
3. examiner
4. accomplice
5. intruder
6. meddled
7. handicap
8. ailment
9. enhancement
10. advantage

11. impediment
12. ensue
13. germinate
14. covert
15. lead
16. ensnare
17. emerge
18. simulate
19. emulate
20. become

Synonyms
A. trespasser ____
B. benefit ____
C. sickness ____
D. cohort ____
E. investigator ____
F. develop ____
G. assisted ____
H. imitate ____
I. grow ____
J. magnification ____
K. inspector ____
L. feign ____
M. proceed ____

Antonyms
A. follow ____
B. aid ____
C. disappear ____
D. set free ____
E. enable ____
F. ignored ____
G. obvious ____

DRILL 20

> **DIRECTIONS:** Match the following words to their appropriate synonym or antonym listed below.

1. exist
2. control
3. develop
4. accumulate
5. congeal
6. evidence
7. story
8. gist
9. plea
10. proof

11. essential
12. accessory
13. basis
14. massive
15. resolute
16. plethora
17. category
18. group
19. abundance
20. core

Synonyms

A. plenty _____
B. dominate _____
C. appeal _____
D. data _____
E. base _____
F. main idea _____
G. classification _____
H. crucial _____
I. ornament _____
J. generate _____
K. fable _____

Antonyms

A. small _____
B. individual _____
C. exterior _____
D. cowardly _____
E. sparsity _____
F. perish _____
G. liquefy _____
H. dispense _____
I. refutation _____

DRILL 21

DIRECTIONS: Match the following words to their appropriate synonym or antonym listed below.

1. recede
2. strangulation
3. suffocation
4. falter
5. shatter
6. attain
7. forfeit
8. accomplish
9. fail
10. fall short

11. accost
12. acrid
13. admonish
14. agitate
15. akin
16. alleviate
17. ambiguous
18. anguish
19. arduous
20. arouse

Synonyms

A. burst ____
B. agony ____
C. subside ____
D. achieve ____
E. blunder (verb) ____
F. chide ____
G. constriction ____
H. fulfill ____
I. relinquish ____
J. asphyxiation ____

Antonyms

A. calm (verb) ____
B. bore (verb) ____
C. complete ____
D. sweet ____
E. act ____
F. defend ____
G. unrelated ____
H. easy ____
I. obvious ____
J. aggravate ____

DRILL 22

DIRECTIONS: Match the following words to their appropriate synonym or antonym listed below.

1.	exacting	11.	skeins
2.	amicable	12.	litter
3.	concentration	13.	nomadic
4.	vigorously	14.	phlegmatic
5.	energetically	15.	vibrate
6.	anchor (verb)	16.	receptive
7.	deprive	17.	sleazy
8.	stun	18.	predator
9.	paralyze	19.	confidant
10.	artifact	20.	metabolism

Synonyms
A. vigorously ____
B. body processes ____
C. coiled yarn ____
D. attention ____
E. secure (verb) ____
F. immobilize ____
G. wandering ____
H. ancient object ____
I. shake ____
J. scatter ____
K. shabby ____
L. shock (verb) ____

Antonyms
A. prey ____
B. lenient ____
C. sluggishly ____
D. bestow ____
E. adversary ____
F. energetic ____
G. antagonistic ____
H. closed-minded ____

DRILL 23

DIRECTIONS: Match the following words to their appropriate synonym or antonym listed below.

1. fugitive
2. palatable
3. foremost
4. indexed (verb)
5. transcribe
6. superceded
7. perforated

8. tranquility
9. cruel
10. inquisitive
11. enterprise
12. venture
13. revenue
14. repugnant

Synonyms
A. risk (noun) ____
B. punctured ____
C. appetizing ____
D. project ____
E. replaced ____
F. listed (verb) ____
G. record (noun) ____
H. refugee ____
I. profits ____

Antonyms
A. uninterested ____
B. attractive ____
C. kind ____
D. tumult ____
E. minor ____

DRILL 24

DIRECTIONS: Match the following words to their appropriate synonym or antonym listed below.

1. objective
2. premise
3. foster
4. neglect
5. apparatus
6. excessive
7. symbolize
8. bail (noun)
9. augment
10. arrogance

11. interactive
12. orbit
13. stagnate
14. seasoned
15. mature
16. immature
17. ripe
18. determinant
19. guarantee
20. ordeal

Synonyms
A. represent ____
B. revolution ____
C. assumption ____
D. decay ____
E. warranty ____
F. material ____
G. security ____
H. factor ____
I. mature ____
J. goal ____
K. developed ____
L. experienced ____
M. joint (adj.) ____

Antonyms
A. humility ____
B. moderate ____
C. neglect ____
D. diminish ____
E. relief ____
F. attend to ____
G. adult ____

DRILL 25

1. deliberately
2. adroitly
3. melancholy
4. scrutiny
5. conscientious
6. savage

7. wrath
8. forbearance
9. abject
10. congenial
11. intrepid
12. invalid

Synonyms
A. careful ____
B. patience ____
C. patient (noun) ____
D. inquiry ____
E. rage ____
F. primitive (noun) ____

Antonyms
A. clumsily ____
B. fearful ____
C. joyful ____
D. accidentally ____
E. hopeful ____
F. unpleasant ____

VOCABULARY DRILLS

ANSWER KEY

DRILL 1

1. remnant
2. squash
3. strain
4. tentative
5. sympathy
6. substance
7. vibrant
8. morbid
9. sluggish
10. diagnosis

11. anomaly
12. zone
13. dominant
14. inferior
15. appreciable
16. negligible
17. inconsequential
18. origin
19. inception
20. canal

Synonyms

A. examination ___10___
B. struggle ___3___
C. region ___12___
D. noticeable ___15___
E. source ___18___
F. fragment ___1___
G. irregularity ___11___
H. start (noun) ___19___
I. flatten ___2___
J. insignificant ___16___
K. matter ___6___
L. waterway ___20___

Antonyms

A. permanent ___4___
B. cheerful ___8___
C. submissive ___13___
D. unconcern ___5___
E. superior ___14___
F. drab ___7___
G. energetic ___9___
H. significant ___17___

DRILL 2

1. automaton
2. mundane
3. digress
4. maintain
5. cessation
6. capacious
7. clumsy
8. inept
9. amateur
10. injustice

11. trauma
12. therapy
13. loot
14. elicit
15. infamous
16. notorious
17. tangible
18. elusive
19. unique
20. atop

Synonyms

A. remedy ___12___
B. inequality ___10___
C. extract ___14___
D. plunder ___13___
E. detectable ___17___
F. stray ___3___
G. disturbance ___11___
H. on ___20___
I. robot ___1___
J. unusual ___19___
K. preserve ___4___ •

Antonyms

A. beginning ___5___
B. competent ___8___
C. honorable ___15___
D. small ___6___
E. noble ___16___
F. straightforward ___18___
G. graceful ___7___
H. exciting ___2___
I. expert ___9___

DRILL 3

1. output
2. prosecute
3. promulgate
4. abandon
5. discontinue
6. indict
7. subject
8. shield
9. expose
10. exempt

11. subordinated
12. seemingly
13. ostensibly
14. genuinely
15. authentic
16. selective
17. impeded
18. facilitate
19. impinged
20. hampered

Synonyms
A. apparently   13
B. excuse   10
C. blocked   17
D. guard   8
E. product   1
F. evidently   12
G. stop   5
H. intruded   19
I. announce   3
J. honestly   14
K. genuine   15
L. submit   7

Antonyms
A. defend   2
B. helped   20
C. clear   6
D. rescue   4
E. conceal   9
F. hinder   18
G. indiscriminate   16
H. dominated   11

DRILL 4

1. nadir
2. apex
3. self-reliance
4. contingence
5. parasitic
6. advocated
7. petition
8. indurate
9. volatile
10. inflammable

11. terse
12. disposal
13. stable
14. vacillate
15. tenuous
16. stimulate
17. ecosystem
18. lapses
19. senility
20. persist

Synonyms

A. summit __2__
B. dependent __5__
C. combustible __10__
D. infirmity __19__
E. mistakes __18__
F. possibility __4__
G. ask __7__
H. lowest point __1__
I. hardened __8__
J. discarding __12__
K. environment __17__
L. waver __14__

Antonyms

A. opposed __6__
B. stable __9__
C. stifle __16__
D. quit __20__
E. wordy __11__
F. dependence __3__
G. solid __15__
H. changeable __13__

DRILL 5

1. transact
2. penetrate
3. skeptical
4. mutual
5. durable
6. recite
7. random
8. get across
9. spill
10. probe

11. refine
12. behavior
13. prevalent
14. divulge
15. get rid of
16. deviate
17. prior
18. static
19. turn to
20. recluse

Synonyms

A. investigation   10
B. widespread   13
C. stray   16
D. perform   1
E. shared   4
F. narrate   6
G. drop   9
H. convey   8
I. rely on   19
J. conduct (noun)   12
K. improve   11

Antonyms

A. convinced   3
B. subsequent   17
C. flimsy   5
D. conceal   14
E. withdraw   2
F. regular   7
G. preserve   15
H. active   18
I. socialite   20

DRILL 6

1. foresee
2. globose
3. orb-like
4. angular
5. decrepit
6. agile
7. longitudinal
8. resolute
9. breadthwise
10. lengthwise

11. extravagant
12. held
13. derided
14. abhorred
15. menaced
16. argue
17. quality
18. track
19. characteristic
20. species

Synonyms
A. trait ___17___
B. breed ___20___
C. threatened ___15___
D. anticipate ___1___
E. globular ___2___
F. sharp-cornered ___4___
G. clutched ___12___
H. trait ___19___
I. round ___3___
J. path ___18___
K. up and down ___7___

Antonyms
A. loved ___14___
B. across ___10___
C. doubtful ___8___
D. awkward ___6___
E. frugal ___11___
F. admired ___13___
G. agree ___16___
H. vertical ___9___
I. sturdy ___5___

DRILL 7

1. perish
2. composite
3. scarce
4. tract
5. masonry
6. utilitarian
7. acuity
8. tactile
9. imaging
10. surname

11. genealogy
12. jilted
13. spurn
14. consummate
15. documentation
16. corroborate
17. turmoil
18. tranquil
19. inaugurated
20. ridiculed

Synonyms
A. region   4
B. portray   9
C. useful   6
D. inducted   19
E. sharpness   7
F. die   1
G. construction   5
H. concrete   8
I. combination   2
J. last name   10
K. evidence   15
L. ancestry   11
M. fulfill   14

Antonyms
A. welcomed (verb)   12
B. praised   20
C. abundant   3
D. turbulent   18
E. respect   13
F. refute   16
G. order   17

DRILL 8

1. imminent
2. chaos
3. conventional
4. traverse
5. prelude
6. depict
7. compulsory
8. trivial
9. prudent
10. eradicate

11. blizzard
12. captive
13. surmise
14. deprecate
15. fraction
16. extensive
17. rivalry
18. bring about
19. intricate
20. prolific

Synonyms
A. describe __6__
B. eliminate __10__
C. piece __15__
D. comprehensive __16__
E. guess __13__
F. criticize __14__
G. produce __18__
H. snowstorm __11__
I. cross (verb) __4__
J. hostage __12__
K. fruitful __20__

Antonyms
A. significant __8__
B. distant __1__
C. simple __19__
D. unorthodox __3__
E. order __2__
F. friendship __17__
G. voluntary __7__
H. finale __5__
I. foolish __9__

DRILL 9

1.	schedule		11.	verify
2.	pessimist		12.	haphazard
3.	equivocal		13.	tolerant
4.	decrepit		14.	credulous
5.	negligent		15.	induce
6.	ultimate		16.	confide
7.	taciturn		17.	luminous
8.	evolve		18.	sporadic
9.	loathe		19.	callous
10.	bribe		20.	flee

Synonyms

A.	escape	20
B.	glowing	17
C.	trusting	14
D.	utmost	6
E.	payoff	10
F.	reveal	16
G.	plan	1
H.	develop	8
I.	random	12
J.	confirm	11

Antonyms

A.	talkative	7
B.	love	9
C.	careful	5
D.	robust	4
E.	optimist	2
F.	strict	13
G.	clear	3
H.	tender	19
I.	steady	18
J.	prevent	15

DRILL 10

1. generic
2. specific
3. non-trademark
4. expensive
5. brand name
6. exotic
7. patent
8. asset
9. prescription
10. accommodation

11. license
12. situated
13. barricaded
14. located
15. synchronize
16. concocted
17. devise
18. ponder
19. condone
20. create

Synonyms
A. blocked ___13___
B. common ___1___
C. permit ___11___
D. design (verb) ___17___
E. generic ___3___
F. label ___5___
G. lodge ___10___
H. formulated ___16___
I. copyright ___7___
J. positioned ___12___
K. written direction ___9___
L. coordinate ___15___

Antonyms
A. forget ___18___
B. cheap ___4___
C. destroy ___20___
D. general ___2___
E. native ___6___
F. lost ___14___
G. liability ___8___
H. disapprove ___19___

DRILL 11

1.	chore	11.	compassion
2.	flimsy	12.	raze
3.	deterioration	13.	take after
4.	tumult	14.	pact
5.	detect	15.	diligent
6.	scatter	16.	commerce
7.	menace	17.	pollute
8.	incisive	18.	hectic
9.	soothe	19.	eccentric
10.	discern	20.	hoax

Synonyms

A. sympathy __11__
B. comprehend __10__
C. frantic __18__
D. task __1__
E. penetrating __8__
F. prank __20__
G. exchange __16__
H. treaty __14__
I. threat __7__
J. decay __3__

Antonyms

A. lazy __15__
B. sturdy __2__
C. build __12__
D. gather __6__
E. overlook __5__
F. serenity __4__
G. differ __13__
H. typical __19__
I. cleanse __17__
J. upset __9__

DRILL 12

1. lament
2. malign
3. grudge
4. postpone
5. tranquil
6. infest
7. extinct
8. molest
9. condone
10. meticulous

11. shrewd
12. facile
13. repel
14. placate
15. tumble
16. synchronize
17. inhabit
18. vary
19. concoct
20. confiscate

Synonyms
A. resentment __3__
B. calm (verb) __14__
C. delay __4__
D. fall __15__
E. dwell __17__
F. clever __11__
G. assault __8__
H. match __16__
I. infect __6__
J. create __19__
K. seize __20__

Antonyms
A. difficult __12__
B. celebrate __1__
C. attract __13__
D. living __7__
E. maintain __18__
F. praise __2__
G. careless __10__
H. stormy __5__
I. disapprove __9__

DRILL 13

1.	hypothesis	11.	omit
2.	defect	12.	esteem
3.	cogent	13.	cut down
4.	shatter	14.	reconcile
5.	limb	15.	erosion
6.	retard	16.	blame
7.	cryptic	17.	simulate
8.	obscure	18.	perforated
9.	diminutive	19.	perilous
10.	incessant	20.	explicit

Synonyms

A. copy ___17___
B. constant ___10___
C. diminish ___13___
D. theory ___1___
E. reunite ___14___
F. unclear ___8___
G. dangerous ___19___
H. flaw ___2___
I. branch ___5___
J. deterioration ___15___

Antonyms

A. include ___11___
B. quicken ___6___
C. mend ___4___
D. sealed ___18___
E. vindicate ___16___
F. unconvincing ___3___
G. obvious ___7___
H. big ___9___
I. ambiguous ___20___
J. scorn (noun) ___12___

DRILL 14

1. emit
2. grievance
3. assuage
4. feud
5. aversion
6. exasperate
7. hilarious
8. dissect
9. revenue
10. blandishment

11. leisure
12. contaminated
13. scorn
14. brittle
15. ominous
16. dubious
17. ignorant
18. fret
19. perpetual
20. chasm

Synonyms

A. threatening   15
B. crevasse   20
C. doubtful   16
D. analyze   8
E. complaint   2
F. worry   18
G. flattery   10
H. dislike   5
I. comical   7
J. emanate   1
K. relaxation   11

Antonyms

A. purified   12
B. truce   4
C. sturdy   14
D. informed   17
E. sporadic   19
F. soothe   6
G. aggravate   3
H. loss   9
I. admire   13

DRILL 15

1. effects
2. blight
3. allure
4. merger
5. consequences
6. tailored
7. adapt
8. illuminate
9. aggravate
10. confine

11. deficiency
12. feebleness
13. prevalence
14. lack
15. irritation
16. soluble
17. dissolvable
18. exorbitant
19. penetrable
20. absorbant

Synonyms

A. adjust _7_
B. passable _19_
C. plague _2_
D. fragility _12_
E. results _1_
F. dissoluble _17_
G. alliance _4_
H. suited _6_
I. solvent _16_
J. predomination _13_
K. bibulous _20_

Antonyms

A. surplus _14_
B. causes _5_
C. abundance _11_
D. obscure _8_
E. repel _3_
F. release _10_
G. alleviate _9_
H. pleasure _15_
I. cheap _18_

DRILL 16

1.	enhance	11.	placate
2.	seize	12.	terminate
3.	coerce	13.	drought
4.	audacious	14.	exhaust
5.	harsh	15.	creed
6.	wither	16.	futile
7.	greed	17.	molest
8.	bewilder	18.	castigate
9.	obsolete	19.	decade
10.	culpable	20.	integrate

Synonyms

A. severe   5
B. outdated   9
C. intensify   1
D. combine   20
E. drain   14
F. discontinue   12
G. ten years   19
H. compel   3
I. belief   15
J. wilt   6
K. bold   4

Antonyms

A. flood   13
B. release   2
C. worthy   16
D. clarify   8
E. defend   17
F. compliment (verb)   18
G. innocent   10
H. agitate   11
I. release   2

DRILL 17

1.	accrued	11.	phenomenon
2.	ample	12.	desire
3.	approximate	13.	enticement
4.	abated	14.	fact
5.	accumulate	15.	occurrence
6.	investment	16.	destiny
7.	dependable	17.	fascinate
8.	unreliable	18.	predetermine
9.	affluent	19.	synchronize
10.	antique	20.	disseminate

Synonyms

A. reliable _7_
B. captivate _17_
C. wish _12_
D. event _15_
E. fate _16_
F. collected _1_
G. match _19_
H. irresponsible _8_
I. miracle _11_
J. predestine _18_
K. contribution _6_

Antonyms

A. insufficient _2_
B. poor _9_
C. modern _10_
D. repellent _13_
E. exact _3_
F. disperse _5_
G. increased _4_
H. assemble _20_
I. fiction _14_

DRILL 18

1. chilly
2. assert
3. fraud
4. dangle
5. vulnerable
6. ban
7. purify
8. aspire
9. fascinate
10. glitter

11. lush (adj.)
12. blunder
13. sagacity
14. lament
15. cabal
16. cryptic
17. culpable
18. elucidate
19. enervate
20. decency

Synonyms
A. aim _8_
B. trickery _3_
C. affirm _2_
D. shrewdness _13_
E. illuminate _18_
F. suspend _4_
G. enthrall _9_
H. sparkle _10_
I. error _12_
J. conspiracy _15_

Antonyms
A. permit _6_
B. arid _11_
C. obvious _16_
D. celebrate _14_
E. vulgarity _20_
F. warm _1_
G. innocent _17_
H. strengthen _19_
I. pollute _7_
J. impenetrable _5_

DRILL 19

1. abetted
2. analyst
3. examiner
4. accomplice
5. intruder
6. meddled
7. handicap
8. ailment
9. enhancement
10. advantage

11. impediment
12. ensue
13. germinate
14. covert
15. lead
16. ensnare
17. emerge
18. simulate
19. emulate
20. become

Synonyms
A. trespasser   5
B. benefit   10
C. sickness   8
D. cohort   4
E. investigator   2
F. develop   20
G. assisted   1
H. imitate   19
I. grow   13
J. magnification   9
K. inspector   3
L. feign   18
M. proceed   12

Antonyms
A. follow   15
B. aid   11
C. disappear   17
D. set free   16
E. enable   7
F. ignored   6
G. obvious   14

DRILL 20

1. exist
2. control
3. develop
4. accumulate
5. congeal
6. evidence
7. story
8. gist
9. plea
10. proof

11. essential
12. accessory
13. basis
14. massive
15. resolute
16. plethora
17. category
18. group
19. abundance
20. core

Synonyms
A. plenty   _19_
B. dominate   _2_
C. appeal   _9_
D. data   _6_
E. base   _13_
F. main idea   _8_
G. classification   _17_
H. crucial   _11_
I. ornament   _12_
J. generate   _3_
K. fable   _7_

Antonyms
A. small   _14_
B. individual   _18_
C. exterior   _20_
D. cowardly   _15_
E. sparsity   _16_
F. perish   _1_
G. liquefy   _5_
H. dispense   _4_
I. refutation   _10_

DRILL 21

1.	recede	11.	accost
2.	strangulation	12.	acrid
3.	suffocation	13.	admonish
4.	falter	14.	agitate
5.	shatter	15.	akin
6.	attain	16.	alleviate
7.	forfeit	17.	ambiguous
8.	accomplish	18.	anguish
9.	fail	19.	arduous
10.	fall short	20.	arouse

Synonyms

A. burst __5__
B. agony __18__
C. subside __1__
D. achieve __6__
E. blunder (verb) __9__
F. chide __13__
G. constriction __2__
H. fulfill __8__
I. relinquish __7__
J. asphyxiation __3__

Antonyms

A. calm (verb) __14__
B. bore(verb) __20__
C. complete __10__
D. sweet __12__
E. act __4__
F. defend __11__
G. unrelated __15__
H. easy __19__
I. obvious __17__
J. aggravate __16__

DRILL 22

1. exacting
2. amicable
3. concentration
4. vigorously
5. energetically
6. anchor (verb)
7. deprive
8. stun
9. paralyze
10. artifact

11. skeins
12. litter
13. nomadic
14. phlegmatic
15. vibrate
16. receptive
17. sleazy
18. predator
19. confidant
20. metabolism

Synonyms
A. vigorously __5__
B. body processes __20__
C. coiled yarn __11__
D. attention __3__
E. secure (verb) __6__
F. immobilize __9__
G. wandering __13__
H. ancient object __10__
I. shake __15__
J. scatter __12__
K. shabby __17__
L. shock (verb) __8__

Antonyms
A. prey __18__
B. lenient __1__
C. sluggishly __4__
D. bestow __7__
E. adversary __19__
F. energetic __14__
G. antagonistic __2__
H. closed-minded __16__

DRILL 23

1. fugitive
2. palatable
3. foremost
4. indexed (verb)
5. transcribe
6. superceded
7. perforated

8. tranquility
9. cruel
10. inquisitive
11. enterprise
12. venture
13. revenue
14. repugnant

Synonyms
A. risk (noun) __12__
B. punctured __7__
C. appetizing __2__
D. project __11__
E. replaced __6__
F. listed (verb) __4__
G. record (verb) __5__
H. refugee __1__
I. profits __13__

Antonyms
A. uninterested __10__
B. attractive __14__
C. kind __9__
D. tumult __8__
E. minor __3__

DRILL 24

1. objective
2. premise
3. foster
4. neglect
5. apparatus
6. excessive
7. symbolize
8. bail (noun)
9. augment
10. arrogance

11. interactive
12. orbit
13. stagnate
14. seasoned
15. mature
16. immature
17. ripe
18. determinant
19. guarantee
20. ordeal

Synonyms
A. represent   7
B. revolution   12
C. assumption   2
D. decay   13
E. warranty   19
F. material   5
G. security   8
H. factor   18
I. mature   17
J. goal   1
K. developed   14
L. experienced   15
M. joint (adj.)   11

Antonyms
A. humility   10
B. moderate   6
C. neglect   3
D. diminish   9
E. relief   20
F. attend to   4
G. adult   16

DRILL 25

1. deliberately
2. adroitly
3. melancholy
4. scrutiny
5. conscientious
6. savage

7. wrath
8. forbearance
9. abject
10. congenial
11. intrepid
12. invalid

Synonyms
A. careful   5
B. patience   8
C. patient (noun)   12
D. inquiry   4
E. rage   7
F. primitive (noun)   6

Antonyms
A. clumsily   2
B. fearful   11
C. joyful   3
D. accidentally   1
E. hopeful   9
F. unpleasant   10

Chapter 6

The Sample Tests

Test of English as a Foreign Language
TEST 1
ANSWER SHEET

Section 1:
Listening Comprehension

1. Ⓐ Ⓑ Ⓒ Ⓓ
2. Ⓐ Ⓑ Ⓒ Ⓓ
3. Ⓐ Ⓑ Ⓒ Ⓓ
4. Ⓐ Ⓑ Ⓒ Ⓓ
5. Ⓐ Ⓑ Ⓒ Ⓓ
6. Ⓐ Ⓑ Ⓒ Ⓓ
7. Ⓐ Ⓑ Ⓒ Ⓓ
8. Ⓐ Ⓑ Ⓒ Ⓓ
9. Ⓐ Ⓑ Ⓒ Ⓓ
10. Ⓐ Ⓑ Ⓒ Ⓓ
11. Ⓐ Ⓑ Ⓒ Ⓓ
12. Ⓐ Ⓑ Ⓒ Ⓓ
13. Ⓐ Ⓑ Ⓒ Ⓓ
14. Ⓐ Ⓑ Ⓒ Ⓓ
15. Ⓐ Ⓑ Ⓒ Ⓓ
16. Ⓐ Ⓑ Ⓒ Ⓓ
17. Ⓐ Ⓑ Ⓒ Ⓓ
18. Ⓐ Ⓑ Ⓒ Ⓓ
19. Ⓐ Ⓑ Ⓒ Ⓓ
20. Ⓐ Ⓑ Ⓒ Ⓓ
21. Ⓐ Ⓑ Ⓒ Ⓓ
22. Ⓐ Ⓑ Ⓒ Ⓓ
23. Ⓐ Ⓑ Ⓒ Ⓓ
24. Ⓐ Ⓑ Ⓒ Ⓓ
25. Ⓐ Ⓑ Ⓒ Ⓓ
26. Ⓐ Ⓑ Ⓒ Ⓓ
27. Ⓐ Ⓑ Ⓒ Ⓓ
28. Ⓐ Ⓑ Ⓒ Ⓓ
29. Ⓐ Ⓑ Ⓒ Ⓓ
30. Ⓐ Ⓑ Ⓒ Ⓓ
31. Ⓐ Ⓑ Ⓒ Ⓓ
32. Ⓐ Ⓑ Ⓒ Ⓓ
33. Ⓐ Ⓑ Ⓒ Ⓓ
34. Ⓐ Ⓑ Ⓒ Ⓓ
35. Ⓐ Ⓑ Ⓒ Ⓓ
36. Ⓐ Ⓑ Ⓒ Ⓓ
37. Ⓐ Ⓑ Ⓒ Ⓓ
38. Ⓐ Ⓑ Ⓒ Ⓓ
39. Ⓐ Ⓑ Ⓒ Ⓓ
40. Ⓐ Ⓑ Ⓒ Ⓓ
41. Ⓐ Ⓑ Ⓒ Ⓓ
42. Ⓐ Ⓑ Ⓒ Ⓓ
43. Ⓐ Ⓑ Ⓒ Ⓓ
44. Ⓐ Ⓑ Ⓒ Ⓓ
45. Ⓐ Ⓑ Ⓒ Ⓓ
46. Ⓐ Ⓑ Ⓒ Ⓓ
47. Ⓐ Ⓑ Ⓒ Ⓓ
48. Ⓐ Ⓑ Ⓒ Ⓓ
49. Ⓐ Ⓑ Ⓒ Ⓓ
50. Ⓐ Ⓑ Ⓒ Ⓓ

Section 2:
Structure and Written Expression

1. Ⓐ Ⓑ Ⓒ Ⓓ
2. Ⓐ Ⓑ Ⓒ Ⓓ
3. Ⓐ Ⓑ Ⓒ Ⓓ
4. Ⓐ Ⓑ Ⓒ Ⓓ
5. Ⓐ Ⓑ Ⓒ Ⓓ
6. Ⓐ Ⓑ Ⓒ Ⓓ
7. Ⓐ Ⓑ Ⓒ Ⓓ
8. Ⓐ Ⓑ Ⓒ Ⓓ
9. Ⓐ Ⓑ Ⓒ Ⓓ
10. Ⓐ Ⓑ Ⓒ Ⓓ
11. Ⓐ Ⓑ Ⓒ Ⓓ
12. Ⓐ Ⓑ Ⓒ Ⓓ
13. Ⓐ Ⓑ Ⓒ Ⓓ
14. Ⓐ Ⓑ Ⓒ Ⓓ
15. Ⓐ Ⓑ Ⓒ Ⓓ
16. Ⓐ Ⓑ Ⓒ Ⓓ
17. Ⓐ Ⓑ Ⓒ Ⓓ
18. Ⓐ Ⓑ Ⓒ Ⓓ
19. Ⓐ Ⓑ Ⓒ Ⓓ
20. Ⓐ Ⓑ Ⓒ Ⓓ
21. Ⓐ Ⓑ Ⓒ Ⓓ
22. Ⓐ Ⓑ Ⓒ Ⓓ
23. Ⓐ Ⓑ Ⓒ Ⓓ
24. Ⓐ Ⓑ Ⓒ Ⓓ
25. Ⓐ Ⓑ Ⓒ Ⓓ
26. Ⓐ Ⓑ Ⓒ Ⓓ
27. Ⓐ Ⓑ Ⓒ Ⓓ
28. Ⓐ Ⓑ Ⓒ Ⓓ
29. Ⓐ Ⓑ Ⓒ Ⓓ
30. Ⓐ Ⓑ Ⓒ Ⓓ
31. Ⓐ Ⓑ Ⓒ Ⓓ
32. Ⓐ Ⓑ Ⓒ Ⓓ
33. Ⓐ Ⓑ Ⓒ Ⓓ
34. Ⓐ Ⓑ Ⓒ Ⓓ
35. Ⓐ Ⓑ Ⓒ Ⓓ
36. Ⓐ Ⓑ Ⓒ Ⓓ
37. Ⓐ Ⓑ Ⓒ Ⓓ
38. Ⓐ Ⓑ Ⓒ Ⓓ
39. Ⓐ Ⓑ Ⓒ Ⓓ
40. Ⓐ Ⓑ Ⓒ Ⓓ

321

Section 3:
Reading Comprehension
and Vocabulary

1. Ⓐ Ⓑ Ⓒ Ⓓ
2. Ⓐ Ⓑ Ⓒ Ⓓ
3. Ⓐ Ⓑ Ⓒ Ⓓ
4. Ⓐ Ⓑ Ⓒ Ⓓ
5. Ⓐ Ⓑ Ⓒ Ⓓ
6. Ⓐ Ⓑ Ⓒ Ⓓ
7. Ⓐ Ⓑ Ⓒ Ⓓ
8. Ⓐ Ⓑ Ⓒ Ⓓ
9. Ⓐ Ⓑ Ⓒ Ⓓ
10. Ⓐ Ⓑ Ⓒ Ⓓ
11. Ⓐ Ⓑ Ⓒ Ⓓ
12. Ⓐ Ⓑ Ⓒ Ⓓ
13. Ⓐ Ⓑ Ⓒ Ⓓ
14. Ⓐ Ⓑ Ⓒ Ⓓ
15. Ⓐ Ⓑ Ⓒ Ⓓ
16. Ⓐ Ⓑ Ⓒ Ⓓ
17. Ⓐ Ⓑ Ⓒ Ⓓ
18. Ⓐ Ⓑ Ⓒ Ⓓ

19. Ⓐ Ⓑ Ⓒ Ⓓ
20. Ⓐ Ⓑ Ⓒ Ⓓ
21. Ⓐ Ⓑ Ⓒ Ⓓ
22. Ⓐ Ⓑ Ⓒ Ⓓ
23. Ⓐ Ⓑ Ⓒ Ⓓ
24. Ⓐ Ⓑ Ⓒ Ⓓ
25. Ⓐ Ⓑ Ⓒ Ⓓ
26. Ⓐ Ⓑ Ⓒ Ⓓ
27. Ⓐ Ⓑ Ⓒ Ⓓ
28. Ⓐ Ⓑ Ⓒ Ⓓ
29. Ⓐ Ⓑ Ⓒ Ⓓ
30. Ⓐ Ⓑ Ⓒ Ⓓ
31. Ⓐ Ⓑ Ⓒ Ⓓ
32. Ⓐ Ⓑ Ⓒ Ⓓ
33. Ⓐ Ⓑ Ⓒ Ⓓ
34. Ⓐ Ⓑ Ⓒ Ⓓ
35. Ⓐ Ⓑ Ⓒ Ⓓ
36. Ⓐ Ⓑ Ⓒ Ⓓ
37. Ⓐ Ⓑ Ⓒ Ⓓ
38. Ⓐ Ⓑ Ⓒ Ⓓ
39. Ⓐ Ⓑ Ⓒ Ⓓ

40. Ⓐ Ⓑ Ⓒ Ⓓ
41. Ⓐ Ⓑ Ⓒ Ⓓ
42. Ⓐ Ⓑ Ⓒ Ⓓ
43. Ⓐ Ⓑ Ⓒ Ⓓ
44. Ⓐ Ⓑ Ⓒ Ⓓ
45. Ⓐ Ⓑ Ⓒ Ⓓ
46. Ⓐ Ⓑ Ⓒ Ⓓ
47. Ⓐ Ⓑ Ⓒ Ⓓ
48. Ⓐ Ⓑ Ⓒ Ⓓ
49. Ⓐ Ⓑ Ⓒ Ⓓ
50. Ⓐ Ⓑ Ⓒ Ⓓ
51. Ⓐ Ⓑ Ⓒ Ⓓ
52. Ⓐ Ⓑ Ⓒ Ⓓ
53. Ⓐ Ⓑ Ⓒ Ⓓ
54. Ⓐ Ⓑ Ⓒ Ⓓ
55. Ⓐ Ⓑ Ⓒ Ⓓ
56. Ⓐ Ⓑ Ⓒ Ⓓ
57. Ⓐ Ⓑ Ⓒ Ⓓ
58. Ⓐ Ⓑ Ⓒ Ⓓ
59. Ⓐ Ⓑ Ⓒ Ⓓ
60. Ⓐ Ⓑ Ⓒ Ⓓ

TOEFL

TEST 1

Section 1:
LISTENING COMPREHENSION

TIME: 35 Minutes
50 Questions

Part A

> **DIRECTIONS:** In Part A you will hear short conversations between two speakers. At the end of each conversation, a third person will ask a question about what was said. **You will hear each conversation just one time.** Therefore, you must listen carefully to understand what each speaker says. After you hear a conversation and the question about it, read the four possible answers in your test book and decide which one is the best answer to the question you heard. Then on your answer sheet, find the number of the question and fill in the space that corresponds to the answer you have chosen.

1. (A) He does not like the hat.
    (B) He suggests that she try on a different hat.
    (C) He thinks the hat looks good on her.
    (D) He doesn't like the hat because it is green.

2. (A) The woman thinks they will lose the game.
    (B) The woman thinks the team is doing very poorly this season.
    (C) The woman thinks the team will tie the game.
    (D) The woman thinks the team has a very good chance of winning.

3. (A) She forgot to lock the door.
    (B) The man was supposed to have locked the door on his way out.
    (C) She did lock the door.
    (D) She remembered seeing him lock the door.

4. (A) No, she did not get there on time.
    (B) No, the show was cancelled.
    (C) No, she only saw the band, but did not meet them.
    (D) Yes, she did meet the band.

5. (A) The janitor did not clean.
    (B) The janitor did clean.
    (C) The janitor had the day off.
    (D) The janitor cleaned but did not empty her wastebasket.

6. (A) She does not care for his company.
    (B) She was unaware of his call.
    (C) She did not have the time to call him.
    (D) When she received the message that he called, it was too late to call him back.

7. (A) Late papers are acceptable.
    (B) Late papers will be accepted, but will receive a lower grade.
    (C) Late papers will not be accepted.
    (D) The professor is not concerned when the papers are done, as long as they are well done.

8. (A) The smoke is not a cause for concern.
    (B) The smoke could be coming from his grandmother's house.
    (C) There is a store on fire.
    (D) Someone should call the fire department.

9. (A) She thinks the electricity failed.
    (B) She does not know what is wrong with the computer.
    (C) She thinks that one of the connections is loose.
    (D) The whole computer system is experiencing difficulties, it is not just his computer.

10. (A) They do not allow pets in their apartment building.
    (B) She has not seen the man as often as she once did.
    (C) She saw a moving van outside his apartment.
    (D) He told her he had plans to move soon.

11. (A) She does not like going out.
    (B) She cannot go because she has to write a paper.
    (C) She could not finish the paper, because she went to the show.
    (D) She loves writing papers.

12. (A) In a bookstore   (C) In a library
    (B) In a classroom   (D) In a shopping mall

13. (A) She does not intend to give him notes.
    (B) She thinks he should read the history books himself.
    (C) The new teacher did not want anyone to take notes.
    (D) She did not take notes because she did not think anything important was discussed.

14. (A) This restaurant buys food from a deli.
    (B) They can eat in the restaurant once every week without affecting their budget.
    (C) They are afraid of getting weak if they eat there regularly.
    (D) The restaurant guarantees satisfaction.

15. (A) She wants to do the least amount of reading.
    (B) Though she is not fully prepared, she will take the test.
    (C) She has been reading for the test for a long time.
    (D) She does not want to take the test.

16. (A) She will cook dinner.
    (B) They will go to a party.
    (C) They will skip dinner because they ate too much last night.
    (D) They will eat the food left from last night's party.

17. (A) The man did not attend the meeting.
    (B) He should have talked to her after coming out.
    (C) If he disagreed with the proposals, he should have expressed his views on the spot.
    (D) He did not get time to speak at the meeting.

18. (A) He is not sure whether he should give a birthday gift to Tom.
    (B) A gift certificate is a better gift than a book.
    (C) Tom likes to read different books than him.
    (D) He is not confident about his ability to select.

19. (A) A person should always be careful about his eyes.
    (B) The man should talk to a doctor immediately.
    (C) The man should use contact lenses.
    (D) It is the man's right to consult a doctor.

20. (A) Yes, but he is not the manager.
    (B) No, because the woman is not his boss.
    (C) Yes, but he needs a letter of permission to do that.
    (D) No. He suggests that the woman should get help from the manager.

21. (A) The man should try to learn how to fly.
    (B) Air travel is sometimes less expensive than train travel.
    (C) The man can save some time if he takes a flight.
    (D) Train authorities are not fair.

22. (A) Lisa   (C) Cathy
    (B) A Mechanic   (D) Cathy's friend

23. (A) Drawing a map   (C) Giving orders
    (B) Writing an address (D) Giving directions

24. (A) Mark is no longer young.
    (B) Mark is a good speaker.
    (C) Mark has been kind to people since he was young.
    (D) Mark was given the prize because he was young.

25. (A) Dr. Warner does not like slow people.
     (B) Decisions taken in haste are always good.
     (C) Dr. Warner takes his classes in small rooms.
     (D) If the man waits, he might not get admission to Dr. Warner's course.

Part B

DIRECTIONS: In Part B you will hear extended conversations between two speakers. At the end of each conversation, a third person will ask several questions about what was said. **You will hear each conversation and the questions about it just one time.** They will not be written out for you. Therefore, you must listen carefully to understand what each speaker says. After you hear a conversation and the question about it, read the four possible answers in your test book and decide which one is the best answer to the question you heard. Then on your answer sheet, find the number of the question and fill in the space that corresponds to the answer you have chosen.

26. (A) A play   (C) An opera
     (B) A sports game   (D) A movie

27. (A) He wanted to walk out on it.
     (B) He liked it a lot.
     (C) He would not wait for a ticket.
     (D) He hated it.

28. (A) An hour   (C) He did not wait.
     (B) Two hours   (D) Just a few minutes

29. (A) Two hours
     (B) One hour
     (C) There was no one in front of him.
     (D) He did not wait in line.

30. (A) Monday or Tuesday
    (B) Wednesday or Thursday
    (C) Saturday or Sunday
    (D) Tonight

31. (A) Their families
    (B) High school graduation
    (C) University graduation.
    (D) Business.

32. (A) No, because she is not sure if her parents can attend it.
    (B) Yes, because this is a very important occasion in her life.
    (C) No, because she thinks high school graduation is more fun.
    (D) Yes, because she has waited too long to get her degree.

33. (A) Because they look upon him as a bright student.
    (B) Because they like people with degrees.
    (C) Because he is the first one in the family to get a degree.
    (D) Because they have to travel only 30 miles.

34. (A) Texas
    (B) New York
    (C) Virginia
    (D) Georgia.

35. (A) In a month
    (B) Tomorrow
    (C) Next week
    (D) Tonight

36. (A) Make yardsticks
    (B) Build a farm house
    (C) Make some gardening tools
    (D) Make a fence

37. (A) Because he has his own house.
    (B) Because he was brought up on farms.
    (C) Because he loves fresh vegetables.
    (D) Because he never had a chance to go to school.

38. (A) Vegetables
    (B) Rose plants
    (C) Seeds
    (D) Oil

39. (A) In the man's yard
    (B) In the woman's house
    (C) On the street
    (D) In the garden shop

40. (A) To get some money for helping in the garden
    (B) To get some guidance in gardening
    (C) To ask him to work for their garden
    (D) To ask him to keep a watch on their yard

Part C

DIRECTIONS: In Part C you will hear short talks. At the end of each talk, a second person will ask several questions about what was said. **You will hear each talk and the questions about it just one time.** They will not be written out for you. Therefore, you must listen carefully to understand what each speaker says. After you hear a question, read the four possible answers in your test book and decide which one is the best answer to the question you heard. Then on your answer sheet, find the number of the question and fill in the space that corresponds to the answer you have chosen.

WAIT

41. (A) George Washington   (C) Grover Cleveland
    (B) Abraham Lincoln   (D) Woodrow Wilson

42. (A) Minister   (C) Politician
    (B) Doctor   (D) Farmer

43. (A) Rutgers   (C) Yale
    (B) Harvard   (D) Princeton

44. (A) Massachusetts   (C) New Hampshire
    (B) New Jersey   (D) New York

45. (A) John Adams   (C) Bill Clinton
     (B) Grover Cleveland   (D) George Bush

46. (A) Because it is like a dreamland
     (B) Because it has a short history
     (C) Because Europeans like it
     (D) Because it accommodates thousands of immigrants every year from all over
          the world

47. (A) Political oppression in native countries of the immigrants
     (B) Search for employment
     (C) Love for nature and wildlife
     (D) Exploration of business possibilities

48. (A) From Africa, Asia, and Mexico only
     (B) From all parts of the world
     (C) From Mexico only
     (D) From Asia and Mexico only

49. (A) Business and knowledge
     (B) Political oppression
     (C) Disappointment
     (D) Freedom and opportunity

50. (A) No, they face a lot of disappointments and failures before they are success-
          ful.
     (B) Yes, they get whatever they are looking for as soon as they enter the United
          States.
     (C) Yes, because America is a dreamland.
     (D) No, it involves advanced knowledge.

STOP

If time still remains, you may review work only in this section.
When the time allotted is up, you may go on to the next section.

Section 2:
STRUCTURE AND WRITTEN EXPRESSION

TIME: 25 Minutes
40 Questions

DIRECTIONS: Questions 1-15 are incomplete sentences. Beneath each sentence are four words or phrases marked (A), (B), (C), and (D). Choose the **one** word or phrase which best completes the sentence. Then, on your answer sheet, find the number of the question and fill in the space that corresponds to the answer you have chosen.

---

1.   When he was going away for the weekend, he _____ his neighbor water the lawn.
   (A)   got   (C)   requested
   (B)   has   (D)   had

2.   Not only did many people volunteer to bring food for the picnic, _____

   _____.
   (A)   but also drinks and games.
   (B)   many people offered to bring drinks and games.
   (C)   many people did not offer to bring drinks and games.
   (D)   they brought food.

3.   Vasco Núñez de Balboa _____ the Pacific Ocean in 1513.
   (A)   was discovered
   (B)   had discover
   (C)   discovered
   (D)   discover

4.   While my brother has excellent eyesight, he _____ hard of hearing.
   (A)   has   (C)   was
   (B)   is   (D)   isn't

5.   My cousin lives _____ a farm.
   (A)   at   (C)   in
   (B)   on   (D)   within

331

6. When she was a young girl, she used to wish she _____ a princess.
   (A)   were
   (B)   was
   (C)   is
   (D)   became

7. Travelers checks are useful when one is travelling because _____ people refuse to accept them.
   (A)   quite a few
   (B)   a few
   (C)   few
   (D)   many

8. We usually expect that _____ bring bad news.
   (A)   a telegram
   (B)   telegrams
   (C)   telegram
   (D)   the telegrams

9. If we _____ salt, the soup would have been tastier.
   (A)   add
   (B)   could add
   (C)   don't add
   (D)   had added

10. For a variety of reasons, many American young adults are returning home or are not leaving home at all, _____.
    (A)   which has made families to react in different ways.
    (B)   which makes families react in different ways to this.
    (C)   to which makes families react in different ways.
    (D)   which is making families react in different ways.

11. Had I run out of gas, I _____ called the garage.
    (A)   had
    (B)   would have
    (C)   would
    (D)   should have

12. Paterson was angry _____ his friend and threw a book at him.
    (A)   with
    (B)   at
    (C)   on
    (D)   about

13. You _____ better study a lot next week, if you want to get through that exam.
    (A)   should
    (B)   had
    (C)   will
    (D)   must

14. Your friends won't be late, _____?

    (A) won't they   (C) isn't it
    (B) will they   (D) is it

15. _____ guns had been made by skilled

    gunsmiths, one at a time.

    (A) In 1798, Eli Whitney came up with a new idea,
    (B) In 1798, when Eli Whitney came up with a new idea,
    (C) Since 1798 Eli Whitney had been working on a new idea,
    (D) Until 1798, when Eli Whitney came up with a new idea,

---

DIRECTIONS: In questions 16-40 each sentence has four underlined words or phrases, marked (A), (B), (C), and (D). Choose the **one** word or phrase which is incorrect and must be changed to make the sentence correct. Then, on your answer sheet, find the number of the question and fill in the space that corresponds to the answer you have chosen.

16. The lab's conversational desk top is a voice-controlled computer system that acts
         A   B   C

     like an automatic receptionist, personal secretary, and travel agent which screening
                                                              D

     all calls, taking messages, and making airline reservations.

17. Even among the general public, consciousness has been raised high enough so that
                                                A   B

     anyone sporting finery made from the skins of an endangered animal run the risk
                                                                      C

     of at least a verbal assault.
                D

18. Coastal erosion is the only natural process that has altered the world's shorelines
                       A   B   C

     ever since the oceans formed first some three billion years ago.
                              D

19. Surveys note however, that the elderly are frequent victims of certain types of
                      A

     crimes, like purse-snatching.
        B   C   D

20. Noise is external and excessive stimulus that increases rather than decreases
                  A   B   C   D

     your tension.

21. Although teachers around the world are separated by thousands of miles, their
         A   B

     methods of trying to encourage children to write springs from a common source.
             C   D

22. The professor managed to attending to the needs of his family while working day
                      A   B   C

    and night for the prestigious award.
             D

23. Jan later laughs about having fell into the pond, although she was very
               A   B   C

    embarrassed about it then.
           D

24. Only one egg hatched after twenty-eight days, while all the others hatched after
                                  A   B C

    twenty-ninth day.
         D

25. A few and the 50 stamps that my sister had were either for sale or trade.
        A B   C   D

26. My grandmother could never understand why I preferred a 20-stories building
                                        A   B

    to a rambling house in the fields.
       C   D

27. "The Starlight Cafe" is a good place for order seafood but not to order meat.
             A   B   C D

28. The legendary Robin Hood used to steal from the rich people to give to all poor.
      A   B   C   D

29. Although the poor families are fast learning the new trade, the lack of education
                           A   B

    are hampering their advancement.
       C   D

30. In the event something happening to the family, the lawyer assured her that the
          A   B   C
    house would go to her friend.
              D

31. The entire city except the western section is being plunge into darkness for
            A   B   C   D
    the night.

32. Frank and Anna Johnson had a daughter who were born in 1950, but who died
                              A   B   C
    a few years later.
              D

33. Americans tend to embody to what many is a curious combination of admiration
                            A   B
    for their political system in general and disdain for its particular operations.
    C   D

34. I have been having headaches so often later that I think I ought to see a doctor.
      A   B C   D

35. Thousands years ago, the world had several ice ages; or periods of time when the
    A   B   C
    climate was very cold and thick sheets of ice covered much of the earth.
                                                   D

36. Hunger is not an unavoidable phenomena as are death and taxes.
      A   B   C   D

37. Peter Weir, the prominent Australian filmmaker and screenplay writer, and
                    A   B
    was planning to visit the United States to make a film.
      C   D

38. While most Americans may admire a person who speaks more than one language,
—— A ————————————— themselves B —
most of them do not place any value on learning another language themself.
—————————————————————————— C ———————————————————————————— D

39. Having spent his childhood longing for books, Andrew Carnegie realized their
————— A
value and went on to become the largest donor of funds the American public
———————————— B —————————————————————————————— C
library system has ever had donors.
———————————————— D

40. The survival instinct of cockroaches are so great that they are known to reproduce
——— A ——————————————— is B ————————————— C
even within a ring of fire.
——————— D

(**STOP**)

If time still remains, you may review work only in this section.
When the time allotted is up, you may go on to the next section.

Section 3:
READING COMPREHENSION
AND VOCABULARY

TIME: 55 Minutes
         60 Questions

> **DIRECTIONS**: In this section you will read several passages. Each one is followed by several questions about it. You are to choose the best answer to each question, marked (A), (B), (C), and (D). Then, on your answer sheet, find the number of the question and fill in the space that corresponds to the answer you have chosen.

Questions 1–10 refer to the following passage.

1   As viewed from space, Earth's distinguishing characteristics are its blue waters and white clouds. Enveloped by an ocean of air consisting of 78% nitrogen and 21% oxygen, the planet is the only one in our solar system known to harbor life. Circling the Sun at an average distance of 149 million km (93 million miles), Earth is the third planet from the Sun and the
5   fifth largest planet in the solar system.
    Its rapid spin and molten nickel-iron core give rise to an extensive magnetic field which, coupled with the atmosphere, shields us from nearly all of the harmful radiation coming from the Sun and other stars. Most meteors burn up in the Earth's atmosphere before they can strike the surface. The planet's active geological processes have left no evidence of
10   the ancient pelting it almost certainly received soon after it was formed.
    The Earth has a single natural satellite—the Moon.

1.   Approximately how much of the Earth's atmosphere is nitrogen?
    (A)   One-fourth
    (B)   One-half
    (C)   Three-fourths
    (D)   All of it

2.   Which of the following helps to create Earth's magnetic fields?
    (A)   Its blue waters
    (B)   Its nitrogen atmosphere
    (C)   Its molten metal core
    (D)   The Moon

3. What two factors help protect the Earth from radiation?
   (A) Magnetic field and atmosphere
   (B) Rapid spin and molten iron-nickel core
   (C) The Sun and the Moon
   (D) Blue waters and white clouds

4. In line 2, "consisting" most nearly means
   (A) hardening.   (C) withholding.
   (B) containing.   (D) shortening

5. Why does the Earth show almost no signs of having been hit by numerous meteors in the past?
   (A) Humans have built over most of the craters.
   (B) Most meteors fell into the ocean and not on land.
   (C) Earth's magnetic field repelled most meteors.
   (D) Earth's natural geologic activity has eliminated most traces.

6. The main idea of this passage is that
   (A) there are life-supporting characteristics on Earth.
   (B) Earth is predominantly water.
   (C) Earth has no common characteristics with other planets.
   (D) Earth is the only planet with a moon.

7. The word "distinguishing" as it is used in this selection means
   (A) elevating in nature.
   (B) devastating in nature.
   (C) characteristics like all other planets.
   (D) characteristics that set it apart from other planets.

8. It's probable that the next paragraph would discuss
   (A) people on planets.
   (B) the solar system as a whole.
   (C) the Earth's natural satellite—the Moon.
   (D) rings around Saturn.

9. As used in this selection, the word "harbor" is synonymous with
   (A) support   (C) water
   (B) surround   (D) include

βxC

10. This selection leads one to believe that
   (A) Earth never gets hit by meteors.
   (B) Earth always gets hit by meteors.
   (C) Earth was hit by meteors in some past time period.
   (D) Earth may be bombarded by meteors in the near future.

Questions 11–20 refer to the following passage

1   Since life began eons ago, thousands of creatures have come and gone. Some, such as
the dinosaurs, became extinct due to naturally changing ecologic conditions. More recent
threats to life forms are humans and their activities. Man has drained marshes, burned
prairies, damned and diverted rivers. Some of the more recent casualties of man's expansion
5 have been the dodo, great auk, passenger pigeon, Irish elk, and Steller's sea cow.
       Sadly, we can no longer attribute the increasing decline in our wild animals and plant
species to "natural" processes. Many species are dying out because of exploitation, habitat
alteration or destruction, pollution, or the introduction of new species of plants and animals
to an area. As mandated by Congress, protecting endangered species, and restoring them to
10 the point where their existence is no longer jeopardized, is the primary objective of the U.S.
Fish and Wildlife Service's Endangered Species Program.

11. In line 1, "eons" most nearly means
   (A) ages.   (C) animals.
   (B) particles.   (D) conditions.

12. Which of the following is a form of man's habitat alteration?
   (A) Glacial encroachment
   (B) Hurricanes
   (C) Damned rivers
   (D) Snowstorms

13. Which of the following have become extinct due to man's destruction?
   (A) African elephants
   (B) Irish elk
   (C) Giant panda
   (D) White bengal

14. Which of the following would be a likely theme for the next paragraph?
   (A) Naturally changing ecological conditions
   (B) Animals that have become extinct
   (C) Achievements of the government Endangered Species Program
   (D) Programs that have destroyed natural habitats

15. In line 6, "attribute" most nearly means
    (A) assign.   (C) introduce.
    (B) characteristic.   (D) change.

16. The tone of this passage is
    (A) nationalistic   (C) anti-wildlife
    (B) pro-wildlife   (D) feminist

17. "Habitat alteration" as used in this paragraph means
    (A) changing clothes.
    (B) changing animals' environments.
    (C) changing humans' environments.
    (D) climate change.

18. According to this passage,
    (A) man is the cause of some animal extinction.
    (B) animals often bring about their own extinction.
    (C) Congress can absolutely end extinction of animals.
    (D) a law is more important than human responsibility.

19. Which of the following is NOT a cause of increasing decline of wild animal population?
    (A) Exploitation
    (B) Pollution
    (C) Habitat alteration
    (D) Congressional law

20. The primary objective of the U.S. Fish and Wildlife Service's Endangered Species Program can be stated as
    (A) custodial care of endangered species.
    (B) enforcement of Congressional law.
    (C) education of the public.
    (D) stopping pollution.

Questions 21–30 refer to the following passage.

1   With the sudden onset of severe psychotic symptoms, the individual is said to be experiencing acute schizophrenia. "Psychotic" means out of touch with reality, or unable to separate real from unreal experiences. Some people have only one such psychotic episode; others have many episodes during a lifetime but lead relatively normal lives during interim

5 periods. The individual with chronic (continuous or recurring) schizophrenia often does not fully recover normal functioning and typically requires long-term treatment, generally including medication, to control the symptoms. These symptoms may include hallucinations, incoherence, delusions, lack of judgment, deterioration of the abilities to reason and feel emotion, and a lack of interaction between the patient and his environment. The hallucina-

10 tions may be of a visual, auditory, or tactile variety. Some chronic schizophrenic patients may never be able to function without assistance of one sort or another.

21.   In line 3, "episode" most nearly means
      (A)   program.   (C)   treatment.
      (B)   experience.   (D)   assistance.

22.   Which of the following is NOT a symptom of schizophrenia?
      (A)   Hallucinations   (C)   Incoherence
      (B)   Delusions   (D)   Vertigo

23.   According to the passage, how many different types of hallucinations are there?
      (A)   1   (C)   3
      (B)   2   (D)   4

24.   In line 4, "interim" most nearly means
      (A)   temporary.   (C)   constant.
      (B)   continuous.   (D)   unreal.

25.   In line 10, "tactile" most nearly means
      (A)   touch.   (C)   sight.
      (B)   smell.   (D)   taste.

26.   "Acute" as used to describe schizophrenia in the passage means
      (A)   chronic.   (C)   severe.
      (B)   recurring.   (D)   mild.

27. It can be inferred from the passage that a person experiencing acute schizophrenia most likely
    (A)   cannot live without medication .
    (B)   cannot go on living.
    (C)   can hold a full-time job.
    (D)   cannot distinguish real from unreal.

28. According to this passage, thinking that one can fly might be an example of
    (A)   medicine overdose.
    (B)   being out of touch with reality.
    (C)   recovering normal functioning.
    (D)   symptom control.

29. The passage suggests that the beginning of severe psychotic symptoms of acute schizophrenia may be any of the following EXCEPT
    (A)   debilitating.
    (B)   sudden.
    (C)   occurring after a long period of normalcy.
    (D)   drug-induced.

30. The passage implies that normal life may be possible for the chronic schizophrenic with the help of
    (A)   medicines.
    (B)   neurotic episodes.
    (C)   psychotic episodes.
    (D)   time.

Questions 31–40 refer to the following passage.

1   Stress is with us all the time. It comes from mental or emotional activity as well as physical activity. It is unique and personal to each of us. So personal, in fact, that what may be relaxing to one person may be stressful to another. For example, if you're a busy executive who likes to keep occupied all of the time, "taking it easy" at the beach on a beautiful day may
5   feel extremely frustrating, nonproductive, and upsetting. You may be emotionally distressed from "doing nothing." Too much emotional stress can cause physical illnesses such as high blood pressure, ulcers, or even heart disease. Physical stress from work or exercise is not likely to cause such ailments. The truth is that physical exercise can help you to relax and to better handle your mental or emotional stress.

31. In line 2, "unique" most nearly means
    (A) stressful.
    (B) distinctive.
    (C) brisk.
    (D) relaxing.

32. Which of the following people would find "taking it easy" stressful?
    (A) Construction worker
    (B) Business executive
    (C) Farm worker
    (D) Truck driver

33. In line 5, "distressed" most nearly means
    (A) upset.
    (B) distinctive.
    (C) relaxed.
    (D) active.

34. In line 8, "ailments" most nearly means
    (A) traits.
    (B) characteristics.
    (C) episodes.
    (D) illnesses.

35. Which of the following would be a determinant as to what people find stressful?
    (A) Personality
    (B) Education
    (C) Marital status
    (D) Shoe size

36. This article, published by the Department of Health and Human Services, probably came from the
    (A) Federal Bureau of Investigation.
    (B) Alcohol, Drug Abuse, and Mental Health Administration.
    (C) Education Administration.
    (D) Communicable Diseases Administration.

37. Stress is
    (A) optional.
    (B) relaxing.
    (C) manageable.
    (D) the same for all people.

38. A source of stress NOT specifically mentioned in this passage is
    (A) educational activity.
    (B) physical activity.
    (C) mental activity.
    (D) emotional activity.

39. Physical problems caused by emotional stress can appear as all of the following except
    (A) ulcers.   (C) heart disease.
    (B) pregnancy.   (D) high blood pressure.

40. One method mentioned to help handle stress is
    (A) physical exercise.   (C) drugs.
    (B) tranquilizers.   (D) taking it easy.

Questions 41–50 refer to the following passage.

1   The "Karat" marking on jewelry tells you what proportion of gold is mixed with other
metals. If 14 parts of gold are mixed with 10 parts of base metal, the combination is called
14 Karat (14K) gold. The higher the Karat rating, the higher the proportion of gold in the
object. The lowest Karat gold that can be marketed in the United States is 10 Karat. Jewelry
5 does not have to be marked with its Karat quality, but most of it is. If there is a Karat quality
mark, next to it must be the U.S. registered trademark of the person or company that will stand
behind the mark, as required by the National Gold and Silver Stamping Act.

41. In line 1, "proportion" most nearly means
    (A) ratio.   (C) registered.
    (B) mix.   (D) quality.

42. If a ring is stamped 24K, it has
    (A) 204 parts gold.
    (B) 24 parts gold.
    (C) two and four-tenths parts gold.
    (D) 10 parts gold.

43. In line 6, "registered" most nearly means
    (A) documented.   (C) mixed.
    (B) marketed.   (D) stamped.

44. According to the passage, the phrase "stand behind" most nearly means
    (A) not in front.   (C) back up.
    (B) to the side.   (D) give up.

45. In line 4, "marketed" most nearly means
    (A) engraved.   (C) mixed.
    (B) registered.   (D) sold.

46. "Karat," as it used in the jewelry industry, refers to the
    (A) jeweler's appraisal.
    (B) U.S. registered trademark.
    (C) amount of gold mixed with other metals.
    (D) money value.

47. Gold which is 10 Karat in proportion
    (A) represents the highest grade of gold in the U.S.
    (B) cannot be sold in the U.S.
    (C) never carries a Karat quality mark.
    (D) represents the lowest-grade gold marketable in the U.S.

48. If gold is marked with a Karat quality mark, it must also
    (A) bear a national gold and silver stamp.
    (B) bear the registered trademark of the entity standing behind the mark.
    (C) bear a "made in the USA" mark.
    (D) bear a percentage mark.

49. If the jewelry is marked, 14 parts of gold mixed with 10 parts of base metal will always bear
    (A) a 14K mark.
    (B) a 10K mark.
    (C) an 18K mark.
    (D) a platinum mark.

50. This paragraph conveys to the consumer
    (A) important buying information.
    (B) a challenge to buy more gold.
    (C) a debate over gold prices.
    (D) advice about buying silver.

Questions 51–60 refer to the following passage.

1   Mr. Faugel was convinced that student nervousness had affected their scores; to reduce the anxiety of those students who had already been tested, he gave 22 of them a beta blocker before readministration of the test. Their scores improved significantly. The other 8 students (who did not receive the beta blockers) improved only slightly. Second-time test-
5 takers nationwide had average improvements which were similar to those in Faugel's non-beta blocker group.
       Beta blockers are prescription drugs which have been around for 25 years. These medications, which interfere with the effects of adrenaline, have been used for heart conditions

and for minor stress such as stage fright. Now they are used for test anxiety. These drugs seem
10   to help test-takers who have low scores because of test fright, but not those who do not know
the material. Since there can be side effects from these beta blockers, physicians are not ready
to prescribe them routinely for all test-takers.

51.   In line 2, "reduce" most nearly means
    (A)   increase.   (C)   lessen.
    (B)   maximize.   (D)   build up.

52.   Beta blockers have been around since approximately what year?
    (A)   1790   (C)   1950
    (B)   1907   (D)   1970

53.   Where is the only place a person can obtain beta blockers?
    (A)   Supermarket
    (B)   Convenience store
    (C)   Stationery store
    (D)   Doctor's office

54.   In line 8, "interfere" most nearly means
    (A)   hinder.   (C)   help.
    (B)   aid.   (D)   prescribe.

55.   Why are beta blockers not prescribed regularly?
    (A)   Students are expected to do poorly.
    (B)   There are side effects.
    (C)   The drugs are only 25 years old.
    (D)   They cause test anxiety.

56.   According to the passage
    (A)   all people can take beta blockers.
    (B)   beta blockers are widely prescribed.
    (C)   beta blockers work only on test anxiety.
    (D)   beta blockers work only to improve test scores if the test-taker truly
            knows the material.

57. "Readministration" in this passage refers to
    (A) giving the test again to people without administering beta blockers.
    (B) giving the test again to both groups after beta blockers have been administered to one group.
    (C) giving the test to both groups of test-takers and then giving them beta blockers.
    (D) giving the beta blockers without retesting.

58. What possible use for beta blockers was NOT discussed in this passage?
    (A) Test anxiety   (C) Minor stress
    (B) Pain relief   (D) Heart conditions

59. Beta blockers work on some physical and emotional symptoms because they
    (A) fool a person into a healthier stance.
    (B) interfere with the side effects of adrenaline.
    (C) produce side effects worse than the symptoms.
    (D) primarily change human thought processes.

60. Faugel's research showed that beta blockers given to his sample
    (A) increased scores less than the national average.
    (B) increased scores the same as the national average.
    (C) decreased scores.
    (D) increased scores much more than the national average.

STOP

If time still remains, you may review your work only in this section.

TEST 1

ANSWER KEY

SECTION 1: LISTENING COMPREHENSION

1.	(C)	14.	(B)	26.	(D)	39.	(A)
2.	(D)	15.	(B)	27.	(B)	40.	(B)
3.	(B)	16.	(D)	28.	(A)	41.	(C)
4.	(D)	17.	(C)	29.	(A)	42.	(A)
5.	(A)	18.	(C)	30.	(C)	43.	(D)
6.	(B)	19.	(B)	31.	(C)	44.	(B)
7.	(C)	20.	(D)	32.	(B)	45.	(A)
8.	(B)	21.	(B)	33.	(C)	46.	(D)
9.	(C)	22.	(C)	34.	(A)	47.	(C)
10.	(B)	23.	(D)	35.	(C)	48.	(B)
11.	(B)	24.	(B)	36.	(D)	49.	(D)
12.	(C)	25.	(D)	37.	(B)	50.	(A)
13.	(D)			38.	(C)		

SECTION 2: STRUCTURE AND WRITTEN EXPRESSION

1.	(D)	11.	(B)	21.	(D)	31.	(D)
2.	(A)	12.	(A)	22.	(A)	32.	(B)
3.	(C)	13.	(B)	23.	(B)	33.	(A)
4.	(B)	14.	(B)	24.	(D)	34.	(B)
5.	(B)	15.	(D)	25.	(A)	35.	(A)
6.	(A)	16.	(D)	26.	(B)	36.	(C)
7.	(C)	17.	(C)	27.	(B)	37.	(B)
8.	(B)	18.	(D)	28.	(D)	38.	(D)
9.	(D)	19.	(B)	29.	(C)	39.	(D)
10.	(D)	20.	(A)	30.	(A)	40.	(B)

SECTION 3: READING COMPREHENSION AND VOCABULARY

1.	(C)	16.	(B)	31.	(B)	46.	(C)
2.	(C)	17.	(B)	32.	(B)	47.	(D)
3.	(A)	18.	(A)	33.	(A)	48.	(B)
4.	(B)	19.	(D)	34.	(D)	49.	(A)
5.	(D)	20.	(A)	35.	(A)	50.	(A)
6.	(A)	21.	(B)	36.	(B)	51.	(C)
7.	(D)	22.	(D)	37.	(C)	52.	(D)
8.	(C)	23.	(C)	38.	(A)	53.	(D)
9.	(A)	24.	(A)	39.	(B)	54.	(A)
10.	(C)	25.	(A)	40.	(A)	55.	(B)
11.	(A)	26.	(C)	41.	(A)	56.	(D)
12.	(C)	27.	(D)	42.	(B)	57.	(B)
13.	(B)	28.	(B)	43.	(A)	58.	(B)
14.	(C)	29.	(D)	44.	(C)	59.	(B)
15.	(A)	30.	(A)	45.	(D)	60.	(D)

Detailed Explanations
of Answers

TEST 1

Section 1:
LISTENING COMPREHENSION

Part A

1.   **(C)**   The question asked was, "What does the man mean?" The correct answer is (C)—He thinks the hat looks good on her. The woman said to the man, "I'm not sure if I like this hat on me. Do you like it?" The man replied, "I think it brings out the green in your eyes. Look in the mirror and see for yourself." He meant that he thought the hat was very becoming.

2.   **(D)**   The question asked was, "What does the woman think about the team?" The correct answer is (D)—The woman thinks the team has a very good chance of winning. When asked if she thinks the team will win the game, she replied, "They are only 10 points behind now. If they can keep playing this well, they certainly will."

3.   **(B)**   The question asked was, "What does the woman mean?" The correct answer is (B)—The man was supposed to have locked the door on his way out. When asked if she remembers if the door was locked, the woman replied, "Well, I didn't lock the door. You were the last one out!"

4.   **(D)**   The question asked was, "Did the woman meet the rock band?" The correct response is (D)—Yes she did meet the band. The man asked the woman, "Did you get to meet the rock and roll band?" The woman responded, "Everyone except the drummer autographed my album, and the lead singer kissed my cheek." If she had not met the band, she would not have been able to get her album autographed.

5. **(A)** The question asked was, "What does the woman mean?" The correct answer is (A)—The janitor did not clean. When asked if she thought the janitor cleaned last night, the woman replied, "Well, there was still trash in my wastebasket when I arrived this morning." The woman implied that the janitor did not clean.

6. **(B)** The question asked was, "Why didn't the woman return the man's call?" The correct answer is (B)—She was unaware of his call. The woman implies that, had she known that he called, she would have returned his phone call.

7. **(C)** The question asked was, "What does the woman mean?" The correct answer is (C)—Late papers will not be accepted. The man said, "Do you think that the professor will allow me to hand it [the paper] in late?," and the woman replied, "Dr. Hatton said that he would not accept any late papers."

8. **(B)** The question asked was, "What is the man thinking?" The correct answer is (B)—The smoke could be coming from his grandmother's house. When the woman noticed the smoke and said, "I bet there is a fire," the man replied, "That is the direction of Grandma's house!!"

9. **(C)** The question asked was, "What does the woman think is wrong with the computer?" The correct answer is (C)—She thinks one of the connections is loose. When the man asked the woman what was wrong with his computer, the woman replied "Have you checked all the connections in the back? Maybe one is loose."

10. **(B)** The question asked was, "Why does the woman think the man has moved?" The correct response is (B)—She has not seen the man as often as she once did. The woman said, "I rarely see you around here any more, I thought you moved."

11. **(B)** The question asked was, "What does the woman mean?" The answer is (B)— She cannot go because she has to write a paper. The woman clearly states, "I would have loved to go, but I still have not finished writing my paper...."

12. **(C)** The question asked was, "Where did this conversation probably take place?" The answer is (C)—In a library. The woman was looking for a book. The man said "Maybe somebody already borrowed it. Let's check the subject catalog." A library has catalogs and books for borrowing.

13. **(D)** The question asked was, "What is the woman trying to say?" The answer is (D)—She did not take notes because she did not think anything important was discussed. The woman said "I didn't take any.... I thought I could find them (dates) in any history book."

14. **(B)** The question asked was, "What do they think of the restaurant?" The answer is (B)—They can eat in the restaurant once every week without affecting their budget. The man said, "We can afford to eat here once a week...." And the woman responded "Oh yes! I agree one hundred percent."

15. **(B)** The question asked was, "What does the woman mean?" The answer is (B)— Though she is not fully prepared, she will take the test. When the man asked if she was prepared for the test the woman answered, "Not really.... But I will take the test anyway."

16. **(D)** The question asked was, "What will they probably do about dinner?" The answer is (D)—They will eat the food left from last night's party. When the woman asked if she should cook some dinner, the man answered, "I don't think so. There is enough left over from the party last night.

17. **(C)** The question asked was, "What does the woman think?" The answer is (C)— If he disagreed with the proposals, he should have expressed his views on the spot. The man said, "...But I didn't agree with most of their proposals." The woman's response was, "Well, why didn't you speak out at that time?" She meant he should have expressed his views at that moment.

18. **(C)** The question asked was, "What does the man mean?" The answer is (C)— Tom likes to read different books than him. The man said, "I am not sure he cares for the type of books that we would select."

19. **(B)** The question asked was, "What does the woman suggest?" The answer is (B)—The man should talk to a doctor immediately. The woman remarked, "...You should contact a doctor right away."

20. **(D)** The question asked was, "Is the man willing to help?" The answer is (D)— No. He suggests that the woman should get help from the manager. When asked to pick up a bottle, the man answered, "I don't work here. Maybe you can get a ladder from the manager."

21. **(B)** The question asked was, "What does the woman mean?" The answer is (B)— Air travel is sometimes less expensive than train travel." The woman said, "Airfares are sometimes much cheaper than train fares."

22. **(C)** The question asked was, "Who fixed the toaster?" The answer is (C)—Cathy. The woman said, "No, she had it fixed by her friend Cathy." This means her friend Cathy fixed it for her.

23. **(D)** The question asked was, "What is the woman doing?" The answer is (D)— Giving directions. The woman said, "Go straight and make a right on Morris Street. The bank is right on the corner." It is while giving directions one may tell people where to turn left or right and where a place is located.

24. **(B)** The question asked was, "What does the woman think about Mark?" The answer is (B)—Mark is a good speaker. The woman said, "…He (Mark) had been good at public speaking since he was young."

25. **(D)** The question asked was, "What is the woman's opinion?" The answer is (D)—If the man waits, he might not get admission to Dr. Warner's course." The woman said, "Dr. Warner does not allow more than 15 students in his class. If you want to do it (take a course with him), you'd better make your decision fast."

Part B

26. **(D)** The question asked was, "What did the man go see?" The correct response is (D)—A movie. The woman asks, "Was it any good?" The man then proceeds to explain how he waited in line for it. The listener can infer from the conversation that he did go to see the movie

27. **(B)** The question asked was, "What did the man think of the movie?" The correct response is (B)—He liked it a lot. He told her, "The acting was fantastic and the plot had me on the edge of my seat." To be "on the edge of your seat" is to be waiting with anticipation for the events that are about to occur.

28. **(A)** The question asked was, "How long did the man wait in line?" The correct response is (A)—An hour. He told the woman, "I had to wait in line over an hour to get a ticket."

29. **(A)**   The question asked was, "How long did the people in front of him wait in line?" The correct answer is (A)—Two hours. The people in front of him waited on line for an hour before he arrived, and you have to add to that the hour he waited on line before they began to sell the tickets.

30. **(C)**   The question asked was, "When will the woman go to see the movie?" The correct response is (C)—Saturday or Sunday. The woman told the man, "I think I will try to go this weekend." The weekend is normally considered to be Saturday and Sunday. The other answer choices are all weekdays.

31. **(C)**   The question asked was, "What are these people talking about?" The answer is (C)—University graduation. In the conversation, the woman said that she missed her high school graduation so this was to be a big event for her. The man said, "I am the first one in the family to graduate from a university...," which hints of a college graduation.

32. **(B)**   The question asked was, "Is the woman looking forward to her graduation?" The answer is (B)—Yes, because this is a very important occasion in her life. When the man asked, "Aren't you excited about it?", she replied, "Of course, I am. I couldn't attend my high school graduation, so this is a really big event for me."

33. **(C)**   The question asked was, "Why is the man's graduation important to his family?" The answer is (C)—Because he is the first one in the family to get a degree. The man said, "I am the first one in the family to graduate from a university so they are all looking forward to it."

34. **(A)**   The question asked was, "What state do the woman's parents live in?" The answer is (A)—Texas. The woman said, "...They live in Texas."

35. **(C)**   The question asked was, "When is the graduation?" The answer is (C)—Next week. The man said, "I can't believe it is only a week from now!" The woman asked, "What?" And he replied, "Our college graduation...."

36. **(D)**   The question asked was, "What is the man planning to do with the wood?" The answer is (D)—Make a fence. When the woman asked "...What is all this wood for?," the man answered, "I am planning to make a wooden fence for my yard."

37. **(B)**   The question asked was, "Why does the man have an interest in gardening?" The answer is (B)—Because he was brought up on farms. When the woman was surprised to learn of the man's gardening experience, the man's response was, "I grew up on farms." What he implied was, "It is natural, because I grew up on farms."

38. **(C)**   The question asked was, "What is the man's father going to send?" The answer is (C)—Seeds. In the conversation, the man mentioned that he was going to get some seeds for vegetables from his father.

39. **(A)**   The question asked was, "Where did this conversation probably take place?" The answer is (A)—In the man's yard. The conversation took place in the man's yard because the woman remarked upon the pile of wood which was to be used to build the new fence.

40. **(B)**   The question asked was, "Why would the woman go to Mike if John agreed to have a garden?" The answer is (B)—To get some guidance in gardening. Towards the end of the conversation, the woman said, "…and if he agrees to have a little garden in our yard, I will come to you for gardening tips." Tips here means guidance or suggestions and not money.

Part C

41. **(C)**   The question asked was, "Who was the first democrat elected after the Civil War?" The correct response is (C)—Grover Cleveland. The speaker said, "Woodrow Wilson was only the second democrat (Grover Cleveland was the first) elected president since the Civil War."

42. **(A)**   The question asked was, "What did Woodrow Wilson's father do?" The correct response is (A)—Minister. The speaker said that Wilson was "the son of a Presbyterian minister."

43. **(D)**   The question asked was, "Where did Woodrow Wilson earn his doctoral degree?" The correct response is (D)—Princeton. The speaker said, "After earning a doctorate at Johns Hopkins University, he taught history and political science at Princeton, and in 1902 became the president of that university.

44. **(B)** The question asked was, "Which state did Woodrow Wilson govern?" The correct response is (B)—New Jersey. The speaker says, "In 1910 he was elected governor of New Jersey as a reform or progressive Democrat." You know that Wilson was elected president and that he would govern the United States, but the question asks specifically for a single state.

45. **(A)** The question asked was, "Who was the last person before Woodrow Wilson to personally address Congress?" The correct response is (A)—John Adams. The speaker's final sentence is "On April 8, 1913 he became the first president since John Adams to appear personally before Congress to promote his program."

46. **(D)** The question asked was, "Why is the United States a unique nation?" The answer is (D)—Because it accommodates thousands of immigrants every year from all over the world. The first statement in the essay was, "The United States is a unique nation in that it absorbs thousands of immigrants every year...."

47. **(C)** The question asked was, "Which one of the following is not a reason for immigration?" The answer is (C)—Love for nature and wildlife. This choice was not mentioned in the essay as a reason for immigration.

48. **(B)** The question asked was, "From where do people emigrate to the United States?" The answer is (B)—From all parts of the world. In the essay you heard, "...People emigrate here from all parts of the world"—not from strictly one country or continent.

49. **(D)** The question asked was, "To the immigrants, what does America stand for?" The answer is (D)—Freedom and opportunity. In the essay you heard "Still, to every immigrant, America stands for freedom and opportunity."

50. **(A)** The question asked was, "Is the transition easy for immigrants?" The answer is (A)—No, they face a lot of disappointments and failures before they are successful. In the talk you heard "...of course, most of the immigrants have to meet with a lot of disillusionment before they are successful."

Section 2:
STRUCTURE AND WRITTEN EXPRESSION

1. **(D)** (A) is incorrect because **got** should be followed by **to water the lawn.** The structure is **getting someone to do something.** (B) is incorrect, as the sentence talks about an incident that took place in the past, when he went away for the weekend. (C) is incorrect because **requested,** like **got,** has to be followed by **to do something.** (D) is the correct answer. The structure is **have someone do something** for the person. As the sentence is in the past tense, the verb should be **had.**

2. **(A)** (A) is the correct answer. **Not only... but also** is the structure. They not only offered to bring food, but also drinks and games. (B) is incorrect because **many people** is redundant and **not only** would not be necessary if the sentence is simply about what people offered to bring. (C) is incorrect because **not only** suggests immediately that people offered more than to bring just food for the picnic. (D) is incorrect for the same reason as (C).

3. **(C)** (A) is incorrect, as it suggests that Núñez de Balboa was discovered, rather than the ocean. (B) is incorrect because **had** must be followed by the past participle of the verb. (C) is the correct answer. The simple past tense must be used to describe an action that took place on a specific date. (D) is incorrect because the verb has not been put in the right tense.

4. **(B)** (B) is the correct answer. The structure is **to be hard of hearing.** So in use, the structure would read **He is hard of hearing, The old men are hard of hearing.** (A) is incorrect because **has** is used with **poor vision.** (C) is incorrect because the sentence is in the present. (D) is incorrect because **while** is used when comparing the brother's senses—**While one is good, the other is poor.**—and not to suggest that both are good.

5. **(B)** (A) is incorrect because **at** suggests nearness rather than exactness with reference to places. (B) is correct because the accepted preposition used with **farm** is **on.** (C). Although this would be the obvious choice as in **live in a house,** or **live in New York,** it is incorrect when used with **farm.** (D) is incorrect because it suggests confinement to a place.

6. **(A)** (A) is the correct answer. Wishes are always used with **were,** whether in the past or present, e.g., **I wish I were a....** (B) is incorrect. Although this would be the obvious choice because third person singular is used with **was,** the verb **wish** changes

that to **were**. (C) is incorrect because the entire sentence is in the past. (D) is incorrect because the young girl can only wish she **could become** (the future past tense).

7.   **(C)**   (A) is incorrect because it contradicts the sentence. Why would they be useful if quite a few people don't accept them? (B) is incorrect. Here it is important to pay attention to the difference between **few** and **a few**. **Few** signifies a lesser number than **a few**. In this sentence the least number is preferred. (C) is correct. Few used without an article means that there are **very few people** who would accept the checks. (D) is incorrect for the same reason as (A).

8.   **(B)**   (A) is incorrect because the verb is conjugated to the third person plural, while the subject is in the third person singular. (B) is the correct answer. The plural noun is used to represent the entire class of telegrams. (C) is incorrect for the same reason as (A). (D) is incorrect because when referring to telegrams as a class, it is not required to use **the**.

9.   **(D)**   (A) is incorrect because the sentence is in the past as indicated by the verb **would have**. (B) is incorrect. **Could add** means that the salt could be added later, but the sentence is in the past. (C) is incorrect. If we **had not added** the salt, the soup would have been tastier. The verb **don't add** is inconsistent with the sentence. (D) is correct. Since the first action should have taken place before the second action, the tense to be used is past perfect. **If we had added salt, the soup would have been tastier.**

10.   **(D)**   (A) is incorrect. The use of the present perfect in the second half of the sentence is not consistent with the correct tense throughout. The use of the preposition **to** is incorrect also. The correct structure is **make families react to something.** (B) is incorrect. **To this** is redundant because of the presence of **which,** a relative pronoun. (C) is incorrect because of the use of both **to which** and **which makes.** It can only be either, not both. (D) is correct. To keep consistent with the tense throughout the sentence, it must read, **which is making families....**

11.   **(B)**   (A) is incorrect because **had called** suggests that the action already took place, whereas the whole sentence is speculative, **if it had happened to me...** (B) is correct. **If I had run out of gas, I would have called the garage** (speculation in the past). (C) is incorrect. **Would** cannot be used with a past participle alone without the auxiliary verb. (D) is incorrect. **Should have** can be used if the incident really happened, as in **when I ran out of gas, I should have called the garage.**

12. **(A)** (A) is correct. One can be angry **with** a person and angry **at** a situation or thing. (B) is incorrect. Although it is an accepted colloquially, it is incorrect to say that a person was **angry at someone.** (C) is incorrect. **On** is not an accepted preposition to be used with **angry.** (D) is incorrect. **About** is also an unacceptable preposition with **angry.**

13. **(B)** (A) is incorrect because of the presence of **better.** It is, however, correct to say **you should study, if...** (B) is the correct answer. **Had better study** is a structure used to warn or to make a strong suggestion, e.g., **you had better take an umbrella today, it looks like rain.** (C) is incorrect, because of the presence of **better. Will** also does not have that element of warning or precaution. (D) is incorrect because of **better** in the middle of the verb. **You must study a lot** is correct by itself.

14. **(B)** (A) is incorrect because a negative question always has a positive tag question. (B) is the correct answer. The negative question has a positive tag, e.g., They are not coming today, **are they?** (C) is incorrect. It is important to watch for the main verb in the question, when adding a tag, as it is easy to make a mistake and add **isn't it?** (D) is incorrect because the auxiliary verb in the question is **won't.**

15. **(D)** (A) is incorrect because the clause **Eli Whitney came up with a new idea,** does not have a relative pronoun which makes the sentence complete. (B) is incorrect because the act of making guns should be described in the past continuous tense rather than the past perfect. The sentence would then read, **In 1798, when Eli Whitney came up with a new idea, guns were being made by skilled gunsmiths one at a time.** (C) is incorrect because there is no conjunction between the first and second parts of the sentence. (D) is the correct answer. Until Eli Whitney came up with a new idea, guns had been made by gunsmiths.

16. **(D)** (D) shows incorrect usage. **Which** is unnecessary because of the use of **that** earlier in the sentence.

17. **(C)** (C) shows incorrect usage. **Anyone** is used with the third person singular form of the verb. Therefore, it would be correct to say **Anyone runs the risk....**

18. **(D)** (D) shows incorrect usage. The adjectives in most cases precede the noun. Therefore, it should read, **...since the oceans first formed.**

19. **(B)** (B) shows incorrect usage. Crime is an uncountable noun. The sentence should read **...victims of certain types of crime.**

20. **(A)** (A) shows incorrect usage. Although there are two adjectives, the first one should carry the article **an.**

21. **(D)** (D) shows incorrect usage. It is an error in number. **Their methods...spring** is correct.

22. **(A)** (A) shows incorrect usage. The structure is **attending to** a person's needs, a person's problem, etc. The correct sentence would read, **The professor managed to attend to the needs of his family....**

23. **(B)** (B) shows incorrect usage. **Having fallen** should be the correct tense of the verb. The sentence describes an action that took place in the past, but is being talked about in the present.

24. **(D)** (D) shows incorrect usage. The definite article **the** should be placed before the specific day.

25. **(A)** (A) shows incorrect usage. **And** should be replaced by **of.**

26. **(B)** (B) shows incorrect usage. It is an example of a compound noun, where the noun is always in the singular. It should read a **20-story building;** other examples: a four-door car, a three-room apartment.

27. **(B)** (B) shows incorrect usage. The main verb is **order** and it should be in the infinitive, **to** order, when preceded by **a good place.**

28. **(D)** (D) shows incorrect usage. Since there is no repetition of **people,** the definite article should be used with **rich.** It should read **...to give to all the poor.**

29. **(C)** (C) shows incorrect usage. **Lack of education** is singular and should be followed by **is hampering....**

30. **(A)** (A) shows incorrect usage. The preposition **of** should follow **in the event,** when followed by the verb in the -ing form. Otherwise, it would have been correct to read it as **in the event something happens to....**

31. **(D)**   (D) shows incorrect usage. The past participle of the main verb should be used: **plunged,** as the sentence is in the passive voice.

32. **(B)**   (B) shows incorrect usage. This sentence requires a detailed look: **who** refers to the daughter that Frank and Anna had, and so the verb should be **was.**

33. **(A)**   (A) shows incorrect usage. It is a case of reversal of the relative pronoun and the preposition. Americans tend to embody <u>what to</u> many appears to be a **curious combination...**

34. **(B)**   (B) shows incorrect usage. **Later** has been wrongly used instead of the correct adverb of time, **lately.**

35. **(A)**   (A) shows incorrect usage. When there is no clear indication of how many thousand years ago, it is correct to say **thousands <u>of</u> years ago,** in general.

36. **(C)**   (C) shows incorrect usage. The singular **phenomenon** should be used to describe the singular noun **hunger.**

37. **(B)**   (B) shows incorrect usage because **and** is unnecessary. If the adjectival clause, **the prominent Australian filmmaker and screenplay writer,** were removed, the sentence should read **Peter Wier was planning to visit the U.S. to make a film.** In such a case, **and** is simply redundant.

38. **(D)**   (D) shows incorrect usage. The plural reflexive pronoun is **themselves.**

39. **(D)**   (D) shows incorrect usage. **Donors** at the end of the sentence is redundant. In such a case, the rule of ellipsis enables us to drop repeated information. **Largest donor** suggests that he donated the maximum amount of money among donors, so it is unnecessary to repeat **donors.**

40. **(B)**   (B) shows incorrect usage. The subject is the **survival instinct,** not **cockroaches,** so the verb should be **is.**

Section 3:
READING COMPREHENSION
AND VOCABULARY

1. **(C)** The answer to this question is found in the sentence, "Enveloped by an ocean of air consisting of 78% nitrogen and 21% oxygen, the planet is the only one in our solar system known to harbor life." Seventy-eight percent is approximately equivalent to three-fourths. The other answer choices do not convey the correct percentage.

2. **(C)** In order to answer this question, you must know that a nickel-iron core is a metal core. The answer comes from the first sentence of the second paragraph "Its rapid spin and molten nickel-iron core give rise to an extensive magnetic field which, coupled with its atmosphere, shields us from nearly all the harmful radiation coming from the Sun and other stars." Choice (B) nitrogen atmosphere—mentioned in the same sentence, but it is not a reference to the magnetic field. Choices (A) and (D) are also not part of the magnetic field.

3. **(A)** The answer to this question appears in the same sentence as the previous question. It is the "magnetic field, coupled with the atmosphere," that protects the Earth from radiation. Choice (B) "Rapid spin and molten nickel-iron core" contribute to the magnetic field and therefore indirectly protect the Earth from radiation, but this is not the best choice from the answers given. Choices (C) and (D) are simply wrong.

4. **(B)** The best choice for the meaning of "consisting" is "containing." The air contains nitrogen and oxygen. It does not (A) harden, (C) withhold, or (D) shorten the oxygen and nitrogen.

5. **(D)** The last sentence of the second paragraph holds the answer to this question. "The planet's active geological processes have left almost no evidence of the ancient pelting it almost certainly received soon after it was formed." In this case "left almost no evidence" is synonymous with "has eliminated most traces." Also in this question, "processes" is equivalent to "activity." The other choices are not mentioned in the passage.

6. **(A)** In the first paragraph there is the statement, "the planet is the only one in our solar system known to harbor life." Coupled with the statement in the second paragraph that Earth is shielded from radiation rays, they show why life is possible on Earth.

Although Earth's moon (D) is mentioned, the passage says nothing about the existence of moons near other planets. There are no facts given to support choices (B) or (C).

7. **(D)** Basic knowledge enables the reader to know that not all planets are covered with blue oceans. This characteristic is unique to the Earth, making (D) "characteristics that set it apart from other planets" the correct answer.

8. **(C)** Since paragraph three discusses the Moon, it may be assumed that further discussion of the Moon will follow, making (C) "the Earth's natural satellite—the Moon" the next probable paragraph. "People on planets" (A) and "rings around Saturn" (D) are not mentioned, and (B) "the solar system as a whole" is too unspecific.

9. **(A)** One definition of "harbor" is "support." (B) and (D) are not relevant. Another meaning of harbor is as a body of water. That is not the correct meaning in this case, as can be discerned by examining the context of the word within the passage.

10. **(C)** The words in the last paragraph, "the planet's active geological processes have left no evidence of the ancient pelting it almost certainly received soon after it formed," lead the reader to believe that Earth was hit by meteors in some past time period. (A) "Earth never gets hit by meteors" is directly opposite to this. (B) "Earth always gets hit by meteors" is probably false, and (D) "Earth may be bombarded by meteors in the near future" is not discussed in the passage.

11. **(A)** In this sentence, "eons" most nearly means "ages." The answer can be obtained from the context of the sentence from which it was taken. "Since life began eons ago, thousands of creatures have come and gone." Neither choice (B)—particles, choice (C)—animals, nor choice (D)—conditions fit within the context of the sentence.

12. **(C)** The answer to this comes directly from the passage. "Man has drained marshes, burned prairies, damned and diverted rivers." The other answer choices are also forms of habitat alteration, but they are natural occurrences. The question asks specifically for what man does to habitats.

13. **(B)** This answer is taken directly from the reading. "Some of the more recent casualties of man's expansion have been the dodo, great auk, passenger pigeon, Irish elk, and Stellar's sea cow." The other choices are all animals that are currently on the endangered species list, but are not mentioned in the passage.

14. **(C)** The last sentence of the passage describes the role of the Endangered Species Program. This provides a logical transition to the achievements of the program as mentioned in choice (C). Choices (A), (B), and (D) would all have fit somewhere in the first paragraph.

15. **(A)** In this sentence, "attribute" is used as a verb. In this case it most closely means "assign." Choice (B)—characteristic, is a definition of "attribute" when it is used as noun, but in this case that is the wrong answer. The other choices are just wrong.

16. **(B)** "Pro-wildlife" is the correct answer, since everything said favors the protection of wildlife. Words such as "sadly" infer sympathy towards the cause. (A) "nationalistic" is not discernible nor is (D) "feminist." (C) "anti-wildlife" cannot be correct because of the use of "sadly" in connection with certain wildlife due to human factors.

17. **(B)** "Changing animals' environments" is correct. (A) is incorrect because the paragraph does not refer to members of religious orders whose articles of clothing are called "habits." (C) "changing humans' environments" is not correct because the word "habitat" does not usually apply to human environments. (D) is not correct because the phrase does not apply to weather.

18. **(A)** The words "more recent threats by humans" implies that "Man is the cause of some animal extinction." Animals are not mentioned as a cause (B). Congress can only pass laws, not guarantee their success (C), and (D) "a law is more important" is directly opposite to the truth.

19. **(D)** (A) "exploitation," (B) "pollution," and (C) "habitat alteration" are all mentioned in the passage as reasons why many species are dying out. Only Congressional law is mentioned as mandating protection.

20. **(A)** Choice (A) is mentioned as the primary objective of the U.S. Fish and Wildlife Service's Endangered Species Program. While (B) "law enforcement," (C) "education," and (D) "stopping pollution" are all methods of protection, the main goal of the service is custodial care.

21. **(B)** This comes from the sentence, "Some people have only one such psychotic episode; others have many episodes during a lifetime but lead relatively normal lives during interim periods." In this sentence, "episode" refers to an "experience." The other choices refer to help that a person having a psychotic episode can receive.

22. **(D)** The answer to this question appears in the sentence, "These symptoms may include hallucinations, incoherence, delusions, lack of judgment, deterioration of the abilities to reason and feel emotion, and a lack of interaction between the patient and his environment." Only choice (D)—vertigo is not listed as a symptom. In fact, vertigo is a type of phobia that is another mental illness.

23. **(C)** This is another direct content question. It only requires you to know how many items were in a list. The answer is in the sentence, "The hallucinations may be of a visual, auditory, or tactile variety." There are three items listed as types of hallucinations.

24. **(A)** The answer for this question is found in the following sentence, "Some people have only one such psychotic episode; others have many episodes during a lifetime but lead relatively normal lives during interim periods." The best choice is (A)—temporary. Choices (B) and (C) are the opposite of the meaning of the sentence because the non-psychotic periods are not long-term episodes. Choice (D) is also incorrect because the interim periods are the times when things are real for the patient.

25. **(A)** The question tests your knowledge of vocabulary. From the content of the sentence, you can guess that the answer is probably going to be one of the senses. Unfortunately, all the answer choices are senses. The correct answer is (A)—touch. The other three choices are incorrect.

26. **(C)** The word "acute" in the first sentence is a clue that (C) "severe" is the correct answer. The word "sudden" in the first sentence shows that (A) "chronic" could not be correct. (B) "recurring" means "happening again" so it is not correct. (D) "mild" is the opposite of the correct answer.

27. **(D)** This choice is correct as stated in the passage. (A) is wrong, as the passage states that only chronic schizophrenics necessarily need medication. (B) is incorrect, as nothing is said about dying. (C) is incorrect, since chronic schizophrenics have employment problems.

28. **(B)** "Being out of touch with reality" is correct. (A) "medicine overdose" is never discussed. (C) "recovering normal functioning" is the opposite of thinking that one could fly and (D) "symptom control" refers to the absence of symptoms; reality distortion is a symptom.

29. **(D)** "Drug-induced" is the only possibility not discussed so it is the correct answer. (A) "debilitating," (B) "sudden," and (C) "occurring after a long period of normalcy" are all given as possibilities.

30. **(A)** "Medicines" is the correct answer. (B) "neurotic episodes" are not mentioned. (C) "psychotic episodes" are mentioned as abnormal, and (D) "time," without treatment methods, will not permit a long-term normal life.

31. **(B)** "Distinctive" is the correct answer. According to the passage, stress is unique and personal. It follows that the answer needed would be one that was capable of describing stress. The other choices are not able to do that.

32. **(B)** According to the passage, "a busy executive who likes to keep occupied all of the time, 'taking it easy' at the beach on a beautiful day may feel extremely frustrating, nonproductive, and upsetting." The other choices may be correct, but there is no indication of that from the passage.

33. **(A)** "Upset" is the correct answer. This word comes from the sentence, "You may be emotionally distressed from 'doing nothing.'" When the word or phrase is put into quotes within a passage, and the item in quotes is not repeating what someone else wrote, then it usually means that the item in quotes is not going to be used in the literal sense. In the case of this sentence, you would think doing nothing would be relaxing, choice (C), but when taken in the context of the previous sentence, it actually would be the opposite, which is choice (A). Choices (B) and (D) do not fit into the context of the sentence.

34. **(D)** "Illnesses" is the correct choice. Ailments refer back to the list of diseases in the previous sentence. Because "high blood pressure, ulcers, and heart disease" are all health problems, choices (A), (B), and (C) are not the best choices for the context.

35. **(A)** To answer this question, you will need to infer from the passage which of the choices would be correct. There is no sentence which will give you the answer. The passage talks about mental stress and emotional stress. It also explains how each person feels differently about what causes stress. This should lead to the conclusion that personality is the determinant. Choices (B)—education and (C)—marital status both may cause stress and both are part of a person's personality, but the best choice is (A) because it encompasses both (B) and (C). Choice (D) is just wrong.

36. **(B)** The "Alcohol, Drug Abuse, and Mental Health Administration" is the correct answer as stress falls under the category of mental health. (A) Federal Bureau of Investigation, (C) Education Administration, or (D) Communicable Disease Administration would not publish an article on this topic.

37. **(C)** Physical exercise is mentioned as a method to reduce stress, thus making it manageable. (A) "optional" implies that we have a choice, which is not true, since everyone experiences stress at some time. (B) "relaxing" may help to relieve stress, but it does not define it. The words "it is unique and personal to each of us" shows that (D) "the same for all people" is not correct.

38. **(A)** "Educational activity" is the only source of stress that is not mentioned. (B) "physical activity," (C) "mental activity," and (D) "emotional activity" are all mentioned.

39. **(B)** "Pregnancy" is the only condition not mentioned, so it is the correct answer. (A) "ulcers," (B) "heart disease," and (D) "high blood pressure" are all mentioned.

40. **(A)** "Physical exercise" is mentioned as a stress handler. (B) "tranquilizers" and (C) "drugs" are not mentioned. (D) "taking it easy" is mentioned as actually causing stress in some individuals.

41. **(A)** "Ratio" is the correct answer. A proportion is how much of each item are in a combination. In the case of this passage, how much gold is mixed with base metal. Proportion refers to the ratio of ingredients and not the actual mix, so choice (B) is wrong. Choices (C) and (D) refer to other parts of the passage.

42. **(B)** The answer to this question is simply being able to identify that 24K translates to 24 parts gold. Choice (A) would be 204 parts, choice (C) would be 2.4 parts, and choice (D) refers to the base metal content and not the gold.

43. **(A)** "Documented" is the correct response. To register an item, whether it be a car or a name, means to have it legally documented with the proper government agency. Choices (B), (C), and (D) are all verbs used within the passage, but they do not refer to "registered."

44. **(C)** To "stand behind" a mark, means to pledge that what is stamped on the gold is accurate. Although in this passage "stand behind" does not mean "in back of," a phrase similar to "stand behind" is (C) "back up." Choices (A) and (B) are phrases of position, which are not correct for the context of this passage. Choice (D) refers to surrendering and also does not work in this passage.

45. **(D)** "Sold" is the correct answer. To market an item means to put it up for sale. The other choices given do not fit within the context of the sentence.

46. **(C)** The first sentence defines Karat as the proportion of gold mixed with other metals. (A) "jeweler's appraisal" refers to the worth of the gold and other metals. (B) "U.S. registered trademark" refers to a symbol announcing authenticity. (D) "money value" is very unspecific and could refer to any item, not necessarily gold.

47. **(D)** The sentence, "the lowest Karat gold that can be marketed in the U.S. is 10 Karat" shows (D) to be the correct answer. (A) "represents the highest grade of gold sold in the U.S." cannot be the answer as no "highest grade" is given in the passage. (B) "cannot be sold in the U.S." is untrue according to the passage. (C) "never carries a Karat quality mark" is not correct; although some jewelry may be unmarked, not all of it is.

48. **(B)** The sentence, "If there is a Karat quality mark, next to it must be the U.S. registered trademark of the person or the company that stands behind the mark" shows (B) to be correct. (A) cannot be correct as there is no mention of a national gold and silver stamp. (C) is not correct, as only the person or company is required to be stamped. (D) is not correct because the measure is in Karats and not in percentages.

49. **(A)** A 14K mark is defined in the second sentence. "If 14 parts of gold are mixed with 10 parts of base metal, the combination is called 14 Karat (14K) gold." (B) "a 10K mark" refers to 10 parts of gold. (C) "an 18K mark" refers to 18 parts of gold. (D) "a platinum mark" is not discussed in the passage.

50. **(A)** "Important buying information" is the correct answer, as a consumer educated about gold marking is a more skilled gold buyer. (B) "a challenge to buy more gold," (C) "a debate over gold prices," and (D) "advice about buying silver" are never mentioned.

51. **(C)** "Lessen" is the correct response. To reduce an item means to decrease it. Choices (A)—increase, (B)—maximize, and (D)—build up are all the opposite of the

context of the sentence. The students did not need to have their anxiety increased, but decreased.

52. **(D)** The first sentence of the second paragraph says that beta blockers have been around for approximately 25 years. Simple subtraction from the current year puts the approximate date at choice (D)—1970. The other choices are too far in the past to be correct.

53. **(D)** The first sentence of the second paragraph says, "Beta blockers are prescription drugs which have been around for 25 years." If a drug is obtained through a prescription, then it can only be obtained from a doctor. Therefore, choice (D)—doctor's office is correct. The other choices do not involve doctors, therefore, they are incorrect.

54. **(A)** "Hinder" is the correct response. To interfere is to prevent something from doing what it is doing or expected to do. Choice (B)—aid and (C)—help are opposites of what is intended of the sentence. Choice (D) is incorrect in this sentence.

55. **(B)** The answer to this question is lifted directly from the reading. "Since there can be side effects from these beta blockers, physicians are not ready to prescribe them routinely for all test-takers." Choice (A) is not mentioned in the passage. Choice (C) is accurate in describing the drug, but is not the answer to the question. Choice (D) is the opposite effect of what the drug does.

56. **(D)** "Not those who do not know the material" implies that beta blockers will only work with test-takers who know the material. The last sentence implies that (A) "all people" and (B) "are not widely prescribed" are not correct. The second sentence of the second paragraph, "have been used for heart conditions..." shows that (C) "work only on test anxiety" is not correct.

57. **(B)** Improvements are noted in both groups, indicating all people were retested whether or not they took the beta blockers. (A) "without beta blockers" and (C) "testing and then giving beta blockers" are incorrect. (D) "without retesting" is incorrect.

58. **(B)** Pain relief is the only one not discussed. All other answers (A) "test anxiety," (C) "minor stress," and (D) "heart conditions" were discussed.

59. **(B)** "Interfere with the effects of adrenaline" is mentioned in the second sentence of the second paragraph. (A), (C), and (D) are not presented or explained fully.

60. **(D)** The passage states that the beta blocker group had significant improvement in their test scores. It also states that the non-beta blocker group showed only a slight improvement, which was similar to the nationwide average for second-time test-takers. From this it can be determined that the beta blockers "increased scores much more than the nationwide average." Choices (A), (B), and (C) are incorrect.

Test of English as a Foreign Language
TEST 2
ANSWER SHEET

Section 1:
Listening Comprehension

1. Ⓐ Ⓑ Ⓒ Ⓓ
2. Ⓐ Ⓑ Ⓒ Ⓓ
3. Ⓐ Ⓑ Ⓒ Ⓓ
4. Ⓐ Ⓑ Ⓒ Ⓓ
5. Ⓐ Ⓑ Ⓒ Ⓓ
6. Ⓐ Ⓑ Ⓒ Ⓓ
7. Ⓐ Ⓑ Ⓒ Ⓓ
8. Ⓐ Ⓑ Ⓒ Ⓓ
9. Ⓐ Ⓑ Ⓒ Ⓓ
10. Ⓐ Ⓑ Ⓒ Ⓓ
11. Ⓐ Ⓑ Ⓒ Ⓓ
12. Ⓐ Ⓑ Ⓒ Ⓓ
13. Ⓐ Ⓑ Ⓒ Ⓓ
14. Ⓐ Ⓑ Ⓒ Ⓓ
15. Ⓐ Ⓑ Ⓒ Ⓓ
16. Ⓐ Ⓑ Ⓒ Ⓓ
17. Ⓐ Ⓑ Ⓒ Ⓓ
18. Ⓐ Ⓑ Ⓒ Ⓓ
19. Ⓐ Ⓑ Ⓒ Ⓓ
20. Ⓐ Ⓑ Ⓒ Ⓓ
21. Ⓐ Ⓑ Ⓒ Ⓓ
22. Ⓐ Ⓑ Ⓒ Ⓓ
23. Ⓐ Ⓑ Ⓒ Ⓓ
24. Ⓐ Ⓑ Ⓒ Ⓓ
25. Ⓐ Ⓑ Ⓒ Ⓓ
26. Ⓐ Ⓑ Ⓒ Ⓓ
27. Ⓐ Ⓑ Ⓒ Ⓓ
28. Ⓐ Ⓑ Ⓒ Ⓓ
29. Ⓐ Ⓑ Ⓒ Ⓓ
30. Ⓐ Ⓑ Ⓒ Ⓓ

31. Ⓐ Ⓑ Ⓒ Ⓓ
32. Ⓐ Ⓑ Ⓒ Ⓓ
33. Ⓐ Ⓑ Ⓒ Ⓓ
34. Ⓐ Ⓑ Ⓒ Ⓓ
35. Ⓐ Ⓑ Ⓒ Ⓓ
36. Ⓐ Ⓑ Ⓒ Ⓓ
37. Ⓐ Ⓑ Ⓒ Ⓓ
38. Ⓐ Ⓑ Ⓒ Ⓓ
39. Ⓐ Ⓑ Ⓒ Ⓓ
40. Ⓐ Ⓑ Ⓒ Ⓓ
41. Ⓐ Ⓑ Ⓒ Ⓓ
42. Ⓐ Ⓑ Ⓒ Ⓓ
43. Ⓐ Ⓑ Ⓒ Ⓓ
44. Ⓐ Ⓑ Ⓒ Ⓓ
45. Ⓐ Ⓑ Ⓒ Ⓓ
46. Ⓐ Ⓑ Ⓒ Ⓓ
47. Ⓐ Ⓑ Ⓒ Ⓓ
48. Ⓐ Ⓑ Ⓒ Ⓓ
49. Ⓐ Ⓑ Ⓒ Ⓓ
50. Ⓐ Ⓑ Ⓒ Ⓓ

Section 2:
Structure and
Written Expression

1. Ⓐ Ⓑ Ⓒ Ⓓ
2. Ⓐ Ⓑ Ⓒ Ⓓ
3. Ⓐ Ⓑ Ⓒ Ⓓ
4. Ⓐ Ⓑ Ⓒ Ⓓ
5. Ⓐ Ⓑ Ⓒ Ⓓ
6. Ⓐ Ⓑ Ⓒ Ⓓ
7. Ⓐ Ⓑ Ⓒ Ⓓ

8. Ⓐ Ⓑ Ⓒ Ⓓ
9. Ⓐ Ⓑ Ⓒ Ⓓ
10. Ⓐ Ⓑ Ⓒ Ⓓ
11. Ⓐ Ⓑ Ⓒ Ⓓ
12. Ⓐ Ⓑ Ⓒ Ⓓ
13. Ⓐ Ⓑ Ⓒ Ⓓ
14. Ⓐ Ⓑ Ⓒ Ⓓ
15. Ⓐ Ⓑ Ⓒ Ⓓ
16. Ⓐ Ⓑ Ⓒ Ⓓ
17. Ⓐ Ⓑ Ⓒ Ⓓ
18. Ⓐ Ⓑ Ⓒ Ⓓ
19. Ⓐ Ⓑ Ⓒ Ⓓ
20. Ⓐ Ⓑ Ⓒ Ⓓ
21. Ⓐ Ⓑ Ⓒ Ⓓ
22. Ⓐ Ⓑ Ⓒ Ⓓ
23. Ⓐ Ⓑ Ⓒ Ⓓ
24. Ⓐ Ⓑ Ⓒ Ⓓ
25. Ⓐ Ⓑ Ⓒ Ⓓ
26. Ⓐ Ⓑ Ⓒ Ⓓ
27. Ⓐ Ⓑ Ⓒ Ⓓ
28. Ⓐ Ⓑ Ⓒ Ⓓ
29. Ⓐ Ⓑ Ⓒ Ⓓ
30. Ⓐ Ⓑ Ⓒ Ⓓ
31. Ⓐ Ⓑ Ⓒ Ⓓ
32. Ⓐ Ⓑ Ⓒ Ⓓ
33. Ⓐ Ⓑ Ⓒ Ⓓ
34. Ⓐ Ⓑ Ⓒ Ⓓ
35. Ⓐ Ⓑ Ⓒ Ⓓ
36. Ⓐ Ⓑ Ⓒ Ⓓ
37. Ⓐ Ⓑ Ⓒ Ⓓ
38. Ⓐ Ⓑ Ⓒ Ⓓ
39. Ⓐ Ⓑ Ⓒ Ⓓ
40. Ⓐ Ⓑ Ⓒ Ⓓ

Section 3:
Reading Comprehension
and Vocabulary

1. Ⓐ Ⓑ Ⓒ Ⓓ
2. Ⓐ Ⓑ Ⓒ Ⓓ
3. Ⓐ Ⓑ Ⓒ Ⓓ
4. Ⓐ Ⓑ Ⓒ Ⓓ
5. Ⓐ Ⓑ Ⓒ Ⓓ
6. Ⓐ Ⓑ Ⓒ Ⓓ
7. Ⓐ Ⓑ Ⓒ Ⓓ
8. Ⓐ Ⓑ Ⓒ Ⓓ
9. Ⓐ Ⓑ Ⓒ Ⓓ
10. Ⓐ Ⓑ Ⓒ Ⓓ
11. Ⓐ Ⓑ Ⓒ Ⓓ
12. Ⓐ Ⓑ Ⓒ Ⓓ
13. Ⓐ Ⓑ Ⓒ Ⓓ
14. Ⓐ Ⓑ Ⓒ Ⓓ
15. Ⓐ Ⓑ Ⓒ Ⓓ
16. Ⓐ Ⓑ Ⓒ Ⓓ
17. Ⓐ Ⓑ Ⓒ Ⓓ
18. Ⓐ Ⓑ Ⓒ Ⓓ
19. Ⓐ Ⓑ Ⓒ Ⓓ
20. Ⓐ Ⓑ Ⓒ Ⓓ
21. Ⓐ Ⓑ Ⓒ Ⓓ
22. Ⓐ Ⓑ Ⓒ Ⓓ
23. Ⓐ Ⓑ Ⓒ Ⓓ
24. Ⓐ Ⓑ Ⓒ Ⓓ
25. Ⓐ Ⓑ Ⓒ Ⓓ
26. Ⓐ Ⓑ Ⓒ Ⓓ
27. Ⓐ Ⓑ Ⓒ Ⓓ
28. Ⓐ Ⓑ Ⓒ Ⓓ
29. Ⓐ Ⓑ Ⓒ Ⓓ
30. Ⓐ Ⓑ Ⓒ Ⓓ
31. Ⓐ Ⓑ Ⓒ Ⓓ
32. Ⓐ Ⓑ Ⓒ Ⓓ
33. Ⓐ Ⓑ Ⓒ Ⓓ
34. Ⓐ Ⓑ Ⓒ Ⓓ
35. Ⓐ Ⓑ Ⓒ Ⓓ
36. Ⓐ Ⓑ Ⓒ Ⓓ
37. Ⓐ Ⓑ Ⓒ Ⓓ
38. Ⓐ Ⓑ Ⓒ Ⓓ
39. Ⓐ Ⓑ Ⓒ Ⓓ
40. Ⓐ Ⓑ Ⓒ Ⓓ
41. Ⓐ Ⓑ Ⓒ Ⓓ
42. Ⓐ Ⓑ Ⓒ Ⓓ
43. Ⓐ Ⓑ Ⓒ Ⓓ
44. Ⓐ Ⓑ Ⓒ Ⓓ
45. Ⓐ Ⓑ Ⓒ Ⓓ
46. Ⓐ Ⓑ Ⓒ Ⓓ
47. Ⓐ Ⓑ Ⓒ Ⓓ
48. Ⓐ Ⓑ Ⓒ Ⓓ
49. Ⓐ Ⓑ Ⓒ Ⓓ
50. Ⓐ Ⓑ Ⓒ Ⓓ
51. Ⓐ Ⓑ Ⓒ Ⓓ
52. Ⓐ Ⓑ Ⓒ Ⓓ
53. Ⓐ Ⓑ Ⓒ Ⓓ
54. Ⓐ Ⓑ Ⓒ Ⓓ
55. Ⓐ Ⓑ Ⓒ Ⓓ
56. Ⓐ Ⓑ Ⓒ Ⓓ
57. Ⓐ Ⓑ Ⓒ Ⓓ
58. Ⓐ Ⓑ Ⓒ Ⓓ
59. Ⓐ Ⓑ Ⓒ Ⓓ
60. Ⓐ Ⓑ Ⓒ Ⓓ

TOEFL

TEST 2

Section 1:
LISTENING COMPREHENSION

TIME: 35 Minutes
50 Questions

Part A

> **DIRECTIONS:** In Part A you will hear short conversations between two speakers. At the end of each conversation, a third person will ask a question about what was said. **You will hear each conversation just one time.** Therefore, you must listen carefully to understand what each speaker says. After you hear a conversation and the question about it, read the four possible answers in your test book and decide which one is the best answer to the question you heard. Then on your answer sheet, find the number of the question and fill in the space that corresponds to the answer you have chosen.

1. (A) He's glad the woman got into a car accident.
    (B) That the accident was a terrible thing, but more damage could have occurred.
    (C) The man thinks the woman is lying about the accident.
    (D) The man is angry, because the woman was driving his car at the time of the accident.

2. (A) The money belongs to the two little girls.
    (B) The girls should take better care of their earnings.
    (C) They should give the money to the little girls immediately.
    (D) They should keep the money because they don't know if it belongs to the little girls.

3. (A) Put the steak in the microwave oven to defrost it.
    (B) Cook the steak anyway.
    (C) Order a pizza.
    (D) Go to a fast food restaurant.

4. (A) It's too early in the year to have Halloween decorations up.
    (B) It's three months after Halloween, and the decorations should have been removed by now.
    (C) The decorations are in poor taste.
    (D) The woman did not notice the Halloween decorations.

5. (A) She didn't even notice Susan walking by.
    (B) She just saw Susan the day before and had nothing to say to her.
    (C) She and Susan had a disagreement and are no longer speaking to one another.
    (D) The woman he saw was not Susan.

6. (A) The woman used the computer and erased his term paper.
    (B) The woman corrected his term paper.
    (C) The woman did not use the computer.
    (D) The woman moved the man's term paper to another computer.

7. (A) The man did not follow the recipe.
    (B) The man did follow the recipe.
    (C) The cookies taste great.
    (D) The man should have used a different recipe.

8. (A) Husband and wife
    (B) Brother and sister
    (C) Cousins
    (D) Friends

9. (A) A gym   (C) An office
    (B) A movie theater   (D) An ice cream parlor

10. (A) Several months ago
    (B) Two weeks ago
    (C) Last year
    (D) They have never watched that movie before.

11. (A) Susan's exam is over.
    (B) Susan could have kept the book since he has another copy.
    (C) Susan could have made a copy of the book.
    (D) He can give another book to Susan.

12. (A) The battery of the man's car is dead.
    (B) The man is not lucky.
    (C) The car is not reliable.
    (D) It is difficult to get help.

13. (A) The college campus is very dirty.
    (B) He does not like the college bulletin.
    (C) The editorial in the college bulletin is not good.
    (D) There should be no editorials in the college bulletin.

14. (A) At a patient's home
    (B) In a doctor's office
    (C) In a research laboratory
    (D) In a store

15. (A) He does not like school.
    (B) He does not have good clothes.
    (C) He is still ironing his clothes.
    (D) He is very depressed.

16. (A) She has done enough work.
    (B) The man should be fair to her.
    (C) They should do equal amounts of work.
    (D) The suggestion sounds good to her.

17. (A) At four-thirty
    (B) After five-thirty
    (C) Earlier than four-thirty
    (D) Any time that he likes

18. (A) Professor Miller offered more help than he had expected.
    (B) Professor Miller will not discuss the topic with him.
    (C) He asked Professor Miller for some books.
    (D) Professor Miller gave him more books than he had requested.

19. (A) On the desk
    (B) In the woman's purse
    (C) In the drawer
    (D) In the man's wallet

20. (A) Stephanie
    (B) Stephanie's friend
    (C) Her sister
    (D) Her friend's sister

21. (A) He is happy that the woman thanked him.
    (B) He is always ready to help.
    (C) The woman is noble.
    (D) He is happy to donate to a worthy cause.

22. (A) She has a big nose.
    (B) She makes a lot of noise.
    (C) She is very inquisitive.
    (D) She does not know anything.

23. (A) Because she can always get another job.
    (B) Because she is rich.
    (C) Because there is plenty of time.
    (D) Because there is another train in ten minutes.

24. (A) Happy   (C) Sorry
    (B) Apathetic   (D) Angry

25. (A) The man should work in a bank to get money.
    (B) The man should withdraw all his money from the bank.
    (C) The man should try to borrow money from other students.
    (D) The man should try to get a loan from a bank.

Part B

DIRECTIONS: In Part B you will hear conversations between two speakers. At the end of each conversation, a third person will ask several questions about what was said. **You will hear each conversation and the questions about it just one time.** They will not be written out for you. Therefore, you must listen carefully to understand what each speaker says. After you hear a conversation and the question about it, read the four possible answers in your test book and decide which one is the best answer to the question you heard. Then on your answer sheet, find the number of the question and fill in the space that corresponds to the answer you have chosen.

WAIT

26. (A) Jill
    (B) The woman
    (C) His teacher
    (D) Clem

27. (A) She was sick.
    (B) She was on vacation.
    (C) She was in class.
    (D) She avoided Jill.

28. (A) He skipped class.
    (B) He was on a field trip.
    (C) He did not listen in class.
    (D) He was sick.

29. (A) Math
    (B) History
    (C) English
    (D) Science

30. (A) She was not taking the test.
    (B) She was not in the class.
    (C) She had already studied.
    (D) She wanted to fail.

31. (A) Theatrical groups
    (B) Performing arts
    (C) The woman's performance
    (D) Nervousness

32. (A) Because she was afraid of criticism.
    (B) Because the role she was going to play was challenging.
    (C) Because she had never acted before.
    (D) Because she did not know much about acting.

33. (A) By doing small child roles for a theatrical group
    (B) By acting for school plays
    (C) By joining a school for acting
    (D) By working for a T.V. program

34. (A) He is a director.   (C) He is an editor.
    (B) He is an actor.   (D) He is a student.

35. (A) Because she likes writers.
    (B) Because she thought he can recommend him to another director.
    (C) Because she was never praised before.
    (D) Because his opinion was valuable as a critic.

36. (A) Reading a book.
    (B) Cleaning the garage.
    (C) Making a writing desk.
    (D) Selecting a design for a desk.

37. (A) In the garage   (C) In the kitchen
    (B) In the library   (D) On the lawn

38. (A) Because he is a carpenter.
    (B) Because he does not like to waste time.
    (C) Because he likes to work on a Sunday.
    (D) Because he thinks that by doing so he can have a choice in material and design and save some money.

39. (A) From a furniture showroom
    (B) From the woman
    (C) From a book
    (D) From a friend

40. (A) Read it.
    (B) Hide it away till winter.
    (C) Throw it away.
    (D) Give it to her friend.

Part C

DIRECTIONS: In Part C you will hear short talks. At the end of each talk, a second person will ask several questions about what was said. **You will hear each talk and the questions about it just one time.** They will not be written out for you. Therefore, you must listen carefully to understand what each speaker says. After you hear a question, read the four possible answers in your test book and decide which one is the best answer to the question you heard. Then on your answer sheet, find the number of the question and fill in the space that corresponds to the answer you have chosen.

WAIT

41. (A) Dardanelle   (C) Constantinople
    (B) Mamara   (D) Hippodrome

42. (A) 150   (C) 15,000
    (B) 1,500   (D) 15

43. (A) Greeks   (C) Arabs
    (B) Constantine   (D) Romans

44. (A) Byzantium   (C) Hippodrome
    (B) Greek colonists (D) Constantine

45. (A) Forums and temples (C) Houses
    (B) Stores (D) Channels

46. (A) Fluttering wings of a butterfly
    (B) The blades of a machine
    (C) A soft musical note
    (D) Noise

47. (A) Because we are too busy.
    (B) Because we need special lessons to be able to do it.
    (C) Because we don't loose music
    (D) Because we are surrounded by a lot of other noise.

48. (A) Music
    (B) The ability to communicate with nature
    (C) Driving
    (D) Teaching

49. (A) Because it has a lot to offer our senses.
    (B) Because we can listen to different types of music in the midst of nature.
    (C) Because nature is all powerful.
    (D) Because it relieves our minds of a lot of stress.

50. (A) Trees (C) Children
    (B) Butterflies (D) Teachers

(STOP)

If time still remains, you may review work only in this section.
When the time allotted is up, you may go on to the next section.

Section 2:
STRUCTURE AND WRITTEN EXPRESSION

TIME: 25 Minutes
         40 Questions

DIRECTIONS: Questions 1-15 are incomplete sentences. Beneath each sentence are four words or phrases marked (A), (B), (C), and (D). Choose the **one** word or phrase which best completes the sentence. Then, on your answer sheet, find the number of the question and fill in the space that corresponds to the answer you have chosen.

---

1. _____ aspects of his talk have global applications.
   - (A) One of the
   - (B) Some of
   - (C) Any of the
   - (D) Although some of the

2. The American way of life _____.
   - (A) has admired and criticized.
   - (B) has been admired and criticized.
   - (C) have been admired and criticized.
   - (D) has been the object of admiring and criticizing.

3. After a day's work in the lab, all the _____ were covered with iodine.
   - (A) student's hands
   - (B) students hands
   - (C) students' hands
   - (D) student's hand

4. Special airplane fares for tourists make travel _____ than ever before.
   - (A) expensive and attractive
   - (B) less expensive and more attractive
   - (C) less expensive but attractive
   - (D) less expensive therefore attractive

383

5. _____ people study Latin seriously, while most seem to prefer Spanish, Italian and the like.
   - (A) Little
   - (B) Few
   - (C) Many
   - (D) Much of

6. _____ the less interested we have become in our religion, nationality, and family life.
   - (A) The further the century progressed,
   - (B) The further the century has progressed,
   - (C) The more the century progressed,
   - (D) As the century progressed,

7. We cannot believe that he is the man _____ saved you from drowning.
   - (A) that
   - (B) whom
   - (C) who
   - (D) whose

8. John and Pamela hated _____ for not being by their little sister's side at the hospital.
   - (A) herself
   - (B) they
   - (C) themself
   - (D) themselves

9. The only thing _____ stopped her from going to study abroad was the pleading of her grandmother.
   - (A) who
   - (B) which
   - (C) whom
   - (D) why

10. _____ is a way of life for them, not something that terrorizes them.
    - (A) Living with deadly snakes
    - (B) Having lived with deadly snakes
    - (C) Living deadly snakes
    - (D) Deadly snakes

11. She also wrote poetry _____ articles for the local newspaper.
    (A) alongside she wrote
    (B) beside writing
    (C) as well as writing
    (D) besides writing

12. The department ordered _____ new furniture to redecorate its offices.
    (A) many
    (B) a large number of
    (C) a large amount of
    (D) several

13. Since the beginning of time, women _____ of as inferior to men.
    (A) are thought
    (B) have been thought
    (C) are thoughtful
    (D) were thought

14. _____ about the need to educate people on recycling, the speaker stressed the importance of conserving paper.
    (A) During talking
    (B) While talking
    (C) In the event of talking
    (D) A talk

15. A metaphor, _____ compares two things that are different, but have something in common.
    (A) often used in poetry,
    (B) has use in poetry,
    (C) is used in poetry,
    (D) has uses in poetry,

DIRECTIONS: In questions 16-40 each sentence has four underlined words or phrases marked (A), (B), (C), and (D). Choose the **one** word or phrase which is incorrect and must be changed to make the sentence correct. Then, on your answer sheet, find the number of the question and fill in the space that corresponds to the answer you have chosen.

16. Foreigners who understand the styles of American communication will

    far less likely be to contribute to misunderstandings and negative feelings, and
        A   B
    their opportunities for constructive interaction will be much greater.
      C   D

17. Once the province of aging screen stars and wealthy, cosmetic surgery now
        A   B
    attracts middle-class office workers, many in their 30s and 40s, and many of
                                 C
    them men.
       D

18. Self-educated philosopher and orphan who wearily travelled China advocating
           A   B
    the traditional Chinese way of life, Confucius survived all three of his children

    and never fulfilled his life-long search for a government post in which he could
        C   D
    demonstrate his teachings.

19. Neither too much rest nor a diet of rich food are good for the body.
            A   B C   D

20. Associated with African-American music has been the lively and sentimental
    A   B   C

    minstrel songs written by composers such as Stephen Foster and James Bland.
    D

21. Once considered a luxury, the video recorder has become a necessary even for
                    A   B   C   D

    middle class people all over America.

22. Columbus landed on an island in the Caribbean Sea, off the coast of North America,
               A   B

    in October 12, 1492 and thought he had reached India.
    C   D

23. The commission's report suggested to the agricultural countries that continue with
    A   B   C

    their own farming methods instead of blindly adopting the methods of developed,
                                 D

    industrial countries.

24. The Classic Maya who considered the numbers and the days in their calendar as a
                    A   B

    procession of Gods who marched along an eternal trail with no beginning and no end.
                    C   D

25. Like most other modern instruments, the European lute was merely a refinement of
                                            A

    a Near Eastern model which reached at Europe during the Middle Ages through
    B   C   D

    Spain and the Islamic conquests.

26. For years, Somerset Maugham was the most popular short-story writer in English,
                                                                              A

    and his stories, like those of Maupassant is directness and firm structure, are still
                        B   C

    widely read.
        D

27. Most animals feed is made from a mixture of corn and wheat chaff rather than
             A   B   C   D

    chemicals.

28. Almost 20 percent of Finland's population, closely 900,000 people, live in the
             A   B

    ten-region metropolitan area of Helsinki.
        C   D

29. An American's faith in the rule of law explains the conviction which many held, and
                A   B

    many foreigners could not understand, that President Nixon should be removed
                                           C

    from office as a result of his behavior in connection with what was called the
        D

    "Watergate Scandal."

30. As small talk, housewives, whose numbers are steadily decreasing in American
    A   B

    society, are liking to talk about their children, if they have any, or about household
                 C   D

    matters or personal care.

31. The dam <u>used</u> as a drinking water reservoir until recently, <u>when</u> the oil spill from
          A   B

    an exploding tanker made the water <u>unusable</u>.
          C   D

32. Each specialized group <u>coins</u> new words: <u>while</u> some of these spread quickly,
                            A   B

    <u>especially</u> when they are picked up by newspapers and the television and radio
          C

    media, <u>others of these</u> may become popular only in one city or geographic region.
                  D

33. On the basis of annual flow combined with <u>considerable</u> height, Guaira, <u>located</u>
      A   B

    <u>between</u> Brazil and Paraguay, is the world's <u>greater</u> waterfall.
      C   D

    while she was faxed   becas she have to fax the

34. <u>By having faxed</u> the synopsis, she <u>only needed</u> to follow <u>it up</u> with the <u>full-length</u>
      A   B   C   D
    manuscript.

35. When given a choice <u>between</u> a microwave and an <u>exercise</u> machine, Patricia said
                      A   B

    she <u>could rather</u> have the <u>former</u>.
          C   D

36. <u>If early</u> arrival of the doctor or ambulance <u>is expected</u>, try not to <u>administering</u>
       A   B   C

    medical assistance <u>on your own</u>.
                 D

37. A recent <u>study</u> of woodpeckers <u>may have solved</u> <u>their</u> mystery of why these birds
          A   B   C

    do not suffer brain damage or concussions <u>as</u> they hammer.
                                          D

38. It <u>had been</u> a long tradition <u>between</u> the Montague family and the Capulet family
        A   B
    to quarrel <u>with</u> one <u>another</u>.
            C   D

39. <u>Wholely</u> the book was less <u>interesting than</u> the individual <u>sections</u> describing the
    A   B   C
    struggles <u>faced</u> by the cavemen.
             D

40. Although the justices <u>have been</u> tolerant in the past, in recent years the majority
                              A
    <u>have voted</u> to permit the search of <u>student possessions</u> without a warrant, <u>a result</u>
       B   C   D
    of the excessive drug abuse in school campuses.

(STOP)

If time still remains, you may review work only in this section.
When the time allotted is up, you may go on to the next section.

Section 3:
READING COMPREHENSION
AND VOCABULARY

4/3 Correct
17 incorrect.

TIME: 55 Minutes
60 Questions

DIRECTIONS: In this section you will read several passages. Each one is followed by several questions about it. You are to choose the best answer to each question, marked (A), (B), (C), and (D). Then, on your answer sheet, find the number of the question and fill in the space that corresponds to the answer you have chosen.

Questions 1–10 refer to the following passage.

1   During the past three years, the staff members of the Smithsonian Institution's Family Folklore Project have interviewed hundreds of persons about their family folklore. To prepare for these interviews we drew upon our academic backgrounds in folklore and American studies, and upon our personal backgrounds as members of families. In addition,
5   we reviewed the major instruction guides in genealogy, oral history, family history, and folklore fieldwork. Although these publications were all helpful in some way, no single book was completely adequate since family folklore combines aspects of all the above disciplines. Over time we have developed guidelines and questions that have proven successful for us; we hope that the following suggestions will be helpful to anyone who wishes to collect the
10 folklore of his or her own family.

1.   In line 6, "publications" most nearly means
     (A)   members.   (C)   schools.
     (B)   backgrounds.   (D)   journals.

2.   In line 7, "adequate" most nearly means
     (A)   sufficient.   (C)   boring.
     (B)   unhelpful.   (D)   genealogical.

3.   What would be the topic of the paragraph that would follow this one?
     (A)   How to gather family folklore
     (B)   History of the Smithsonian Institution
     (C)   A description of genealogy
     (D)   Useful books on family folklore

4. What can be inferred about the researchers who conducted the interviews?
   (A) They were mathematicians and physicists.
   (B) They were historians and sociologists.
   (C) They had children.
   (D) They wrote books.

5. The purpose of this passage is to
   (A) motivate.
   (B) berate.
   (C) instruct.
   (D) cajole.

6. The assumption of this passage is that
   (A) anyone can successfully interview people about their family folklore without prior training.
   (B) American history is inherent in the family folklore of Americans.
   (C) American history and folklore of Americans have no connections.
   (D) no guidelines are needed in the interviews.

7. According to the passage, which kind of instructional guide was NOT consulted as a source?
   (A) Clinical sociology
   (B) Genealogy guides
   (C) Oral history
   (D) Folklore fieldwork

8. "Academic background" in this passage refers to
   (A) life experience.
   (B) college/university study.
   (C) fieldwork.
   (D) travel.

9. One definition of family folklore represents it as
   (A) not historical in nature.
   (B) not traditional in nature.
   (C) not academic in nature.
   (D) interdisciplinary in nature.

10. The final decision of the Smithsonian Institution's Family Folklore Project was to
    (A) use only a fieldwork guide to proceed with their work.
    (B) trust only already published guides on how to proceed.
    (C) use only historical accounts on how to collect family folklore.
    (D) write their own guidelines on how to collect family folklore.

Questions 11–20 refer to the following passaghe.

1   The most popular organic gem is the pearl. A pearl is the response of a marine mollusk to the presence of an irritating impurity accidentally introduced into its body; a cultured pearl is the result of the intentional insertion of a mother-of-pearl bead into a live mollusk. Whether introduced accidentally or intentionally, the pearl-making process is the same: the mollusk
5   coats the irritant with a substance called nacre. Nacre is composed chiefly of calcium carbonate. Because very few natural pearls are now on the market, most pearls used in fine jewelry are cultured. These include "Biwa" pearls and most other freshwater pearls. Cultured pearls are not easily distinguished from natural pearls except by an expert.

11.   Which of the following people could tell the difference between a cultured pearl and an organic pearl?
(A)   Scuba diver
(B)   Fisherman
(C)   Jeweler
(D)   Clerk

12.   In line 2, "impurity" most nearly means
(A)   mollusk.
(B)   contaminant.
(C)   pearl.
(D)   diver.

13.   In line 5, "irritant" most nearly means
(A)   annoyance.
(B)   aid.
(C)   relief.
(D)   jewelry.

14.   What is the chief component of nacre?
(A)   Sand
(B)   Bead
(C)   Calcium carbonate
(D)   Biwa

15.   In line 3, "intentional" most nearly means
(A)   deliberate.
(B)   accidental.
(C)   unconscious.
(D)   forceful.

16.   A pearl is
(A)   a rock.
(B)   a gemstone.
(C)   a mineral.
(D)   an organic gem.

17.   The difference between a pearl and a cultured pearl is the nature of the
(A)   color.
(B)   introduction of the irritating impurity.

    (C)   coating material.

    (D)   irritating impurity.

18.   Nacre is a substance that is

    (A)   mechanically manufactured.

    (B)   the result of laboratory testing.

    (C)   organically secreted by the mollusk.

    (D)   present in the chemical composition of freshwater ponds.

19.   The main idea in this passage is that

    (A)   most marketable pearls are cultured because nature does not produce enough of its own to satisfy the market.

    (B)   cultured pearls are of a higher quality than natural pearls.

    (C)   there are two major methods of pearl-making.

    (D)   a natural "drought" of pearl production is taking place.

20.   A mollusk, while not defined in this passage, must be

    (A)   any animal.

    (B)   a land animal.

    (C)   the water organism which produces the pearl.

    (D)   all the above.

Questions 21–30 refer to the following passage.

1   From the dawn of civilization, the gaze of humanity has been drawn to the stars. The stars have been relied upon to direct travelers, to make agricultural predictions, to win wars, and to awaken love in the hearts of men and women.

        Ancient stargazers pondering the nighttime sky saw definite star patterns emerge. The
5 names for many of these star patterns retain the names given to them by the Greeks which were most often derived from mythology. The Greeks only knew 48 star patterns. Today's astronomers have charted 88 of these patterns, or constellations, which may be viewed from different parts of the world at different times of the year.

21.   Stars have been relied upon for all of the following EXCEPT

    (A)   as directional aids.

    (B)   for crop predictions.

    (C)   as medical cures.

    (D)   as war omens.

22. In line 5, "retain" most nearly means
    (A) keep.
    (B) eliminate.
    (C) know.
    (D) view.

23. Approximately how many new patterns have been discovered since the time of the ancient Greeks?
    (A) 40
    (B) 48
    (C) 88
    (D) 136

24. In line 6, "derived" most nearly means
    (A) written.
    (B) gazed.
    (C) drawn.
    (D) learned.

25. Which of the following might share a name with a constellation?
    (A) A U.S. president
    (B) A country in the Middle East
    (C) An ancient Greek hero
    (D) A farmer

26. The passage states that
    (A) man never depends on the stars.
    (B) stars are only for beautifying our skies.
    (C) man has depended on stars at times.
    (D) moons are the same as stars.

27. The author states that
    (A) only adults are intrigued with the stars and constellations.
    (B) stars have scientific significance only.
    (C) only children are intrigued with the stars and constellations.
    (D) people have been intrigued with the stars and constellations since ancient times.

28. "Predictions" in this passage refer to
    (A) crop fertility.
    (B) war success.
    (C) Cupid's progress.
    (D) travel directions.

29. The word "charted" in this passage means
   (A) admired.
   (B) identified according to composition and location.
   (C) illustrated.
   (D) named.

30. Which two words are used synonymously in the passage?
   (A) Humanity-astronomers
   (B) Different parts-different times
   (C) Stargazers-travelers
   (D) Patterns-constellations

Questions 31–40 refer to the following passage.

1   Try to make the Visitor Center your first stop at any park. There you will find information on attractions, facilities, and activities such as scenic drives, nature trails, and historic tours. Descriptive films, literature, and exhibits will acquaint you with the geology, history, and plant and animal life of the area. The park staff will answer questions about
5 accommodations, services, and the attractions. Most of the parks described in this book do not offer meals and lodging.

   Many parks can provide assistance for those who have visual, auditory, or other physical limitations. Most have parking lots, restrooms, and other features that are accessible to disabled persons. If accessibility is important to you, however, inquire in advance.

31. What do most parks NOT offer?
   (A) Lodging   (C) Nature trails
   (B) Restrooms   (D) Exhibits

32. Which of the following park areas might have special facilities for a handicapped person?
   (A) Nature trail   (C) Restroom
   (B) Historic tour   (D) Restaurant

33. Why should the Visitor Center be your first stop?
   (A) It will offer detailed information on the park and its activities.
   (B) The Visitor Center always has free food.
   (C) It is the only place with a bathroom.
   (D) The Visitor Center is the only place to buy park passes.

34. In line 3, "descriptive" most nearly means
     (A) natural.   (C) beautiful.
     (B) comely.   (D) representative.

35. In line 9, "inquire" most nearly means
     (A) demand.   (C) ignore.
     (B) ask.   (D) pay.

36. In this passage "accessibility" means
     (A) availability of admission tickets to certain areas.
     (B) availability of park staff to assist people.
     (C) the ease with which a physically disabled person can get to and through a park.
     (D) in what direction one drives to get to a particular attraction.

37. The implication for handicapped people is that
     (A) they are welcome but not provided for in most parks.
     (B) they are welcome and provided for in most parks.
     (C) they are not really welcome in most parks.
     (D) there are no facilities for them in most parks.

38. The background material described includes all the following EXCEPT
     (A) interviews with inhabitants.
     (B) exhibits.
     (C) literature.
     (D) films.

39. What is meant by "accommodations"?
     (A) Scenic drives-nature trails
     (B) Geology-history
     (C) Meals-lodging
     (D) Plant life-animal life

40. What limitations does the author NOT consider with respect to requiring special assistance?
     (A) Visual limitations
     (B) Auditory limitations
     (C) Physical limitations
     (D) Mental limitations

Questions 41–50 refer to the following passage.

1   The use of asbestos millboard in wall and floor protection is a controversial issue because of the health hazard of asbestos fibers in the manufacturing, preparation, and handling of the millboard. The National Fire Protection Association is currently initiating the process of removing asbestos as a standard protection for reduced clearances. Since the
5   process is a lengthy one, this new standard will probably not be in effect until early 1981. We strongly encourage the use of an alternative protection whenever one is available. However, if you must use the asbestos millboard, use it cautiously. We recommend painting the asbestos to keep the fibers from coming loose. If the board must be cut, do not inhale the dust; do the work outdoors, using a breathing mask.

41.   Where should the millboard be cut?
    (A)   In a closed room
    (B)   Outdoors
    (C)   Under a tarp
    (D)   Under a clearance

42.   What precaution should be taken when cutting millboard?
    (A)   Wear gloves
    (B)   Paint the board first
    (C)   Wear a breathing mask
    (D)   Wear overalls

43.   In line 2, "hazard" most nearly means
    (A)   danger.   (C)   aid.
    (B)   benefit.   (D)   enhancer.

44.   This passage serves as a(n)
    (A)   instruction.   (C)   aid.
    (B)   benefit.   (D)   warning.

45.   In line 5, "standard" most nearly means
    (A)   asbestos.   (C)   criterion.
    (B)   flag.   (D)   millboard.

46.   The overall implication of the passage is
    (A)   asbestos is as safe as other building materials.
    (B)   only touching the asbestos fibers with your hands is harmful.
    (C)   asbestos can be harmful to one's health.
    (D)   using asbestos in building materials is all right.

47. The National Fire Protection Association is
    (A) promoting asbestos as a safe building material.
    (B) becoming active in the removal of asbestos as a standard building material.
    (C) taking a "wait-and-see" position on asbestos as a building material.
    (D) staying out of the asbestos controversy completely.

48. "Controversial" as used in this passage means
    (A) without pro and con sides in the question of its use.
    (B) an issue about which there are strong opinions on both the pro and con sides.
    (C) an issue about which there is agreement.
    (D) something no one really cares about.

49. "Inhale" in this passage means
    (A) breathe into either nose or mouth.
    (B) take in air through eyes.
    (C) get fibers under fingernails.
    (D) get fibers in open cuts and sores.

50. What can be used as a deterrent to the hazard of asbestos?
    (A) Water   (C) Air
    (B) Boards   (D) Paint

Questions 51–60 refer to the following passage.

1   The term "verbal dyspraxia" is used by some scientists and clinicians to describe the inability to produce the sequential, rapid, and precise movements required for speech. Nothing is wrong with the child's vocal apparatus, but the child's brain cannot give correct instructions for the motor movements involved in speech. This disorder is characterized by
5   many sound omissions. Some verbally dyspraxic children, for instance, speak only in vowels, making their speech nearly unintelligible. One little boy trying to say "My name is Billy" can only manage "eye a eh ee-ee." These children also have very slow, halting speech with many false starts before the right sounds are produced. Their speech errors may be similar to those children with phonological impairment.

51. In line 3, "apparatus" most nearly means
    (A) device.   (C) brain.
    (B) child.   (D) speech.

52. In line 4, "characterized" most nearly means
(A) appeared.
(B) described.
(C) emoted.
(D) spoken.

53. What is a characteristic of speech in children with verbal dyspraxia?
(A) Rapid
(B) Clear
(C) Concise
(D) Halting

54. In line 6, "unintelligible" most nearly means
(A) clear.
(B) unstoppable.
(C) unrecognizable.
(D) slow.

55. In line 9, "impairment" most nearly means
(A) repair.
(B) problem.
(C) speech.
(D) instructions.

56. A person suffering from verbal dyspraxia cannot produce
(A) precise speech sounds.
(B) vowel sounds.
(C) more than one sound in a series.
(D) any human sounds.

57. Sound omissions in verbally dyspraxic children are
(A) only occasional.
(B) very rare.
(C) nonexistent.
(D) common.

58. Similarity of speech errors exists between
(A) stroke victims and verbal dyspraxics.
(B) heart attack victims and verbal dyspraxics.
(C) verbal dyspraxics and children with phonological impairment.
(D) mutes and verbal dyspraxics.

59. The implication about consonants in this passage is that
(A) they are not necessary for intelligent human speech.
(B) without them human speech is unintelligible.
(C) lack of them causes stuttering.
(D) lack of them slows down human speech.

60. The real source in the disability of verbal dyspraxia is
    (A) vocal apparatus.
    (B) the brain's inability to give instructions for motor movements involved in speech.
    (C) the child's personality.
    (D) a physical disability.

STOP

If time still remains, you may review work only in this section.

TEST 2

ANSWER KEY

SECTION 1: LISTENING COMPREHENSION

1.	(B)	14.	(B)	26.	(A)	39.	(C)
2.	(D)	15.	(C)	27.	(C)	40.	(B)
3.	(C)	16.	(D)	28.	(D)	41.	(C)
4.	(B)	17.	(B)	29.	(D)	42.	(B)
5.	(C)	18.	(A)	30.	(C)	43.	(A)
6.	(A)	19.	(C)	31.	(C)	44.	(D)
7.	(A)	20.	(A)	32.	(B)	45.	(A)
8.	(B)	21.	(D)	33.	(A)	46.	(C)
9.	(D)	22.	(C)	34.	(D)	47.	(D)
10.	(B)	23.	(D)	35.	(D)	48.	(B)
11.	(B)	24.	(A)	36.	(C)	49.	(D)
12.	(A)	25.	(D)	37.	(A)	50.	(C)
13.	(C)			38.	(D)		

SECTION 2: STRUCTURE AND WRITTEN EXPRESSION

1.	(B)	11.	(D)	21.	(C)	31.	(A)
2.	(B)	12.	(C)	22.	(C)	32.	(D)
3.	(C)	13.	(B)	23.	(C)	33.	(D)
4.	(B)	14.	(B)	24.	(A)	34.	(A)
5.	(B)	15.	(A)	25.	(C)	35.	(C)
6.	(B)	16.	(A)	26.	(C)	36.	(C)
7.	(C)	17.	(B)	27.	(A)	37.	(C)
8.	(D)	18.	(A)	28.	(B)	38.	(D)
9.	(B)	19.	(D)	29.	(B)	39.	(A)
10.	(A)	20.	(B)	30.	(C)	40.	(B)

SECTION 3: READING COMPREHENSION AND VOCABULARY

1.	(D)	16.	(D)	31.	(A)	46.	(C)
2.	(A)	17.	(B)	32.	(C)	47.	(B)
3.	(A)	18.	(C)	33.	(A)	48.	(B)
4.	(B)	19.	(C)	34.	(D)	49.	(A)
5.	(C)	20.	(C)	35.	(B)	50.	(D)
6.	(B)	21.	(C)	36.	(C)	51.	(A)
7.	(A)	22.	(A)	37.	(B)	52.	(B)
8.	(B)	23.	(A)	38.	(A)	53.	(D)
9.	(D)	24.	(C)	39.	(C)	54.	(C)
10.	(D)	25.	(C)	40.	(D)	55.	(B)
11.	(C)	26.	(C)	41.	(B)	56.	(A)
12.	(B)	27.	(D)	42.	(C)	57.	(D)
13.	(A)	28.	(A)	43.	(A)	58.	(C)
14.	(C)	29.	(B)	44.	(D)	59.	(B)
15.	(A)	30.	(D)	45.	(C)	60.	(B)

Detailed Explanations of Answers

TEST 2

Section 1:
LISTENING COMPREHENSION

Part A

1.   **(B)**   The question asked was, "What does the man mean?" The correct answer is (B)—That the accident was a terrible thing, but more damage could have occurred. When the woman complained about her car accident, the man replied, "Well, it could have been worse."

2.   **(D)**   The question asked was, "What is the man implying?" The correct answer is (D)—They should keep the money because they don't know if it belongs to the little girls. When the woman spotted the money on the ground, and asked if they should give it to the little girls running the lemonade stand, the man replied, "No, we don't know for certain that it belongs to them."

3.   **(C)**   The question asked was, "What does the woman want to do about dinner?" The correct answer is (C)—Order a pizza. When the man asked the woman what they should do about dinner, the woman answered, "Let's order out for a pizza."

4.   **(B)**   The question asked was, "What does the woman mean?" The correct answer is (B)—It's three months after Halloween and the decorations should have been removed by now. The woman said, "...I can't believe they still have Halloween decorations up! It's the end of January!" Halloween occurs on October 31. By the end of January, Halloween has been over for three months.

5.   **(C)**   The question asked was, "What does the woman mean?" The correct answer is (C)—She and Susan had a disagreement, and are no longer speaking to one another. When the man asked the woman why she did not say hello to her friend Susan, the woman replied, "Susan and I are no longer on speaking terms."

6.   **(A)**   The question asked was, "What is the man implying?" The correct answer is (A)—The woman used the computer and erased his term paper. The man said, "I had saved the term paper on the hard drive of this computer. Have you used it recently?"

7.   **(A)**   The question asked was, "What is the woman implying?" The correct answer is (A)—The man did not follow the recipe. The woman said, "These cookies taste funny. Are you sure you added enough sugar?" If the recipe was followed correctly, enough sugar would have been added, and the cookies would not have tasted funny.

8.   **(B)**   The question asked was, "What is the most probable relationship between these two people?" The correct answer is (B)—Brother and sister. The woman said, "I broke mom's favorite vase!" and the man said, "…Just wait until Dad gets home!" The most probable relationship between these two people is "brother and sister," because both people collectively refer to "Mom" and "Dad."

9.   **(D)**   The question asked was, "Where does this conversation most likely take place?" The correct response is (D)—An ice cream parlor. The woman said, "I'd like mint chocolate chip in a cup with rainbow sprinkles and whipped cream, please," and the man said, "I'd like a banana split." These are both things which would be ordered at an ice cream parlor.

10.   **(B)**   The question asked was, "How long ago does the woman think they watched the movie?" The correct answer is (B)—Two weeks ago. The woman said, "Why did you rent that movie again? We just watched it two weeks ago."

11.   **(B)**   The question asked was, "What does the man mean?" The correct answer is (B)—Susan could have kept the book, he has another copy. The man said, "I have another copy. She could have kept it till her test was over." He didn't mean that Susan could have made another copy or that he could give her another book.

12.   **(A)**   The question asked was, "What seems to be the problem?" The correct answer is (A)—The battery of the man's car is dead. The man said, "Oh, no! Looks like the battery went down."

13. **(C)**   The question asked was, "What is the man's opinion?" The correct answer is (C)—The editorial in the college bulletin is not good. When the woman asked the man about the editorial in the college bulletin, he said, "…it stinks." This expression is used to show disgust for something. (A) and (B) are not correct because the man was not referring to the college campus or the college bulletin but the editorial in the college bulletin. (D) is not correct because the man was not making a general statement; he was referring to a specific editorial.

14. **(B)**   The question asked was, "Where did this conversation take place?" Choices (A), (C), and (D) are incorrect, because the woman said, "Dr. Johnson is with another patient." Only in a doctor's office, (B), would this conversation take place.

15. **(C)**   The question asked was, "Why is Mike not ready yet?" The correct answer is (C)—He is still ironing his clothes. The man said, "No, he is still in the laundry room pressing his clothes." It does not mean he is depressed or does not like school.

16. **(D)**   The question asked was, "What is the woman's response to the man's suggestion?" The correct answer is (D)—The suggestion sounds good to her. The woman said, "Fair enough!" It means it is satisfactory.

17. **(B)**   The question asked was, "What time will the man pick up the woman?" The correct answer is (B)—after five-thirty. When the man asked, "…Is four-thirty good?" The woman said, "That will be too early. My class is over at five-thirty. Any time after that is good." So the man cannot pick her up at four-thirty or earlier than that or any time. He will pick her up after five-thirty.

18. **(A)**   The question asked was, "What does the man mean?" The correct answer is (A)—Professor Miller offered more help than he had expected. When the woman asked, "Did Professor Miller agree to discuss the topic again with you?", the man said, "Yes. Not only that, he offered to give me some books on the topic. That was more than I could ask for."

19. **(C)**   The question asked was, "Where were the tickets?" The correct answer is (C)—In the drawer. The woman said, "You said you kept them on the desk. Thank goodness I checked the drawer…." This means that though the man said he had kept the tickets on the desk, they were not there. They were in the drawer.

20. **(A)**   The question asked was, "Who gave the pen to the woman?" The correct answer is (A)—Stephanie. The woman said, "My sister's friend Stephanie gave it to me on my birthday." Her sister's friend, whose name is Stephanie, gave it to her.

21. **(D)**   The question asked was, "What does the man imply?" The correct answer is (D)—He is happy to donate to a worthy cause. The man said, "I am glad I could offer some help for a noble cause." He is happy to offer help for the good work.

22. **(C)**   The question asked was, "What is the man's opinion of Mrs. Wood?" The correct answer is (C)—She is very inquisitive. The man said, "She is really nosy, isn't she?" "Nosy" means inquisitive, not having a big nose or being noisy.

23. **(D)**   The question asked was, "Why does the man ask the woman not to worry?" The correct answer is (D)—Because there is another train in ten minutes. When the man said, "Don't worry! There is another in ten minutes," he was referring to a train and not a job.

24. **(A)**   The question asked was, "How does the man feel about the woman's decision?" The correct answer is (A)—Happy. The man said, "Really? What a pleasant surprise!" This expression is used when one hears unexpected good news.

25. **(D)**   The question asked was, "What does the woman suggest?" The correct answer is (D)—The man should try to get a loan from the bank. The woman said, "I would advise you to approach a bank. They have plenty of loans available for students." She suggests that the man should go to a bank and try to get a loan. It does not mean he should work in a bank or get money from other students.

Part B

26. **(A)**   The question asked was, "Who was the man looking for?" The correct response is (A)—Jill. The man asked the woman, "Have you seen Jill today?" This implies that he is looking for her and not just wanting to know if the woman has seen her.

27. **(C)**   The question asked was, "Why did the woman not see Jill?" The correct response is (C)—She was in class. The woman responds to the man's inquiry by stating, "No, I have been in class all day and have not seen her."

28. **(D)** The question asked was, "How come the man did not get the notes for class?" The correct response is (D)—He was sick. The man told the woman that, "She was supposed to give me the class notes from when I was sick and I need them to study for the test tomorrow."

29. **(D)** The question asked was, "What class were the notes for?" The correct answer is (D)—Science. For this question the listener will have to know that chemistry is a science class and not one of the other choices. The woman asked, "What class are the notes for?" The man replied, "Chemistry."

30. **(C)** The question asked was, "Why did the woman not need her notes?" The correct response is (C)—She had already studied. The man is willing to borrow her notes, but only if it is not inconvenient for her. Inconvenient means not too much trouble. The woman replied, "I studied for the test last night so I will not need my notes tonight."

31. **(C)** The question asked was, "What were these people talking about?" The correct answer is (C)—The woman's performance. The conversation started in reference to the woman's performance. And though there were references to theatrical groups and nervousness in the conversation, the main topic was the woman's performance.

32. **(B)** The question asked was, "Why was the woman nervous?" The correct answer is (B)—Because the role she was going to play was challenging. The woman said, "This role was a challenge and I was very nervous before the performance." So, the reason for her being nervous was that the role was difficult.

33. **(A)** The question asked was, "How did the woman start acting?" The correct answer is (A)—By doing small child roles for a theatrical group. When the man asked, "Have you been acting long?" the woman said, "Since I was five. My father was associated with an amateur theatrical group. I started acting by doing small child roles for them."

34. **(D)** The question asked was, "What does this man do?" The correct answer is (D)—He is a student. In the conversation the man said, "I am not an actor. I am a student of art history."

35. **(D)** The question asked was, "Why did the woman feel flattered upon realizing that the man wrote critiques of theatrical events?" The correct answer is (D)—Because his opinion was valuable as a critic. The woman said to the man, "You sound like you

know a lot about acting." In response to that the man let her know that he wrote critiques of theatrical events. Then she exclaimed, "Isn't that nice to know! I am really flattered by your compliments." She is happy to be praised for acting by someone who knows about acting.

36. **(C)**   The question asked was, "What are these people doing?" The correct answer is (C)—Making a writing desk. In the conversation the man said, "Just a few more minutes and we will have a perfect little writing desk here."

37. **(A)**   The question asked was, "Where are they working?" The correct answer is (A)—In the garage. Towards the end of the conversation the woman said, "I don't want to waste another nice Sunday in the garage making some piece of furniture." This means they are in the garage now and the woman does not enjoy it.

38. **(D)**   The question asked was, "Why does the man like making furniture?" The correct answer is (D)—Because he thinks that by doing so he can have a choice in material and design and save some money. When the woman expressed her inability to understand how anyone could enjoy making a writing desk on a Sunday, the man pointed out the advantages of making something oneself: "…you can choose your own design…you can save money on labor."

39. **(C)**   The question asked was, "From where did the man get the idea?" The correct answer is (C)—From a book. When the woman exclaimed, "I wonder who gives you such fantastic ideas!" the man said, "Nobody, I just bought an easy-to-make furniture manual. It has many such wonderful designs." So he found the idea and design from the book he bought. Obviously, neither the woman nor a friend gave him the idea.

40. **(B)**   The question asked was, "What does the woman want to do with the book?" The correct answer is (B)—Hide it away till winter. When the man asked, "Want to have a look at it?" the woman said, "No, I want to hide it till winter." The woman does not sound very interested in making furniture, so she wouldn't want to read it. Nor does she want to throw it away or give it away. She only wants to hide it till winter. Maybe she doesn't mind making furniture in winter.

Part C

41. **(C)** The question asked was, "What is the capital of the Byzantine empire?" The correct response is (C)—Constantinople. This is given in the first line of the paragraph. The other choices are all names that also appeared in the short talk.

42. **(B)** The question asked was, "How many cities compose the empire's infrastructure?" The correct response is (B)—1500. The listener for this question must be able to differentiate the different numbers that appear in the answer choices. The listener should know that "one thousand five hundred" looks like 1500. English does not always put an "and" between numbers.

43. **(A)** The question asked was, "Who founded the city?" The correct response is (A)—Greeks. The answer to this question comes for the line, "Founded by Greek colonists, the city's location at the mouth of the Dardanelles gave it access to the Black Sea and the Sea of Mamara" To "found" a city is another way of saying to establish or create. Constantine moved his capital to it and changed the name but he did not create it.

44. **(D)** The question asked was, "Who changed the name of the city?" The correct response is (D)—Constantine. This question is asking for a "who" and not "what" the name was changed to. The answer is found in the line, "The city's name was changed from Byzantium to Constantinople when Constantine moved his capital to the site."

45. **(A)** The question asked was, "What was constructed during the expansion of the city?" The correct response is (A)—Forums and temples. The other choices in this answer may all be correct, but it cannot be learned from the information given. "Forums and temples" is the best choice to the question.

46. **(C)** The question asked was, "What does a breeze passing through trees sound like?" The correct answer is (C)—A soft musical note. The talk started with a question about the sound of a breeze passing through a thick cluster of trees and the statement following was, "...it is so rhythmic and sonorous that it sounds like a soft musical note." "It" here refers to the sound of a breeze.

47. **(D)** The question asked was, "Why do we find it difficult to listen to the music of a breeze in our everyday lives?" The correct answer is (D)—Because we are surrounded by a lot of other noise. In the talk you heard, "In our everyday hectic lives, we don't hear it (the music of a breeze) because there is so much other noise around us—from ma-

chines, from cars and buses, from people." It is this noise that does not allow us to pay attention to that music.

48. **(B)** The question asked was, "What is an important skill for a healthy life according to this talk?" The correct answer is (B)—The ability to communicate with nature. In the talk there was a statement, "In fact, one can actually learn to communicate with nature." According to the talk communication with nature can take a lot of stress off our minds. And that is why, according to this talk, "the ability to communicate with nature is an important skill for a healthy life."

49. **(D)** The question asked was, "Why is the effect of nature so soothing?" The correct answer is (D)—Because it relieves our minds of a lot of stress. Though there were references to different types of music found in nature in the talk, why the effect of nature is soothing is because it relieves our minds of stress. In the talk you heard "...it is very soothing. It takes a lot of stress off our minds."

50. **(C)** The question asked was, "Who does the author want to teach the music of nature to?" The correct response is (C)—Children. In the last line of the talk, the reader says, "It would be wonderful if we could teach our children such an important skill for a healthy life." The other answer choices are mentioned in the passage, but do not answer the question.

Section 2:
STRUCTURE AND WRITTEN EXPRESSION

1. **(B)**   (A) is incorrect because while the subject is in the singular, **one of the,** the main verb is in the plural, **have.** (B) is the correct answer. The subject is plural and so is the corresponding verb. (C) is incorrect. It is unacceptable to use **any** while writing a sure statement. **Any** can be used if the sentence reads as follows: **Any** of the aspects of his talk **may** have global applications. (D) is incorrect. If the sentence is begun with (D), it remains incomplete. **Although** is used only to juxtapose two different ideas.

2. **(B)**   (A) is incorrect because the sentence has no object. The sentence leaves us asking **The American way of life has admired and criticized what?** (B) is correct. It is a passive sentence. (C) is incorrect because the subject is singular, but the verb is in the plural form. (D) is incorrect because the nouns **admiration** and **criticism** have been wrongly used.

3. **(C)**   (A) is incorrect because it indicates that only one **student's** hands were dirty. (B) is incorrect because there is no indication of possession, as denoted by apostrophes. (C) is correct. When the apostrophe is placed after the plural marker, it shows that **all** the students' hands were dirty. (D) is incorrect. All the students cannot have only one hand.

4. **(B)**   (A) is incorrect. Air fare that is expensive cannot be attractive too. (B) is correct. **Less...more...than ever before** is the structure. It is a comparison of fares that have become less expensive, and therefore more attractive than before. (C) and (D) are incorrect because the second part of the clause does not fit in with the **...than ever before.** It has to be **more attractive than ever before.**

5. **(B)**   (A) is incorrect because **little** is used with uncountable nouns. (B) is correct. **Few** without an article suggests the small number of people who study Latin and compares it in this sentence to **most** of the people who seem to prefer Spanish and the like. (C) is incorrect, because in a comparison it is necessary to have a conjunction such as **but** when using **many** and **most.** (D) is incorrect because **much** is used with uncountable nouns.

6. **(B)**   (A) is incorrect because of the inconsistency of tense in the sentence. The first part of the sentence is in the simple past, while the second is in the present perfect. (B) is correct. The tenses are correct for both parts of the sentence. (C) is incorrect

because of the same reason as (A). (D) is incorrect because the first part of the sentence does not lend itself to comparison as does the second part. The structure in this case is **the further...the less.**

7. **(C)** (A) is incorrect. Although it is accepted in spoken American English, **that** is used only in reference to ideas, things, and nonpeople nouns. (B) is incorrect because **whom** is used with a preposition such as **to whom, with whom, from whom,** etc. (C) is correct. The relative pronoun **who** refers to the man who saved you from drowning. (D) is incorrect. **Whose** is a relative pronoun used to show possession, such as **whose bag,** etc.

8. **(D)** (A) is incorrect because the subject is plural and **herself** is a reflexive pronoun in third person singular. (B) is incorrect because **they** is unacceptable usage here. It can only be **them.** (C) is incorrect. The reflexive pronoun for **them** is **themselves,** in plural. (D) is the correct answer: third person plural reflexive pronoun.

9. **(B)** (A) is incorrect. The relative pronoun **who** is used only to refer to people. In this case, reference is to **pleading.** (B) is the correct answer. The relative pronoun for an idea or thing is **which.** (C) is incorrect. Refer to answer (B). (D) is incorrect. If the reason was the subject of the sentence, **why** would have been acceptable. But the sentence begins with **The only thing....**

10. **(A)** (A) is the correct answer. **Living** is a gerund, a verb that can be used as a noun. (B) is incorrect because of the lack of the pronoun **it,** after **Having lived with deadly snakes.** Without the pronoun, we will have to ask, **what** is a way of life? (C) and (D) are incorrect because the verb of the sentence is in the singular, while the subject is in the plural.

11. **(D)** (A) is incorrect. There is an unnecessary repetition of **she wrote.** (B) is incorrect because **beside** is used to show proximity rather than addition. (C) is incorrect because **also** and **as well as** are repetitions of the same thing. (D) is correct. It is important to pay attention to the difference between **beside** and **besides. Besides** refers to ideas such as **other than.** Other than writing articles for the local newspaper, she wrote poetry.

12. **(C)** (A) and (B) are incorrect because **furniture** is an uncountable noun, while **many** is used only with countable nouns. (C) is the correct answer. Furniture can be ordered in large quantities and amounts, as they are uncountable. (D) is incorrect.

13. **(B)** (A) is incorrect because **are thought of** shows that the thought prevails now and not since the beginning of time. (B) is the correct answer. Present perfect in the passive voice is the correct tense form to show that from the very beginning of time, people have thought of women as being inferior to men. (C) is incorrect because **thoughtful** is an adjective which means **considerate.** Although it has the same root word, thought, it means something quite different. (D) is incorrect because **were thought** can be used only if the thought **used to prevail** and it no longer exists. But the first part of the sentence suggests that things have not changed and that from the very beginning, up to the present time, they are still thought of the same way.

14. **(B)** (A) is incorrect because **during** can be used only in reference to a period of time, e.g., **during the recess, during the talk, during the performance.** It is incorrect to use it with actions, like during talking, during dancing. (B) is the correct answer. In the process of talking about recycling, the speaker also stressed paper conservation. (C) is incorrect because **in the event** suggests **as a result of talking,** but the meaning is **while talking.** (D) is incorrect because the subject of the sentence is the speaker's stressing the importance of recycling and paper conservation. Therefore, the sentence can only begin, **While talking about....**

15. **(A)** (A) is correct. The clause refers to the metaphor and adds the information that they are often used in poetry. (B), (C), and (D) are incorrect because they contribute a main verb, **has use,** which is unnecessary. The sentence already has a main verb, **compares.**

16. **(A)** (A) is incorrect. The main verb is **will be.** Although main verbs may be broken up to accommodate an adverb, in this case, it distorts the meaning. The sentence should read **...will be far less likely to contribute....**

17. **(B)** (B) is the incorrect answer. As the reference here is to all the wealthy in general, it should be **the wealthy.**

18. **(A)** (A) is incorrect. It should read **A self-educated philosopher and orphan.** The sentence is a simple case of reversed subject and adjectival clause. It is a reversal of **Confucius, a self-educated philosopher and orphan....** Therefore, the article **a** is necessary.

19. **(D)** (D) is incorrect. The **neither...nor** structure is one that must be paid close attention. The verb that follows the structure is always in the singular. It is common to make the mistake of using the plural from when the sentence is perceived as having two

subjects. The sentence should read, **Neither too much rest nor a diet of rich food is good for the body.**

20. **(B)**   (B) is incorrect. This sentence calls for careful reading. If we ask the question, **"What is associated with African-American music?"**—the answer is in the plural form, lively and sentimental minstrel songs. Therefore, the verb should be put in the plural form to read, **have been.**

21. **(C)**   (C) is incorrect. The correct part of speech to be used here is the noun form of the word: **necessity.** The video recorder has become a necessity.

22. **(C)**   (C) is incorrect. When the date includes a number, such as 12th, 31st, or a day, such as Monday or Friday, the pronoun that goes with it is **on.**

23. **(C)**   (C) is incorrect. With **suggested to,** the verb that follows should be in the infinitive, **to continue.** The sentence would therefore read **...report suggested to the agricultural countries that they continue with...**

24. **(A)**   (A) is incorrect. The first relative pronoun, **who,** is not needed. The Maya people **considered the numbers and days in their calendar as a procession of gods who marched along an eternal trail with no beginning and no end.** The second **who** is necessary because it is the gods who marched, not the Maya people.

25. **(C)**   (C) is incorrect. The preposition is not necessary when used with **reached.** However, if the verb was **arrived, at** would be needed. The lute **reached** Europe during the Middle Ages.

26. **(C)**   (C) is incorrect. Maugham's stories are like those of Maupassant in their directness and firm structure; e.g., she is like me **in** her dislike for seafood, is another way of saying that we both dislike seafood.

27. **(A)**   (A) is incorrect. **Animal feed** is a compound word and comes under the category of words like **man hunt, animal farm,** etc. Although it may stand for plural nouns, it is used in the singular.

28. **(B)**   (B) is incorrect. Although it would have been acceptable to use **nearly** in that

place, **close** does not become **closely**. It should read **...Finland's population, close to 900,000...**

29. **(B)**   (B) is incorrect. There should also be a relative pronoun here, **which.** It is part of the clause, **and which many foreigners could not understand.**

30. **(C)**   (C) is incorrect. **Liking** can easily be mistaken for being part of the verb **are liking,** but it really is an adverb there and should read, **are likely to talk about their children.**

31. **(A)**   (A) is incorrect. If the second part of the sentence were taken away, the first part would be left without a verb. It should read **The dam was used as a drinking water reservoir....**

32. **(D)**   (D) is incorrect. **Of these** is redundant because of the presence of **others. Others** by itself means **other new words.**

33. **(D)**   (D) is incorrect. **Greater** can be used here only if the comparison is between two rivers. It is obviously a comparison of all the big rivers in the world, so **greatest** is the correct answer.

34. **(A)**   (A) is incorrect. By doing something is the correct structure, e.g., **by faxing the synopsis, by writing the memo,** etc. In this case, there is no need for **by** before **having faxed.** The expression means that the act has been done.

35. **(C)**   (C) is incorrect. **Would** is the modal for showing preference as Patricia did here. She would rather have the microwave.

36. **(C)**   (C) is incorrect. **To administer** should be the correct conjugation of the verb. The sentence is in the imperative: **try** not to administer is the important thing to note here.

37. **(C)**   (C) is incorrect. Although the mystery may pertain to the wood woodpeckers, it does not become the woodpeckers' mystery. So it suffices to say **the mystery.**

38. **(D)** (D) is incorrect. It should read **each other.** Although at a glance it may appear correct, the important thing to note here is that the nouns are two in number. In such a case, it should be **each other.** If there were three families or more, it would be **one another.**

39. **(A)** (A) is incorrect. It is often easy to mistake words that are made from the common root word, as in this case. **On the whole** does not mean the same thing as **wholly.** Wholly means totally; while **On the whole** means globally, or in the surface.

40. **(B)** (B) is incorrect. This sentence is another that has to be studied carefully. The sentence began with a plural noun, **justices,** but it later talks about the **majority,** which is a singular noun. Therefore, the verb should be singular and should read **has voted.**

Section 3:
READING COMPREHENSION
AND VOCABULARY

1. **(D)** "Journals" is the answer. "Publications" refers back to "instruction guides" and of the four choices, only (D) is a written item. The other choices are all references to items in the passage, but they are not applicable to the question.

2. **(A)** "Sufficient" is the correct answer. The sentence where this word is found begins with "although." This usually means that the first half of the sentence will be the opposite of the second half. The first half of the sentence informs the reader of the helpfulness of the publications. It follows that the second half would describe how the books were not helpful. Choice (B) "unhelpful" might seem like the correct choice, but the second half of the sentence begins with a negative so "adequate" would need to be a positive word, in this case (A) "sufficient.' Choices (C) and (D) are not applicable to this sentence.

3. **(A)** Although this type of question may seem like a lot of work, the answer to this one is given in the last sentence of the passage. "Over time we have developed guidelines and questions that have proven successful for us; we hope that the following suggestions will be helpful to anyone who wishes to collect the folklore of his or her family." The phrase, "the questions that follow" indicates that what follows would be (A) "How to gather family folklore." The other choices are all topics discussed in the passage, but not what would follow.

4. **(B)** The answer to this question can be found in the sentence, "To prepare for these interviews we drew upon our academic backgrounds in folklore and American studies, and upon our personal backgrounds as members of families." That their academic backgrounds were in folklore and American studies suggests that (B) "They were historians and sociologists." Even though they had families, it does not mean (C) "They had children." Choices (A) and (D) are not mentioned in the passage.

5. **(C)** The purpose of this passage is to (C) "instruct." The passage was written as an introduction to a "how-to" on compiling family folklore. The passage does not (A) "motivate," (B) "berate or insult," or (D) "cajole or flatter."

6.   **(B)**   "American history is inherent in the family folklore in America" is correct. (A) "anyone can successfully interview people about their family folklore without prior training," may appear to be true, but one must then realize that the results will not be as comprehensive and effective as compared to an interview carried out by someone with prior training. (C) "American history and folklore of Americans have no connections" is implied as incorrect by the words "background in folklore and American studies," showing a connection according to the staff at the Smithsonian Institution. (D) "no guidelines are needed in the interviews" is false, as demonstrated by the Smithsonian group, who felt the need to write their own.

7.   **(A)**   "Clinical sociology guides" are the only ones not discussed in the passage. (B) "genealogy guides," (C) "oral history," and (D) "folklore fieldwork," are all mentioned.

8.   **(B)**   The implication is that staff members of the Smithsonian Institution's Family Folklore Project are most likely college graduates. (A) "life experience," (C) "fieldwork," and (D) "travel," do not necessarily take place in a college setting.

9.   **(D)**   The phrase "no single book was completely adequate since folklore combines aspects of all the above disciplines" clearly shows that "interdisciplinary" is correct. As the passage does state that the definition does represent it as historical, traditional, and academic in nature. (A), (B), and (C) are not correct.

10.   **(D)**   "Over time, we have developed guidelines and questions that have proved successful for us" indicates that "write their own guidelines on how to collect family folklore" was their decision. (A) "use only a fieldwork guide to proceed with their work," (B) "to trust only already published guides on how to proceed," and (C) "to use only historical accounts on how to collect family folklore," are disproved by the statement that they did develop their own guidelines and questions.

11.   **(C)**   The answer to this question is in the sentence, "Cultured pearls are not easily distinguished from natural pearls except by an expert." Of the four choices, only (C) "jeweler," would have the expert knowledge of pearls.

12.   **(B)**   "Contaminant" is the correct answer. In this sentence, an "impurity" is a particle that has invaded the shell of the mollusk. Choices (A) and (D) do not make sense in the sentence. Choice (C) "pearl," is not correct because the pearl is created after the contaminant has irritated the mollusk.

13. **(A)** "Annoyance" is the correct response. An irritant is something that causes uncomfortableness or annoyance. Choices (B) "aid" and (C) "relief" are the opposite in meaning. Choice (D) is not relevant to this sentence.

14. **(C)** The answer to this question is provided in the sentence, "Nacre is composed chiefly of calcium carbonate." The other answer choices are items mentioned within the passage, but not components of nacre.

15. **(A)** "Deliberate" is the correct response. To do something intentionally is to do it deliberately or with forethought. Choices (B) "accidental" and (C) "unconscious" are the opposite in meaning. Choice (D) has no relationship to the answer.

16. **(D)** "Organic gem" is mentioned in the first sentence. While (B) "a gemstone," is a partial answer, it is not complete. (A) "a rock," and (C) "a mineral" are not mentioned at all.

17. **(B)** "The introduction of the irritating impurity" is described in the second sentence as the difference between a pearl and a cultured pearl. (A) "color" is not mentioned in the passage. (C) The "coating material" is nacre for both a cultured and a natural pearl. (D) "irritating impurity" is not correct because it is not a complete answer.

18. **(C)** "Organically secreted by the mollusk" can be inferred by the statement "The mollusk (i.e., the organism) coats the irritant with a substance called nacre." (A) "mechanically manufactured," (B) "the result of laboratory testing," and (D) "present in the chemical composition of freshwater ponds" are not correct.

19. **(C)** The passage discusses two forms of pearl-making. (B) The allusion that cultured pearls are of a higher quality than natural pearls is never mentioned. Choices (A) and (D) both refer to a lack of supply of natural pearls. While it is possible that this "drought" is taking place, the passage does not state clearly **why** there are more cultured pearls being used; this may be the result of the lesser cost of the cultured pearls, or perhaps because they can be made more quickly and easily.

20. **(C)** "The water organism" is the correct answer, taken from the statement, "a cultured pearl is the result of the intentional insertion of a mother-of-pearl bead into a live marine mollusk." (A) "any animal" is much too broad to be correct, as a mollusk is a specific animal. (B) "a land animal" is totally incorrect as pearls are grown in the water. The word "marine" in the second sentence is an important clue. (D) "all of the above," cannot be true if some of the answers are incorrect.

21. **(C)** The answer to this question is given in the list of the first paragraph. The only item not listed is (C) "as medical cures." The other three are mentioned in order in the second sentence.

22. **(A)** "Keep" is the correct answer. To retain something is to keep it in this case. The constellations are keeping the names given to them by the Greeks. Choice (B) "eliminate" is the opposite in meaning to the sentence. Choices (C) and (D) have nothing to do with the sentence.

23. **(A)** The answer to this question requires some simple math. The ancient Greeks discovered 48 star patterns. Astronomers now know of 88 such patterns. When you subtract 48 from 88, your remainder is (A) "40." Do not try to add the two numbers since the question asks for the number found between then and now.

24. **(C)** "Drawn" is the correct answer. Although "drawing" usually refers to pictures, it also means "to be obtained from." In this sentence, the star patterns are obtaining their names from Greek mythology. The other choices are not appropriate to this question.

25. **(C)** The passage states, "The names for many of these star patterns retain the names given to them by the Greeks which were most often derived from mythology." Of the four choices, the one that would most likely be a figure from Greek mythology would be (C)—an ancient Greek hero.

26. **(C)** "Man has depended on the stars at times" is clearly stated by the words "the stars have been relied upon." (A) "man never depends on the stars" is the opposite of this statement and is therefore incorrect. (B) "stars are only for beautifying our skies" is proved incorrect by the words "relied upon" and (D) "moons are the same as stars" is never mentioned.

27. **(D)** References to "the dawn of civilization" and "ancient stargazers" imply a long-time fascination. (A) "only adults are intrigued with the stars and constellations" is disproved by the use of "humanity," indicating all age groups. (B) "stars have scientific significance only" is disproved by "the stars have been relied upon to direct travelers, to make agricultural predictions, to win wars and to awaken love in the hearts of men and women." (C) is also disproved by the use of "humanity," and the knowledge that adults travel, make predictions, and participate in wars.

28. **(A)** "Predictions" refers to "crop fertility" as seen in the words "agricultural predictions." (B) "war success" is modified by the word "win," not "predict." (C) "Cupid's

421

progress" is implied by and preceded by the word "awaken." (D) "travel directions" is preceded by the words "relied upon."

29. **(B)** "Charted" means identified according to composition and location, as seen in the words "definite star patterns." (A) "admired" means to be looked at favorably. (C) "illustrated" implies picture form without words. (D) "named" refers merely to the calling of something by a specific name.

30. **(D)** "Patterns-constellations" are synonymous as seen in the phrase "patterns or constellations" in the last sentence. (A) "humanity-astronomers" are not always the same. (B) "different parts-different times" are two different things. (C) "stargazers-travelers" are also two different kinds of people.

31. **(A)** According to the passage, "Most of the parks described in this book do not offer meals and lodging." The correct answer is (A) "lodging." The other three choices are all things that parks do provide according to the passage.

32. **(C)** The answer for this question is taken directly from the passage. "Most have parking lots, restrooms, and other features that are accessible to disabled persons." In this sentence, "disabled" means "handicapped." Choices (A), (B), and (D) may be accessible to a handicapped person, but they are not mentioned in the passage.

33. **(A)** According to the passage, "There you will find information on attractions, facilities, and activities such as scenic drives, nature trails, and historic tours." This question is a simple content question, and the information is found in the second sentence of the passage. The other choices are not mentioned as being part of the Visitor's Center.

34. **(D)** "Representative" is the correct response. A description offers a representation of a person, place or thing. Do not think that because a description deals with appearance, that choice (B) "comely" or choice (C) "beautiful" is correct. Choice (A) "natural" is also incorrect. Do not think that because the passage is discussing nature that "natural" is a possibility.

35. **(B)** "Ask" is the correct response. To inquire is to ask. Choice (A) "demand" is the opposite of the intended meaning. The other choices are not synonyms for "inquire."

36. **(C)** "The ease with which a physically disabled person can get to and through a

park" is implied in the second paragraph. (A) "availability of admission tickets to certain areas" implies that tickets may or may not be available. (B) "availability of park staff to assist people" is not an issue of actual accessibility. (D) "in what direction one drives to get to a particular attraction" does not imply accessibility, but rather necessary knowledge to get there. The context of the word usage is important for this answer.

37. **(B)** "They are welcome and provided for in most parks" is seen in the sentence, "Many parks can provide assistance for those who have visual, auditory, or other physical handicaps." (A) "they are welcome but not provided for," is incorrect. (C) "they are not really welcome in most parks" is not true as implied by the words, "most parks can provide assistance." (D) "there are no facilities for them in most parks" is not true, as implied by the phrase "many parks can provide assistance."

38. **(A)** "Interviews with inhabitants" is not mentioned in the first paragraph as are (B) "exhibits," (C) "literature," and (D) "films."

39. **(C)** Meals and lodging describe the word "accommodations" as seen in the last sentence of the first paragraph. (A) "scenic drives-nature trails," (B) "geology-history," and (D) "plant life-animal life" have nothing to do with accommodations.

40. **(D)** The first sentence of the second paragraph does not include mental limitations in its list of special assistance provisions. All others are included in the author's list of limitations and are, therefore, incorrect.

41. **(B)** According to the last sentence of the passage, "If the board must be cut, do not inhale the dust; do the work outdoors, using a breathing mask." The correct response is (B) "outdoors." All the other choices are opposite to what is supposedly needed, which is an open space.

42. **(C)** According to the last sentence of the passage, "If the board must be cut, do not inhale the dust; do the work outdoors, using a breathing mask." The correct response is (C) "wear a breathing mask." Choice (B) "paint the board first" is recommended to keep the fibers from coming loose. If the board is being cut then the fibers will come loose anyway and the paint will not be effective. Choices (A) and (D) are not mentioned in the passage as safety precautions.

43. **(A)** "Danger" is the correct response. There are not context clues to the meaning of the word within the sentence itself, but from the overall tone of the passage, the reader

should be able to determine that asbestos is dangerous. Therefore, if asbestos is a health hazard, it is probably a danger to your health. Choices (B), (C), and (D) are all opposite to the meaning of "hazard."

44. **(D)** "Warning" is the correct choice. Choices (A) "instruction" and (C) "aid" are both potentially correct, but do not offer as strong a message as (D) "warning." The authors' word choice within the passage includes, "hazard," "strongly recommended", and "cautiously." These are all very strong words, so there tone is one of warning and not just aid or instruction.

45. **(C)** "Criterion" is the correct choice. A standard could be a (B) "flag," but it does not fit in the context of this passage. Choices (A) and (D) are references to topics discussed within the passage, but they do not refer to "standards."

46. **(C)** "Asbestos can be harmful to one's health" is implied in such terms as "health hazard," "as a standard protection," "alternate protection," "use it cautiously," "do not inhale," and "use a breathing mask." (A) "asbestos is as safe as other building materials" is not correct in light of the words, "health hazard of asbestos fibers." (B) is not correct because "do not inhale the dust" implies that the dust is a hazard to your lungs, too. (D) "using asbestos in building materials is all right" is qualified by the words of caution, "if you must use the asbestos millboard."

47. **(B)** "Becoming active" is implied by the statement "initiating the process of removing asbestos as a standard protection." (A) "promoting asbestos as a safe building material" is directly opposite the statement "initiating the process of removing asbestos." (C) "taking a 'wait and see' position on asbestos as a building material" is directly opposite the idea implied through the use of word "initiating." (D) "staying out of the asbestos controversy completely" is in direct opposition to the idea implied through the use of the word "initiating."

48. **(B)** There are strong opinions on both sides because, although the material is hazardous, its use is widespread, and it would be costly to substitute. (A) and (C) are similar incorrect choices, meaning that there is no controversy. (D) also implies a lack of controversy, but this time it is because of a lack of concern.

49. **(A)** "Breathe into either nose or mouth" is the correct answer, as a breathing mask is suggested to stop this hazard. (B) "take in air through the eyes" is not discussed in the paragraph. (C) "get fibers under fingernails" is not discussed, nor is (D) "get fibers in open cuts and sores."

50. **(D)**   Paint is offered as a deterrent to the hazard of asbestos in the statement, "We recommend painting the asbestos to help keep the fibers from coming loose." (A) "water," (B) "boards," and (C) "air" are not discussed in the passage as possible deterrents.

51. **(A)**   "Device" is the correct choice. Within the sentence "apparatus" is described by both "vocal" and child's," therefore, it is unlikely that either (B) "child" or (D) "speech" would be the correct choices. A noun is almost never used to describe itself. Choice (C) can be eliminated because you cannot have a vocal "brain."

52. **(B)**   "Described" is the correct response. The "characteristic" of anything are the qualities of the item. When used as a verb, "characterize," it means to describe the qualities. The other choices are not synonyms of "characterized."

53. **(D)**   The answer to this question is in the sentence, "These children have very slow, halting speech with many false starts before the right sounds are produced." The other three choices mentioned are all contrary to the description of the characteristics of verbal dyspraxia.

54. **(C)**   "Unrecognizable" is the correct answer. In describing the speech of children with verbal dyspraxia, it is never (A) "clear" or (B) "unstoppable." From the context of the sentence "unintelligible" is in and the one that follows, (D) "slow" can be eliminated because the sample of speech given is (C) "unrecognizable" as speech.

55. **(B)**   "Problem" is the correct choice. Choice (A) "repair" is the opposite of the meaning of the sentence. If it was repaired, then there would be no difficulties with speech. Choices (C) "speech" and (D) "instructions" are referred to in the passage, but they are not synonyms to "impairment."

56. **(A)**   Produce "precise speech sounds" is described in the words "inability to produce the sequential, rapid and precise movements required for speech." (B) "vowel sounds" is incorrect because the passage states that some children speak only in vowel sounds. (C) "more than one sound in a series" is incorrect because the passage shows the little boy could make more than one sound at a time with his "eye a eh ee-ee." (D) "any human sounds" is incorrect because the child described can make vowel sounds as well as exhibit "halting speech."

57. **(D)**   "Common" is synonymous to the description of sound omissions in the sentence "This disorder is characterized by many sound omissions." (A) "only occasional,"

(B) "very rare," and (C) "nonexistent" are all disproven by the word "many" in the above sentence.

58. **(C)** "Verbal dyspraxics and children with phonological impairment" can have similar problems, as noted in the last sentence. (A) "stroke victims," (B) "heart attack victims," and (D) "mutes" are not mentioned.

59. **(B)** "Without consonants human speech is unintelligible" is implied by the phrase "speak only in vowels making their speech unintelligible." (A) "they are not necessary for intelligent human speech" is disproved by the words "speak only in vowels, making their speech nearly unintelligible." (C) "lack of them causes stuttering" is not discussed in the passage. (D) "lack of them slows down human speech" may be true, but is not the entire answer.

60. **(B)** "The brain's inability to give instructions for motor movements involved with speech" is found in the phrase "but the child's brain cannot give correct instructions." (A) "vocal apparatus," (C) "the child's personality," and (D) "a physical disability" are all incorrect as the "brain's inability" is given as the "real culprit."

Test of English as a Foreign Language
TEST 3
ANSWER SHEET

Section 1:
Listening Comprehension

1. Ⓐ Ⓑ Ⓒ Ⓓ
2. Ⓐ Ⓑ Ⓒ Ⓓ
3. Ⓐ Ⓑ Ⓒ Ⓓ
4. Ⓐ Ⓑ Ⓒ Ⓓ
5. Ⓐ Ⓑ Ⓒ Ⓓ
6. Ⓐ Ⓑ Ⓒ Ⓓ
7. Ⓐ Ⓑ Ⓒ Ⓓ
8. Ⓐ Ⓑ Ⓒ Ⓓ
9. Ⓐ Ⓑ Ⓒ Ⓓ
10. Ⓐ Ⓑ Ⓒ Ⓓ
11. Ⓐ Ⓑ Ⓒ Ⓓ
12. Ⓐ Ⓑ Ⓒ Ⓓ
13. Ⓐ Ⓑ Ⓒ Ⓓ
14. Ⓐ Ⓑ Ⓒ Ⓓ
15. Ⓐ Ⓑ Ⓒ Ⓓ
16. Ⓐ Ⓑ Ⓒ Ⓓ
17. Ⓐ Ⓑ Ⓒ Ⓓ
18. Ⓐ Ⓑ Ⓒ Ⓓ
19. Ⓐ Ⓑ Ⓒ Ⓓ
20. Ⓐ Ⓑ Ⓒ Ⓓ
21. Ⓐ Ⓑ Ⓒ Ⓓ
22. Ⓐ Ⓑ Ⓒ Ⓓ
23. Ⓐ Ⓑ Ⓒ Ⓓ
24. Ⓐ Ⓑ Ⓒ Ⓓ
25. Ⓐ Ⓑ Ⓒ Ⓓ
26. Ⓐ Ⓑ Ⓒ Ⓓ
27. Ⓐ Ⓑ Ⓒ Ⓓ
28. Ⓐ Ⓑ Ⓒ Ⓓ
29. Ⓐ Ⓑ Ⓒ Ⓓ
30. Ⓐ Ⓑ Ⓒ Ⓓ
31. Ⓐ Ⓑ Ⓒ Ⓓ
32. Ⓐ Ⓑ Ⓒ Ⓓ
33. Ⓐ Ⓑ Ⓒ Ⓓ
34. Ⓐ Ⓑ Ⓒ Ⓓ
35. Ⓐ Ⓑ Ⓒ Ⓓ
36. Ⓐ Ⓑ Ⓒ Ⓓ
37. Ⓐ Ⓑ Ⓒ Ⓓ
38. Ⓐ Ⓑ Ⓒ Ⓓ
39. Ⓐ Ⓑ Ⓒ Ⓓ
40. Ⓐ Ⓑ Ⓒ Ⓓ
41. Ⓐ Ⓑ Ⓒ Ⓓ
42. Ⓐ Ⓑ Ⓒ Ⓓ
43. Ⓐ Ⓑ Ⓒ Ⓓ
44. Ⓐ Ⓑ Ⓒ Ⓓ
45. Ⓐ Ⓑ Ⓒ Ⓓ
46. Ⓐ Ⓑ Ⓒ Ⓓ
47. Ⓐ Ⓑ Ⓒ Ⓓ
48. Ⓐ Ⓑ Ⓒ Ⓓ
49. Ⓐ Ⓑ Ⓒ Ⓓ
50. Ⓐ Ⓑ Ⓒ Ⓓ

Section 2:
Structure and
Written Expression

1. Ⓐ Ⓑ Ⓒ Ⓓ
2. Ⓐ Ⓑ Ⓒ Ⓓ
3. Ⓐ Ⓑ Ⓒ Ⓓ
4. Ⓐ Ⓑ Ⓒ Ⓓ
5. Ⓐ Ⓑ Ⓒ Ⓓ
6. Ⓐ Ⓑ Ⓒ Ⓓ
7. Ⓐ Ⓑ Ⓒ Ⓓ
8. Ⓐ Ⓑ Ⓒ Ⓓ
9. Ⓐ Ⓑ Ⓒ Ⓓ
10. Ⓐ Ⓑ Ⓒ Ⓓ
11. Ⓐ Ⓑ Ⓒ Ⓓ
12. Ⓐ Ⓑ Ⓒ Ⓓ
13. Ⓐ Ⓑ Ⓒ Ⓓ
14. Ⓐ Ⓑ Ⓒ Ⓓ
15. Ⓐ Ⓑ Ⓒ Ⓓ
16. Ⓐ Ⓑ Ⓒ Ⓓ
17. Ⓐ Ⓑ Ⓒ Ⓓ
18. Ⓐ Ⓑ Ⓒ Ⓓ
19. Ⓐ Ⓑ Ⓒ Ⓓ
20. Ⓐ Ⓑ Ⓒ Ⓓ
21. Ⓐ Ⓑ Ⓒ Ⓓ
22. Ⓐ Ⓑ Ⓒ Ⓓ
23. Ⓐ Ⓑ Ⓒ Ⓓ
24. Ⓐ Ⓑ Ⓒ Ⓓ
25. Ⓐ Ⓑ Ⓒ Ⓓ
26. Ⓐ Ⓑ Ⓒ Ⓓ
27. Ⓐ Ⓑ Ⓒ Ⓓ
28. Ⓐ Ⓑ Ⓒ Ⓓ
29. Ⓐ Ⓑ Ⓒ Ⓓ
30. Ⓐ Ⓑ Ⓒ Ⓓ
31. Ⓐ Ⓑ Ⓒ Ⓓ
32. Ⓐ Ⓑ Ⓒ Ⓓ
33. Ⓐ Ⓑ Ⓒ Ⓓ
34. Ⓐ Ⓑ Ⓒ Ⓓ
35. Ⓐ Ⓑ Ⓒ Ⓓ
36. Ⓐ Ⓑ Ⓒ Ⓓ
37. Ⓐ Ⓑ Ⓒ Ⓓ
38. Ⓐ Ⓑ Ⓒ Ⓓ
39. Ⓐ Ⓑ Ⓒ Ⓓ
40. Ⓐ Ⓑ Ⓒ Ⓓ

Section 3:
Reading Comprehension
and Vobcabulary

1. (A) (B) (C) (D)
2. (A) (B) (C) (D)
3. (A) (B) (C) (D)
4. (A) (B) (C) (D)
5. (A) (B) (C) (D)
6. (A) (B) (C) (D)
7. (A) (B) (C) (D)
8. (A) (B) (C) (D)
9. (A) (B) (C) (D)
10. (A) (B) (C) (D)
11. (A) (B) (C) (D)
12. (A) (B) (C) (D)
13. (A) (B) (C) (D)
14. (A) (B) (C) (D)
15. (A) (B) (C) (D)
16. (A) (B) (C) (D)
17. (A) (B) (C) (D)
18. (A) (B) (C) (D)

19. (A) (B) (C) (D)
20. (A) (B) (C) (D)
21. (A) (B) (C) (D)
22. (A) (B) (C) (D)
23. (A) (B) (C) (D)
24. (A) (B) (C) (D)
25. (A) (B) (C) (D)
26. (A) (B) (C) (D)
27. (A) (B) (C) (D)
28. (A) (B) (C) (D)
29. (A) (B) (C) (D)
30. (A) (B) (C) (D)
31. (A) (B) (C) (D)
32. (A) (B) (C) (D)
33. (A) (B) (C) (D)
34. (A) (B) (C) (D)
35. (A) (B) (C) (D)
36. (A) (B) (C) (D)
37. (A) (B) (C) (D)
38. (A) (B) (C) (D)
39. (A) (B) (C) (D)

40. (A) (B) (C) (D)
41. (A) (B) (C) (D)
42. (A) (B) (C) (D)
43. (A) (B) (C) (D)
44. (A) (B) (C) (D)
45. (A) (B) (C) (D)
46. (A) (B) (C) (D)
47. (A) (B) (C) (D)
48. (A) (B) (C) (D)
49. (A) (B) (C) (D)
50. (A) (B) (C) (D)
51. (A) (B) (C) (D)
52. (A) (B) (C) (D)
53. (A) (B) (C) (D)
54. (A) (B) (C) (D)
55. (A) (B) (C) (D)
56. (A) (B) (C) (D)
57. (A) (B) (C) (D)
58. (A) (B) (C) (D)
59. (A) (B) (C) (D)
60. (A) (B) (C) (D)

TOEFL

TEST 3

Section 1:
LISTENING COMPREHENSION

TIME: 35 Minutes
50 Questions

Part A

DIRECTIONS: In Part A you will hear short conversations between two speakers. At the end of each conversation, a third person will ask a question about what was said. **You will hear each conversation just one time.** Therefore, you must listen carefully to understand what each speaker says. After you hear a conversation and the question about it, read the four possible answers in your test book and decide which one is the best answer to the question you heard. Then on your answer sheet, find the number of the question and fill in the space that corresponds to the answer you have chosen.

(WAIT)

1. (A) Give the woman a cigarette
    (B) Not give the woman a cigarette
    (C) Offer to light the woman's cigarette
    (D) Tell the woman that he quit smoking

2. (A) Daughter
    (B) Sister
    (C) Niece
    (D) Nephew

3.   (A) He would not like to go to the theater with the woman.
     (B) He would like to go see a play at the theater, but not with the woman.
     (C) He would like to go see a play at the theater with the woman, but he would like to invite other people as well.
     (D) He would not like to go to the theater, but he already saw that particular play.

4.   (A) The beach
     (B) A swimming pool
     (C) A health club
     (D) The gym

5.   (A) In a classroom
     (B) In a doctor's office
     (C) At a dentist's office
     (D) At the department of motor vehicles

6.   (A) She would love to take care of his cat.
     (B) She hates cats.
     (C) She could not take his pet because she is allergic to cats.
     (D) She already has a dog, and doesn't think it would get along with the cat.

7.   (A) She will share her books with the man.
     (B) She can't share her books with the man, because she no longer has them.
     (C) She never took that class.
     (D) She used different books when she had that class.

8.   (A) The entire office is empty because everyone called out sick.
     (B) The woman is the only person who is not feeling well.
     (C) The woman has probably caught the same illness that many other people in the office have.
     (D) The woman is infecting the whole office with her illness.

9.   (A) The man's
     (B) The woman's
     (C) The woman's grandmother's
     (D) The pie was bought in a store

10. (A) The man should solve all his problems over the weekend.
    (B) The man should do something relaxing and enjoyable over the weekend, and not think about his problems at work.
    (C) The man should work during the weekend.
    (D) The man should quit his job this weekend.

11. (A) She is sorry that the back door is not locked.
    (B) The area they live in is not safe.
    (C) The man should get two locks for the back door.
    (D) They should recheck that the back door is locked for the sake of safety.

12. (A) Seventy miles per hour
    (B) Fifty miles per hour
    (C) Fifteen miles per hour
    (D) Forty miles per hour

13. (A) Because she thinks he is a strong man
    (B) Because he has missed meetings for two weeks
    (C) Because he has to read a will
    (D) Because he is a man of strong determination

14. (A) He is sick.
    (B) He thinks that the days are getting longer.
    (C) He had too much work at the office.
    (D) His office is very far from his home.

15. (A) In a bank
    (B) Near a pay phone
    (C) In a car
    (D) In an office

16. (A) One
    (B) Two
    (C) Three
    (D) Four

17. (A) The woman is very fond of shopping.
    (B) The woman is tired.
    (C) Shopping with the woman is very boring.
    (D) He has to buy a tire for his car.

18. (A) She is surprised.
    (B) She is happy.
    (C) She is relieved.
    (D) She is angry.

19. (A) In her office
    (B) In the library
    (C) In the laboratory
    (D) In the conference room

20. (A) Auto mechanic
    (B) Electrician
    (C) Car salesman
    (D) Insurance agent

21. (A) She has a problem to take care of.
    (B) She does not like the people who arranged the party.
    (C) She usually does not like to go to parties.
    (D) She is afraid people will not be friendly with her.

22. (A) The man will lose his job if he doesn't work hard.
    (B) The man should feel excited about the interview.
    (C) The man should try everything to get the job.
    (D) The man should at least take the opportunity to appear for the interview.

23. (A) He has a good mind.
    (B) He can achieve anything, if he is determined.
    (C) He cannot complete any course because he is not brilliant.
    (D) He does not mind doing anything in order to complete his course.

24. (A) At five o'clock
    (B) At three o'clock
    (C) At two o'clock
    (D) At six o'clock

25. (A)   She is not a lucky person.
     (B)   She never had good luck with her jobs.
     (C)   She will never take another job.
     (D)   She is very happy with her new job.

Part B

WAIT

26. (A)   At the garage
     (B)   At home
     (C)   On the side of the road
     (D)   Driving to work

27. (A)   Flat tire
     (B)   Engine problems
     (C)   No gas
     (D)   Earthquake

28. (A)   She did
     (B)   Her husband
     (C)   A mechanic
     (D)   The man

29. (A)   She grew up working on cars.
     (B)   She took a class.
     (C)   She guessed.
     (D)   She used to race cars.

30. (A) He knows the engine inside and out.
    (B) He also works as a mechanic.
    (C) He can just about change a flat tire.
    (D) He used to race cars.

31. (A) Because he is very forgetful
    (B) Because he doesn't trust the woman
    (C) Because it is unusual for them to have extra money at the end of the month
    (D) Because they received many bills this month

32. (A) They have not paid their bills.
    (B) The woman didn't take the piano lessons this month.
    (C) They didn't buy the bookshelf.
    (D) They decided to save money.

33. (A) Buy a bookshelf
    (B) Not to take piano lessons any more
    (C) Buy a piano
    (D) Pay all her bills

34. (A) The woman has to pay the bills in time.
    (B) The woman has to stop taking piano lessons.
    (C) The woman has to forget about the bookshelf.
    (D) The woman has to help save some money next month.

35. (A) Because they don't intend to pay their bills
    (B) Because they won't go to the showroom
    (C) Because they don't have to pay for the woman's piano lessons next month also
    (D) Because he is going to get some extra money

36. (A) Get a photocopy of her dissertation
    (B) Get a hundred pages typed
    (C) Get her picture taken
    (D) Get her thesis written

37. (A) Fifteen dollars
    (B) Ten dollars
    (C) One hundred dollars
    (D) Twenty dollars

38. (A) Because he is a good man
    (B) Because the woman has about a hundred pages for photocopying
    (C) Because he doesn't have to do it today
    (D) Because he likes students

39. (A) One page
    (B) Fifteen pages
    (C) Ten pages
    (D) One hundred pages

40. (A) She is waiting for her professor's review.
    (B) She is waiting for the man to still lower the charge.
    (C) She is waiting for some money.
    (D) She is waiting to finish typing.

Part C

DIRECTIONS: In Part C you will hear short talks. At the end of each talk, a second person will ask several questions about what was said. **You will hear each talk and the questions about it just one time.** They will not be written out for you. Therefore, you must listen carefully to understand what each speaker says. After you hear a question, read the four possible answers in your test book and decide which one is the best answer to the question you heard. Then on your answer sheet, find the number of the question and fill in the space that corresponds to the answer you have chosen.

(WAIT)

41. (A) Middle Ages
    (B) Renaissance
    (C) Twentiety century
    (D) 1100s

42. (A) 60%
    (B) 70%
    (C) 80%
    (D) 90%

43. (A) Islamic and Byzantine
    (B) German and Italian
    (C) Russian and Norwegian
    (D) American and Chinese

44. (A) The illiterate
    (B) Merchants
    (C) Intellectuals
    (D) Artists

45. (A) Agriculture and manufacturing
    (B) Philosophy and science
    (C) Shipping and sailing
    (D) Fitness and nutrition

46. (A) Trees and shrubs
    (B) Paint and color
    (C) Some steps for satisfactory painting
    (D) Sash brushes

47. (A) Because many a time colors look different in the daylight than under artificial light
    (B) Because paints are expensive
    (C) Because no one can afford to paint their house every year
    (D) Because some colors don't adhere to walls

48. (A) Hot and humid
    (B) Cold and windy
    (C) Warm and dry
    (D) Chilly and dry

49. (A) Because it is the speaker's opinion
     (B) Because we may forget to finish it later on
     (C) Because it saves a lot of paint
     (D) Because, if we don't, the paint will dry unevenly

50. (A) By using the paint sparingly
     (B) By being careful about selection
     (C) By filming it with solvent, sealing it, and keeping it in a warm dry place
     (D) By using a good sash brush

STOP

If time still remains, you may review work only in this section.
When the time allotted is up, you may go on to the next section.

Section 2:
STRUCTURE AND WRITTEN EXPRESSION

TIME: 25 Minutes
         40 Questions

DIRECTIONS: Questions 1-15 are incomplete sentences. Beneath each sentence are four words or phrases marked (A), (B), (C), and (D). Choose the **one** word or phrase which best completes the sentence. Then, on your answer sheet, find the number of the question and fill in the space that corresponds to the answer you have chosen.

---

1. _____ must pay the admission fee.
    (A)   Everyone who doesn't have a free ticket
    (B)   No one who doesn't have a free ticket
    (C)   No one who has free tickets
    (D)   Anyone who has free tickets

2. When I last saw them, the police _____ the robbers down Columbus Street.
    (A)   were chasing
    (B)   was chasing
    (C)   chased
    (D)   were on a chase

3. Erosion _____, but it constantly changes the features on the surface of the earth.
    (A)   which is a slow process
    (B)   although a slow process
    (C)   being a slow process
    (D)   is a slow process

4. When an organism is completely encapsulated and preserved, it becomes a fossil, _____ turning into evidence of things that once lived.
    (A)   thereby
    (B)   as a result of
    (C)   so
    (D)   in the end

5. The pictures of the Loch Ness Monster show a remarkable resemblance to a plesiosaur, a large water reptile of the Mesozoic era _____ to be extinct for more than 70 million years.
    (A) presumably
    (B) presumed
    (C) presumptuous
    (D) is presumed

6. In our own galaxy, the Milky Way, there are perhaps 200 billion stars, _____ probably have planets on which life is feasible.
    (A) a small fraction in which
    (B) a small fraction of which
    (C) a small fraction which
    (D) which a fraction of

7. _____ John F. Kennedy requested sweeping civil rights legislation from Congress and successfully managed the Cuban missile crisis in 1962.
    (A) He was the youngest man ever elected president,
    (B) The youngest man ever elected president,
    (C) Because he was the youngest man ever elected president,
    (D) The youngest man ever elected president he was,

8. _____, Parliament passed a series of new acts, or laws, for the colonies.
    (A) About 1764 and 1773
    (B) On 1764 and 1773
    (C) Between 1764 and 1773
    (D) Before 1764 and 1773

9. He is _____, if not taller, than his uncle.
    (A) tall
    (B) as tall
    (C) as tall as
    (D) the tallest

10. The trapeze artist who ran away with the clown _____ the lion tamer's heart.
    (A) broke away
    (B) broke down
    (C) broke
    (D) broken down

11. His heavy drinking _____ makes him a poor role model.
    (A) and the fact that he gambles
    (B) and that he gambles
    (C) and he gambles which
    (D) and gambling

12. Depression that inflicts people who become conscious of the lack of content in their lives when the rush of the busy week stops _____ as Sunday Neurosis.
    (A) has been referred to by a prominent psychiatrist
    (B) has been referred to as by a prominent psychiatrist
    (C) a prominent psychiatrist has referred to it
    (D) it has been referred to by a prominent psychiatrist

13. Just as there are occupations that require college degrees, _____ occupations for which technical training is necessary.
    (A) so to there are
    (B) so also there are
    (C) so there are
    (D) so too are there

14. Most of the older civilizations which flourished during the fifth century B.C. _____.
    (A) they have died out
    (B) has died out
    (C) have died out
    (D) they had died out

15. The student asked her professor if he would have gone on the space ship _____ earlier.
    (A) if he knew
    (B) if he knows
    (C) he had known
    (D) had he known

DIRECTIONS: In questions 16-40 each sentence has four underlined words or phrases, marked (A), (B), (C), and (D). Choose the **one** word or phrase which is incorrect and must be changed to make the sentence correct. Then, on your answer sheet, find the number of the question and fill in the space that corresponds to the answer you have chosen.

16. Even after having their grandchildren live with them for ten years, the
                    A   B
     couple felt that rising children these days was the most difficult of all
                    C   D
     family matters.

17. The most important cash crop of the farmers in Iraq is dates, which Iraq
                                    A   B   C
     is the world's leading exporter.
                    D

18. More has been learned about the Moon that any other of the Earth's
     A   B
     neighbors in space because of the Apollo program, which enabled men
                                                              C
     to walk on the Moon and bring back hundreds of pounds of rocks.
                                        D

19. Despite the variety that the average family has in meat, fish, poultry, and
          A   B   C
     vegetarian recipes, they find most meals unexciting.
                    D

20. The speaker ought not have criticized the paraprofessionals, knowing fully
                            A   B
     well that they were seated in the audience.
                        C   D

21. Although there are 48 sounds in the spoken English language, there are
          A   B
     26 letters only to express these sounds in the written language.
                    C   D

441

22. Iceland has the oldest parliament, which goes as far back to 930 A.D.,
    —A—   —B—
    when "Althing," the legislative assembly, was established.
         ©   D

23. The young woman often wondered where at the estuary did the river formed
    ————————————————   ————   —   ——————
              A   B C   D
    little rivulets.

24. The only problem with the debate last week was that it had beginning to
    —————————————   —————————————
           A   ®
    sound more like a personal attack than a dispassionate, intellectual
    —————   ——————————
        C   D
    argument.

25. Susan Jones was at the bus stop well on time to catch the 7:01 bus, but had
                  —   ——————   ————
                  Ⓐ   B   C
    to miss her breakfast to do it.
    —————————
         D

26. As her father could not drive her to the airport, she requested her uncle
    —   ———————   ——————————————
    A taking her   B
    take her instead of her father.
    ————   ——————————
     ©   D

27. Plays that stress the illogical or irrational aspects of experience usually
              —————   —————
    show   A   B
    to show the pointlessness of modern life.
    —————
     ©   D

28. A famous collection of Persian, Indian, and Arabian folktales, the *Arabian*
    —
    A
    Nights it was supposedly told by the legendary queen Scheherazade to her
            was
          ——————   ————————————————
            ®   C
    husband every night for 1001 days.
    ————————————
         D

29. What may the oldest fossil foot print yet found was discovered in
        A   B   C
    June 1968 by William J. Meister, an amateur fossil collector.
                                               D

30. Most of us think of sharks as danger, due to a lack of information
                              A   B   C
    rather than fear.
        D

31. When ionizing radiation penetrates living tissue, it wreaks havoc on the
                                        A
    atoms and molecules in its path, setting off a chain of events that can
                    B   C
    destroy living cells, or make them function abnormal.
                                      D

32. Numerous differences in skeletons and musculature distinguish the two
        A   B
    groups, along the fact that loons, unlike waterfowl, cannot walk well on
            C   D
    land.

33. Most women have the capacity of bearing children even after the age of
                        A   B
    30, but doctors advise them to have children sooner.
                C   D

34. The discovery of the connection between aspirin and Reye's syndrome, a
            A   B
    rare and deadly disease, is a recent example of the caution which drugs
                    C   D
    must be used, even for medical purposes.

35. My parents moved out of their old home sometimes last year after they
    _____
      A   B
    had celebrated their fiftieth anniversary there.
    _____
         C   D

36. The library she worked in borrowed books, magazines, audio cassettes, and
    _____
         A   B
    maps to its patrons, who could keep them for four weeks.
    ____   ____
     C   D

37. The most common question that people ask a fiction writer is whether
    ____   ____   ____
     A   B
    or not has he experienced what he has written about.
    _____
     C   D

38. At the World Literacy Center, an organization that works to help people
    ____   ____
     A   B
    read, the volunteers work hardly, enabling them to successfully reach
                            ____   ____
                             C   D
    their goals.

39. The officers made it clear that they were leaving her go only on the
    _____   _____   ____
         A   A   B
    grounds that she was old and not because she was above suspicion.
    ____   ____
     C   D

40. The book, which is a useful guide for today's young people, is dealing with
              _____   _____
                A   B
    many questions and problems that confront them at school and at home as
                                     _____   _____
                                        C   D
    well as in society.

(STOP)

If time still remains, you may review work only in this section.
When the time allotted is up, you may go on to the next section.

444

Section 3:
READING COMPREHENSION
AND VOCABULARY

TIME: 55 Minutes
60 Questions

DIRECTIONS: In this section you will read several passages. Each one is followed by several questions about it. You are to choose the best answer to each question, marked (A), (B), (C), and (D). Then, on your answer sheet, find the number of the question and fill in the space that corresponds to the answer you have chosen.

Questions 1 to 10 refer to the following passage:

1   Awarded the Nobel prize for physics in 1918, German physicist Max Planck is best remembered as the originator of the quantum theory. His work helped usher in a new era in theoretical physics and revolutionized the scientific community's understanding of atomic and subatomic processes.

5   Planck introduced an idea that led to the quantum theory, which became the foundation of twentieth century physics. In December 1900, Planck worked out an equation that described the distribution of radiation accurately over the range of low to high frequencies. He had developed a theory which depended on a model of matter that seemed very strange at the time. The model required the emission of electromagnetic radiation in
10   small chunks or particles. These particles were later called quantums. The energy associated with each quantum is measured by multiplying the frequency of the radiation, v, by a universal constant, h. Thus, energy, or E, equals hv. The constant, h, is known as Planck's constant. It is now recognized as one of the fundamental constants of the world.

      Planck announced his findings in 1900, but is was years before the full consequences
15   of his revolutionary quantum theory were recognized. Throughout his life, Planck made significant contributions to optics, thermodynamics and statistical mechanics, physical chemistry, and other fields. In 1930 he was elected president of the Kaiser Wilhelm Society, which was renamed the Max Planck Society after World War II. Though deeply opposed to the fascist regime of Adolf Hitler, Planck remained in Germany throughout the war. He died
20   in Gottingen on October 4, 1947.

$v + h = hv$

1.   In which of the following fields did Max Planck NOT make a significant contribution?
        (A)   Optics
        (B)   Thermodynamics

445

      (C)   Statistical mechanics

      (D)   Biology

2.   The word "revolutionary," as used in line 15, means

      (A)   dangerous.

      (B)   extremist.

      (C)   momentous.

      (D)   militarist.

3.   It can be inferred from the passage that Planck's work led to the development of which of the following?

      (A)   The rocket

      (B)   The atomic bomb

      (C)   The internal combustion engine

      (D)   The computer

4.   The particles of electromagnetic radiation given off by matter are known as

      (A)   quantums.

      (B)   atoms.

      (C)   electrons.

      (D)   valences.

5.   The word "universal," as used in line 12, most nearly means

      (A)   planetary.

      (B)   cosmic.

      (C)   worldwide.

      (D)   always present.

6.   The implication in this passage is that

      (A)   only a German physicist could discover such a theory.

      (B)   quantum theory, which led to the development of twentieth century physics, is basically a mathematical formula.

      (C)   Planck's constant was not discernible before 1900.

      (D)   radiation was hard to study.

7.   "An idea" as used in line 5, refers to

      (A)   a model of matter.

      (B)   emission of electromagnetic radiation.

      (C)   quantums.

(D)   the equation that described the distribution of radiation accurately over the range of low to high frequencies.

8.   The word "emission" as used in line 9 means
     (A)   giving off.
     (B)   holding on to.
     (C)   throwing away.
     (D)   taking back.

9.   Planck's constant, expressed in a mathematical formula, is
     (A) $e = v/h$
     (B) $E = h/v$
     (C) $e = h - v$
     (D) $E = hv$

10. What is known as Planck's constant?
     (A) v
     (B) h
     (C) e
     (D) E

Questions 11 to 20 refer to the following passage:

1   There has been much speculation about the origin of baseball. In 1907 a special commission decided that the modern game was invented by Abner Doubleday, a West Point cadet, at Cooperstown, N.Y., in 1839. One hundred years later the National Baseball Museum was opened at Cooperstown to honor Doubleday. Historians, however, disagree about the
5   origin of baseball. Some say that baseball comes from bat-and-ball games of ancient times.
         It is a matter of record that in the 1700s English boys played a game they called base ball. Americans have played a kind of baseball since about 1800. At first the American game had different rules and different names in various parts of the country—town ball, rounders, or one old cat. Youngsters today still play some of these simplified forms of the game.
10   Baseball did not receive a standard set of rules until 1845, when Alexander Cartwright organized the Knickerbocker Baseball Club of New York City. The rules Cartwright set up for his nine-player team were widely adopted by other clubs and formed the basis of modern baseball. The game was played on a "diamond" infield with the bases 90 feet apart. The first team to score 21 runs was declared the winner. By 1858 the National Association of Base Ball
15   Players was formed with 25 amateur teams. The Cincinnati Red Stockings began to pay players in 1869.

11. Which of the following is true about the origins of baseball?
    (A) Historians agree that baseball was invented by Abner Doubleday.
    (B) Baseball, as played in the early nineteenth century, differed very little from today's game.
    (C) As early as the 1700s, English boys played a came called "base ball."
    (D) The first standard set of baseball rules was established at the turn of the century.

12. What was the first professional baseball team?
    (A) New York Knickerbockers
    (B) Milwaukee Braves
    (C) Cincinnati Red Stockings
    (D) Brooklyn Dodgers

13. Who first gave baseball a standard set of rules?
    (A) Abner Doubleday
    (B) Alexander Cartwright
    (C) Albert Spalding
    (D) Babe Ruth

14. Which of the following was not a predecessor of baseball?
    (A) Rounders
    (B) Town ball
    (C) Cricket
    (D) One old cat

15. In what year was the National Baseball Museum opened?
    (A) 1939
    (B) 1907
    (C) 1839
    (D) 1845

16. The word "adopted" in line 12 means
    (A) established.
    (B) accepted.
    (C) rejected.
    (D) abolished.

17.   The word "standard" in line 10 means
    (A)   normal.
    (B)   disputed.
    (C)   conclusive.
    (D)   official.

18.   According to the passage, where is the National Baseball Museum located?
    (A)   Cooperstown
    (B)   New York City
    (C)   Cincinnati
    (D)   West Point

19.   The tone of the passage is
    (A)   persuasive.
    (B)   informative.
    (C)   biased.
    (D)   argumentative.

20.   The passage implies that until 1869, baseball was played for all of the following reasons EXCEPT
    (A)   exercise.
    (B)   leisure.
    (C)   profit.
    (D)   socializing.

Questions 21 to 30 refer to the following passage:

1   The blue of the sea is caused by the scattering of sunlight by tiny particles suspended in the water. Blue light, being of short wavelength, is scattered more efficiently than light of longer wavelengths.
         Although waters of the open ocean are commonly some shade of blue, especially in
5   tropical or subtropical regions, green water is commonly seen near coasts. This is caused by yellow pigments being mixed with blue water. Phytoplankton are one source of the yellow pigment. Other microscopic plants may color the water brown or brownish-red. Near the shore silt or sediment in suspension can give waters a brownish hue; outflow of large rivers can often be observed many miles offshore by the coloration of suspended soil particles.
10   Marine phytoplankton (Greek for "plant wanderers") are microscopic single-celled plants that include diatoms, dinoflagellates, coccolithophorids, green algae, and blue-green algae, among others. The growth of these organisms, which photosynthesize light, depends on a delicate balance between nutrient enrichment by vertical mixing, often limited by the availability of nitrogen and light. Diatoms are one-celled plants with patterned glass
15   coverings. Each glass, or silicon dioxide box, is ornamented with species-specific designs,

pits, and perforations making them popular with microscopists and, more recently, scanning electron microscopists.

Some of the thousands of kinds of phytoplankton swim feebly by lashing a whiplike thread appendage called a flagellum. The dinoflagellates are known for their bioluminescence, or phosphorescence, a "cold light" similar to that of fireflies.

20

21.   The growth of phytoplankton is often limited by the availability of
(A)   oxygen.
(B)   hydrogen.
(C)   nitrogen.
(D)   carbon dioxide.

22.   Which of the following is not a type of phytoplankton?
(A)   Green algae
(B)   Diatoms
(C)   Blue-green algae
(D)   Amoeba

23.   Many phytoplankton use an appendage called a flagellum for
(A)   reproduction.
(B)   propulsion.
(C)   digestion.
(D)   respiration.

24.   What color pigment is phytoplankton a source of?
(A)   Red
(B)   Green
(C)   Yellow
(D)   Blue

25.   What can give waters a brownish hue near the shore?
(A)   Sediment
(B)   Phytoplankton
(C)   Blue pigment
(D)   Diatoms

26.   All ocean water is the same shade of blue
(A)   in all places.
(B)   at all times.

    (C)   hardly ever.

    (D)   because all light waves are the same length.

27.   Blue light is

    (A)   a short wavelength.

    (B)   a long wavelength.

    (C)   about equal to all other wavelengths.

    (D)   not scatterable.

28.   Green water near coastlines is almost always caused by

    (A)   sand color.

    (B)   red pigments in coastal waters.

    (C)   blue pigment.

    (D)   reflected light and yellow pigment from plant life.

29.   Phytoplankton are

    (A)   short light rays.

    (B)   suspended soil particles.

    (C)   microscopic floating plants.

    (D)   long light rays.

30.   The main idea of this passage is

    (A)   light causes sea color.

    (B)   sea coloration is varied because of a combination of length of light waves and microscopic plant life and silt.

    (C)   microscopic plant life causes sea color.

    (D)   water composition causes sea color.

Questions 31 to 40 refer to the following passage:

1   Biomass is organic material such as trees, crops, manure, seaweed, and algae. Biomass captures and stores energy though a process called photosynthesis.

        Carbon dioxide from the air enters the leaf through the stomata. Water travels to the leaf cells from the soil through the xylem in the roots and stems. The captured light energy

5 is then used to break down the water into oxygen molecules and hydrogen atoms and to join these hydrogen atoms to the carbon dioxide molecules to make sugar molecules. Six molecules of oxygen are produced as a waste product and are released into the air through the stomata.

        This energy can be released from any form of biomass through conversion processes

10 to produce a variety of useful energy forms—gas, steam, hydrogen, charcoal, methane, and synthetic oils with by-products for food, fertilizers, and chemicals as a bonus. These energy

forms, in turn, can be used to produce electricity, heat, and transportation fuels, reducing the use of conventional nonrenewable energy sources.

31. Which of the following is NOT an energy form produced by the conversion of biomass?
    (A) Methane
    (B) Steam
    (C) Oxygen
    (D) Synthetic oils

32. What is the name of the specialized structures in green plants that carries out photosynthesis?
    (A) Enzymes
    (B) Chlorophyll
    (C) Stomata
    (D) Chloroplasts

33. Which of the following is NOT an essential "ingredient" for photosynthesis to occur?
    (A) Sunlight
    (B) Carbon dioxide
    (C) Oxygen
    (D) Water

34. In line 11, "synthetic" most nearly means
    (A) artificial.
    (B) natural.
    (C) useful.
    (D) organic.

35. How many molecules of oxygen are produced by photosynthesis?
    (A) Four
    (B) Eight
    (C) Six
    (D) Two

36. The main idea of this passage is that biomass
    (A) is inorganic material.
    (B) uses energy.

(C)   is the beginning of many natural energy forms that conserve use of conventional energy sources.

(D)   uses photosynthesis to transport fuels.

37.   Which of the following is not mentioned in the passage as an organic material?
(A)   Metal
(B)   Crops
(C)   Manure
(D)   Algae

38.   In this passage "photosynthesis" is the
(A)   process needed to create algae.
(B)   reason nonrenewable energy sources can be saved.
(C)   method of producing electricity.
(D)   process biomass uses to capture and store energy.

39.   The conversion process is considered what part of the biomass continuum?
(A)   Beginning point
(B)   Release valve
(C)   End point
(D)   Shut-off valve

40.   "Bonus" in this passage refers to
(A)   by-products.
(B)   biomass.
(C)   photosynthesis.
(D)   conversion.

Questions 41 to 50 refer to the following passage:

1   The United States government publishes guidelines for appropriate nutrient intakes. These are known as the Recommended Dietary Allowances (RDAs) and are updated regularly based on new research in the science of nutrition. RDAs are suggested amounts of calories, protein, and some minerals and vitamins for an adequate diet. For other dietary
5   substances, specific goals must await further research. However, for the U.S. population as a whole, increasing starch and fiber in our diets and reducing calories (primarily from fats, sugar, and alcohol) is sensible. These suggestions are especially appropriate for people who have other factors for chronic diseases such as family history of obesity, premature heart disease, diabetes, high blood pressure, and high blood cholesterol, or for those who use
10   tobacco.
        Snacks can furnish about one-fourth of the calorie requirements among teenagers.

Those snacks should also furnish much of the day's allowances for protein, minerals, and vitamins. Sandwiches, fruit, and milk make good snacks for active teenagers.

15   Food from the food pyramid may be part of any meal. A grilled cheese sandwich or a bowl of whole-grain cereal is just as nutritious in the morning as it is at noon. In addition, a good breakfast consists of any foods that supply about one-fourth of the necessary nutrients for the day.

41.   The passage directly states that most of the U.S. population should increase their intake of
    (A)   protein.
    (B)   fats.
    (C)   starch and fiber.
    (D)   sandwiches.

42.   A good breakfast should supply about what percentage of the necessary nutrients for the day?
    (A)   One-half
    (B)   One-third
    (C)   One-fourth
    (D)   Less than one-fourth

43.   The passage implies which of the following?
    (A)   The time of day when food is consumed affects its nutritive value.
    (B)   Different foods can be combined to increase total nutrition value.
    (C)   It can be detrimental to your health to eat breakfast foods later in the day.
    (D)   When food is eaten has no bearing on its nutritive effects.

44.   In line 4, "adequate" most nearly means
    (A)   superior.
    (B)   sufficient.
    (C)   long-lasting.
    (D)   adult.

45.   Why are RDAs regularly updated?
    (A)   New discoveries in the science of nutrition are constantly being made.
    (B)   American's diets are constantly changing.
    (C)   As people age, their nutritional needs change.
    (D)   Very little is currently known about nutrition.

46. In this passage RDAs refers to
    (A) types of vitamins.
    (B) types of protein.
    (C) types of minerals.
    (D) amounts of energy, protein, vitamins, and minerals.

47. One implication in this passage is that
    (A) all RDAs have been established.
    (B) not all RDAs have been established yet.
    (C) it's not important to know RDAs.
    (D) RDAs are necessary only for sick people.

48. Most of the U.S. population would do well to include in their diets more
    (A) alcohol.
    (B) sugars.
    (C) fats.
    (D) starch and fiber.

49. "Chronic" as used in line 8 means
    (A) continuing.
    (B) intermittent.
    (C) acute.
    (D) curable.

50. The reduction of calories in the diet is particularly good for people who suffer from
    (A) obesity.
    (B) premature heart disease and diabetes.
    (C) high blood pressure and cholesterol levels.
    (D) All of the above

Questions 51 to 60 refer to the following passage:

1   Once flourishing in grassy marshlands and bogs, the whooping crane almost disappeared as people's croplands and cities altered its natural habitat.
     In the late 1940s, only one flock of fewer than 20 whooping cranes was left in the world. No one knew where the whooper went to lay its eggs but after a long search, scientists
5   found the whooping crane's nesting grounds in Canada's remote Wood Buffalo Park in 1954. It was a crucial discovery, enabling biologists to begin a comprehensive program to save the great white birds.
     Strenuous efforts are made by Canada and the United States to protect this magnificent

bird. The education of the hunter along with its flyway is important. The cranes are impressive
10 in flight—great white birds with a seven-foot (2-meter) spread between their black wing tips.
There are other large white birds with black wing tips, however—the white pelican, wood
ibis, and snow goose. And the young birds, mottled with rusty brown, could be mistaken for
the more common sandhill cranes. The federal authorities, therefore, are urging hunters to
adopt the slogan, "Don't Shoot Any Large White Bird."

51.   The whooping crane almost disappeared because of
        (A)   disease.
        (B)   alteration of its habitat.
        (C)   overeating.
        (D)   change in climate.

52.   The whooping crane is similar in appearance to
        (A)   the while pelican.
        (B)   the wood ibis.
        (C)   the snow goose.
        (D)   All of the above.

53.   The whooping crane nests in
        (A)   Yosemite National Park.
        (B)   the Gulf coast of Florida.
        (C)   Wood Buffalo Park.
        (D)   Mexico.

54.   The young whooping crane could be mistaken for
        (A)   a sandhill crane.
        (B)   a bald eagle.
        (C)   a seagull.
        (D)   a vulture.

55.   It can be inferred from the author's tone that he/she feels which of the following?
        (A)   Whooping cranes should be allowed to become extinct.
        (B)   Whooping cranes are overabundant .
        (C)   Whooping cranes should be protected.
        (D)   Whooping cranes should be hunted.

56. The implication here was that at one time the whooping crane was almost
    (A) extinct.
    (B) nesting.
    (C) overabundant.
    (D) wiped out by disease.

57. The main idea in this passage is that whooping cranes
    (A) are extinct.
    (B) nest in Canada.
    (C) would not have been saved if their nesting grounds had not been found.
    (D) are egg laying.

58. The word "altered" in this passage refers to
    (A) left unchanged.
    (B) changed by encroaching civilizations.
    (C) fixed.
    (D) moved.

59. The word "crucial" in line 6 means
    (A) of little consequence.
    (B) mildly important.
    (C) least important.
    (D) most important.

60. "Remote" in line 5 means
    (A) on the edge of the wilderness.
    (B) close to civilization.
    (C) easily accessible.
    (D) far away from civilization.

If time still remains, you may review work only in this section.

TEST 3

ANSWER KEY

SECTION 1: LISTENING COMPREHENSION

1.	(B)	14.	(C)	26.	(C)	39.	(D)
2.	(C)	15.	(B)	27.	(B)	40.	(D)
3.	(C)	16.	(C)	28.	(A)	41.	(A)
4.	(A)	17.	(A)	29.	(A)	42.	(D)
5.	(B)	18.	(B)	30.	(C)	43.	(A)
6.	(C)	19.	(D)	31.	(C)	44.	(C)
7.	(B)	20.	(A)	32.	(B)	45.	(B)
8.	(C)	21.	(C)	33.	(A)	46.	(C)
9.	(C)	22.	(D)	34.	(D)	47.	(A)
10.	(B)	23.	(B)	35.	(C)	48.	(C)
11.	(D)	24.	(A)	36.	(A)	49.	(D)
12.	(A)	25.	(D)	37.	(B)	50.	(C)
13.	(D)			38.	(B)		

SECTION 2: STRUCTURE AND WRITTEN EXPRESSION

1.	(A)	11.	(D)	21.	(C)	31.	(D)
2.	(A)	12.	(A)	22.	(B)	32.	(C)
3.	(D)	13.	(D)	23.	(D)	33.	(A)
4.	(A)	14.	(C)	24.	(B)	34.	(D)
5.	(B)	15.	(D)	25.	(B)	35.	(B)
6.	(B)	16.	(C)	26.	(D)	36.	(B)
7.	(B)	17.	(C)	27.	(C)	37.	(D)
8.	(C)	18.	(B)	28.	(B)	38.	(C)
9.	(C)	19.	(D)	29.	(A)	39.	(A)
10.	(C)	20.	(A)	30.	(B)	40.	(B)

SECTION 3: READING COMPREHENSION AND VOCABULARY

1.	(D)	16.	(B)	31.	(C)	46.	(D)
2.	(C)	17.	(D)	32.	(D)	47.	(B)
3.	(B)	18.	(A)	33.	(C)	48.	(D)
4.	(A)	19.	(B)	34.	(A)	49.	(A)
5.	(D)	20.	(C)	35.	(C)	50.	(D)
6.	(B)	21.	(C)	36.	(C)	51.	(B)
7.	(D)	22.	(D)	37.	(A)	52.	(D)
8.	(A)	23.	(B)	38.	(D)	53.	(C)
9.	(D)	24.	(C)	39.	(B)	54.	(A)
10.	(B)	25.	(A)	40.	(A)	55.	(C)
11.	(C)	26.	(C)	41.	(C)	56.	(A)
12.	(C)	27.	(A)	42.	(C)	57.	(C)
13.	(B)	28.	(D)	43.	(D)	58.	(B)
14.	(C)	29.	(C)	44.	(B)	59.	(D)
15.	(A)	30.	(B)	45.	(A)	60.	(D)

Detailed Explanations of Answers

TEST 3

Section 1:
LISTENING COMPREHENSION

Part A

1. **(B)** The question asks, "What will the man most likely do?" The correct answer is (B)—Not give the woman a cigarette. When the woman asked for a cigarette, the man replied, "Yes, I do. But I thought the doctor told you that you were supposed to quit smoking. I don't want to contribute to your bad health."

2. **(C)** The question asks, "What is the baby's relationship to the woman?" The correct answer is (C)—Niece. The man asked, "Did your sister give birth to her baby yet?" The woman responded, "Yes, she had a baby girl last week." The relationship between the woman and her sister's daughter is that of aunt to niece.

3. **(C)** The question asks, "What is the man implying?" The correct answer is (C)— He would like to go see a play at the theater with the woman, but he would like to invite other people as well. The woman asked, "Would you like to go to see a play at the theater with me?" The man responded, "Yes, but why don't we see if anyone else would like to come with us as well."

4. **(A)** The question asks: "Where did this conversation most likely take place?" The correct response is (A)—The beach. The man said, "Could you pass me the suntan lotion? I think I am burning." The woman responded, "Get the bottle of suntan lotion yourself. I have to get this sand out of my bathing suit."

5. **(B)** The question asks, "Where did this conversation most likely take place?" The correct answer is (B)—In a doctor's office. The man said, "Ouch! That hurts! Do you think I broke my ankle?" The woman replied, "No, I think it is probably only a sprain. Let's run some x-rays and then we will know for sure."

6. **(C)** The question asks, "What does the woman mean?" The correct answer is (C)—She could not take his pet because she is allergic to cats. The man said, "I just moved into my new apartment, and they don't allow pets. Would you like to have my cat?" The woman responded, "Oh, I'd love to, but I'm allergic to cats."

7. **(B)** The question asks, "What does the woman mean?" The correct answer is (B)—She can't share her books with the man, because she no longer has them. The man said, "The books required for this class are awfully expensive! Do you think I could just borrow your books?" The woman replied, "I took that class last semester, and I sold the books back at the end of the term."

8. **(C)** The question asks, "What does the man mean?" The correct answer is (C)—The woman has probably caught the same illness that many other people in the office have. The woman said, "I don't feel very well. I have a headache, and a cough, and my nose is running." The man replied, "Yes, it seems as though the whole office is sick. There is something going around." The phrase, "something going around," means that a virus, cold, or some other contagious illness is infecting many people.

9. **(C)** The question asks, "Whose recipe was used to make the apple pie?" The correct answer is (C)—The woman's grandmother. The woman said, "I made an apple pie using the recipe that my grandmother gave me."

10. **(B)** The question asks, "What does the woman mean?" The correct answer is (B)—The man should do something relaxing and enjoyable over the weekend, and not think about his problems at work. The man said, "Work has been very stressful lately. There are too many problems to deal with right now." The woman responded, "Well, this weekend you should find something to do to keep your mind off things."

11. **(D)** The question asks, "What does the woman mean?" The correct answer is (D)—They should recheck that the back door is locked for the sake of safety. The woman said, "Please go and double check for me. Better to be safe than sorry." "Double check" means recheck.

12. **(A)** The question asks, "At what speed is the man driving?" The correct answer is (A) — Seventy miles per hour. The woman said, "...The speed limit here is fifty-five miles per hour and you were going fifteen miles over it." Fifty-five plus fifteen is seventy.

13. **(D)** The question asks, "Why is the woman certain that Mr. Holden will come?" The correct answer is (D) — Because he is a man of strong determination. The woman said, "...He is a man of strong will." "Strong will" means strong determination and not strong body.

14. **(C)** The question asks, "What is the man's problem?" The correct answer is (C) — He had too much work at the office. The man said, "...I just had a long day at the office." The expression "to have a long day" means to have a lot of work.

15. **(B)** The question asks, "Where did this conversation most probably take place?" The correct answer is (B) — Near a pay phone. The woman said, "...I need twenty more cents for this call." Obviously, she was making a call from a pay phone.

16. **(C)** The question asks, "How may people live in the apartment?" The correct answer is (C) — Three. The man asked, "Does Gloria rent this apartment alone?" The woman responded, "No. She shares it with two of her friends." So, it is Gloria and her two friends—three people living in the apartment.

17. **(A)** The question asks, "What does the man mean?" The correct answer is (A) — The woman is very fond of shopping. The woman said, "One more thing from this store and I am done." This means she has been shopping for quite a while. In response to that, the man asked, "Don't you ever get tired of shopping?" The question was asked only to emphasize that she does not get tired of shopping.

18. **(B)** The question asks, "How does the woman feel about the proposal?" The correct answer is (B) — She is happy. Her response to the proposal was, "Wonderful! That's my idea of a relaxing weekend." The exclamation "Wonderful!" is used when a person is pleased.

19. **(D)** The question asks, "Where could the man find Dr. Gordon?" The correct answer is (D) — In the conference room. The woman said, "...She thought she had to meet you in the conference room." Dr. Gordon was waiting for the man in the conference room.

20. **(A)** The question asks, "What kind of a job does John probably have?" The correct answer is (A) — Auto mechanic. The woman mentioned a problem with her car and the man said, "I will ask John to have a look at it tomorrow." Only an auto mechanic would be able to help in the situation.

21. **(C)** The question asks, "What does the woman mean?" The correct answer is (C) — She usually does not like to go to parties. When the man said, "Why aren't you coming to the party? I promise you won't feel left out.", the woman answered, "That's not the problem. I am just not a party person." It means she is not concerned about being left out, she just doesn't like parties.

22. **(D)** The question asks, "What does the woman imply?" The correct answer is (D) — The man should at least take the opportunity to appear for the interview. When the man said, "I don't feel very excited about this interview," the woman said, "Just give it a try. What do you have to lose?"; meaning even if he is not successful he is not going to lose anything.

23. **(B)** The question asks, "What is the man's opinion about Willie?" The correct answer is (B) — He can achieve anything, if he is determined. The man said, "I knew he could accomplish anything, if he put his mind to it."

24. **(A)** The question asks, "Approximately at what time should the woman be able to get her watch back?" The correct answer is (A) — At five o'clock. The man said, "It is two o'clock now. I should be able to fix it in about three hours." Three hours after two would be five o'clock.

25. **(D)** The question asks, "What does the woman mean?" The correct answer is (D) — She is very happy with her new job. The woman said, "I have never been luckier with my job." It means she has not been so lucky with her jobs before. She is happy with her job.

Part B

26. **(C)** The question asks, "Where did the man see the woman?" The correct response is (C)—On the side of the road. The man's first statement of the conversation was, "I saw you stopped on the side of the road this morning."

27. **(B)**   The question asks, "Why was the woman stopped?" The correct response is (B)—Engine problems. The woman says, "She stopped her car because it started shaking." This does not shed any light on the answer to the question. But, later in the conversation she says, "One of the cables to the spark plugs had come loose." Even without knowing the workings of an engine, the listener can eliminate the three other choices based on the information given.

28. **(A)**   The question asks, "Who fixed the woman's car?" The correct response is (A)—She did. When the man asks if she had a mechanic look at the car, she says, "No, it was easy to just reconnect the cables so the car could run."

29. **(A)**   The questions asks, "How did the woman know about car engines?" The correct response is (A)—She grew up working on cars. The listener can infer from the fact that she grew up working on cars that she knew about the engines.

30. **(C)**   The question asks, "How much did the man know about cars?" The correct response is (C)—He can just about change a flat tire. The man says, "I can barely change a flat tire." This means that he knows how to do it, but does not know anything more complicated.

31. **(C)**   The question asks, "Why does the man think that they have missed a bill?" The correct answer is (C) — Because it is unusual for them to have extra money at the end of the month. In the conversation the man said, "It is almost the end of the month and I was wondering how come we still have some extra money in our account."

32. **(B)**   The question asks, "What is the reason why they have some extra money in their account?" The correct answer is (B) — The woman didn't take the piano lessons this month. When the man said, "...I was wondering how come we have some extra money in our account," the woman said, "I know why. We didn't have to pay for my piano lessons this month."

33. **(A)**   The question asks, "What does the woman plan to do?" The correct answer is (A) — Buy a bookshelf. The woman said, "...it would be a good idea to use that money for that bookshelf that we saw last week..."

34. **(D)**   The question asks, "What promise does the man ask for?" The correct answer is (D) — The woman has to help save some money next month. In the conversation the man said, "...You have to promise to help save some money next month."

35. **(C)**   The question asks, "Why does the man think they can save some money next month?" The correct answer is (C) — Because they don't have to pay for the woman's piano lessons next month also. Towards the end of the conversation the man said, "Your piano teacher is going to be away next month also..." It means that the woman cannot take her piano lessons next month and they don't have to pay for it.

36. **(A)**   The question asks, "What does the woman want to get done?" The correct answer is (A) — Get a photocopy of her dissertation. In the beginning of the conversation, the woman asked the charge for photocopying. And when the man asked, "Approximately how many do you have?", the woman answered, "...It is my dissertation, which will be about a hundred pages."

37. **(B)**   The question asks, "Approximately how much would the woman have to pay for the photocopying of her dissertation?" The correct answer is (B) — Ten dollars. The man agreed to charge ten cents per page, and her dissertation would be about a hundred pages. So she would have to pay about ten dollars.

38. **(B)**   The question asks, "Why did the man lower the charge?" The correct answer is (B) — Because the woman has about a hundred pages for photocopying. When the woman first asked about the charge, he said, "fifteen cents per page." But when she said, "...it is my dissertation which will be about a hundred pages," he lowered the charges saying, "In that case, I will do it for ten cents per page." He gave a discount for more work.

39. **(D)**   The question asks, "About how long is the woman's dissertation?" The correct answer is (D) — One hundred pages. In the conversation the woman said, "...it is my dissertation which will be about a hundred pages."

40. **(D)**   The question asks, "What is the woman waiting for?" The correct answer is (D) — She is waiting to finish typing. Towards the end of the conversation the woman said, "...But I am not through typing yet. I should be able to finish it within four or five days." Only after she finishes typing, she can bring it for photocopying.

Part C

41. **(A)**   The question asks, "During what period were most Europeans illiterate?" The correct response is (A)—Middle Ages. The answer to this question is in the first line of the talk, "During the Middle Ages the majority of Europeans were illiterate." Do not be confused by the line about the eleventh century which refers to the 1000s not the 1100s.

42. **(D)** The question asks, "Approximately what percentage of people continued to live off the land?" The correct response is (D)—90%. This question is answered in the line, "Probably more than ninety percent of the population continued to live off the land." You have to know that ninety refers to 90 and not 19.

43. **(A)** The question asks, "What empires did the Europeans come into contact with?" The correct response is (A)—Islamic and Byzantine. The answer for this question comes straight from the line, "The growth in commerce between East and West offered Europeans contact with the Islamic and Byzantine civilizations.

44. **(C)** The question asks, "Who did the cultural awakening affect?" The correct response is (C)—Intellectuals. This question is answered in the line, "The cultural awakening of the high Middle Ages affected only a small number of intellectuals.

45. **(B)** The question is "Advances in which subjects had long-range consequences?" The correct response is (B)—Philosophy and science. The answer to this question comes from a list of several items which had consequences. "Nevertheless, the advances in education, philosophy, science, literature, and the arts that unfolded during this period had long-range consequences." The listener must be able to distinguish parts of a list from the list as a whole.

46. **(C)** The question asks, "What was the main topic of the talk?" The correct answer is (C)—Some steps for satisfactory painting. Though there were references to trees and shrubs, paint and color and sash brush in the talk, the main purpose of the speaker was to give some tips in painting.

47. **(A)** The question asks, "Why should we take extra care in selecting colors?" The correct answer is (A)—Because many a time colors look different in the daylight than under artificial light. In the talk you heard, "...Another area in which you need to take extra care is colors. Colors often look different under artificial light than in daylight...."

48. **(C)** The question asks, "What type of weather is good to start painting?" The correct answer is (C)—Warm and dry. The speaker said, "...Once you are ready with the paint, select a warm and dry day to start painting."

49. **(D)** The question asks, "Why should we paint an entire section at one time?" The correct answer is (D)—Because, if we don't, the paint will dry unevenly. In the talk you

heard, "…paint an entire section at one time. Don't stop half way through the section, otherwise the paint will dry unevenly."

50. **(C)**   The question ask, "How can we keep extra paint for years?" The correct answer is (C)—By filming it with solvent, sealing it, and keeping it in a warm dry place. The last two sentences in the talk were, "…when you are done painting, float a thin layer of solvent on the surface of the remaining paint, seal the can and store it in a warm, dry place. It will last for years."

Section 2:
STRUCTURE AND WRITTEN EXPRESSION

1. **(A)** (A) is the correct answer. All the people who do not have free tickets must pay the admission fee. (B) is incorrect. The use of **no one** makes this possibility wrong. It makes for two negatives in the sentence and creates an imbalance in meaning. (C) is incorrect. If the sentence had read **...need pay the admission fee,** instead of **must pay,** (C) would have been the correct choice. Paying the admission fee is not mandatory (as implied by **must**), for those who have free tickets. So it is incorrect. (D) is incorrect. It is illogical for one who has free tickets to pay an admission fee.

2. **(A)** (A) is the correct answer. Past continuous tense is the right tense. The sentence is a description of a past continuous act. (B) is incorrect because **the police** is representative of the whole force and is therefore considered a plural noun. It is incorrect to use a singular verb conjugation for a plural noun. (C) is incorrect because the act of chasing is a continuous act. It would be more appropriate to use the continuous tense. (D) is incorrect because **on a chase** makes the sentence complete and therefore **the robbers down the street** is redundant.

3. **(D)** (A) is incorrect because it is only a clause, whereas the sentence needs a main verb. (B) is incorrect. **Although** sets the note of contrast, and this is further contradicted by **but**. It is unacceptable to have two contradictory terms in a sentence. (C) is incorrect. It too is also a subordinate clause that does not provide the main verb for the sentence. (D) is the correct answer. It makes a statement. **Is** is the main verb, and the second part of the sentence adds the necessary information.

4. **(A)** (A) is the correct answer. **Thereby** means **thus,** it suggests result. (B) is incorrect because of the **of** in the end. **When...it becomes a fossil, as a result, turning into evidence of things that once lived.** (C) is incorrect. So must be followed by the pronoun in the first part of the sentence, and therefore the verb should change to **turns.** (D) is incorrect. **In the end** is an inaccurate expression for the lengthy process of fossilization.

5. **(B)** (A) is incorrect. The adverb **presumably** should not be followed by the infinitive of the verb. It can only be **presumably dead, presumably extinct.** (B) is correct. This presumption has been held for many years. It is a case of ellipsis, where the **which is** of **which is presumed to be extinct** is dropped. (C) is incorrect. It is an

adjective that does not fit here. (D) is incorrect because of the absence of the relative pronoun **which.**

6.   **(B)**   (A) is incorrect. **A small fraction** is part of a whole, so the preposition that should follow is **of.** (B) is correct. In a small fraction of the 200 billion stars, life is possible. (C) is incorrect because of the lack of a preposition. (D) is incorrect because the relative pronoun **which** should refer to the fraction, not to the 200 billion stars.

7.   **(B)**   (A) is incorrect. The pronoun **he** and the noun J.F. Kennedy are too close together and therefore one of them becomes redundant. (B) is correct. Another way of writing this sentence would be: **J.F. Kennedy, the youngest man ever to be president, requested sweeping civil rights**.... Instead of the clause coming after the noun, it comes before. (C) is incorrect. Although structurally acceptable, JFK's youth had nothing to do with his request for sweeping legislation from Congress. (D) is incorrect for the same reason as (A).

8.   **(C)**   (A) is incorrect because **about** is not a word used with specific years. (B) is incorrect. **On** is also not used except when referring to a specific date in the year. (C) is the correct answer. **Between** the two years, a period of nine years, the parliament passed laws. (D) is incorrect. **Before** can be associated only with one date at a time. It is incorrect to give two different years with **before.**

9.   **(C)**   (A) is incorrect because of the lack of **as** to show comparison. At a glance (B) may seem like the correct choice, but the lack of a second **as** makes it incorrect. (C) is the correct answer. **His uncle** is put at the end of the sentence because it is common for both parts of the sentence. He is as tall as his uncle, if not taller than his uncle. (D) is incorrect. If he is the tallest, there is no comparison with his uncle.

10.   **(C)**   (A) is incorrect. Broke **away** is taking a piece from the whole. (B) is incorrect. Broke **down** is breaking down into smaller parts. (C) is correct. A person **breaks** someone's heart, i.e., is hurting someone badly. (D) is incorrect because of the tense and the inappropriate preposition.

11.   **(D)**   (A), (B), and (C) are incorrect because the verbs are not in the same tense as they should be drinking and gambling. (D) is the correct answer. His two vices, drinking and gambling, make him a poor role model.

12.   **(A)**   (A) is the correct answer. The depression has been **referred to** by a prominent psychiatrist. The preposition that goes with **refer** is **to.** (B) is incorrect. **As is**

redundant because it follows in the sentence later. Choice (C) is not connected to the first part of the sentence through any conjunction, therefore, it is incorrect. (D) is incorrect. The pronoun **it** is unnecessary because the subject is **depression,** and the second part of the sentence is not separate from the first.

13. **(D)** (A) is incorrect because the comparative word **too** has been replaced by **to.** (B) is incorrect. **Too** is preferred over **also** in most cases. For example, I speak English too. They would like to come with us too. (C) is incorrect. There is no addition if **so** is used. It only suggests result. (D) is the correct answer. Just as there are jobs that require college degrees, there are occupations for which technical training is needed.

14. **(C)** (A) is incorrect. There is no need for the pronoun **they**; it is redundant. (B) is incorrect. The verb should be in the third person plural, not singular. (C) is the correct answer. **Have died out** is the present perfect tense, signifying that most of the older civilizations have disappeared. (D) is incorrect because of the pronoun and the tense. **Up to now they have died out** is the meaning. So it should be in the present perfect tense.

15. **(D)** (A) is incorrect. There are too many **ifs** in the sentence. (B) is incorrect. **Knows** and **earlier** don't go together. (C) is incorrect. An inversion is required to make the structure correct. For example, I would have gone had I known earlier. In an attempt not to repeat the **if**, the inversion becomes necessary. (D) is the correct answer. There are two actions in the past. One is the student asking her professor and the other the professor's knowing earlier. The latter action took place earlier than the former. So it should be in the past perfect tense. The inversion of **he had known** into **had he known** is the result of **The student asked her professor if....**

16. **(C)** (C) is incorrect. Careful attention must be paid to the difference between **rising** and **raising.** The former is **getting up** while the latter means **bringing up.**

17. **(C)** (C) is incorrect. There is a missing preposition **of**. The sentence should read **...farmers in Iraq is dates, of which Iraq is the world's leading exporter.**

18. **(B)** (B) is incorrect. The structure is **more...than,** not **that. More** has been learned about the Moon **than**.... The meaning is that we have learned more about the Moon than any other planet.

19. **(D)** (D) is incorrect. The pronoun should refer to the **average family,** which is singular. So it should be **it finds most meals unexciting.**

20. **(A)**   (A) is incorrect. There is a missing **to** in the infinitive form of the verb, **have.** If the sentence were in the affirmative, it would read, **The teacher ought to have criticized.** Similarly, the negative should be **ought not to have.**

21. **(C)**   (C) is incorrect. It is the position of **only** that is questionable. It should come before the noun, which is **twenty-six letters.** In written English, it will be considered appropriate to read it as: **there are only 26 letters to express....**

22. **(B)**   (B) is incorrect. The structure is **to go as far back as,** not **as far back to.** There would be no need for a comparison if the sentence just read, **which goes back to 930 A.D.**

23. **(D)**   (D) is incorrect. The past tense of the verb **does (did)** is not necessary in this sentence. The sentence should read: **The young woman often wondered where at the estuary the river formed little rivulets.**

24. **(B)**   (B) is incorrect. The tense to be used is the past perfect, **had begun,** instead of **had beginning.**

25. **(B)**   (B) is incorrect. A person is usually **on** time, if it is understood earlier on in the sentence at what time he/she has to be there. But when there is an action that has to be performed at a particular time, and the person has to be there before that, **in** has to be used. For example, I was well **in** time **to catch the ten o'clock bus.** I am usually punctual with my meetings. I shall be **on** time.

26. **(D)**   (D) is incorrect because it is redundant. **Instead** automatically includes the idea that her father was not the one who was going to take her to the airport.

27. **(C)**   (C) is incorrect. The verb should be conjugated in the third person plural, not left in the infinitive. It should be **that show the pointlessness....**

28. **(B)**   (B) is incorrect. There is no need for the pronoun **it.** The first part of the sentence, including the clause, is the subject.

29. **(A)**   (A) is incorrect. The modal, **may,** is incomplete without the main verb, **be.** It should read, **what may be the oldest fossil....**

30. **(B)**   (B) is incorrect. The adjective form of **danger** should be used. **Most of us think of sharks as dangerous** is the correct form.

31. **(D)**   (D) is incorrect. The adverbial form of the word **abnormal** should be used. The verb is **function**. It is qualified by **abnormally**.

32. **(C)**   (C) is incorrect. It should read **among them**. The meaning is **among numerous differences in skeletons and musculature, one is that loons cannot walk well on land.**

33. **(A)**   (A) is incorrect. The structure is **having the capacity to do something.** For example, she has the capacity to do better in her exams.

34. **(D)**   (D) is incorrect. This sentence has a missing preposition. The structure is **with caution:** Drugs must be used with caution. The sentence is reversed to read **is an example of the caution with which drugs must be used.**

35. **(B)**   (B) is incorrect. **Sometimes** means **a few times.** In this case, the person is unsure of when the parents moved out and so has to use **sometime.** For example, we should get together sometime next week.

36. **(B)**   (B) is incorrect. **To borrow** is used when a person **takes** something for a period of time and later returns it. **To lend** is when a person **gives** something for a period of time. The library **lends its books to a borrower.**

37. **(D)**   (D) is incorrect. In reported speech, it is necessary to reverse the subject-verb positions. For example, **whether or not he has experienced....** In a regular question it would be, **Has he experienced anything?**

38. **(C)**   (C) is incorrect. **Hard** remains **hard** when it becomes an adverb. It does not follow the usual rules of taking on **ly** in the end, as do most adjectives: e.g., quick-quickly. **Hard** is an exception, as is **fast.** So, the sentence should read, **they work hard, enabling them to reach their goals.**

39. **(A)**   (A) is incorrect. The expression is **letting someone go.** Although **leave** and **let** have similar meanings, they express different ideas. For example, **I will not let you go to the party alone. I want to leave my child at the day-care center.**

40. **(B)** (B) is incorrect. The verb should be in the simple present tense when talking about a generality, such as what a book deals with. It is not an action that will change; it will remain constant. The verb should be **the book deals with many questions.**

Section 3:
READING COMPREHENSION
AND VOCABULARY

1.　**(D)**　The last paragraph of the passage clearly lists four fields in which Planck made significant contributions. Biology is not mentioned as one of these.

2.　**(C)**　As used within the context of the passage, "revolutionary" most nearly means "momentous," since the implication here is that Planck's discovery was a major and positive one. The other choices have either negative or war-like connotations.

3.　**(B)**　The first paragraph states that Planck's work "revolutionized the scientific community's understanding of atomic and subatomic processes." It can thus be inferred that his work helped pave the way for the atomic bomb. The other inventions were not the direct result of Planck's work.

4.　**(A)**　The passage directly states that the particles are called quantums. The other choices are terms related to atomic processes, but are all incorrect.

5.　**(D)**　In the context of Planck's theories, the correct meaning of "universal" is "always present," as in a constant. The other choices have geographic or astronomical connotations which do not apply here.

6.　**(B)**　The fact that the quantum theory is capable of mathematical translation is seen in the sentence, "Thus energy, or E, equals hv."

7.　**(D)**　The "idea" is defined later in the passage as the "equation" presented in choice (D). Although the other choices are mentioned, they do not define "idea."

8.　**(A)**　"Giving off" is the motion described in the phrase, "required the emission of electromagnetic radiation in small chunks or particles."

9. **(D)** "$E = hv$" is presented in the words, "Thus, energy, or E, equals hv."

10. **(B)** "h" is the correct answer as seen in the sentence, "The constant, h, is known as Planck's constant."

11. **(C)** The only true statement among the choices is that English boys played a game they called "base ball" in the 1700s. Historians dispute that Doubleday invented the game (A). There are many differences between today's game and the nineteenth-century game (B). The first set of rules was established well before the turn of the century, in 1845 (D).

12. **(C)** The passage states the "the Cincinnati Red Stockings began to pay players in 1869," which would make them the first professional baseball team. The New York Knickerbockers (A) was an early baseball club, but it was not a professional team. The Milwaukee Braves (B) and Brooklyn Dodgers (D) were teams appearing later.

13. **(B)** The passage states that Alexander Cartwright set up the rules when he formed his Knickerbocker Baseball Club in 1845. Abner Doubleday (A) was involved with the early development of baseball. Albert Spalding (C) and Babe Ruth (D) are not mentioned in the passage.

14. **(C)** The only game not mentioned in the passage as an early forerunner of baseball is cricket, an English game not unlike baseball.

15. **(A)** The first paragraph states that the museum opened 100 years after 1839.

16. **(B)** "Adopt" means "to accept." In this case, the other teams accepted Cartwright's set of rules. Established (A), rejected (C), and abolished (D) all violate the meaning of the sentence.

17. **(D)** "Standard" means official. In this context, official is correct because standard is referring to rules. Normal (A) is not as precise as official. Disputed (B) is the opposite of standard. Conclusive (C) is too vague in this context.

18. **(A)** The passage clearly states that the museum is in Cooperstown, NY. The other sites are related to the early history of baseball, but are incorrect here.

19. **(B)** The passage is simply an objective presentation of facts. The objective tone of the passage obviously refutes "biased" (C) as the correct answer. There is no attempt to be persuasive (A) or argumentative (D).

20. **(C)** The fact that the first professional team was not established until 1869 indicates that baseball was not played for profit before that time. All of the other choices are reasons for which the game was played.

21. **(C)** The third paragraph states that phytoplankton growth is often limited by the availability of nitrogen. The other substances are not mentioned in the passage.

22. **(D)** An amoeba is not a plant and is not mentioned in the passage.

23. **(B)** The passage states that many kinds of phytoplankton use flagellum to swim.

24. **(C)** The yellow pigment of the phytoplankton mixes with the blue water to form green water commonly found near coasts.

25. **(A)** The passage states that silt or sediment, usually as outflow from a large river, can cause a brownish hue.

26. **(C)** "Hardly ever" is implied in the words, "some shade of blue," meaning there are many shades.

27. **(A)** A "short wavelength" is the descriptor directly following "blue light" in the first paragraph of the passage.

28. **(D)** "Reflected light and yellow pigment from plant life" directly follows mention of green water in the passage preceded by the words, "This is caused by." (A) sand color, (B) red pigment and (C) blue pigment are never mentioned.

29. **(C)** The words "microscopic floating plants" are directly followed by the parenthetical term phytoplankton.

30. **(B)** "Sea coloration variation" is the topic discussed. The other choices are elements of that variation, but do not encompass the subject of the entire passage.

31. **(C)** The first sentence of the third paragraph lists energy forms produced by the conversion of biomass. Oxygen is not mentioned as one of them.

32. **(D)** The passage states that "photosynthesis is carried out in specialized structures...called chloroplasts." The other choices are involved in the process, but are not the specialized structure itself.

33. **(C)** Oxygen is not a component of photosynthesis, but one of its products. The other choices are all necessary for photosynthesis to occur.

34. **(A)** "Synthetic" most nearly means (A)—artificial. There are no context clues to provide the answer to this question. Since the passage discusses plant material, you may think that either (B)—natural or (D)—organic is the correct answer, but both are the opposite of the meaning of "synthetic." Choice (C) is also incorrect.

35. **(C)** The last sentence of the passage directly states, "Six molecules of oxygen are produced as a waste product and are released into the air through the stomata."

36. **(C)** That biomass is the beginning of natural energy forms conserving other forms is the main idea stated in the last sentence of the first paragraph.

37. **(A)** "Metal" is the one answer not stated, and therefore is the correct answer.

38. **(D)** Photosynthesis is the process biomass uses to capture and store energy and is directly stated in the second sentence of the passage.

39. **(B)** "Release valve" is stated in the words, "Can be released from any form of biomass through conversion."

40. **(A)** The words "byproducts for food, fertilizers, and chemicals as a bonus" shows this to be the answer.

41. **(C)** The passage directly states that most people would benefit from an increased intake of starch and fiber, not protein (A), fats (B), or sandwiches (D).

42. **(C)** The last sentence of the passage directly states that one-fourth of the day's nutrients should come from breakfast.

43. **(D)** The passage states that "a grilled cheese sandwich or a bowl of whole-grain cereal is just as nutritious in the morning as it is at noon." This certainly implies that the time of day food is eaten has no bearing on its nutritional value. Therefore, (A) and (C) are clearly incorrect. (B) may be true, but is not mentioned in the passage.

44. **(B)** The definition of "adequate" is "capable of meeting a need or requirement." Here, an "adequate" diet is one that meets the Recommended Dietary Allowances. The other choices make no sense.

45. **(A)** The passage indicates that RDAs are updated as more is known about the science of nutrition. While both (B) and (C) may be correct, they do not affect RDAs. Choice (D) is absolutely false—very much is currently known about nutrition.

46. **(D)** The word "amounts" is directly preceded by the words "Recommended Daily Allowances (RDAs)."

47. **(B)** The answer, "not all RDAs have been established yet," is shown in the words "must await further research."

48. **(D)** "More starch and fiber" is suggested in the words, "increasing starch and fiber in our diets."

49. **(A)** The word "continuing" is synonymous with the word "chronic." The diseases mentioned, such as heart disease and diabetes, are usually not (B) intermittent, (C) acute, or (D) curable.

50. **(D)** All of the above answers are included in the last two sentences under the categories of disease whose sufferers benefit from reduced caloric intake.

51. **(B)** The first sentence of the passage states that the whooping crane almost disappeared because of the alteration of its habitat.

52. **(D)** The third paragraph mentions (A) the white pelican, (B) the wood ibis, and (C) the snow goose as other large white birds with black wing tips.

53. **(C)** The second paragraph states that scientists found the whooping crane's nesting ground in Canada's remote Wood Buffalo Park in 1954. The other locations were not mentioned in the passage.

54. **(A)** The third paragraph says that the young whooping crane, mottled with rusty brown, could be mistaken for the more common sandhill cranes. The other birds were not mentioned in the passage.

55. **(C)** The author's use of the terms "great white birds" and "magnificent bird" implies that the author believes that the birds should be protected. Also, the statement that the discovery of the nesting ground "was a crucial discovery" also supports this answer.

56. **(A)** "Extinct" is the correct answer. (C) "overabundant" is the opposite, (B) refers to where the crane lays its eggs, and (D) is not mentioned.

57. **(C)** The phrase "It was a crucial discovery" in the last sentence of the second paragraph introduces this idea.

58. **(B)** "Changed by encroaching civilizations" is synonymous with the words in the passage "as people's croplands and cities altered its natural habitat."

59. **(D)** The words "enabling biologists to begin a comprehensive program to save the great white birds" in the last sentence of the second paragraph defines "crucial" as "more important."

60. **(D)** "Remote" is defined as "far away from civilization." The other choices imply that the nesting grounds are nearby.

Test of English as a Foreign Language
TEST 4
ANSWER SHEET

Section 1:
Listening Comprehension

1. Ⓐ Ⓑ Ⓒ Ⓓ
2. Ⓐ Ⓑ Ⓒ Ⓓ
3. Ⓐ Ⓑ Ⓒ Ⓓ
4. Ⓐ Ⓑ Ⓒ Ⓓ
5. Ⓐ Ⓑ Ⓒ Ⓓ
6. Ⓐ Ⓑ Ⓒ Ⓓ
7. Ⓐ Ⓑ Ⓒ Ⓓ
8. Ⓐ Ⓑ Ⓒ Ⓓ
9. Ⓐ Ⓑ Ⓒ Ⓓ
10. Ⓐ Ⓑ Ⓒ Ⓓ
11. Ⓐ Ⓑ Ⓒ Ⓓ
12. Ⓐ Ⓑ Ⓒ Ⓓ
13. Ⓐ Ⓑ Ⓒ Ⓓ
14. Ⓐ Ⓑ Ⓒ Ⓓ
15. Ⓐ Ⓑ Ⓒ Ⓓ
16. Ⓐ Ⓑ Ⓒ Ⓓ
17. Ⓐ Ⓑ Ⓒ Ⓓ
18. Ⓐ Ⓑ Ⓒ Ⓓ
19. Ⓐ Ⓑ Ⓒ Ⓓ
20. Ⓐ Ⓑ Ⓒ Ⓓ
21. Ⓐ Ⓑ Ⓒ Ⓓ
22. Ⓐ Ⓑ Ⓒ Ⓓ
23. Ⓐ Ⓑ Ⓒ Ⓓ
24. Ⓐ Ⓑ Ⓒ Ⓓ
25. Ⓐ Ⓑ Ⓒ Ⓓ
26. Ⓐ Ⓑ Ⓒ Ⓓ
27. Ⓐ Ⓑ Ⓒ Ⓓ
28. Ⓐ Ⓑ Ⓒ Ⓓ
29. Ⓐ Ⓑ Ⓒ Ⓓ
30. Ⓐ Ⓑ Ⓒ Ⓓ

31. Ⓐ Ⓑ Ⓒ Ⓓ
32. Ⓐ Ⓑ Ⓒ Ⓓ
33. Ⓐ Ⓑ Ⓒ Ⓓ
34. Ⓐ Ⓑ Ⓒ Ⓓ
35. Ⓐ Ⓑ Ⓒ Ⓓ
36. Ⓐ Ⓑ Ⓒ Ⓓ
37. Ⓐ Ⓑ Ⓒ Ⓓ
38. Ⓐ Ⓑ Ⓒ Ⓓ
39. Ⓐ Ⓑ Ⓒ Ⓓ
40. Ⓐ Ⓑ Ⓒ Ⓓ
41. Ⓐ Ⓑ Ⓒ Ⓓ
42. Ⓐ Ⓑ Ⓒ Ⓓ
43. Ⓐ Ⓑ Ⓒ Ⓓ
44. Ⓐ Ⓑ Ⓒ Ⓓ
45. Ⓐ Ⓑ Ⓒ Ⓓ
46. Ⓐ Ⓑ Ⓒ Ⓓ
47. Ⓐ Ⓑ Ⓒ Ⓓ
48. Ⓐ Ⓑ Ⓒ Ⓓ
49. Ⓐ Ⓑ Ⓒ Ⓓ
50. Ⓐ Ⓑ Ⓒ Ⓓ

Section 2:
Structure and
Written Expression

1. Ⓐ Ⓑ Ⓒ Ⓓ
2. Ⓐ Ⓑ Ⓒ Ⓓ
3. Ⓐ Ⓑ Ⓒ Ⓓ
4. Ⓐ Ⓑ Ⓒ Ⓓ
5. Ⓐ Ⓑ Ⓒ Ⓓ
6. Ⓐ Ⓑ Ⓒ Ⓓ
7. Ⓐ Ⓑ Ⓒ Ⓓ

8. Ⓐ Ⓑ Ⓒ Ⓓ
9. Ⓐ Ⓑ Ⓒ Ⓓ
10. Ⓐ Ⓑ Ⓒ Ⓓ
11. Ⓐ Ⓑ Ⓒ Ⓓ
12. Ⓐ Ⓑ Ⓒ Ⓓ
13. Ⓐ Ⓑ Ⓒ Ⓓ
14. Ⓐ Ⓑ Ⓒ Ⓓ
15. Ⓐ Ⓑ Ⓒ Ⓓ
16. Ⓐ Ⓑ Ⓒ Ⓓ
17. Ⓐ Ⓑ Ⓒ Ⓓ
18. Ⓐ Ⓑ Ⓒ Ⓓ
19. Ⓐ Ⓑ Ⓒ Ⓓ
20. Ⓐ Ⓑ Ⓒ Ⓓ
21. Ⓐ Ⓑ Ⓒ Ⓓ
22. Ⓐ Ⓑ Ⓒ Ⓓ
23. Ⓐ Ⓑ Ⓒ Ⓓ
24. Ⓐ Ⓑ Ⓒ Ⓓ
25. Ⓐ Ⓑ Ⓒ Ⓓ
26. Ⓐ Ⓑ Ⓒ Ⓓ
27. Ⓐ Ⓑ Ⓒ Ⓓ
28. Ⓐ Ⓑ Ⓒ Ⓓ
29. Ⓐ Ⓑ Ⓒ Ⓓ
30. Ⓐ Ⓑ Ⓒ Ⓓ
31. Ⓐ Ⓑ Ⓒ Ⓓ
32. Ⓐ Ⓑ Ⓒ Ⓓ
33. Ⓐ Ⓑ Ⓒ Ⓓ
34. Ⓐ Ⓑ Ⓒ Ⓓ
35. Ⓐ Ⓑ Ⓒ Ⓓ
36. Ⓐ Ⓑ Ⓒ Ⓓ
37. Ⓐ Ⓑ Ⓒ Ⓓ
38. Ⓐ Ⓑ Ⓒ Ⓓ
39. Ⓐ Ⓑ Ⓒ Ⓓ
40. Ⓐ Ⓑ Ⓒ Ⓓ

Section 3:
Reading Comprehension
and Vocabulary

1. Ⓐ Ⓑ Ⓒ Ⓓ
2. Ⓐ Ⓑ Ⓒ Ⓓ
3. Ⓐ Ⓑ Ⓒ Ⓓ
4. Ⓐ Ⓑ Ⓒ Ⓓ
5. Ⓐ Ⓑ Ⓒ Ⓓ
6. Ⓐ Ⓑ Ⓒ Ⓓ
7. Ⓐ Ⓑ Ⓒ Ⓓ
8. Ⓐ Ⓑ Ⓒ Ⓓ
9. Ⓐ Ⓑ Ⓒ Ⓓ
10. Ⓐ Ⓑ Ⓒ Ⓓ
11. Ⓐ Ⓑ Ⓒ Ⓓ
12. Ⓐ Ⓑ Ⓒ Ⓓ
13. Ⓐ Ⓑ Ⓒ Ⓓ
14. Ⓐ Ⓑ Ⓒ Ⓓ
15. Ⓐ Ⓑ Ⓒ Ⓓ
16. Ⓐ Ⓑ Ⓒ Ⓓ
17. Ⓐ Ⓑ Ⓒ Ⓓ
18. Ⓐ Ⓑ Ⓒ Ⓓ

19. Ⓐ Ⓑ Ⓒ Ⓓ
20. Ⓐ Ⓑ Ⓒ Ⓓ
21. Ⓐ Ⓑ Ⓒ Ⓓ
22. Ⓐ Ⓑ Ⓒ Ⓓ
23. Ⓐ Ⓑ Ⓒ Ⓓ
24. Ⓐ Ⓑ Ⓒ Ⓓ
25. Ⓐ Ⓑ Ⓒ Ⓓ
26. Ⓐ Ⓑ Ⓒ Ⓓ
27. Ⓐ Ⓑ Ⓒ Ⓓ
28. Ⓐ Ⓑ Ⓒ Ⓓ
29. Ⓐ Ⓑ Ⓒ Ⓓ
30. Ⓐ Ⓑ Ⓒ Ⓓ
31. Ⓐ Ⓑ Ⓒ Ⓓ
32. Ⓐ Ⓑ Ⓒ Ⓓ
33. Ⓐ Ⓑ Ⓒ Ⓓ
34. Ⓐ Ⓑ Ⓒ Ⓓ
35. Ⓐ Ⓑ Ⓒ Ⓓ
36. Ⓐ Ⓑ Ⓒ Ⓓ
37. Ⓐ Ⓑ Ⓒ Ⓓ
38. Ⓐ Ⓑ Ⓒ Ⓓ
39. Ⓐ Ⓑ Ⓒ Ⓓ

40. Ⓐ Ⓑ Ⓒ Ⓓ
41. Ⓐ Ⓑ Ⓒ Ⓓ
42. Ⓐ Ⓑ Ⓒ Ⓓ
43. Ⓐ Ⓑ Ⓒ Ⓓ
44. Ⓐ Ⓑ Ⓒ Ⓓ
45. Ⓐ Ⓑ Ⓒ Ⓓ
46. Ⓐ Ⓑ Ⓒ Ⓓ
47. Ⓐ Ⓑ Ⓒ Ⓓ
48. Ⓐ Ⓑ Ⓒ Ⓓ
49. Ⓐ Ⓑ Ⓒ Ⓓ
50. Ⓐ Ⓑ Ⓒ Ⓓ
51. Ⓐ Ⓑ Ⓒ Ⓓ
52. Ⓐ Ⓑ Ⓒ Ⓓ
53. Ⓐ Ⓑ Ⓒ Ⓓ
54. Ⓐ Ⓑ Ⓒ Ⓓ
55. Ⓐ Ⓑ Ⓒ Ⓓ
56. Ⓐ Ⓑ Ⓒ Ⓓ
57. Ⓐ Ⓑ Ⓒ Ⓓ
58. Ⓐ Ⓑ Ⓒ Ⓓ
59. Ⓐ Ⓑ Ⓒ Ⓓ
60. Ⓐ Ⓑ Ⓒ Ⓓ

TOEFL

TEST 4

Section 1:
LISTENING COMPREHENSION

TIME: 35 Minutes
50 Questions

Part A

DIRECTIONS: In Part A you will hear short conversations between two speakers. At the end of each conversation, a third person will ask a question about what was said. **You will hear each conversation just one time.** Therefore, you must listen carefully to understand what each speaker says. After you hear a conversation and the question about it, read the four possible answers in your test book and decide which one is the best answer to the question you heard. Then, on your answer sheet, find the number of the question and fill in the space that corresponds to the answer you have chosen.

---

1.   (A)   She did watch the same television program that the man saw.
     (B)   She watched a different television program last night.
     (C)   She couldn't watch anything on television, because her television is out for repairs.
     (D)   She watched the program at a friend's house.

2.   (A)   1966
     (B)   1968
     (C)   1970
     (D)   1972

3. (A) The bumper cars
   (B) The roller coaster
   (C) The ferris wheel
   (D) The Tilt-a-Whirl

4. (A) A birthday party
   (B) A funeral
   (C) A baby shower
   (D) A wedding

5. (A) Nine
   (B) Seven
   (C) Five
   (D) Three

6. (A) Sam never promised to meet the woman.
   (B) Sam probably got lost on his way to the meeting place.
   (C) Sam probably forgot the meeting because he has been so busy.
   (D) Sam said he would meet the woman at 11:00.

7. (A) A bakery
   (B) A hospital
   (C) A deli
   (D) A beauty parlor

8. (A) He had to work late the day before.
   (B) He woke up early in the morning.
   (C) He went to sleep late the night before.
   (D) A dog barking kept him awake most of the night.

9. (A) He does not like being in the library.
   (B) The library is closing.
   (C) He only has five sources.
   (D) He is unable to find enough sources that he needs to complete his paper.

10. (A) She does not know where the man's coat is.
    (B) She put the man's coat in the closet.
    (C) She saw the man put his coat in the closet when he arrived.
    (D) She thinks the man left his coat on a chair.

11. (A) Yes, because they thought he was the right candidate.
    (B) No, because the hospital does not have any positions available at the moment.
    (C) No, because he did not call the right person to get the job.
    (D) Yes, because he approached them at the right time.

12. (A) It is fruitful.
    (B) He doesn't have enough time to work on it.
    (C) He is tired of working on it.
    (D) It is taking too long to finish.

13. (A) Giving directions
    (B) Giving orders
    (C) Giving her address
    (D) Taking an oath

14. (A) He lost money in his insurance business.
    (B) He had to pay a lot of money to his insurance company.
    (C) He had a sudden loss in his weight.
    (D) He does not enjoy doing business.

15. (A) At a car dealer's
    (B) At an auto garage
    (C) In a house
    (D) Near a police station

16. (A) They should have better light in their dining area.
    (B) He didn't like the dinner.
    (C) He cannot eat anything.
    (D) He doesn't want to have a heavy dinner.

17. (A) Clare is very poor.
    (B) Clare will not get admission in a good school.
    (C) Clare could have scored better.
    (D) Clare's score is very bad.

18. (A) Susan has not arrived yet.
    (B) David has not come in yet.
    (C) Both Susan and David have not arrived.
    (D) The meeting is scheduled at ten o'clock and it is not ten yet.

19. (A) Julie is not good with names.
    (B) Not Al but Mr. Alexander Robbins is the vice president of this organization.
    (C) In place of Al, Mr. Robbins will see them at three o'clock.
    (D) Al is Alexander's familiar name.

20. (A) Sixteen
    (B) Twenty
    (C) Four
    (D) Twelve

21. (A) Her brother drove at a tremendous speed.
    (B) She does not trust her brother's driving.
    (C) She could not believe that they arrived in time.
    (D) She did not believe in driving at high speed.

22. (A) They quarreled with some people.
    (B) She is tired of them.
    (C) They are happily married.
    (D) They are very good people.

23. (A) The man has to take a test for his music course.
    (B) She wishes him good luck for his test.
    (C) Only great people love classical music.
    (D) The man has the ability to appreciate really good music.

24. (A) Monday
    (B) Sunday
    (C) Saturday
    (D) Friday

25. (A) She does not have any regard for the man.
    (B) The man must have made a mistake in paying the bill.
    (C) She is sorry that the man has disregarded their notice.
    (D) If the man has paid his bill, he should not pay attention to the notice.

Part B

WAIT

26. (A) A sweater
    (B) A blazer
    (C) Shoes
    (D) A suit

27. (A) She thought it was too big.
    (B) She liked it on him.
    (C) She did not like the color.
    (D) She did not like the blazer.

28. (A) 25%
    (B) 50%
    (C) 75%
    (D) 90%

29. (A) They did not fit properly.
    (B) They cost too much.
    (C) She did not like the colors.
    (D) She did not like the stores.

30. (A) About 5 p.m.
    (B) About 2 p.m.
    (C) About noon
    (D) About 9 a.m.

31. (A) The man's qualifications
    (B) The man's interview
    (C) The man's knowledge
    (D) The man's ability

32. (A) His qualifications are not good.
    (B) He doesn't have up-to-date knowledge.
    (C) There were many other qualified candidates.
    (D) He does not have enough work experience.

33. (A) The ability to apply knowledge to work
    (B) Good qualifications
    (C) Experience
    (D) Theoretical knowledge

34. (A) They are better than the interviewers expected.
    (B) They are poor.
    (C) They are fairly good.
    (D) They are not compatible with the position.

35. (A) They have very good experience.
    (B) They are experts in this field.
    (C) They have good qualifications.
    (D) They were impressed by him.

36. (A) The man
    (B) The whole earth
    (C) The eighth-grade students
    (D) The woman herself

37. (A) Because there are many festivals in the spring
    (B) Because it is hot and humid
    (C) Because it is colorful and pleasant
    (D) Because she lives in a tropical country

38. (A) He does not like flowers.
    (B) He likes the winter.
    (C) He lives in a cold country.
    (D) He gets sick in the spring.

39. (A) Cold
    (B) Tropical
    (C) Hot
    (D) Humid

40. (A) Intelligent
    (B) Funny
    (C) Stupid
    (D) Boring

Part C

WAIT

41. (A) Northern
    (B) Southern
    (C) Eastern
    (D) Western

42. (A) Zenith and nadir
    (B) Alderan and Betelgeuse
    (C) Alembic and alchemy
    (D) Soda and syrup

43. (A) Germanic invasions
    (B) Greek invasions
    (C) Islamic invasions
    (D) Roman invasions

44. (A) Germans'
    (B) Greeks'
    (C) Arabs'
    (D) Italians'

45. (A) Philosophy and education
    (B) Art and literature
    (C) Agriculture and sailing
    (D) Medicine and science

46. (A) Because 90 percent of the ice on the earth lies there
    (B) Because it is a land of fierce winds
    (C) Because the conditions there are hostile to human inhabitation
    (D) Because it has an average annual temperature of –70°F

47. (A) There would be no scarcity of fresh water in the world.
    (B) The sea level would rise about 60 feet.
    (C) There would be thunderstorms all over the world.
    (D) The Antarctic would become more hospitable to human life.

48. (A) Two hundred miles per hour
    (B) Sixty miles per hour
    (C) Seventy miles per hour
    (D) Ninety miles per hour

49. (A) Because it has 90 percent of the planet's ice
    (B) Because it is hostile to human life
    (C) Because it has the world's largest populations of wildlife
    (D) Because it is the windiest continent

50. (A) Seal
    (B) Whale
    (C) Penguin
    (D) Elephant

STOP

If time still remains, you may review work only in this section.
When the time allotted is up, you may go on to the next section.

Section 2:
STRUCTURE AND WRITTEN EXPRESSION

TIME: 25 Minutes
          40 Questions

DIRECTIONS: Questions 1-15 are incomplete sentences. Beneath each sentence are four words or phrases marked (A), (B), (C), and (D). Choose the **one** word or phrase which best completes the sentence. Then, on your answer sheet, find the number of the question and fill in the space that corresponds to the answer you have chosen.

1.   Grover Cleveland was the first president _____ in the White House.
     (A)   got married
     (B)   to get married
     (C)   has got married
     (D)   was married

2.   If cauliflowers _____ from extreme temperatures, the heads get discolored.
     (A)   were not protected
     (B)   are not protected
     (C)   are not being protected
     (D)   will not be protected

3.   The first nuclear power reactor was designed _____ in 1942.
     (A)   by Fermi
     (B)   through Fermi
     (C)   with Fermi
     (D)   to Fermi

4.   Greenland is the main source of cryolite, _____ soft mineral used in the production of aluminum.
     (A)   that is a
     (B)   which is a
     (C)   it is a
     (D)   who is a

5. _____ is the science of making artificial replacements for parts of the human body.
   (A) Prosthetics
   (B) Prosthetic
   (C) A prosthetic
   (D) The prosthetics

6. Rice is the staple diet of _____.
   (A) a large amount of Asians
   (B) much Asians
   (C) most Asians
   (D) number of Asians

7. William Byrd was the owner of _____ library in colonial times.
   (A) the most large
   (B) a larger
   (C) a largest
   (D) the largest

8. Exobiology is the study of life _____.
   (A) in other planets
   (B) at other planets
   (C) on other planets
   (D) to other planets

9. The Declaration of Independence, _____ the Constitution of the United States, was drawn up with the help of Benjamin Franklin.
   (A) and
   (B) also
   (C) as well as
   (D) so too

10. It was from the Lowell Laboratory that _____.
    (A) Pluto was sighted 1930
    (B) Pluto in 1930 was sighted
    (C) Pluto was in 1930 sighted
    (D) Pluto was sighted in 1930

11. The rodent, comprising of the mouse, rat, guinea pig, and porcupine, _____ with incisor-like teeth in both jaws.
   (A)   are mammals
   (B)   is a mammal
   (C)   is the mammal
   (D)   are the mammals

12. _____ into oceans and rivers is a serious form of pollution.
   (A)   Having dumped sewage
   (B)   Being dumped sewage
   (C)   Dumped sewage
   (D)   Dumping sewage

13. Products which are made from natural earths and are _____ are known as ceramics.
   (A)   being subject to high temperatures
   (B)   subjected to high temperatures
   (C)   subject to high temperatures
   (D)   having been subjected to high temperatures

14. _____ called melanin protects the underlying layers of skin from sun rays.
   (A)   A color pigment
   (B)   A colorful pigment
   (C)   The pigment
   (D)   A pigment

15. Oranges are a _____ source of vitamin C.
   (A)   well
   (B)   better
   (C)   good
   (D)   very

> **DIRECTIONS**: In questions 16-40 each sentence has four underlined words or phrases, marked (A), (B), (C), and (D). Choose the **one** word or phrase which is incorrect and must be changed to make the sentence correct. Then, on your answer sheet, find the number of the question and fill in the space that corresponds to the answer you have chosen.

used.

16.   Walt Disney was used to make numerous visits to Disneyland to find out what the
                    (A)   B   C

needs and interests of the public were.
                                    D

had not taken

17.   If James B. Connolly would not take part in the first modern Olympic Games, in
                                (A)   B C

1896, he might have graduated from Harvard.
                                    D

18.   Margaret Sanger made the people to see the need *of* for birth control.
                                    A   B   (C)   D

will

19.   If we continue to exploit nature there should not be enough resources left for
                        A   (B)   C   D

future generations.

20.   I have not learned cycling as I have been afraid of falling and hurting me.
            A   B   C   (D)

21.   It is imperative that all processed food be approving by the Food and Drug
                A   B   (C)
Administration for hygenic standards.
                        D

many

22.   Not much scientists have the time or the verbal skills required to become
            (A)   B   C   D

literary writers.

has

23. Although coal has to been in use since prehistoric times, it is only since the
               A   B   C

    18th century that coal mining has become a major industry.
               D

24. For best results eggs and cheese should be cooked over gentle heat, isn't it?
          A   B   C   D

    aren't they

25. Although it started life as an apprentice to a soap boiler, William Colgate
             A   B

    was to become immortalized in toilet products.
          C   D

26. The kinds of trees that shed their leaves in autumn are known as deciduous trees.
          A   B   C   D

27. The plants make their own food through a process called photosynthesis.
        A   B   C   D

28. Science has transformed the planet but literature has not paid
                        A   B

    enough amount of attention to how scientists have lived and worked.
            C   D

29. The prime meridian which passes through Greenwich, in England, is the same
                 A   B   C   D

    the Greenwich meridian.

30. There is usually no charge for using a library but however for overdue charges and
      A   B   C   D

    certain specialized services.

31. Tom <u>does not</u> agree that TV watching <u>is</u> in any way <u>useful</u> and <u>so does</u> Harry.
         A   B   C   D

32. A cuckoo <u>always</u> <u>never</u> hatches <u>its</u> eggs but leaves <u>them</u> in another bird's nest to
               A   B   C   D
     be hatched by that bird.

33. Recalling his interview <u>with</u> the actor, Henabery Brownlow says that he
                            A
     <u>does not expect</u> the actor <u>to talk</u> for <u>four hours</u>.
           B   C   D

34. Chaplin had wanted some reels of <u>his films</u> to be destroyed <u>but</u> <u>he</u> had been saved
                                        A   B C
     by <u>his manager</u>.
        D

35. <u>For to commemorate</u> the dog Nipper, <u>whose</u> <u>picture</u> appears on old gramophone
            A   B   C
     records, a brass plaque <u>marks</u> his grave.
                       D

36. Businesses <u>are finding</u> a word processor <u>invaluable</u> as text <u>can be</u> stored in it,
                   A   B   C
     reused indefinitely and <u>modification</u> easily.
                          D

37. The <u>ginko</u> is an <u>ornamental decorative</u> tree that <u>was first imported</u> from China
           A B   C   D
     and Japan.

38. <u>Leavening</u> agents such <u>as</u> baking powder <u>are</u> used to make bread and cake <u>raise</u>.
          A   B   C   D

were agreed.

39. Most neighborhood agreed that there should not be a shopping mall
    <u>A</u>   (B)   <u>C</u>

    next to the park.
    <u>D</u>

40. Peristalsis is the squeeze movement of the muscles in the gullet.
    <u>A</u>   <u>the squeeze</u> <u>movement</u> <u>of the muscles</u> <u>in the gullet.</u>
       A   (B)   C   D

STOP

If time still remains, you may review work only in this section.
When the time allotted is up, you may go on to the next section.

Section 3:
READING COMPREHENSION
AND VOCABULARY

TIME: 55 Minutes
        60 Questions

DIRECTIONS: In this section you will read several passages. Each one is followed by several questions about it. You are to choose the best answer to each question, marked (A), (B), (C), and (D). Then, on your answer sheet, find the number of the question and fill in the space that corresponds to the answer you have chosen.

Questions 1 to 10 refer to the following passage:

1   The most familiar speleothems (from the Greek word *spelaion* for cave and *thema* for deposit), the decorative dripstone features found in caves, are stalactites and stalagmites. Stalactites hang downward from the ceiling of the cave and are formed as drop after drop of water slowly trickles through cracks in the cave roof. Stalagmites grow upward from the floor
5   of the cave, generally as a result of water dripping from an overhead stalactite. A column forms when a stalactite and a stalagmite grow until they join. A "curtain" or "drapery" begins to form on an inclined ceiling when drops of water trickle along a slope.

       Natural openings on the surface that lead to caves are called sinkholes, or swallow holes. Streams sometimes disappear down these holes and flow through the cavern. Rivers
10   may flow from one mountain to another through a series of caves. Some caverns have sinkholes in their floors. Water often builds up a rim of dripstone around the edge of the hole. Dripping water often contains dissolved minerals as well as acid. These minerals too will be deposited; and they may give rich coloring to the deposits. If minerals in the water change, layers of different colors may be formed.

1.   Stalagmites are formed by
      (A)   drops of water which enter through cracks in the ceiling.
      (B)   underground rivers which flow through the cave.
      (C)   water dripping from an overhead stalactite.
      (D)   water which trickles down a slope.

2.   Sinkholes are
      (A)   the decorative dripstone features found in caves.

    (B)   natural openings on the surface that lead to caves.
    (C)   colorful layers of mineral deposits.
    (D)   None of the above

3.   Which speleothem grows upward from the floor?
    (A)   Stalagmites
    (B)   Stalactites
    (C)   Sinkholes
    (D)   Curtains

4.   An "inclined ceiling" is one which
    (A)   is straight.
    (B)   is crooked.
    (C)   is slanted.
    (D)   is wet.

5.   Which of the following are NOT caused by dripping water?
    (A)   Stalagmites
    (B)   Stalactites
    (C)   Slopes
    (D)   Curtains

6.   The information in the passage is most relevant to which field of study?
    (A)   Geography
    (B)   Archaeology
    (C)   Physics
    (D)   Geology

7.   "Curtains" can also be called
    (A)   columns.
    (B)   draperies.
    (C)   stalagmites.
    (D)   rims.

8.   The word *speleothem* comes from which language?
    (A)   Latin
    (B)   French
    (C)   Greek
    (D)   English

9.   Stalagmites are formed by
       (A)   drops of water which enter the cave through cracks in the ceiling.
       (B)   underground rivers which flow through the cave.
       (C)   water which seeps through the cave floor.
       (D)   water which trickles down a slope.

10.   Which speleothem hangs from the ceiling of a cave?
       (A)   Stalagmites
       (B)   Stalactites
       (C)   Columns
       (D)   Rimstones

Questions 11 to 20 refer to the following passage:

1   Horse owners who plan to breed one or more mares should have a working knowledge
    of heredity and know how to care for breeding animals and foals. The number of mares bred
    that actually conceive varies from about 40 to 85 percent, with the average running less than
    50 percent. Some mares that do conceive fail to produce living foals. This means that, on
5   average, two mares are kept a whole year to produce one foal, and even then, some foals are
    disappointments from the standpoint of quality.
           By careful selection, breeders throughout history have developed various kinds of
    horses with a wide variety of characteristics to suit many different needs. The Great Horse
    of the Middle Ages, for example, was bred for size and strength to carry a heavily armored
10 knight. The massive horses of such breeds are often called "cold blooded." The Arabs bred
    lithe desert horses that were small and swift. These animals are often referred to as "hot
    blooded." Cross-breeding of hot-blooded and cold-blooded horses for certain characteristics
    produced breeds ranging from riding horses to draft horses.
           The Thoroughbred is considered by many to be the highpoint of elegance and fine
15 selective breeding. Many persons mistakenly apply the name Thoroughbred to any purebred
    horse. But a Thoroughbred is a distinct breed of running horses that traces its ancestry through
    the male line directly back to three Eastern stallions: the Byerly Turk, the Darley Arabian,
    and the Godolphin Barb.
           For convenience the breeds of horses are often divided into three major groups: (1)
20 ponies, (2) heavy, or draft horses, and (3) light horses.

11.   Which of the following is not an example of an Eastern stallion?
       (A)   Byerly Turk
       (B)   Darley Arabian
       (C)   Thoroughbred
       (D)   Godolphin Barb

12. Which of the following was NOT a characteristic of the Great Horse of the Middle Ages?
    (A) Large size
    (B) Swiftness
    (C) Strength
    (D) "Cold-bloodedness"

13. It can be inferred from the passage that cold-blooded and hot-blooded horses were cross-bred for what reason?
    (A) Such cross-breeding was a safer means of reproduction.
    (B) Cross-bred horses were preferred by Arabs.
    (C) By cross-breeding, horses with desirable mixed characteristics could be produced.
    (D) Cross-breeding produced Thoroughbred horses.

14. In line 11, "lithe" most nearly means
    (A) graceful.
    (B) clumsy.
    (C) massive.
    (D) bulky.

15. Which of the following is NOT one of the major divisions of horse breeds?
    (A) Draft horses
    (B) Ponies
    (C) Foals
    (D) Light horses

16. According to the passage, which of the following horses is considered to be the finest purebred?
    (A) Darley Arabian
    (B) Thoroughbred
    (C) Godolphin Barb
    (D) Byerly Turk

17. To conceive is to
    (A) become sick.
    (B) become pregnant.
    (C) die.
    (D) be born.

18. A foal is a
    (A)   male horse.
    (B)   female horse.
    (C)   old horse.
    (D)   baby horse.

19. The average amount of mares bred which actually conceive is less than what percent?
    (A)   40
    (B)   85
    (C)   50
    (D)   75

20. A mare is a
    (A)   male horse.
    (B)   baby horse.
    (C)   female horse.
    (D)   old horse.

Questions 21 to 30 refer to the following passage:

1   Animals that produce large amounts of offspring depend upon the sheer size of the litter for the perpetuation of their species. The young mature very quickly and are not educated, as the parents are usually involved with obtaining their own food and with reproduction. Should some of the offspring become endangered, the parent will not interfere,
5 because it is not expected that all the young survive, which is the reason for a large litter.

        One animal that produces large litters is the hamster. A female hamster is able to bear young when she is six weeks to two months old. The gestation period is about 16 days. Although an average litter size is from five to ten, hamsters commonly have as few as three or as many as a dozen offspring at a time. Mothers will sometimes eat their own young,
10 particularly when the number of offspring is large. Females may produce litters up to an age of about 15 months at monthly intervals. The blind, hairless young begin to grow fur in two to three days. Their eyes open after about two weeks. After ten days they begin eating solid food, though the mother will continue to nurse them for about two more weeks. In captivity, a typical hamster may live for two to three years.

21. The gestation period for hamsters is about
    (A)   nine months.
    (B)   one month.
    (C)   16 days.
    (D)   six weeks.

22. Female hamsters will sometimes eat their young for what reason?
    (A) Hunger
    (B) Because of a large number of offspring
    (C) Deformed babies
    (D) The young mature too quickly

23. Female hamsters may reproduce as young as
    (A) six weeks old.
    (B) six months old.
    (C) 15 months old.
    (D) two weeks old.

24. "Perpetuation" in line 2 means
    (A) extinction.
    (B) annihilation.
    (C) variation.
    (D) continuation.

25. Hamsters can produce offspring until what age?
    (A) two years
    (B) six weeks
    (C) 15 months
    (D) 16 days

26. What is the tone of the passage?
    (A) Argumentative
    (B) Informative
    (C) Biased
    (D) Farcical

27. What is the BEST title for this passage?
    (A) "Endangered Animal Litters"
    (B) "Reasons for Large Litters"
    (C) "Parents of Large Litters"
    (D) "Educating Litters"

28.   What is a litter?
   (A)   The amount of parents an animal has
   (B)   The amount of garbage an animal has
   (C)   The amount of offspring an animal has
   (D)   The amount of siblings an animal has

29.   Why would an animal parent not be able to care for its litter?
   (A)   It is busy reproducing and food gathering.
   (B)   It is busy educating the litter.
   (C)   It interferes with the litter.
   (D)   It is busy playing.

30.   Which of the following is NOT a reason for a large litter?
   (A)   The young are not expected to live.
   (B)   The young are educated.
   (C)   The parents are too busy to protect them.
   (D)   The young mature quickly.

Questions 31 to 40 refer to the following passage:

1   Juan Ponce de León was the first Spaniard to touch the shores of the present United
States. As Columbus had not remotely realized the extent of his momentous discovery, so de
León never dreamed that his "island" of Florida was a peninsular extension of the vast North
American continent. After coming to the New World with Columbus in 1493, he had led the
5   occupation of Puerto Rico in 1508 and governed it from 1509 to 1512. In 1509, de León
started a colony at Caparra, later abandoned in favor of San Juan. He was one of the first
adelantados—men who "advanced" the Spanish Empire by conquest, subjugation of the
Indians, and establishment of a semi-military government.
     In Puerto Rico he heard a legend about an island called Bimini, where there was said
10   to be a spring that restored youth to all who bathed in it. It is said he was seeking this spring
when he discovered Florida.
     He sailed from Puerto Rico in March 1513. On Easter Sunday he sighted the coast. A
few days later he landed on Florida's east coast, near what is now St. Augustine. He named
the place La Florida after the Spanish term for Easter Sunday—Pascua florida, or "flowery
15   feast." He then sailed around the peninsula and up the west coast. He returned to Florida in
1521.

31.   In what year did de León discover Florida?
   (A)   1508
   (B)   1513
   (C)   1521
   (D)   1492

32. What was the title of the first colony started by Ponce de León in Puerto Rico?
    (A) San Juan
    (B) La Florida
    (C) Caparra
    (D) St. Augustine

33. What was the name of the legendary island where the fabled Fountain of Youth was said to be?
    (A) Cuba
    (B) Bimini
    (C) Atlantis
    (D) Bermuda

34. Which of the following is implied by the passage?
    (A) Ponce de León was the true discoverer of the North American continent.
    (B) Ponce de León rejected the philosophy of the *adelantados*.
    (C) Ponce de León may have discovered Florida "by accident."
    (D) Ponce de León's greatest contribution was his discovery of the Fountain of Youth.

35. *Pascua florida* is the Spanish term for which holiday?
    (A) Easter Sunday
    (B) Christmas
    (C) Thanksgiving
    (D) Palm Sunday

36. According to the passage, which of the following was NOT a means of advancement of the Spanish Empire in the New World?
    (A) Conquest
    (B) Subjugation of Indians
    (C) Establishment of semi-military governments
    (D) Treaties and negotiation

37. From the passage, it can be assumed that a "peninsula" is
    (A) a volcanic island.
    (B) an island completely surrounded by water.
    (C) an extension of land surrounded almost completely by water.
    (D) an island inhabited by Indians.

38.   The tone of the word "advanced" in line 7 suggests that

(A)   *adelantados* favor progress.

(B)   progress could not have occurred without subjugation.

(C)   progress is related to conquest and subjugation.

(D)   conquest, subjugation, and semi-military government are not progress.

39.   According to the passage, Ponce de León believed the land he discovered was

(A)   part of the Bahamas.

(B)   the new "island" of Florida.

(C)   the mainland of the United States.

(D)   Puerto Rico.

40.   Ponce de León was classified as an *adelantado* because he

(A)   was a great explorer.

(B)   was the first Spaniard to see the shores of the United States.

(C)   conquered and ruled by military force.

(D)   claimed Florida for the King of Spain.

Questions 41 to 50 refer to the following passage:

1   Any list of the greatest thinkers in history contains the name of the brilliant physicist
Albert Einstein. His theories of relativity led to entirely new ways of thinking about time,
space, matter, energy, and gravity. Einstein's work led to such scientific advances as the
control of atomic energy, even television as a practical application of Einstein's work.

5   In 1902 Einstein became an examiner in the Swiss patent office at Bern. In 1905, at
age 26, he published the first of five major research papers. The first one provided a theory
explaining Brownian movement, the zig-zag motion of microscopic particles in suspension.
The second paper laid the foundation for the photon, or quantum, theory of light. In it he
proposed that light is composed of separate packets of energy, called quanta or photons, that
10   have some of the properties of particles and some of the properties of waves. A third paper
contained the "special theory of relativity" which showed that time and motion are relative
to the observer, if the speed of light is constant and the natural laws are the same everywhere
in the universe. The fourth paper was a mathematical addition to the special theory of
relativity. Here Einstein presented his famous formula, $E = m(cc)$, known as the energy mass
15   equivalence. In 1916, Einstein published his general theory of relativity. In it he proposed that
gravity is not a force, but a curve in the space-time continuum, created by the presence of
mass.

        Einstein spoke out frequently against nationalism, the exalting of one nation above all
others. He opposed war and violence and supported Zionism, the movement to establish a
20.   Jewish homeland in Palestine. When the Nazis came to power in 1933, they denounced his
ideas. He then moved to the United States. In 1939 Einstein learned that two German chemists
had split the uranium atom. Einstein wrote to President Franklin D. Roosevelt warning him
that this scientific knowledge could lead to Germany developing an atomic bomb. He
suggested the United States begin its own atomic bomb research.

41.   Einstein's primary work was in the area of
      (A)   chemistry.
      (B)   biology.
      (C)   physics.
      (D)   engineering.

42.   Which of the following inventions is mentioned in the passage as a practical application of Einstein's discoveries?
      (A)   Radio
      (B)   Automobiles
      (C)   Computers
      (D)   Television

43.   According to the passage, Einstein supported all of the following except
      (A)   the establishment of a Jewish homeland in Palestine.
      (B)   nationalism.
      (C)   atomic bomb research in the United States.
      (D)   the defeat of the Nazis.

44.   In which country was Einstein born?
      (A)   Switzerland
      (B)   United States
      (C)   Germany
      (D)   Israel

45.   What is "Brownian movement"?
      (A)   The zig-zag motion of microscopic particles in suspension
      (B)   The emission of electrons from solids when struck by light
      (C)   The motion of photons in light
      (D)   The basis of the theory of relativity

46.   Einstein was a citizen of all of the following countries EXCEPT
      (A)   Belgium.
      (B)   Germany.
      (C)   United States.
      (D)   Switzerland.

47. It is clear from the tone of the passage that the author feels
    (A) Einstein's work in physics was somewhat tarnished by his conservative political views.
    (B) Albert Einstein was one of the most brilliant thinkers in history.
    (C) Einstein's work in physics, though theoretically impressive, led to few practical applications.
    (D) Einstein's theories have been consistently proven incorrect.

48. According to Einstein's special theory of relativity,
    (A) all properties of matter and energy can be explained in a single mathematical formula.
    (B) light is composed of separate packets of energy.
    (C) time and motion are relative to the observer.
    (D) some solids emit electrons when struck by light.

49. In line 18, the word "exalting" most nearly means
    (A) elevation.
    (B) criticism.
    (C) support.
    (D) elimination.

50. According to Einstein, light is composed of separate packets of energy called
    (A) electrons.
    (B) photoelectrons.
    (C) quanta.
    (D) gamma rays.

Questions 51 to 60 refer to the following passage:

1   We believe the Earth is about 4.6 billion years old. At present we are forced to look to other bodies in the solar system for hints as to what the early history of the Earth was like. Studies of our moon, Mercury, Mars, and the large satellites of Jupiter and Saturn have provided ample evidence that all these large celestial bodies were bombarded by smaller
5   objects in a wide variety of sizes shortly after the larger bodies had formed. This same bombardment must have affected Earth as well. The lunar record indicates that the rate of impacts decreased to its present low level about 4 billion years ago. On Earth, subsequent erosion and crustal motions have obliterated the craters that must have formed during this epoch.
10   Scientists estimate the Earth's age by measuring the ratios of various radioactive elements in rocks. The oldest Earth rocks tested thus far are about $3^{1}/_{3}$ billion years old. But no one knows whether these are the oldest rocks on Earth. Tests on rocks from the moon and on meteorites show that these are about 4.6 billion years old. Scientists believe that this is the true age of the solar system and probably the true age of the Earth.

51. In line 8, the word "obliterated" means
    (A) created.
    (B) destroyed.
    (C) changed.
    (D) eroded.

52. According to this passage, how do scientists estimate the age of the Earth?
    (A) By measuring the ratios of radioactive elements in rocks
    (B) By examining fossils
    (C) By studying sunspots
    (D) By examining volcanic activity

53. Scientists estimate the age of the Earth as
    (A) $3^1/_3$ billion years old.
    (B) 4 billion years old.
    (C) 4.6 billion years old.
    (D) 6 billion years old.

54. Which of the following processes led to the obliteration of the craters formed by the bombardment of the Earth by celestial bodies?
    (A) Volcanic activity
    (B) Solar radiation
    (C) Gravity
    (D) Crustal motions

55. According to the passage, why are scientists forced to look at other bodies in the solar system to determine the early history of the Earth?
    (A) Human alteration of the Earth
    (B) Erosion and crustal motions
    (C) Solar flares
    (D) Deforestation

56. What is the BEST title for this passage?
    (A) "Determining the Age of the Earth"
    (B) "Determining the Age of the Solar System"
    (C) "Erosion and Crustal Motion of Earth"
    (D) "Radioactive Elements in Rocks"

57. Which of the following bodies was NOT studied to give evidence that the Earth was bombarded in its early history?
    (A) Mars
    (B) Mercury
    (C) Jupiter
    (D) Earth's moon

58. Bombardment of the Earth at one time by various sized bodies is
    (A) inferred from what happened on other planetary bodies.
    (B) documented fact.
    (C) proven by the lunar record.
    (D) indicated by erosion.

59. The level of impacts of the bombardments of Earth have
    (A) decreased to below normal.
    (B) increased to a current high.
    (C) increased after a periodic low.
    (D) decreased to a current low.

60. In line 6, the word "bombardment" means
    (A) an avoidance.
    (B) an assault.
    (C) an effect.
    (D) a cause.

STOP

If time still remains, you may review work only in this section.

TEST 4

ANSWER KEY

SECTION 1: LISTENING COMPREHENSION

1.	(C)	14.	(A)	26.	(D)	39.	(A)
2.	(C)	15.	(B)	27.	(B)	40.	(B)
3.	(C)	16.	(D)	28.	(B)	41.	(D)
4.	(D)	17.	(C)	29.	(A)	42.	(B)
5.	(B)	18.	(B)	30.	(A)	43.	(A)
6.	(C)	19.	(D)	31.	(B)	44.	(B)
7.	(A)	20.	(B)	32.	(D)	45.	(D)
8.	(C)	21.	(A)	33.	(A)	46.	(D)
9.	(D)	22.	(D)	34.	(C)	47.	(B)
10.	(A)	23.	(D)	35.	(B)	48.	(A)
11.	(B)	24.	(D)	36.	(B)	49.	(C)
12.	(A)	25.	(D)	37.	(C)	50.	(D)
13.	(C)			38.	(D)		

SECTION 2: STRUCTURE AND WRITTEN EXPRESSION

1.	(B)	11.	(B)	21.	(C)	31.	(D)
2.	(B)	12.	(D)	22.	(A)	32.	(A)
3.	(A)	13.	(B)	23.	(A)	33.	(B)
4.	(B)	14.	(D)	24.	(D)	34.	(C)
5.	(A)	15.	(C)	25.	(A)	35.	(A)
6.	(C)	16.	(A)	26.	(A)	36.	(D)
7.	(D)	17.	(A)	27.	(A)	37.	(C)
8.	(C)	18.	(A)	28.	(C)	38.	(D)
9.	(C)	19.	(B)	29.	(D)	39.	(A)
10.	(D)	20.	(D)	30.	(D)	40.	(B)

SECTION 3: READING COMPREHENSION AND VOCABULARY

1.	(C)	16.	(B)	31.	(B)	46.	(A)
2.	(B)	17.	(B)	32.	(C)	47.	(B)
3.	(A)	18.	(D)	33.	(B)	48.	(C)
4.	(C)	19.	(C)	34.	(C)	49.	(A)
5.	(C)	20.	(C)	35.	(A)	50.	(C)
6.	(D)	21.	(C)	36.	(D)	51.	(B)
7.	(B)	22.	(B)	37.	(C)	52.	(A)
8.	(C)	23.	(A)	38.	(D)	53.	(C)
9.	(A)	24.	(D)	39.	(B)	54.	(D)
10.	(B)	25.	(C)	40.	(C)	55.	(B)
11.	(C)	26.	(B)	41.	(C)	56.	(A)
12.	(B)	27.	(B)	42.	(D)	57.	(C)
13.	(C)	28.	(C)	43.	(B)	58.	(A)
14.	(A)	29.	(A)	44.	(C)	59.	(D)
15.	(C)	30.	(B)	45.	(A)	60.	(B)

Detailed Explanations
of Answers

TEST 4

Section 1:
LISTENING COMPREHENSION

Part A

1.   **(C)**   The question asks, "What does the woman mean?" The correct answer is (C) — She couldn't watch anything on television, because her television is out for repairs. The man says, "There was a great television show on last night. It was a documentary about the history of the space program. Did you see it?" The woman replies, "My television is at the repair shop."

2.   **(C)**   The question asks, "What year was the woman born?" The correct answer is (C) — 1970. When the man asks how old the woman's sister was, the woman responds, "My sister is two years older than I am. She was born in 1968." The woman was born two years after her sister was, which would make the year of her birth 1970.

3.   **(C)**   The question asks, "What ride will they probably go on next?" The correct answer is (C) — The ferris wheel. The man says, "Well, the line for the bumper cars is very long, but the line for the ferris wheel looks relatively short."

4.   **(D)**   The question asks, "Where is this conversation most likely taking place?" The correct response is (D) — A wedding. The woman says, "The gown she is wearing was her mother's," and the man says, He makes a handsome groom."

5.   **(B)**   The question asks, "How many days does the man have to get his project done?" The correct answer is (B) — Seven. The man says, "I have to get this project done by the twenty-first of the month. What day is it today?" The woman replies, "Today is the fourteenth."

513

6.   **(C)**   The question asks, "What does the man mean?" The correct answer is (C) — Sam probably forgot the meeting because he has been so busy. The man says, "He has had a busy schedule."

7.   **(A)**   The question asks, "Where is this conversation most likely taking place?" The correct answer is (A) — A bakery. The woman says, "Were these muffins made fresh this morning?" The man answers, "Of course, ma'am, we bake them every day."

8.   **(C)**   The question asks, "Why is the man tired?" The correct answer is (C) — He went to sleep late the night before. The woman says to the man, "You should not have stayed up so late last night."

9.   **(D)**   The question asks, "Why is the man aggravated?" The correct answer is (D) — He is unable to find enough sources that he needs to complete his paper. The man says, "I have been in this library for hours, but I cannot find enough sources of information for my term paper."

10.   **(A)**   The question asks, "What does the woman mean?" The correct answer is (A) — She does not know where the man's coat is. The woman asks, "How am I supposed to know where your things are?"

11.   **(B)**   The question asks, "Does Bill have a job in the hospital?" The correct answer is (B) — No, because the hospital does not have any positions available at the moment. The woman says, "...they don't have any openings right now." "Openings" means available positions.

12.   **(A)**   The question asks, "How does the man feel about his new project?" The correct answer is (A) — It is fruitful. In the conversation the man says, "...I think it is well worth the time and effort." It means that the time and energy spent on it are not wasted.

13.   **(C)**   The question asks, "What was the woman doing?" The correct answer is (C) — Giving her address. The woman says, "Send it to me. Ms. Gloria Gessner, 147 Washington Avenue, Burlington, New York, Zip 11340." It is while giving an address that you give the street address, the town, the state, and the ZIP code one after the other.

14.   **(A)**   The question asks, "What was the reason for Richard's depression?" The

rect answer is (A) — He lost money in his insurance business. The man says, "I heard he suffered some heavy losses in his insurance business."

15. **(B)** The question asks, "Where did this conversation most probably take place?" The correct answer is (B) — At an auto garage. The woman says, "...Can you please check my brake fluid? I am afraid of getting into an accident." The man's response is, "Sure. Can you open the hood please?" It is obvious that the woman wants to get the brakes of her car checked which is most likely to be done at an auto garage.

16. **(D)** The question asks, "What does the man mean?" The correct answer is (D) — He doesn't not want to have a heavy dinner. When the woman asks, "What would you like to have for dinner?", the man answers, "Anything light would be good..." What he means by "light" is "not heavy." He is not referring to the light in the dining area.

17. **(C)** The question asks, "What was the woman's opinion?" The correct answer is (C) — Clare could have scored better. The woman says, "...score is too poor for her." It means the score could be good for others but Clare is capable of scoring better.

18. **(B)** The question asks, "Why can't they start the meeting?" The correct answer is (B) — Because David has not come in yet. When the man suggests to check if Susan has arrived in order to start the meeting, the woman says, "Susan came in ten minutes ago. We still have to wait for David, though." So, it is David who has not arrived yet.

19. **(D)** The question asks, "What does the woman mean?" The correct answer is (D) — Al is Alexander's familiar name. The woman said, "His name is Alexander Robbins. Al is his nickname..." "Nickname" means familiar name or pet name.

20. **(B)** The question asks, "How many people came for lunch?" The correct answer is (B) — Twenty. The man says, "I thought you had ordered lunch for 16 people." The woman responded, "Yes. But we have four more unexpected guests." Sixteen people were expected and four more people came which means there were 20 people.

21. **(A)** The question asks, "What does the woman mean?" The correct answer is (A) — Her brother drove at a tremendous speed. The woman says, "The speed at which my brother drove was unbelievable." "Unbelievable speed" means very high speed.

22. **(D)** The question asks, "What is the woman's opinion about her new neighbors?"

The correct answer is (D) — They are very good people. The woman says, "They are wonderful people… I was tired of the quarrelsome couple that lived here before." "Wonderful" is used as a compliment. The quarrelsome couple is the one that lived there before.

23. **(D)** The question asks, "What does the woman mean?" The correct answer is (D) — The man has the ability to appreciate really good music. The woman says, "You have great taste in music." "Taste" here means artistic appreciation.

24. **(D)** The question asks, "On what day did this conversation take place?" The correct answer is (D) — Friday. The woman asks, "Are they closed already?…" The man answers, "Yes. They close at five on Fridays. And they are closed even on weekends." This means the conversation took place on a Friday after five o'clock.

25. **(D)** The question asks, "What does the woman mean?" The correct answer is (D) — If the man has paid his bill, he should not pay attention to the notice. The woman says, "If you have paid it, just disregard the notice." "Disregard" here means not to pay attention to.

Part B

26. **(D)** The question asks, "What did the man buy?" The correct response is (D) — A suit. This is taken directly from the conversation. The man says, "I just bought this new suit." Choice (B) "A blazer" is what the woman says she is looking to buy. Choices (A) and (C) are not mentioned in the conversation.

27. **(B)** The question asks, "What did the woman think of the man's new clothing?" The correct response is (B) — She liked it on him. The woman says, "It looks very good on you." Choices (A), (C), and (D) are not part of the conversation that was heard.

28. **(B)** The question asks "What was the discount the man received on his clothing?" The correct response is (B) — 50%. The man says, "I have a friend who owns a clothing store and he gives me all my clothes at half off regular price." Half off is a 50 percent discount. Choice (A) "25%" is one-fourth off. Choice (C) "75%" is three-fourths off. Choice (D) "90%" is nine-tenths off (a phrase that is almost never used).

29. **(A)** The questions asks, "How come the woman could not wear most clothes?" The correct response is (A) — They did not fit properly. She says, "Most off-the-rack

clothing does not fit me well; does he do any tailoring?" The phrase "off-the-rack" refers to all clothes that are not tailor made for the individual. The clothes that are purchased in most department stores or brand-name clothing stores are "off the rack."

30. **(A)** The question asks, "When were they going to the store?" The correct response is (A) — About 5 p.m. This question requires you to make an inference based upon the conversation. First, the man is in a suit, so you can infer that he works in an office environment. The man also suggests that he and the woman go to the store after work. The office hours for most businesses are 9 a.m. to 5 p.m. From the answer choices given, "about 5 p.m." is the best response.

31. **(B)** The question asks, "What were these people talking about?" The correct answer is (B) — The man's interview. During the conversation the man says, "I hope my interviewers feel that way." The focus of the whole conversation was the interview for which the man has just appeared.

32. **(D)** The question asks, "Why is the man not confident about getting the job?" The correct answer is (D) — He does not have enough work experience. The man says, "My qualifications are O.K. But I don't have the experience of working on a project like this. That's why I am not so sure about getting this job."

33. **(A)** The question asks, "What is an important quality for good work according to the woman?" The correct answer is (A) — The ability to apply knowledge to work. The woman says, "I think what matters is that you have the ability to ply your knowledge to your work."

34. **(C)** The question asks, "How does the man feel about his qualifications?" The correct answer is (C) — They are fairly good. In the conversation the man says, "My qualifications are O.K...."

35. **(B)** The question asks, "What is the man's opinion about his interviewers?" The correct answer is (B) — They are experts in this field. In the conversation the man says, "...All of them are authorities in this field."

36. **(B)** The question asks, "Who seems to be in a festive mood in the spring according to the woman?" The correct answer is (B) — The whole Earth. While explaining why she likes the spring, the woman says, "...I love flowers and colors. You can see so many of them in the spring; as if the whole Earth is in a festive mood."

37. **(C)**   The question asks, "Why is the spring the favorite season of the woman?" The correct answer is (C) — Because it is colorful and pleasant. When the man asks, "...which is your favorite season?", the woman answers, "...the spring." When the man asks "Why?", the woman answers, "Because I love flowers and colors. You can see so many of them in the spring... Also, it's the most pleasant weather."

38. **(D)**   The question asks, "What is the reason why the man cannot appreciate the spring?" The correct answer is (D) — He gets sick in the spring. When the woman asks him why the spring is not his favorite season, he answers, "Because I get terrible allergies in the spring."

39. **(A)**   The question asks, "What type of country is Norway?" The correct answer is (A) — Cold. In the conversation the man says, "If I am in a cold country like Norway, it would be the summer...."

40. **(B)**   The question asks, "How does the woman find the man's explanation?" The correct answer is (B) — Funny. When the man explains why his favorite season would differ from country to country, the woman exclaims, "Aren't you funny?"

Part C

41. **(D)**   The question asks, "On what civilization did medieval Islamic culture leave a lasting impression?" The correct response is (D) — Western. This is given in the first line of the paragraph. "Medieval Islamic culture left a lasting imprint on the development of Western civilization."

42. **(B)**   The question asks, "Which stars have their names from Arabic words?" The correct response is (B) — Alderan and Betelgeuse. This sentence requires you to distinguish from a list of words and to interpret pauses in speaking to separate different groups of words. The sentence reads, "The terms zenith, nadir, zero, and the names of stars like Alderan and Betelgeuse, along with amalgam, alembic, alchemy, alkali, soda, and syrup all have their origin in Arabic." The pauses created by the commas indicate that only Alderan and Betelgeuse are stars.

43. **(A)**   The question asks, "Why was western Europe languishing?" The correct response is (A) — Germanic invasions. This information was given in the sentence, "While western Europe was languishing in the wake of the Germanic invasions, the Islamic people were vibrant and creative." Choices (B) and (C) were other culture's

mentioned in the text, but are not involved in invasions. Choice (D) does not appear in the text.

44. **(B)** The question asks, "Whose philosophy did the Islamic people keep alive?" The correct response is (B) — Greeks'. This answer to this question comes from the sentence, "They kept alive the philosophy of the Greeks and made numerous advances in medicine and science." Choices (A) and (C) are other culture's mentioned in the reading, but are not mentioned in conjunction with philosophy. Choice (D) is not in the passage.

45. **(D)** The question asks, "In what areas did the people of Islamic culture make advances?" The correct response is (D) — Medicine and science. The answer to this question appears in the same sentence as the answer to the previous question. The other choices given may have been correct, but they do not appear in the reading.

46. **(D)** The question asks, "Why is the Antarctic the world's coldest continent?" The correct answer is (D) — Because it has an average annual temperature of minus seventy degrees Fahrenheit. The first statement in the talk is, "The world's coldest continent, the Antarctic, has a mean annual temperature of $-70°F$."

47. **(B)** The question asks, "What would happen if ice on the Antarctic ever melted?" The correct answer is (B) — The sea level would rise about 60 feet. In the talk you heard, "If the ice lying there ever melted, it would raise the sea level by approximately 60 feet."

48. **(A)** The question asks, "At what speeds do the most fierce winds in the Antarctic blow?" The correct answer is (A) — Two hundred miles per hour. In the talk you heard, "The most fierce gusts of the wind there are nearly 200 miles per hour."

49. **(C)** The question asks, "Why would a biologist find the Antarctic an interesting continent?" The correct answer is (C) — Because it has the world's largest population of wildlife. In the talk you heard, "...the Antarctic has plenty to offer for a biologist's study."

50. **(D)** The question asks, "Which animal is not an inhabitant of the Antarctic?" The correct answer is (D) — Elephant. In the last sentence of the talk, the animals living in the Antarctic are mentioned and the elephant is not one of them.

Section 2:
STRUCTURE AND WRITTEN EXPRESSION

1. **(B)**   (B) is correct because the infinitive performs the function of the adjective to qualify **president.** (A) lacks the relative pronoun **who** to form an adjectival clause that can qualify **president.** (C) is incorrect because the present tense does not agree with the past tense **was** in the main clause. In addition, it lacks **who** to form an adjectival clause. (D) lacks the relative pronoun **who.**

2. **(B)**   (B) is correct because the simple present tense agrees with the simple present tense **get** in the main clause, and scientific facts and results are normally stated in simple present tense. (A) is incorrect because the past tense does not agree with the present tense **get** in the main clause. (C) is incorrect because the present continuous tense does not agree with **get** in the main clause; **get** must be in the future tense. (D) The future tense does not agree with **get** and so it is wrong.

3. **(A)**   (A) is correct because **by** denotes agent (person/thing) responsible for event in this passive voice sentence. (B) **Through** is used to denote the means of doing something. (C) **with** is used to denote the means of doing something. (D) **to** is a preposition of direction or introduces a purpose or intent.

4. **(B)**   (B) is correct because the relative pronoun **which** introduces an (adjectival) subordinate clause. (A) **that** is a relative pronoun but has a restrictive or classifying meaning (only a mineral that is ...), so it is wrong. (C) The personal pronoun **it** cannot refer to a preceding noun, so it is wrong. (D) The relative pronoun **who** can refer only to persons, so it is wrong.

5. **(A)**   (A) is correct. Prosthetics is a non-count noun and singular in agreement with the verb **is.** (B) is an adjective and therefore not suitable. (C) is an adjective and therefore not suitable. (D) The article **the** is not required.

6. **(C)**   (C) is correct because **most** is a numeral adjective, denoting an unspecified large number. (A) **A large amount** refers to a quantity of non-count nouns. **Asians** is a count noun. (B) **Much** refers to a quantity of non-count nouns. (D) You must have the indefinite article **a** before **number of Asians.**

7.   **(D)**   (D) is the right answer; it is in the superlative degree. (A) The superlative degree of **large** is **largest** not **most large**. (B) indicates comparative degree. There is no indication of a comparison in the sentence. (C) The superlative degree must be preceded by the definitive article **the.**

8.   **(C)**   (C) is the right answer; **on** is used to locate objects on a two-dimensional space or surface. A planet is perceived as a surface. (A) **in** is used to locate objects in a three-dimensional space or a location perceived as three-dimensional. (B) **at** is used to denote a specific point on a linear dimension. (D) **to** is a preposition of direction and therefore unsuitable here.

9.   **(C)**   (C) is the right answer; **as well as** combines the two items **Declaration** and **Constitution** in an inclusive way to form a single subject. This is in agreement with the singular verb **was.** (A) **and** joins two words/phrases of equal rank and so there will be two subjects; this does not agree with the singular verb **was.** (B) **also** cannot join the two items **Declaration** and **Constitution**; it can add a statement to another. (D) **so too** cannot join two nouns; it can only add a statement to another.

10.   **(D)**   (D) is the right answer; it is a phrase denoting time in the right place. (A) The preposition **in** is missing before **1930.** (B) This order of words is not normal in prose; it may occur in poetry. (C) This order of words is not normal in prose; it may occur in poetry.

11.   **(B)**   (B) is the right answer; the singular verb is in agreement with the subject. **Comprising** is an inclusive term and so **the rodent** is a single subject. (A) is a plural verb not in agreement with the singular subject **rodent.** (C) **mammal** must be preceded by the indefinite article **a.** (D) The tense and article are incorrect.

12.   **(D)**   (D) is the right answer; **dumping** is a gerundial (50% noun + 50% verb) noun, and the subject of the sentence. **Sewage** is the object of **dumping.** (A) **having dumped** is a perfect participle which should precede another action in the past. (B) **being dumped** is a participle qualifying the following noun making it a subject. **Sewage** is not the subject of the sentence. (C) **dumped** is a past participle qualifying **sewage** and making it a subject, which it is not.

13.   **(B)**   (B) is the right answer; the past participle **subjected** agrees with the past participle **made** in the first clause. The verbs in a series must agree. (A) The participle **being** following the conjunction **and** must agree with the verb **made** in the first clause but does not. (C) **Subject** is an adjective, not agreeing with **made.** (D) The present continuous participle does not agree with **made.**

14. **(D)** (D) is the right answer; no redundancy. (A) Color is redundant; the idea of **color** is inherent in **pigment.** (B) **Colorful** is redundant. (C) The definitive article **the** is incorrect here.

15. **(C)** (C) is the right answer; it is an attributive adjective qualifying **source.** (A) **well** is an adverb modifying a verb. As an adjective it qualifies health in the predicative. (B) is an adjective of comparative degree unsuitable here. (D) is an intensifier adverb which modifies an adjective or another adverb.

16. **(A)** (A) is the right answer. The sentence must read "Walt Disney *used to* make...." A habitual action in the past is denoted by **used to.** (B) is a numeral adjective qualifying **visits.** (C) is an infinitive of purpose functioning as an adjective to qualify **visits.** (D) The conjunction joins the two nouns **needs** and **interests.**

17. **(A)** (A) is the right answer. **If** at the beginning of the sentence signifies a conditional sentence. The right form of the conditional verb is **had not taken** which will agree with the result **might have graduated.** A condition or hypothesis in past time must be denoted by the past perfect tense. (B) relates a person/thing to a condition or event. (C) The definitive article is in agreement with the specific event **Olympic Games.** (D) **From** when it follows the verb **graduate** denotes completion of a course of studies.

18. **(A)** (A) is the right answer. The infinitive should be used without **to** when it complements the causative verb **make.** (B) The definitive article is in agreement with **need,** specified later in the context. (C) The preposition **for** is correctly used in modifying **need.** (D) The compound noun tells us what the people needed.

19. **(B)** (B) is the right answer. The first word in the sentence, **if,** signifies a conditional sentence. A condition in the present tense, **continue** must have its result expressed in the future tense. The answer should be **will.** (A) The infinitive is the object of the verb **continue.** (C) Denotes the existence of resources. (D) **For** expresses intent to give something to someone.

20. **(D)** (D) is the right answer. **Me** must be replaced by the reflexive pronoun **myself.** When the agent of the action is also the object of the action, the object must be expressed by a reflexive pronoun. (A) Present perfect is in agreement with the present perfect **have been.** (B) is the gerundial object of **learnt.** (C) is the gerundial complement of **have been afraid.**

21. **(C)** (C) is the right answer. **Approving** must be replaced by the past participle **approved** to denote passive voice. (A) **Imperative** means important and is therefore appropriate. (B) The past participle form functions as an adjective qualifying **food.** (D) is an adjective qualifying the noun **standards.**

22. **(A)** (A) is the right answer. **Much** is an adjective of quantity used to refer to non-count nouns. It must be replaced by **many** a numeral adjective, to qualify the count-noun **scientists.** (B) expresses a choice between **time** and **skills.** (C) is an adjective qualifying **skills.** (D) **To become** is an infinitive of purpose complementing **required.**

23. **(A)** (A) is the right answer. **To** in **has to been** is an ungrammatical addition. There is no such verbal form. **Has been** expresses duration of time from prehistoric times to the present. (B) **Since** is an appropriate preposition for signifying the starting point, in the past, of a duration of time. (C) **Only** is a restrictive adverb limiting **coal mining** to a certain starting point in time. (D) is a gerundial compound noun functioning as subject of the verb **has been.**

24. **(D)** (D) is the right answer. The tag question should be **shouldn't they?; shouldn't** agrees with **should** in the main clause; **they** agrees with the two nouns **eggs** and **cheese.** (A) The superlative is not preceded by the definite article **the;** in the absence of the article, **results** is the appropriate noun number, not **result.** (B) **Should** expresses an obligation to be performed for the desired results. (C) is a preposition relating **cooked** to **heat.**

25. **(A)** (A) is the right answer. The personal pronoun **it** cannot refer to William Colgate, a person. It must be replaced by the personal pronoun **he.** (B) **Apprentice** is preceded by the appropriate article **an** and followed by the appropriate preposition **to.** (C) **was to become** denotes a future event from a point of view in the past. (D) The adjective **toilet** is not preceded by the indefinite article **a** so the qualified noun must be in the plural.

26. **(A)** (A) is the right answer because **kinds** must be replaced by **kind** as the trees that shed their leaves form one class or type. (B) The simple present tense is used to denote a scientific fact. (C) The plural possessive pronoun **their** refers to the plural noun **trees.** (D) The simple present tense, in passive voice, is in agreement with **shed.**

27. **(A)** (A) is the right answer. Food production by photosynthesis is common to the whole genre of plants. While talking of a whole genre, the definite article **the** is not required. (B) The simple present tense is used to denote a scientific fact. (C) The preposi-

tional phrase modifies the verb **make**. (D) The past participle **called** denotes the passive voice which is the appropriate verb form for the object **photosynthesis**.

28. **(C)**   (C) is the right answer. There is a redundant use of the adjectives of quantity. The answer should be **enough attention;** enough denotes unspecified quantity just short of the desired limit. **Amount of** is a certain quantity which needs to be qualified, such as **great amount of.**

29. **(D)**   (D) is the right answer. **The same** qualifies **Greenwich meridian** but does not relate it to **prime meridian.** The two terms refer to the same thing. Only **the same as** denotes that both are the same thing. (A) is the simple present tense, used to denote scientific fact. (B) **Through** denotes path of movement. (C) **In** is the appropriate preposition for locating objects in a large segment of space (town, country, etc.).

30. **(D)**   (D) is the right answer. **But for** makes an exception to what is stated earlier: **no charges for using the library. However** is a conjunction that must introduce a clause contrasting with the main clause. There is just one clause in this sentence. The answer should be **but for.** (A) The indefinite pronoun **there** is usually used to begin a sentence when the real subject is to follow. (B) **Usually** is an adverb modifying the verb **is.** (C) The preposition **for** denotes the purpose of **charge.**

31. **(D)**   (D) is the right answer. **So does** denotes affirmative agreement. When the main verb is in the negative **does not,** the agreement of Harry with Tom's opinion must also be expressed in the negative; this is called negative agreement. The answer should be **neither does Harry.** (A) The singular verb is in agreement with the singular noun **Tom.** (B) The expression of an opinion is normally expressed in the simple present tense. (C) The adjective **useful** complements the verb **is.**

32. **(A)**   (A) is the right answer. **Always** and **never** are contradictory terms and so cannot be used together. The answer is **never.** (B) The simple present tense has been used to denote a scientific fact. (C) The possessive plural refers to **cuckoo.** (D) **Them** is an object pronoun; it is the object of the verb **leaves,** referring to **eggs.**

33. **(B)**   (B) is the right answer. The present tense **does not** does not agree with the participle **recalling** which implies that the interview took place in the past. The answer should be **had not expected;** the past perfect locates the **expectation** in a past time before the **interview.** The answer could also be **did not expect** which also denotes past time. (A) **With** denotes the inclusion of the noun **actor** in the interview. (C) is the complement of **expect.** (D) denotes duration of time.

34. **(C)** (C) is the right answer. The pronoun must refer to **films. He** is a masculine, singular pronoun not agreeing with films. The answer must be **they,** a plural pronoun. (A) is the object of the verb **wanted.** (B) **But** denotes a contrast to Chaplin's wish. (D) Denotes agent of **saved.**

35. **(A)** (A) is the right answer. It contains a redundant use of **for. To commemorate** denotes purpose of the **brass plaque.** (B) is the possessive form of the relative pronoun **who.** (C) **Picture** is the object of **whose.** (D) is the finite verb of the clause **a brass plaque marks....**

36. **(D)** (D) is the right answer. The adverb **easily** must be preceded by a verb which will parallel the series **stored, reused....** The answer should be **modified.** (A) The present continuous tense denotes something happening nowadays. (B) is an adjective qualifying **word processor.** (C) The simple present tense (in the passive voice) is used to express a general fact.

37. **(C)** (C) is the right answer. **Ornamental** and **decorative** mean the same thing, so their combined use is redundant. Only one of them is required to qualify the noun **tree.** (A) A definite article is required to specify a particular kind of tree. (B) is the simple present tense used to denote a general fact. (D) The relative pronoun **that** refers to **tree; was** is the finite verb of the subordinate clause **that...Japan.**

38. **(D)** (D) is the right answer. **Raise** is a transitive verb requiring an object. The answer should be **rise.** The causative verb **make** should be followed by an infinitive without **to.** (A) is a participle functioning as an adjective to qualify the noun **agents.** (B) **Such as** is used to give examples of the preceding noun **agents.** (C) The plural verb is in agreement with the noun **agents.**

39. **(A)** (A) is the right answer. **Most** is an indefinite numeral adjective denoting part of a whole. So we must say **most of the neighborhood.** (B) is a finite verb completing the main clause **most...agreed.** (C) The noun (the real subject of the subordinate clause) is anticipated by the impersonal pronoun **there.** (D) shows position of the shopping mall.

40. **(B)** (B) is the right answer. **Squeeze** is a verb. **Movement** must be qualified by the participle **squeezing.** (A) Simple present tense denotes a scientific fact. (C) **Of** denotes possession; relates **movement** to **muscles.** (D) is an adverbial phrase denoting where the **movement** takes place.

Section 3:
READING COMPREHENSION
AND VOCABULARY

1.   **(C)**   The passage states that stalagmites grow "as a result of water dripping from an overhead stalactite. Choice (A) is how a stalactite is formed, the opposite of a stalagmite. Underground rivers (B) do not result in mineral deposits. Water which trickles down a slope, (D), results in a curtain.

2.   **(B)**   The second paragraph begins with the definition of sinkholes — "natural openings on the surface that lead to caves."

3.   **(A)**   Stalagmites grow upward from the floor. Stalactites (B) hang from the ceiling of a cave. Sinkholes (C) are openings that lead to caves. Curtains (D) form when drops of water trickle along a slope.

4.   **(C)**   In the term "inclined ceiling," the word "inclined" means sloped, or slanted. Therefore, slanted is the correct answer. (A), (B), and (D) are incorrect.

5.   **(C)**   Slopes are not caused by dripping water. They are part of the natural shape of the cave, so (C) is the correct choice. Stalagmites (A) and stalactites (B) are both caused by dripping water; these choices are incorrect. Curtains (D) are formed out of stalactites and stalagmites, which are created by dripping water. Therefore, (D) is incorrect.

6.   **(D)**   Geology includes the study of rocks, including speleothems. (D) is the right answer. Geography (A) is the study of all the Earth's features, not just caves, and is incorrect. Archaeology (B) is the study of ancient civilizations and their remains; (B) is also incorrect. Physics (C) is the science of energy and matter; (C) is an incorrect answer.

7.   **(B)**   In this passage, another term for "curtain" is "drapery." Choice (B) "draperies," the plural form of "drapery," is the correct answer. (A) "columns," (C) "stalagmites," and (D) "rims" are incorrect.

8. **(C)** The passage states that the word *speleothem* comes from the Greek language. Therefore, (A) Latin, (B) French, and (D) English are all incorrect.

9. **(A)** The passage says specifically that stalactites "are formed as drop after drop of water slowly trickles through cracks in the cave roof." This is restated in choice (A), the correct answer. There is no mention of underground rivers in the passage, so (B) is an incorrect choice. Water which seeps through the floor of the cave (C) is the opposite of the correct answer and should not be chosen. Curtains, not stalactites, are formed by water dripping down a slope. Therefore, (D) is incorrect.

10. **(B)** Stalactites grow from the ceiling, and, therefore, (B) is the correct answer. Stalagmites (A) grow from the cave floor. (A) is incorrect. Columns (C) are the union of stalactites and stalagmites; they do not grow from ceilings. (C) is incorrect. Rimstones (D) are not mentioned in the passage. (D) is incorrect.

11. **(C)** The passage lists three examples of Eastern stallions: Byerly Turk, Darley Arabian, and Godolphin Barb. According to the passage, the Thoroughbred is a distinct breed that traces its ancestry to Eastern stallions, but is not technically an Eastern stallion itself.

12. **(B)** According to the passage, the Great Horse of the Middle Ages was bred for all of the listed characteristics except swiftness. It was the horse bred by the Arabs, in fact, that showed swiftness.

13. **(C)** The passage states that "cross-breeding of hot- and cold-blooded horses for certain characteristics produced breeds ranging from riding horses to draft horses." Choices (A), (B), and (D) are all factually incorrect within the passage.

14. **(A)** The clue here is in the description of the horses as "small and swift," which would most likely mean they were also "graceful." The horses, then, would certainly not be "clumsy" (B), "massive" (C), or "bulky" (D).

15. **(C)** A "foal," or baby horse, is not one of the major divisions of horse breeds.

16. **(B)** The passage states, "the Thoroughbred is considered by many to be the high point of elegance and fine selective breeding." The other choices are earlier ancestors of the Thoroughbred.

17. **(B)** A breeder is someone who raises horses in order to have them reproduce. Bred mares become pregnant when they conceive. (B) is the correct answer. Although a horse may become sick when it conceives, (A) is not the correct answer. To die (C) is not the correct answer. To be born (D) is the result of conception, not the definition of conception. Therefore, (D) is also incorrect.

18. **(D)** A foal is a baby horse. A male horse (A) is a stallion, and a female horse (B) is a mare. There is no a term for an old horse (C). Therefore, (A), (B), and (C) are incorrect.

19. **(C)** According to the passage, the average amount of mares which actually conceive is less than 50 percent (50%). (A) 40 and (B) 85 are the percentages of variation in horses' conception, not the average. (D) 75 is not mentioned in the passage at all.

20. **(C)** A mare is a female horse. A male horse (A) is a stallion. A baby horse (B) is a foal. There is no term for an old horse (D). Therefore, (A), (B), and (D) are incorrect.

21. **(C)** The second paragraph states that the gestation period for hamsters is about 16 days.

22. **(B)** The second paragraph states that female hamsters may eat their own young when the litter is large. Hunger (A), deformity (C), and quick maturation (D) are not listed as possible reasons.

23. **(A)** The passage states that a female hamster can bear young when she is six weeks to two months old.

24. **(D)** The word perpetuation in this context means that the animals need a large litter to continue their species. Extinction (A) and annihilation (B) both are opposites of perpetuation. Variation (C) would mean that they wanted diversity in the litter.

25. **(C)** The second paragraph states that the female hamster may produce litters up to an age of 15 months.

26. **(B)** The tone of the passage could best be described as informative because of the extensive information about large litters and especially hamsters.

27. **(B)** Since the passage's main idea is about why animals have large litters, "Reasons for Large Litters" is the best choice. Although the passage says that some of the offspring of the litter can be endangered, it is not the main theme, so the title in choice (A), "Endangered Animal Litters," is not the best choice. While the passage does discuss the parents of large litters, they are not the main topic. Therefore (C), "Parents of Large Litters," is an incorrect answer. Since the passage states that litters are not educated, choice (D), "Educating Litters," is a wrong answer.

28. **(C)** A litter is the amount of offspring, or babies, an animal has. The amount of parents an animal has (A) does not vary. Therefore, (A) is incorrect. Although "litter" can also mean "garbage," (B) it is the wrong meaning for this passage. A litter is the number of children an animal has, not how many brothers and sisters (siblings) it has, therefore, (D) is an incorrect choice.

29. **(A)** The passage states that the parents of the litter spend most of their time reproducing and food gathering. (A), which restates the passage, is the correct answer. The passage specifically states that the litter is uneducated, so (B) is incorrect. The parents of the litter are too busy to interfere with the litter. Therefore, (C) is incorrect. The passage does not mention playing, so (D) is an incorrect choice.

30. **(B)** (A), (C), and (D) are all reasons to have large litters as stated in the passage. Only (B) is incorrect, for the passage says litters are uneducated. Since the question asked for the incorrect answer, (B) is the right choice.

31. **(B)** The third paragraph clearly states that de León landed on Florida's east coast in March, 1513. The other choices, then, are obviously incorrect.

32. **(C)** According to the passage, Ponce de León started a colony in Caparra in 1509 and later abandoned it in favor of San Juan (A). La Florida (B) is the name de León gave to the peninsular extension of North America, and St. Augustine (D) is the name later given to the area in Florida where he landed in 1513.

33. **(B)** The second paragraph clearly states that the legendary island was named "Bimini." The other choices are thus incorrect.

34. **(C)** The passage states, "it is said he was seeking this spring [The Fountain of Youth] when he discovered Florida." None of the other statements are supported by the passage.

35. **(A)** The second paragraph states that "he named the place La Florida after the Spanish term for Easter Sunday — Pascua florida."

36. **(D)** Nowhere in the passage is it stated that the Spanish Empire was advanced through negotiations — only by subjugation and force.

37. **(C)** If you can imagine what Florida looks like on a map, you know that three of its sides are surrounded by water, while the top part is attached to the rest of the North American continent. Such a land formation is called a "peninsula." Choice (C), which restates this definition, is the correct answer. Choice (A) is incorrect because the passage mentions nothing about volcanoes in Florida. Choice (B), an island, is what de León *thought* Florida was; he did not realize it was part of a huge continent. And choice (D) is incorrect because the shape of the land mass, incorrectly called an island, has nothing to do with its inhabitants.

38. **(D)** This question asks you about the intent (or tone) of a word, instead of its meaning. Because the word "advanced" is in quotations in the passage itself, we can assume that the author of the passage had a different meaning in mind for the word, implying that the way *adelantados* "advanced" the Spanish Empire was wrong. Choice (A), which states that *adelantados* favor progress, is true, but it does not give a negative meaning to "advanced." (A) is incorrect. (B), progress could not have occurred without subjugation (repression), may be the way the *adelantados* felt, but not how the author feels. (B) is incorrect. (C) is also incorrect. Although progress may be related to conquest and subjugation, it is not what the tone of "advanced" suggests. (D) is correct because the quotations around "advanced" suggest the author's feelings that what *adelantados* believe is progress really is not.

39. **(B)** According to the passage, de León believed he had discovered a new island called Florida. (B), which restates this, is the correct answer. (A), (C), and (D) are therefore incorrect.

40. **(C)** Although de León was a great explorer and was the first Spaniard to see the shores of the United States, that is not what *adelantado* means, so choices (A) and (B) are incorrect. The passage does not state that de León claimed Florida for the King of Spain, so (D) is incorrect. The passage states that an *adelantado* is one who "'advanced' the Spanish Empire by conquest, subjugation of the Indians, and establishment of a semi-military government." (C), conquered and ruled by military force, restates the passage, and therefore is correct.

41. **(C)** The passage focuses primarily on Einstein's work in physics and does not mention chemistry (A), biology (B), or engineering (D).

42. **(D)** The passage discusses television as being a practical application of Einstein's theory of light. None of the other inventions are discussed.

43. **(B)** The passage states that "Einstein spoke out frequently against nationalism, the exalting of one nation above all others." According to the passage, Einstein supported Zionism (A), U.S. atomic bomb research (C), and the defeat of the Nazis (D).

44. **(C)** Einstein was born in Ulm, Germany. He later lived in Switzerland (A) and the United States (B). Israel (D) was not a nation when he was born.

45. **(A)** Brownian movement is the zig-zag motion of microscopic particles in suspension. Choices (B) and (C) relate to Einstein's later work, not to Brownian movement. Brownian movement did not form the basis of the theory of relativity (D).

46. **(A)** Nowhere in the passage is it mentioned that Einstein ever lived in Belgium, much less became a citizen there. He was, however, a citizen of the United States (C) and Switzerland (D). He was always obviously a citizen of Germany (B), having been born there.

47. **(B)** It is obvious from the passage that the author greatly respects Albert Einstein's work and considers him "one of the greatest thinkers in history." Nowhere does the author pass judgment on Einstein's political views (A). Choices (C) and (D) are directly opposite of the facts in the passage.

48. **(C)** Einstein's special theory of relativity directly states that time and motion are relative to the observer, given a constant speed of light and natural laws. The other choices are also Einstein theories, but are not related to his special theory of relativity.

49. **(A)** In this context, nationalism refers to the "elevation" of one nation over all others. This eliminates (B) and (D) as possibilities. "Support" (C) would be a good second choice, but does not have as strongly positive a connotation as "elevation."

50. **(C)**   The passage states that Einstein's second paper "proposed that light is composed of separate packets of energy, called quanta." None of the other terms is discussed in the passage.

51. **(B)**   In this context, "obliterated" would mean "destroyed." "Created" (A) is the opposite of "obliterated." "Changed" (C) and "eroded" (D) are not meanings for "obliterated."

52. **(A)**   The second paragraph states that scientists estimate the Earth's age by measuring the ratios of various radioactive elements in rocks. The other methods are not mentioned in the passage.

53. **(C)**   Scientists estimate that the Earth is 4.6 billion years old by testing rocks found on the moon and meteorites. (A) $3^1/_3$ billion years old, is the age of the oldest rock found on Earth. The other choices are incorrect.

54. **(D)**   The passage indicates that the craters were obliterated by crustal motions and erosion. None of the other answers were mentioned in the passage.

55. **(B)**   Erosion and crustal motions are mentioned in the passage as the cause for the obliteration of the craters that formed from celestial bombardment of the Earth. Human alteration (A) and deforestation (D) are both man-made processes of recent occurrence.

56. **(A)**   "Determining the Age of the Earth" would be the primary focus of the passage. "Determining the Age of the Solar System" (B) is mentioned but is not the focus of the passage. "Erosion and Crustal Motion of Earth" (C) is a process that hampered scientific determining of the Earth's age. "Radioactive Elements in Rocks" (D) help determine the age of the Earth.

57. **(C)**   Choices (A), (B), and (D) were all studied to determine if Earth was bombarded in its early history. The satellites of Jupiter were studied, according to the passage. Jupiter, choice (C), was not studied, however. Therefore, (C) is the correct answer.

58. **(A)**   The passage says that there is evidence that the other planetary bodies were bombarded; from that evidence, one can infer that Earth was bombarded as well. There is no mention in the passage that bombardment of Earth is documented fact, so choice (B) is incorrect. The lunar record is discussed in the passage as indicating the decrease of bombardment, not whether it actually happened, so choice (C) is incorrect. The passage

states that erosion has gotten rid of any evidence that Earth was bombarded, so (D) is incorrect.

59. **(D)**   The passage states that the number of bombardments "decreased to its current low about 4 billion years ago." Choices (A), (B), and (C) are incorrect because they state that information incorrectly.

60. **(B)**   "Assault" is the best answer because it is closest to the meaning of "bombardment," which is an attack or battering. An "avoidance" (A) is the opposite of a bombardment, so (A) is a wrong answer. Choices (C) and (D), effect and cause, have nothing to do with the meaning of bombardment.

Test of English as a Foreign Language
TEST 5
ANSWER SHEET

Section 1:
Listening Comprehension

1. Ⓐ Ⓑ Ⓒ Ⓓ
2. Ⓐ Ⓑ Ⓒ Ⓓ
3. Ⓐ Ⓑ Ⓒ Ⓓ
4. Ⓐ Ⓑ Ⓒ Ⓓ
5. Ⓐ Ⓑ Ⓒ Ⓓ
6. Ⓐ Ⓑ Ⓒ Ⓓ
7. Ⓐ Ⓑ Ⓒ Ⓓ
8. Ⓐ Ⓑ Ⓒ Ⓓ
9. Ⓐ Ⓑ Ⓒ Ⓓ
10. Ⓐ Ⓑ Ⓒ Ⓓ
11. Ⓐ Ⓑ Ⓒ Ⓓ
12. Ⓐ Ⓑ Ⓒ Ⓓ
13. Ⓐ Ⓑ Ⓒ Ⓓ
14. Ⓐ Ⓑ Ⓒ Ⓓ
15. Ⓐ Ⓑ Ⓒ Ⓓ
16. Ⓐ Ⓑ Ⓒ Ⓓ
17. Ⓐ Ⓑ Ⓒ Ⓓ
18. Ⓐ Ⓑ Ⓒ Ⓓ
19. Ⓐ Ⓑ Ⓒ Ⓓ
20. Ⓐ Ⓑ Ⓒ Ⓓ
21. Ⓐ Ⓑ Ⓒ Ⓓ
22. Ⓐ Ⓑ Ⓒ Ⓓ
23. Ⓐ Ⓑ Ⓒ Ⓓ
24. Ⓐ Ⓑ Ⓒ Ⓓ
25. Ⓐ Ⓑ Ⓒ Ⓓ
26. Ⓐ Ⓑ Ⓒ Ⓓ
27. Ⓐ Ⓑ Ⓒ Ⓓ
28. Ⓐ Ⓑ Ⓒ Ⓓ
29. Ⓐ Ⓑ Ⓒ Ⓓ
30. Ⓐ Ⓑ Ⓒ Ⓓ

31. Ⓐ Ⓑ Ⓒ Ⓓ
32. Ⓐ Ⓑ Ⓒ Ⓓ
33. Ⓐ Ⓑ Ⓒ Ⓓ
34. Ⓐ Ⓑ Ⓒ Ⓓ
35. Ⓐ Ⓑ Ⓒ Ⓓ
36. Ⓐ Ⓑ Ⓒ Ⓓ
37. Ⓐ Ⓑ Ⓒ Ⓓ
38. Ⓐ Ⓑ Ⓒ Ⓓ
39. Ⓐ Ⓑ Ⓒ Ⓓ
40. Ⓐ Ⓑ Ⓒ Ⓓ
41. Ⓐ Ⓑ Ⓒ Ⓓ
42. Ⓐ Ⓑ Ⓒ Ⓓ
43. Ⓐ Ⓑ Ⓒ Ⓓ
44. Ⓐ Ⓑ Ⓒ Ⓓ
45. Ⓐ Ⓑ Ⓒ Ⓓ
46. Ⓐ Ⓑ Ⓒ Ⓓ
47. Ⓐ Ⓑ Ⓒ Ⓓ
48. Ⓐ Ⓑ Ⓒ Ⓓ
49. Ⓐ Ⓑ Ⓒ Ⓓ
50. Ⓐ Ⓑ Ⓒ Ⓓ

Section 2:
Structure and
Written Expression

1. Ⓐ Ⓑ Ⓒ Ⓓ
2. Ⓐ Ⓑ Ⓒ Ⓓ
3. Ⓐ Ⓑ Ⓒ Ⓓ
4. Ⓐ Ⓑ Ⓒ Ⓓ
5. Ⓐ Ⓑ Ⓒ Ⓓ
6. Ⓐ Ⓑ Ⓒ Ⓓ
7. Ⓐ Ⓑ Ⓒ Ⓓ
8. Ⓐ Ⓑ Ⓒ Ⓓ
9. Ⓐ Ⓑ Ⓒ Ⓓ
10. Ⓐ Ⓑ Ⓒ Ⓓ
11. Ⓐ Ⓑ Ⓒ Ⓓ
12. Ⓐ Ⓑ Ⓒ Ⓓ
13. Ⓐ Ⓑ Ⓒ Ⓓ
14. Ⓐ Ⓑ Ⓒ Ⓓ
15. Ⓐ Ⓑ Ⓒ Ⓓ
16. Ⓐ Ⓑ Ⓒ Ⓓ
17. Ⓐ Ⓑ Ⓒ Ⓓ
18. Ⓐ Ⓑ Ⓒ Ⓓ
19. Ⓐ Ⓑ Ⓒ Ⓓ
20. Ⓐ Ⓑ Ⓒ Ⓓ
21. Ⓐ Ⓑ Ⓒ Ⓓ
22. Ⓐ Ⓑ Ⓒ Ⓓ
23. Ⓐ Ⓑ Ⓒ Ⓓ
24. Ⓐ Ⓑ Ⓒ Ⓓ
25. Ⓐ Ⓑ Ⓒ Ⓓ
26. Ⓐ Ⓑ Ⓒ Ⓓ
27. Ⓐ Ⓑ Ⓒ Ⓓ
28. Ⓐ Ⓑ Ⓒ Ⓓ
29. Ⓐ Ⓑ Ⓒ Ⓓ
30. Ⓐ Ⓑ Ⓒ Ⓓ
31. Ⓐ Ⓑ Ⓒ Ⓓ
32. Ⓐ Ⓑ Ⓒ Ⓓ
33. Ⓐ Ⓑ Ⓒ Ⓓ
34. Ⓐ Ⓑ Ⓒ Ⓓ
35. Ⓐ Ⓑ Ⓒ Ⓓ
36. Ⓐ Ⓑ Ⓒ Ⓓ
37. Ⓐ Ⓑ Ⓒ Ⓓ
38. Ⓐ Ⓑ Ⓒ Ⓓ
39. Ⓐ Ⓑ Ⓒ Ⓓ
40. Ⓐ Ⓑ Ⓒ Ⓓ

Section 3:
Reading Comprehension
and Vocabulary

1. Ⓐ Ⓑ Ⓒ Ⓓ
2. Ⓐ Ⓑ Ⓒ Ⓓ
3. Ⓐ Ⓑ Ⓒ Ⓓ
4. Ⓐ Ⓑ Ⓒ Ⓓ
5. Ⓐ Ⓑ Ⓒ Ⓓ
6. Ⓐ Ⓑ Ⓒ Ⓓ
7. Ⓐ Ⓑ Ⓒ Ⓓ
8. Ⓐ Ⓑ Ⓒ Ⓓ
9. Ⓐ Ⓑ Ⓒ Ⓓ
10. Ⓐ Ⓑ Ⓒ Ⓓ
11. Ⓐ Ⓑ Ⓒ Ⓓ
12. Ⓐ Ⓑ Ⓒ Ⓓ
13. Ⓐ Ⓑ Ⓒ Ⓓ
14. Ⓐ Ⓑ Ⓒ Ⓓ
15. Ⓐ Ⓑ Ⓒ Ⓓ
16. Ⓐ Ⓑ Ⓒ Ⓓ
17. Ⓐ Ⓑ Ⓒ Ⓓ
18. Ⓐ Ⓑ Ⓒ Ⓓ

19. Ⓐ Ⓑ Ⓒ Ⓓ
20. Ⓐ Ⓑ Ⓒ Ⓓ
21. Ⓐ Ⓑ Ⓒ Ⓓ
22. Ⓐ Ⓑ Ⓒ Ⓓ
23. Ⓐ Ⓑ Ⓒ Ⓓ
24. Ⓐ Ⓑ Ⓒ Ⓓ
25. Ⓐ Ⓑ Ⓒ Ⓓ
26. Ⓐ Ⓑ Ⓒ Ⓓ
27. Ⓐ Ⓑ Ⓒ Ⓓ
28. Ⓐ Ⓑ Ⓒ Ⓓ
29. Ⓐ Ⓑ Ⓒ Ⓓ
30. Ⓐ Ⓑ Ⓒ Ⓓ
31. Ⓐ Ⓑ Ⓒ Ⓓ
32. Ⓐ Ⓑ Ⓒ Ⓓ
33. Ⓐ Ⓑ Ⓒ Ⓓ
34. Ⓐ Ⓑ Ⓒ Ⓓ
35. Ⓐ Ⓑ Ⓒ Ⓓ
36. Ⓐ Ⓑ Ⓒ Ⓓ
37. Ⓐ Ⓑ Ⓒ Ⓓ
38. Ⓐ Ⓑ Ⓒ Ⓓ
39. Ⓐ Ⓑ Ⓒ Ⓓ

40. Ⓐ Ⓑ Ⓒ Ⓓ
41. Ⓐ Ⓑ Ⓒ Ⓓ
42. Ⓐ Ⓑ Ⓒ Ⓓ
43. Ⓐ Ⓑ Ⓒ Ⓓ
44. Ⓐ Ⓑ Ⓒ Ⓓ
45. Ⓐ Ⓑ Ⓒ Ⓓ
46. Ⓐ Ⓑ Ⓒ Ⓓ
47. Ⓐ Ⓑ Ⓒ Ⓓ
48. Ⓐ Ⓑ Ⓒ Ⓓ
49. Ⓐ Ⓑ Ⓒ Ⓓ
50. Ⓐ Ⓑ Ⓒ Ⓓ
51. Ⓐ Ⓑ Ⓒ Ⓓ
52. Ⓐ Ⓑ Ⓒ Ⓓ
53. Ⓐ Ⓑ Ⓒ Ⓓ
54. Ⓐ Ⓑ Ⓒ Ⓓ
55. Ⓐ Ⓑ Ⓒ Ⓓ
56. Ⓐ Ⓑ Ⓒ Ⓓ
57. Ⓐ Ⓑ Ⓒ Ⓓ
58. Ⓐ Ⓑ Ⓒ Ⓓ
59. Ⓐ Ⓑ Ⓒ Ⓓ
60. Ⓐ Ⓑ Ⓒ Ⓓ

TOEFL

TEST 5

Section 1:
LISTENING COMPREHENSION

TIME: 35 Minutes
50 Questions

Part A

DIRECTIONS: In Part A you will hear short conversations between two speakers. At the end of each conversation, a third person will ask a question about what was said. **You will hear each conversation just one time.** Therefore, you must listen carefully to understand what each speaker says. After you hear a conversation and the question about it, read the four possible answers in your test book and decide which one is the best answer to the question you heard. Then, on your answer sheet, find the number of the question and fill in the space that corresponds to the answer you have chosen.

$$\boxed{\text{WAIT}}$$

1. (A) 8:00   (C) 6:30
    (B) 7:30   (D) 7:00

2. (A) An airport   (C) A train station
    (B) A bus depot   (D) A marina

3. (A) A drug store   (C) A post office
    (B) A deli   (D) A boutique

537

4. (A) He knows but will not tell the woman.
    (B) He had to leave early so he does not know who won.
    (C) He was unable to attend the ceremony and does not know who won.
    (D) He does not know but thinks that the woman should know who won.

5. (A) She thinks the gypsy's fortunes are too expensive.
    (B) She thinks it would be fun to get her fortune told.
    (C) She thinks the man is being humorous.
    (D) She thinks the gypsy is a fraud.

6. (A) Three   (C) Five
    (B) One   (D) Two

7. (A) He has also read a novel by Toni Morrison.
    (B) He is unfamiliar with Toni Morrison.
    (C) He is presently reading a novel by Toni Morrison.
    (D) He, himself, is an author.

8. (A) The Caribbean
    (B) The South Pacific
    (C) Florida
    (D) California

9. (A) Cereal   (C) French toast
    (B) Pancakes   (D) Eggs

10. (A) Boss and employee
    (B) Husband and wife
    (C) Teacher and student
    (D) Parent and child

11. (A) Harry is not interested in his boss.
    (B) Harry does not care about his boss's opinion.
    (C) Harry has a good boss.
    (D) Harry really takes good care to impress his boss.

12. (A) The man
    (B) The woman
    (C) The doctor
    (D) The woman's uncle

13. (A) In a department store
    (B) In a bank
    (C) At an electrician's
    (D) At a train station

14. (A) There was an accident.
    (B) It was very difficult to find the place.
    (C) It rained heavily.
    (D) Everyone returned immediately because there were hard feelings among people.

15. (A) The woman should go to the head of the department to get the permission.
    (B) The woman should turn right to go to the library.
    (C) The woman can go to the library without him.
    (D) The woman can use his library because he doesn't need it till six o'clock.

16. (A) Subways are suffocating in the summer.
    (B) Subways are disgusting.
    (C) She hates some of the people travelling on subways.
    (D) You can't carry a lot of stuff on subways.

17. (A) Literary masterpieces
    (B) Silk fabric
    (C) Paintings
    (D) Some printed material on fabric painting

18. (A) Four o'clock
    (B) Three thirty
    (C) Three o'clock
    (D) Four thirty

19. (A) She broke a glass vase.
     (B) She does not want to remember the glass vase.
     (C) She cannot purchase it right now because she does not have any money.
     (D) She does not want to buy the vase because it is broken.

20. (A) Physics
     (B) Biology
     (C) Math
     (D) Chemistry

21. (A) Because it is too late in the evening.
     (B) Because there is too much traffic on the route they are taking.
     (C) Because they got into an accident.
     (D) Because their tickets were for yesterday's concert.

22. (A) She doesn't like history.
     (B) It is a relief to know that the test has been postponed.
     (C) History tests should always be on Mondays.
     (D) She will not take the test.

23. (A) Because he cares a lot about Valerie.
     (B) Because Valerie seems to be extremely disturbed.
     (C) Because Valerie fell down from a staircase.
     (D) Because it is his nature to worry.

24. (A) It is difficult.
     (B) It is interesting.
     (C) It is easy.
     (D) She regrets that she didn't take it.

25. (A) The lady at the front counter looked strangely at her.
     (B) The lady at the front counter is dirty.
     (C) The lady at the front counter came in very late.
     (D) The lady at the front counter gave her dirty socks.

Part B

(**WAIT**)

26. (A) Her uncle   (C) The man
     (B) Her brother   (D) Her father

27. (A) United States   (C) Austria
     (B) Germany   (D) Canada

28. (A) Pictures   (C) Cans
     (B) Suitcases   (D) Coins

29. (A) $1,000   (C) $10
     (B) $10,000   (D) $100

30. (A) Drink them   (C) Crush them
     (B) Sell them   (D) Recycle them

31. (A) In a home   (C) In an office
     (B) In a post office   (D) In a store

32. (A) Her daughter's   (C) Teri's
     (B) Her husband's   (D) Mr. Smith's

33. (A) It's her daughter's birthday.
    (B) She has a meeting with Mr. Smith.
    (C) She has to go out.
    (D) She has to take care of a couple of things.

34. (A) He will wish the woman's daughter a "Happy Birthday."
    (B) He will surprise the woman.
    (C) He will leave a message for the woman.
    (D) He will ask Terri to talk to Mr. Smith.

35. (A) The man   (C) Her daughter
    (B) Mr. Smith   (D) Teri

36. (A) Night   (C) Evening
    (B) Morning   (D) Afternoon

37. (A) Jogging
    (B) Talking
    (C) Walking
    (D) Going to a health club

38. (A) Seven   (C) Four
    (B) Three   (D) Two

39. (A) Because she does not have to pay for jogging.
    (B) Because she can talk to people while jogging.
    (C) Because she can get some fresh air while jogging.
    (D) Because jogging is the best exercise.

40. (A) You can do it any time you like.
    (B) You can get fresh air while jogging.
    (C) It is enjoyable.
    (D) You don't have to follow someone's instructions in jogging.

Part C

WAIT

41. (A) Construction
    (B) Stock market
    (C) Cars
    (D) Airplanes

42. (A) 3.6 million
    (B) 8 million
    (C) 26 million
    (D) 25,000

43. (A) Model A
    (B) Model E
    (C) Model T
    (D) Edsel

44. (A) Ford Model T
    (B) Automobiles
    (C) Gerald Ford
    (D) Henry Ford

45. (A) Steel and rubber
    (B) Lumber and coal
    (C) Fishing and canning
    (D) Banking and investing

46. (A) High protein in soybean
    (B) Bean curd made from soybean
    (C) Experiments with soybean products
    (D) The growing popularity of soybean

47. (A) Bean sprouts and cooking oil
    (B) Hot dogs and soybean ice cream
    (C) Tofu and soybean milk
    (D) Soybean milk and bean sprouts

48. (A) China   (C) Japan
    (B) United States   (D) Argentina

48. (A) Milk   (C) Curd
    (B) Oil   (D) Meat

50. (A) Because it was planted 3,000 years ago.
    (B) Because tofu is made out of soybean.
    (C) Because it can be used in a variety of ways.
    (D) Because it is rich in protein.

(**STOP**)

If time still remains, you may review work only in this section.
When the time allotted is up, you may go on to the next section.

Section 2:
STRUCTURE AND WRITTEN EXPRESSION

TIME: 25 Minutes
40 Questions

DIRECTIONS: Questions 1-15 are incomplete sentences. Beneath each sentence are four words or phrases marked (A), (B), (C), and (D). Choose the **one** word or phrase which best completes the sentence. Then, on your answer sheet, find the number of the question and fill in the space that corresponds to the answer you have chosen.

1. Chicory _____ and mixed with coffee to make a darker beverage.
   (A) is grinded
   (B) is grind
   (C) is ground
   (D) is grinden

2. When Walt Disney watched his children play in the park, he wished that there _____ be a park where parents and children could have fun together.
   (A) would
   (B) should
   (C) must
   (D) will

3. Since ancient times, silver _____ to human beings.
   (A) is known
   (B) has been known
   (C) is being known
   (D) has been knowing

4. President Polk worked so hard that his _____ away from his desk was a rare occurrence.
   (A) has been
   (B) was
   (C) being
   (D) to be

545

5. _____ was revolutionized by the advent of the radio which gave distant events an immediacy.
   (A) News report
   (B) News reporting
   (C) To news report
   (D) To news reporting

6. A rocket propellant consists of a fuel and _____ oxidizer.
   (A) a
   (B) the
   (C) an
   (D) another

7. Yesterday I felt a little ill and today I feel _____ .
   (A) more ill
   (B) most ill
   (C) worse
   (D) worst

8. The three business partners decided to end their partnership due to a dispute _____ them.
   (A) between
   (B) in the middle of
   (C) among
   (D) by

9. Henry Ford not only revolutionized the automobile industry, _____ established the Ford Foundation, the biggest charitable organization.
   (A) he is also
   (B) but also
   (C) also
   (D) as well as

10. Paperbacks sell _____ , as people can afford to buy them any time.
    (A) quicker
    (B) fastly
    (C) readily
    (D) with ready

11. Through one's lethargy _____ could lose the opportunities to succeed in life.
   (A) we
   (B) he
   (C) they
   (D) one

12. Snow, sleet, frost, and hail are _____ forms of ice.
   (A) different
   (B) different from
   (C) differing from
   (D) no different

13. You'd better _____ from work tomorrow.
   (A) not be absent
   (B) not to absent
   (C) not to be absent
   (D) not absenting

14. In 1871, a fire in Chicago destroyed _____ 1,800 buildings.
   (A) many
   (B) the same as
   (C) just as
   (D) as many as

15. Please _____ a one-inch margin on the left and top of your answer sheets.
   (A) let
   (B) let be
   (C) leave
   (D) leave out

DIRECTIONS: In questions 16-40 each sentence has four underlined words or phrases, marked (A), (B), (C), and (D). Choose the **one** word or phrase which is incorrect and must be changed to make the sentence correct. Then, on your answer sheet, find the number of the question and fill in the space that corresponds to the answer you have chosen.

16. Jute is used to making yarn, twines, and ropes and is blended with hard fibers
    A   B   C

    to produce, stronger types of rope.
    D

17. When radium decays, it will produce a gas called radon.
    A   B   C   D

18. Education professionals are now trying to get parents take more interest in their
                                        A   B   C

    children's academic development.
    D

19. If water is found on Mars' moon, its components, hydrogen and oxygen,
                  A   B   C

    can be used as a source of fuel.
    D

20. Walt Disney saw his amusement park as an incomplete thing that will continually
                                                          A   B   C

    get additions as long as there was imagination left in the world.
                                 D

21. It was an uneventful four days journey for Apollo 11 from Cape Kennedy,
                             A   B

    in Florida, to the moon.
    C   D

22. The Kennedy Center for the Performing Arts honors every year American artists
                                                    A   B

    for their achievements.
    C   D

23. It was only a little years ago that literary feminism spearheaded by female
           A   B

    scholars made its appearance on campuses.
              C   D

24. Chaplin would never finalize a scene till he had tried it over and over again,
            A   B C

    wouldn't he?
       D

25. Goneril protested that it was not her but her husband who was responsible for the
                                     A   B   C

    inhospitality shown to her father.
                       D

26. The sheeps from Australia are the biggest source of natural wool.
           A   B   C   D

27. Some of the American presidents, Andrew Johnson was a tailor
      A   B   C

    before becoming president.
           D

28. The salesman's introduction was enough interesting to get me curious about
                                        A   B

    what he had to say further.
       C   D

29. Many amusement parks similar with Disneyland are being established in
       A   B   C

    different parts of the world.
              D

30. Signals picked up by several antennas would be integrated into one image as if a
                                    A   B

    single antenna had been used, except many.
                        C   D

31. A recent study on health and nutrition recommends that we avoid high-fat diets

                                                                     A

    for that the risk of heart diseases may be reduced.

       B   C   D

32. Once of the space station Freedom is ready, eight international crew members

     A   B

    will undertake a preliminary study tour to the station.

         C   D

33. The writer Thomas Easley says, I wanted to be a writer and that he still has the

                              A   B   C

    urge to be one.

         D

34. The bunch of roses in the vase, by my bed, have surprisingly remained fresh for

                         A   B   C   D

    more than a week.

35. The teacher warned the indifferent student that he was better improve his study

                                               A   B

    habits or he would fail the grade.

      C   D

36. In ancient times man found gold unsuitable for making weapons because its

                      A   B   C

    softness and therefore used it for adornment.

                            D

37. Joan Williams, the novelist, she has taught at colleges and universities and now

                                   A   B

    conducts a writing workshop for adults.

      C   D

38. When the Europeans landed in America, they found that vast natural resources lie

     A   B   C   D

    unexploited before them.

39. Eleanor Roosevelt was the primary president's wife to travel by plane to a
                        (A)   B   C D

    foreign country.

40. Radar technology has made great advances, so as it is now possible
                   A   (B)

    for astronomers to discover hitherto unknown facts about the universe.
              C   D

STOP

If time still remains, you may review work only in this section.
When the time allotted is up, you may go on to the next section.

Section 3:
READING COMPREHENSION
AND VOCABULARY

TIME: 55 Minutes
         60 Questions

DIRECTIONS: In this section you will read several passages. Each one is followed by several questions about it. You are to choose the best answer to each question, marked (A), (B), (C), and (D). Then, on your answer sheet, find the number of the question and fill in the space that corresponds to the answer you have chosen.

Questions 1 to 10 refer to the following passage:

1   Bumblebees are found throughout the world, primarily in the temperate and northern regions. The bumblebees are considered to be the most primitive of the social bees. Their colonies lack much of the structure and highly evolved behavior of the honey bees; however, like the honey bees, the bumblebees are plant feeders and important pollinators of crops. A
5 typical colony consists of at least one queen, several males, and numerous workers. Only young fertilized queens survive the winter to establish new colonies the next spring. The nests are normally located deep in undisturbed ground, like fence rows, and are supplied with a mixture of pollen and honey. During late summer, a colony usually contains between 100 and 500 bees. Although bumblebees are two to three times larger than honey bees, they are
10 neither as aggressive nor as abundant as the honey bees, and therefore not as dangerous.

1.   Why are bumblebees considered the most primitive of the social bees?
    (A)   They are two to three times larger than honey bees.
    (B)   Their colonies are not as structured and highly evolved as those of honey bees.
    (C)   They are plant feeders.
    (D)   They are not as abundant as honey bees.

2.   Where are bumblebees primarily found?
    (A)   Near the equator
    (B)   Mexico
    (C)   The temperate and northern regions
    (D)   The Western Hemisphere

3. During which time of year do bumblebee queens form their nests?
    (A) Spring
    (B) Late summer
    (C) Early fall
    (D) Winter

4. In line 2, the word "primitive" most nearly means
    (A) tiny.
    (B) uncivilized.
    (C) undeveloped.
    (D) original.

5. According to the passage, bumblebees are different from honey bees because
    (A) bumblebees are less primitive than honey bees.
    (B) bumblebees are more abundant than honey bees.
    (C) honey bees are more dangerous than bumblebees.
    (D) bumblebees are plant feeders but honey bees are not.

6. In the passage, "plant feeders" means that bumble bees
    (A) pollinate plants.
    (B) feed plants.
    (C) eat plants.
    (D) sting plants.

7. A typical bumblebee colony consists of
    (A) two queens, numerous males, few workers.
    (B) one queen, no males, numerous workers.
    (C) one queen, several males, no workers.
    (D) one queen, several males, numerous workers.

8. Bumblebee nests are located
    (A) hanging from fences.
    (B) deep underground.
    (C) on the ground.
    (D) hanging from trees.

9. What is the main topic of the passage?
    (A) Why honey bees are better than bumblebees
    (B) The differences between honey bees and bumblebees
    (C) A description of the bumblebee
    (D) The size of a bumblebee colony

10. Bumble bee colonies usually consist of how many bees?
    (A) Between 50 and 100
    (B) Between 100 and 500
    (C) 600
    (D) Over 500

Questions 11 to 20 refer to the following passage:

1   The chief figure of the scientific revolution of the seventeenth century was Sir Isaac Newton. He was a physicist and mathematician who laid the foundations of calculus, extended the understanding of color and light, studied the mechanics of planetary motion, and discovered the law of gravitation. Isaac Newton's supreme scientific work was his system of
5   universal gravitation. He went to his farm in 1665 to avoid the plague, and during this time he worked out the law of gravity and its consequences for the solar system. This law arose from Newton's question: what keeps the moon in its regular path around the Earth? He concluded that only their attraction for each other could account for it. He later remarked to a friend that he got the idea while watching an apple fall from a tree in his orchard. Every
10   particle of matter in the universe, he wrote, attract every other particle with a force varying in inverse proportion to the square of the distance between them, and directly proportional to the product of their masses.

11. The word "law" in line 4 most nearly means
    (A) principle.   (C) legislation.
    (B) rule.   (D) decree.

12. Which of the following was NOT a contribution made by Newton?
    (A) Laying the foundation of calculus
    (B) Discovering the law of gravitation
    (C) Establishing the theory of relativity
    (D) Extending the understanding of color and light

13. The word "revolution" in line 1 most nearly means
    (A) uprising.   (C) battle.
    (B) rotation.   (D) upheaval.

14. The word "supreme" in line 4 most nearly means
    (A) god-like.   (C) greatest.
    (B) ideal.   (D) dominating.

15. Newton's law of gravity can be applied to which of the following celestial bodies?
    (A) Venus and Earth
    (B) Earth and the moon
    (C) Mars and Jupiter
    (D) Saturn and Mercury

16. Which of the following scientific fields benefitted the most from Newton's work?
    (A) Biology   (C) Geology
    (B) Chemistry   (D) Astronomy

17. In the passage, the phrase "every particle of matter attracts every other particle" means that every particle
    (A) repels other particles.
    (B) seeks other particles.
    (C) draws other particles to itself.
    (D) evades other particles.

18. According to the passage, the system of universal gravitation is Newton's
    (A) least important scientific work.
    (B) most disputed scientific work.
    (C) most misunderstood scientific work.
    (D) most important scientific work.

19. Isaac Newton can best be described as a
    (A) biologist.   (C) physicist.
    (B) geologist.   (D) physician.

20. Newton discovered the system of universal gravitation in which century?
    (A) Sixteenth   (C) Eighteenth
    (B) Seventeenth   (D) Nineteenth

Questions 21 to 30 refer to the following passage:

1   Someone with a great desire to learn is said to be highly motivated. Motivation is very important in what one learns and how quickly one learns it. A motivated person will generally learn faster and more efficiently than an unmotivated one. To learn efficiently, a person must intend to learn (intentional learning). However, incidental learning—learning that is not
5   intended but which results simply from exposure to material—sometimes does occur. The degree of incidental learning does not approach that of intentional learning in real-life situations.

To what extent motives aid learning is undecided. Motives do contribute as incentives to performance of what has been learned. If an individual expects to be rewarded for doing
10 well, performance (perhaps on a test) may improve. It also may worsen, if the fear and anxiety over not passing is great enough. Human motives in relation to learning are so varied and complex that controlled experiments to analyze them are virtually impossible.

21. According to the passage, which of the following is true about incidental learning?
(A) More learning is incidental rather than intentional.
(B) Incidental learning is caused by a desire to become more educated.
(C) Less learning is incidental rather than intentional.
(D) Incidental learning is superior to intentional learning.

22. According to the passage, which of the following is true about motivation and learning?
(A) The connection between motives and learning is clearly known.
(B) The expectation of reward always leads to increased performance.
(C) The connection between motives and learning is too complex to precisely analyze.
(D) There is absolutely no connection between motives and learning.

23. Which of the following situations is an example of incidental learning?
(A) Studying for an exam
(B) Reading a book about astronomy
(C) Going to a lecture about art history
(D) Seeing newspaper headlines while waiting for the bus

24. In line 8, "incentives" most nearly means
(A) motivators.   (C) obstacles.
(B) rewards.   (D) payments.

25. Which of the following summarizes the author's opinions about learning?
(A) Incidental learning is superior to intentional learning.
(B) Intentional learning, while more efficient than incidental learning, is far less prevalent.
(C) Intentional learning is a more efficient and superior means of learning.
(D) There is essentially no difference between intentional and incidental learning.

26. Which of the following would be the best title for this passage?
    (A) "Motivation and School Performance"
    (B) "Incidental Learning in the Classroom
    (C) "The Connection Between Motivation and Learning"
    (D) "Experiments in Intentional Learning"

27. In line 3, what is the closest meaning of "efficiently"?
    (A) Effectively   (C) Cheaply
    (B) Quickly   (D) Proficiently

28. The passage implies that if a student studies for an exam, he is practicing
    (A) incidental learning.
    (B) intentional learning.
    (C) residual learning.
    (D) motivational learning.

29. In line 1, "motivation" means
    (A) dread.
    (B) repulsion.
    (C) neglect.
    (D) impulsion.

30. According to the passage, in order to learn by intentional learning, one must be
    (A) highly motivated.
    (B) unmotivated.
    (C) tired of learning.
    (D) in need of learning.

Questions 31 to 40 refer to the following passage:

1   The earliest vertical windmills were used in Persia more than 2,000 year ago for the
grinding of grain. Windmills were adopted for pumping water in North America by the
middle of the nineteenth century. Their use declined drastically in the 1930s when inexpensive electricity reached the rural areas. A renewed interest in the use of windpower to generate
5 electricity followed the energy crisis of the 1970s. A program of the United States
Department of Energy encouraged the development of new machines, the construction of
wind farms, and an evaluation of the economic effect of a large-scale use of wind power.
        Public acceptance of wind energy conversion systems is an important consideration
in planning for the widespread application of wind energy. Studies have shown that the
10 environmental impact of such systems is relatively small compared to conventional electric
power systems. Wind-powered systems do not require the flooding of large land areas or the

alteration of the natural ecology, as do hydroelectric systems. Furthermore, they produce no waste products or thermal or chemical effluents, as fossil-fueled and nuclear-fueled systems do.

31. Which of the following events led to renewed interest in the use of wind power?
     (A) World War II
     (B) The energy crisis of the 1970s
     (C) The Three Mile Island crisis
     (D) The advent of electricity

32. Which of the following is NOT an advantage of wind energy?
     (A) Wind energy does not require the flooding of large land areas.
     (B) Wind energy produces no waste products.
     (C) The availability of wind energy is not dependent on the weather.
     (D) Wind energy does not produce thermal or chemical effluents.

33. According to the passage, which of the following was wind energy first used for?
     (A) Pumping water
     (B) Electricity
     (C) Propelling ships
     (D) Grinding grain

34. In line 12, what is the closest meaning of "alteration"?
     (A) Conversion
     (B) Changing
     (C) Elimination
     (D) Enhancing

35. The United States Department of Energy has advocated all of the following EX-CEPT
     (A) the elimination of windmills as a means of pumping water.
     (B) the development of new wind energy machines.
     (C) an evaluation of the economic effects of a large-scale use of wind power.
     (D) the construction of wind farms.

36. Which of the following most led to a decreased use of windmills in the U.S.?
     (A) The advent of nuclear energy
     (B) Increased environmental awareness
     (C) The availability of inexpensive electricity in rural areas
     (D) A long-term shift in wind currents

37.   According to the passage
      (A)   wind energy is more efficient than electric power.
      (B)   wind energy is less expensive than electric power.
      (C)   wind energy does not have as much environmental impact as electric power.
      (D)   wind energy is more expensive than electric power.

38.   From the passage it can be assumed that wind energy is better because
      (A)   it is cheaper than electric power.
      (B)   it does not alter the environment as much as other types of power.
      (C)   it lasts longer than electric power.
      (D)   it is more efficient than electric power.

39.   In the passage, "environmental impact" means
      (A)   importance of nature.
      (B)   effect on man.
      (C)   importance of environment.
      (D)   effect on nature.

40.   The BEST title for this passage is
      (A)   "The Public's Response to Wind Energy."
      (B)   "The Benefits of Wind Energy."
      (C)   "How Wind Energy Works."
      (D)   "Wind Energy vs. Other Types of Power."

Questions 41 to 50 refer to the following passage:

1   The symptoms of Alzheimer's disease were long dismissed as normal consequences
of human aging, but in the 1980s the disease came to be recognized as the most common cause
of intellectual deterioration in the elderly and middle-aged. It is characterized by the death
of nerve cells in the cerebral cortex—the part of the brain involved in complex functions.

5   The major debilitating symptoms of Alzheimer's disease include serious forgetfulness—particularly about recent events—and confusion. At first, the individual experiences
only minor and almost imperceptible symptoms that are often attributed to emotional upsets
or other physical illnesses. Gradually, however, the person becomes more forgetful, and this
may be reported by anxious relatives. The person may neglect to turn off the oven, may
10   misplace things, may recheck to see if a task was done, may take longer to complete a chore
that was previously routine, or may repeat already answered questions. As the disease
progresses, memory loss and such changes in personality, mood, and behavior, such as
confusion, irritability, restlessness, and agitation, are likely to appear. Judgment, concentration, orientation, writing, reading, speech, motor behavior, and naming of objects may also
15   be affected. Even when a loving and caring family is available to give support, the victim of
Alzheimer's disease is most likely to spend his or her last days in a nursing home or long-term
care institution. At this time, there is no cure.

41. In line 7, "imperceptible" means
     (A) unnoticeable.
     (B) microscopic.
     (C) intangible.
     (D) imponderable.

42. According to the passage, which of the following is NOT true about Alzheimer's disease?
     (A) In the past, Alzheimer's disease has often been mistaken as normal human aging.
     (B) Victims of Alzheimer's disease rarely need to be institutionalized.
     (C) There is currently no cure for Alzheimer's disease.
     (D) The primary symptoms are serious forgetfulness and confusion.

43. According to the passage, which of the following causes Alzheimer's disease?
     (A) Severe emotional stress
     (B) Nutritional deficiency
     (C) The death of nerve cells in the cerebral cortex
     (D) Severe head trauma

44. In line 3, "deterioration" means
     (A) decline.
     (B) ruin.
     (C) strengthening.
     (D) detachment.

45. The BEST title for this passage would be
     (A) "A Cure for Alzheimer's Disease."
     (B) "The Effect of Alzheimer's Disease on the Family."
     (C) "A History of Alzheimer's Disease."
     (D) "The Progressive Effects of Alzheimer's Disease."

46. This passage implies that victims of Alzheimer's disease may
     (A) not remember childhood events.
     (B) suffer a gradual worsening of cognitive functions.
     (C) incur personality and behavioral changes.
     (D) spend their last days in a long-term care facility.

47. Symptoms of Alzheimer's disease include
    (A) enhanced motor skills.
    (B) loss of appetite.
    (C) forgetfulness and confusion.
    (D) laziness.

48. In line 5, "debilitating" means
    (A) to make feeble.
    (B) capability.
    (C) to strengthen.
    (D) stamina.

49. The cure for Alzheimer's disease is
    (A) bedrest.
    (B) hospitalization.
    (C) not found yet.
    (D) long-term care.

50. According to the passage, a person with Alzheimer's disease might not be able to
    (A) walk.
    (B) remember the answer to a question which was already asked.
    (C) remain awake.
    (D) drive a car.

Questions 51 to 60 refer to the following passage:

1   From the beginning of beekeeping in the 1600s until the early 1800s, honey was largely an article of local trade. Many farmers and villagers kept a few colonies of bees in box hives to supply their own needs and those of some friends, relatives, and neighbors. Moses Quimby of New York State was the first commercial beekeeper in the United States, as his
5 sole means of livelihood was producing and selling honey. Other beekeepers in Quimby's neighborhood used his methods and began to produce honey on a commercial scale. As the use of improved hives and new honey-gathering methods became more widespread, commercial beekeeping spread into other states.

51. According to the passage, what was the primary reason people kept bee colonies prior to the advent of commercial beekeeping?
    (A) As a recreational activity
    (B) As a profit-making venture
    (C) To supply honey for themselves and neighbors
    (D) To scare away wild animals

52. According to the passage, which of the following is a reason for the spread of commercial beekeeping?
    (A) A dramatic increase in demand for honey
    (B) The use of improved hives and honey-gathering methods
    (C) An increase in bee populations in the Northeast
    (D) The coming of the Industrial Revolution

53. In line 2, the word "article" means
    (A) object.
    (B) element.
    (C) assembly.
    (D) piece.

54. According to the passage, which of the following is NOT true about commercial beekeeping?
    (A) Commercial beekeeping is done for profit.
    (B) Commercial beekeepers supply a large number of consumers with honey.
    (C) Commercial beekeepers use more advanced honey-gathering methods than private beekeepers.
    (D) Commercial beekeeping began to spread during the seventeenth century.

55. In line 6, what does the phrase "on a commercial scale" mean?
    (A) A heavier, thicker form of honey
    (B) Subject to government regulation
    (C) In large amounts for many consumers
    (D) Purely for personal consumption

56. In line 5, "livelihood" means
    (A) a hobby.
    (B) employment.
    (C) the length of one's life.
    (D) entertainment.

57. The BEST title for this passage would be
    (A) "A History of Beekeeping."
    (B) "The Development of Commercial Beekeeping."
    (C) "Moses Quimby—Commercial Beekeeper."
    (D) "Beekeeping in New York State."

58. According to the passage, commercial beekeeping began
    (A) before 1600.
    (B) between 1600 and 1800.
    (C) in the early 1800s.
    (D) in 1750.

59. According to the passage, Moses Quimby made a living by
    (A) making honey for friends, relatives, and neighbors.
    (B) building improved hives.
    (C) creating new honey-gathering techniques.
    (D) producing and selling honey.

60. What kind of information would follow this paragraph?
    (A) A discussion of Moses Quimby's beekeeping business.
    (B) A discussion of the honey-gathering methods.
    (C) A discussion of what happened when beekeeping spread to other states.
    (D) A discussion of how bees make honey.

STOP

If time still remains, you may review work only in this section.

TEST 5

ANSWER KEY

SECTION 1: LISTENING COMPREHENSION

1.	(D)	14.	(C)	26.	(A)	39.	(C)
2.	(A)	15.	(D)	27.	(B)	40.	(D)
3.	(C)	16.	(A)	28.	(C)	41.	(C)
4.	(B)	17.	(D)	29.	(D)	42.	(A)
5.	(A)	18.	(B)	30.	(B)	43.	(C)
6.	(D)	19.	(C)	31.	(C)	44.	(D)
7.	(B)	20.	(A)	32.	(D)	45.	(A)
8.	(C)	21.	(D)	33.	(A)	46.	(D)
9.	(D)	22.	(B)	34.	(D)	47.	(B)
10.	(A)	23.	(B)	35.	(C)	48.	(A)
11.	(B)	24.	(D)	36.	(B)	49.	(D)
12.	(D)	25.	(A)	37.	(A)	50.	(C)
13.	(A)			38.	(C)		

SECTION 2: STRUCTURE AND WRITTEN EXPRESSION

1.	(C)	11.	(D)	21.	(A)	31.	(B)
2.	(A)	12.	(A)	22.	(B)	32.	(A)
3.	(B)	13.	(A)	23.	(A)	33.	(A)
4.	(C)	14.	(D)	24.	(D)	34.	(C)
5.	(B)	15.	(C)	25.	(A)	35.	(A)
6.	(C)	16.	(A)	26.	(A)	36.	(C)
7.	(C)	17.	(C)	27.	(A)	37.	(A)
8.	(C)	18.	(B)	28.	(A)	38.	(D)
9.	(B)	19.	(D)	29.	(B)	39.	(A)
10.	(C)	20.	(B)	30.	(D)	40.	(B)

SECTION 3: VOCABULARY AND READING COMPREHENSION

1.	(B)	16.	(D)	31.	(B)	46.	(A)
2.	(C)	17.	(C)	32.	(C)	47.	(C)
3.	(A)	18.	(D)	33.	(D)	48.	(A)
4.	(C)	19.	(C)	34.	(B)	49.	(C)
5.	(C)	20.	(B)	35.	(A)	50.	(B)
6.	(C)	21.	(C)	36.	(C)	51.	(C)
7.	(D)	22.	(C)	37.	(C)	52.	(B)
8.	(B)	23.	(D)	38.	(B)	53.	(A)
9.	(C)	24.	(A)	39.	(D)	54.	(D)
10.	(B)	25.	(C)	40.	(D)	55.	(C)
11.	(A)	26.	(C)	41.	(A)	56.	(B)
12.	(C)	27.	(A)	42.	(B)	57.	(B)
13.	(D)	28.	(B)	43.	(C)	58.	(C)
14.	(C)	29.	(D)	44.	(A)	59.	(D)
15.	(B)	30.	(A)	45.	(D)	60.	(C)

2717

15/50

Detailed Explanations of Answers

TEST 5

Section 1:
LISTENING COMPREHENSION

Part A

1.   **(D)**   The question asks, "At what time should they have had their newspaper delivered?" The correct answer is (D) — 7:00. The woman says, "It's 7:30. The newspaper should have been delivered a half an hour ago."

2.   **(A)**   The question asks, "Where does this conversation most likely take place?" The correct answer is (A) — An airport. The man asks, "What time is the next flight to Mesa?", and the woman replies, "Oh, I'm sorry sir, that plane left ten minutes ago..."

3.   **(C)**   The question asks, "Where does this conversation most likely take place?" The correct choice is (C) — A post office. The man says, "I need to send this package to Boston. How much will that cost?" The woman replies, "That will depend upon the weight of the package and how quickly you want it to arrive."

4.   **(B)**   The question asks, "Does the man know who won the award?" The correct answer is (B) — He had to leave early so he does not know who won. The woman asks, "Do you know who won the award last night?" The man replies, I wasn't able to stay at the banquet until the winner was announced, but I believe that you can find the winner in this morning's paper."

5.   **(A)**   The question asks, "What does the woman mean?" The correct answer is (A) — She thinks the gypsy's fortunes are too expensive. The man says, "That gypsy over there says she will read our fortune for ten dollars." The woman replies, "You cannot be serious, that is highway robbery."

6.   **(D)**   The question asks, "How many more sodas would the woman need to keep her promise to Katie?" The correct answer is (D) — Two. The man says, "I saw three in there when I looked before." The woman then says, "Oh, I promised Katie I would give her five bottles."

7.   **(B)**   The question asks, "What does the man mean?" The correct answer is (B) — He is unfamiliar with Toni Morrison. The woman says, "I have just read the most wonderful novel by Toni Morrison." The man replies, "Who is she?"

8.   **(C)**   The question asks, "Where will they probably go on their summer vacation?" The correct answer is (C) — Florida. The man says, "I think we either should go to the South Pacific or the Caribbean for our summer vacation." The woman replies, "Oh, honey, we have to think of the cost and we have a voucher to save 20 percent off a vacation in Florida."

9.   **(D)**   The question asks, "What will they probably have for breakfast?" The correct answer is (D) — Eggs. The woman comments, "Oh, I was really in the mood for either pancakes or French toast. Could we have one of those instead?" The man informs her, "We don't have the ingredients for those things."

10.   **(A)**   The question asks, "What is the most likely relationship between these people?" The correct answer is (A) — Boss and employee. The woman says, "This report was due yesterday. If you continue to work at this pace, your position here will be in danger."

11.   **(B)**   The question asks, "What does the man mean?" The correct answer is (B) — Harry does not care about his boss's opinion. When the woman said, "I don't think Harry is in good with his boss," the man asked, "Do you think Harry really cares?" It means Harry really doesn't care if he is in good favor with his boss.

12.   **(D)**   The question asks, "'Who might need an operation?" The correct answer is (D) — The woman's uncle. The woman said, "…My uncle got into an accident last night. The doctor said he might have to be operated on."

13.   **(A)**   The question asks, "Where did this conversation most probably take place?" The correct answer is (A) — In a department store. The woman wanted to return a lamp and the man said, "If you are returning something, you have to go to the customer service counter." We can return something that we bought only in a department store.

14. **(C)** The question asks, "What happened at the picnic?" The correct answer is (C) — It rained heavily. The woman said, "...It rained so heavily, we came back all drenched."

15. **(D)** The question asks, "What does the man mean?" The correct answer is (D) — The woman can use his library because he doesn't need it till six o'clock. When the woman asked, "Can I use your library for awhile?", the man answered, "Go right ahead. I am not going to work there till six o'clock this evening." "Go ahead" is an expression used to convey permission to do something.

16. **(A)** The question asks, "What is the woman's opinion about the subways?" The correct answer is (A) — Subways are suffocating in the summer. The woman said, "I hate subways in the summer. They are so stuffy!" "Stuffy" means suffocating.

17. **(D)** The question asks, "What is the man going to send to the woman?" The correct answer is (D) — Some printed material on fabric painting. The man said, "...if you leave your address, I will send you some literature on fabric painting." "Literature" here means printed material and not literary masterpieces.

18. **(B)** The question asks, "Around what time did this conversation take place?" The correct answer is (B) — Three thirty. The woman said, "...it doesn't start till four o'clock. We still have half an hour to prepare our points." This means that the conversation took place half an hour before four o'clock which is three thirty.

19. **(C)** The question asks, "What does the woman mean?" The correct answer is (C) — She cannot purchase it right now because she does not have any money. The woman said, "...I have to forget about it this time. I am totally broke." "Broke" means penniless.

20. **(A)** The question asks, "What will these people study first?" The correct answer is (A) — Physics. The woman said, "...I think we should start with physics. It is more difficult than biology, or math, or even chemistry." And the man agreed, "As you please."

21. **(D)** The question asks, "Why can't these people attend the concert?" The correct answer is (D) — Because their tickets were for yesterday's concert. The man said, "...But if we don't hit the traffic, we can still make it to the concert, can't we?" The woman answered, "No. We can't. Our tickets were for yesterday."

22. **(B)** The question asks, "What does the woman mean?" The correct answer is (B) — It is a relief to know that the test has been postponed. When the man said, "Our history test has been postponed until next Monday," the woman exclaimed, "What a relief!" It means that she was relieved to know that the test was postponed.

23. **(B)** The question asks, "Why is this man worried about Valerie?" The correct answer is (B) — Because Valerie seems to be extremely disturbed. The man said, "…It looks like she is falling apart." The expression "falling apart" means extremely disturbed.

24. **(D)** The question asks, "How does the woman feel about the course?" The correct answer is (D) — She regrets that she did not take it. The woman said, "Now I regret not taking it (the course)."

25. **(A)** The question asks, "What does the woman mean?" The correct answer is (A) — The lady at the front counter looked strangely at her. The woman said, "The lady at the front desk gave me such a dirty look for coming in so late." "To give a dirty look to someone" means to look strangely at someone, usually with contempt.

Part B

26. **(A)** The question asks, "Who did the woman have a picture of on her desk?" The correct response is (A) — "Her uncle." When asked, "Who is that a picture of on your desk?" she replied, "That is my Uncle Floyd."

27. **(B)** The question is, "What country did the man in the picture go to?" The correct response is (B) — "Germany." The woman says, "The picture was taken last month when he went to Germany." None of the other choices is mentioned in the conversation.

28. **(C)** The question is, "What did the man in the picture collect?" The correct response is (C) — "Cans." The woman says, "He collects beer cans from around the world. Choices (A) "Pictures" and (D) "Coins" are two other types of common collectibles, but neither of them are what the woman's uncle collects. Choice (B) "Suitcases" are what the man brought the cans home in.

29. **(D)** The question asks, "How much are some cans worth?" The correct answer is (D) — "$100." She says, "He said that some people will pay up to one hundred dollars

for one." This question requires the listener to recognize "one hundred dollars" as $100. Choice (A) "$1,000" is one thousand dollars. Choice (B) "$10,000" is ten thousand dollars. Choice (C) "$10" is ten dollars.

30. **(B)** The question asks, "What was thé man in the picture going to do with the cans?" The correct response is (B) — "Sell them." When the man asks, "What is he going to do with all those cans?", she responds, "He's going to sell them, of course." The other choices are other things that can be done with cans, but none of them are mentioned in the paragraph.

31. **(C)** The question asks, "Where did this conversation most probably take place?" The correct answer is (C) — In an office. These people were talking about the woman's day off and there was also a reference to a meeting with Mr. Smith. The most likely place where people talk about these things is in an office.

32. **(D)** The question asks, "Whose call is the women expecting?" The correct answer is (D)—Mr. Smith's. In the conversation the women said, "...and if Mr. Smith calls, can you please set a time for our meeting on Tuesday?"

33. **(A)** The question asks, "Why does the woman have a day off?" The correct answer is (A) — It's her daughter's birthday. When the man asked, "...Are you going out?" the women answered, "No. It's my daughter's birthday and I want to surprise her by being at home."

34. **(D)** The question asks, "What would the man do if he left early on the woman's day off?" The correct answer is (D) — He will ask Terri to talk to Mr. Smith. Toward the end of the conversation the man said, "...I might leave early tomorrow. If Mr. Smith doesn't call before that, I will ask Terri to speak to him."

35. **(C)** The question asks, "Who does the woman want to surprise?" The correct answer is (C) — Her daughter. The woman said, "...It's my daughter's birthday and I want to surprise her by being at home."

36. **(B)** The question asks, "In what part of the day did this conversation take place?" The correct answer is (B) — Morning. The conversation started with the woman greeting the man with a "Good morning!"

37. **(A)** The question asks, "What activity are these people interested in?" The correct answer is (A) — Jogging. The main topic of their conversation was jogging and both of them expressed their liking for it.

38. **(C)** The question asks, "About how many times does the women try to jog in a week?" The correct answer is (C) — Four. In the conversation the woman said, "I try (jogging) at least four times a week."

39. **(C)** The question asks, "Why does the woman prefer jogging to going to a health club?" The correct answer is (C) — Because she can get some fresh air while jogging. In the conversation the woman said, "I used to go to a health club before. But I prefer jogging because I love fresh air."

40. **(D)** The question asks, "What advantage does the man see in jogging?" The correct answer is (D) — You don't have to follow someone's instructions in jogging. Towards the end of the conversation, when the woman explained why she preferred jogging to going to a health club, the man said, "Besides, there is no one to tell you what to do and how many times."

Part C

41. **(C)** The question asks, "What was the major factor of the economy of the 1920s?" The correct response is (C) — Cars. This is given in the first line of the reading. The listener needs to know that "automobiles" are the same as "cars."

42. **(A)** The question asks, "Approximately how many cars were produced each year during the 1920s?" The correct response is (A) — 3.6 million. This question requires the listener to distinguish three numbers all referring to the number of cars in the 1920s. Choice (B) "8 million" was the number of cars registered in 1920. Choice (C) "6 million" was the number of cars registered in 1929. Choice (D) "25,000" does not refer to cars, but to how much money Ford made each day.

43. **(C)** The question asks, "Which Ford car had its price reduced to $290?" The correct response is (C) — Model T. This information was taken from the line, "By 1925 the price of a Ford Model T had been reduced to $290, less than three months pay for the average worker."

44. **(D)** The question asks. "Who averaged $25,000 per day in the 1920s?" The correct response is (D) — Henry Ford. In order to answer this question the listener must realize that "who" refers to a person and not a thing. Once that is determined, choices (A) "Ford Model T" and (B) "automobiles" can be eliminated. Choice (C) "Gerald Ford" was not an automaker, but the 38th president of the United States.

45. **(A)** The question is, "What other industries benefited from automobile production?" The correct response is (A) — Steel and rubber. This question requires that the listener distinguish parts of a longer list.

46. **(D)** The question asks, "What is a good sign according to the speaker?" The correct answer is (D) — The growing popularity of soybean. The first statement in the talk was, "The growing popularity of soybean is a good sign because they are very high in protein."

47. **(B)** The question asks, "What soybean recipes are popular in the United States?" The correct answer is (B) — Hot dogs and soybean ice cream. In the talk you heard, "It is possible to get soybean hot dogs and cholesterol-free soybean ice cream in American supermarkets."

48. **(A)** The question asks, "Where was the soybean first planted?" The correct answer is (A) — China. In the talk you heard, "These beans were first planted in China about 3,000 years ago."

49. **(D)** The question asks, "What is "Tofu" a substitute for?" The correct answer is (D) — Meat. In the talk you heard, "Tofu is a substitute for meat for all nutritional purposes."

50. **(C)** The question asks, "Why is the soybean called a bean of a thousand guises?" The correct answer is (C) — Because it can be used in a variety of ways. The last statement in this talk was, "Due to the various uses of soybean, it is called a bean of a thousand guises."

Section 2:
STRUCTURE AND WRITTEN EXPRESSION

1. **(C)**   (C) is the right answer; **ground** is the past participle form of **grind.** In a passive voice sentence the main verb must be in the past participle form. (A) **Grinded** is not the right form of the past participle of **grind.** (B) **Grind** is not a past participle. (D) **Grinden** is not the right past participle form of **grind.**

2. **(A)**   (A) is the right answer; the past tense of **wish** in the main clause must be followed by **would** in the subordinate clause. (B) **Should** is an obligation agreeing with an order, not a wish. (C) **Must** is an obligation, not agreeing with **wished.** (D) is incorrect because it is in the future tense and, thus, does not agree with the past tense of **wished.**

3. **(B)**   (B) is the right answer; the present perfect tense agrees with **since;** both denote a time duration beginning at a point in the past and continuing up to the present. (A) Simple present tense **is** does not agree with **since.** (C) Present continuous tense does not agree with **since.** (D) The sentence is in the passive voice; **has been** is in the active voice.

4. **(C)**   (C) is the right answer; **being** is a gerund (part verb and part noun). As a noun it can follow the possessive pronoun **his.** As a verb it can precede the adverb **away.** (A) **Has been** is a finite verb; it cannot follow a possessive pronoun—only nouns and personal pronouns. (B) **Was** is a finite verb. (D) Infinitives cannot follow a possessive pronoun.

5. **(B)**   (B) is the right answer; **reporting** is a gerundial noun meaning a whole system of disseminating information. (A) denotes a particular item; **revolutionize** is to bring about great changes in a system, not a single item. (C) **To report news** may form a noun but does not denote a system. (D) It appears from here that **news report** is a verb, but such a verb is not in use.

6. **(C)**   (C) is the right answer; **an** is the form of the indefinite article **a** that should be used before words beginning with a vowel *sound* (not just a vowel letter). (A) is not the right form of the indefinite article. (B) The definite article **the** does not parallel the indefinite article in **a fuel.** (D) **Another** can function as a pronoun or as an adjective; in

either case it adds an item to another of the same class. In this sentence there is mention of just one oxidizer.

7. **(C)** (C) is the right answer; **worse** is the right form of the comparative degree of **ill.** (A) **More ill** is not the right form of the comparative degree of **ill.** (B) There is no need for a superlative degree here; only two states of health are compared, **most ill** is not the right superlative form. (D) The superlative form of **ill** is not required here.

8. **(C)** (C) is the right answer; **among** is used to relate persons or things numbered more than two. (A) **Between** is used with reference to two persons or things. (B) **In the middle of** refers to a central position on something. (D) **By** does not relate two items but may show the position of one with reference to the other (e.g., the table is by the window).

9. **(B)** (B) is the right answer; the conjunction **but also** is always paired with **not only.** Each is dependent on the other. (A) **He is also** is incorrect because **is** is in the present tense while **established** is in the past tense. (C) **Also** does not work in conjunction with **not only.** (D) **As well as** does not work in conjunction with **not only.**

10. **(C)** (C) is the right answer; **readily** is an adverb of manner modifying the verb **sell.** (A) A comparative degree (adjective) is not required here. (B) **Fast** is an adverb; **ly** is an erroneous addition. (D) **Ready** is an adjective; it cannot follow the preposition **with.**

11. **(D)** (D) is the right answer; the indefinite pronoun **one** agrees with **one's.** (A) The personal pronoun **we** does not agree with **one's.** (B) The personal pronoun **he** does not agree with **one's.** (C) The personal pronoun **they** does not agree with **one's.**

12. **(A)** (A) is the right answer; **different** is an adjective qualifying the noun **forms.** (B) **Different from** compares two dissimilar things. (C) **Differing** is a verb denoting that something is unlike another. (D) **No different** must be followed by **from.** It compares two things that are alike.

13. **(A)** (A) is the right answer. The infinitive without **to** is the right form to follow imperative sentences beginning with **you better/had better.** (B) **To** is not required. (C) **To** is not required; **absent** is an adjective and cannot come before a reflexive pronoun (himself). (D) **Absenting** is not an infinitive.

14. **(D)**   (D) is the right answer; an adjectival phrase used to denote number approximating to the given number. (A) **Many** is an indefinite numeral and so does not agree with the specific number **1800.** (B) is used for comparison; there is no comparison in this sentence. (C) is used for comparison; there is no comparison in this sentence.

15. **(C)**   (C) is the right answer; it is a finite verb completing the sentence. (A) is an infinitive without **to.** (B) **Let** is a finite verb followed by the infinitive **be** without **to.** (D) **Leave out** implies the exclusion of something that is already present but the **margin** is not already there.

16. **(A)**   (A) is the right answer; **to making** is not a verbal form in use. The answer should be **in making.** (B) The present tense, passive form, parallels **is used.** (C) denotes an act of combining. (D) is an infinitive of purpose, complementing the verb **is blended.**

17. **(C)**   (C) is the answer. A scientific fact is normally stated in the simple present tense. **Will produce** is future tense. The answer must be **produces.** (A) denotes the time at which an event takes place. (B) is a personal pronoun, referring to **radium.** (D) is a past participle qualifying **radon.**

18. **(B)**   (B) is the answer. The causative verb needs an infinitive to complement it. The answer must be **to take.** (A) is the present continuous tense denoting something happening currently. (C) is a possessive pronoun used to relate children to parents. (D) is a possessive form of children to show relationship with **academic development.**

19. **(D)**   (D) is the answer. When a condition is expressed in the present tense, then its consequence must be expressed by **would** or **could.** So the answer must be **could be used. Could** here denotes a possibility. (A) is the preposition used to locate objects on a surface such as a planet. (B) is the possessive form of Mars to show relationship with **moon.** (C) is the possessive form of the personal pronoun **it** to denote relationship of **components** with **water.**

20. **(B)**   (B) is the answer. **Will** is not in agreement with the past tense verb **saw.** The answer should be **would** which denotes futurity from a point of view in the past. (A) is a relative pronoun introducing an adjectival clause. (C) is an adverb meaning **frequently.** (D) is the past tense in keeping with the past tense **saw.**

21. **(A)**   (A) is the answer. **Days** is not an independent noun qualified by **four.** The answer must be **four days. Four day** is a compound adjective qualifying **journey.** (B)

denotes point of departure. (C) denotes a large segment of space. (D) is a preposition of direction.

22. **(B)**   (B) is the answer. The adverbial phrase **every year** is not in the right position in the sentence. It could appear at the beginning of the sentence; otherwise it must appear after **American artists. American artists** being the object of the verb **honors** must immediately follow it.

23. **(A)**   (A) is the answer. The adjective of quantity, **little,** denotes a small quantity. It cannot qualify the count noun **years. Few** is a numeral adjective denoting an indefinite small number. The answer should be **a few years.** (B) denotes the agent responsible for the event. (C) is a finite verb completing the subordinate clause, and past tense agreeing with the past tense **was** in the main clause. (D) is a possessive pronoun showing relationship between **literary feminism** and **appearance.**

24. **(D)**   (D) is the answer. **Wouldn't he** is not the right form of the tag question. Since the verb in the main clause is in the negative, the tag question must be in the affirmative. The answer must be **would he?** (A) is an auxiliary of **finalize** denoting a habitual action in the past. (B) is a past participle forming part of the verb group **had tried.** (C) is a personal pronoun referring to **scene.**

25. **(A)**   (A) is the answer. The possessive pronoun **her** is not the right form of the pronoun to be used here. The answer must be **she,** the feminine personal pronoun in the singular. The impersonal pronoun **it** refers to **she** in anticipation. (B) The possessive pronoun **her** relates **husband** to **Goneril.** (C) The relative pronoun **who** introduces the adjectival clause **who was…father.** (D) denotes the direction taken by **inhospitality.**

26. **(A)**   (A) is the answer. **Sheeps** is not the right plural form of **sheep.** The plural form is also **sheep.** (B) The definite article must precede an adjective in the superlative degree. (C) is the complement of the verb **are.** (D) relates **natural wool** to source.

27. **(A)**   (A) is the answer. **Some** is an indefinite numeral adjective. It cannot, then, refer to **Andrew Jackson.** A definite numeral must be used. The answer should be **one of. Of the** denotes that **one** is a part of a bigger number. (B) The singular verb is in agreement with the subject. (C) complements the verb **was.** (D) is an adverbial phrase modifying **was.**

28. **(A)**   (A) is the answer. The adjective **enough** cannot precede another adjective but must follow it. The answer should be **interesting enough.** (B) is an infinitive functioning

as a verb. (C) **What** is a pronoun referring in anticipation to the salesman's talk. (D) is the infinitive object of the verb **had.**

29. **(B)** (B) is the answer. The word **similar** must be followed by the preposition **to.** The answer must be **similar to.** (A) is a numeral adjective qualifying **parks.** (C) The plural verb is in agreement with the plural subject **parks.** (D) is a noun, meaning *locations.*

30. **(D)** (D) is the answer. **Except** is inappropriate here. The adjective to be used is **not.** The answer should be **rather than many.** (A) The plural is in agreement with the numeral adjective **several.** (B) is a compound conjunction connecting the two clauses, **signals...image** and **as if...many.** (C) The past perfect tense locates this event at a point before the hypothetical event.

31. **(B)** (B) is the answer. **For that** is an inappropriate way of expressing reason. The answer should be **so that.** (A) Verbs like **recommend** and **suggest** are always followed by the infinitive form without **to.** (C) The definitive article is appropriate, as **risk** is stated later in the text. (D) is the possibility expressed in the passive voice.

32. **(A)** (A) is the answer. **Once** means **at a point in time. Of** denotes a part of something and is inappropriate here. The conjunction **one** will serve to join **once...ready** and **eight...station.** (B) is the subject of **will undertake.** (C) The future tense is in agreement with present tense hypothetical statement. (D) is the adverbial of place, denoting the destination of the tour.

33. **(A)** (A) is the answer. **I** is not the right personal pronoun here. The sentence is in reported speech. The first person pronoun in direct speech must be changed to an appropriate third person pronoun in reported speech. In the answer **I** must be changed to **he.** (B) The past tense is the right form when reporting the words of the speaker. (C) The present tense of the verb is appropriate as the **urge** continues in the present. (D) The pronoun **one** refers to the noun **artist.**

34. **(C)** (C) is the answer. The subject of the sentence is **bunch,** not **roses.** The plural verb **have** does not agree with **bunch** which is a singular noun. The answer should be **has.** (A) denotes three-dimensional location (vase). (B) **By** means **beside.** (D) denotes duration of time.

35. **(A)** (A) is the answer. The verb **warned** must be followed by **had better,** not **was.** (B) The possessive pronoun relates **study** to **student.** (C) denotes a choice between

improve his daily habits and **fail.** (D) **Would** is used to express future consequence of a hypothetical situation.

36. **(C)** (C) is the answer. **Because** is a conjunction joining two clauses. **Because its softness** is not a clause. The answer should be **because of,** meaning **due to.** (A) is past tense agreeing with **ancient times.** (B) **For** is the right preposition to follow **suitable/unsuitable.** (D) The past tense is in agreement with the past tense **found.**

37. **(A)** (A) is the answer. **She** is a repetition of the subject and is not required. (B) **At** is the preposition normally used to refer to working places and educational institutions. (C) The singular verb is in agreement with the single subject **Joan Williams.** (D) is the object of the verb **conducts.**

38. **(D)** (D) is the answer. The present tense **lie** is not in agreement with the past tense verb **found.** The answer must be **lay,** the past tense of **lie.** (A) is a certain point in time. (B) is the preposition used to denote a large segment of space. (C) The past tense is in agreement with the past tense **landed.**

39. **(A)** (A) is the answer. **Primary** means the first stage of something, so it cannot qualify **president's wife;** the answer is **first.** (B) is the complement of the verb **was.** (C) is the adverbial of the phrase modifying **to travel.** (D) is the preposition of **direction.**

40. **(B)** (B) is the answer. **So as** cannot function as a conjunction to join the two clauses **radar...advances** and **it...universe.** The answer should be **so that.** (A) The present perfect tense denotes a duration of time from past to the present. (C) is the complement of the verb **is.** (D) The definitive article is used to refer to something that is the only one of its kind.

Section 3:
READING COMPREHENSION
AND VOCABULARLY

1. **(B)** The reason bumblebees are considered more primitive than honey bees is that their colonies are not as highly developed. All the other choices are facts stated in the passage, but they do not have anything to do with bumblebees' more primitive nature.

2. **(C)** While the other choices may be areas where bumblebees can be found, the passage clearly states that bumblebees are found "primarily in the temperate and northern regions." Choice (C) is therefore correct.

3. **(A)** The passage tells us that "young fertilized queens…establish new colonies the next spring." This statement clearly eliminates all other choices.

4. **(C)** In this context, the word "primitive" most nearly means "undeveloped." The second sentence indicates that the structure of bumblebee colonies is not as highly developed as that of honey bees. "Primitive" (A) in no way means "tiny." Both "uncivilized" (B) and "original" (D) are other meanings of "primitive," but do not make sense here.

5. **(C)** Bumblebees are described by the passage as less dangerous than honey bees, so therefore we can say that honey bees are more dangerous than bumblebees. The passage states that bumblebees are the most primitive of the social bees, so (A) is an incorrect answer. The passage also states that honey bees are more abundant (plentiful) than bumblebees, so answer (B) is incorrect as well. Answer (D) is incorrect because both honey bees and bumblebees feed on plants.

6. **(C)** A plant feeder eats plants, so (C) is the right answer. Although the passage says that bees do pollinate (A), the question asks what is specifically meant by the term "plant feeders." (A), therefore, is incorrect. Choice (B) feed plants is the opposite of eating plants and is thus incorrect. Since plants do not harm bees, which is why bees sting, they do not sting the plants. (D) is an incorrect choice.

7. **(D)** The passage states that a colony is made up of "at least one queen, several males, and numerous workers." Choice (D), which lists them in the same way, is the right answer. Choices (A), (B), and (C) are incorrect because they do not list the members of the colony in the right amounts.

8. **(B)** Although the passage says that the colonies are situated "like fence rows," that is not where they are located, which is deep underground (B). Therefore, answers (A), (C), and (D) are incorrect because they misinterpret what the passage says.

9. **(C)** While all the choices are definitely mentioned in the passage, only one is the main topic—a description of the bumblebee. This is a very general topic which includes all of the other answer choices, which are more specific.

10. **(B)** The passage specifically states that a colony usually contains "between 100 and 500 bees." Choices (A), (C), and (D) are all incorrect because they do not state the correct amount.

11. **(A)** A "principle" is a basic truth about something—here, about gravity. It is therefore the best synonym for "law" in this context. The other choices are definitions of "law" that apply in other contexts, but not here.

12. **(C)** The first paragraph lists some of Newton's contributions to science. Establishing the theory of relativity (C) is not among them. This theory was in fact established by Albert Einstein.

13. **(D)** The most precise synonym in this context is "upheaval," which is what Newton and his contemporaries caused in scientific thinking in the seventeenth century. "Uprising" (A) and "battle" (C) have militaristic connotations, and "rotation" (B) is an entirely different meaning of the word.

14. **(C)** The passage discusses the law of gravity as being Newton's most important, or "greatest" contribution to science. "God-like" (A) is clearly not appropriate, and "ideal" (B) and "dominating" (D) violate the meaning of the sentence.

15. **(B)** It can be deduced from the information given that Newton's law of gravity would apply to a body that orbits another body, as the moon orbits the Earth.

16. **(D)** The passage clearly indicates that much of Newton's work was motivated by a desire to learn more about planetary motion. Therefore, astronomy, the study of the universe beyond Earth, would have benefitted the most from his work.

17. **(C)** Choice (C) is the right answer because it is the definition of "attracts." The key word in this phrase is the word "attracts," which means to draw something near. Choice (A) is the opposite of this definition and is an incorrect answer. Choice (B) is wrong because if the particle seeks other particles, then it is not attracting them. Choice (D) is incorrect because "evading" is the opposite of "attracting."

18. **(D)** In the first sentence it says that "Isaac Newton's supreme scientific work was his system of universal gravitation." This means that his system was his best and most famous. Only choice (D) states that Newton's system was his most important scientific discovery, which is the same meaning as the word "supreme" in the sentence. Therefore, (D) is the right answer. Choices (A), (B), and (C) all state the opposite of the word "supreme" and are therefore incorrect.

19. **(C)** A physicist (C) is one who studies physics, or the laws of matter and energy. We know from the passage that Newton was studying gravity, which is an important part of physics. Therefore, (C) is the correct choice. A biologist (A) is one who studies the science of living things. Although Newton did observe living things he was not a biologist. (A) is incorrect. A geologist (B) studies rocks, which is not what Newton did, so (B) is incorrect as well. (D), a physician, may sound like physicist, but is really a medical doctor. (D) is incorrect.

20. **(B)** The year of Newton's discovery is stated in the passage as 1665. This year is part of the seventeenth century, so choice (B) is the correct answer. You may have chosen choice (A), the sixteenth century. But that is incorrect, because a century is always numbered ahead of the years it represents. For example, the years 1900 to 1999 are called the twentieth century, even though they begin with 1900. So 1665 is part of the seventeenth (not the sixteenth) century, even though it begins with 1600. Choices (C) and (D) are incorrect because they come much too late in history.

21. **(C)** The passage clearly states that "the degrees of incidental learning does not approach that of intentional learning." Choices (A), (B), and (D) directly contradict statements in the passage.

22. **(C)** The second paragraph indicates that the connection between motives and learning is too complex to precisely evaluate. This immediately eliminates choice (A), as well as (B). Although the relationship between motives and learning is complex and not

easily understood, the passage certainly implies that the connection is there, so choice (D) is incorrect.

23. **(D)** The passage states that incidental learning is not intended and results simply from exposure to material. This points to choice (D) as the correct answer. The other choices show an intentional and motivated desire to learn.

24. **(A)** In the context of the sentence and the passage, the best definition of "incentives" is "motivators." An incentive motivates a person to do something. Choices (B) and (D) are examples of incentives, not synonyms. Choice (C) is opposite in meaning.

25. **(C)** The author makes two statements that point to his or her opinion: first, that intentional learning comes from motivation, and secondly, that "a motivated person will generally learn faster and more efficiently than an unmotivated one." The connection between these two statements indicates that (C) is the correct answer.

26. **(C)** The primary focus of the passage is on the connection between motivation and learning, making (C) the best title. School performance (A) and experiments (D) are only briefly discussed. Choice (B) ignores intentional learning as an important part of the discussion.

27. **(A)** While choices (B), (C), and (D) are often considered ways of being efficient, only choice (A) clearly defines the word "efficient" in the context of learning.

28. **(B)** The passage describes someone who is motivated as someone who intends (or plans) to learn. A student who studies for an exam is motivated to do well on the exam, and therefore that student plans, or intends, to study for that exam. Studying for an exam, then, is practicing intentional learning. Choice (A) is wrong because someone who learns incidentally did not plan to do so. Residual learning, choice (C), is not even mentioned in the passage and is therefore wrong. Motivational learning (D) is not the best answer because it does not describe the student's intention to study.

29. **(D)** Impulsion means the same as "motivation." Therefore, (D) is the right answer. Dread (A), repulsion (B), and neglect (C) are all opposites of the meaning of the word "motivation," which is a desire, or impulsion, to do something.

30. **(A)** As discussed in the explanation for question 28, one must be motivated to practice intentional learning. Therefore, choice (A), which restates this idea, is the correct

answer. The other choices are incorrect because they are the opposite of what one must be in order to use intentional learning.

31. **(B)**   The passage clearly states that the energy crisis of the 1970s led to "a renewed interest in the use of wind power to generate electricity."

32. **(C)**   Choice (C) is correct for two reasons. First, the passage mentions all other choices as explicit advantages of wind energy. Secondly, logic dictates that weather is the primary factor leading to the availability of wind energy.

33. **(D)**   The passage states that "the earliest vertical windmills were used in Persia more than 2,000 years ago for the grinding of grain." They were used later for pumping water (A) and electricity (B). The passage does not mention the use of windmills for propelling ships (C).

34. **(B)**   Here, the closest synonym is "changing." The passage discusses the effect of other sources of energy on the environment as having a negative impact. The other choices do not fit the meaning of the sentence.

35. **(A)**   The last sentence of the first paragraph lists the recommendations of the U.S. Department of Energy regarding wind power. The elimination of windmills as a means of pumping water is not mentioned.

36. **(C)**   The first paragraph clearly states that the use of windmills "declined drastically in the 1930s when inexpensive electricity reached the rural areas." None of the other choices are discussed as being factors in the decreased use of windmills.

37. **(C)**   Although the passage compares wind energy to electric energy at one point, electric energy is not a main topic. But the one time it is mentioned, the passage states that wind power's environmental impact is "relatively small" compared to electric power's impact. So choice (C), which states this, is the correct answer. All the other choices restate the comparison incorrectly and should not be chosen.

38. **(B)**   The comparison to electric power in the passage does not include any reasons why wind energy may be better than electric. But the passage does state what choice (B) says, that wind energy does not alter the environment as much as other powers, such as hydroelectric or nuclear-fueled systems. The other choices all have to do with electric power and are incorrect for that reason.

39. **(D)** Only (D), the effect on nature, has the same meaning as the term "environmental impact." "Impact" is another way of saying "effect," and the environment is another term for nature in general. The importance of nature (A), the effect on man (B), and the importance of the environment (C) are all important, but they are not specifically mentioned in the passage.

40. **(D)** Because wind energy is compared throughout the passage to other forms of energy, the title "Wind Energy vs. Other Types of Power" is the best title, since it encompasses the main point of the entire passage. The public's response to wind energy is mentioned in the first sentence of the passage, but it is not the main topic and should not be included in the title. (A) is incorrect. Many benefits of wind energy are discussed, but they too are not the main topic, and therefore they do not belong in the title either. (B) is incorrect. There is no discussion in the passage at all about how wind energy works, so (C) is a wrong answer.

41. **(A)** Although the other choices are also synonyms of "imperceptible," the most precise meaning here is "unnoticeable." The passage discusses the early symptoms of Alzheimer's disease as being difficult to notice.

42. **(B)** The statement in choice (B) is directly contradicted by the passage: "The victim of Alzheimer's disease is most likely to spend his or her last days in a nursing home or long-term care institution." All the other statements are supported by the passage.

43. **(C)** The second sentence of the passage clearly states that Alzheimer's disease is "characterized by the death of nerve cells in the cerebral cortex." This eliminates all other possible answer choices.

44. **(A)** The best synonym here is "decline," as in a lessening of intellectual power. Choice (B), "ruin," is too strong a word. Choices (C) and (D) are not correct definitions of the word.

45. **(D)** Choice (D) is the best possible title, since the passage tracks the progressive nature of symptoms in Alzheimer's disease. Choice (A) is clearly incorrect since there is no cure for the disease. The passage only briefly mentions the family's role, so choice (B) is a weak choice. Choice (C) is incorrect because the main focus of the passage is not on the history of the disease, but of its effects on the individual.

46. **(A)** Since this question uses the word "implies," you must look for the answer which is not specifically stated in the passage. Choices (B), (C), and (D) are specifically mentioned in the passage, and therefore should not be chosen. Only choice (A) is not specifically stated. The passage says, in the first sentence, "The major debilitating symptoms of Alzheimer's disease include serious forgetfulness." It can therefore be assumed, or implied, that a person who has Alzheimer's disease may not remember childhood events.

47. **(C)** Forgetfulness and confusion are stated in the very first sentence of the paragraph. (C) is the correct answer. Enhanced motor skills (A), is the opposite of the symptoms of Alzheimer's, so (A) should not be chosen. (B) and (D) are not even mentioned in the passage and are therefore incorrect.

48. **(A)** A debilitating disease, such as Alzheimer's, is one which makes a person weak, or feeble. Choice (A), therefore, is the correct answer. Choices (B) and (D) are nouns, not adjectives like "debilitating," and are therefore incorrect answers. To strengthen is the opposite of "to make feeble."

49. **(C)** The passage states in the last sentence that there is no cure for Alzheimer's disease. There is no mention of bedrest (A) as a cure for Alzheimer's disease. While (B) and (D) are stated in the passage as ways to care for the Alzheimer's patient, they are not cures.

50. **(B)** Choice (B) is mentioned in the passage as one of the aspects of forgetfulness. While choices (A), (C), and (D) may be true, they are not specifically stated in the passage. Therefore, they are incorrect choices.

51. **(C)** According to the passage, "many farmers and villages kept a few colonies of bees in box hives to supply their own needs and those of some friends, relatives, and neighbors." This obviously eliminates choice (B) as a possibility. Nowhere is it mentioned that bees were kept for recreation (A) or to scare away wild animals (D).

52. **(B)** The last sentence of the paragraph clearly states that "as the use of improved hives and new honey-gathering methods became more widespread, commercial beekeeping spread into other states." None of the other choices are mentioned in the passage.

53. **(A)** In this context, honey is an "object" of local trade. None of the other choices are synonyms of "article"; thus, they violate the meaning of the sentence.

54. **(D)**   The passage states that until the early 1800s, "honey was largely an article of local trade." This rules out the possibility that commercial beekeeping was prominent in the seventeenth century. All of the other choices are facts either explicitly stated or implied within the passage.

55. **(C)**   The passage explains that commercial beekeeping involves the production of larger amounts of honey, for more than just personal needs and those of friends, relatives, and neighbors. This obviously rules out choice (D). In addition, the phrase used here has nothing to do with the weight of the honey (A) or regulation by government (B).

56. **(B)**   Choice (B), employment, is correct. A livelihood can be defined as a means of support or employment. Choices (A) and (D) are thus incorrect because hobbies and entertainment are not means of support. Choice (C) is also incorrect, for a livelihood is not a measure of how long one's life is.

57. **(B)**   "The Development of Commercial Beekeeping" encompasses the topic of the passage. (B), therefore, is the correct answer. While the passage does give some history of beekeeping, it is not the main point. Therefore, answer (A) is incorrect. Moses Quimby is discussed as the beginner of commercial beekeeping, but the passage is not specifically about him, so choice (C) is incorrect. "Beekeeping in New York State" (D) is not the main topic of the passage, so (D) is incorrect.

58. **(C)**   The passage states that local beekeeping ended around the "early 1800s." (A) is incorrect because the passage implies that beekeeping began after 1600. (B) is incorrect because between 1600 and 1800, *local* beekeeping was most widespread. (D) is wrong because 1750 is not mentioned in the passage.

59. **(D)**   While Moses Quimby performed all of these tasks, only (D) explains how he made his living. (A) was what all local beekeepers did. (B) and (C) were accomplishments of Quimby's, but they are not stated in the passage of how he made his living. Only (D) is the correct answer, since it responds to what the question asks.

60. **(C)**   Since the end of the passage states that "commercial beekeeping spread into other states," it follows that if another paragraph was added, it would discuss the effects of beekeeping's moving into other states. Since (C) restates this, it is the correct answer. Choices (A) and (B) were already discussed in the passage, so these choices are incorrect. Choice (D), how bees make honey, is not relevant to the topic and should not be chosen.

Test of English as a Foreign Language
TEST 6
ANSWER SHEET

Section 1:
Listening Comprehension

1. (A) (B) (C) (D)
2. (A) (B) (C) (D)
3. (A) (B) (C) (D)
4. (A) (B) (C) (D)
5. (A) (B) (C) (D)
6. (A) (B) (C) (D)
7. (A) (B) (C) (D)
8. (A) (B) (C) (D)
9. (A) (B) (C) (D)
10. (A) (B) (C) (D)
11. (A) (B) (C) (D)
12. (A) (B) (C) (D)
13. (A) (B) (C) (D)
14. (A) (B) (C) (D)
15. (A) (B) (C) (D)
16. (A) (B) (C) (D)
17. (A) (B) (C) (D)
18. (A) (B) (C) (D)
19. (A) (B) (C) (D)
20. (A) (B) (C) (D)
21. (A) (B) (C) (D)
22. (A) (B) (C) (D)
23. (A) (B) (C) (D)
24. (A) (B) (C) (D)
25. (A) (B) (C) (D)
26. (A) (B) (C) (D)
27. (A) (B) (C) (D)
28. (A) (B) (C) (D)
29. (A) (B) (C) (D)
30. (A) (B) (C) (D)

31. (A) (B) (C) (D)
32. (A) (B) (C) (D)
33. (A) (B) (C) (D)
34. (A) (B) (C) (D)
35. (A) (B) (C) (D)
36. (A) (B) (C) (D)
37. (A) (B) (C) (D)
38. (A) (B) (C) (D)
39. (A) (B) (C) (D)
40. (A) (B) (C) (D)
41. (A) (B) (C) (D)
42. (A) (B) (C) (D)
43. (A) (B) (C) (D)
44. (A) (B) (C) (D)
45. (A) (B) (C) (D)
46. (A) (B) (C) (D)
47. (A) (B) (C) (D)
48. (A) (B) (C) (D)
49. (A) (B) (C) (D)
50. (A) (B) (C) (D)

Section 2:
Structure and
Written Expression

1. (A) (B) (C) (D)
2. (A) (B) (C) (D)
3. (A) (B) (C) (D)
4. (A) (B) (C) (D)
5. (A) (B) (C) (D)
6. (A) (B) (C) (D)
7. (A) (B) (C) (D)

8. (A) (B) (C) (D)
9. (A) (B) (C) (D)
10. (A) (B) (C) (D)
11. (A) (B) (C) (D)
12. (A) (B) (C) (D)
13. (A) (B) (C) (D)
14. (A) (B) (C) (D)
15. (A) (B) (C) (D)
16. (A) (B) (C) (D)
17. (A) (B) (C) (D)
18. (A) (B) (C) (D)
19. (A) (B) (C) (D)
20. (A) (B) (C) (D)
21. (A) (B) (C) (D)
22. (A) (B) (C) (D)
23. (A) (B) (C) (D)
24. (A) (B) (C) (D)
25. (A) (B) (C) (D)
26. (A) (B) (C) (D)
27. (A) (B) (C) (D)
28. (A) (B) (C) (D)
29. (A) (B) (C) (D)
30. (A) (B) (C) (D)
31. (A) (B) (C) (D)
32. (A) (B) (C) (D)
33. (A) (B) (C) (D)
34. (A) (B) (C) (D)
35. (A) (B) (C) (D)
36. (A) (B) (C) (D)
37. (A) (B) (C) (D)
38. (A) (B) (C) (D)
39. (A) (B) (C) (D)
40. (A) (B) (C) (D)

Section 3:
Reading Comprehension
and Vocabulary

1. (A) (B) (C) (D)
2. (A) (B) (C) (D)
3. (A) (B) (C) (D)
4. (A) (B) (C) (D)
5. (A) (B) (C) (D)
6. (A) (B) (C) (D)
7. (A) (B) (C) (D)
8. (A) (B) (C) (D)
9. (A) (B) (C) (D)
10. (A) (B) (C) (D)
11. (A) (B) (C) (D)
12. (A) (B) (C) (D)
13. (A) (B) (C) (D)
14. (A) (B) (C) (D)
15. (A) (B) (C) (D)
16. (A) (B) (C) (D)
17. (A) (B) (C) (D)
18. (A) (B) (C) (D)

19. (A) (B) (C) (D)
20. (A) (B) (C) (D)
21. (A) (B) (C) (D)
22. (A) (B) (C) (D)
23. (A) (B) (C) (D)
24. (A) (B) (C) (D)
25. (A) (B) (C) (D)
26. (A) (B) (C) (D)
27. (A) (B) (C) (D)
28. (A) (B) (C) (D)
29. (A) (B) (C) (D)
30. (A) (B) (C) (D)
31. (A) (B) (C) (D)
32. (A) (B) (C) (D)
33. (A) (B) (C) (D)
34. (A) (B) (C) (D)
35. (A) (B) (C) (D)
36. (A) (B) (C) (D)
37. (A) (B) (C) (D)
38. (A) (B) (C) (D)
39. (A) (B) (C) (D)

40. (A) (B) (C) (D)
41. (A) (B) (C) (D)
42. (A) (B) (C) (D)
43. (A) (B) (C) (D)
44. (A) (B) (C) (D)
45. (A) (B) (C) (D)
46. (A) (B) (C) (D)
47. (A) (B) (C) (D)
48. (A) (B) (C) (D)
49. (A) (B) (C) (D)
50. (A) (B) (C) (D)
51. (A) (B) (C) (D)
52. (A) (B) (C) (D)
53. (A) (B) (C) (D)
54. (A) (B) (C) (D)
55. (A) (B) (C) (D)
56. (A) (B) (C) (D)
57. (A) (B) (C) (D)
58. (A) (B) (C) (D)
59. (A) (B) (C) (D)
60. (A) (B) (C) (D)

TOEFL
TEST 6

Section 1:
LISTENING COMPREHENSION

TIME: 35 Minutes
50 Questions

Part A

> **DIRECTIONS**: In Part A you will hear short conversations between two speakers. At the end of each conversation, a third person will ask a question about what was said. **You will hear each conversation just one time.** Therefore, you must listen carefully to understand what each speaker says. After you hear a conversation and the question about it, read the four possible answers in your test book and decide which one is the best answer to the question you heard. Then, on your answer sheet, find the number of the question and fill in the space that corresponds to the answer you have chosen.

(**WAIT**)

1. (A) She really likes the song.
   (B) She really dislikes the song.
   (C) She does not get to hear the song often enough.
   (D) She has heard the song too much.

2. (A) Man   (C) Melisa
   (B) Woman   (D) Erik

3. (A) They have already eaten.
    (B) They will eat later when they are more hungry.
    (C) They will leave now to go to eat at a restaurant.
    (D) They will eat a lunch now that the man prepares.

4. (A) Give it stitches.
    (B) Nothing, it is merely a scratch.
    (C) Perform an operation.
    (D) Bandage it.

5. (A) The woman is usually careless when packing.
    (B) Missing little things when packing is a common occurrence.
    (C) The woman is always packing.
    (D) He is the one who had missed the little things when packing.

6. (A) Ten   (C) Three
    (B) Two   (D) Five

7. (A) The man did not wash the dishes.
    (B) The man was reading.
    (C) The man did not attend the meeting with her.
    (D) The meeting did not go as planned.

8. (A) Go out in the sailboat if there are thunder showers
    (B) Watch the weather forecast herself
    (C) Go out in the sailboat if the weather is nice
    (D) Buy a sailboat if the weather is nice

9. (A) Three   (C) Five days
    (B) A week   (D) One month

10. (A) He gets his fortune told regularly, and things it is worthwhile.
    (B) He has never had his palm read by a fortune teller.
    (C) He has had his fortune told, but thinks it is worthless to do so.
    (D) He enjoys spending the time and money to have his palm read by a fortune teller.

11. (A) The woman doesn't need summer clothes.
     (B) They should have started looking for summer clothes earlier.
     (C) Weekend is not a good time for shopping.
     (D) It's not time yet to look for summer clothes.

12. (A) Three fifteen   (C) Two Thirty
     (B) Three o'clock   (D) Three thirty

13. (A) One   (C) Three
     (B) Two   (D) Four

14. (A) It is not surprising that Tim was happy.
     (B) Tim's salary is not wonderful.
     (C) Tim never thought about his salary.
     (D) Tim was not happy or surprised.

15. (A) He does not like to talk.
     (B) He talks nonstop.
     (C) He is pleasant to talk with.
     (D) He always talks about boxing.

16. (A) Dr. Sampson
     (B) The man
     (C) Dr. Jones
     (D) Both Dr. Jones and Dr. Sampson

17. (A) Onions   (C) Mushroom soup
     (B) Tomato soup   (D) French onion soup

18. (A) In a stadium   (C) In a movie theater
     (B) At a concert   (D) In a house

19. (A) She does not like talking to the man.
     (B) She is not the right person to talk to.
     (C) She does not have time at the moment but she can talk tomorrow.
     (D) She can talk if he can finish fast.

20. (A) He has an unfriendly attitude.
    (B) He is friendly.
    (C) He is a quiet person.
    (D) No one in the office is as unpopular as Rick is.

21. (A) The article has many good ideas.
    (B) They should finish reading the article.
    (C) The man has no idea how bad the article is.
    (D) It would be nice to take a break.

22. (A) Watching a TV program
    (B) Going through files
    (C) Discussing a project
    (D) Working on a computer

23. (A) Her pie is excellent.
    (B) Her mother and her aunt made better pies than this.
    (C) Her mother made better pies than her aunt.
    (D) Her mother and her aunt gave her more compliments.

24. (A) The bank   (C) The school
    (B) The post office   (D) On the road

25. (A) Gary is crazy.
    (B) The house was not built to Gary's satisfaction.
    (C) He was surprised that Gary sold the house.
    (D) Gary had to sell his house to pay his debts.

Part B

DIRECTIONS: In Part B you will hear extended conversations between two speakers. At the end of each conversation, a third person will ask several questions about what was said. **You will hear each conversation and the questions about it just one time.** They will not be written out for you. Therefore, you must listen carefully to understand what each speaker says. After you hear a question, read the four possible answers in your test book and decide which one is the best answer to the question you heard. Then on your answer sheet, find the number of the question and fill in the space that corresponds to the answer you have chosen.

WAIT

26. (A) His siblings (C) His parents
    (B) His cousins (D) His grandparents

27. (A) Weekend (C) Afternoon
    (B) Evening (D) Morning

28. (A) Home (C) Aquarium
    (B) Amusement park (D) Studio tour

29. (A) Only new movies (C) Only school movies
    (B) Only bad movies (D) Only famous movies

30. (A) At school (C) At work
    (B) At home (D) At a park

31. (A) He got a job in Italy.
    (B) He was here only for studies; so legally, he cannot stay any longer.
    (C) He misses his country.
    (D) He failed in many subjects.

32. (A) Get a job for him (C) Teach him English
    (B) Take his picture (D) Give him a parting gift

33. (A) Because Mike himself was planning to take a picture of the class
    (B) Because he doesn't like the woman
    (C) Because he has already bought something else
    (D) Because Mike is more fond of books

34. (A) Dictionaries published by different publishing houses
    (B) Hardbound editions of good dictionaries
    (C) Dictionaries not available in Italy
    (D) Different dictionaries serving various purposes

35. (A) She doesn't like it.
    (B) She agrees to it as dictionaries are always useful.
    (C) She does not understand what he said.
    (D) She is impressed by the man's greatness.

36. (A) They had a long day.
    (B) They should not attend the meeting.
    (C) There are some good restaurants around.
    (D) Food is an interesting subject.

37. (A) At home   (C) In a motel
    (B) In a hotel   (D) At her sister's

38. (A) Swiss restaurant across the street
    (B) French restaurant on Dublin Street
    (C) Italian restaurant around the corner
    (D) Oriental restaurant on the main street

39. (A) He has lived there all his life.
    (B) He is fond of good food.
    (C) He owns some of these restaurants.
    (D) He has friends working for these restaurants.

40. (A) On the main street
    (B) On Dublin Street
    (C) Two blocks away
    (D) Across the street

Part C

(WAIT)

41. (A) 1
    (B) 2
    (C) 3
    (D) 4

42. (A) Blood
    (B) Salt
    (C) Thalium
    (D) Water

43. (A) Respiratory
    (B) Digestive
    (C) Excretory
    (D) Circulatory

44. (A) Dry mouth
    (B) Concentration of salt
    (C) Fluid in blood stream
    (D) Rise in body temperature

45. (A) Hearts and veins
    (B) Lungs and trachea
    (C) Mouth and stomach
    (D) Liver and kidneys

46. (A) The distinct atmosphere of each section
    (B) Special sound effects
    (C) Flashing traffic lights
    (D) The extraordinary views of the zookeeper

47. (A) Because the zookeeper kept on giving commentary
     (B) Because there were cars running through the zoo
     (C) Because each section had a distinct atmosphere
     (D) Because there were animals from all over the world

48. (A) To keep the animals under control
     (B) To have music for the visitors
     (C) To provide the animals with special sound effects of their natural surround-
          ings
     (D) To record the conversations of the visitors

49. (A) Because if the animals weren't caged, the roads would look like jungles.
     (B) Because our roads are as dangerous for animals as dark jungles are for us.
     (C) Because there are so many accidents on roads every day.
     (D) Because roads pass through jungles.

50. (A) A lover of animals
     (B) A student of sound effects
     (C) An authority on jungles
     (D) A true friend

STOP

If time still remains, you may review work only in this section.
When the time allotted is up, you may go on to the next section.

Section 2:
STRUCTURE AND WRITTEN EXPRESSION

TIME: 25 Minutes
        40 Questions

DIRECTIONS: Questions 1-15 are incomplete sentences. Beneath each sentence are four words or phrases marked (A), (B), (C), and (D). Choose the **one** word or phrase which best completes the sentence. Then, on your answer sheet, find the number of the question and fill in the space that corresponds to the answer you have chosen.

1. *The Scarlet Letter* _____ a novel about a woman who commits adultery.
    (A) is
    (B) has been
    (C) to be
    (D) which is

2. It is important that all luggage _____ for identification, before being loaded into the aircraft.
    (A) to be labelled
    (B) must be labelled
    (C) should be labelled
    (D) be labelled

3. Metallic paints are used to paint bridges, _____.
    (A) isn't it?
    (B) isn't that so?
    (C) no?
    (D) aren't they?

4. The _____ purpose of the jury system is to allow people to participate in the judicial process, not to inconvenience citizens.
    (A) most
    (B) least
    (C) very
    (D) much

597

5. The _____ Neil Armstrong on the moon was a momentous event in the history of mankind.
   (A) first
   (B) walking
   (C) landing
   (D) landing of

6. _____ obtained by heating coal in the absence of air is known as coal gas.
   (A) A gas
   (B) A gas that
   (C) The gas that
   (D) The gas

7. The U.S. team to the first modern Olympics in 1896 reached the venue just in time for the games but performed much _____ than expected.
   (A) well
   (B) better
   (C) good
   (D) least

8. The Yellowstone National Park, in Wyoming, was started _____ in order to protect the natural wonders of that region.
   (A) during 1872
   (B) at 1872
   (C) in 1872
   (D) on 1872

9. It is not outdoor pollution, _____ indoor pollution that must be given more attention as people spend most of their time indoors.
   (A) on the contrary
   (B) actually
   (C) but
   (D) also

10. Early European settlers found that the Indians popped corn _____ of heating them on stones.
    (A) with
    (B) through
    (C) by
    (D) by means

11. _____ Adolf Meyer, the Swiss-American psychiatrist, who coined the term "mental hygiene."

    (A) It seems
    (B) It is
    (C) It is believed
    (D) It is said that

12. _____ we manage the environment better, there will not be adequate supplies of natural resources for future generations.

    (A) As long as
    (B) Not until
    (C) Till such time
    (D) Unless

13. One respect in which Disneyland _____ other amusement parks is in referring to its paying customers as guests.

    (A) is different
    (B) different from
    (C) differs from
    (D) more different

14. Thousands of years ago giraffes had much _____ necks than they have now.

    (A) short
    (B) shorter
    (C) less short
    (D) least short

15. Different libraries have different periods of time for which members may _____ books.

    (A) charge
    (B) lend
    (C) buy
    (D) borrow

DIRECTIONS: In questions 16-40 each sentence has four underlined words or phrases, marked (A), (B), (C), and (D). Choose the **one** word or phrase which is incorrect and must be changed to make the sentence correct. Then, on your answer sheet, find the number of the question and fill in the space that corresponds to the answer you have chosen.

16. Long ago, I gave up to try to learn swimming as I could not get over my fear
    (A)   (B) (C)   (D)
    of water.

17. Every year during autumn, careful gardeners have been removing certain plants
                                                        (A)
    to be potted and nurtured indoors till spring.
    (B)   (C)   (D)

18. Having children to accompany their parents to the supermarket is more educative
                    (A)   (B)   (C)
    than trying to teach them directly.
    (D)

19. Sondheim's musical "Into the Woods" explores what ought happen to some of the
    (A)   (B)
    famous fairy tale characters after they were happily married.
                (C)   (D)

20. Little Nicky wished that he could not have to get up so early in the morning, in
                            (A)   (B)   (C)
    winter, to go to school.
    (D)

21. The two competitors looked intensely at one other, each trying to gauge the
    (A)   (B) (C)
    other's strengths and weaknesses.
            (D)

22. Unlike modern clocks, most old-fashioned clocks need to wind manually
    (A)   (B)   (C)
    in order to show time.
    (D)

23. According to space scientists, astronauts will have to land on Mars in the year
                                        (A)   (B)
    2007, after a reconnaissance trip has been made by an unmanned ship.
                              (C)   (D)

24. A large amount of people have suddenly become interested in gardening as it
       (A)   (B)(C)
    provides a more purposeful exercise than workouts.
              (D)

25. William Taylor's coverage of the America's Cup Races in 1934 won to him the
                                           (A)   (B)   (C)
    first Pulitzer Prize given for sports writing.
                         (D)

26. We had fried chickens for dinner, after which we went to an ice cream parlor
                   (A)   (B) (C)
    for dessert.
    (D)

27. Only a little meals can be prepared without the use of fats.
         (A)   (B)   (C)   (D)

28. Of Cicely Tyson's powerful roles in "Roots" and "Sounder," one can't say which
       (A)   (B)
    one is better than the another.
    (C)   (D)

29. Citrine, which is a light yellow quartz, looks alike topaz but is softer than
                    (A)   (B) (C)   (D)
    true topaz.

30. A major source of indoor pollution is the combustion of fuels as kerosene, natural
          (A)   (B)(C)
    gas, and wood.
         (D)

31. When a space station <u>has been established</u>, then <u>it becomes</u> possible to go <u>very far</u>
    <u>out into</u> space.

32. An engineer tries to <u>exploit</u> natural resources to the maximum to <u>serve a particular</u>
    end, <u>so also</u> an ecologist tries <u>to preserve</u> the ecosystem.

33. In 1962, Kennedy <u>said that</u> the nation should <u>aspire to land a man on the moon</u>
    <u>by the end</u> of <u>this decade</u>.

34. <u>Seemingly</u> <u>that</u> the American Library Association <u>is</u> <u>the oldest</u> and largest library
    <u>association</u> in the world.

35. I <u>could rather</u> have a good <u>night's sleep</u> than watch a movie, however good, <u>if it is</u>
    <u>late</u> in the night.

36. <u>Despite</u> of <u>the absence</u> of specific rules for the purpose, an experienced <u>player</u>
    <u>knows</u> how to get out of dangerous situations in a game.

37. Due to an awakening of interest in nutritious food, it is easier <u>to come at</u> a <u>variety</u>
    <u>fruits</u> and vegetables now than it used to be.

38. Some children with <u>an</u> attention deficit disorder find it difficult to concentrate
    on <u>their</u> work or <u>set</u> for <u>long periods</u> at their desks.

602

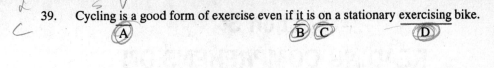

39.   Cycling is a good form of exercise even if it is on a stationary exercising bike.
           A   B C   D

40.   With judicious planning, TV watching can be controlled so as, instead of
               A   B   C   D
       passive watchers, we become intelligent viewers.

STOP

If time still remains, you may review work only in this section.
When the time allotted is up, you may go on to the next section.

Section 3:
READING COMPREHENSION
AND VOCABULARY

TIME: 55 Minutes
60 Questions

DIRECTIONS: In this section you will read several passages. Each one is followed by several questions about it. You are to choose the best answer to each question, marked (A), (B), (C), and (D). Then, on your answer sheet, find the number of the question and fill in the space that corresponds to the answer you have chosen.

Questions 1 to 10 refer to the following passage:

1 In the late 1980s, the American Speech-Language-Hearing Association estimated that about five percent of the population of the United States suffered from some form of speech or language disorder. It is believed that the incidence of speech disorders follows similar patterns among other Western nations. Speech problems develop from a variety of causes.
5 These may include physical injury or abnormality, disease, or emotional or psychological problems.

Speech-language pathologists generally define children as disordered if they lag significantly behind their age peers in reaching certain speech and language milestones. The importance of this lag is determined by a thorough professional examination. British studies
10 show that the normal range for early language acquisition is enormous. Most normal children speak their first word at anywhere from 6 to 18 months, and combine words into phrases for the first time at anywhere from 10 to 24 months. It takes a skilled practitioner to distinguish between a slow child who will eventually catch up and a child with a true delay.

1. According to the passage, which of the following is NOT a cause of speech problems?
    (A) Physical injury
    (B) Disease
    (C) Emotional problems
    (D) Nutritional deficiency

2. In line 12, the word "practitioner" means
    (A) professional.   (C) trainer.
    (B) doctor.   (D) laborer.

3. According to the passage, a speech pathologist would most likely be concerned if a child had not spoken his first word by which of the following ages?

    (A)   six months   (C)   two years
    (B)   one year   (D)   eight months

4. According to the passage, which of the following is true about language acquisition?

    (A)   Most children learn to speak and form words at roughly the same age.
    (B)   A child who has not spoken his first word by the age of six months is most likely disordered.
    (C)   Most children begin to combine words into phrases by the age of eight months.
    (D)   The normal range for language acquisition can vary widely among children.

5. In line 10, "enormous" means

    (A)   outrageous.   (C)   bloated.
    (B)   vast.   (D)   tiny.

6. Which of the following would be the BEST title for this passage?

    (A)   "Adolescent Speech Disorders"
    (B)   "A Cure for Speech Disorders"
    (C)   "The Early Detection of Speech Disorders"
    (D)   "The Role of Nutrition in Preventing Speech Disorders"

7. According to the passage, which of the following is true about the incidence of speech and language disorders worldwide

    (A)   Approximately 10 percent of the population worldwide suffers from a speech or language disorder.
    (B)   The rate of speech and language disorder is significantly higher in the U.S. than in other Western nations.
    (C)   The U.S. has the lowest incidence of speech and language disorders among Western nations.
    (D)   The incidence of speech and language disorders is around five percent for the U.S. and other Western nations.

8. The inherent implication of this passage is that

    (A)   only a skilled speech-language pathologist should be consulted about matters of speech and language.
    (B)   there is no difference between a slow child and a truly language-delayed child.

(C)   ranges in language development are so close only a pathologist can see the differences.

(D)   examinations do not necessarily show differences.

9.   The word "significantly" as it is used in line 8 means

(A)   not enough to worry about.

(B)   a great deal.

(C)   too much to measure quantitatively.

(D)   more than one month below normal.

10.   The pattern of growth in language, as stated in this passage, is

(A)   babbling to silence.

(B)   silence to syllables.

(C)   silence to some sound.

(D)   words to phrases.

Questions 11 to 20 refer to the following passage:

1   The most common nutritional deficiency in the world caused by a chronic lack of protein in the diet is kwashiorkor. Originally identified in Ghana in 1960, kwashiorkor is now known to be rampant in most developing nations. Children with this disease suffer severe growth retardation, vulnerability to illness, swelling of the abdomen with water, and marked 5   apathy. Kwashiorkor patients lose so much responsiveness to events around them that the treated youngster who eventually smiles is considered to be on the road to recovery.

11.   The word "apathy" in line 5 means

(A)   disinterest.

(B)   hyperactivity.

(C)   concern.

(D)   regard.

12.   Which of the following is the main cause of kwashiorkor?

(A)   High-fat diets

(B)   Lack of vitamin C

(C)   Chronic lack of protein

(D)   Unsanitary living conditions

13.   In line 6, "recovery" means

(A)   renewal.   (C)   retrieval.

(B)   improvement.   (D)   restoration.

14. Which of the following would be the BEST title for this passage?
    - (A) "The Kwashiorkor Epidemic in Ghana"
    - (B) "A Solution to Kwashiorkor"
    - (C) "Kwashiorkor: Its Cause and Its Symptoms"
    - (D) "Nutritional Deficiencies in Developed Nations"

15. Which of these discussions would best follow this paragraph?
    - (A) How kwashiorkor was discovered
    - (B) A history of nutritional deficiencies
    - (C) Current research into kwashiorkor
    - (D) Long-term treatment of kwashiorkor patients

16. The word "chronic" in line 1 means
    - (A) prolonged.
    - (B) immediate.
    - (C) habitual.
    - (D) gradual.

17. One inference that can be drawn from this passage is that
    - (A) starvation happens only in developing nations.
    - (B) established nations are not sending enough protein to developing nations.
    - (C) kwashiorkor has been well-known since the beginning of this century.
    - (D) most developing nations do not have enough protein sources to feed their populations.

18. The word "rampant" in line 3 means
    - (A) widespread
    - (B) not throughout any given population
    - (C) just in children
    - (D) just in adults

19. Which of the following is not a stated symptom of kwashiorkor?
    - (A) Severe growth retardation
    - (B) Depressed ability to fight disease
    - (C) Apathy
    - (D) Red blotches

20. The main idea of this passage is that
    - (A) kwashiorkor is a disease of malnutrition with observable causes, symptoms, and cures.
    - (B) kwashiorkor should be a United Nations problem.

(C)   kwashiorkor is killing off large populations.

(D)   kwashiorkor is destroying Ghana's future.

Questions 21 to 30 refer to the following passage:

1   Humans have long been studying the flight of birds and trying to imitate it. Not until
the twentieth century did engineers fully understand the principles of flight that birds have
been using for millions of years.

        Birds are adapted in their body structure, as no other creatures, to life in the air. Their
5   wings, tails, hollow bones, and internal air sacs all contribute to this great faculty. These
adaptations make it possible for birds to seek out environments most favorable to their needs
at different times of the year. This results in the marvelous phenomenon we know as
migration—the regular, seasonal movement of entire populations of birds from one geographic location to another.

10   Each year with great regularity most species of birds return to their summer homes,
court and choose mates, build their nests, lay eggs, and rear their young. In the late summer
and fall they acquire their new plumage. Then they join with others of their kind in large and
small flocks, feeding and storing up fat in their bodies. Thus they prepare for the hardships
of winter, whether they remain in the cold northlands or make the strenuous journey to the
15   south.

21. ' Which of the following is NOT an activity of birds in the summer?
       (A)   Building nests
       (B)   Laying eggs
       (C)   Traveling southward
       (D)   Choosing mates

22.   In line 7, "phenomenon" most nearly means
       (A)   miracle.   (C)   celebration.
       (B)   event.   (D)   milestone.

23.   The BEST title for this passage would be
       (A)   "The Migration of the Hummingbird."
       (B)   "How Birds Fly."
       (C)   "The Annual Migration of Birds."
       (D)   "Courting and Mating Rituals of Birds."

24.   Which of the following is implied by the passage?
       (A)   Because birds have not properly adapted to changes in climate, they are
              forced to endure cold winters.
       (B)   Each individual bird has its own pattern of migration.

608

    (C)   The migration of birds is a "social" undertaking.

    (D)   All birds fly south for the winter.

25.   Which of the following would best follow this passage?

    (A)   A specific discussion of migratory flight patterns

    (B)   A description of how birds fly

    (C)   A discussion of when birds return to their summer homes

    (D)   A discussion of birds' feeding patterns

26.   The word "faculty" In line 5 most nearly means

    (A)   strength.   (C)   endowment.

    (B)   knack.   (D)   ability.

27.   The word "adaptations" in this passage refers to

    (A)   coloration.

    (B)   size.

    (C)   physical properties of the bird.

    (D)   reproductive practices.

28.   The main idea of this passage is that

    (A)   birds are built the same as other creatures.

    (B)   birds are built to fly.

    (C)   birds need to migrate to survive.

    (D)   birds need to be told when to migrate.

29.   The phrase "for birds to seek out environments" means that

    (A)   birds stay in the same place year-round.

    (B)   migration is a function of bird keepers.

    (C)   birds travel where and when they feel the need to do so.

    (D)   birds prefer only one geographic zone all year.

30.   Which adaptation is NOT a stated help to flight?

    (A)   Internal air sacs

    (B)   Hollow bones

    (C)   Tails

    (D)   Coloration

Questions 31 to 40 refer to the following passage:

1   Each child has his individual pattern of social, as well as physical, development. Some of it depends on his home life and his relationships with the people who love him. Children in large families learn how to get along with others through normal brother-sister play and tussles. An only child, on the other hand, may have to learn his lessons in social living through
5 hard experiences on the playground or in the classroom. Twins who always have one another to lean on may be slow in responding to others because they do not need anyone else.

A child who is constantly scolded and made to feel he does everything wrong may have a difficult time developing socially. He may be so afraid of displeasing the adults around him that he keeps to himself (where he can't get into trouble), or he may take the opposite route
10 and go out of his way to create trouble. Like the isolated child, he too may return to infantile pleasures, developing habits that will satisfy him, but create barriers toward social contact.

31. The passage implies that which of the following may have the easiest time learning to get along with others?
(A) An only child
(B) A child from a large family
(C) Twins
(D) Children who are continually scolded

32. In line 10, "infantile" most nearly means
(A) undeveloped.   (C) childish.
(B) idle.   (D) babyish.

33. Which of the following would be the BEST title for this passage?
(A) "The Social Development of the Only Child"
(B) "Physical Development of Children"
(C) "The Role of Family Structure in the Social Development of Children"
(D) "Early Social Development: A Case Study"

34. Which of the following is implied by the passage?
(A) Excessive scolding of children may impede their social development
(B) Children who are constantly scolded develop alternative methods for social development.
(C) Isolated children often exhibit quicker social development.
(D) All children develop socially in identical ways.

35. In line 11, "barriers" most nearly means
(A) boundaries.   (C) obstacles.
(B) passages.   (D) paths.

36. The main idea in this passage is that
    (A) twins are slower in developing than single children.
    (B) only children take longer to develop.
    (C) children develop socially, physically, and developmentally according to an individual pattern.
    (D) secure children take longer to develop.

37. The social development of a child can be affected by
    (A) habits.
    (B) infantile pleasures.
    (C) patterns.
    (D) the number of siblings.

38. One inference that can be drawn from this passage is that
    (A) continual scolding is not harmful to the child.
    (B) continual scolding inhibits healthy social development.
    (C) continual scolding does not affect physical development.
    (D) continual scolding has adverse effects on the disciplinarian.

39. Where does the passage say the only child learns his social lessons?
    (A) Home and school
    (B) Playground and classroom
    (C) Playground and home
    (D) All of the above

40. Home life and people who live with the child affect his development
    (A) partially.
    (B) at no time.
    (C) totally.
    (D) in no noticeable ways.

Questions 41 to 50 refer to the following passage:

1   Accidents seldom "just happen," and many can be prevented. Accidental injuries become more frequent and serious in later life. Thus, attention to safety is especially important for older persons.

    Several factors make people in this age group prone to accidents. Poor eyesight and
5 hearing can decrease awareness of hazards. Arthritis, neurological diseases, and impaired coordination and balance can make older people unsteady.

    Various diseases and medications, alcohol, and preoccupation with personal problems can result in drowsiness, distraction, or poor physical conditioning.

When accidents occur, older persons are especially vulnerable to severe injury and
10 tend to heal slowly. Particularly in women, the bones often become thin and brittle with age,
causing seemingly minor falls to result in broken bones.

Many accidents can be prevented by maintaining mental and physical health and
conditioning, and by cultivating good safety habits.

41. The word "cultivating," as used in line 13, means
    (A) discontinuing.   (C) disrupting.
    (B) beginning.   (D) encouraging.

42. In old age, women often appear more accident prone, because
    (A) women are always more accident prone than men.
    (B) women suffer the most marked decrease in eyesight.
    (C) women's bones often become thin and brittle with age, causing more fre-
         quent instances of broken bones and fractures.
    (D) women are generally more clumsy than men.

43. According to the passage, which of the following would NOT help elderly people
    prevent accidents?
    (A) Maintaining physical health
    (B) Maintaining mental health
    (C) Cultivating good safety habits
    (D) Entering a nursing home

44. Poor eyesight and hearing in the elderly can decrease awareness of
    (A) hazards.
    (B) injury.
    (C) drowsiness.
    (D) arthritis.

45. The underlying assumption in this passage is that
    (A) young people have more accidents than other groups.
    (B) infants are the most accident prone.
    (C) accidents happen equally to all age groups.
    (D) old age brings more propensity to accidents.

46. "Just happen" refers to
    (A) by chance.
    (B) by being a victim.

(C) with cause.

(D) with warning.

47. Accident prone is a condition not brought about by which of the following?

(A) Arthritis

(B) Neurological diseases

(C) Poor eyesight and hearing

(D) Wealth

48. "Vulnerability" in this passage refers to the elderly population's

(A) unconquerability.

(B) susceptibility.

(C) invincibility.

(D) indestructibility.

49. Which physical problem is not mentioned as a cause of unsteadiness in the elderly?

(A) Neurological diseases

(B) High blood pressure

(C) Arthritis

(D) Coordination problems

50. Drowsiness or distraction, which can cause accidents, can frequently be caused by any of the following factors EXCEPT

(A) medications.

(B) alcohol.

(C) too much TV viewing.

(D) preoccupation with personal problems.

Questions 51 to 60 refer to the following passage:

1   Cacti and other succulent plants originate in areas where water is available only occasionally, and therefore are conditioned to deal with long periods of drought. They possess structural modifications enabling them to store moisture for use in times of scarcity. The storage areas include thickened leaves and stems. Leaves, which transpire precious
5 moisture, may be eliminated altogether (with the stem taking over the process of photosynthesis), or the moisture in the leaves may be protected by a leathery surface or covered with wiry or velvety hairs, thick spines, or even a powdery coating.

Cacti grow chiefly in the arid regions of the southwestern United States, Mexico, Central America, and southern South America. Many curious and beautiful varieties are
10 prized as houseplants. As a consequence many rare species have been overcollected and about 20 face extinction.

51. According to the passage, which of the following factors has led to some species of cacti facing extinction?
    (A) Long-term droughts in the Southwest
    (B) The use of some cacti as houseplants
    (C) An inability of cacti to adapt to changing weather conditions
    (D) The overcollection of cacti for food

52. According to the passage, which of the following is NOT an area where cacti usually grow?
    (A) Southwestern U.S.
    (B) Mexico
    (C) Australia
    (D) Southern South America

53. In line 8, "arid" means
    (A) a very dry climate.
    (B) a desolate area.
    (C) extremely hot.
    (D) a rainy climate.

54. From this passage, it can be assumed that photosynthesis
    (A) requires leaves.
    (B) is not necessary to the cactus' survival.
    (C) occurs only in the rainy season, not in the dry season.
    (D) can be carried out by more than one part of the plant.

55. In line 4, "transpire" means
    (A) collect.   (C) expel.
    (B) create.   (D) absorb.

56. From this passage, it can be assumed that cacti
    (A) grow near deep rivers.
    (B) grow in areas of high rainfall.
    (C) grow only in captivity.
    (D) grow where it rains occasionally.

57. What kind of coverings do cacti have to retain moisture?
    (A) Transparent tissue
    (B) Thick spines and velvety hairs

(C)   Grainy coating
(D)   Leaves and stems

58.   Why do cacti store moisture?
(A)   To water other cacti
(B)   For use when it is very rainy
(C)   For use during dry seasons
(D)   To keep stems and leaves thick

59.   A drought is
(A)   an exceptionally cold season.
(B)   an exceptionally wet season.
(C)   an exceptionally cloudy season.
(D)   an exceptionally dry season.

60.   In line 1, "succulent" means
(A)   dry.
(B)   water-retaining.
(C)   water-releasing.
(D)   leaf-transpiring.

STOP

If time still remains, you may review your work only in this section.

TEST 6

ANSWER KEY

SECTION 1: LISTENING COMPREHENSION

1.	(D)	14.	(A)	26.	(C)	39.	(B)
2.	(D)	15.	(B)	27.	(B)	40.	(B)
3.	(B)	16.	(C)	28.	(D)	41.	(C)
4.	(D)	17.	(D)	29.	(D)	42.	(B)
5.	(B)	18.	(C)	30.	(A)	43.	(D)
6.	(D)	19.	(C)	31.	(B)	44.	(A)
7.	(A)	20.	(A)	32.	(D)	45.	(C)
8.	(C)	21.	(D)	33.	(A)	46.	(D)
9.	(A)	22.	(D)	34.	(D)	47.	(C)
10.	(C)	23.	(B)	35.	(B)	48.	(C)
11.	(D)	24.	(A)	36.	(A)	49.	(B)
12.	(B)	25.	(D)	37.	(C)	50.	(A)
13.	(C)			38.	(D)		

SECTION 2: STRUCTURE AND WRITTEN EXPRESSION

1.	(A)	11.	(B)	21.	(C)	31.	(B)
2.	(D)	12.	(D)	22.	(C)	32.	(C)
3.	(D)	13.	(C)	23.	(A)	33.	(D)
4.	(C)	14.	(B)	24.	(A)	34.	(A)
5.	(D)	15.	(D)	25.	(C)	35.	(A)
6.	(D)	16.	(A)	26.	(A)	36.	(A)
7.	(B)	17.	(A)	27.	(A)	37.	(C)
8.	(C)	18.	(A)	28.	(D)	38.	(C)
9.	(C)	19.	(B)	29.	(C)	39.	(D)
10.	(D)	20.	(A)	30.	(C)	40.	(C)

SECTION 3: READING COMPREHENSION AND VOCABULARY

1.	(D)	16.	(A)	31.	(B)	46.	(A)
2.	(A)	17.	(D)	32.	(D)	47.	(D)
3.	(C)	18.	(A)	33.	(C)	48.	(B)
4.	(D)	19.	(D)	34.	(A)	49.	(B)
5.	(B)	20.	(A)	35.	(C)	50.	(C)
6.	(C)	21.	(C)	36.	(C)	51.	(B)
7.	(D)	22.	(B)	37.	(D)	52.	(C)
8.	(A)	23.	(C)	38.	(B)	53.	(A)
9.	(B)	24.	(C)	39.	(B)	54.	(D)
10.	(D)	25.	(A)	40.	(A)	55.	(C)
11.	(A)	26.	(D)	41.	(D)	56.	(D)
12.	(C)	27.	(C)	42.	(C)	57.	(B)
13.	(B)	28.	(B)	43.	(D)	58.	(C)
14.	(C)	29.	(C)	44.	(A)	59.	(D)
15.	(D)	30.	(D)	45.	(D)	60.	(B)

Detailed Explanations
of Answers

TEST 6

Section 1:
LISTENING COMPREHENSION

Part A

1. **(D)** The question asks, "What does the woman think of the song?" The correct answer is (D)—She has heard the song too much. The woman says, "Don't you think they play it too much on the radio?"

2. **(D)** The question asks, "Who will most likely buy the birthday present?" The correct response is (D)—Erik. The woman says, "Tomorrow is Melisa's birthday and I still have not bought her a present yet." The man says, "Erik said that he was going to take care of Melisa's birthday present this year, so don't worry about it."

3. **(B)** The question asks, "What will they do for lunch?" The correct response is (B)—They will eat later when they are more hungry. The man asks, "Do you want me to make lunch now?" The woman replies, "I'm not hungry right now. Maybe later, okay?"

4. **(D)** The question asks, "What will they probably do for the cut?" The correct response is (D)—Bandage it. The woman asks, "Doctor, do you think this cut will require stitches?" The man responds, "Well, actually, all it requires is a good bandage."

5. **(B)** The question asks, "What does the man mean?" The correct answer is (B)—Missing little things when packing is a common occurrence. The woman states, "I thought I was through packing everything, but I keep finding little things that I have missed." The man replies, "Stuff like that always happens."

6. **(D)** The question asks, "How many hours will the man have to wait if he it at the end of the repairman's list?" The correct answer is (D)—Five. The woman says, "He could be at your house as early as 10:00 a.m. However, if you are at the end of his list, he will not arrive there until 3:00 p.m. You should wait at home the entire time, though."

7. **(A)** The question asks, "Why is the woman angry?" The correct answer is (A)—The man did not wash the dishes. The woman says, "You were supposed to have washed the dishes by the time I got home from the meeting."

8. **(C)** The question asks, "What does the woman want to do?" The correct answer is (C)—Go out in the sailboat if the weather is nice. The woman said, "If the weather is nice tomorrow, I was hoping to go out in the sailboat…"

9. **(A)** The question asks, "How many days late was the man's newspaper article?" The correct answer is (A)—"Three." When the man handed in his newspaper article, the woman said, "Thank you. But unfortunately, it's too late. Your deadline for that article was Tuesday. Today is Friday." Friday is three days later than Tuesday.

10. **(C)** The question asks, "What does the man mean?" The correct response is (C)—he has had his fortune told, but thinks it is worthless to do so. The woman said, "I had my palm read by the fortune teller on the boardwalk. Have you ever done that?" The man replied, "Yes, but I think that is a complete waste of time and money."

11. **(D)** The question asks, "What does the man mean?" The correct answer is (D)—It's not time yet to look for summer clothes. When the woman said, "I am going to look for some winter clothes this weekend," the man asked, "Don't you think it's a little too early for that?" The question was asked only to suggest that it is really early to look for winter clothes.

12. **(B)** The question asks, "At what time is Ms. White expected?" The correct answer is (B)—Three o'clock. The woman said, "It's quarter to three. Do you think I should start arranging the table?" The man answered, "Yes. Ms. White should be here in 15 minutes. She is known for her punctuality." The conversation took place at quarter to three, and if Ms. White is punctual and is expected to arrive in 15 minutes, that time would be three o'clock.

13. **(C)** The question asks, "How many buses will the man ride to get to the museum?" The correct answer is (C)—Three. The woman said, "You will have to change

twice. Once at the zoo and then near the courthouse." It means the man will take the first bus to the zoo, the second bus from the zoo to the courthouse, and the third bus from near the courthouse to the museum.

14. **(A)** The question asks, "What does the woman need?" The correct answer is (A)—It is not surprising that Tim was happy. The man said, "Tim got a really good raise in his salary." The woman responded, "No wonder he looked so happy." "No wonder" means it is not surprising.

15. **(B)** The question asks, "What is the man's opinion about Peter?" The correct answer is (B)—He talks nonstop. The man said, "...I think he is a chatterbox." "Chatterbox" means a person who talks nonstop.

16. **(C)** The question asks, "Who is the woman's favorite teacher?" The correct answer is (C)—Dr. Jones. When the man asked, "Why didn't you take the criticism course this semester?", the woman answered, "I would have taken it if Dr. Jones was teaching it, but since it is Dr. Sampson I decided to skip it." It is obvious that the woman likes Dr. Jones better as a teacher.

17. **(D)** The question asks, "What would the woman like to have?" The correct answer is (D)—French onion soup. When the man asked, "Would you like to have some tomato or mushroom soup?", the woman answered, "I would rather have some French onion soup."

18. **(C)** The question asks, "Where are these people?" The correct answer is (C)—In a movie theater. When the woman asked, "Do you see any empty seats?", the man said, "The theater is packed. This is an award winning movie." It means that they are in a movie theater.

19. **(C)** The question asks, "What does the woman mean?" The correct answer is (C)—She does not have time at the moment but she can talk tomorrow. When the man asked, "Can I talk to you for a few minutes?", the woman answered, "I am in a rush right now. Is it O.K. if we talk tomorrow?" "To be in a rush" means "to be in a hurry." She does not have time right now as she is in a hurry.

20. **(A)** The question asks, "What does the man think about Rick?" The correct answer is (A)—He has an unfriendly attitude. When the woman asked, "Why is Rick so unpopular in this office?", the man answered, "It's his attitude. He never talks to anyone in a friendly manner."

21. **(D)**   The question asks, "What does the woman mean?" The correct answer is (D)—It would be nice to take a break. When the man suggested, "How about taking a break after we finish reading this article?", the woman responded, "Not a bad idea." She was referring to taking a break and not to the article or the work.

22. **(D)**   The question asks, "What are these people doing?" The correct answer is (D)—Working on a computer. When the woman asked, "Do you know the format to pull up files?…," the man said, "Let me try. My computer is programmed a little bit differently." Apparently, they were working on a computer.

23. **(B)**   The question asks, "What does the woman mean?" The correct answer is (B)—Her mother and her aunt made better pies than this. When the man complimented the woman on the pie, the woman said, "Thanks. But still it can't beat my mother's or my aunt's." It means that it does not compare to her mother's or aunt's pie.

24. **(A)**   The question asks, "Where will these people stop first?" The correct answer is (A)—The bank. When the woman asked the man if he could give her a ride, the man answered, "I don't mind. But I am stopping first at the bank and then at the post office. Is that a problem?" The woman said, "Not at all." So, they will first stop at the bank.

25. **(D)**   The question asks, "What does the man mean?" The correct answer is (D)—Gary had to sell the house to pay his debts. When the woman expressed her surprise that Gary had sold his house, the man said, "He had no choice. He had to do it to pay his debts." What he meant was Gary had no other alternative.

Part B

26. **(C)**   The question asks, "Who was coming to visit the man?" The correct response is (C)—His parents. The man says, "I just received a letter from my mother. She and my father are planning on taking a trip to visit me." His mother and father are his parents. Choice (A) "His siblings" would be brothers and sisters. Choice (B) "His cousins" would be the children of his aunts and uncles. Choice (D) "his grandparents" would be the parents of his parents.

27. **(B)**   The question asks, "Which classes is the man going to miss?" The correct response is (B)—Evening. The man told the woman, "I am only going to be taking off from my night classes."Another word for "night" is "evening." Choice (A) "Weekend" is normally considered to be Saturday and Sunday. Choice (C) "Afternoon" is considered to

be the time during the middle of the day. Choice (D) "Morning" is the opposite of evening and is the time of day when most people are waking up.

28. **(D)**   The question asks, "Where did the woman go?" The correct response is (D)—Studio tour. She says, I went on the studio tour." The other choices are places that the man plans on having his parents go.

29. **(D)**   The question asks, "What does the tour cover?" The correct answer is (D) — Only famous movies. The man asks, "Did the tour just cover things from new movies?" The woman responds, "No, they had a little bit on all their famous movies from the 1940s to the present."

30. **(A)**   The question asks, "Where did this conversation probably take place?" The correct response is (A)—At school. This question requires the listener to make a conclusion based on given facts. Of the four choices, choice (A) "At school" is the best response because the man refers to his classes and his professors while talking to the woman. Although any of the three other choices could be correct, there are no hints given that the two people are at any of these places.

31. **(B)**   The question asks, "Why does Mike have to go back to Italy?" The correct answer is (B)—He was here only for studies; so legally, he cannot stay any longer. In the conversation the woman said, "…I thought he was looking for a job." The man said, "No. He was here only for studies. He has to go back now. His visa expires soon."

32. **(D)**   The question asks, "What are these people planning for Mike?" The correct answer is (D)—Give him a parting gift. During the conversation the man said, "…We were thinking of giving him a gift to remember us by. Would you like to contribute?" The woman answered, "Sure…."

33. **(A)**   The question asks, "Why didn't the man accept the suggestion of giving Mike a picture of their class?" The correct answer is (A)—Because Mike himself was planning to take a picture of the class. When the woman suggested, "How about a framed picture of our whole class?", the man said, "Mike mentioned the other day that he himself is going to take one next week."

34. **(D)**   The question asks, "What does the man mean by a set of dictionaries?" The correct answer is (D)—Different dictionaries serving various purposes. When the woman asked, "What do you mean by a set?", the man explained, "Like one regular, another for usage, one from English to Italian, and one from Italian to English."

35. **(B)** The question asks, "What is the woman's response to the man's suggestion?" The correct answer is (B)—She agrees to it as dictionaries are always useful. When the man explained what he meant by a "set of dictionaries," the woman exclaimed, "That sounds great! He can use them and remember us for his whole life."

36. **(A)** The question asks, "On what point do these people agree?" The correct answer is (A)—They had a long day. In the beginning of the conversation the woman said, "After this meeting I am not staying here for a minute. The day has dragged. It was too much work." The man responded, "I agree. I also want to get this meeting over with...." "The day had dragged" means they had a lot of work.

37. **(C)** The question asks, "Where is the woman staying?" The correct answer is (C)—A hotel. During the conversation the man mentioned, "...There is an excellent French restaurant on Dublin Street by your hotel..." This means that the woman is staying in a hotel.

38. **(D)** The question asks, "What place would the man suggest if the woman liked spicy food?" The correct answer is (D)—Oriental restaurants on the main street. In the conversation the man mentioned, "...If you like spicy food, there are some really good Asian restaurants on the main street..."

39. **(B)** The question asks, "How does the man know about so many restaurants in the town?" The correct answer is (B)—He is fond of good food. When the woman said, "...You seem to know all of them (restaurants) by heart," the man answered, "Well, food is my favorite subject."

40. **(B)** The question asks, "Where is the good French restaurant?" The correct response is (B)—On Dublin Street. This is taken directly from the conversation. The Asian restaurants are located (A) on the main street. The Italian restaurant is located (C) two blocks away. The Swiss restaurant is located (D) across the street.

Part C

41. **(C)** The question asks, "How many mechanisms produce thirst?" The correct response is (C)—3. This is given in the first line of the paragraph. "Three primary mechanisms produce thirst."

42. **(B)** The question asks, "What causes the hypothalamus to trigger thirst?" The

correct response is (B)—Salt. This comes straight from the line, "First, when the concentration of salt cells in the body reaches a certain level, the hypothalamus is triggered to act in a way that results in the experience of thirst."

43. **(D)** The question asks, "A decrease in the fluid of which system also causes thirst?" The correct response is (D)—Circulatory. The answer to this question is in the line, "A decrease in the total volume of fluid in the circulatory system also causes the sense of thirst."

44. **(A)** The question asks, "What is not a cause of thirst?" The correct response is (A)—Dry mouth. This comes from the line, "The dry mouth that accompanies thirst is a symptom of the need for water but not the cause."

45. **(C)** The question asks, "Where is the water meter for water consumption located?" The correct response is (C)—Mouth and stomach. The answer to this question is in the last line of the reading. "The body does seem to have a kind of water meter in the mouth and stomach, however, that monitors the amount of water that has been consumed and immediately informs drinkers when they have had enough liquid to meet their needs.

46. **(D)** The question asks, "What made the speaker's visit to the zoo a unique experience?" The correct answer is (D)—The extraordinary views of the zookeeper. The first two sentences of the talk were, "Last week, I visited a zoo with a friend. It was a unique experience because the zookeeper there had extraordinary views about zookeeping."

47. **(C)** The question asks, "Why was the tour like moving from one continent to another?" The correct answer is (C)—Because each section had a distinct atmosphere. In the talk the speaker said, "We were surprised to see that each section had a distinct atmosphere. It was like moving from continent to continent."

48. **(C)** The question asks, "What was the purpose of microphones in the wall?" The correct answer is (C)—To provide the animals with special sound effects of their natural surroundings. In the talk the speaker said, "The zookeeper explained that they were trying their best to provide the animals with their natural surroundings. Not only did they have trees and plants brought from all over the world, but also they had speakers attached to walls in order to provide special sound effects to each animal."

49. **(B)** The question asks, "Why did the zookeeper refer to roads as jungles?" The correct answer is (B)—Because our roads are as dangerous for animals as dark jungles

are for us. When the speaker expressed surprise at the zookeeper's referring to the roads as jungles, he explained, "Our roads, with flashing traffic lights and rushing cars, are as frightening for them as the darkest jungles in the world are for us."

50. **(A)** The question asks, "How would you describe the zookeeper?" The correct answer is (A)—A lover of animals. In the talk the zookeeper showed concern for animals. This implies that he cares about their well-being.

Section 2:
STRUCTURE AND WRITTEN EXPRESSION

1.   **(A)**   (A) is the right answer; the finite verb completes the sentence. The story of a novel is for all time and therefore the simple present tense (covering past, present and future) is appropriate. (B) is a finite verb but the present perfect tense denotes a duration of time from past to present only. (C) An infinitive verb cannot complete the sentence. (D) introduces an adjectival subordinate clause not required here.

2.   **(D)**   (D) is the right answer. A subjunctive (obligation/need) in the active voice is expressed by an infinitive, without **to,** which functions as a finite verb; in the passive voice, the verb is **be + past participle.** The clause **all luggage be identified** is in the passive voice. (A) **To** is not required in the infinitive. (B) is a finite verb not agreeing with the main clause **it is important.** (C) is a finite verb not agreeing with the main clause.

3.   **(D)**   (D) is the right answer; **aren't** agrees with **are** in the main clause and **they** with **paints** in the main clause. (A) does not agree with the verb **are** in the main clause. (B) is not the right form for a tag question. (C) is not the right form for a tag question.

4.   **(C)**   (C) is the right answer; **very** is an intensifier adjective, emphasizing the noun **purpose.** (A) A degree of comparison is not required here. (B) A degree of comparison is not required here. (D) **Much** functions as an adjective or adverb of quantity and so is not required here.

5.   **(D)**   (D) is the right answer; the gerund **landing** is the subject of the sentence. (A) A numeral adjective cannot be the subject. (B) A present participle verb cannot be the subject. (C) A present participle verb cannot be the subject.

6.   **(D)**   (D) is the right answer; the definite article **the** is the right article as the gas has been specified later in the sentence. (A) The indefinite article is not right. (B) **That** introduces a clause that is not required here. (C) **That** introduces a clause that is not required here.

7.   **(B)**   (B) is the right answer; the comparative adverb is appropriate. There is a comparison between what was performed and what was expected. (A) The positive degree is not required. (C) The positive degree is not suitable. (D) The superlative degree is not suitable here.

8. **(C)** (C) is the right answer; **in** is used to denote a segment of time bigger than a **day,** such as a month or year. The implication is that the park was **started** at some point in time not specified here but in the year 1872. (A) denotes a stretch of time; **starting** happens at a particular point in time, not over a stretch of time. (B) **At** is used to denote a specific moment in time but a **year** is a large segment of time, so the two are incompatible. (D) **On** is used to locate an event in the time segment called **day.**

9. **(C)** (C) is the right answer; the conjunction **but** not only joins **indoor pollution** and **outdoor pollution** but also serves to contrast them. (A) denotes contrast but does not function as a conjunction. (B) is an adverbial modifier, not a conjunction. (D) **Also** is a conjunction that adds something to a statement and therefore is not suitable.

10. **(D)** (D) is the right answer; **by means** along with **of** in the sentence denotes how something is done. (A) **With** denotes an instrument used in an event. (B) **Through** denotes the means of doing something. (C) **By** denotes an agent responsible for the event.

11. **(B)** (B) is the right answer; the impersonal pronoun **it** anticipates the complement **Adolf Meyer. It is** completes the main clause **It is…psychiatrist.** (A) requires a subordinate clause; it will not complete the main clause **…psychiatrist.** (C) requires a subordinate clause; as is, it will not complete the main clause. (D) requires a subordinate clause; as is, it will not complete the main clause.

12. **(D)** (D) is the right answer. **Unless** is a conjunction of condition; **unless we** means **if we do not.** It joins the subordinate clause to the main clause. In this sentence the subordinate clause is at the beginning. (A) is a conjunction denoting a duration of time. (B) **Not until** negatively denotes a duration of time. (C) denotes a duration of time.

13. **(C)** (C) is the right answer; the finite verb **differs** contrasts **other parks** from **Disneyland.** (A) lacks the preposition **from** to complete the sentence. (B) lacks a finite verb to complete the sentence. (D) **Different** has no comparative form.

14. **(B)** (B) is the right answer; it is an adjective in the comparative degree, comparing two states of the giraffe's neck. (A) is an adjective in the positive degree; not appropriate here. (C) is not the right comparative form of **short.** (D) is not the right superlative form of **short,** nor is the superlative degree required here.

15. **(D)** (D) is the right answer; **borrow** means to get temporary possession of something. (A) **Charge** means to ask a price; the meaning is not appropriate to the sentence.

(B) **Lend** means to give possession of something for a limited time; the meaning is not appropriate to the sentence. (C) **Buy** is to pay a price for something to get possession of it, so it is not appropriate here.

16. **(A)**   (A) is the answer. The verb **give up** denotes ceasing to do something one has been doing over a period of time. The infinitive limits the action to a single point in time (implying a single act). The gerundial form **trying** implies a continuity. So the answer should be **trying**. (B) is a conjunction meaning **because** connecting the two clauses **Long ago...swimming** and **I could...water.** (C) The past tense of **can** is in agreement with **gave up.** (D) is the principal verb of the verb group **could not get over.**

17. **(A)**   (A) is the answer. An event/action repeated at intervals must be expressed in the simple present tense. Since the context implies an annual action, the answer should be **remove.** (B) indicates the purpose expressed in the passive. (C) is a past participle that parallels **potted.** (D) is an adverb of **place** modifying **potted** and **nurtured.**

18. **(A)**   (A) is the answer. The causative verb **have** must be followed by an action expressed in the plain infinitive (without **to**). The answer should be **accompany.** (B) is a preposition of directionality. (C) is the complement of the verb **is.** (D) The gerundial form parallels **having,** the two methods that are compared.

19. **(B)**   (B) is the answer. **Ought** must be followed by **to** but is still inappropriate here, as it denotes obligation. The answer should be **might have happened** as it denotes a past probability. (A) is the possessive form denoting a relationship with **musical.** (C) The plural form is in agreement with **they.** (D) is past tense to indicate a past event and has a plural verb in agreement with **characters.**

20. **(A)**   (A) is the answer. A wish contrary to fact must be expressed in the past tense. We know that **getting up early** is a fact from the adverb **so,** which denotes the degree to which something is being experienced. The answer should be **did not.** (B) is a preposition referring to one of the large segments of time a day is divided into. (C) **In** is used to denote month/year/seasons. (D) is a preposition of directionality.

21. **(C)**   (C) is the answer. **One other** is an irregular combination. The standard phrase is **each other** and **one another.** (A) The definite article is used to differentiate two competitors from others. (B) **At** denotes a specific point in space. (D) is a conjunction joining **strengths** and **weaknesses.**

22. **(C)** (C) is the answer. When the object of the verb **need** denotes repairs, improvements, and regular attention, it must be expressed in the gerundial form. The answer should be **to be wound.** (A) **Unlike** means **different from** and qualifies the compound noun **modern clocks.** (B) is an adjective of quantity qualifying **old-fashioned clocks.** (D) The phrase means **for the purpose of.**

23. **(A)** (A) is the answer. **Will have to land** expresses obligation and is therefore inappropriate here. The answer should be **will have landed,** (prediction). (B) is the preposition used for referring to **year.** (C) The perfect tense denotes that **trip** is completed before **landing:** events seen as past from a point in the future. (D) denotes the agent making the **trip.**

24. **(A)** (A) is the answer. **Amount** is an adjective of quantity and so cannot refer to count nouns (persons). The answer should be **a large number.** (B) is a conjunction meaning **because** connecting the clauses **a large…gardening** and **it provides….** (C) is a personal pronoun standing for **gardening.** (D) is a comparative determiner of **purposeful.**

25. **(C)** (C) is the answer. A preposition is not required to show the direction of the **prize.** The object of the verb **won** is automatically the receiver; the sentence should read "won him the first…" (A) is the preposition used for referring to **year.** (B) is a finite verb predicating **coverage.** (D) The preposition denotes the purpose of the **Prize.**

26. **(A)** (A) is the answer. The plural form of **chicken** is used only to denote the animal (a count noun). The meat of animals is a mass noun and cannot be pluralized. The answer should be **chicken.** (B) is a past tense verb agreeing with the past tense **had.** (C) is a preposition of directionality. (D) is a preposition denoting purpose.

27. **(A)** (A) is the answer. **Little** is an adjective of quantity. **Meals** being a count noun, the answer should be **only a few. Few** is a numeral adjective. (B) is a finite verb predicating **meals.** (C) is a preposition denoting a lack of something. (D) forms a noun phrase with **fats.**

28. **(D)** (D) is the answer. **Another** is a pronoun used to refer to an additional item of a class already mentioned. Therefore, **another** is inappropriate here. The answer should be **other** referring to the remaining item in a set (the two roles). (A) is a preposition of reference to a part of something. (B) is an indefinite pronoun referring to anyone. (C) is an indefinite pronoun standing for **any one** of two roles.

29. **(C)**   (C) is the answer. **Alike** is an adjective used predicatively (i.e., after a verb, e.g., citrine and quartz are alike). **Like** is an adjective used attributively, i.e., preceding a noun (topaz). So the answer should be **like.** (A) is a relative pronoun introducing an adjectival clause **which is a light yellow quartz.** (B) is a finite verb predicting **Citrine.** (D) is a comparative adjective qualifying **Citrine.**

30. **(C)**   (C) is the answer. **As** is a conjunction meaning **because** and is therefore inappropriate here. The answer should be **such as** which means **for example.** (A) is the subject of the verb **is.** (B) is the complement of the verb **is.** (D) is a conjunction connecting **gas** and **wood.**

31. **(B)**   (B) is the answer. The simple present tense denotes a habitual or existing scientific fact but the space station is not ready yet. Therefore, **it becomes** is inappropriate. The answer should be **will become.** (A) The perfect tense locates the event at a point in time before another event in the future. (C) is an adjective intensifying the adverb **far.** (D) is a preposition of direction towards a three-dimensional or large location.

32. **(C)**   (C) is the answer. **So also** denotes agreement but the context implies a contrast of two events taking place over a stretch of time as expressed by the simple present tense. The answer should be **while** because it denotes two events happening simultaneously. (A) is a finite verb predicating **engineer.** (B) is the infinitive of purpose. (D) is a finite verb paralleling **tries to exploit.**

33. **(D)**   (D) is the answer. **This** refers to something nearby. In this context **decade** refers to the **sixties** and so the answer should be **that decade.** (A) The past tense is in agreement with **1962.** (B) A preposition (denoting surface) and definite article (denoting one of its kind) are appropriate. (C) is a preposition meaning **not larger than.**

34. **(A)**   (A) is the answer. **Seemingly** is an adverb and cannot precede **that** which introduces a subordinate clause in this sentence. There must be a main clause before **that,** so the answer is **it seems.** (B) is a definite article to refer to only one of its kind. (C) is a finite verb of the clause **the American....** (D) is the superlative degree paralleling **largest.**

35. **(A)**   (A) is the answer. **Could** expresses ability and **rather** expresses preference. So the two are incompatible. The answer should be **would** which expresses desire/wish. (B) is the possessive form showing a relationship with **sleep.** (C) is a personal pronoun standing for **movie.** (D) is a preposition used to refer to a large segment of time.

36. **(A)** (A) is the answer. **Despite** does not require the preposition **of. In spite** requires the preposition **of.** So the answer should be **despite** or **in spite of.** (B) is denoting what is not present. (C) is the right form of the indefinite article before a noun beginning with a vowel sound. (D) is a finite verb predicating **player.**

37. **(C)** (C) is the answer. **Come at** means to arrive at something and so is inappropriate here. The answer should be **to come by.** The prepositional idiom **to come by** means **to obtain.** (A) is an adjective qualifying **food.** (B) is a comparative adjective qualifying a period of time (now). (D) is a conjunction connecting **fruits** and **vegetables.**

38. **(C)** (C) is the answer. **Set** is not the appropriate verb here because it means **to arrange** or **to put** something somewhere. The answer should be **sit.** (A) is the appropriate form of the indefinite article **a** as it precedes a noun beginning with a vowel sound. (B) **On** relates **attention** to **work.** Scheduled activities like studying and tests are denoted by **on.** The possessive adjective **their** qualifies **work.** (D) is a preposition denoting a specific location.

39. **(D)** (D) is the answer. The present participle preceding a noun makes the noun the actor of the action denoted by the present participle. The bike does not do the exercise but is used for exercise. So the answer should be **exercise bike** (a compound noun). (A) is a finite verb predicating the subject **cycling.** (B) is the personal pronoun **it** standing for **cycling.** (C) is the appropriate preposition to denote a surface (the seat of a bike).

40. **(C)** (C) is the answer. **Such as** means **for example. Such that** means **with the result that.** The answer should be **such that.** (A) is a preposition meaning **by means of.** (B) is the subject of the verb **can be controlled.** (D) The phrase means **in the place of.**

Section 3:
READING COMPREHENSION
AND VOCABULARY

1.   **(D)**   The last sentence of the first paragraph lists several causes of speech pathology. Nutritional deficiency (D) is not among them.

2.   **(A)**   A professional is an individual trained in a specific area. In this case, the "practitioner" is someone trained in the field of speech pathology. Although this person may be a doctor (B), the term is too specific for the context of this sentence. The other two choices, (C) and (D), do not make sense here.

3.   **(C)**   The passage indicates that studies show most children speak their first word anywhere from 6 to 18 months. Therefore, a child at two years who had not yet spoken his first word would be cause for concern.

4.   **(D)**   The passage states the following: "British studies show that the normal range for early language acquisition is enormous." This clearly makes choice (D) the correct answer. The other choices are contradictory to facts stated in the passage.

5.   **(B)**   The passage discusses the large range of ages when children reach significant language milestones. The closest synonym, therefore, is "vast." The other choices do not make sense in this context.

6.   **(C)**   The primary focus of the passage is on the use of early language milestones as a means of detecting speech disorders. Therefore, choice (C) is the best potential title. Adolescent speech disorders (A), a possible cure (B), and nutrition (D) are not discussed in the passage.

7.   **(D)**   The passage states that about five percent of the population of the U.S. suffers from speech or language disorder and that "the incidence of speech disorders follows similar patterns among other Western nations." This clearly establishes (D) as the only possible answer.

8.   **(A)**   The words "it takes a skilled practitioner to distinguish" implies that only a skilled speech-language pathologist should be consulted.

9. **(B)** The words "normal range for early language acquisition is enormous" indicate that (A) and (D) cannot be true. (C) is untrue and makes no sense since the time it takes a child to learn to speak can always be measured.

10. **(D)** The sentence, "Normal children speak their first word at anywhere from 6 to 18 months, and combine words into phrases for the first time at anywhere from 10 to 24 months" indicates that "words to phrases" is the correct order and answer.

11. **(A)** The context clue here is the statement that "patients lose...responsiveness to events around them." This shows "disinterest," which is the only synonym for "apathy" among the four choices. Choices (B), (C), and (D), in fact, are all opposite in meaning to "apathy."

12. **(C)** The first line of the passage clearly states that kwashiorkor is caused by "chronic lack of protein." High-fat diets (A), lack of vitamin C (B), and unsanitary living conditions (D) are not mentioned as factors.

13. **(B)** The most precise synonym for "recovery" in this context is "improvement," as in an improvement in the patient's condition. "Renewal" is too strong a word, since the patient is just beginning to get better. "Retrieval" (C) is the recovery of a possession, and "restoration" (D) is the regaining of original condition.

14. **(C)** The passage is a very general overview of the cause and symptoms of kwashiorkor, so choice (C) would be the best potential title. The passage mentions that the disease was discovered in Ghana (A), but that nation is not the focus. Neither specific solutions (B) nor nutritional deficiencies in developed nations (D) are discussed.

15. **(D)** Since the paragraph ends with the statement "the treated youngster who eventually smiles is considered to be on the road to recovery," a discussion of further long-term treatment would be most appropriate. The other choices would all cause jarring shifts in the logical progression of the passage.

16. **(A)** The best synonym here is "prolonged." A nutritional deficiency as severe as kwashiorkor would require a long-term lack of protein. "Immediate" (B), therefore, is incorrect. "Habitual" (C) is a synonym of chronic, but a lack of protein is not said to be a habit. "Gradual" (D) is not as precise in this context.

17. **(D)** While it is nearly directly stated, "developing nations do not have enough protein sources to feed their populations" is the reason, as stated in the first sentence "by a chronic lack of protein." (A) is not necessarily true, (B) is incorrect because there was no mention of responsibility for the other nations to take up the supply issue, and (C) is incorrect because 1960 is not near the beginning of this century.

18. **(A)** "Widespread" is the most correct answer. (B) is incorrect. Kwashiorkor *is* throughout a certain protein-lacking population. (C) "children" or (D) "adults" are not correct because, although the passage talks about children, there is no mention that it is restricted to them.

19. **(D)** Only "red blotches" is not mentioned as a stated symptom.

20. **(A)** "Kwashiorkor is a disease of malnutrition with observable causes and symptoms" can be inferred from the passage. (B) "United Nations" is never mentioned. (C) is stated but not inclusive enough to be the main idea, nor is (D).

21. **(C)** The passage indicates that all of the choices except for (C) are done when birds return to their summer homes. Birds travel southward (C) in the fall and early winter, not in the summer.

22. **(B)** The most appropriate synonym in this context is "event." The words "miracle" (A), "celebration" (C), and "milestone" (D) are not appropriate for the meaning of this sentence.

23. **(C)** Since the passage is a general overview of the annual migration patterns of birds, (C) is the best potential title for the passage. Hummingbirds (A) are not even mentioned. Although the process of flight (B) and courting and mating (D) are briefly discussed, they are by no means the primary focus here.

24. **(C)** The third paragraph states that birds "join with others of their kind in large and small flocks," indicating that (C) is the correct answer and thereby negating (B). Choice (A) completely contradicts the main idea of the passage. Choice (D) is incorrect because the last sentence indicates that some birds "remain in the cold northlands."

25. **(A)** Since the passage ends with a mention of birds' "strenuous journey to the south," it would make most sense to follow this with a discussion of migratory patterns. Choice (B) would be redundant, since this is already discussed in the first paragraph.

Choice (C) would also cause an abrupt shift in the chronology of the discussion. Choice (D) is not relevant to the discussion of migration in the passage.

26. **(D)** The best synonym for "faculty" in this context is "ability," as in birds' *ability* to fly. The other choices are also synonyms for "ability," but are not as precise in this context.

27. **(C)** "Physical properties" is the correct answer. (A) "coloration" and (B) "size" are examples of adaptation and (D) "reproductive practices" are never mentioned.

28. **(B)** "Birds are built to fly" is the main idea as it is the adaptation which produces migration and not the other way around. (C) "Birds need to migrate to survive" is a secondary idea. (A) is disproven by the words "as no other creatures" and (D) is disproven by the word "phenomenon."

29. **(C)** "Birds travel where and when they feel the need to do so" is the correct answer as it defines the words "seek out."

30. **(D)** Internal air sacs, hollow bones, and tails are all mentioned. Only coloration is not mentioned, making it the correct answer.

31. **(B)** The passage states that "children in large families learn how to get along with others through normal brother-sister play and tussles." This implies that social and physical development for these children take place in the home, and, therefore, relatively quickly. By contrast, the passage indicates that only children (A), twins (C), and children who are continually scolded (D) adapt slower.

32. **(D)** The best synonym in this context is "babyish." Since the sentence says that "he too may *return* to infantile pleasures," the correct choice must indicate an age younger than a child. This rules out "childish" (C). "Undeveloped" (A) and "idle" (B) are too vague to be correct.

33. **(C)** The passage primarily focuses on how only children, twins, and children from large families differ in their social adaptations. This makes (C) the best potential title. Choice (A) is incorrect because the passage does not solely focus on only children. Choice (B) is incorrect because physical development is not discussed. Choice (D) implies that the focus of the passage is on one particular child.

34. **(A)**   The first sentence of the second paragraph clearly states that "a child who is constantly scolded...may have a difficult time developing socially." The other choices are all directly contradicted by statements in the passage.

35. **(C)**   An obstacle is something which must be overcome to achieve a desired goal. In this context, infantile habits are a "barrier" toward social contact. "Boundaries" (A) is not correct in this context. "Passages" (B) and "paths" (D) are opposite in meaning from "barriers."

36. **(C)**   The main idea is stated in the first sentence. (A) is stated but is not the main idea. (B) is not stated in the passage. (D) is not discussed.

37. **(D)**   Examples of various amounts of siblings are given in the first paragraph.

38. **(B)**   That continual scolding inhibits the child is stated in the second paragraph. (A) "continual scolding is not harmful" and (C) "continual scolding does not affect" are disproved in the second paragraph. (D) That "continual scolding has adverse effects on the disciplinarian" is not discussed.

39. **(B)**   "Playground and classroom" is stated in the fourth sentence.

40. **(A)**   As some things are learned outside the home only (A) "partially" can be correct. (B) "at no time," (C) "totally," and (D) "in no noticeable ways" are incorrect.

41. **(D)**   "Encouraging" is the correct answer. "Cultivating," as it is used in the passage, is best defined as the act of fostering or encouraging growth and development, making choice (D) the correct response. Answer choices (A), (B), and (C) are not synonyms of the word "cultivating," and therefore are incorrect.

42. **(C)**   The correct answer is (C), "Women's bones often become thin and brittle with age, causing more frequent instances of broken bones and fractures." The passage states, "Particularly in women, the bones often become thin and brittle with age, causing seemingly minor falls to result in broken bones." The passage does not mention anything about women being more accident prone (A), suffering the most marked decrease in eyesight (B), or women being more clumsy (D) than men. These choices are incorrect.

43. **(D)** The passage does not mention anything about entering a nursing home therefore, choice (D) is the correct answer. The passage does mention that (A) maintaining physical health, (B) maintaining mental health, and (C) cultivating good safety habits are ways to help elderly people prevent accidents.

44. **(A)** The correct answer is "hazards." The passage states, "Poor eyesight and hearing can decrease awareness of hazards." Answer choices (B) injury, (C) drowsiness, and (D) arthritis are not mentioned in the passage as results of poor eyesight and hearing.

45. **(D)** This assumption is stated in "several factors make people in this age group prone to accidents" and the repeated reference to old people makes "old age brings more propensity to accidents" correct.

46. **(A)** "By chance" is the correct answer. (B) "by being a victim" is off the topic. (C) "with cause" and (D) "with warning" preclude the idea of chance.

47. **(D)** "Wealth" is the only answer not stated, so therefore is the correct answer. All others are mentioned as factors.

48. **(B)** "Susceptibility" is synonymous with "vulnerability." (A) "unconquerability," (C) "invincibility," and (D) "indestructibility" are therefore incorrect.

49. **(B)** "High blood pressure" is not mentioned. (A) "neurological diseases," (C) "arthritis," and (D) "coordination problems" are all mentioned.

50. **(C)** "Too much TV viewing" is the only cause not mentioned and is therefore correct. All other chances are mentioned.

51. **(B)** The second paragraph states that "many rare species have been overcollected and about 20 face extinction." Choices (A) and (C) are contradicted by the statement that cacti "are conditioned to deal with long periods of drought." The use of cacti for food (D) is not mentioned in the passage.

52. **(C)** Australia is not mentioned within the passage as an area where cacti usually grow. The Southwestern U.S. (A), Mexico (B), and southern South America (D) are all mentioned, however.

53. **(A)** Since the passage discusses cacti as being conditioned to growing in areas "where water is available only occasionally," we can assume that "arid" describes a very dry climate. Although this climate may also be very hot (C) or desolate (B), it does not necessarily have to be arid. Choice (D) is the opposite in meaning and is therefore incorrect.

54. **(D)** The passage states that without leaves, the stem of the cactus takes over the process of photosynthesis; therefore, (A) is incorrect. Since photosynthesis is the process by which plants produce food, it is clearly necessary to the survival of the plant, so (B) is incorrect. Nothing in the passage suggests that photosynthesis occurs only in certain seasons, so (C) is incorrect.

55. **(C)** The passage states that leaves may be eliminated because they "transpire precious water." From this we can assume that this means to "expel," or get rid of water. In its dry climate, the cactus certainly would not want to eliminate leaves that collect, create, or absorb water, so (A), (B), and (D) are incorrect.

56. **(D)** The passage states "Cacti and other succulent plants originate in areas where water is available only occasionally." (A) and (B) are incorrect. Plants which grow near deep rivers would have a constant supply of water, so would plants in areas of high rainfall. (C) is incorrect. The passage mentions nothing about cacti in captivity. (D) is the correct answer because it restates that cacti grow in areas where it rains occasionally.

57. **(B)** Answers (A), (C), and (D) are incorrect because they are not mentioned in the passage as coverings for retaining moisture. Only thick spines and velvety hairs (B) are specifically mentioned in the passage as a coating which helps cacti retain moisture. Therefore, (B) is the correct answer.

58. **(C)** Cacti store moisture in order to survive during dry seasons when there is little water available. To water other cacti (A) is not a reason to retain water, so (A) is incorrect. (B) is the opposite of why cacti retain water, so it is incorrect. Leaves and stems are thick (D) as a result of storing water; they are not the reason for storing water. Therefore, (D) is incorrect.

59. **(D)** A drought is an exceptionally dry season requiring plants to store moisture to survive. Therefore, answers (A), (B), and (C) are incorrect. Although coldness, wetness, and cloudiness do occur, they are not reasons which require plants to retain water.

60. **(B)** Because the term "succulent plants" is coupled with "cacti," it can be assumed that both can survive in long dry seasons by retaining moisture. Therefore, dry (A) is an incorrect meaning for succulent. Water-retaining (B) is the correct answer. Water-releasing (C) is incorrect because succulent plants must retain water to survive, not release it. Leaf-transpiring (D) is incorrect because all plants, succulent or not, transpire through their leaves.

Chapter 7

Transcripts for the Listening Comprehension Sections of the Diagnostic Test and Tests 1 – 6

This is the transcript for the Diagnostic Test for TOEFL,
the Test of English as a Foreign Language.

DIAGNOSTIC TEST
PART A

> **DIRECTIONS**: In Part A you will hear short conversations between two speakers. At the end of each conversation, a third person will ask a question about what was said. **You will hear each conversation and question about it just one time.** Therefore, you must listen carefully to understand what each speaker says. After you hear a conversation and the question about it, read the four possible answers in your test book and decide which one is the best answer to the question you heard. Then on your answer sheet, find the number of the question and fill in the space that corresponds to the answer you have chosen.

Man: Do you want to drive your car to the movie theater, or should I drive mine?

Woman: Well, I wouldn't mind driving, but I don't have enough gas in my car.

Question 1.

What will they probably do about driving to the movies?

Man: Do you like my new tie?

Woman: Yes, but I prefer the one you wore yesterday.

Question 2.

What is the woman trying to say?

Woman: Look at the shopping mall! It's three stories high with eight major department stores! Is it new?

Man: Probably. When I was a kid there was a field here. We would come and play ball after school.

Question 3.

Where did this conversation probably take place?

Man:	That piano piece sounds as though it could use some work. You played several wrong notes. Did you practice last week?
Woman:	Well, I was very busy last week. I probably should've practiced more, but I really didn't think it sounded that bad.

Question 4.

What does the woman mean?

Man:	Would you like a piece of chocolate cake?
Woman:	Oh, although I love chocolate cake, I'm on a diet. But I suppose a tiny slice wouldn't really hurt.

Question 5.

What will the woman probably do?

Man:	I just bought this book. It got great reviews and is number one on the best-seller list. Have you read it yet?
Woman:	I started reading that book, but I couldn't get into it.

Question 6.

What does the woman mean?

Woman:	Sir, I'm afraid there is a problem with the bouquet you ordered. We no longer have daisies, daffodils, and pink carnations in stock.
Man:	Well, do you have any red, long-stemmed roses in stock?
Woman:	Oh yes, we have plenty of those.

Question 7.

What will the man probably do?

Woman:	I love this shirt. But when I tried on the "small," it fit too tightly, and when I tried on the "large," it fit too loosely. Do you have this shirt in a "medium"?
Man:	No, not right now. But if you can wait a week, that size will be shipped to us.

Question 8.

What will the woman probably do?

Woman: The food at that restaurant was very good, but I thought the service was poor. Do you agree?

Man: Yes, we should have left the waiter a smaller tip.

Question 9.

What does the man think about the restaurant?

Woman: I have to get the milk, butter, and eggs in aisle 8. While I'm doing that, will you please go and get the flour, oatmeal, and chocolate chips?

Man: Sure. What aisles can I find those items in?

Question 10.

Where did this conversation probably take place?

Woman: Do you think we can afford a new television right now?

Man: Maybe, if we pool all our resources together.

Question 11.

What does the man mean?

Man: Did you send all the invitations today?

Woman: I sent ten of them today, and I will send five tomorrow. Then I will be done.

Question 12.

How many total invitations does the woman have to send?

Woman: How long would you take to develop this film?

Man: Three working days. You can pick up the pictures on Thursday.

Question 13.

Where did this conversation take place?

Woman: I don't feel like working overtime today.

Man: You can't do that to me. I am counting on you to finish this work.

Question 14.

What does the man imply?

Woman: I think Shawn is going to feel very badly about not getting this job.
Man: Don't worry about him. He is a happy-go-lucky man.

Question 15.

What is the man's opinion of Shawn?

Woman: They said the train is 15 minutes late. It has been more than half an hour since then.
Man: All we can do is wait.

Question 16.

What are these people doing?

Man: Many, many happy returns of the day! And here is a small birthday gift for you from all of us.
Woman: Thank you so much everyone.

Question 17.

On what day did this conversation take place?

Woman: Are you going to grant a day off to Linda?
Man: Will you please mind your own business?

Question 18.

What does the man mean?

Man: Can we eat the cake now? I would like to see how successful my first attempt at baking is.
Woman: Just a minute. Let me call Kathy and Johnny.

Question 19.

Who baked the cake?

Woman: This looks like an old building.
Man: Yes. It was built in the last decade of the nineteenth century.

Question 20.

About how long ago was the building built?

Woman: I don't believe Donald behaved like a stranger with us.
Man: He is not the same man that went to school with us.

Question 21.

What does the man mean?

Man: Do you think we should hire Ms. Emerson for this decorating job?
Woman: I think she would be a perfect choice.

Question 22.

What does the woman think about Ms. Emerson?

Woman: How could Bill make such a big mistake?
Man: He fell prey to his friend's show of sympathy.

Question 23.

What does the man mean?

Man: Can you help me with some typing?
Woman: Let me finish making this soup. Then, let's have dinner. After dinner,
          I can do all the typing.

Question 24.

What is the woman doing?

Woman: Did you call Dr. James yet?
Man: I did. But you said his number was in our telephone book; it was not. I
          couldn't find it in the directory either. At last, I called the operator and
          got it.

Question 25.

How did the man find Dr. James's number?

This is the end of the Diagnostic Test, Part A.

PART B

Questions 26 through 30 are based on the following conversation.

Man:	Did you notice if it was snowing outside?
Woman:	No, I have been working in my office all morning, and I do not have a window. Why did you want to know?
Man:	An announcement was made that if it started to snow we would all be allowed to leave early.
Woman:	That would be great, but I could not leave because I have too much work to do.
Man:	I would have to leave if the snow started getting heavy. I live over an hour away and the roads can get very bad when it snows.
Woman:	I live very far away too. Will they pay us if we have to leave early?
Man:	Only if they decide to close the building.
Woman:	If it snows I hope they do decide to close the building. I could always take the work home with me, but I cannot afford to go without pay.
Man:	I know how you feel. I need every penny of my paycheck.
Woman:	Let me know if you see it starting to snow.

Question 26.

Why could the woman not answer the man's question?

Question 27.

Why did the man have to leave if it snowed?

Question 28.

Under what condition would the employees get paid if it snowed?

Question 29.

Why did the woman not want to leave early?

Question 30.

What did the man say he needed?

Questions 31 through 35 are based on the following conversation.

Man:	Did you see the list of books for this course?
Woman:	Yes, Dr. Downs said he expects us to have the first five on the list. He is going to discuss them in detail.
Man:	Are you going to buy them?
Woman:	I don't know. These books are expensive. And I don't have a lot of money on me.
Man:	How about sharing them with me?
Woman:	Sounds good.
Man:	Let's do this. I will buy three and you buy two of them.
Woman:	I would rather do it this way: we pay fifty-fifty for the books now. And at the end of the course you can take the books you find more interesting and I will take the ones I like.
Man:	What if we both like the same books?
Woman:	Come on, we are not going to argue over that. Are we?
Man:	I was just joking. It's definitely a better idea.
Woman:	Then let's get the books at the earliest.

Question 31.

What are these people concerned about?

Question 32.

How many books do they have to buy?

Question 33.

Why does Dr. Downs want his students to have these five books?

Question 34.

How do these people plan to solve their problem about the books?

Question 35.

How does the woman want to share the books?

Questions 36 through 40 are based on the following conversation.

Man:	I have never seen such an exotic idol before. Did you buy it from an antique auction?

Woman:	No. I bought this in Nepal last summer. I went there for my vacation.
Man:	That is interesting. Is this very expensive?
Woman:	You won't believe the price I paid for it. It is less than 25 dollars.
Man:	Really? That is amazing.
Woman:	Yes, it is. In some of the Oriental countries, the traditional art products are so beautiful, they could be easily sold for hundreds of dollars.
Man:	Is that so? Actually, I was planning a trip to the Orient myself.
Woman:	You must take it. Many of the countries have very interesting cultures. And some of the spots are quite rich in natural beauty.
Man:	I think I will talk to my travel agent next week.

Question 36.

From where did the woman get the idol?

Question 37.

How much did she pay for the idol?

Question 38.

What could be sold for hundreds of dollars?

Question 39.

Why does the woman recommend a trip to the Oriental countries?

Question 40.

Who is planning a trip to the Orient?

This is the end of the Diagnostic Test, Part B.

PART C

Questions 41 through 45 are based on the following short talk.

The Works Progress Administration (WPA) was started in May 1935 following the passage of the Emergency Relief Appropriations Act of April 1935. The WPA employed people from the relief rolls for 30 hours of work a week at pay double the relief payment but less than private employment. There was not enough money to hire all of the unemployed, and the numbers varied from time to time, but an average of 2.1 million people per month were employed. By the end of the program in 1941, 8.5 million people had worked at some time for the WPA at a total cost of $11.4 billion.

Question 41.

What does WPA stand for?

Question 42.

When was the Emergency Relief Appropriations Act begun?

Question 43.

How many hours per week did the WPA employ people for?

Question 44.

When did the WPA program end?

Question 45.

How much did the WPA program cost?

Questions 46 through 50 are based on the following short talk.

If I had to name a single great invention of mankind, I would say language. There has been no greater invention, because if there was no language, most of man's inventions would not have been made. Though there are other means of communication like signals in war, signs made with hands, and facial expressions, they are not as powerful as language. The communication possible through these means is limited. Language made it possible for man to share his thoughts, his questions, and his knowledge with his fellow beings. Knowledge gained by one generation could become the basis of inventions of the next generation only because of language. The written word and the printed word were the two next greatest inventions. Can you imagine our world with everything else but without printed pages? The modern world functions on the strength of the printed word. There would be no universities, no business contracts, no political treaties, and no newspapers, if we did not have the printed word.

Question 46.

For what reason is language the greatest invention of mankind?

Question 47.

What makes language the greatest means of communication?

Question 48.

What would be the condition of the world if there was no printed word?

Question 49.

How does the knowledge gained by one generation become a basis for the inventions of the next?

Question 50.

What was the main topic of the talk?

This is the end of the Diagnostic Test, Part C.

THIS IS THE END OF THE DIAGNOSTIC TEST

This is the transcript of the recording program for TOEFL,
the Test of English as a Foreign Language.

TEST 1

PART A

Woman: I'm not sure if I like this hat on me. Do you like it?

Man: I think it brings out the green in your eyes. Look in the mirror and see for yourself.

Question 1.

What does the man mean?

Man: The team is making a remarkable comeback. Do you think they will win the game?

Woman: They are only 10 points behind now. If they can keep playing this well, they certainly will.

Question 2.

What does the woman think about the team?

Man: I can't remember if I locked the door on the way out of the house. Do you remember locking it?

Woman: Well, I didn't lock the door. You were the last one out!

Question 3.

What does the woman mean?

Man: Hey, I heard you were going to that record signing. Did you get to meet the rock and roll band?

Woman: Everyone except the drummer autographed my album, and the lead singer kissed my cheek.

Question 4.

Did the woman meet the rock and roll band?

Man: Did you notice if the janitor cleaned last night?

Woman: Well, there was still trash in my wastebasket when I arrived this morning.

Question 5.

What does the woman mean?

Man: I telephoned you last night. Why didn't you return my call?

Woman: You called?

Question 6.

Why didn't the woman return the man's call?

Man: I didn't finish my term paper because the electricity in the library failed last night. Do you think the professor will allow me to hand it in late?

Woman: Dr. Hatton said that he would not accept any late papers.

Question 7.

What does the woman mean?

Woman: Look at all that smoke coming from over that hill. I bet there is a fire.

Man: That is the direction of Grandma's house! I hope she is okay.

Question 8.

What is the man thinking?

Man: My computer screen went blank. What do you think happened?

Woman: Have you checked all the connections in the back? Maybe one is loose.

Question 9.

What does the woman think is wrong with the computer?

Woman: I rarely see you around here any more. I thought you moved.
Man: I've just been staying at a friend's house so that I can take care of his pets while he is away.

Question 10.

Why does the woman think the man has moved?

Man: Are you going to the show tonight?
Woman: I would have loved to go, but I still have not finished writing my paper which is due tomorrow.

Question 11.

What does the woman mean?

Woman: Professor Nelson said that I should find the book in this section. But nothing even similar to that book is here.
Man: Maybe somebody already borrowed it. Let's check the subject catalog.

Question 12.

Where did this conversation probably take place?

Man: Can I borrow your history notes? I didn't attend the class yesterday.
Woman: I didn't take any notes. The teacher just read dates from her notes to us, and I thought I could find them in any history book.

Question 13.

What is the woman trying to say?

Woman: The food in this restaurant is really delicious. And it is not very expensive.
Man: We can afford to eat here once a week, can't we?
Woman: Oh yes! I agree one hundred percent.

Question 14.

What do they think of the restaurant?

Man: Are you ready for your final exam next week?

Woman: Not really, the reading list is too long. But I will take the test anyway.

Question 15.

What does the woman mean?

Woman: Do you think I should cook some dinner now?

Man: I don't think so. There is enough left over from the party last night.

Question 16.

What will they probably do about dinner?

Woman: Were you present at the meeting this morning?

Man: Yes, but I didn't agree with most of their proposals. I think they are making admission rules too rigid.

Woman: Well, why didn't you speak out at the time?

Question 17.

What does the woman think?

Woman: Do you think we should buy Tom a book for his birthday?

Man: I am not sure he cares for the type of book that we would select. I would rather give him a gift certificate.

Question 18.

What does the man mean?

Woman: Why are your eyes so red? Studying hard these days?

Man: No, I accidentally sprayed some glass-cleaner into my eyes.

Woman: I don't think you should neglect this. You should contact a doctor right away.

Question 19.

What does the woman suggest?

Woman: I am trying to pick up that bottle on the top shelf. Would you mind helping me with it?

Man: I don't work here. Maybe you can get a ladder from the manager.

Question 20.

Is the man willing to help?

Man: I have an interview in Detroit on the tenth, but the train fare is incredibly high.
Woman: You should try flying. Airfares are sometimes much cheaper than train fares.

Question 21.

What does the woman mean?

Man: Did Lisa fix the toaster herself?
Woman: No, she had it fixed by her friend Cathy.

Question 22.

Who fixed the toaster?

Man: How do I get to the bank from here?
Woman: Go straight and make a right on Morris Street. The bank is right on the corner.

Question 23.

What is the woman doing?

Man: Do you know who won the prize for debating?
Woman: I think Mark did. He had been good at public speaking since he was young.

Question 24.

What does the woman think about Mark?

Man: I am thinking of taking a course with Dr. Warner.
Woman: Dr. Warner does not allow more than 15 students in his class. If you want to do it, you'd better make your decision fast.

Question 25.

What is the woman's opinion?

This is the end of sample Test 1, Part A.

PART B

Questions 26 through 30 are based on the following conversation.

Man: Have you seen that new hit movie?

Woman: No I have not. Was it any good?

Man: I had to wait over an hour in line to get a ticket, but it was worth it. The acting was fantastic, and the plot had me on the edge of my seat.

Woman: How come you had to wait an hour for a ticket?

Man: I arrived at the theater early because I had heard the movie kept selling out and I did not want to miss it.

Woman: And did the movie sell out?

Man: Yes. In fact, by the time they opened the doors, the line had stretched around the corner of the building.

Woman: So, were you the first one in line?

Man: No. There were people ahead of me who had been waiting for almost an hour before I arrived.

Woman: It must be a good movie if all these people are going to see it. I think I will try and go this weekend.

Question 26.

What did the man go to see?

Question 27.

What did the man think of the movie?

Question 28.

How long did the man wait in line?

Question 29.

How long did the people in front of him wait in line?

Question 30.

When will the woman go to see the movie?

Questions 31 through 35 are based on the following conversation.

Man: I can't believe it is only a week from now!
Woman: What?
Man: Our college graduation! Aren't you excited about it?
Woman: Of course I am! I couldn't attend my high school graduation, so this is really a big event for me.
Man: Are your parents coming for your graduation?
Woman: I am not sure. They live in Texas, so it is very hard for them. But my father will be calling me tonight to let me know. He has a business trip to New York next week, but hopefully he will adjust it somehow and come. Is your family coming?
Man: Yes, they are. They live only 30 miles from here. Besides, I am the first one in the family to graduate from a university. So they are all looking forward to it.
Woman: Isn't that wonderful?

Question 31.

What are these people talking about?

Question 32.

Is the woman looking forward to her graduation?

Question 33.

Why is the man's graduation important to his family?

Question 34.

What state do the woman's parents live in?

Question 35.

When is the graduation?

Questions 36 through 40 are based on the following conversation.

Woman: Hi Mike! What is all this wood for?

Man: I am planning to make a wooden fence for my yard. And then, in the summer, I want to pick up on my gardening again.

Woman: I didn't know you were interested in gardening.

Man: I grew up on farms. My father is a farmer. After I left for school I didn't get a chance to do any gardening. But now that I have my own house, I thought I would recreate some of the farm life here.

Woman: That's interesting. What do you plan to grow?

Man: I have ordered some rose plants, some tulip bulbs, and some marigold plants from a nursery. And I am also getting some seeds for vegetables from my father. He was here last week, so he knows what can grow in this soil.

Woman: Well, I wish you good luck! I will talk to John, and if he agrees to have a little garden in our yard, I will come to you for gardening tips.

Man: Any time!

Question 36.

What is the man planning to do with the wood?

Question 37.

Why does the man have an interest in gardening?

Question 38.

What is the man's father going to send?

Question 39.

Where did this conversation probably take place?

Question 40.

Why would the woman go to Mike if John agreed to have a garden?

This is the end of sample Test 1, Part B.

PART C

Questions 41 through 45 are based on the following short talk.

Woodrow Wilson was only the second Democrat (Grover Cleveland was the first) elected president since the Civil War. He was born in Virginia in 1856, the son of a Presbyterian minister, and was reared and educated in the South. After earning a doctorate at Johns Hopkins University, he taught history and political science at Princeton, and in 1902 became president of that university. In 1910 he was elected governor of New Jersey as a reform or progressive Democrat. In 1912 he was elected president of the United States. On April 8, 1913 he became the first president since John Adams to appear personally before Congress to promote his program.

Question 41.

Who was the first Democrat elected president after the Civil War?

Question 42.

What did Woodrow Wilson's father do?

Question 43.

Where did Woodrow Wilson earn his doctoral degree?

Question 44.

Which state did Woodrow Wilson govern?

Question 45.

Who was the last president before Wilson to personally address Congress?

Questions 46 through 50 are based on the following short talk.

The United States is a unique nation in that it absorbs thousands of immigrants every year. People migrate here from all parts of the world—from Europe, from Asia, from Africa, from Latin America. They have different reasons for migrating to this country. Some leave their countries due to political oppression, some come to America to explore business opportunities, some of them can't find employment in their native lands, and some arrive here in search of advanced education. People are ready to take any risk to be able to enter the United States. Of course, most of the immigrants meet with a lot of frustration and disillusionment before they are successful. Isn't it wonderful that a nation with so comparatively short a history should become such a dreamland for people all over the world?

Question 46.

Why is the United States a unique nation?

Question 47.

Which one of the following is not a reason for immigration?

Question 48.

From where do people emigrate to the United States?

Question 49.

To the immigrants, what does America stand for?

Question 50.

Is the transition easy for the immigrants?

This is the end of sample Test 1, Part C.

THIS IS THE END OF SAMPLE TEST 1.

This is the transcript of the recording program for TOEFL,
the Test of English as a Foreign Language.

TEST 2

PART A

Woman: I'm so upset! I got into a car accident yesterday. The back end of my car is smashed in, but at least it still runs.

Man: Well, it could have been worse.

Question 1.

What does the man mean?

Woman: Do you think that five dollar bill on the ground belongs to those two little girls at the lemonade stand? Maybe we should give it to them.

Man: No, we don't know for certain that it belongs to them.

Question 2.

What is the man implying?

Man: The steak that I set aside for dinner hasn't fully defrosted yet. What should we do?

Woman: Let's order out for a pizza.

Question 3.

What does the woman want to do about dinner?

Man: Did you see that house we just passed by?
Woman: Yes. I can't believe they still have Halloween decorations up! It's the end of January!

Question 4.

What does the woman mean?

Man: I thought I just saw your friend Susan walk by. Why didn't you stop and say "Hello"?
Woman: Susan and I are no longer on speaking terms.

Question 5.

What does the woman mean?

Man: I had saved my term paper on the hard drive of this computer. Have you used it recently?
Woman: Yes, I used that computer yesterday.

Question 6.

What is the man implying?

Woman: These cookies taste funny. Are you sure you added enough sugar?
Man: I thought I followed the recipe exactly.

Question 7.

What is the woman implying?

Woman: I broke Mom's favorite vase!
Man: She told you not to play ball in the house! Just wait until Dad gets home!

Question 8.

What is the most probable relationship between these two people?

Woman: I'd like mint chocolate chip in a cup with rainbow sprinkles and whipped cream, please.
Man: And I'd like a banana split.

Question 9.

Where does this conversation most likely take place?

Woman: Why did you rent that movie again? We just watched it two weeks ago.
Man: This happens to be my favorite movie, and the last time we saw it was several months ago.

Question 10.

How long ago does the woman think they watched the movie?

Woman: Susan was here earlier to return your book.
Man: I have another copy. She could have kept it till her test was over.

Question 11.

What does the man mean?

Man: Oh no! Looks like the battery went down. I don't seem to have good luck with this car.
Woman: Calm down! Let's try to get some help.

Question 12.

What seems to be the problem?

Woman: Did you read the editorial in our college newspaper?
Man: Yes, did you like it? I think it stinks.

Question 13.

What is the man's opinion?

Man: Good Morning! I have an appointment with Dr. Johnson at 9 o'clock.
Woman: Dr. Johnson is with another patient. He should be available in a few minutes.

Question 14.

Where did this conversation take place?

Man: Is Mike ready to go to school?
Woman: No, he is in the laundry room, pressing his clothes.

Question 15.

Why is Mike not ready yet?

Man: Since you did the laundry this week, I will clean the house.
Woman: Fair enough!

Question 16.

What is the woman's response to the man's suggestion?

Man: What time should I pick you up? Is 4:30 good?
Woman: That will be too early. My class is over at 5:30. Any time after that is
              good.

Question 17.

What time will the man pick the woman up?

Woman: Did Professor Miller agree to discuss the topic again with you?
Man: Yes. Not only that, he offered to give me some books on the topic.
              That was more than I could ask for.

Question 18.

What does the man mean?

Man: Did you find the tickets? Hurry up! We're going to be late.
Woman: You said you kept them on the desk. Thank goodness I checked the
              drawer. How could we go without the tickets?

Question 19.

Where were the tickets?

Man: That's a nice pen.
Woman: Thank you! My sister's friend Stephanie gave it to me on my birthday.

Question 20.

Who gave the pen to the woman?

Woman: Thank you very much for your generous donation to our institution!
Man: I am glad I could offer some help for a noble cause.

Question 21.

What does the man imply?

Woman: Mrs. Wood was asking me if we have invited the Moors to the party.
Man: She really is nosy, isn't she?

Question 22.

What is the man's opinion about Mrs. Wood?

Woman: I missed the train by one minute. Now I will be late to work.
Man: Don't worry! There is another in ten minutes. You will get there in time.

Question 23.

Why does the man tell the woman not to worry?

Woman: I have finally decided to go to the picnic.
Man: Really? What a pleasant surprise! Everybody was sorry that you were planning to cancel.

Question 24.

How does the man feel about the woman's decision?

Man: I didn't get financial aid. I don't think I can take any courses this semester.
Woman: I would advise you to approach a bank. They have plenty of loans available for students.

Question 25.

What does the woman suggest?

This is the end of sample Test 2, Part A.

PART B

DIRECTIONS: In Part B you will hear extended conversations between two speakers. At the end of each conversation, a third person will ask several questions about what was said. **You will hear each conversation and the question about it just one time.** They will not be written out for you. Therefore, you must listen carefully to understand what each speaker says. After you hear a question, read the four possible answers in your test book and decide which one is the best answer to the question you heard. Then on your answer sheet, find the number of the question and fill in the space that corresponds to the answer you have chosen.

Questions 26 through 30 are based on the following conversation.

Man	Have you seen Jill today?
Woman:	No, I have been in class all day and have not seen her.
Man:	If you do see her, will you tell her that I am looking for her?
Woman:	I will. Is it anything important?
Man:	She was supposed to give me the class notes from when I was sick, and I need them to study for the test tomorrow.
Woman:	What class are the notes for?
Man:	Chemistry.
Woman:	If you want you can borrow my notes. I have been in class all week and they are complete.
Man:	Thanks. I will as long as it is not inconvenient for you.
Woman:	I studied for that test last night so I will not need my notes tonight.

Question 26.

Who was the man looking for?

Question 27.

Why did the woman not see Jill?

Question 28.

How come the man did not get the notes for class?

Question 29.

What class were the notes for?

Question 30.

Why did the woman not need her notes?

Questions 31 through 35 are based on the following conversation.

Man: Your performance last night was excellent. Congratulations!

Woman: Thank you. I am glad to hear that. This role was a challenge and I was very nervous before the performance.

Man: You were absolutely fantastic! Have you been acting long?

Woman: Since I was five. My father was associated with an amateur theatrical group. I started acting by doing small child roles for them.

Man: No wonder your acting was so mature.

Woman: Thank you again. But you sound like you know a lot about acting yourself.

Man: A little. I am not an actor. I am a student of art history. But I sometimes write critiques on theatrical events for the student newspaper.

Woman: Isn't that nice to know! I am really flattered by your compliments.

Question 31.

What were these people talking about?

Question 32.

Why was the woman nervous?

Question 33.

How did the woman start acting?

Question 34.

What does the man do?

Question 35.

Why did the woman feel flattered upon realizing that the man wrote critiques of theatrical events?

Questions 36 through 40 are based on the following conversation.

Woman: Can we take a break now? It has been more than three hours since we had our coffee.

Man: Just a few more minutes and we will have a perfect little writing desk here. Pass me the toolbox and hold this board tight for a minute, will you please?

Woman: Do I have a choice? I don't understand how anyone can enjoy making a writing desk on a Sunday.

Man: Actually, making anything yourself has many advantages. First of all, you know that you are using quality material. Secondly, you can choose your own design. And thirdly, you can save some money on labor.

Woman: I wonder who gives you such fantastic ideas!

Man: Nobody. I just bought an easy-to-make furniture manual. It has many such wonderful designs.

Woman: Where is it?

Man: In the library. Want to have a look at it?

Woman: No. I want to hide it till winter. I don't want to waste another nice Sunday in the garage making some piece of furniture.

Question 36.

What are these people doing?

Question 37.

Where are they working?

Question 38.

Why does the man like making furniture?

Question 39.

From where did the man get the idea?

Question 40.

What does the woman want to do with the book?

This is the end of sample Test 2, Part B.

PART C

Questions 41 through 45 are based on the following short talk.

Constantinople was the capital of the Byzantine Empire. It was the administrative and economic center of the 1,500 cities that composed the Empire's infrastructure. Founded by Greek colonists, the city's location at the mouth of the Dardenelles gave it access to the Black Sea and the Sea of Mamara. The city's name was changed from Byzantium to Constantinople when Constantine moved his capital to this site. Constantine expanded the city, ordering the construction of a forum, temples, and an enlarged Hippodrome on the city's seven hills.

Question 41.

What was the capital of the Byzantine Empire?

Question 42.

How many cities composed the empire's infrastructure?

Question 43.

Who founded the city?

Question 44.

Who changed the name of the city?

Question 45.

What was constructed during the expansion of the city?

Questions 46 through 50 are based on the following short talk.

Have you ever listened closely to the sound of a breeze passing through a thick cluster of trees? It is so rhythmic and sonorous that it sounds like a soft musical note. In our everyday hectic lives, we don't hear it because there is so much noise around us— from machines, from cars and buses, from people. But on quiet summer nights, sitting by an open window, it is possible to listen to the music of a breeze. Even fluttering wings of a butterfly or raindrops dropping gently from a leaf have their own music. Nature has a lot to offer to our senses, if we keep them open. In fact, one can actually learn to communicate with nature; it is very soothing. It takes a lot of stress off our minds. It would be wonderful if we could teach our children such an important skill for a healthy life.

Question 46.

What does a breeze passing through trees sound like?

Question 47.

Why do we find it difficult to listen to the music of a breeze in our everyday lives?

Question 48.

According to this talk, what is an important skill for a healthy life?

Question 49.

Why is the effect of nature soothing?

Question 50.

Who does the author want to teach the music of nature to?

This is the end of sample Test 2, Part C.

THIS IS THE END OF SAMPLE TEST 2.

This is a transcript of the recording program for TOEFL, the Test of English as a Foreign Language.

TEST 3

PART A

Woman: Do you have a cigarette that you could give to me?
Man: Yes, I do. But I thought the doctor told you that you were supposed to quit smoking. I don't want to contribute to your bad health.

Question 1.

What will the man most likely do?

Man: Did your sister give birth to her baby yet?
Woman: Yes, she had a baby girl last week.

Question 2.

What is the baby's relationship to the woman?

Woman: Would you like to go to see a play at the theater with me?
Man: Yes, but why don't we see if anyone else would like to come with us as well.

Question 3.

What is the man implying?

Man: Could you pass me the suntan lotion? I think I am burning.
Woman: Get the bottle of suntan lotion yourself. I have to get this sand out of my bathing suit.

Question 4.

Where did this conversation probably take place?

Man: Ouch! That hurts! Do you think I broke my ankle?
Woman: No, I think it is probably only a sprain. Let's run some x-rays and then we will know for sure.

Question 5.

Where did this conversation most likely take place?

Man: I just moved into my new apartment, and they don't allow pets. Would you like to have my cat?
Woman: Oh, I'd love to, but I'm allergic to cats.

Question 6.

What does the woman mean?

Man: The books required for this class are awfully expensive! Do you think I could just borrow your books?
Woman: I took that class last semester, and I sold the books back at the end of the term.

Question 7.

What does the woman mean?

Woman: I don't feel very well. I have a headache, and a cough, and my nose is running.
Man: Yes, it seems as though the whole office is sick. There is something going around.

Question 8.

What does the man mean?

Woman: I made an apple pie using the recipe that my grandmother gave me. Would you like to try a slice?
Man: Of course, you know I love apple pie.

Question 9.

Whose recipe was used to make the apple pie?

Man: Work has been very stressful lately. There are too many problems to deal with right now.

Woman: Well, this weekend you should find something to do to keep your mind off things.

Question 10.

What does the woman mean?

Woman: Are you sure you locked the back door?

Man: I am sure I did.

Woman: Please go and double-check for me. Better to be safe than sorry.

Question 11.

What does the woman mean?

Man: Do you think I am going too fast?

Woman: Definitely. The speed limit here is 55 miles per hour, and you are going 15 miles over it.

Question 12.

At what speed is the man driving?

Man: I think Mr. Holden is still too weak to come for the meeting.

Woman: And I am positive he will come. He is a man of strong will.

Question 13.

Why is the woman certain that Mr. Holden will come?

Woman: You look terrible. Are you all right?

Man: Yes, I am. I just had a long day at the office.

Question 14.

What is the man's problem?

Woman: Can I borrow a quarter from you? I need 20 more cents for this call.
Man: You sure can. Calling people is getting expensive.

Question 15.

Where did this conversation probably take place?

Man: Does Gloria rent this apartment alone?
Woman: No. She shares it with two other friends.

Question 16.

How many people live in the apartment?

Woman: One more thing from this store and I am done.
Man: Don't you ever get tired of shopping?

Question 17.

What does the man mean?

Man: How would you like to go fishing this weekend?
Woman: Wonderful! That's my idea of a relaxing weekend.

Question 18.

How does the woman feel about the proposal?

Man: Do you know where I can find Dr. Gordon? I have been looking for her
         in the library, in her office, and in the laboratory.
Woman: Goodness! She thought she had to meet you in the conference room.

Question 19.

Where could the man find Dr. Gordon?

Woman: My car seems to have a problem picking up speed.
Man: I will ask John to have a look at it tomorrow.

Question 20.

What kind of a job does John probably have?

Man: Why aren't you coming to the party? I promise you won't feel left out.
Woman: That's not the problem. I'm just not a party person.

Question 21.

What does the woman mean?

Man: I don't feel very excited about this interview.
Woman: Just give it a try. What do you have to lose?

Question 22.

What does the woman imply?

Woman: Did you hear that Willie got "A's" in all his major subjects?
Man: I knew he could accomplish anything if he put his mind to it.

Question 23.

What is the man's opinion about Willie?

Woman: Do you think you can fix this watch today?
Man: Yes Ma'am! It is two o'clock now. I should be able to fix it in about three hours.

Question 24.

Approximately at what time should the woman be able to get her watch back?

Man: So, how is your new job?
Woman: I have never been luckier with my job.

Question 25.

What does the woman mean?

This is the end of sample Test 3, Part A.

PART B

Questions 26 through 30 are based on the following conversation.

Man: I saw you stopped on the side of the road this morning. What happened?
Woman: I was driving to pick up my husband and the car suddenly started shaking. I pulled off the road to see what was wrong.
Man: Was it anything serious?
Woman: One of the cables to the spark plugs had come loose.
Man: Did you have anyone look at it?
Woman: No, it was easy to just reconnect the cable so the car could run.
Man: If my car starts to make any noises I bring it straight to a mechanic. I don't know anything about engines.
Woman: My family has owned a garage for many years. I grew up working on cars.
Man: You are lucky. I can barely change a flat tire.
Woman: Well, if you want any lessons on cars just let me know.

Question 26.

Where did the man see the woman?

Question 27.

Why was the woman stopped?

Question 28.

Who fixed the woman's car?

Question 29.

How did the woman know about car engines?

Question 30.

How much did the man know about cars?

Questions 31 through 35 are based on the following conversation.

Man: Do you know if we have missed any bills this month?
Woman: No. I am sure I have paid them all.
Man: It is almost the end of the month, and I was wondering how come we still have some extra money in our account.
Woman: I know why. We didn't have to pay for my piano lessons this month.
Man: Oh yes! I forgot all about it.
Woman: I think it would be a good idea to use that money for that bookshelf we saw last week in the showroom. We really need it.
Man: I may agree to that on one condition.
Woman: And what is that?
Man: Your piano teacher is going to be away next month also. You have to promise to help save some money next month.
Woman: You have a promise!

Question 31.

Why does the man think that they have missed a bill?

Question 32.

What is the reason they have some extra money in their account?

Question 33.

What does the woman plan to do?

Question 34.

What promise does the man ask for?

Question 35.

Why does the man think they can save some money next month?

Questions 36 through 40 are based on the following conversation.

Woman: What do you charge for photocopying?
Man: Fifteen cents per page.
Woman: Even for bulk?
Man: Approximately how many pages do you have?
Woman: I don't have them with me right now. But it is my dissertation, which will be about a hundred pages.
Man: In that case, I will do it for ten cents per page. Does that sound fair to you?
Woman: Good enough! But I am not through typing yet. I should be able to finish it within four or five days.

Man: See you in a week then.

Question 36.

What does the woman want to get done?

Question 37.

Approximately how much would the woman have to pay for the photocopy of her dissertation?

Question 38.

Why did the man lower the charge?

Question 39.

About how long is the woman's dissertation?

Question 40.

What is the woman waiting for?

This is the end of sample Test 3, Part B.

PART C

DIRECTIONS: In Part C you will hear short talks. At the end of each talk, a second person will ask several questions about what was said. **You will hear each talk and the questions about it just one time.** They will not be written out for you. Therefore, you must listen carefully to understand what each speaker says. After you hear a question, read the four possible answers in your test book and decide which one is the best answer to the question you heard. Then on your answer sheet, find the number of the question and fill in the space that corresponds to the answer you have chosen.

Questions 41 through 45 are based on the following short talk.

During the early Middle Ages the majority of Europeans were illiterate. Towards the middle of the eleventh century there were signs of a cultural revival. These changes did not touch the lives of most Europeans. Probably more than 90 percent of the population continued to live on the land. The intellectual climate, however, was improving. The growth in commerce between East and West offered Europeans contact with the Islamic and Byzantine civilizations. The cultural awakening of the high Middle Ages affected only a small number of intellectuals. Nevertheless, the advances in education, philosophy, science, literature, and the arts that unfolded during this period had long-range consequences.

Question 41.
During what period were most Europeans illiterate?

Question 42.
Approximately what percentage of the people continued to live off the land?

Question 43.
What empires did the Europeans come into contact with?

Question 44.
Who did the cultural awakening affect?

Question 45.
Advances in which subjects had long-range consequences?

Questions 46 through 50 are based on the following short talk.

If you are planning to paint your house this summer, I have some useful tips on painting. The first step towards satisfactory painting is the selection of the paint and the color. Make sure that the paint you select will adhere to an existing paint. Another area in which you need to take extra care is colors. Colors often look different under artificial light than in daylight. So check the paint chips in the daylight before ordering the paint. Once you are ready with the paint, select a warm and dry day to start painting. Before you start painting, make sure you have trimmed the trees and shrubs away from the house. While painting, paint an entire section at one time. Don't stop halfway through the section; otherwise the paint will dry unevenly. Use a good sash brush for windows. And when you are done painting, float a thin layer of solvent on the surface of the remaining paint, seal the can, and store it in a warm, dry place. It will last for years.

Question 46.

What was the main topic of the talk?

Question 47.

Why should we take extra care in selecting colors?

Question 48.

What type of weather is good to start painting?

Question 49.

Why should we paint an entire section at one time?

Question 50.

How can we keep extra paint for years?

This is the end of sample Test 3, Part C.

THIS IS THE END OF SAMPLE TEST 3.

This is a transcript of the recording program for TOEFL,
the Test of English as a Foreign Language.

TEST 4
PART A

Man: There was a great television show on last night. It was a documentary about the history of the space program. Did you see it?

Woman: My television is at the repair shop.

Question 1.

What does the woman mean?

Man: How old is your sister?

Woman: My sister is two years older than I am. She was born in 1968.

Question 2.

What year was the woman born?

Woman: Wow! That ride was really great! What should we go on next?

Man: Well, the line for the bumper cars is very long, but the line for the ferris wheel looks relatively short.

Question 3.

What ride will they probably go on next?

Woman: Holly looks beautiful. The gown she is wearing was her mother's.
Man: Is it? It fits her so nicely. Dave also looks good. He makes a handsome groom.

Question 4.

Where is this conversation most likely taking place?

Man: I have to get this project done by the twenty-first of the month. What day is it today?
Woman: Today is the fourteenth.

Question 5.

How many days does the man have to get his project done?

Woman: Sam was supposed to meet me here at 9:30. Where do you think he could be?
Man: He has had a busy schedule lately.

Question 6.

What does the man mean?

Woman: Were these muffins made fresh this morning?
Man: Of course, ma'am, we bake them every day.

Question 7.

Where is this conversation most likely taking place?

Man: I am so tired. I don't think I can make it through the whole day.
Woman: You should not have stayed up so late last night.

Question 8.

Why is the man tired?

Man: I have been in this library for hours, but I cannot find enough sources of information for my term paper.
Woman: How many more sources do you need?
Man: Five.

Question 9.

Why is the man aggravated?

Man: Have you seen my coat? I was sure I left it on this chair when I came into the house.

Woman: How am I supposed to know where your things are? You could look for it in the closet.

Question 10.

What does the woman mean?

Man: Did Bill get a job in the hospital?

Woman: He called the personnel office. But they said they don't have any openings right now.

Question 11.

Does Bill have a job in the hospital?

Woman: How is your new project going?

Man: It is quite a lot of work. But I think it is well worth the time and effort.

Question 12.

How does the man feel about the project?

Man: To whom should I send the receipt?

Woman: Send it to me. Ms. Gloria Gessner, 147 Washington Avenue, Burlington, New York 11340.

Question 13.

What was the woman doing?

Woman: Why does Richard look so depressed these days?

Man: I heard he suffered some heavy losses in his insurance business.

Question 14.

What is the reason for Richard's depression?

Man: May I help you?

Woman: Yes. Can you please check my brake fluid? I am afraid of getting into an accident.

Man: Sure. Can you open the hood please?

Question 15.

Where did this conversation probably take place?

Woman: What would you like to have for dinner?
Man: Anything light would be good. I don't feel very well today.

Question 16.

What does the man mean?

Man: Clare's score is good enough to get admitted to the school she likes.
Woman: Yes. But the score is too poor for her.

Question 17.

What is the woman's opinion?

Man: See if Susan is here. If she is, we can start the meeting.
Woman: Susan came in ten minutes ago. We still have to wait for David, though.

Question 18.

Why can't they start the meeting?

Man: Julie said we had to see Al at three. Who is Al?
Woman: His name is Alexander Robins. Al is his nickname. He is the vice president of this organization.

Question 19.

What does the woman mean?

Man: I thought you had ordered lunch for 16 people.
Woman: Yes, but we have four more unexpected guests. Can we order some more food now?

Question 20.

How many people came for lunch?

Man: I am surprised that you made it in time since you started late.
Woman: The speed at which my brother drove was unbelievable.

Question 21.

What does the woman mean?

Man: What is your experience with your new neighbors?
Woman: They are wonderful people. I am happy now. I was really tired of the quarrelsome couple that lived here before.

Question 22.

What is the woman's opinion about her new neighbors?

Man: I went to a fantastic classical music concert last night.
Woman: You have great taste in music!

Question 23.

What does the woman mean?

Woman: Are they closed already? I needed a book urgently.
Man: Yes. They close at five on Fridays. And they are closed even on weekends. The earliest you can get it now will be Monday morning.

Question 24.

On what day did this conversation take place?

Man: Why did I get this notice? I have already paid the bill.
Woman: If you have paid it, just disregard the notice. It must have been a mistake. I am sorry.

Question 25.

What does the woman mean?

This is the end of sample Test 4, Part A.

PART B

DIRECTIONS: In Part B you will hear extended conversations between two speakers. At the end of each conversation, a third person will ask several questions about what was said. **You will hear each conversation and the questions about it just one time.** They will not be written out for you. Therefore, you must listen carefully to understand what each speaker says. After you hear a question, read the four possible answers in your test book and decide which one is the best answer to the question you heard. Then on your answer sheet, find the number of the question and fill in the space that corresponds to the answer you have chosen.

Questions 26 through 30 are based on the following conversation.

Man: I just bought this new suit. What do you think of it?
Woman: It looks very good on you. Was it expensive?
Man: No. I have a friend who owns a clothing store, and he gives me all my clothes at half off the regular price.
Woman: What kinds of clothing does your friend's store carry?
Man: He carries everything: men's, women's, children's, casual, and formal.
Woman: Most off-the-rack clothes do not fit me well. Does he do any tailoring?
Man: Yes, he has five tailors in the store.
Woman: I need to get a new blazer to replace this one that is getting old. Do you think you could get me a discount on it?
Man: I think I could. How about we go when we get done with work today?
Woman: That would be fine. Thank you.

Question 26.

What did the man buy?

Question 27.

What did the woman think of the man's new clothing?

Question 28.

What was the discount the man received on his clothes?

Question 29.

How come the woman could not wear most clothes?

Question 30.

When were they going to the store?

Questions 31 through 35 are based on the following conversation.

Woman: So, how did it go?
Man: Better than I had expected.
Woman: Didn't I tell you that they are not going to get more qualified people than you?
Man: My qualifications are okay, but I don't have the experience of working on a project like this. My knowledge is mostly theoretical. That's why I am not so sure about getting this job.
Woman: I think what matters is that you have the ability to apply your knowledge to your work.
Man: I hope my interviewers feel that way.
Woman: Don't you think they do?
Man: I don't know. All of them are authorities in this field.
Woman: Don't worry. I am sure they will call you.

Question 31.

What were these people talking about?

Question 32.

Why is the man not confident about getting the job?

Question 33.

According to the woman, what is an important quality for good work?

Question 34.

How does the man feel about his qualifications?

Question 35.

What is the man's opinion about the interviewers?

Questions 36 through 40 are based on the following conversation.

Man: I had asked my eighth grade students to write an essay on their favorite season. Eighty percent of them wrote on the spring. Speaking of seasons, which is your favorite season?
Woman: The same. The spring.
Man: Why?
Woman: Because I love flowers and colors. You can see so many of them in the spring; it's as if the whole earth is in a festive mood. Also, it's the most pleasant weather. It is not bitter and chilly like the winter nor humid and hot like the summer. Isn't it your favorite too?
Man: Not exactly.

Woman: Why?
Man: Because I get terrible allergies during the spring.
Woman: Then which is your favorite season?
Man: It depends on where I am and how I am.
Woman: What does that mean?
Man: If I am in a cold country like Norway, it would be the summer. If I am
          in a hot tropical country, it would be the winter. And if I don't get
          allergies, it would be the spring.
Woman: Aren't you funny!

Question 36.

Who seems to be in a festive mood in the spring according to the woman?

Question 37.

Why is the spring the favorite season of the woman?

Question 38.

What is the reason why the man cannot appreciate the spring?

Question 39.

What type of country is Norway?

Question 40.

How does the woman find the man's explanation?

This is the end of sample Test 4, Part B.

PART C

Questions 41 through 45 are based on the following short talk.

Medieval Islamic culture left a lasting imprint on the development of Western civilization. Words tell much of the story. The terms zenith, nadir, zero, and the names of stars like Alderan and Betelgeuse, along with amalgam, alembic, alchemy, alkali, soda, and syrup all have their origin in Arabic. While Western Europe was languishing in the wake of the Germanic invasions, the Islamic peoples were vibrant and creative. They kept alive the philosophy of the Greeks and made numerous advances in medicine and science. It is difficult to overstate the West's debt to the medieval Islamic world.

Question 41.

On which civilization did medieval Islamic culture leave a lasting impression?

Question 42.

Which stars have their names from Arabic words?

Question 43.

Why was Western Europe languishing?

Question 44.

Whose philosophy did the Islamic people keep alive?

Question 45.

In which areas did the people of Islamic culture make advances?

Questions 46 through 50 are based on the following short talk.

The world's coldest continent, the Antarctic, has a mean annual temperature of minus seventy degrees Fahrenheit. Ninety percent of the ice on the earth lies on and around the Antarctic grounds. Seventy percent of the world's fresh water is bound in that ice. If the ice lying there ever melted, it would raise the sea level by approximately 60 feet. The Antarctic is also the windiest continent in the world. The most fierce gusts of winds there are nearly 200 miles per hour. The conditions there are the most hostile to human inhabitation. They seem hostile to any living being. But strangely enough the Antarctic has the largest population of wildlife anywhere in the world. From microscopic sea vegetation to larger animals such as whales, seals, and penguins, the Antarctic has plenty to offer for biologist's study.

Question 46.

Why is the Antarctic the world's coldest continent?

Question 47.

What would happen if the ice on the Antarctic ever melted?

Question 48.

At what speed do the most fierce winds in the Antarctic blow?

Question 49.

Why would a biologist find the Antarctic an interesting continent?

Question 50.

Which animal is not an inhabitant of the Antarctic?

This is the end of sample Test 4, Part C.

THIS IS THE END OF SAMPLE TEST 4.

This is a transcript of the recording program for TOEFL,
the Test of English as a Foreign Language.

TEST 5
PART A

Woman: It is 7:30! The newspaper should have been delivered a half an hour ago.

Man: You're right. The delivery person is always late.

Question 1.

At what time should they have had their newspaper delivered?

Man: What time is the next flight to Mesa?

Woman: Oh, I'm sorry sir, that plane left ten minutes ago. There won't be another leaving until tomorrow.

Question 2.

Where does this conversation most likely take place?

Man: I need to send this package to Boston. How much will that cost?

Woman: That will depend upon the weight of the package and how quickly you want it to arrive.

Question 3.

Where does this conversation take place?

Woman: Do you know who won the award last night?
Man: I wasn't able to stay at the banquet until the winner was announced,
          but I believe that you can find the winner in this morning's paper.
Woman: I looked earlier and I didn't see it.

Question 4.

Does the man know who won the award?

Man: That gypsy over there says that she will read our fortune for ten dollars.
Woman: You cannot be serious; that is highway robbery.

Question 5.

What does the woman mean?

Woman: How many bottles of soda are left in the refrigerator?
Man: I saw three in there when I looked before.
Woman: Oh, I promised Katie I would give her five bottles.

Question 6.

How many more sodas would the woman need to keep her promise to Katie?

Woman: I have just read the most wonderful novel by Toni Morrison.
Man: Who is she?

Question 7.

What does the man mean?

Man: I think we should go either to the South Pacific or the Caribbean for our
          summer vacation.
Woman: Oh, honey, we have to think of the cost and we have a voucher to save
          20 percent off a vacation in Florida.

Question 8.

Where will they probably go on their summer vacation?

Man: Would you like for me to make eggs for breakfast?
Woman: Oh, I was really in the mood for either pancakes or French toast.
          Could we have one of those instead?
Man: We don't have the ingredients for those things.

694

Question 9.

What will they probably have for breakfast?

Woman: This report was due yesterday. If you continue to work at this pace, your position here will be in danger.

Man: I am very sorry. It will not happen again. I thought it was due today.

Question 10.

What is the most likely relationship between these people?

Woman: I don't think Harry is in good with his boss.

Man: Do you think Harry really cares?

Question 11.

What does the man mean?

Man: Why are you at the hospital? Are you all right?

Woman: I am all right. My uncle got into an accident last night. The doctor said he might have to be operated on.

Question 12.

Who might need an operation?

Woman: I want to return this lamp I bought last week.

Man: If you are returning something, you have to go to the customer service counter.

Question 13.

Where did this conversation probably take place?

Man: How was the picnic last Sunday?

Woman: It was a disaster. It rained so heavily we came back all drenched.

Question 14.

What happened at the picnic?

Woman: Can I use your library for a while?
Man: Go right ahead. I'm not going to work there till six o'clock this
         evening.

Question 15.

What does the man mean?

Man: Are you taking the bus or the subway?
Woman: I hate subways in the summer. They are so stuffy!

Question 16.

What is the woman's opinion about the subways?

Woman: Can you tell me if I can use this color on silk material?
Man: I'm not positive. But if you leave your address, I can send you some
         literature on fabric painting.

Question 17.

What is the man going to send to the woman?

Man: Are you sure the meeting is in this room?
Woman: Yes. But it doesn't start till four o'clock. We still have half an hour to
         prepare our points.

Question 18.

Around what time did this conversation take place?

Man: Didn't you say you liked the glass vase very much?
Women: Yes. But I have to forget about it this time. I am totally broke.

Question 19.

What does the woman mean?

Man: Let's start studying biology first. We have a lot to review in it.
Woman: No. I think we should start with physics. It is much more difficult than
         biology or math, or even chemistry.
Man: As you please.

Question 20.

What will these people study first?

Man: I am sorry I'm a little late. But if we don't hit the traffic, we can still make it to the concert, can't we?
Woman: No. We can't. Our tickets were for yesterday.

Question 21.

Why can't these people attend the concert?

Man: Our history test has been postponed until next Monday.
Woman: What a relief!

Question 22.

What does the woman mean?

Woman: How is Valerie?
Man: I'm worried about her. It looks like she's falling apart.

Question 23.

Why is the man worried about Valerie?

Man: You should have taken this course. It's both interesting and easy.
Woman: Now I regret not taking it. But I thought it was too hard for me.

Question 24.

How does the woman feel about the course?

Man: You look a little upset. What happened?
Woman: The lady at the front counter gave me such a dirty look for coming in so late!

Question 25.

What does the woman mean?

This is the end of sample Test 5, Part A.

PART B

Questions 26 through 30 are based on the following conversation.

Man: Who is that a picture of on your desk?

Woman: That is my Uncle Floyd. The picture was taken last month when he went to Germany.

Man: What is that building behind him?

Woman: That is my uncle's favorite brewery. He collects beer cans from around the world. He said that this brewery's cans are some of the toughest to get in the United States. He said that some people will pay up to $100 for one.

Man: That's a lot of money for a can of beer.

Woman: That does not even include the beer. That price is just for the can.

Man: Did your uncle bring one of these cans back with him?

Woman: He brought back a whole suitcase filled with them.

Man: What is he going to do with all those cans?

Woman: He's going to sell them of course.

Question 26.

Who did the woman have a picture of on her desk?

Question 27.

What country did the man in the picture go to?

Question 28.

What did the man in the picture collect?

Question 29.

How much are some cans worth?

Question 30.

What was the man in the picture going to do with the cans?

Questions 31 through 35 are based on the following conversation.

Woman: I am leaving now. Would you mind doing a couple of things for me tomorrow? I have the day off.

Man: What are they?

Woman: Can you please keep all my messages on my desk and if Mr. Smith calls, can you please set a time for our meeting on Tuesday?

Man: That's no problem. Are you going out?

Woman: No. It's my daughter's birthday, and I want to surprise her by being at home.

Man: That's a nice reason to take a day off. By the way, I might leave early tomorrow. If Mr. Smith doesn't call before that, I will ask Terri to speak to him. Please give my birthday wishes to your daughter.

Woman: I sure will.

Question 31.

Where did this conversation probably take place?

Question 32.

Whose call is the woman expecting?

Question 33.

Why does the woman have a day off?

Question 34.

What will the man do if he leaves early on the woman's day off?

Question 35.

Who does the woman want to surprise?

Questions 36 through 40 are based on the following conversation.

Woman: Good morning! Do you jog around here everyday?

Man: Yes. How about you?

Woman: I try at least four times a week. I am not very regular though.

Man: Something is better than nothing. Even if you jog four times a week, it is pretty good exercise.

Woman: I used to go to a health club before. But I prefer jogging outside because I love fresh air.

Man: Besides, there is no one to tell you what to do and how many times.

Woman: Absolutely.

Question 36.

In what part of the day did this conversation take place?

Question 37.

What activity are these people interested in?

Question 38.

About how many times does the woman try to jog every week?

Question 39.

Why does the woman prefer jogging outside to going to a health club?

Question 40.

What advantage does the man see in jogging?

This is the end of sample Test 5, Part B.

PART C

DIRECTIONS: In Part C you will hear short talks. At the end of each talk, a second person will ask several questions about what was said. **You will hear each talk and the questions about it just one time.** They will not be written out for you. Therefore, you must listen carefully to understand what each speaker says. After you hear a question, read the four possible answers in your test book and decide which one is the best answer to the question you heard. Then on your answer sheet, find the number of the question and fill in the space that corresponds to the answer you have chosen.

Questions 41 through 45 are based on the following short talk.

The principal driving force of the economy of the twenties was the automobile. There were over 8 million motor vehicles registered in the United States in 1920 and over 26 million in 1929. Annual output of automobiles reached 3.6 million in 1923 and remained at about that level throughout the decade. By 1925 the price of a Ford Model T had been reduced to $290, less than three months pay for an average worker. Ford plants produced 9,000 Model T's per day, and Henry Ford cleared about $25,000 a day throughout the decade. Automobile manufacturing stimulated supporting industries such as steel, rubber, and glass, as well as gasoline refining and highway construction.

Question 41.

What was the major factor of the economy of the 1920s?

Question 42.

Approximately how many cars were produced every year during the 1920s?

Question 43.

Which Ford car had its price reduced to $290?

Question 44.

Who averaged $25,000 per day in the 1920s?

Question 45.

What other industries benefited from automobile production?

Questions 46 through 50 are based on the following short talk.

The growing popularity of soybeans is a good sign because they are high in protein. These beans were first planted in China about 3,000 years ago. The Chinese have cultivated a variety of ways to take advantage of the goodness of soybeans. They use bean sprouts, flour, and soybean oil, soy milk, and bean curd, or Tofu. "Tofu" is a substitute for meat for all nutritional purposes. In modern times, the United States is a leader in experimenting with soybean recipes. It is possible to get soybean hot dogs and cholesterol-free soybean ice cream in American supermarkets. Due to the various uses of soybean, it is called a bean with a thousand guises.

Question 46.

According to the speaker, what is a good sign?

Question 47.

What soybean recipes are popular in the United States?

Question 48.

Where was soybean first planted?

Question 49.

What is "Tofu" a substitute for?

Question 50.

Why is soybean called a bean of a thousand guises?

This is the end of sample Test 5, Part C.

THIS IS THE END OF SAMPLE TEST 5.

This is a transcript of the recording program for TOEFL,
the Test of English as a Foreign Language.

TEST 6
PART A

Man: That song is great! I love it!
Woman: Don't you think they play it too much on the radio?!

Question 1.

What does the woman think of the song?

Woman: Tomorrow is Melissa's birthday and I still have not bought her a present yet.
Man: Erik said that he was going to take care of Melissa's present this year, so don't worry about it.

Question 2.

Who will most likely buy the birthday present?

Man: Do you want me to make lunch now?
Woman: I'm not hungry right now. Maybe later, okay?

Question 3.

What will they do for lunch?

Woman: Doctor, do you think this cut will require stitches?
Man: Well, actually, all it requires is a good bandage.

Question 4.

What will they probably do for the cut?

Woman: I thought I was through packing everything, but I keep finding little things that I have missed.
Man: Stuff like that always happens.

Question 5.

What does the man mean?

Man: What time do you think I could expect the repairman?
Woman: He could be at your house as early as 10:00 AM. However, if you are at the end of his list, he will not arrive there until 3:00 PM. You should wait at home the entire time, though.

Question 6.

How many hours will the man have to wait if he is at the end of the repairman's list?

Woman: You were supposed to have washed the dishes by the time I got home from the meeting.
Man: I'm sorry. I didn't get to them. I got caught up in this book and lost track of time.

Question 7.

Why is the woman angry?

Woman: If the weather is nice tomorrow, I was hoping to go out in the sailboat. Did you hear the weather forecast?
Man: Yes, there are supposed to be thunder showers all day tomorrow.

Question 8.

What does the woman want to do?

Man: Here is the article I wrote for the newspaper. I was up all night working on it.
Woman: Thank you. But unfortunately, it's too late. Your deadline for that article was Tuesday. Today is Friday.

Question 9.

How many days late was the man's newspaper article?

Woman: I had my palm read by the fortune teller on the boardwalk. Have you ever done that?
Man: Yes, but I think that is a complete waste of time and money.

Question 10.

What the man mean?

Woman: I am going to look for some winter clothes this weekend.
Man: Don't you think it's a little too early for that?

Question 11.

What does the man mean?

Woman: It's quarter to three. Do you think I should start arranging the table?
Man: Yes. Ms. White should be here in 15 minutes. She's known for her punctuality.

Question 12.

At what time is Ms. White expected?

Man: Do you know how to get to the museum by bus?
Woman: You will have to change twice: once at the zoo and then near the courthouse.

Question 13.

How many buses will the man ride to get to the museum?

Man: Tim got a really good raise in his salary.
Woman: No wonder he looked so happy!

Question 14.

What does the woman mean?

Woman: I think Peter likes to talk.
Man: Likes to talk? I think he's a chatterbox.

Question 15.

What is the man's opinion about Peter?

Man: Why didn't you take the criticism course this semester?
Woman: I would have taken it if Dr. Jones was teaching it, but since it is Dr. Sampson I decided to skip it.

Question 16.

Who is the woman's favorite teacher?

Man: Would you like to have some tomato or mushroom soup?
Woman: I would rather have some French onion soup.

Question 17.

What would the woman like to have?

Woman: Do you see any empty seats?
Man: The theater is packed. This is an award-winning movie.

Question 18.

Where are these people?

Man: Can I talk to you for a few minutes?
Woman: I am in a rush right now. Is it okay if we talk tomorrow?

Question 19.

What does the woman mean?

Woman: Why is Rick so unpopular in his office?
Man: It's his attitude. He never talks to anyone in a friendly manner.

Question 20.

What is the man's opinion about Rick?

Man: How about taking a break after we finish reading this article?
Woman: Not a bad idea.

Question 21.

What does the woman mean?

Woman: Do you know the format to pull up files? I need to go back to my first project.
Man: Let me try. My computer is programmed a little bit differently.

Question 22.

What are these people doing?

Man: This pie is excellent. My compliments to you.
Woman: Thanks. But it still can't beat my mother's or my aunt's.

Question 23.

What does the woman mean?

Woman: I need a ride if you are going to the school.
Man: Oh, I don't mind. But I am stopping first at the bank and then at the post office. Is that a problem?
Woman: Not at all.

Question 24.

Where will these people stop first?

Woman: I am surprised Gary sold his house. He was so crazy about it.
Man: He had no choice. He had to do it to pay his debts.

Question 25.

What does the man mean?

This is the end of sample Test 6, Part A.

PART B

Questions 26 through 30 are based on the following conversation.

Man: I just received a letter from my mother. She and my father are planning on taking a trip to visit me.

Woman: That's great. Are you going to ask your professors for time off to spend with them?

Man: I am only going to be taking off from my night classes. My parents will do some sight-seeing during the day and then we will go out to dinner at night.

Woman: What sights are they going to see?

Man: They are planning to go to the theme park and the aquarium. I also gave them information on the movie studio tour.

Woman: I went to the studio tour. It was a lot of fun. You get to see how special effects are designed, and all the workers are in costume.

Man: Did the tour just cover things from new movies?

Woman: No, they had a little bit on all their famous movies from the 1940s to the present.

Man: I think my parents would like that. They love old movies.

Woman: I took my parents and they enjoyed both the old and the new.

Question 26.

Who was coming to visit the man?

Question 27.

Which classes is the man going to miss?

Question 28.

Where did the woman go?

Question 29.

What does the tour cover?

Question 30.

Where did this conversation probably take place?

Questions 31 through 35 are based on the following conversation.

Man:	Did you know Mike is going back to Italy in two weeks?
Woman:	Really? I thought he was looking for a job.
Man:	No. He was here only for studies. He has to go back now. His visa expires soon.
Woman:	We are all going to miss him, aren't we?
Man:	Of course we are. We were thinking of giving him a gift to remember us by. Would you like to contribute?
Woman:	Sure. Have you decided what we are giving?
Man:	Not yet. Do you have any suggestions?
Woman:	How about a framed picture of our whole class?
Man:	Mike mentioned the other day that he is going to take one himself next week. What do you think of a set of dictionaries?
Woman:	What do you mean by a set?
Man:	Like one regular, another for usage, one from English to Italian, and another one from Italian to English.
Woman:	That sounds great! He can use them and remember us for his whole life.

Question 31.

Why does Mike have to go back to Italy?

Question 32.

What are these people planning to do for Mike?

Question 33.

Why didn't the man accept the suggestion of giving Mike the picture of their class?

Question 34.

What does the man mean by "a set of dictionaries"?

Question 35.

What is the woman's response to the man's suggestion?

Questions 36 through 40 are based on the following conversation.

Woman: After this meeting, I'm not staying here for a minute. The day has dragged. It was too much work.

Man: I agree. I also want to get this meeting over with, rush home, and get a good night's sleep.

Woman: You are lucky. I will still have to look for a place to eat. Do you know any good restaurants around?

Man: There are plenty of them on the main street. But if you don't want to go that far, there is a fine Swiss restaurant right across the street.

Woman: That's good for today. Anything interesting downtown? I am here for the whole week; I can try some varieties.

Man: Yes, there is an excellent French restaurant on Dublin Street by your hotel. If you like spicy food, there are some really good Asian restaurants on the main street and there's also a very good Italian restaurant just two blocks from here.

Woman: That's enough for a week. You seem to know all of them by heart.

Man: Well, food is my favorite subject.

Question 36.

On what point do these people agree?

Question 37.

Where is the woman staying?

Question 38.

What place would the man suggest if the woman liked spicy food?

Question 39.

How does the man know about so many restaurants in the town?

Question 40.

Where is the good French restaurant?

This is the end of sample Test 6, Part B.

PART C

Questions 41 through 45 are based on the following short talk.

Three primary internal mechanisms produce thirst. First, when the concentration of salt cells in the body reaches a certain level, the hypothalamus is triggered to act in a way that results in the experience of thirst. A decrease in the total volume of fluid in the circulatory system also causes the sense of thirst. Finally, a rise in body temperature or a significant energy expenditure also produces thirst, probably because of a rise in the salt concentration of the body. The dry mouth that accompanies thirst is a symptom of the need for water but not the cause. The body does seem to have a kind of water meter in the mouth and stomach, however, that monitors the amount of water that has been consumed and immediately informs drinkers when they have had enough liquid to meet their needs.

Question 41.

How many mechanisms produce thirst?

Question 42.

What causes the hypothalamus to trigger thirst?

Question 43.

A decrease in the fluid of which system also causes thirst?

Question 44.

What is not a cause of thirst?

Question 45.

Where is the water meter for water consumption located?

Questions 46 through 50 are based on the following short talk.

Last week, I visited a zoo with a friend. It was a unique experience because the zookeeper there had extraordinary views about zookeeping. Since my friend knew him, he gave us a tour of the zoo. We were surprised to see that each section had a distinct atmosphere. It was like moving from continent to continent. The zookeeper explained that they were trying their best to provide the animals with their natural surroundings. Not only did they have trees and plants brought from all over the world, they also had speakers attached to the walls in order to provide special sound effects to each animal. These sound effects were carefully taped after studying their natural surroundings. As we were passing by the rabbits, he said, "I wouldn't mind unlocking all the cages, except for the carnivores. But I am afraid of their getting lost in the jungle." "The jungle?" we asked. He explained, "Our roads, with flashing traffic lights and rushing cars, are as frightening for them as the darkest jungles in the world are for us."

Question 46.

What made the narrator's visit to the zoo unique?

Question 47.

Why was the tour like moving from one continent to another?

Question 48.

What was the purpose of the speakers attached to the walls?

Question 49.

Why did the zookeeper refer to roads as jungles?

Question 50.

How would you describe the zookeeper?

This is the end of sample Test 6, Part C.

THIS IS THE END OF SAMPLE TEST 6.